D0210021

The Navigator appears in the lower right-hand corner of the screen.

The Previous button (arrow pointing left) takes you to the previous spread.

The Wave button (center button) takes you to the Contents screen.

The bar above these buttons (gray line above buttons) activates the popPanel (see description below).

The Next button (arrow pointing right) takes you to the next spread.

The popPanel has six icons.

The Bookmark (book with red line) button adds a bookmark to the briefcase, allowing you to mark a specific section.

The Glossary (book without red line) button brings up the glossary.

The Web (WWW) button brings up information about the PACE Web site.

The Briefcase (briefcase) button takes you to the briefcase, allowing you to add notes, print your bookmarks, or jump to a bookmarked location.

The Help (question mark) button provides additional instructions for using the program. You may want to refer to this immediately in order to better understand how to use the PACE CD.

The Quit (arrow pointing at door) button quits the PACE program.

Have fun using PACE!

Information Technology

THE BREAKING WAVE

DENNIS P. CURTIN

KIM FOLEY

KUNAL SEN

CATHLEEN MORIN

Irwin
McGraw-Hill

Boston Burr Ridge, IL Dubuque, IA Madison, WI New York San Francisco St. Louis
Bangkok Bogotá Caracas Lisbon London Madrid
Mexico City Milan New Delhi Seoul Singapore Sydney Taipei Toronto

Irwin/McGraw-Hill
A Division of The **McGraw-Hill** *Companies*

INFORMATION TECHNOLOGY: THE BREAKING WAVE

Copyright ©1998 by The McGraw-Hill Companies, Inc. All rights reserved. Printed in the United States of America. Except as permitted under the United States Copyright Act of 1976, no part of this publication may be reproduced or distributed in any form or by any means, or stored in a data base or retrieval system, without the prior written permission of the publisher.

The accompanying PACE CD was developed using Director ® by Macromedia, Inc. DIRECTOR ® COPYRIGHT© 1994 Macromedia, Inc.

This book is printed on acid-free paper.

1 2 3 4 5 6 7 8 9 0 VNH/VNH 9 0 9 8 7

ISBN 0-256-21847-1 (text)
ISBN 0-256-21848-X (PACE CD)

Vice president and editorial director: *Michael W. Junior*
Senior sponsoring editor: *Garrett Glanz*
Development: *Burrston House, Ltd.*
Editorial coordinator: *Carrie Berkshire*
Marketing manager: *James Rogers*
Senior project manager: *Beth Cigler*
Production supervisor: *Heather D. Burbridge*
Designer: *Lucy Lesiak: Lesiak/Crampton Design Inc.*
Cover photo: *©Don King*
Photo research coordinator: *Sharon Miller*
PACE opening movie: *Surfing footage by Stephen Spaulding, ISOMER Productions, Carmel, CA*
Compositor: *GTS*
Typeface: *10/12 ITC Century Light*
Printer: *Von Hoffmann Press, Inc.*

Library of Congress Cataloging-in-Publication Data

Information technology: the breaking wave / Dennis P. Curtin ... [et al.].
p. cm.
ISBN 0-256-21847-1
Includes index.
1. Information technology. I. Curtin, Dennis P., 1941-
T58.5 .I562 1998
004--dc21 97-43356

http://www.mhhe.com

Preface

Anyone who watches TV or reads the newspapers cannot miss the media's coverage of the rapidly growing impact of information technology in our lives. The stories may address seemingly diverse information technology–related topics such as the Internet, digital TV, DVD discs for music and movies, corporate restructurings, privacy of health records, and wireless phones. To a casual observer, it may seem that these innovations and changes are disconnected, or occurring in separate areas. However, they all share to some extent a common denominator: computers and information technology. Developments in these areas are accelerating the change we see around us, and many previously separate and distinct fields are converging. The adjustments that we are experiencing are neither insignificant nor cosmetic. They are as large as those experienced in the industrial revolution of the 1800s when changes in technology moved people away from farms and rural living and into cities. And, they are as significant as the changes at the beginning of this century, when the popularity of the automobile moved masses of people out of those cities and back into the suburbs. Information technology affects us both as individuals and as a society: Our job prospects, as well as options for health care and education, have radically changed and will continue to change, as will even larger issues, like the workings of our government and society.

The goal of this textbook as well as its accompanying multimedia program and Web site is to give you the background you need to understand the technology underlying the changes that are taking place and the issues that arise from those changes.

Fiber-optic cable is the new information superhighway. Courtesy of Corning

Where Did The Subtitle, The Breaking Wave, Come From?

Just over 25 years ago the first microprocessor emerged on the scene. This tiny, inexpensive, mass-produced device made possible revolutionary advances in information technology. Ten years ago, computers had limited uses and many people simply weren't exposed to them. However, like an ocean wave that builds slowly offshore, only to crest and break as it nears the beach, the impact of microprocessor-based information technology is now cresting and breaking in our work and lives. And the wave that has been building for the past quarter-century has just started to break. We have yet to experience the full power of the pounding surf of change, or deal with the backwash. The subtitle was chosen to reflect this impact.

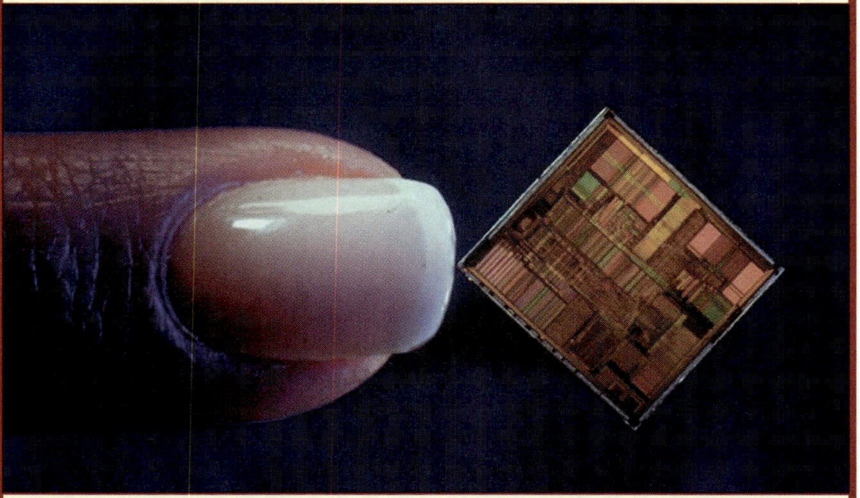

The amazing microprocessor. Courtesy of International Business Machines

The real world

Lots of people have a misconception about professionals in the computer and information technology fields as well as users of the products. They hold stereotypes of "nerds" or highly educated engineers and scientists in white lab coats. These images of computing professionals and computer users were never really accurate but now they are dangerously out of date, as they discourage many students from being interested in computing. Because students don't see themselves fitting the stereotypes, they think information technology isn't for them. But, if they really look around, they will find themselves surrounded by people much like themselves—people who have integrated computers into their work and personal lives, accomplishing things previous generations only dreamed about. People are creating multimedia games and presentations; choreographing dance; composing music, desktop publishing books, magazines and Web sites; and creating business plans. Complicated tasks that used to require efforts of teams of people are now within the grasp of single individuals. But that isn't all: Computers also allow instantaneous communication with people anywhere in the world. Our community is no longer limited by geography, as it is now possible to easily exchange e-mail, photos, music, manuscripts, and even videos with anyone, anywhere. We can even chat in real time or videoconference. These people who use this technology aren't computer experts; they are experts in games, dance, music, and publishing. To them, computers are tools that expand their abilities. They don't consider themselves computer professionals and never will. They learn what they need to about computers to get their job done, but their real interests lie elsewhere. Anyone can join this new class of computer "professionals" by applying information technology in their education or business life.

Pixels. *In the new world of information technology everything is digital—even the dots that form pictures. Here the dots are jelly beans, but you get the idea. Jelly Bean Spirit of '76 courtesy of Herman Goelitz Inc*

A film editor turns raw footage into a finished production. Courtesy of ImMix

Capturing the real world in the classroom

With each technological advance, computing gradually leaked out of the once-prized corporate or university computer room into adjoining offices and classrooms, then into the surrounding community, and finally into our automobiles and living rooms. Technological change continues to advance so rapidly that it is very difficult for anyone to keep up.

The challenge for computer and information technology educators is to present this dynamic field in a way that captures student interest. To do so, we need to accurately convey the flavor and excitement of the new world of computing. Once students interest is captured and preconceived attitudes are changed, we need to establish a foundation of the field of information technology so students can understand subsequent changes as they occur. This text is an attempt to do these things. It is the end result of a two-year effort by a large group of people to turn a vision into reality. What it surely isn't is a new edition of your father's data processing text! It has a multimedia feel to it—a feel that anyone raised on personal computers and video games will recognize. With the material presented in short modules (two facing pages, called a spread) and with over a thousand illustrations in a 320 page book, students will find it an excitingly fast read! However, please don't let the look deceive you, this text has more content than many longer texts.

A multimedia learning system

You'll quickly find that this textbook is only the start when you open to the back cover and find a CD disc that contains an accompanying multimedia program. We believe that our multimedia program is a major production that's both more professional and more comprehensive than anything else in this market. And, as you'll soon see, there is an accompanying Web site that gives you guided access to some of the world's finest online resources. If you want proof that you are using a textbook that reflects the real world of modern computing, please turn to Chapter 1. It's an introduction to the Internet!

All three components—text, CD, and Web site—run in parallel and are designed to reinforce one another. The entire multimedia learning system is called PACE, Program Assisted Computer Education. Now that you know a little about the purpose of PACE, turn the page to the next spread to learn more about it.

A biologist uses satellites and a portable computer to locate her position. Courtesy of Magellan

The PACE Core Text

Information Technology: The Breaking Wave has been developed as an integrated multimedia package for use in an introductory course on information technology. It used to be that a textbook on computing had to be 600-800 pages to capture the essence of the field. For a nonmajors survey course it's been traditional to abbreviate extensive coverage or to water it down. This text tries a different, multifaceted approach: a revolutionary textbook design along with an integrated multimedia component and Web site. With the addition of these two new media, the textbook no longer has to shoulder the entire load. It can become the framework around which other learning experiences are organized. Although the text has been designed so it can stand alone, it is significantly enhanced by use of the accompanying multimedia CD and Web site.

Understanding spreads

One of the first things you'll notice when you browse through this text is that it is organized into highly illustrated modules. Each main topic begins and ends on two facing pages which are called a spread. This is a publishing term for the two facing pages that you see when you open a book or magazine. Most books ignore spreads and just begin new sections wherever the last section ends. They treat the pages in a book as if it were one continuous scroll instead of the series of "posters" that they actually are. Part of the reason spreads are ignored is that writing and laying out a publication in spreads is both time-consuming and expensive. And yet it has been repeatedly proven that organizing a textbook into spreads enhances its educational value. There are a number of reasons for this enhancement.

- By presenting the information in manageable chunks, spreads eliminate the intimidation that many readers feel with the length of traditional chapter sections. This book not only looks easier to read and understand, it *is* easier. The onus for making the book digestible has been placed on the author (where it belongs) and not on the reader.
- Spreads allow this text to be easily correlated to the accompanying multimedia CD and the Web site. If you are reading Spread 3.2 in this text, you'll find related information in Spread 3.2 on the multimedia CD and Spread 3.2 on the Web site.
- Instructors can easily customize their presentation by modifying the sequence in which spreads are covered. This is far more flexible then just assigning chapters in a different order.
- Instructors can refer students to specific topics without elaborate instructions, such as "Read from the middle of page 125 through the end of page 131.
- Spreads allow more frequent illustrations and make it possible to place them right next to the discussion they illustrate. Readers don't have to spend a lot of time looking for the appropriate illustration. In traditional long chapters, art is usually placed at the top or bottom of the page and may even fall on a different page from where it's discussed.

Key features

In addition to spreads, PACE has a number of other unique features. Here are some of the standout features you will notice as you browse through this textbook.

- The text, CD, and Web site all open with a chapter on the Internet. This is done so students have access to this amazing resource throughout the course, not just at the end.
- The text devotes an entire chapter to multimedia, one of the fastest growing and most useful applications of modern computing.
- Anyone who reads lots of computer textbooks soon reaches the conclusion that we often try to teach too much, and this is especially true of those things that rapidly change. You'll find this text relatively free of lists of ever-changing standards and specifications. It's hard for the instructors to keep up with this material let alone expecting students to do so.
- This text focuses on fundamentals of information technology, which change slowly. This not only makes the information remain useful to a student when they graduate, but it also allows us to focus on the foundation concepts on which everything else rests. The PACE Web site provides the latest developments from the rapidly changing world of information technology.

How Students Responded to PACE

When asked about the 2-page spread format of the text, 9 out of 9 students preferred this format over traditional texts. They all believed that 2-page spreads would provide an advantage for studying the material. Some comments were:

"A person can read a particular concept and learn it without reading several pages."

"More concise, easier to understand."

Each spread is identified by a chapter number and a spread number. For example, the 11th spread in Chapter 3 is numbered 3.11. This allows you to quickly refer to the correct concept without using page numbers and ties together the text, the multimedia CD, and the Web site. All three components share this common table of contents and numbering system. This makes it easy to move from one to another, topic by topic.

The layout of the text has a multimedia essence. The heavily illustrated two-page spreads capture the flavor of a well-done interactive multimedia program. The design makes first time computer users more comfortable with the material. On each spread, a concept begins and ends on facing pages. This eliminates the intimidation many readers feel about traditional chapter treatment of topics, where discussion can fill several pages.

All art appears right at the point where it is discussed. No longer do you have to continually refer from a figure number in the narrative to a piece of art somewhere else on the page, or maybe even many pages later in the book.

Boxes contain interesting material that will appeal to students.

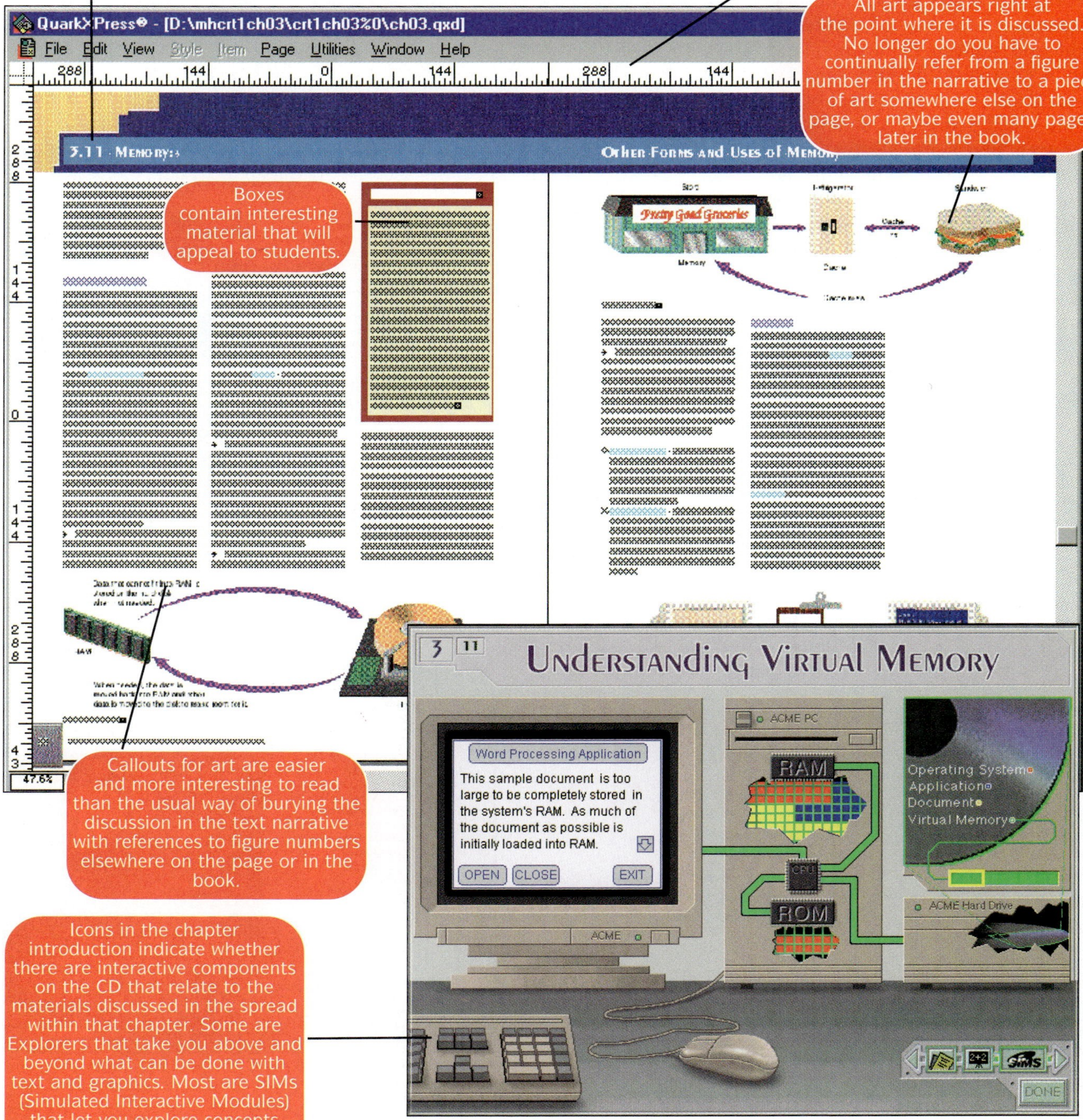

SIM 3-11 from the PACE CD-ROM

Callouts for art are easier and more interesting to read than the usual way of burying the discussion in the text narrative with references to figure numbers elsewhere on the page or in the book.

Icons in the chapter introduction indicate whether there are interactive components on the CD that relate to the materials discussed in the spread within that chapter. Some are Explorers that take you above and beyond what can be done with text and graphics. Most are SIMs (Simulated Interactive Modules) that let you explore concepts interactively.

The PACE CD

Supporting the coverage of the text, and in some cases expanding on it, is a unique multimedia program found on the PACE CD at the back of this book. This interactive program has been designed to illuminate key concepts and provide information beyond what is included in the text. It offers an exciting and interactive new way of combining print and multimedia components into a complete learning environment. Each two-page spread of this highly visual text is accompanied by corresponding material on the CD. This multimedia learning enhancement may be in the form of additional explanations, graphics, video clips, or animations. Being interactive, you don't just read text off the screen—you get involved exploring key concepts. Although this CD has been designed for student use, it can also be used as a lecture aide in situations where students don't have access to multimedia computers.

The PACE CD is the most complete software available for discovering fundamental computer concepts. When combined with this text and the PACE Web site, you are using a fully integrated way of learning about computers—a true multimedia experience.

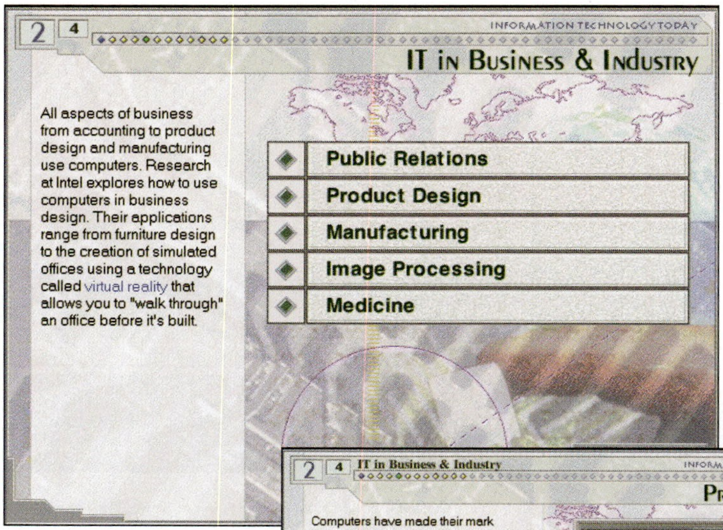

Spreads. *Each spread on the CD has a series of buttons you can click to explore the same topics covered on the same spread in this text.*

Topics. *Clicking any button on a spread displays a topic. Many of these contain text and graphics. Others contain animations, movies, and sounds.*

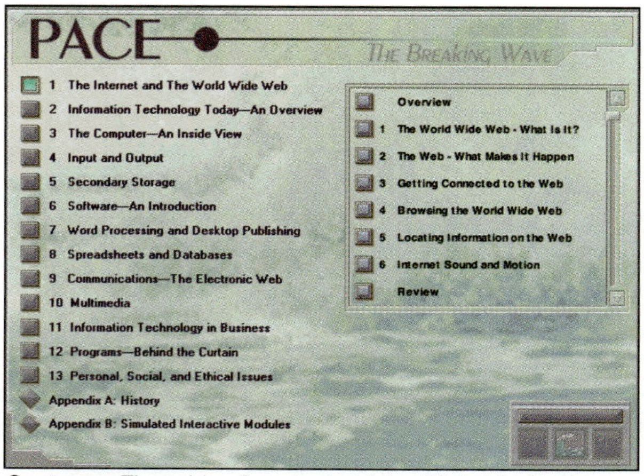

Contents. *The table of contents of the CD is identical to the one in this text so there is a one-to-one correlation. Just start the multimedia program, click a chapter to display its spreads, and then click a spread to jump to the spread you are studying. Nothing could be easier.*

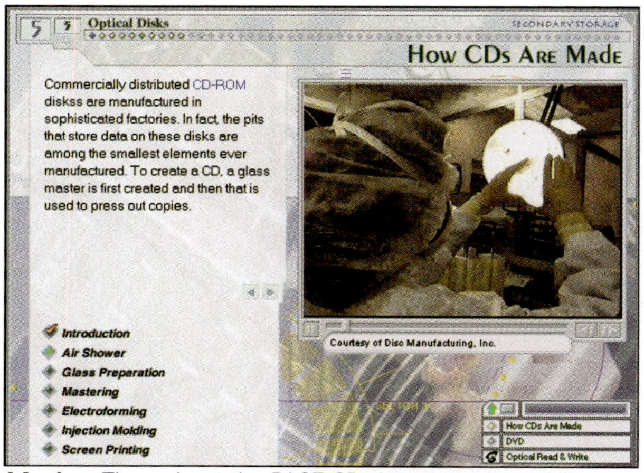

Movies. *Throughout the PACE CD there are about 50 movies illustrating aspects of computers that are hard to convey with still images or words.*

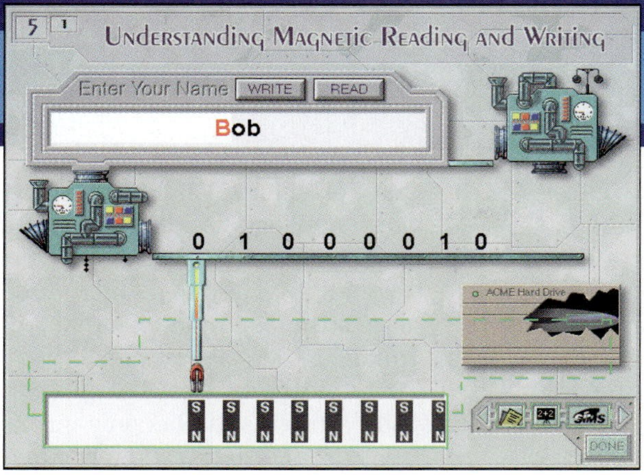

SIMS. *SIMs (Simulated Interactive Modules) demonstrate important concepts interactively. You can change settings, enter or manipulate data and watch the results.*

Explorers. *Explorers are interactive elements that allow you to do such things as simulate working with programs. As you click menu commands or buttons, you see how these programs work and what they do.*

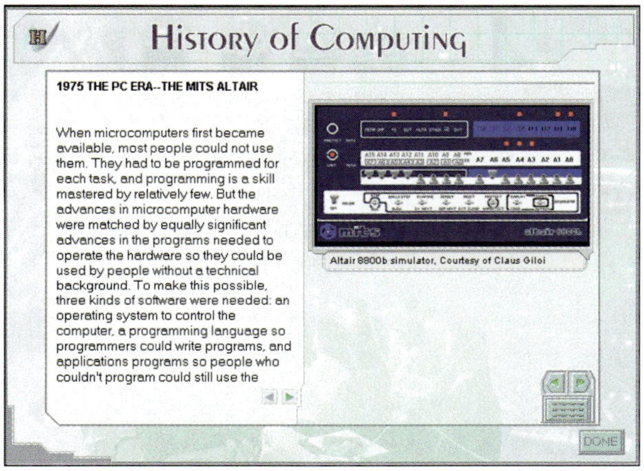

History. *Information technology has a long and interesting history. The history section on the multimedia CD shows the chronology of this history and explains and illustrates key events.*

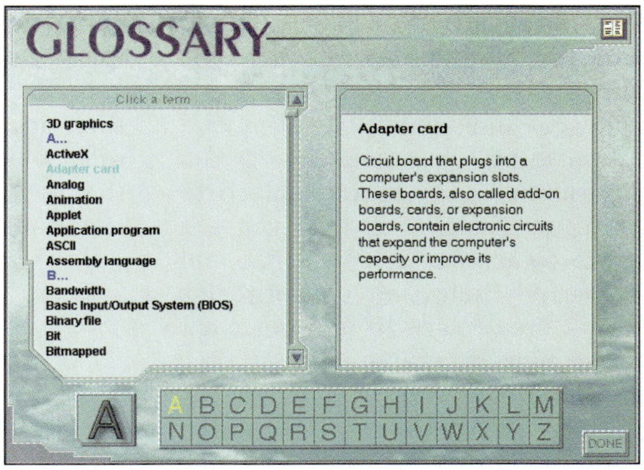

Glossary. *An online glossary lists and describes hundreds of terms used in the text and multimedia program. These terms are hyperlinked wherever they appear in the text and are also accessible from a separate list of terms.*

How Students Responded to PACE

PACE Multimedia CD

ALL liked how PACE correlates and adds to the text discussions.

ALL felt PACE would increase their level of interest and motivation to learn.

Comments:

"Visual examples help connect with the written word."

"Illustrations allow you to see how to do something firsthand."

"Makes it interesting and gives a vivid example."

"Very user-friendly."

"It took my hand & walked me through."

"Watching the simulation while reading about a concept helps me to better understand it."

"The animation will probably be remembered better to help understand and recall later."

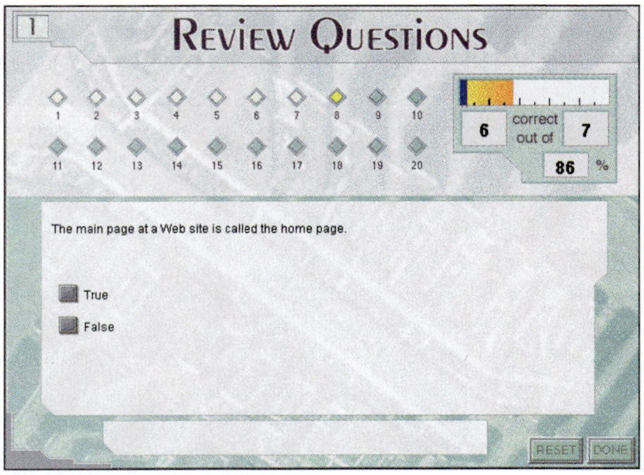

Questions. *At the end of each chapter there are 20 review questions. The results are automatically scored and can be printed out along with instructions on where to go in PACE to review the material covering any missed questions.*

The PACE Web Site and Supplements

In addition to the PACE text and multimedia CD, there is also a fully integrated PACE Web site. The entire PACE learning system is also supported by a full range of supplements for both students and instructors.

The PACE Web site

Text and multimedia programs take months to produce after they have been written. Even the newest book doesn't have the very latest information in it. However, the World Wide Web makes instant publishing possible. All you have to do is write some text and post it on your site, which takes a few minutes at most. Because of the timeliness of Web information, it's an ideal place to turn for breaking news. Because it gives companies such as IBM and Netscape their own platform, it's also a great place to find out what companies are doing and how they are doing it.

The PACE Web site has been designed to extend the coverage and timeliness of this text. Like the multimedia CD, it has an identical table of contents. This allows you to go onto the Web to learn more about any one of the spreads in this text.

1. To access the site, use your browser to go to **http://www.mhhe.com/cit/concepts/pace**.

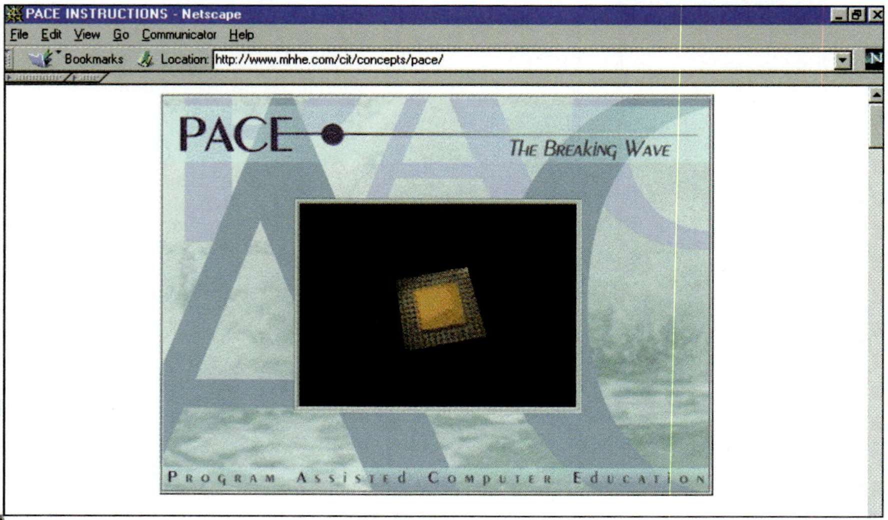

2. Click the contents button to display a list of the chapters in this text.

3. Click any chapter title to display a list of the spreads in that chapter.

4. Click any spread title to display a list of sites you can visit to learn more about the subject discussed in that spread.

Support for students

Applications Software Tutorials Irwin/McGraw-Hill offers five different series of software applications tutorials, which present five different hands-on approaches to learning software. Check with your local sales representative to learn about the specific software covered in each series.

- *The Advantage Series for Computer Education* by Glen Coulthard and Sarah Hutchinson. The Advantage Series offers tutorials for a large number of popular software packages, including the latest versions of Microsoft Office. Designed to teach beyond the basics, these manuals helps students to fully understand the power provided by popular applications and how to use that power. Each session within a manual begins with a case example and concludes with corresponding case problems that show real-world application of the software. Quick-reference guides appear throughout. Boxes introduce more advanced functions that will enhance the user's productivity. *The Advantage Series* will train your students to become proficient users of today's key productivity tools.
- In partnership with MindQ Publishing, Irwin/McGraw-Hill brings you *Advantage Interactive Software Tutorials:* Based on the printed *Advantage Series* texts, these CD-ROMs combine sight, sound, and motion into a truly interactive learning experience. Video clips, simulations, hands-on exercises, and quizzes reinforce every important concept. *Advantage Interactive* CDs are available for Microsoft Office 95 & 97 Professional, and are designed to be used independently or with the corresponding manuals.
- *The O'Leary Series* by Linda and Timothy O'Leary: Designed for application-specific short courses, each manual offers a project-based approach that gives students a sense of the real-world capabilities of software applications. Extensive screen captures provide easy-to-follow visual examples for each major textual step, while visual summaries reinforce the concepts, building upon students' knowledge. *O'Leary Series* manuals are available for a wide variety of software applications, including the latest versions of Microsoft Office.
- *Interactive Computing Skills* by Ken Laudon and Azimuth Multimedia: This series of CD-ROM–based tutorials offer complete introductory coverage of software applications. Each lesson takes 45–60 minutes to complete and is narrated and highly interactive. With up to 4 lessons per disc, you'll find *Interactive Comput-*

ing Skills to be a valuable addition to your courseware package or an excellent self-study tool. Each CD features a SmartQuiz at the end of lessons to actively test software skills within a simulated software environment. Available for Microsoft Office 4.3 and 97.

- *The Effective Series* by Fritz J. Erickson and John A. Vonk: Written specifically for the first-time computer user, the *Effective Series* is based on the premise that success breeds confidence and that confident students learn more effectively. Exercises embedded within each lesson allow students to experience success before moving on to a more advanced topic. The "why" as well as the "how" is always carefully explained. Each lesson features several applications projects and a comprehensive problem for student practice.

Support for the instructor

- The *CIT Classroom Presentation Tool* is a graphics-intensive set of electronic slides created to enhance any lecture. This CD-ROM–based software helps to clarify topics that may otherwise be difficult to present. *Minimum System requirements:* IBM PC or compatible with a Pentium processor, 4X CD-ROM drive and at least 16 MB of RAM, running Windows 3.1 or later. An LCD panel is needed if the images are to be shown to a large audience.
- *Instructor's Resource Guide* This complete guide supports instruction in any course environment.

  For each chapter, the Instructor's Resource Guide provides an overview, chapter outline, lecture notes, notes regarding the boxes from the text, solutions, and suggestions and additional information to enhance the project and critical thinking sections.
- *Test bank* The test bank contains over 1,000 different questions, all referenced to the text. Specifically, it contains true/false, multiple-choice, and fill-in questions, categorized by difficulty and by type; short-essay questions; sample midterm exam; sample final exam; and answers to all questions.
- *Computerized testing software* Called *Computest*, this popular computerized testing software is a user-friendly, menu-driven, microcomputer-based test-generating system that is free to qualified adopters. Containing all the questions from the test bank described above, *Computest* allows instructors to customize tests and generate review quizzes as well as answer keys.

  Available for DOS, Windows, and Macintosh formats, *Computest* has advanced printing features that allow instructors to print all types of graphics; Windows and Macintosh versions use easily remembered icons.

  **Instructors interested in administering networked tests should read the following description of the *McGraw-Hill Learning Architecture*.

  System requirements: IBM PC or compatible with at least 2 MB of RAM running Windows 3.1, or Macintosh with at least 2 MB of RAM running System 6.01 or later; CD-ROM drive or 3.5-inch floppy-disk drives.
- *Videos* A broad selection of 20 video segments from the acclaimed PBS television series *Computer Chronicles* is available to adopters. Each video is 30 minutes long. The videos cover topics ranging from computers and politics to online financial services to the latest developments in PC technology.
- *Instructor support services* Irwin/McGraw-Hill's Technical Support is available to you on any of our software products, such as the PACE CD-ROM or the CIT Classroom Presentation Tool. You can use the Online Helpdesk by linking to **http://www.mhhe.com/helpdesk** If you can't find your answer there, call us at 800-331-5094.
- *McGraw-Hill Learning Architecture (MHLA)* This exciting new Web-based software provides complete course administration. *MHLA* is available to students who use a standard Web browser and allows for content customization, authoring, and delivery. Students can take online quizzes and tests; and their scores are automatically graded and recorded. *MHLA* also includes useful features like e-mail, message boards, chat rooms, and it easily links to other Internet resources. The future of interactive, networked education is here today! Ask your sales representative for more information on the *McGraw-Hill Learning Architecture*.

The PACE Development Story

To capture the essence of today's computing environment and present it in an interesting and informative way is far beyond the ability of any single person. It takes a team working together to create innovative educational materials like these. On this team are writers, producers, programmers, editors (in many flavors), instructors, and students. Here are just some of the people who worked together to bring you this PACE learning System.

The Team

The author team

The author team led the development of this learning system. This team includes the following people (left to right).

Kunal Sen, a graduate of the University of Illinois Phd program in Artificial Intelligence brought understanding of technology and programming to the development of all aspects of the system. If the task was too complicated or difficult for other members of the team, calls were quickly placed to Kunal.

Kim Foley, a graduate of the MIT Media Lab, is the producer of the PACE CD multimedia program. She developed the program's navigation, coordinated its design, and pieced the final product together.

Cathleen Morin tackled the immense task of finding thousands of selections of illustrations, animations, and movies and then got permissions from their owners. When this task was finished, she took the text and illustrations and desktop published them into the textbook you are now reading.

Dennis Curtin has been an author of best-selling computing textbooks for over a decade. He is the author of the PACE text and CD and the developer of the PACE Web site.

The instructors

No educational learning system can be developed without constant feedback from a group of highly committed instructors who spend their days in front of the classroom wrestling with the best way to reach today's students. This project was blessed with a particularly committed group of such teachers. Their support for a new approach and guidance during development shaped PACE.

Albert Harris, Appalachian State U
Carol Pollard, University of Colorado
Catherine Brotherton, Cal State Polytechnic
Cecelia Adams, National College
Darien Hartman, College of Southern Idaho
Denis Titchenell, Los Angeles CC
Elaine Shillito, Clark State CC
Frank Lucente, Westmoreland CC
Frank Whittle, Dutchess CC
Fred Beisse, Lane CC
Fred Wells, DeKalb College, Gwinnett Campus
Fu Yao Wang, Univ. Of West Alabama
Herbert Dershem, Hope College
James McGuffee, Austin CC
Judy Scheeren, Westmoreland County CC
Julie Giles, DeVry DuPage
Larry Booth, Highline CC
Linda Broussard-Mehlinger, Central Mich. State U
Louis Squyres, DeKalb College
Matt Hightower, Bakersfield College
Michael Varano, Villanova
Randy Stolze, Marist College
Rebecca Dawkins, Kean College
Robert Coleman, Pima CC
Robert Crandall, Denver Business College
Robert Treat, Univ. Of Virginia
Russell Lake, Parkland College
Stephen Leach, Florida State Univ.

Steve Holland, New Hampshire Technical Institute
Tim Gottleber, North Lake CC
Wade Graves, Grayson County College
Wanda Grabow, DuPage
William Burkhardt, Carl Sandburg College
William Wagner, Villanova U

The students

During PACE's development, a student focus group was conducted in the Chicago area. Nine students were invited to attend and they spent a day working with the PACE components. Their feedback has been used to improve the text and CD.

Loretta Anderson, Moraine Valley Community College
Cindy Brachle, Joliet Jr. College
Gwentha Butler, South Suburban College
Halina Fuja, Northeastern Illinois University
Diane Greene, College of DuPage
Sarah Kettner, Joliet Jr. College
Jennett Kyler, South Suburban College
Patrick O'Connor, Miami University of Ohio
Francisco Rojas, Joliet Jr. College

The Irwin/McGraw-Hill people

In addition to the teachers and students who guided the development of PACE, a professional staff worked behind the scenes to pull it all together. Without these people, the project would never have come to pass.

Garrett Glanz, Senior Sponsoring Editor. Without his support this project would never have gotton off the ground.
Burrston House, Editorial Development.
Steve Schuetz, Senior New Media Developer
Charles Pelto, New Media Quality Assurance Analyst
Laurie Entringer, Design Coordinator
Heather Burbridge, Production Supervisor
Sharon Miller, Photo Research Coordinator
Beth Cigler, Project Manager. As our day-to-day contact on the project, there isn't enough room to express our appreciation for her patience and professionalism.

How Instructors Responded to PACE

- "This [text] addresses more current topics than my textbook. It is most suitable for my course because it presents a wide variety of topics and covers them in sufficient depth for my students. My overall impression is the [text] is superior to our current textbook."
  Judy Scheeren, Westmoreland County CC
- "When I first looked at the organization of the text and saw that the Internet was to be covered at the beginning I was rather skeptical. Once I started reading and later found the many references to existing Web sites and their relationship to the topics that were covered I was converted, and now I find it to be a very novel approach that, if used correctly, can be a very good teaching tool. Good idea!"
  Matt Hightower, Bakersfield College
- "The introduction of the Web at the beginning of the course and a Web site that parallels the text is a strong selling feature of this book. I like it!"
  Albert Harris, Appalacian State U.
- "The textbook I am currently using does not have an entire chapter devoted to multimedia; *Information Technology: The Breaking Wave* would have the edge."
  Steve Holland, NH Tech Inst.
- "The program was extremely informative. Students will enjoy learning the subject matter using this CD-ROM. It is the best I have seen to date."
  Steve Holland, NH Tech Inst.
- "The product is excellent and it will be very useful to students and instructors. Keep up the good work!"
  Judy Scheeren, Westmoreland County CC

Contents

Contents

Contents

CHAPTER

1 THE INTERNET AND THE

AN OVERVIEW

Imagine all the cities of the world having wonderful streets but no connections between the cities—not even footpaths. It would be an isolated existence for everyone. That was the way the computer world was until a few years ago. Now imagine four-lane superhighways running straight from city to city, creating an interconnected global network or web. You can enter the superhighway at any point and quickly get to any other point. That is the way the computer world is rapidly becoming. Over the past decade, many computers have been linked together in schools and companies so users can exchange files and share printers. Over the past few years, these local groupings, called local area networks, have been connected together into a worldwide network by the Internet—much as cities are connected by superhighways. This vast electronic web has been named cyberspace—a world in which everyone is connected electronically.

One part of the Internet called the World Wide Web, or just the Web, is only a few years old, but it is growing at an astounding rate. Tens of thousands of computers are now connected so you can use your computer's mouse to point and click your way around the world. On a trip through this Web, you can visit colleges, companies, museums, government departments, and other individuals like yourself. As you move through the Web you can read data on almost every imaginable topic. You can visit stores to buy things or transfer movies, pictures, games, and other software to your computer, much of it free.

The World Wide Web is in its infancy, but it may soon become a pipeline for telephone, communications, entertainment, and news—challenging existing technologies. Already you can tune in National Public Radio broadcasts—today's, or any of the shows broadcast over the past few months. Video is a little further behind, but there is already lots to see. In the future, you'll be able to tune in television broadcasts from anywhere in the world.

You might think the World Wide Web would be covered later in the text after you have learned something about the basic technologies that make it possible. However, with the almost limitless resources available on the Web, it makes sense to incorporate it into this course from the beginning. That way you can study things in this fast-moving field we can't even anticipate as these words are written. In this introductory chapter you'll learn what you need to know to use the Web in all your studies.

OBJECTIVES

After completing this chapter, you will be able to:

- Describe the World Wide Web and use it to study information technology.
- Describe the tools you use to browse the World Wide Web and locate information.
- Describe how you get connected to the World Wide Web.
- Describe how text, graphics, sound, and video are used on the World Wide Web.

Internet *n.* 1. the network that connects other networks of computers around the globe into one seamless network. Derived from the phrase interconnected networks.

Network *n.* 1. two or more computers connected to each other and sharing a common language so they can communicate with one another.

ON THE PACE CD ROM

Spread No.	Title
1-4	The Browser
1-4	Uniform Resource Locaters (URLs)
1-5	Search Engines
1-5	Lists
1-5	Tours
1-6	Understanding Communication Bandwidth

World Wide Web

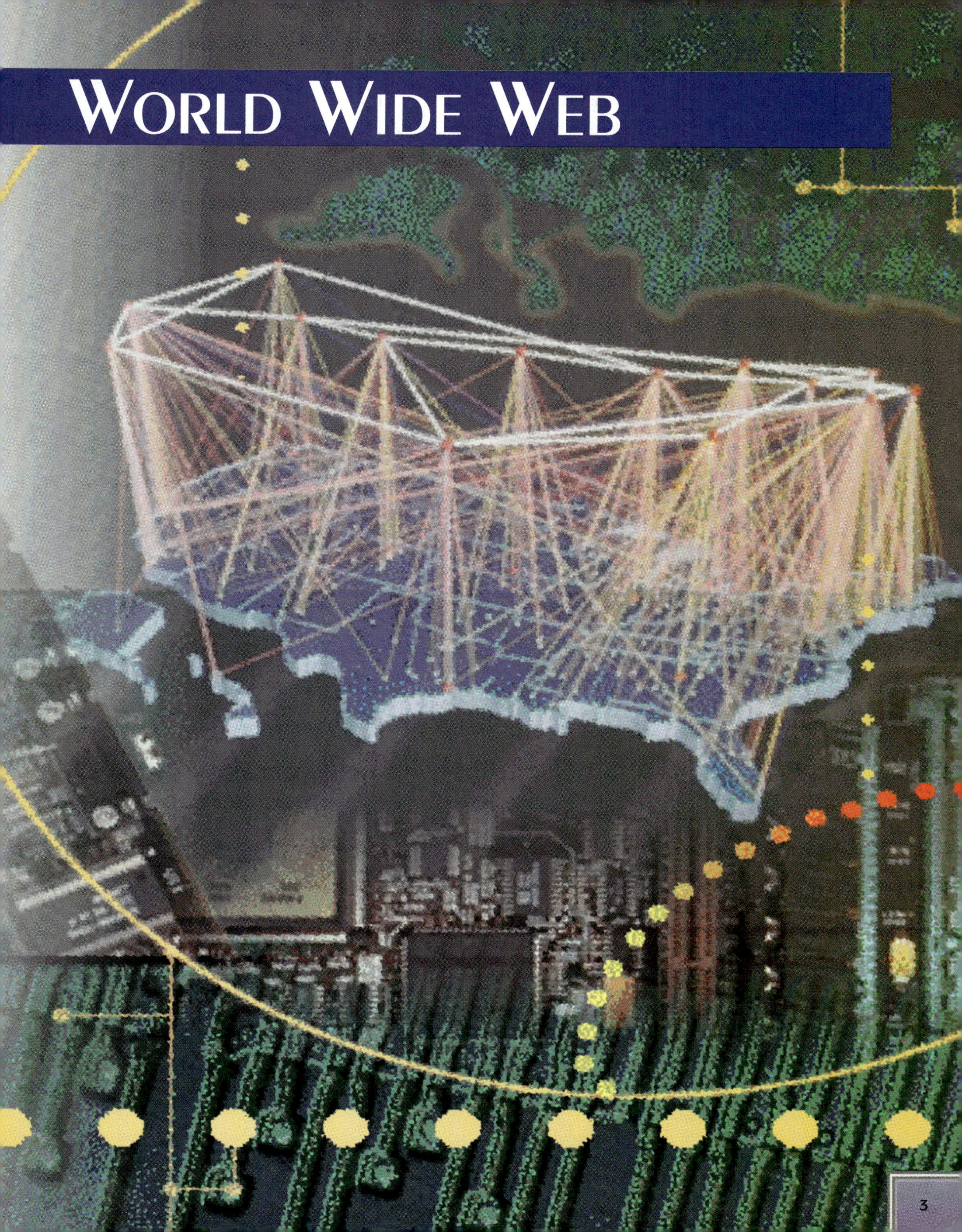

1.1 The World Wide Web—What Is It?

When two or more computers or other devices are connected together so they can communicate with one another, they form a network. If you have used a phone, watched TV, or flipped a light switch, you are already familiar with the power of networks. The largest network in the world is the Internet. This network is not used for phones, TVs, or electricity, but for computers. Any computer connected to this network can communicate with any of the others that are also connected. The Internet has a number of different services but by far the most popular is the World Wide Web, or just the Web, or occasionally WWW or W3. The Web network is the core of what many hope will become the electronic superhighway of the future. In addition to today's text, chat rooms, and sound and video clips, the Internet will soon feature full-screen TV and movies.

What is the Internet?

During the 1960s, computers began to play important roles at major universities and research firms. A U.S. Defense Department agency, the Advance Research Projects Agency (ARPA), decided that everyone would benefit if computers could be linked together so that programs and data could be easily shared. The network was actually developed by Bolt Beranek and Newman (BBN). The first two computers at UCLA and SRI were linked in November 1969. This tiny Defense Department network was the forerunner of today's Internet, the world's largest and fastest growing network. The Internet is a very loosely organized network. Unlike commercial systems, no corporate, government, or educational institution runs the Internet. It is governed only by the Internet Society (ISCO), a group of interested volunteers.

The Internet is so vast it is like an electronic cloud encircling the earth. The numbers one can find vary widely and change from day to day, but there are many tens of millions of users located all over the world. Giving more specific figures is like looking into a rearview mirror. The numbers are immediately outdated. For the next few decades it will be safe to say that the Internet is larger today than it was yesterday, and it'll be larger tomorrow than it is today.

"On the Internet, nobody knows you're a dog."

Cartoon courtesy of The Cartoon Bank

What is the World Wide Web?

The World Wide Web is a recent addition to the Internet. Its popularity has increased dramatically because it's so easy to use, so colorful, and so rich in content. Basically, the Web is a series of interconnected documents stored on computer sites or Web sites. When you use your computer and a software program called a browser to visit a site on the Web, your screen displays a document called a home page, such as the accompanying home page for the United States Mint displayed in a win-

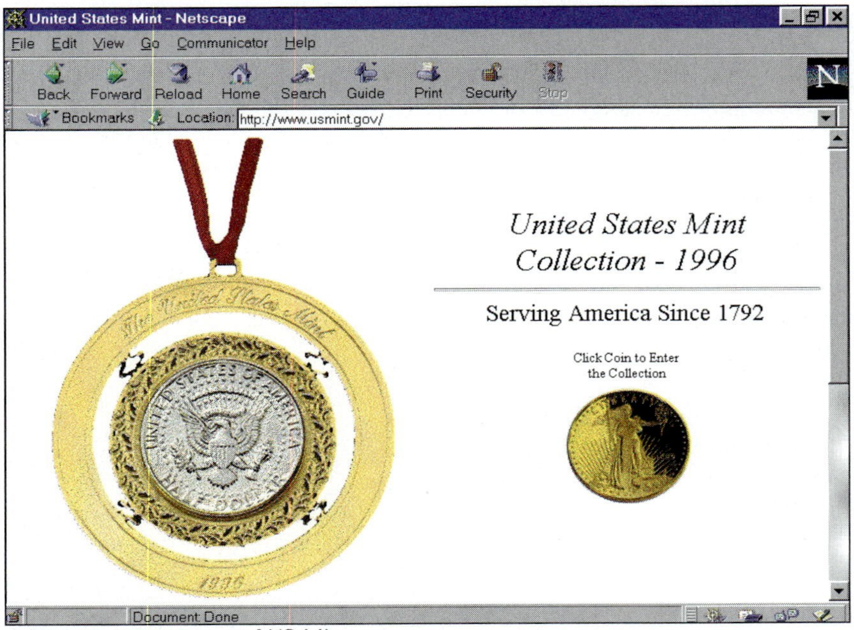

A home page courtesy of US Mint
http://www.usmint.gov

dow in Microsoft's Internet Explorer browser, or the home page for CU-SeeMe at Cornell University.

What's a home page?

Generally a home page gives the name of the organization or individual sponsoring the Web site and displays a list of highlighted words, buttons, or pictures. When you point to one of these highlighted items, the mouse pointer changes to a pointing finger to indicate something you can click. As you've seen, the Web is a network of billions of interlinked documents. These links—called hyper links or links—are the highlighted words, buttons, icons, or pictures. Each link contains the address of another document on the same computer or on another computer anywhere in the world. When you click one of these links you jump to the linked page. You can use the Web to tour the world. In many ways geography and distance have become irrelevant. To make things even more interesting, many of these links are no longer just to other documents. Increasingly, clicking them plays videos, music, 3D animations, or takes you through a virtual reality experience.

Are the Internet and the Web the same thing?

The World Wide Web has received so much publicity that many people think it is the Internet. That isn't the case. The Internet is the network itself and many activities other than the World Wide Web take place on it. Older services such as e-mail, Gopher, ftp, and Usenet news groups are also available separately or access to them has been integrated into the World Wide Web. Middle right you see one of the earliest services, called telnet, still in use by the Library of Congress. It's a service that allows you to log onto other computers over the Internet.

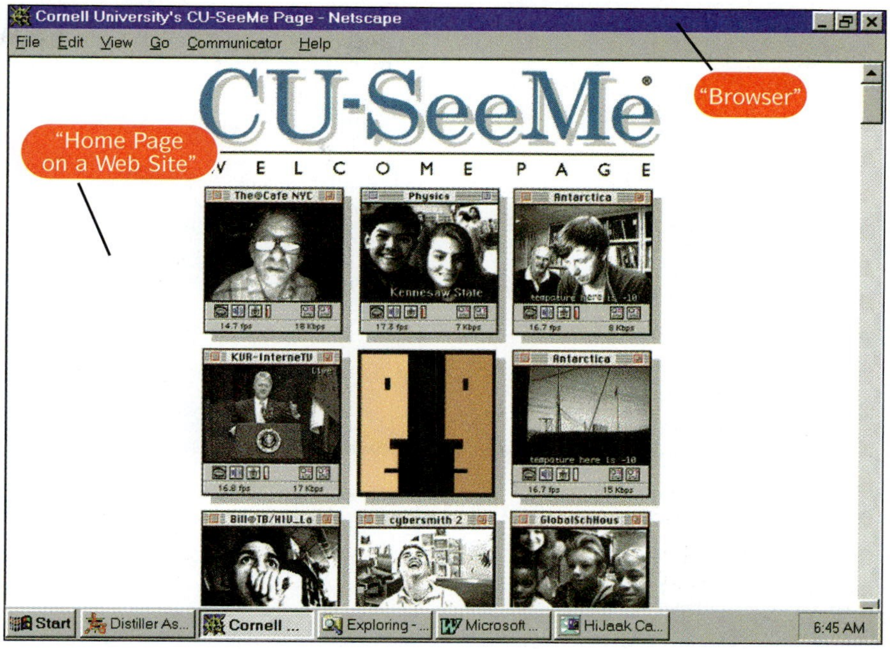

CU-SeeMe home page courtesy of Cornell University
http://cu-seeme.cornell.edu/

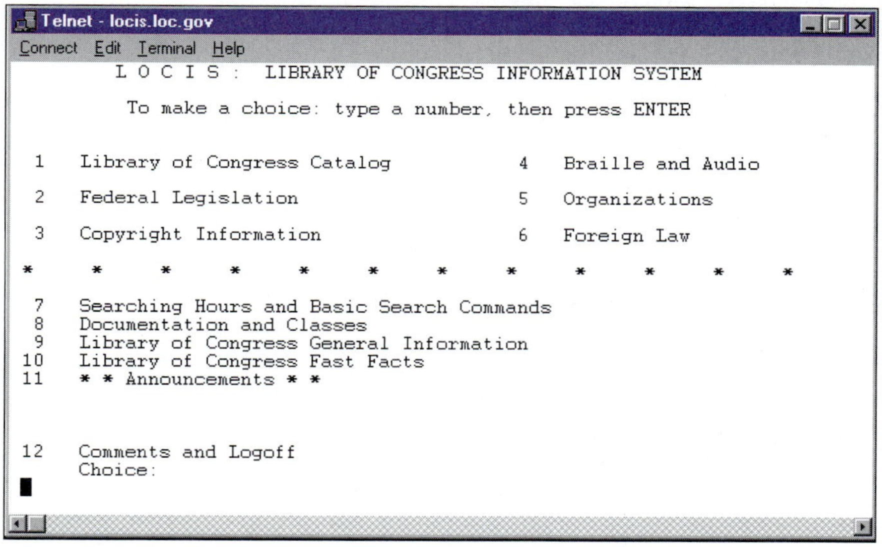

Telnet Site courtesy of the Library of Congress

PROTOCOLS

When you use a computer or the Internet, you are deeply immersed in a sea of rules and regulations that lurk just beneath the surface, usually out of sight and mind. Just as people attending a meeting must follow certain rules of conduct to avoid chaos, so must users of computer systems.

In computing, the common rules are called protocols. Previously, the term "protocols" referred to the "customs and regulation dealing with diplomatic formality, precedence, and etiquette." That definition still fits pretty well when used in the context of computing.

1.2 The Web—What Makes it Happen?

When you first connect to the Web, you're amazed at the variety of information that's available and perhaps can't help wondering where it all came from.

CERN—the birthplace of the Web
http://www1.cern.ch/

Where did the Web come from?

The idea of the Web was conceived by Tim Berners-Lee at CERN (European Particle Physics Laboratory) in 1989 to facilitate the collaboration among scientists working on high-energy physics research. He went on to develop the three standards that made the Web possible. The first described a way for computers to talk to one another over the Internet—called HTTP (Hypertext Transfer Protocol). The second described how to format documents so they can be transferred over the web—HTML (Hypertext Markup Language). The third described a way to give each document a unique address so you can find it on the Web—URL (Uniform Resource Locator).

In 1993, Marc Andreesen at the University of Illinois' National Center for Supercomputer Applications (NCSA) led a team developing the NCSA Mosaic Web browser, a computer program that allows you to view Web pages graphically with colors, interesting typefonts, photographs, and drawings. Eric Bina wrote the actual code.

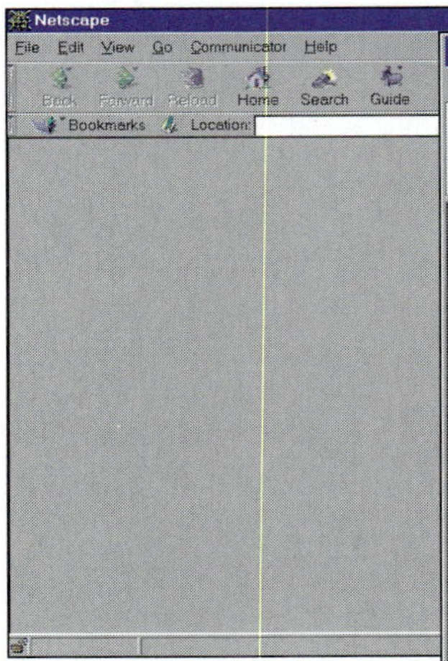

An Empty Browser

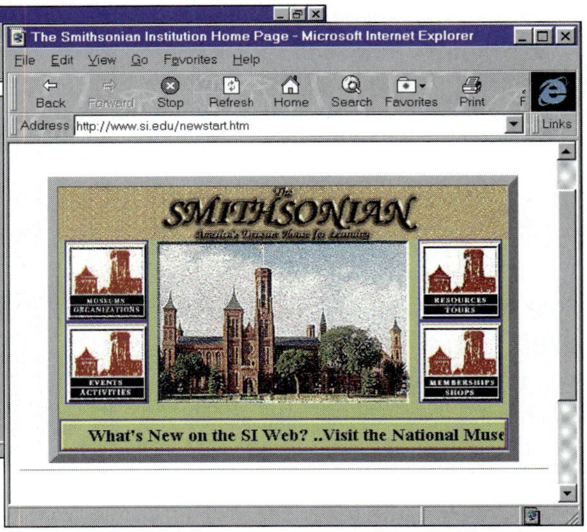

Browser displaying page courtesy of the Smithsonian
http://www.si.edu/newstart.htm

A Word About Words

HTTP, HTML, and URL, are the first computer acronyms in this text and may sound a little too technical because they are unfamiliar jargon. But keep in mind that they are jargon only until you begin using them yourself. You use jargon everyday in your life and aren't afraid of it. When referring to radio, you casually mention FM and AM, or you rush out to get some money from your bank's ATM. Jargon is just a shorthand way of referring to things. It's easier than saying amplitude modulation (AM), frequency modulation (FM), or automatic teller machine (ATM).

Where do Web sites come from?

If you don't hurry, you'll be the last on your block to have a Web site, or at least it sometimes seems that way. Tens of thousands of sites already exist and new ones are being added at an amazing rate.

Setting up a Web site is so easy that almost anyone can do it. However, it takes real skill and technical expertise to put up a large site, especially one with lots of multimedia or interaction. Large companies usually have a person called a webmaster in charge of their site. This person may do a lot of the work but will also call in programmers, graphic designers, and others specialists when needed. Individuals and smaller organizations generally have a more modest approach, putting the site together themselves. As with everything else in computing, things start out being hard to do, but over time tools are developed so anyone with an interest can get the job done. Even though the Web is very young, there are already tools available that make it easy to design a Web site graphically without having to know programming, such as Microsoft's Front Page and NetObjects' Fusion (shown here). You don't even need your own computer permanently connected to the Internet. You can place your Web site on someone else's computer, usually for a modest monthly charge.

Fusion screen display, courtesy of NetObjects
http://www.netobjects.com/html/pagedraw.html

What are Web sites used for?

There are almost as many reasons for being on the Web as there are people browsing it. People use it to locate product information; share research; exchange electronic mail (e-mail); get news, weather, and financial information; do research; look for jobs; chat with others; pursue political or social agendas; transact business; take courses; or just for self-expression. To give you an idea of the scale of activities on the Web, here is a map of the Web sites in the Oakbrook, Illinois, area showing schools, colleges, businesses, government agencies, and even florists.

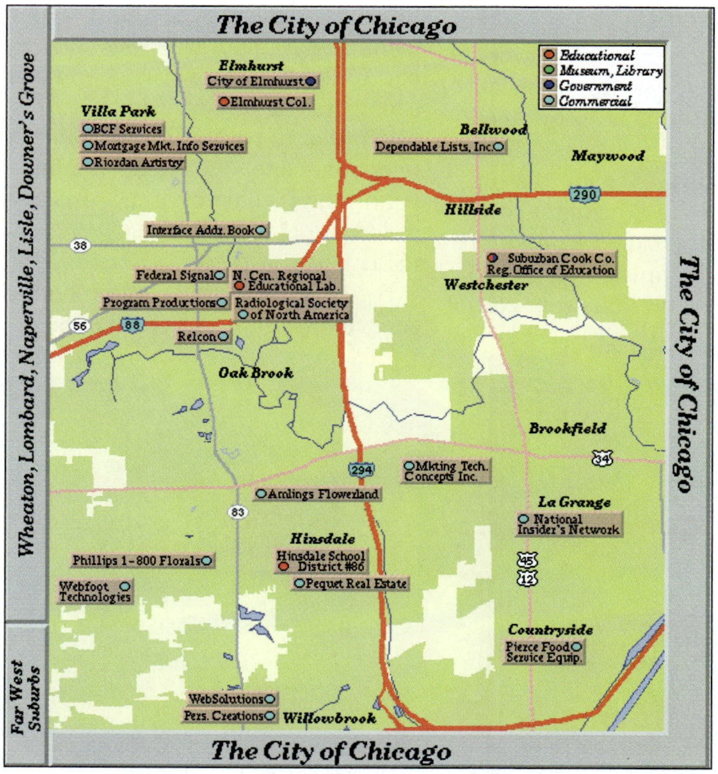

Map courtesy of Christopher Barnard and the Illinois Virtual Tourist
http://www.cs.uchicago.edu/vt/urbcham.html

1.3 Getting Connected to the Web

To use the World Wide Web you need access to the Internet. Everyone from a Fortune 500 company to a home user gets access to the Internet through a service provider, a company with a high-speed direct connection to the Internet. These service providers offer different types of access.

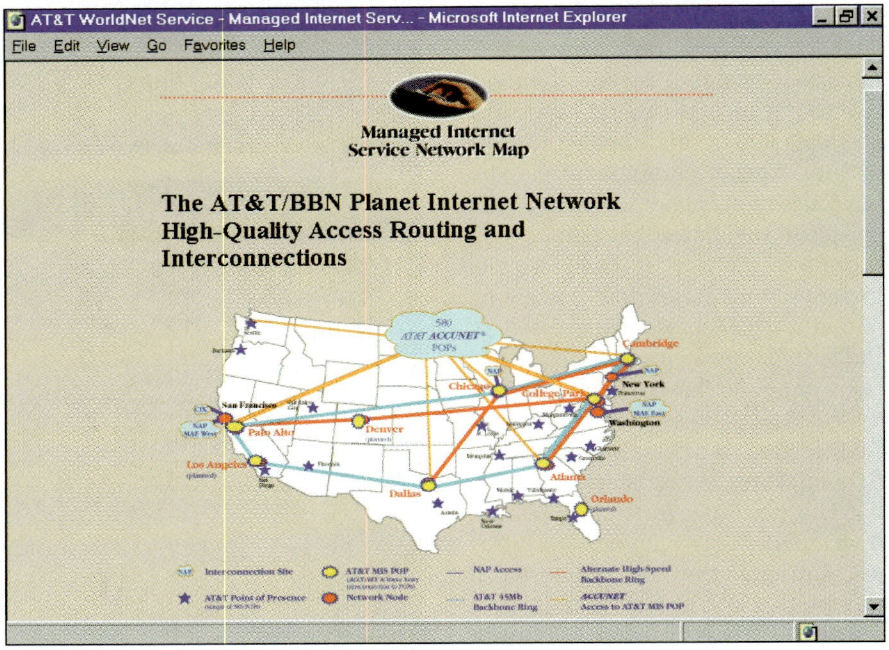

Map of service provider access points courtesy of AT&T
http://www.att.com/worldnet/wmis/misb.html

Presence providers

Businesses and other organizations usually need a permanent presence so people can reach their sites at any time. These sites are directly connected to the Internet through a service called a presence provider or web site host. Your computer at school or work may already be connected in such a way. Shown on the right is a Web site put up by AT&T that illustrates their high-speed lines for business use. Most businesses need such lines to handle the traffic to their sites.

Access providers

Individuals need access only when they want to browse or search for information. To do this, they need what is called dial-up access. There are various ways to gain dial-up access, but the most common way is to use a device called a *modem* between the computer and the phone line. (Modems and other connection devices are discussed in detail in Chapter 9.) When you open your browser, it dials up your service provider for a connection to the Internet. Once connected, your computer temporarily becomes a part of the Internet network and you can access all its services.

To dial in to the Internet over a telephone line, you need a phone connection that uses a protocol called Serial Line Internet Protocol (SLIP) or the newer Point-to-Point Protocol (PPP) that offers better security and faster speeds—making it faster. (Don't let the jargon about protocol put you off. It's not so different from saying you need an FM radio receiver to listen to FM radio stations.)

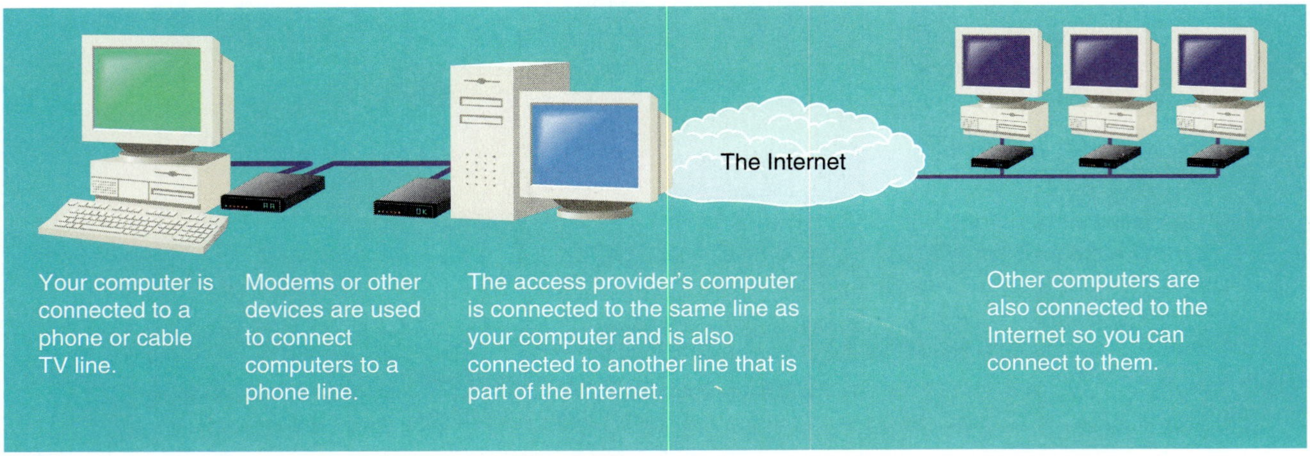

Types of access

There are basically two types of dial-up access: direct service providers and commercial on-line service providers.

- Direct service providers, such as AT&T, give you a connection to the Internet and storage space on their computers so you can use e-mail. Since their computers are permanently connected to the Internet, incoming mail is stored until you dial in to retrieve it. These servers also provide you with customer support and free software. Generally, these connections allow you to choose your own browser. There are hundreds of local and national direct service providers. A site on the Web called "The List" (http://www.thelist.com) lets you search for a provider by area code. Here is a map of the United States with area codes you can click for a list of local access providers.
- Commercial on-line services such as CompuServe, America On-Line, or Microsoft Network can also connect you to the Internet. In addition, they also give you access to their own on-line service and e-mail.

The pricing of these services varies widely and the market is so competitive that pricing changes frequently. Often you can choose from a menu of pricing plans. Some charge a fixed amount for unlimited use. Others charge a lesser fixed monthly amount plus an hourly connect charge. Which plan is best for you depends on how much you use the service.

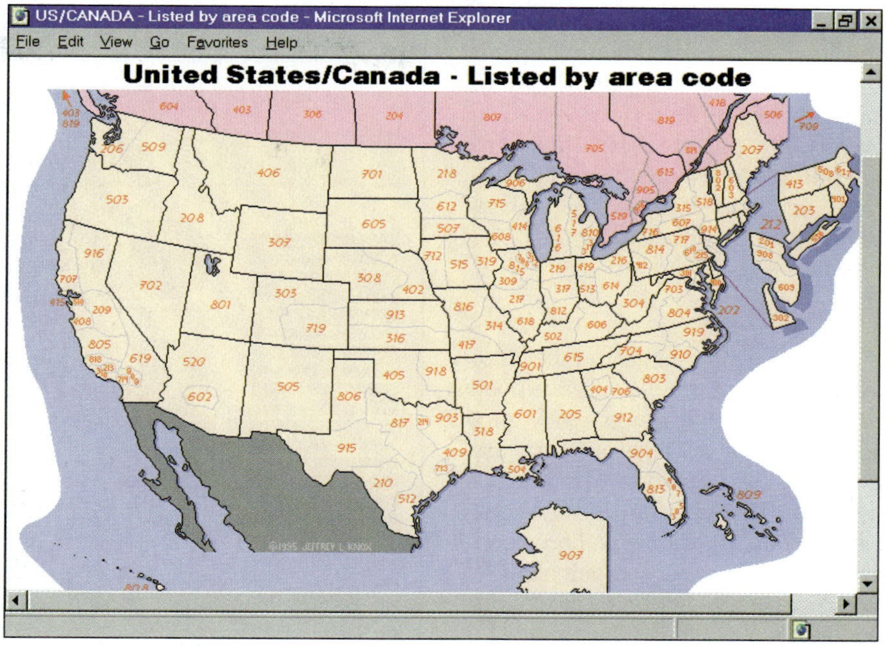

Map courtesy of The List
http://www.thelist.com

Public Internet Access

Not everyone has access to the Internet at home. However, access can often be had through schools, businesses, libraries, and even computer-savvy coffee shops, called cybercafes, which have computers and Internet connections. There are hundreds of coffee shops around the world now offering Internet access along with a cup of coffee.

Libraries increasingly are offering access to the Internet. If your local library doesn't offer this service, they should be able to direct you to one that does.

Cybercafe courtesy of Dennis Curtin

1.4 Browsing the Web

Once you're connected to the Web and your browser is loaded, all you need to do is click hyperlinks to move about the Web. However, to go to a specific page that isn't linked to the one you're viewing, you have to enter an address. Next we look at browsers and addresses.

The browser

As you'll see as you get further into information technology, you need software to make things work on a computer. As we have said, to use the Web, the software you use is a browser. This is an intensely competitive field right now and browsers are undergoing very rapid change. Some are independent software programs such as those developed by Microsoft and Netscape. Others are integrated into application programs such as word processing programs, spreadsheets, and databases.

A browser provides a number of useful functions:

- It allows you to enter the address of the site you want to jump to (called a URL—or uniform resource locator), or to jump there by clicking hotspots, highlighted words, buttons, pictures, or icons called hyperlinks on your screen.
- It formats Web documents for display on your screen.
- It allows you to back up and go forward through pages you have already visited.
- It allows you to copy text from the screen and paste it into a word processing program.
- It allows you to print the document you see on the screen.
- It makes it possible to transfer files—text, graphics, movies, animations, sounds, and programs—from other computers to your computer (called downloading).
- It allows you to send and receive e-mail and other Internet services such as ftp (file transfer protocol), gopher, and Usenet newsgroups, which you'll learn about later.

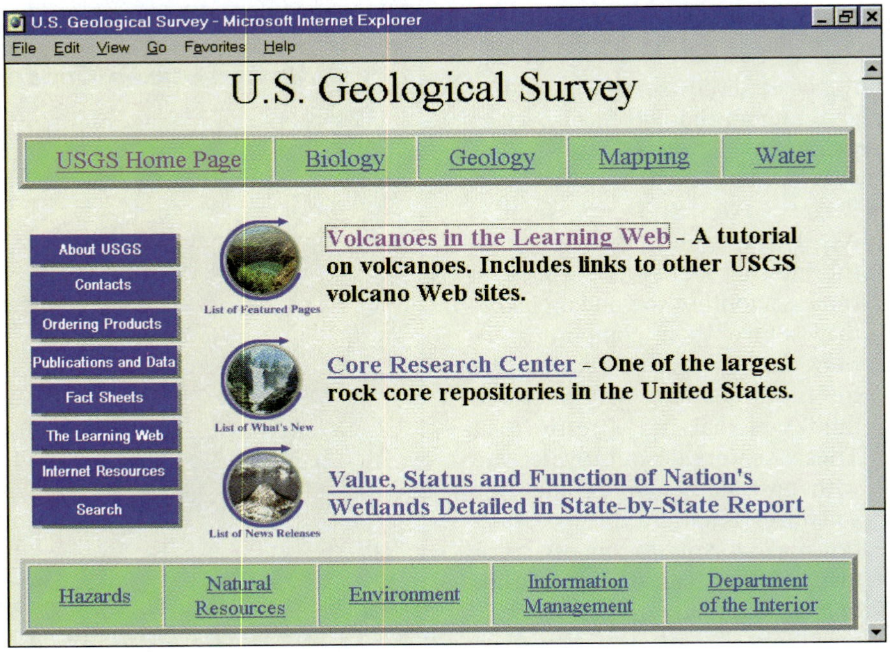

The browser courtesy of Microsoft

Internet addresses—URLs

When you are connected with a site on the Web, you can click hyper links to jump from page to page. As you do so, you'll see addresses displayed by the browser that look like the ones listed here.

When you point to a hyper link, the address that it will jump to may be displayed by your browser on the status line. Clicking the link takes you to that address. When navigating the Web this way, you needn't know anything about addresses because you're jumping from page to page using hyper links. However, to go directly to a site, you type in its address, its uniform resource locator, or URL for short. You see lots of URLs in newspapers and magazines these days. These URLs are basically "pointers" to documents, movies, photos, and so on located on computers somewhere. You may want to visit those sites. Using URLs, if it's out there, you can get to it.

http://www.freesoft.org/Connected/index.html
http://beast.cc.emory.edu/Jargon30/JARGON.HTML
http://www.mckinley.com/browse_bd.cgi?Internet
http://www.freeloader.com/dlfl.htm
http://home.microsoft.com/tutorial/menu.html
http://www.msn.com/tutorial/default.html
http://www.msn.com/tutorial/surfing1c.html
http://www.tiac.net/users/hope/intbib.html
http://www.unitedmedia.com/comics/dilbert/
http://www2.pbs.org/internet/
http://www.ncsa.uiuc.edu/

Typical URLs

Count Your Blessings

While a lucky few million in the rich world amuse themselves in cyberspace, half the human race has never made a telephone call.
The Economist, May 18, 1996, p19.

The anatomy of a URL

Each page on the Web has its own unique URL. Even some elements on a page have separate URLs. For example, a graphic or frame will have a URL that is slightly different from the page it is a part of. URLs have a number of elements including the name of the server (the actual computer), and the path to the file on the computer. Let's look at an example:

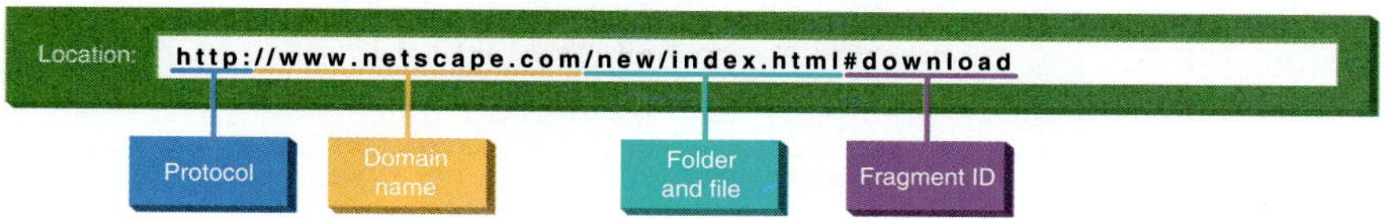

In this example, the URL has the following elements:

- The http specifies the protocol, in this case hypertext transport protocol—the language the World Wide Web uses to tie pages together. A protocol is simply an agreed upon set of standards that allows computers to talk to one another. Since the Web isn't the only Internet service, you may occasionally see addresses that start with ftp: (file transfer protocol), gopher:, telnet:, news: (Usenet news groups), or some other name. The protocol is followed by a colon.
- The www.netscape.com part of the address—called a domain name— is preceded by two slashes. This is the name assigned to a computer located somewhere in the world that is permanently connected to the Web. In the name, www stands for World Wide Web, netscape is the name of the company or organization hosting the site, .com is the identification of the type of organization hosting the site—called the top-most domain. In addition to .com, you'll also find top-most domains such as .edu (educational), .gov (government), .mil (military), .org (organizations), and .net (networks). In countries other than the U.S., the top-most domain name is the two-letter code of the country. For example .fj (Japan), .de (Germany), .uk (United Kingdom), and .il (Israel).
- The /new/index.html is the path to a file—it's saying that the document index.html is stored in a folder named /new.
- The #download part of the name, called a fragment ID, is the name of a specific part of the document.

Once you get used to this addressing system, it's really quite easy. You'll soon see patterns. For example, you can often reach a company's page by entering its name into the address. Using www.kodak.com or www.ibm.com will take you to those companies sites. Entering a school's name may have the same effect. For example, www.mit.edu and www.stanford.edu will take you to MIT or Stanford.

Push or Pull?

Although generally the Web is browsed by clicking links or typing in addresses of sites, as we've described, recently programs have been developed that "broadcast" information from a Web site to your computer without your having to do anything once you set up the program. The first approach is called "pulling" because you pull data off the Internet and the second is called "pushing" because the data is pushed onto your system by someone else. One of the first programs that pushed data was by PointCast. This program puts up news bulletins on your computer's screen when you aren't using it for other tasks.

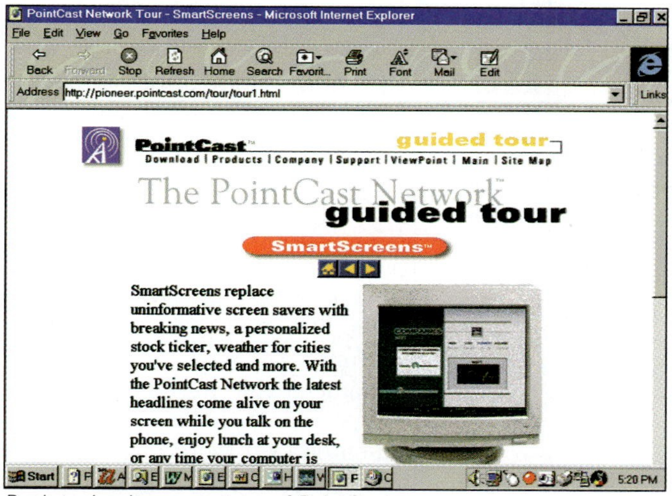

Push technology courtesy of PointCast

It Used To Be a Free Month's Rent

In 1996 a large apartment complex in Anaheim, California, offered new renters 10 hours of free Internet access when they signed a lease. The landlords even offered lessons on using the 'net. Eighty percent of the units were rented within two weeks.

1.5 Locating Information on the Web

Most of us use the Web to search for information, and we can easily follow leads on a topic or jump from topic to topic, free of any concern where the threads may take us. One minute we may be reading a Web page in Italy, the next a page in Australia. The links may lead anywhere, with just the click of the mouse. However, when we're looking for specific information, there are more direct approaches to finding it.

Browsing

People talking about Web often use the terms browsing or surfing which imply a carefree approach to moving from site to site and from topic to topic. This clicking and jumping is fun and there is a certain amount of adventure involved—you never know quite what you are going to run into. There are two ways to browse. The random browse is when you click any link on a page that

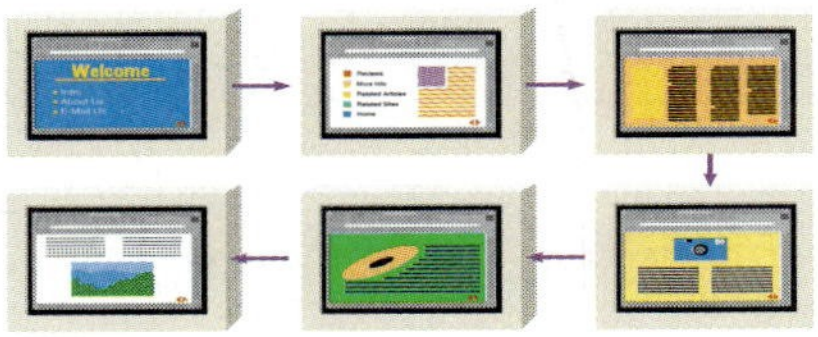

The random browse

catches your attention. In the out and back browse, you click one or more links as in the random browse but then use the browser's Back button to back up to explore another link on a preceding page.

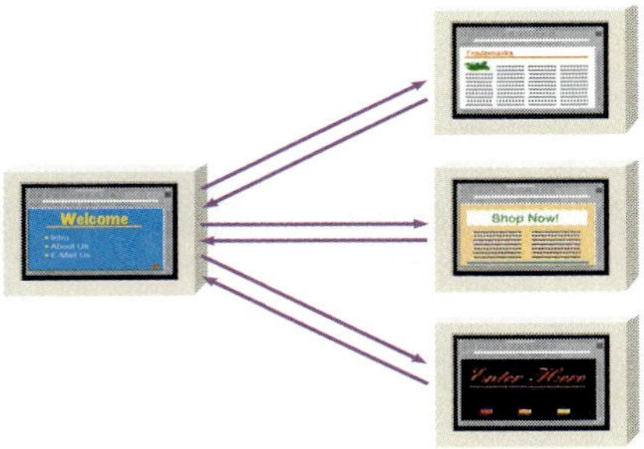

Out and back

Search engines

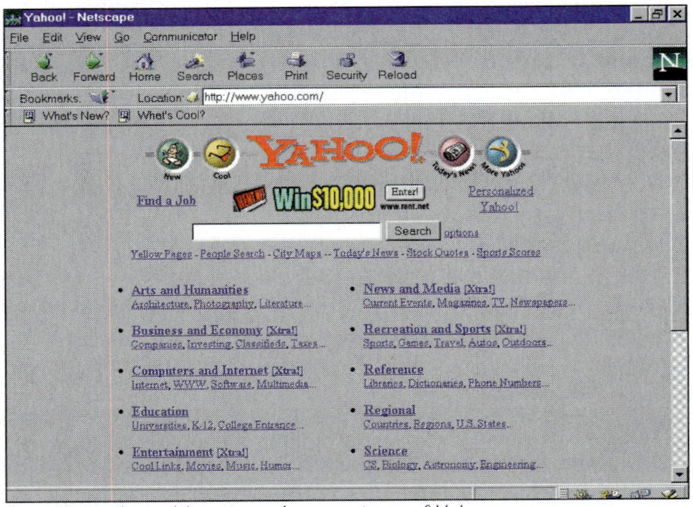

Search engine with categories courtesy of Yahoo
http://www.yahoo.com

It is time-consuming to hop around the world clicking on whatever happens to catch your eye, especially when doing research or looking for specific information. A better way to locate specific information is to use search engines, Web tools that help you find specific sites on the Internet. These are searchable indexes running on powerful computers that let you look up information using key words, words that might be in the document you want to find. When you enter a word or phrase to look up, the search engine locates any documents containing those key words and lists their titles, brief descriptions, and addresses. These listed documents are called "hits" because the computer "hit" on them using your key word. Clicking on the title or address of one of the listed documents jumps you to that page, wherever it is. There are a number of popular search engines on the Web, and each works a little differently.

Some store every word from each site in their databases. When you enter a key word, these engines look up every site containing that word (full-text searches). Other search engines store site names and descriptions and may also offer reviews or ratings. Some are arranged into categories, much like a table of contents in a book. Since each search engine is different, you should explore as many as you can until you get familiar with their strengths and weaknesses.

At one end of the search engine spectrum is the Yahoo Guide (http://www.yahoo.com), designed by David Filo and Jerry Yang while students at Stanford University. Acting as editors, the people at Yahoo make sure you find only the most relevant information much as newspaper editors screen the news and compile only the best into a newspaper. In addition to over thousands of subject entries, Yahoo has a search function and hot lists featuring new and interesting sites. To jump to any of the thousands of listed pages, you just click its name and hyperlinks take you there automatically.

Unlike Yahoo, where the list is edited and polished by people, Alta Vista (http://www.altavista.com) is a search engine that locates documents by brute force. It sends out a program named Scooter to wander the Web and return documents that it finds to the Digital site. As this program, called a Web spider, sends back new documents, an index program at Digital is busy extracting key words from the documents and storing them in a large database along with the addresses of the pages they came from. When you search for key words, Alta Vista looks them up in this database and gives you the addresses where documents containing them can be found. Alta Vista can index 3 million Web pages a day. When you enter a keyword, you may get thousands of hits. A scientist at the World Wide Web Consortium said "Alta Vista is a sort of tribute to brute force. They're sucking the entire Web through a huge pipe. They have more disk space than anyone else."

Lists

In addition to the search engines, there are also subject indexes, directories, or lists of interesting sites created by organizations, companies, or individuals. Frequently, when you visit a well-designed page, you'll find lists of other sites that you can jump off to. The good thing about lists is that they have been screened by someone. If the person is an expert in the field, the chances are the sites are worth visiting. Below is a list of sites recomended by the Library of Congress.

Tours

A tour connects, or threads, a sequence of Web pages into a story. Subject area experts, acting as tour guides, devise sequences of pages, existing and new, that tell stories about their specialties. The accompanying software allows you to move forward and back along the thread of pages. Often the tour is accompanied by narration in the form of text or sound.

Geographical or map directories

You can approach the Web geographically. A number of maps have been developed. Clicking on a country shows its subdivisions such as states or provinces. Clicking one of those shows its cities. At any level of zoom, you can display a list of the Internet resources in that region. CERN's the Virtual Tourist offers a clickable world map listing academic and scientific sites on the Web.

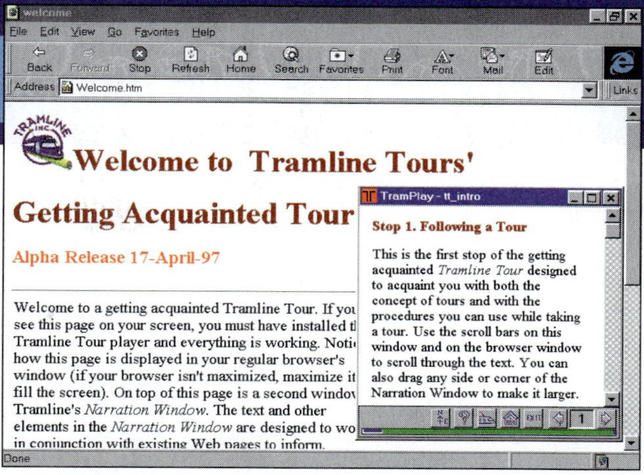

Web tours courtesy of Tramline
www.tramline.com

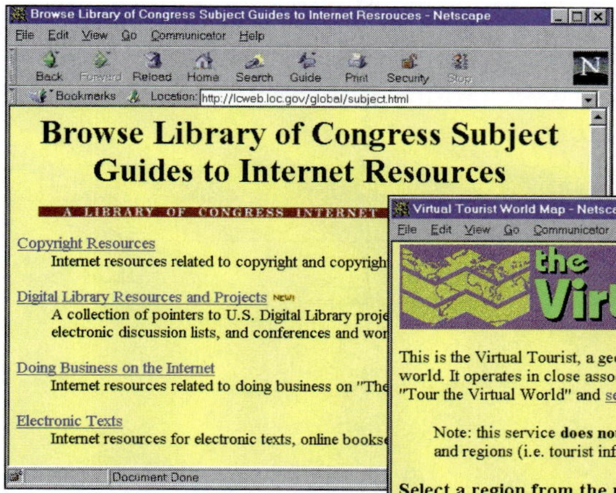

List or directory courtesy of Library of Congress

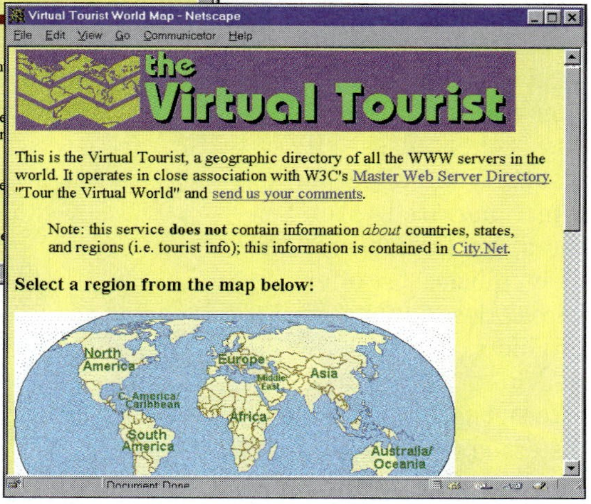

The Virtual Tourist courtesy of Kinesava Geographics
http://www.vtourist.com/webmap/

Web Spiders

A search engine needs a list of key words and a list of the names and addresses of the sites where those words are found. These lists are called indexes because they are much like the indexes in books. Indexes are typically created by software programs called spiders, wanderers, or robots, which crawl the Web. They automatically go to a page and compile a list of all the significant words that it contains, then follow any links on that page to other pages and repeat the procedure. As they move around the Web the spiders process huge amounts of data and compile the results into a database accessible at a single Web site. Thus when you go to that site and look up any word it has indexed, it can display a list of other sites where that word can be found. Spiders and search engines put a strain on the Internet because of the large amounts of data transferred by these programs.

1.6 Web Multimedia

Imagine television in the 1940s. There was almost no programming, the pictures were small and fuzzy, and why "of course" black and white, very few stations were broadcasting, and very few people had sets to view the broadcasts. By the late 50s all this had changed. The Internet today is like television in the 40s. Before too long, it will be richer and more useful than television could ever be. It's already alive with graphics, sound, animations, movies, and even virtual reality—no more than primitive samples of things to come. We'll get into many of these technologies later, but for now here's a sampling of what you might encounter on the Web.

Narrow bandwidth

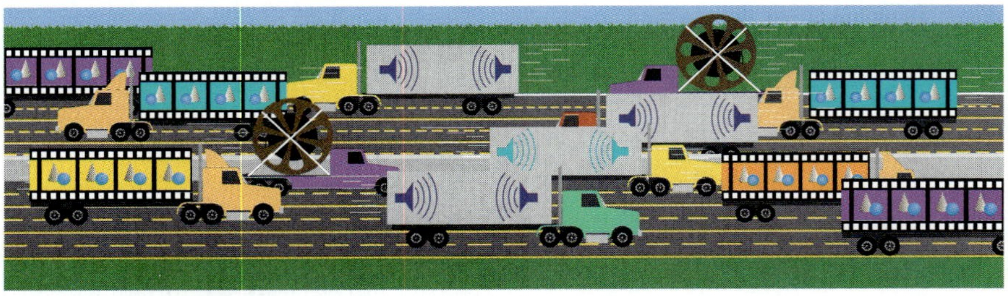

Wide bandwidth

Bandwidth

Bandwidth—How big is your pipe?

For your computer to display any contents of the Web, those contents must first be transferred from the computer they are stored on to your computer. With text, this happens very quickly. However, movies, animations, and sound take a lot longer because their files are larger. Since these files can be huge, you will experience delays because the biggest problem with the Web is its carrying capacity. Think of rush hour traffic on a single-lane dirt road. Now think of it on an 8-lane expressway. One road has a lot more carrying capacity than the other. In computing we refer to carrying capacity such as this as bandwidth (see Chapter 9). Speaking more loosely, it's sometimes referred to as a pipe—as in, "you can see video if you have a big pipe." Text, like that found in memos and letters, can be sent down a dirt road; it doesn't require much bandwidth. However, audio and especially video require a lot of bandwidth, ideally big, wide superhighways. As you'll see in Chapter 10, there are techniques to speed things up. For example, files are compressed so they are smaller and can be sent faster. Also a process called streaming is used so you don't have to wait for an entire file to arrive before you can play it. Streaming receives and stores enough of a broadcast so it has a reservoir to draw on, and then begins playing that part back while the rest of the data is received in the background. The streaming process is a way to give the playback a headstart.

Web sound and video sounds

You can tune into Web radio and TV broadcasts and listen to live broadcasts or call up older ones from the archives. The ability to send sound and video over the Internet also has other uses. It makes it possible to offer narrated Web tours, let buyers preview music, or offer verbal descriptions of products.

Video over the Internet is one of the fastest-growing applications. For companies with high-speed internal networks or expensive connections between offices, on-line video is here now. However, for the rest of us connected over phone lines, video over the Internet still has limited use. It is often just a small, fuzzy, jerky image. It will take more readily available high bandwidth connections from the phone company, the cable company, or others to make it a reality. It's just a matter of time. Intel's Intercast technology shows one possible future for television. It brings together broadcast TV and the Internet. Background information can be fed from an Internet site and displayed on the screen along with the program.

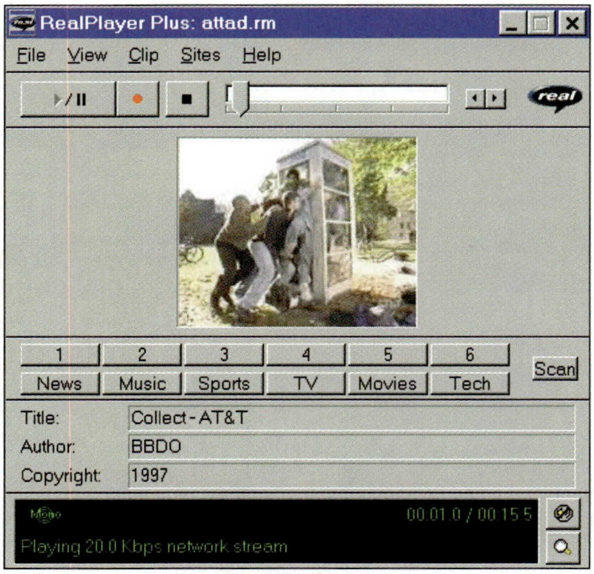

Web video courtesy of RealAudio

Internet phone

With the right software, people can talk over the Internet for the cost of Internet access—there are no additional charges. The only hardware required is a sound card, microphone, and speakers. Older phone programs allow conversations to go only one way at a time, much like CB radio. Others, called duplex, allow them to go both ways at the same time so you can hear the other person while you talk.

Intelicast courtesy of Intel

Multimedia

Full multimedia—graphics, sound, video, and animation—is widely available over the Web. Using technologies such as Shockwave and Java, these presentations can be transferred to your computer and played there. You'll learn more about this form of presentation in Chapter 10. Shown here, a presentation allows you to fly over a part of the San Andreas fault on the San Francisco peninsula. You can play the movie backward and forward at different speeds, play frame-by-frame, or jump to any marked section with a slider control.

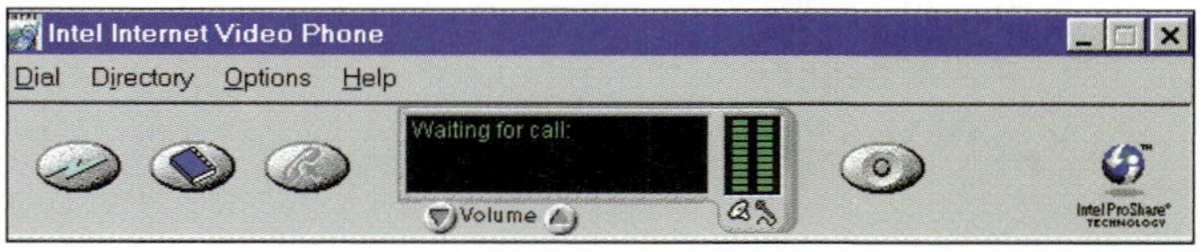

Internet phone courtesy of Intel

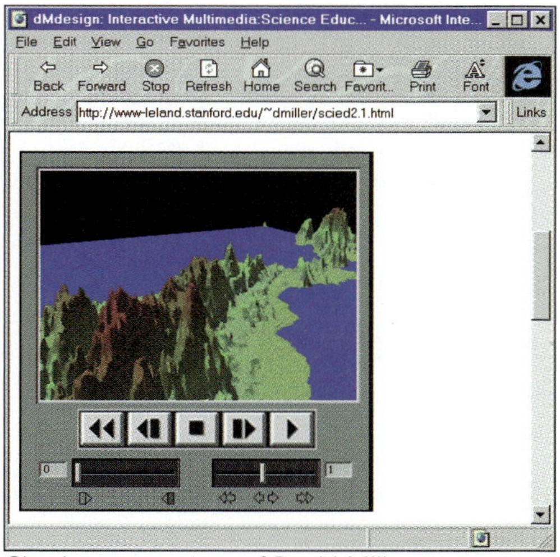

Shockwave courtesy of David Miller
http://www-leland.stanford.edu/~dmiller/scied2.1.html

Helper Applications and Plug-Ins

It wouldn't surprise you to walk into a car dealer's showroom and find that the price of a car doesn't include a stereo, leather upholstery, and various gadgets. You expect to pay extra for them. The same is true of Internet browsers. But you usually don't have to pay for helper applications. To make all the latest technologies available, browsers make provision for improvements and enhancements. After a browser is developed computer companies create helper applications or plug-ins that enhance the browser's capabilities. Eventually, the functions of some of these become popular enough to be absorbed into the main browser and new types of browsers are introduced.

Now It's on Cable!

The Internet is now available in some homes through a subscription with the local cable TV company. These connections can be 100/1000 times faster than using a phone line and a modem. They require a special device called a cable modem. With a cable connection, multimedia and video are displayed as big, bright, fast-moving pictures.

1.7 Enhancing and Testing Your Understanding

Summary

- When two or more computers or other devices are connected together so they can communicate with one another, they form a network. The largest computer network in the world is the Internet.
- The Internet has a number of different services such as e-mail, Gopher, ftp, telnet, and Usenet news groups, but by far the most popular is the World Wide Web, or the Web.
- The Web is a series of interconnected documents stored on a computer somewhere called a site or Web site.
- When you use your computer and a software program called a browser to visit a site on the Web, your screen displays a document called a home page.
- Web pages have highlighted words, buttons, or pictures that are hypertext links or links containing the address of another document. When you click a link you jump to that address.
- HTTP (Hypertext Transfer Protocol) is the protocol used by the Web.
- HTML (Hypertext Markup Language) is the language used to format Web pages.
- Large companies usually have a person called a webmaster in charge of their site.
- To use the World Wide Web you need to be connected to the Internet through a service provider—a company with a high-speed direct connection to the Internet.
- Organizations needing a permanent Web presence are directly connected to the Internet through a service called a presence provider.
- Individuals who need just temporary access to the Web use dial-up access. This can be gained using a modem or other device to connect to an access provider.
- To connect to the Internet over a telephone line, you need a phone connection that uses Serial Line Internet Protocol (SLIP) or Point-to-Point Protocol (PPP).
- Direct service providers, such as AT&T, give you a connection to the Internet and storage space on their computers so you can use e-mail and transfer files.
- Commercial on-line services such as CompuServe, America On-Line, or Microsoft Network can also connect you to the Internet. In addition, they also give you access to their own on-line service and e-mail.
- URLs (Uniform Resource Locators) are addresses of pages on the Web. URLs list a protocol (http), a domain name (www.netscape.com), and/or sometimes the name of a folder and document (/new/index.html).
- Search engines on the Web let you look up information using key words that might be in the document you want to find.
- The index of words in a search engine is compiled by a software program called a spider, wanderer, or robot that wanders the Web looking for documents.
- Movies, sound, and animations are sometimes sent slowly because the Internet lacks sufficient bandwidth.
- Software called helper applications or plug-ins enhances a browser's capabilities.
- The Web offers radio broadcasts, phone service, and multimedia. Television and video are still primitive because of a lack of sufficient bandwidth.

Review Questions

True/False

1. **T F** The largest network in the world is the one called Internet.
2. **T F** The most popular Internet service is the World Wide Web.
3. **T F** The Internet and the World Wide Web are two names for exactly the same thing.
4. **T F** To make a connection to the Internet over the phone lines, you use what's called dial-up access.
5. **T F** Commercial on-line services such as CompuServe, America On-Line, or Microsoft Network don't give you access to the Internet.
6. **T F** Once you have clicked a link to display a new page, you can't back up to the page you jumped off from.
7. **T F** The term surfing refers to the way you click links to move from site to site.
8. **T F** Multimedia is slow over the Web because your connection doesn't have enough bandwidth.
9. **T F** Streaming refers to playing a movie or sound file before all of it has been transferred to your computer.
10. **T F** You can hold phone conversations over the Web.
11. **T F** A number or television networks already are broadcasting live shows over the Web.
12. **T F** To run any multimedia on the Web, the presentation must be transferred to your system and played there.

Fill-In the Blank

1. When two or more computers or other devices are connected together so they can communicate with one another, they are said to form a network.
2. To navigate the Web and display the contents of its pages, you use a software program called a ______________ .
3. When you visit a site on the Web, the first page you often see is called a home page.
4. When you point to a link you can click, your mouse pointer changes to a ______________ .
5. The protocol used by the Web is called HTTP.
6. The language used for format Web pages is called HTML.
7. Web addresses are called URLS.
8. Large companies have a person, called a Webmaster in charge of their site.
9. All connections to the Internet are made through a ______________ .
10. Coffee shops that offer Internet access are called ______________ .
11. Search engines look up the word or words you search for in an ______________ .

Multiple Choice

1. The Web is a series of interconnected documents stored on a computer somewhere called a _____.
   - **a.** Web site **b.** Domain name
   - **c.** Home page **d.** None of the above
2. Pages on the Web have spots you can click called ________.
   - **a.** Hyperlinks **b.** Links
   - **c.** Hot spots **d.** All of the above
3. Links you can click include ________.
   - **a.** Highlighted text **b.** Highlighted graphics
   - **c.** Buttons **d.** All of the above
4. In addition to the Web, the Internet also includes ________.
   - **a.** e-mail **b.** Gopher and ftp
   - **c.** Usenet and telnet **d.** All of the above
5. To put a site on the Web, you need to work with ________.
   - **a.** An access provider **b.** A presence provider
   - **c.** The Internet Authority **d.** A design company
6. For a phone connection to the Web, you need a ________.
   - **a.** PPP or SLIP connection **b.** Modem
   - **c.** Browser **d.** All of the above
7. A browser ________.
   - **a.** Displays Web documents **b.** Allows you to navigate
   - **c.** Allows you to copy, print, and transfer documents
   - **d.** All of the above
8. To locate information on the Web you can ________.
   - **a.** Use a search engine **b.** Select sites from lists
   - **c.** Click any link to browse **d.** All of the above
9. When you use a search engine, the term hit refers to ________.
   - **a.** A popular site **b.** Any site that's listed
   - **c.** Any site that's related to popular music
   - **d.** Any site related to baseball
10. Search engines search indexes of key terms that are often compiled by a software program called ________.
    - **a.** An insect **b.** A spider
    - **c.** A worm **d.** None of the above
11. The term bandwidth refers to ________.
    - **a.** How much data can be sent through a connection
    - **b.** The amount of data in a multimedia file
    - **c.** How fast your computer is
    - **d.** None of the above
12. Browsers are enhanced by installing ________.
    - **a.** Plug-ins **b.** Helper applications
    - **c.** A new version **d.** All of the above

Visual Quiz

1. Circle and label the name of each part of the following URL
   - ~~**a.** Fragment ID~~ ~~**b.** Domain name~~
   - ~~**c.** Folder and filename~~ ~~**d.** Protocol~~

   http://www.freesoft.org/Connected/index.html#page2

   D B C A

Research Projects

1. Locate the name and telephone number of a local Internet access provider. Also get the name, telephone number, and e-mail address of their help desk so they can help if you have any questions getting connected. Ask the following questions:
   - **a.** What is the one-time connect charge, if any?
   - **b.** What is the monthly charge?
   - **c.** How many free hours there are?
   - **d.** What is the cost per hour is after you exceed the maximum free hours?
   - **e.** Do they supply an e-mail address?
   - **f.** What browser is required? Do you have a choice?
2. The PACE Web site at http://www.mhhe.com/PACE contains Web sites directly related to the contents of this chapter. Access that site's home page and select Chapter 1, The Internet and the World Wide Web, to see a list of the topics contained in this chapter. Take each of the tours.

CHAPTER

2 Information Technology

An Overview

After decades of slowly expanding behind the scenes, information technology has suddenly exploded into public view and seems to be everywhere in the popular media. It is like a huge wave that has been building offshore, only to become noticeable as it crests and then breaks on the beach. At the moment, we are all caught in the boiling surf of this breaking wave. It's almost impossible to avoid media stories on such topics as the information superhighway, multimedia, or the Internet. These aspects of information technology are just a few of the thousands of ways in which information technology will affect the way we work, live, and play.

If you'd been a modern Rip Van Winkle, sleeping soundly for the past few years, you would awake and be astounded by the new technology vocabulary and new issues we all have to deal with on a daily basis.

Information technology has changed dramatically. Not long ago, information was processed using electrical or mechanical devices such as typewriters, calculators, and telephones, which stood by themselves as if on information processing islands. Calculations made with a calculator had to be typed into a document. Documents then had to be hand-carried to a copy machine. Secretaries always had to be on hand to answer the phones. Mail could be sent only in printed form. Today, all these devices and procedures have been automated and many of their functions are controlled by built-in microprocessors, computers on chips that give even ordinary devices extraordinary capabilities. But it's not just that individual machines have been improved. The most dramatic change is how all those old information islands are being connected by digital highways. Once information is created in any form, text, sound, pictures, animations, or movies, it can be instantly distributed or changed to other forms in a variety of ways. Technology is advancing so rapidly that previously isolated fields such as television, phone, computers, and radio are all converging into a single field.

Surfing hundreds of digital TV channels for home shopping, infomercials, news, and entertainment won't be all that demanding. But that's only the crest of a huge information technology wave that is rolling into your path. To be ready for this new wave both at home and at work, you have to understand the concepts and applications of digital information technology. In this chapter we continue that journey of understanding.

Objectives

After completing this chapter, you will be able to:

- Compare and contrast information, information technology, information processing, and the information processing cycle.
- Describe hardware, systems, software, and data.
- Identify applications of information technology in business, industry, the home, education, the arts, entertainment, and science.
- Explain how hidden computers are quietly at work without your involvement.
- Describe the role of people in the information technology field.

Information *n.* 1.is the act of informing or the condition of being informed, the communication of knowledge, and knowledge derived from study, experience, or instruction.

Technology *n.* 1. the application of science, especially to industrial or commercial objectives.

TODAY–AN OVERVIEW

2.1 Information Technology-An Introduction

You may hear terms such as information age, information society, and knowledge workers and wonder what they all mean. What these and other such terms refer to is one aspect or another of the increased role that information technology is playing in our lives and careers.

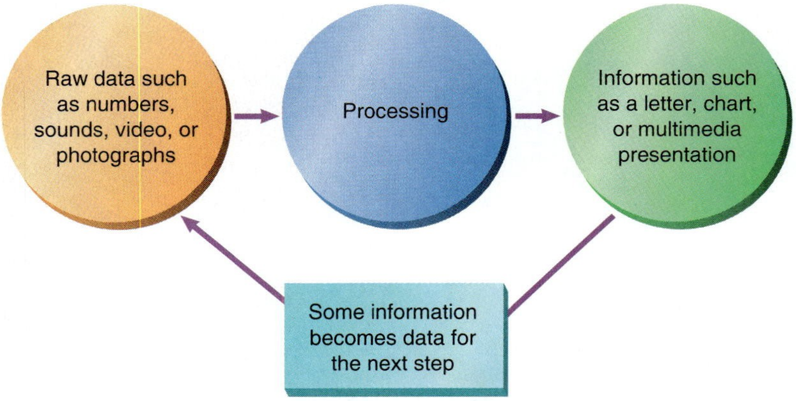

Data versus information

What is information technology?

The phrase information technology (IT) refers to the creation, gathering, processing, storage, and delivery of information and the processes and devices that make all this possible. Think of these processes and devices as tools that make your life and career better or more efficient. The tasks that are handled using information technology continue to increase almost on a daily basis. For example, a few years ago, cinematography and photography didn't use computers at any point in the process. Now, computers are in cameras, processing labs, and the editing room. No matter what field of study you major in, or where you are employed, you'll be sure to find information technology at work.

Information technology can do at least three things:

- Information technology can process raw data into useful information. Imagine taking a series of tests throughout college. The score on each doesn't tell you much. You could be sick the day of a test, or not doing well on the topics currently being covered. Over the semester, you'll get a whole range of test scores between A and F. Each of these is just one bit of raw data. To turn these scores into information, you need to convert them into a grade for the course, useful information because it's a measure of your overall performance. The teacher can now decide if you pass or fail the course.
- Information technology can recycle processed information and use it as data in another processing step. For example, already processed data can be combined with other information to increase its impact. The grade you get in a course can be combined with your other course grades to calculate your quality point average. This is very useful information because it's a single grade based ultimately on hundreds of pieces of data, all the tests you've taken.
- Information technology can package information in a new form so it's easier to understand, more attractive, or more useful. All the quality point averages of your classmates can be sorted into descending order or placed on a chart so you can quickly see how you stand in relation to everyone else.

Hold On, The Ride's Going to Get Faster

Recently, the chief information officer of a large corporation was asked to reflect on the pace of change in the computer field. She responded, "There has been as much change in the last five years as there was in the previous 25. And the frightening thing is that the rate of change is accelerating."

Hardware and software

Information technology stands firmly on two legs: hardware and software.

- The term hardware is applied to any of the physical equipment in a system, usually containing electronic components and performing some kind of function in information processing. Hardware includes not only the computer and devices such as screens and printers, but also all the elements used to tie information systems together. For example, the telephone wires that you see overhead are hardware, as are antennas used for cellular phone calls, and even the familiar television set in your kitchen or dorm room.
- Software is instructions that guide the hardware in the performance of its duties. There is a slogan button floating around that makes this distinction very clear—"Hardware: the part of the computer that you can kick. If you can only curse at it, it's software."

Hardware versus software

The information processing cycle

Processing information is only one step in a larger process called the information processing cycle. This cycle has five steps: input, processing, output, storage and retrieval, and distribution and communication. Computer hardware and software are used in each step. Let's look at each step and the hardware and software that applies to it, as illustrated on the right.

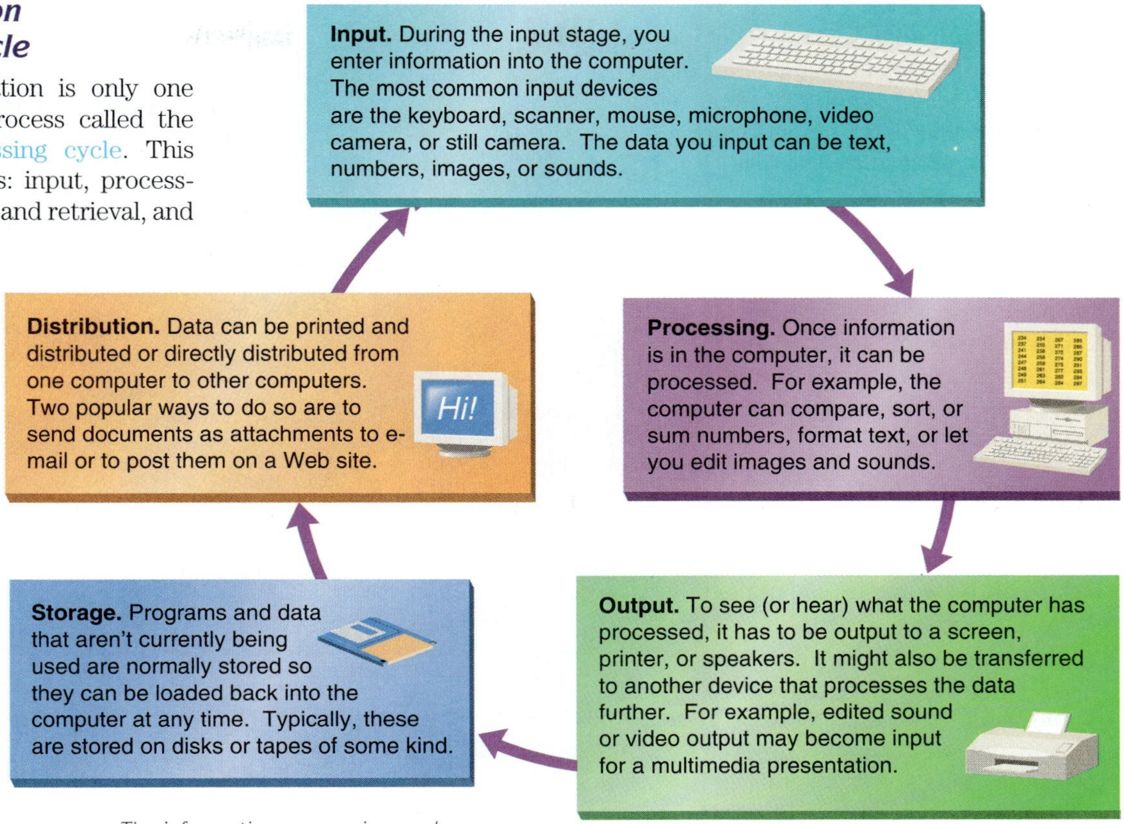

The information processing cycle

Information processing at work

The information processing cycle is put to work every day in an almost endless variety of ways. A typical application is simulating a process instead of actually doing it. For example, in the aircraft industry it's much safer and less expensive to test an airplane on a computer than to actually build one and then fly it to see how it performs. Here a model of an airplane has had sensors mounted on its surface. These can measure such things as temperature or pressure. The output from these sensors is then fed to a computer (input) and converted into a color image (processing) that is easy to interpret. This picture can then be displayed on the screen or printed out (output) and then distributed and stored. Only after an extensive series of such tests has been completed is the plane actually built and flown.

The simulated plane courtesy of International Business Machines

The finished plane courtesy of International Business Machines

2.2 Information Systems

When you interact with information technology you are involved not with a single piece of equipment, but with an ever expanding system of interconnected parts. Let's take a closer look at what information systems are.

UNIVAC courtesy of Hagley Museum and Library

What is a computer?

The computer is at the very heart of modern information technology. It may be in its own air-conditioned room, or sitting on your desktop, or bouncing around in your briefcase, or in your watch—coordinating your activities. Whatever its size, and wherever it is, it's called an electronic digital computer. Let's look at what the three words in this phrase mean.

- Electronic means the computer uses electronic components to process information.
- Digital means the computer processes and stores digital signals that are based on the binary digits, 0 and 1. These two digits can be used in combinations to represent any kind of data including words, numbers, sounds, pictures, and movies.
- Computer means a device that can store and process data based on a set of instructions. The instructions, called a program, are stored in the computer when in use so they can be executed automatically.

What is a system?

A system is a set of related parts that operate together to perform a specific function. You encounter systems every day. For example, as you read this, the parts of your circulatory system, heart, lungs, and blood vessels, are moving blood and energy through your body.

Information systems, like all other systems, are assembled from parts, or components. What you consider to be the components or the system depends on the scale you choose to examine. For example, on a small scale, a personal computer is a system containing such components as a keyboard, a screen, and a printer. However, to an engineer, this system is assembled from smaller systems called subsystems. On a larger scale, the personal computer is a component plugged into a network of other computers and other devices in the organization. That corporate network may in turn be connected to the Internet. It's an unending spiral of small systems being assembled into larger and larger systems. All of these integrated and interconnected components and systems are designed to provide you with the information you need, in the form you need it, when you need it.

Bad Fortune Tellers

Foreseeing the future is never an exact science but these folks couldn't have done much worse with their predictions.

"Computers in the future may weigh no more than 1.5 tons."

Popular Mechanics, forecasting the relentless march of science, 1949.

"I think there is a world market for maybe five computers."

Thomas Watson, chairman of IBM, 1943.

"I have traveled the length and breadth of this country and talked with the best people, and I can assure you that data processing is a fad that won't last out the year."

The editor in charge of business books for Prentice Hall, 1957.

"But what ... is it good for?"

Engineer at the Advanced Computing Systems Division of IBM, 1968, commenting on the microchip.

"There is no reason anyone would want a computer in their home."

Ken Olson, president, chairman and founder of Digital Equipment Corp., 1977.

From the business section of *The Kansas City Star*, Jan. 17, 1995

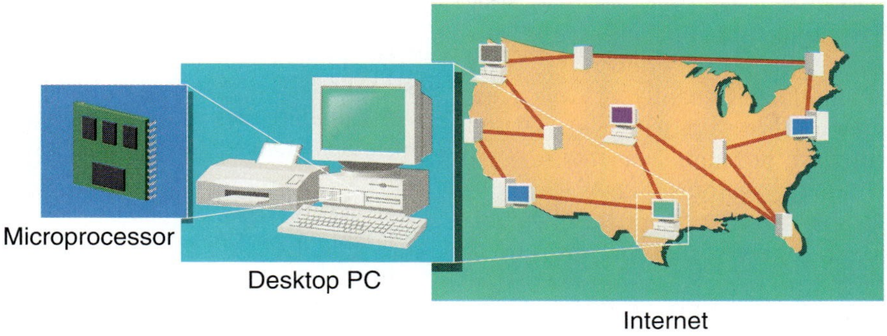

Systems and subsystems

People

Information systems haven't yet gotten to the point where they can think, plan, and react to changing circumstances, so there is still plenty of room for people. George Forrester Colony, a leading consultant, says, “Information in our industry is virtually free. No one will pay you for the information. They will pay you, however, for your analysis of what it means. And that takes a lot of thinking.” Increasingly, the more highly paid jobs are going to people who know how to use information technology to enhance their skills and performance regardless of the field they're in. Only a small minority of these people actually design computers or information technology systems. The vast majority are end-users such as film directors, dancers, athletes, managers, office assistants, and others who use computers in their own fields of endeavor. It's these end-users around whom the entire business of information technology is focused.

You May Know a Computer Personally!

One of the earliest motivations for developing calculating machines was to prepare tables of numbers, first for navigation and then for artillery. Before electronic computers were invented, the people who prepared these tables were called "computers" since they performed computations. If you look in a dictionary from any period before the mid-20th century, the definition of "computer" will refer to a person rather than a machine. Therefore, it's possible that you know someone who was once a computer.

People in computing courtesy of International Business Machines

Its Not a Man's World Anymore

Until very recently, the computer field was almost entirely dominated by men. Initially slower to create change here than in some other fields, women have made amazing progress over the past decade. A survey by *ComputerWorld* in the summer of 1997 reported that women now compose 22% of information systems managers, 30% of systems analysts and computer scientists, 33% or programmers, and 45% of the overall workforce.

2.3 Software and Data

Although the key component in information technology is the computer, it is just an expensive paper weight until you load it with software. It's software—very detailed and precise step-by-step instructions—that allows the computer to perform useful work. In many ways computer hardware is like an actor and the software is like a script. Change the script and an actor performs a new role. Change the software and a computer does the same.

What is software?

What makes a computer so powerful is that a set of instructions called a program or software can be loaded into it so it can process data without your intervention. There are two kinds of software in widespread use: operating system software and application programs.

- An operating system, such as Microsoft Windows, makes it possible for your system to run and perform useful work. It does this by allowing you to load application programs.
- Application programs, such as Microsoft's Word and Excel, or Adobe's Photoshop and PageMaker, are what you use to do word processing, financial planning, photo manipulation, or newsletter layouts. (See at right and below.)

Software from A to Z

The number of application programs from which to choose is truly astounding. Recently, it was estimated there were well over 100,000 software products available for just windows systems. They run the gamut from A (Adobe Photoshop used to edit photographs) to Z (WinZip used to compress large files). Within the huge mountain of choices, the most popular types are:

- Browsers used to navigate the World Wide Web and send e-mail.
- Word processing programs used to write letters, memos, and reports.
- Spreadsheet programs used to manipulate and analyze numbers.
- Database management programs used to store data in a highly structured way.
- Graphics programs used to create line drawings, manipulate photographs, or make presentations to audiences.

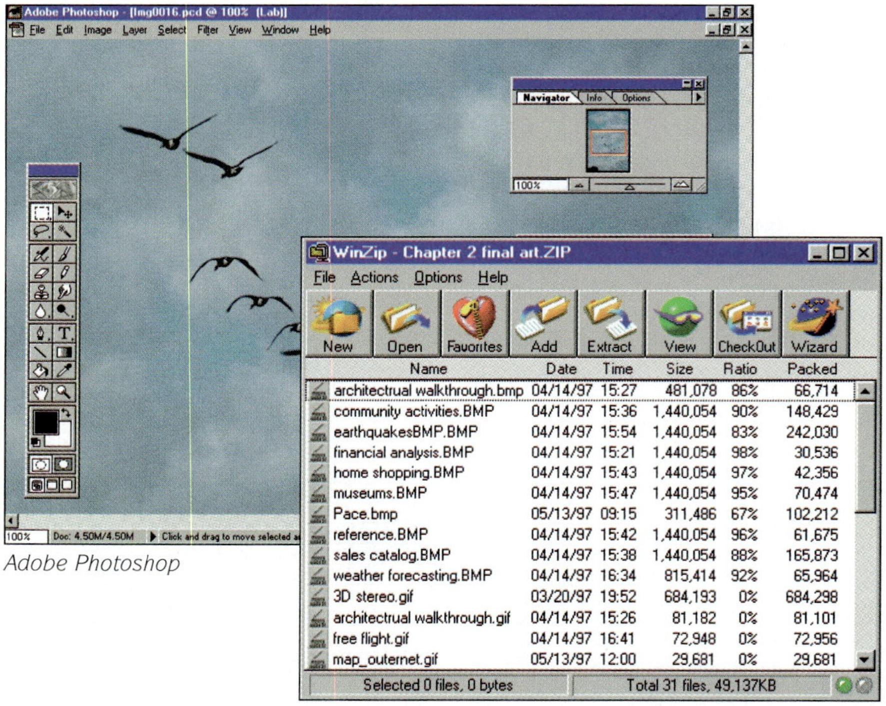
Adobe Photoshop

WinZip

Operating system and application programs

Data Is, Data Are?

Computing is such a fast-moving field that it is sometimes hard to keep up with changes in vocabulary. Until very recently, the term data was always used as a plural and datum as a singular. However, data is increasingly used for both forms of the term. Even a recent ad from Hewlett-Packard used a headline with the phrase Data Is.

What is data?

A dictionary describes data as individual facts, statistics, or items of information. Whatever we call them, data are the raw materials of information processing. Hardware and software are not designed or selected in isolation. Their purpose is to process and present data. A few of the most commonly types of processed data are shown and described on the right. The applications of computers and the variety of data they process are amazing. Data range from letters and numbers, called simple data, to sounds and videos, called complex data.

Data Type	Description
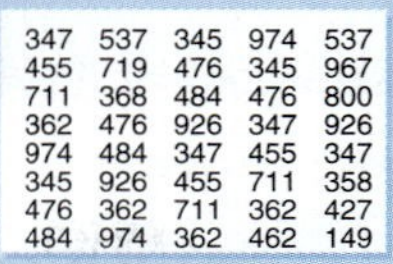	Numeric data, first for the military and then for corporations, was the first data to be widely processed on computers. Currently, data such as inventory, sales, and payrolls are still processed in basically the same way.
	Words are processed into memos, letters, reports, articles, books, and scripts. You can even format them into final form—a process called *desktop publishing*.
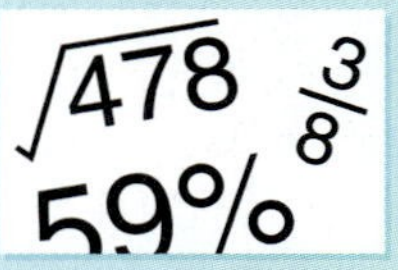	Numbers are used by almost everyone at some time to make calculations. They might be as simple as calculating an annual budget for a year at college or as complex as the budget used to operate the national government.
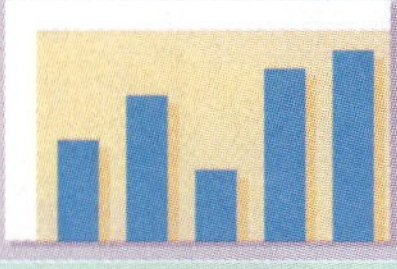	Charts that plot numbers can be used to illustrate and inform more effectively than tables of numbers.
	Photographs and other graphics can be stored, edited, and inserted into other applications to illustrate documents or become part of a multimedia presentation.
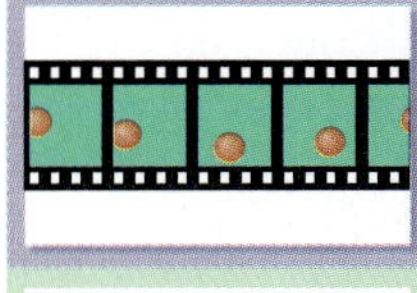	Animated characters and objects move about on the screen to entertain and inform.
	Sounds, such as music, speech, or sound effects, can be stored, edited and played back.
	Videos, such as interviews or movies, are stored as data so they can be edited or played back.

Data isn't what it used to be

Not too long along, the vast majority of information was just lists, integers, times, and characters. Although not at all simple to collect, analyze, and distribute, this kind of data is referred to as simple data (or primitive) because it is relatively simple when compared to some of the other types of computer data now being used. Shown here is a Web page at the Library of Congress where you can search for books. The data that is then displayed is typical of simple data.

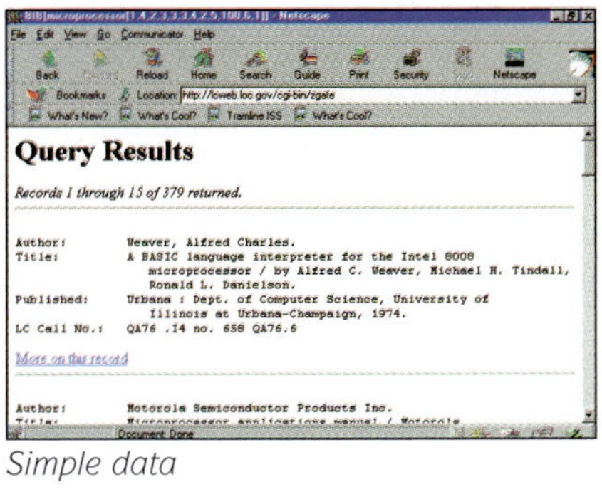

Simple data

Over the past few years there has been explosion of other types of data, complex data, that is much more than just integers and characters. For example, videoconferencing, phone calls, movies, sounds, and animations are routinely used both in business and on the Internet. Handling this diverse information has been made possible by the tremendous increases in computing power over the past decade. Here is a Web page at the Library of Congress that allows you to listen to old recordings and view old movies from the 1870–1920 period of American stage entertainment. This kind of data was not processed and distributed by computer until very recently.

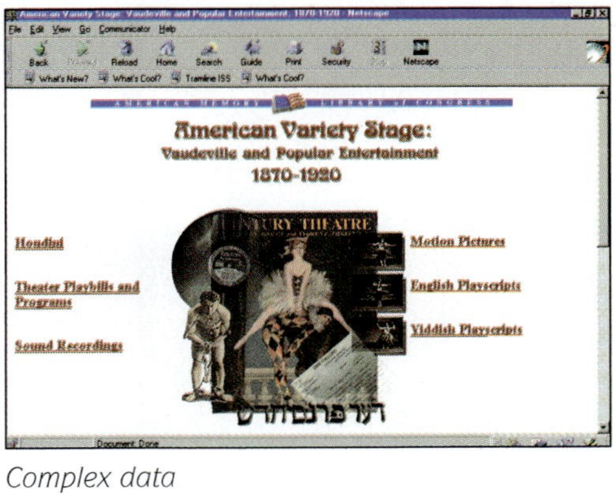

Complex data

2.4 IT in Business and Industry

Home-based work courtesy of International Business Machines

Computers are everywhere and business and industry are using them in new ways unthought of even a decade ago. You could list thousands of these modern uses. Were the power to computers ever shut off, business and industry would almost instantly grind to a halt. Without computers, the modern corporation could not even exist. Computers have become so deeply embedded in information processing and communications systems that almost no activity would be possible without them. Failure of the phone and electrical company's computers would shut off those services. Automated assembly lines and tools would no longer operate. Even many watches, clocks, and stoves in the cafeteria would stop. In fact, many employees' cars wouldn't start so they'd have to walk home.

Computers in business

Let's look at some of the ways computers are integrated into business and industry.

Transaction processing. Most business activities involve transactions with suppliers, employees, or customers. Computers can make these transactions possible.

Home-based workers. Now that it's so easy to connect a computer at home to all of the computers at the office, more and more people are working at home. These telecommuters often work one or more days without the traditional commute. The same ability to communicate so easily makes home-based businesses easier to start and operate.

Desktop publishing. Producing finished business literature is one of the uses of computers in business. Using desktop publishing programs, or even sophisticated word processing programs, people can create sales letters, brochures, price lists, newsletters, and even book-length manuals.

Transaction processing courtesy of International Business Machines

Desktop publishing courtesy of Hewlett-Packard

Financial analysis. Financial analysis is performed throughout the company, from top management on down. People can analyze investments, sales, expenses, markets and other aspects of the business using both numbers and graphs.

Computers in industry

Computers have had a major impact in industries where products are designed and manufactured. Computer-aided design (CAD) is used to develop products. Computer-aided manufacturing (CAM) is used to produce them.

Product design. Designing complicated products can require the efforts of thousands of people working together. This teamwork is greatly enhanced through the use of computerized design.

Factories. Factory floors are becoming increasingly populated by computers used for many purposes including inventory control and planning and process control. Computers are also used to run robots that create, finish, assemble, and test products and their components.

Robot courtesy of Andy Sacks/Tony Stone Images

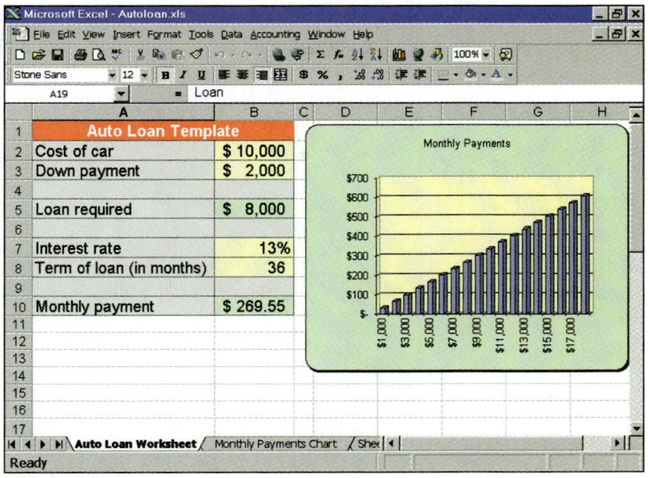

Financial analysis

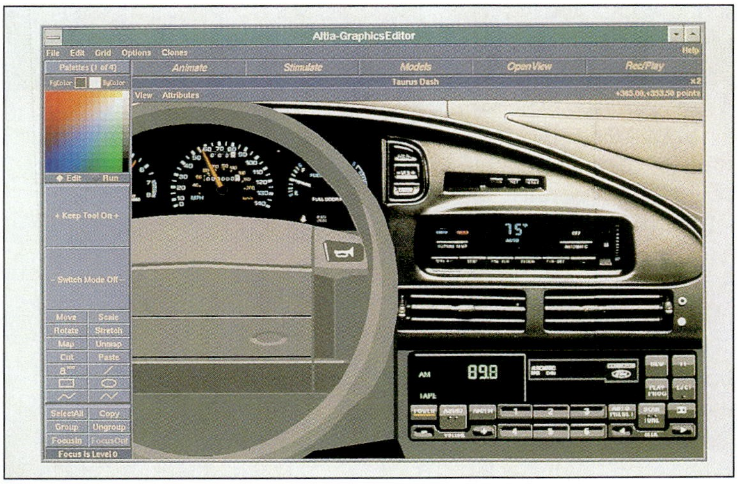

Product design courtesy of Altia

Architectural walk-throughs. To help visualize what a building's design will really be like when it's built, computerized "walk-throughs" are prepared. One application of this technology on the Web is to let you walk through an auditorium or stadium to select a seat for an event. Before you purchase a ticket, you can even "sit" in the seat to see what your angle of view will be like.

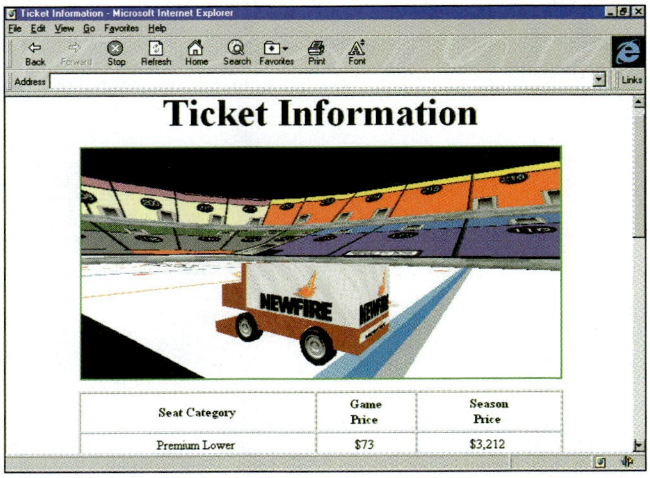

Architectural walk-though courtesy of Newfire
http://www.newfire.com/frames.htm

2.5 IT in the Home and at Play

Recent surveys indicate that computers are in almost one-half of American homes. This is an amazing statistic and it is still rising. Originally, a computer in the home was used to duplicate the role of the computer at work or to play games. However, those simple roles are changing. Home computers are rapidly becoming major information tools.

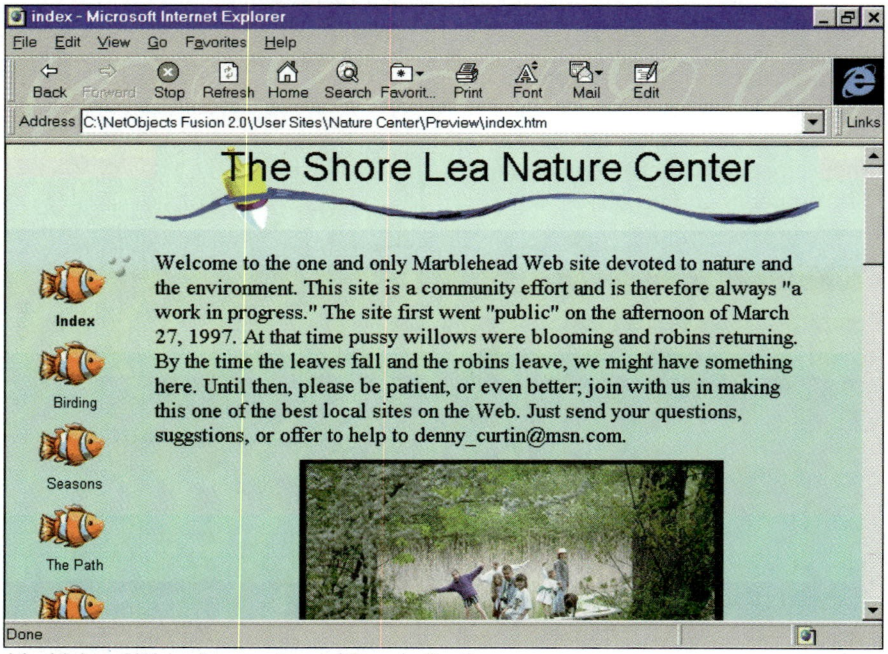

Marblehead Web site courtesy of Dennis Curtin
www.marblehead.org

Computers in the home

When your computer is connected to a CD-ROM drive, encyclopedic information, movies, and animation are instantly available. When your computer is connected to the phone line, you can visit your community or other parts of the world. The lines between work, play, and education are beginning to disappear as resources once available only at work or school become available in the home.

The World Wide Web or on-line services such as CompuServe, America On-Line, and Microsoft Network are only a phone call away. From the comfort of your home you can research school or work assignments, exchange e-mail, join special interest groups, download files, play games, or make airline reservations.

Sales catalogs are now being computerized and many catalogs are even being put on the Web so you can do on-line shopping. You can buy a new pair of hiking boots from L.L. Bean on the Web.

Community activities are listed on a Web site in Marblehead, Massachusetts. Accessible from any computer with an Internet connection, you can read the newspaper, shop want-ads, or read reviews of the movie in town. It's all there, in one easy-to find source.

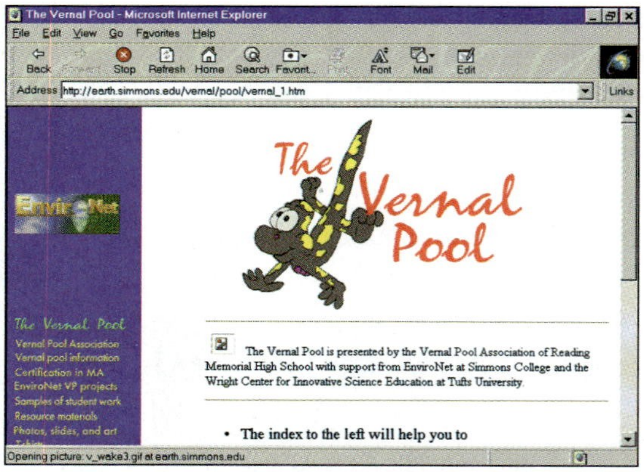

Vernal Pool site courtesy of Leo Kenney
http://earth.simmons.edu/vernal/pool/vernal.htm

Web site courtesy of L.L. Bean
http:\\www.llbean.com

Reference materials from science and engineering data to phone numbers are being digitized. You can get much of this material on CD-ROM discs or over the Internet. Students are often able to research their assignments without leaving their homes or dorms. Here's a popular site on vernal pools and their significance to our environment.

Home shopping and banking are growing areas of computing. The largest on-line bookstore in the world allows you to purchase books and movies, and it even gift wraps. (See display on right.)

Amazon Web site courtesy of Amazon.com

> ## WHAT'S GOING ON HERE?
>
> Here are just a few signs that something big is happening around the home.
>
> A few years ago, the phone came into your house on a wire and the TV signal on an antenna. Now, it's just the opposite.
>
> Now you watch the TV and answer the phone, but it won't be long before you are watching the phone and answering the TV.

Flight Simulator courtesy of Microsoft

Computers at play

For some time games have been played on personal computers, and increasingly the line between education and games is growing happily thin. Below, the Magic School Bus, an educational game for 6-to-10-year-olds, takes them on a tour of the solar system. Computers can add some fun to the learning process.

Above, a flight simulator allows both children and adults to experience being a pilot and to learn about the principles of flying.

Magic School Bus courtesy of Microsoft

2.6 IT in Education and Training

Although they are a long way from fulfilling their potential, computers may become the most amazing teaching tool ever invented. They can pace instruction differently for each student, animate important concepts, and use interactivity to involve students in the learning process. In the future, imagine having immediate access to all the great books and articles ever written, all the great photographs ever taken, and all the great paintings ever painted. Your access to educational resources will seem unlimited by today's standards.

Computers in education

Computers have been used in schools since the first Apples were introduced in the 1970s. However, their impact was limited then because there weren't enough of them and educational computer programming was poor. As technology has advanced, educational software has become a major influence at all levels from elementary schools to universities. The ability to connect computers and students together over a network such as the Internet opens up fantastic educational opportunities.

At colleges computers are increasingly being used to teach courses like the ones you're taking. For example, this text has a computer application integrated into it. For another view of what's discussed here, you can use the PACE CD, a multimedia program that parallels this text. To get more in-depth and up-to-date material, you can use the PACE Web site and tour up-to-the-minute topics that have been preselected for you.

Elementary and secondary schools are using computers to play multimedia educational programs and to teach kids to explore the Web for information.

Museums use interactive multimedia to educate visitors on topics from science to fine art. Increasingly, these exhibits are being put on the Web so you can visit them on your own.

Photo of classroom courtesy of International Business Machines

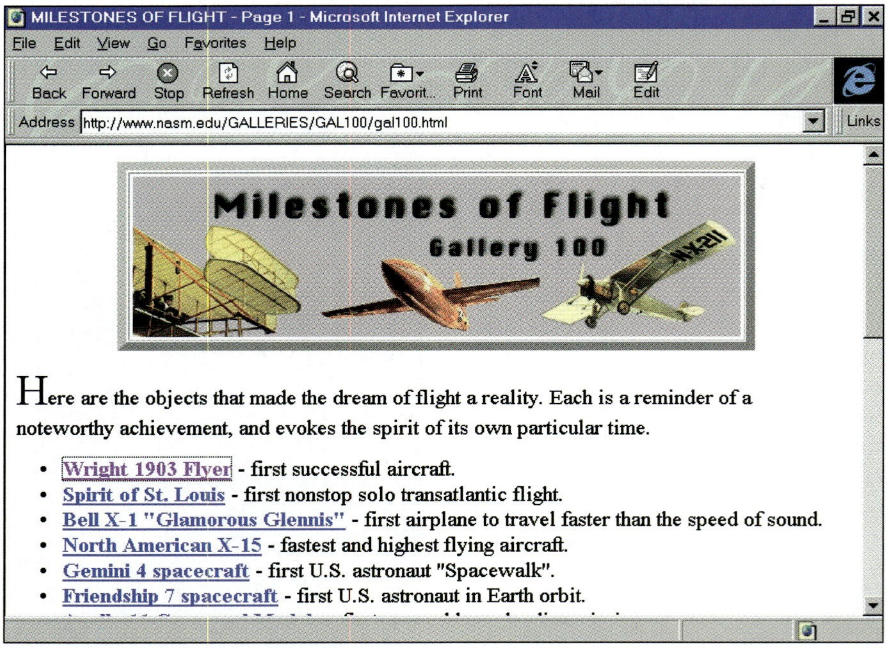

Web museum exhibit courtesy of Smithsonian Institution
http://www.nasm.edu/GALLERIES/GAL100/gal100.html

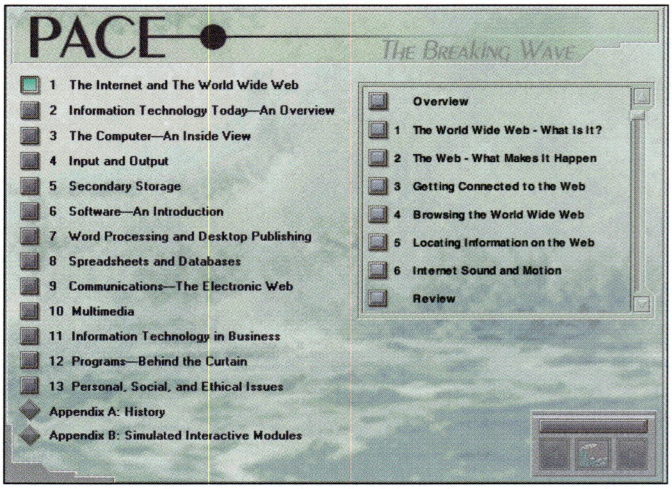

PACE CD that accompanies this text

Computers are especially valuable for students with special needs. A computer's voice recognition capabilities and its connection to the Internet make it possible for special education users to participate in learning experiences from which they may have previously been excluded.

Photo of classroom courtesy of Apple Computer

Computers in training

Training programs in business and various organizations are huge and expensive. To save money and improve performance, companies are using computer-based training (CBT) to train people on procedures and techniques they need to know in their jobs. CBT ranges from relatively simple on-line help systems to sophisticated virtual reality machines such as those used by the military and airlines to train pilots. Training programs in organizations rely heavily on information technology such as video conferencing.

Photo of virtual reality training courtesy of Paradigm Simulation, Inc.

Photo of corporate training courtesy of International Business Machines

Virtual reality is just in its infancy but when developed it will allow you to visit other worlds and feel as if you were really there. It's now used to train pilots by putting them into a cockpit where they can experience the sensations associated with various maneuvers as they learn to handle them.

2.7 IT in Entertainment and the Arts

Information technology isn't limited to the areas where you would most expect to find it such as business and industry. It's also being widely used in the entertainment and arts worlds. From making movies like Pixar's *Toy Story,* the first all digital animated feature film, to modern dance at the local college to professional sports, computers are at work. There are almost as many applications as there are entertainers and artists.

Computers in entertainment

Computers are used in entertainment to create or enhance a production or performance. The tools have become so sophisticated that it's becoming almost impossible to distinguish between the real and the artificial in film and photography.

Movies. Computers are widely used to create special effects in big-budget movies. They are also extensively used behind the scenes to edit film during the production process. Below, in a scene from the movie *Death Becomes Her*, sculpted models of Meryl Streep's head were scanned with a 3D scanner to help create complex twisting motions.

Meryl Streep photo courtesy of Cyberware

Music. Music software allows you to edit recorded music or even create your own. With the computer connected to a stereo or synthesizer, you can be your own composer and audience. Both artists and sound engineers are finding novel applications for computers in their work.

Music courtesy of International Business Machines

Animation courtesy of Ray Dream

Animation. In earlier days, Bugs Bunny, the Road Runner, and Wile E. Coyote were laboriously hand-drawn in the hundreds of thousands of frames needed for each cartoon but now computers are doing much of the repetitious work.

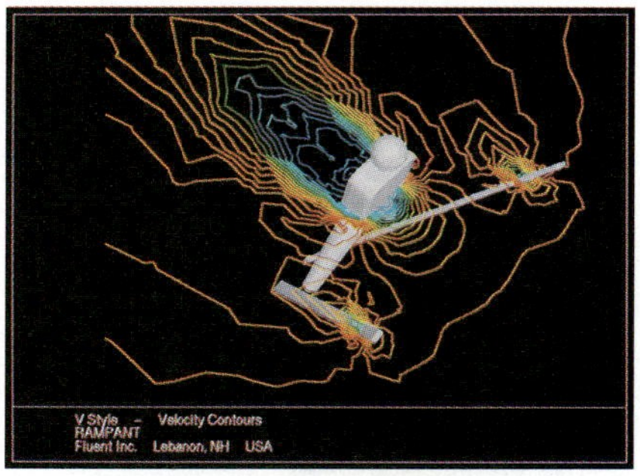

Ski jumper courtesy of Cray

Sports. If there is a perfect way to pitch a baseball, execute a spin on the ice, or take off from a ski jump, computers can find it. By analyzing the motions of the best athletes, sports trainers and kinetic specialists establish profiles. Other athletes can compare themselves to these profiles and try to improve their own styles and moves. Above, a Cray computer has been used to analyze the air flow over and around a ski jumper. Red indicates high speed and blue low.

Computers in the arts

You might think the arts would be the last place to look for computers but you'd be wrong. Computers play a growing role in dance, photography, painting, and many other arts.

Dance. The fluid movements in dance are difficult if not impossible to convey through printed text and drawings. However, with computers the movements can be brought to life through animation. On the right, reflectors are mounted at key points on a dancer's body and the computer compiles a simple animation of her movements for later analysis.

Painting. The computer and the Web allow you to visit most of the art museums in the world from your home. It may not be quite the same as being there, but you have access to much that you might never otherwise see. Computers are also being used by experimental artists. Whenever new tools appear, artists are among the first to use them to explore the frontiers of their medium.

Art courtesy of Suzanne Dougherty

3D stereograms allow you to see a 3D object hidden inside a single image. This process, called a single-image random dot stereogram (SIRD), was developed in 1979 by Christopher Tyler. Seeing the image within the image comes easier to some people than to others. Look at the picture on the right. Focus on a point in the distance and stare blankly. Then move the image into your line of sight without focusing and move it slowly forward and backward. At some point you should be able to bring the image into focus. If this doesn't work, stare at the image and look cross-eyed.

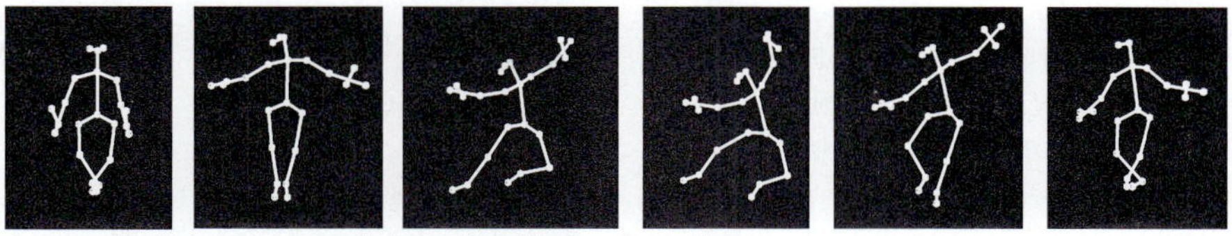

Dance photos courtesy of Adaptive Optics Associates

Photography. Photos can be digitized by dropping them off at your local photo store, or you can take digitized photos with one of the newer digital cameras. Once photos are digitized, you can manipulate them in hundreds of ways. You can cut people from one photo and paste them into another seamlessly. You can no longer trust a photograph to be a "faithful witness," as photos once were called.

Before After
Photos courtesy of Jerry Uelsmann

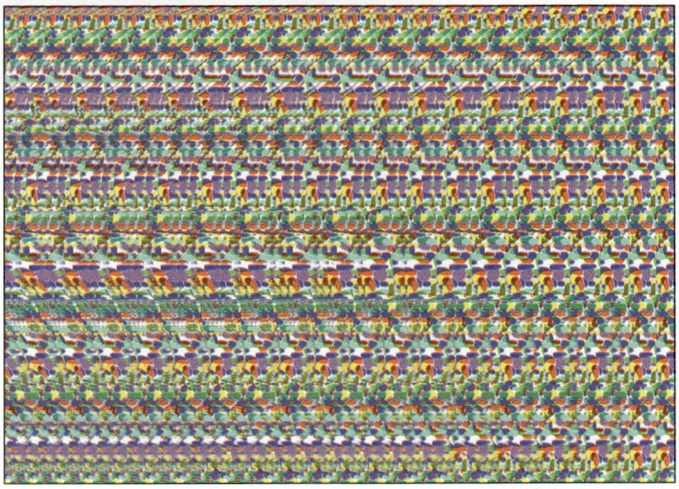

SIRD courtesy of *http://www.softsource.com/s_othcrc.gif*

2.8 IT in Science, Engineering, and Math

Some of the earliest users of information technology were scientists, engineers, and mathematicians. Their reliance on IT has only grown with the development of high powered desktop workstations.

Computers in science and engineering

Powerful computers are used to simulate dynamic processes in the practice of science and engineering.

Chemistry. Supercomputers have numerous applications in chemistry and physics. Below, a chemical process is explored on the computer and colors are used to distinguish between various reactions.

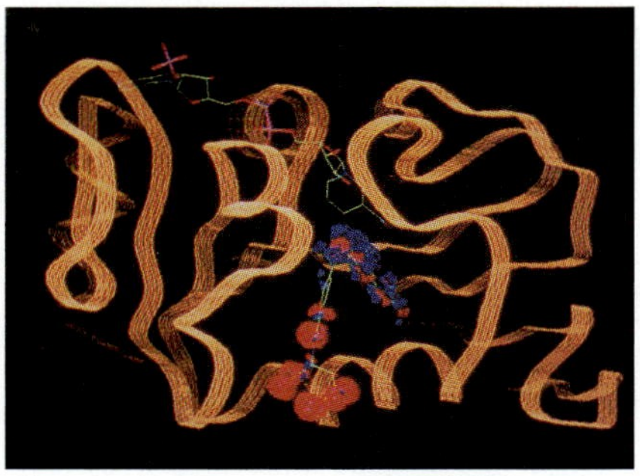

Chemical process courtesy of Cray

Medicine. Physicians use information technology to understand the human body and to diagnose disorders. Below is a computer-generated scan of a human brain.

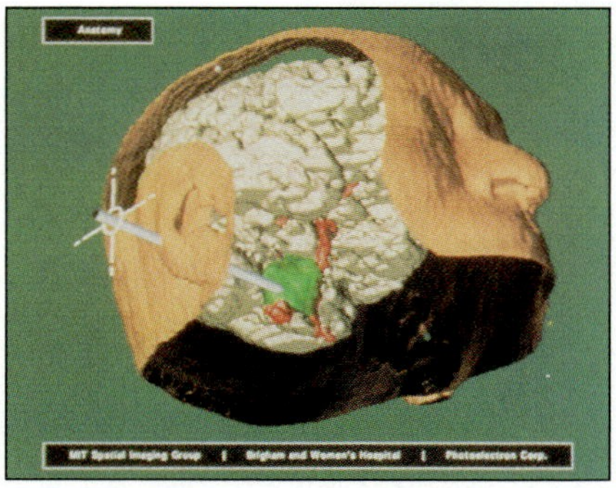

MRI spatial imaging by Stephen Benton courtesy of MIT Media Lab

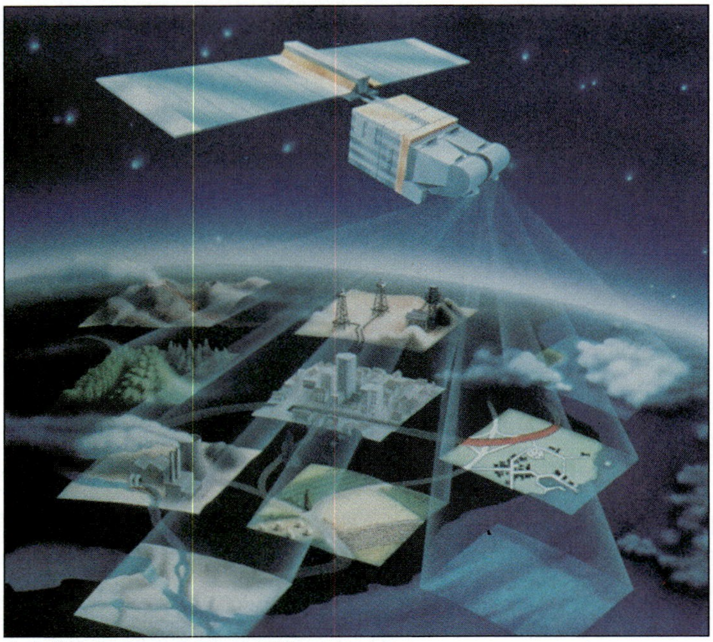

Satellite image courtesy of Spot Image

Satellites. Satellites are commonly used in information technology. They may simply relay signals from one point to another, eliminating the need for wires between two locations. They also broadcast TV and even Internet signals so they can be picked up by small dish antennas.

Topography. Topographic images can be created from raw data supplied by the U.S. Geological Survey. Using a computerized geographic information system, the map below was created after a major oil spill in Alaska for negotiations with a landowner in Prince William Sound. The map indicates what parts of the Orca Narrows viewshed are visible from the specified point of observation.

USGS topography courtesy of ESRI
http://www.esri.com/base/gis/enviro/103azm.html

Seismology. In an attempt to better understand earthquakes, scientists use computers to gather and plot data. To the right, a map of Southern California earthquake activity has been prepared for viewing on the Internet.

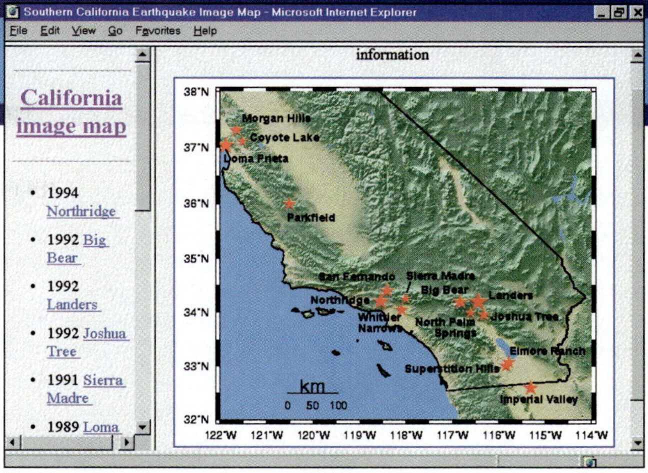

Earthquake map courtesy of USGS
http://www-socal.wr.usgs.gov/slipmodels.html

Astronomy. The Hubble space telescope is one of the most expensive information processing machines ever created. This powerful telescope, launched into orbit around the Earth, is free of the distortions introduced by the atmosphere when ground-based telescopes are used. It can look back almost to the beginning of the universe and transmit the data back to Earth where it is processed and analyzed. Below is one of the thousands of pictures the Hubbletelescope has taken, this one of the Cygnus Loop Supernova Blast Wave.

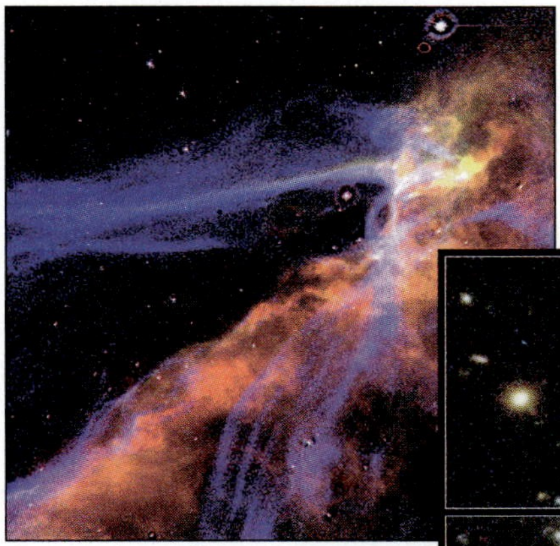

Cygnus Loop Supernova Blast Wave, J. J. Hester (Arizona State University), NASA, STSCI PR-93-01
cloop.tiff from
http://oposite.stsci.edu/pubinfo/tiff/

On the right, three Hubble images show the deepest-ever view of the universe stretching all the way to the visible horizon of the universe. Some of the galaxies may have formed less than one billion years after the Big Bang.

The deepest-ever view of the universe, by the Hubble Telescope
http://oposite.stsci.edu/pubinfo/PR/96/01.html

Computers in mathematics

Here a graphic from Wolfram Research shows some of the visual renderings of mathematical formulas made possible with their Mathematica program. The visual representations make it easier to understand the mathematical and physical principles involved.

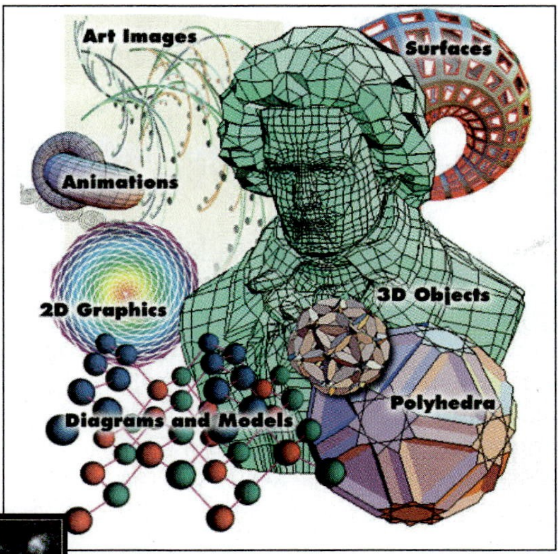

Image courtesy of Wolfram Research
http://www.wolfram.com/look/gallery.html

Fractals are created using simple mathematical functions, but when plotted on a computer, they can be beautiful. What's interesting about fractals is that any small area looks exactly like the entire image. One type of fractal called the Mandelbrot is named after Benoit Mandelbrot, a mathematician who did much of the modern-day pioneering of fractal imaging and applications.

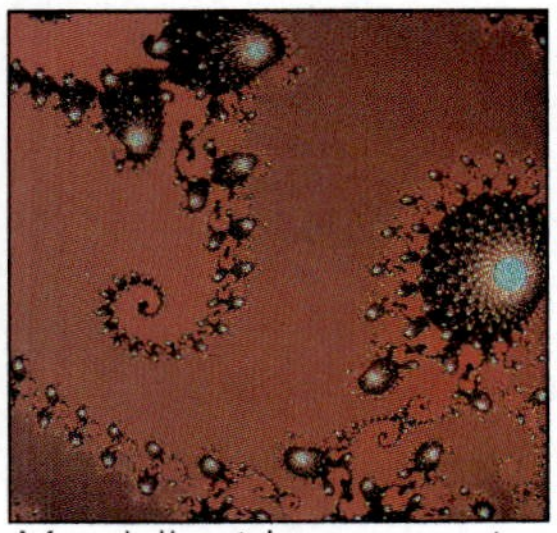

Mandelbrot image courtesy of International Business Machines

2.9 Computers in Hiding

To be a player in the information technology field, you need a lot of training. However, as the field advances, users will need to know less and less about the information technology systems they use. Even today, information technology is at work all around you even when you are unaware of its contributions. In some cases, this is made possible by computers that are embedded in devices. In other cases, the computers work quietly behind the scenes while you interact with a simple interface or just passively watch the results.

Large computer systems you don't see

Many of your daily activities are actually interactions with computers that you don't see.

Airline reservations. When you call to make an airline reservation, an agent enters your request into a computer. The computer then displays all the flights available, the times they depart and arrive, and their fares. If you make a reservation, your request is entered into the computer, and a seat is reserved for you.

Airline reservations office courtesy of American Airlines

Weather forecasting. When you watch or listen to a weather forecast, you're interacting with the output of a massive and powerful system of computers that compile and analyze data from sensors all over the world.

ATMs. When you make a withdrawal from a bank's automatic teller machine, a computer dispenses the money and charges the withdrawal against your account.

Junk mail. When you open your mail, you are likely to find letters automatically generated by computers. Magazines and other businesses often use personalized "computer mail" to try to sell you something.

ATM courtesy of Myrleen Ferguson/PhotoEdit

YOU ARE THE WINNER!!!!

Dear Mr. Smith:

This letter is to inform you that you have won $10,000,000!! All you have to do is return the enclosed card and have it selected from millions of others to claim your prize.

Junk mail

Small computers you don't see

Danny Hillis, founder of Thinking Machines, has been quoted as saying, "I went to my first computer conference at the New York Hilton about 20 years ago. When somebody there predicted the market for microprocessors would eventually be in the millions, someone else said, 'Where are they all going to go? It's not like you need a computer in every doorknob!' Years later, I went back to the same hotel. I noticed the

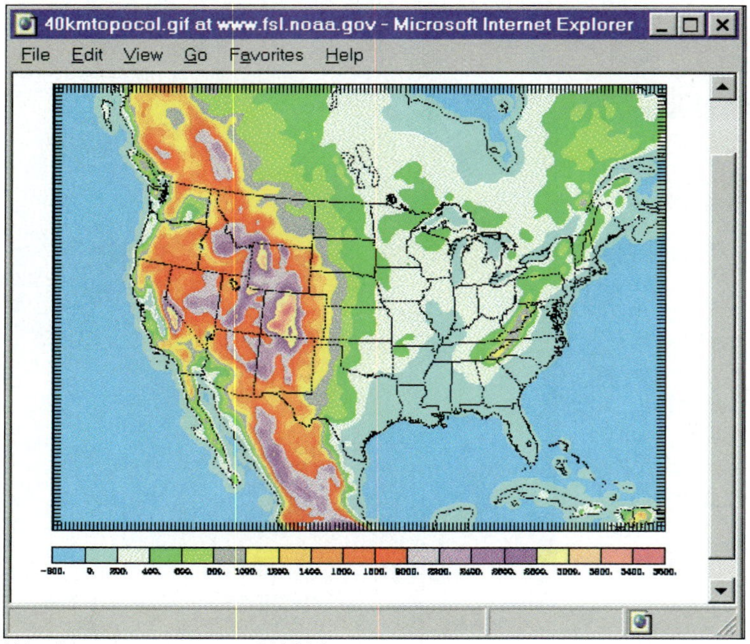

Weather map courtesy of NOAA
http://www.fsl.noaa.gov/frd/maps/40kmtopocol.gif

room keys had been replaced by electronic cards you slide into slots in the doors. There was a computer in every doorknob!" These chips, called embedded microprocessors, are widely used. It's expected that over 100 million a year will be sold by the year 2000.

Automobiles. The chairman of an electronics firm once predicted that by the year 2000, General Motors would be selling more computer power than IBM. In 1970 a car contained about $75 worth of electronics. By the mid-90s this figure had increased to $3,000. Microprocessors, computers on chips, are used to control ignition systems, anti-lock braking systems (ABS), and traction control.

Computer in an automobile courtesy of Delco

Settop box courtesy of DirectTV

Settop boxes may be your connection to the information superhighway. As television becomes digitized and other services are offered over the same line into the house, a computer will be what controls it. Here a settop box for DirectTV may not look like a computer, but it is one.

Watches can calculate your blood pressure or the tides. The one shown here even has a remote control built in so you can check the time while you're surfing the TV channels.

Remote control watch courtesy of Casio

Game machines now have as much power as all but the most powerful desktop computers. They are specially designed to display fast-moving graphics on the screen.

PlayStation courtesy of Sony Computer Entertainment America

Now You Can Use Your Free Hand for Your Cellular Phone

Engineers at the University of Rochester have used a computer chip to create an automatic transmission for a bicycle. It keeps track of how fast you pedal, how fast the wheels are spinning, and how taut the chain is. Using this data and a stored pattern of your preferences, it shifts gears automatically.

2.10 Picture Essay: The Global Positioning System (GPS)

Knowing where you are has always been important. Getting lost has been a matter of life and death for most of human history, as consequences could be fatal. For most of us today "getting lost" means delayed shipments, lost money, higher costs, and frustration. Until recently, navigation required a great deal of experience or very expensive equipment such as that found on airliners. However, with the emergence of Global Positioning System (GPS) technology in 1994, everyone can now locate their position anywhere on the face of the earth for the price of a GPS receiver, which costs as little as a few hundred dollars.

The applications of GPS

The applications of GPS are almost unlimited, even through the system is only a few years old.

Precision farming uses GPS to survey property and guide farming equipment. Satellite images can even be used to analyze property, and then fertilizers and other chemicals can be applied only where they are needed.

Cars and automobiles. GPS is being widely used in ground transportation. GPS units in automobiles can read out audible instructions on when to turn, or they can display your position on moving maps.

Similar devices are used in military vehicles, such as during Operation Desert Storm, when soldiers were able to maneuver in the dark or even in sandstorms when the troops who lived there couldn't.

Tracking commercial vehicles such as railroad cars and delivery trucks is one of the fastest-growing GPS applications, as their positions can be monitored at all times. Police, fire, and emergency medical people are using GPS receivers to determine a response team located closest to an emergency, enabling the quickest possible response in life-or-death situations.

Surveyors can use GPS to help determine locations and positions. When the tunnel under the English Channel was being constructed, one crew started digging from Dover, England and the other from Calais, France. GPS receivers were used to make sure the two tunnels met in the middle.

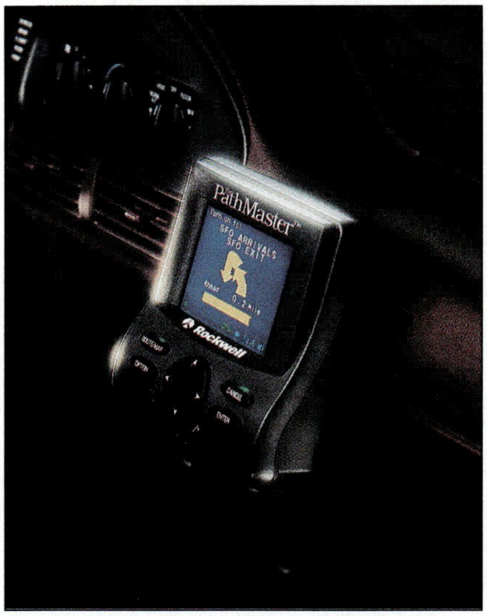

The PathMaster courtesy of Rockwell

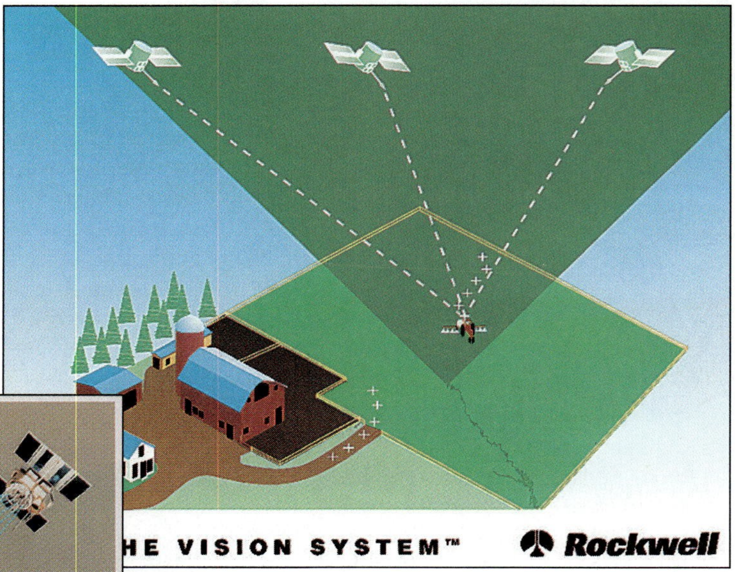

Precision farming courtesy of Rockwell

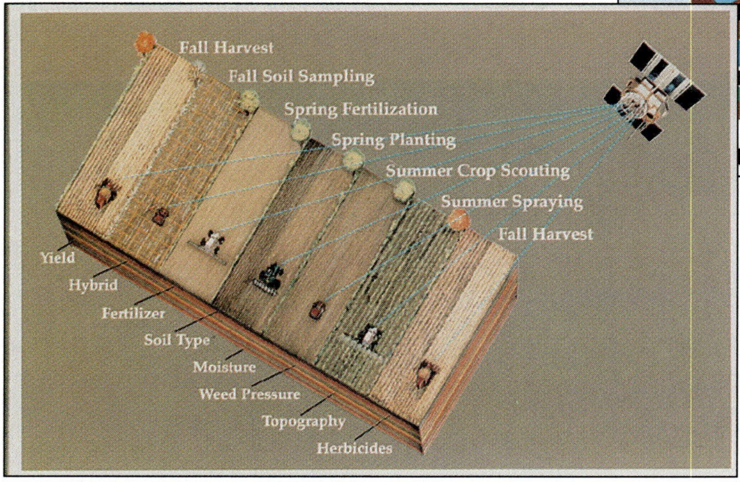

Precision farming courtesy of Rockwell

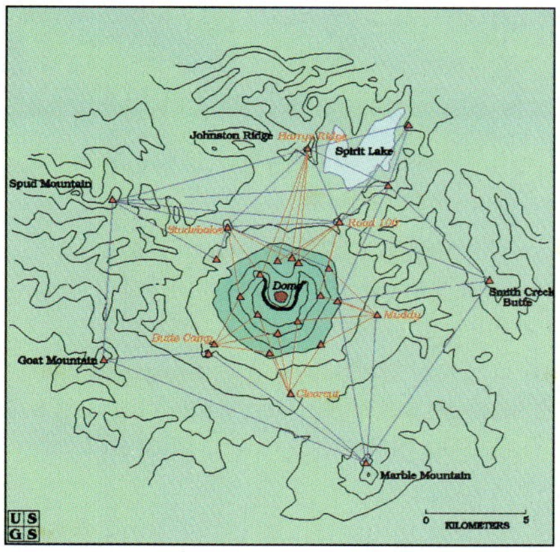

Earthquake monitoring courtesy of USGS
http://vulcan.wr.usgs.gov/Imgs/Gif/Projects/Deformation/MSH/map_outernet.gif

Geologists can use GPS receivers to measure very small shifts in the earth's surface. When mounted on either side of a fault line, they can help detect slippage that would not otherwise be noticeable. When used to surround a volcano, GPS receivers can detect slight movements that might indicate an upcoming eruption.

Air traffic control. A new national system called "free flight" is being developed to control airline flights that use GPS. In free flight, two spatial zones encircle each plane. The smaller zone (shown below in yellow) is called the "protected zone." The protected zone of an aircraft can never meet the protected zone of another aircraft. The larger "alert zone" extends well beyond the protected zone and, upon contact with another aircraft's alert zone (shown in red), signals that action may be required by the air traffic controller and pilot.

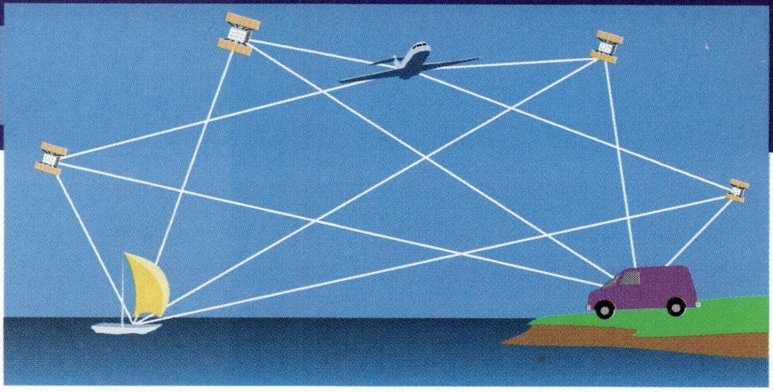

GPS navigational system

Scientists can attach GPS receivers and small transmitters to moving animals such as endangered Montana elk and Mojave Desert tortoises to study their movements and lifestyles. Scientists can even record their observations and positions no matter where they are. Below a biologist in Brazil uses a handheld GPS receiver in wildlife research project.

Biologist using GPS courtesy of Magellan

Free flight courtesy of the federal aviation administration
http://asd.orlab.faa.gov/files/ff_vis.htm

How GPS works

The GPS system has three basic parts: 24 satellites in space, five ground stations that monitor them to make sure they are working, and millions of handheld or mounted receivers.

As the 24 GPS satellites orbit 11,000 miles above the Earth, each takes 12 hours to go around the Earth once. From almost any point on Earth six of the orbiting satellites can be picked up at the same time. Each satellite has a clock that keeps time to within three billionths of a second, and these clocks enable each satellite to broadcast very precise signals.

GPS receiver for a notebook computer courtesy of Delorme

On the ground GPS receivers can calculate how long it takes each signal to arrive from each of the satellites. Even at the speed of light, they will arrive at slightly different times–the closest one arriving first and the furthest last. The receiver then calculates the time differences between the signals and determines the user's latitude, longitude, and altitude.

2.11 Enhancing and Testing Your Understanding

Summary

- News stories on such topics as the information superhighway, multimedia, and the Internet all refer to the new wave of information technology.
- Information technology has changed dramatically during your lifetime as networked computers and other equipment have replaced stand-alone devices such as typewriters, calculators, and telephones.
- Most modern information technology equipment uses built-in microprocessors—computers on chips.
- Once information is created in any form, text, sound, pictures, animations, or movies, it can be instantly distributed to other forms in a variety of ways.
- Technology is advancing so rapidly that previously isolated fields such as television, phone, computers, and radio are all converging into a single field.
- Terms such as information age, information society, and knowledge workers refer to the fact that information and information technology are playing a larger and larger role in our lives and careers.
- The phrase information technology (IT) refers to the creation, gathering, processing, storage, and delivery of information and the processes and devices that make this possible.
- Information technology can process raw data, recycle processed information and use it as data in another processing step, and package information into a new form so it's easier to understand, more attractive, or more useful.
- Hardware is any of the physical equipment in a system and all of the elements used to tie information systems together.
- Software guides the hardware in the performance of its duties. It's these very detailed and precise step by step instructions that allow a computer to perform useful work.
- Processing information is only one step in a larger process called the information processing cycle. This cycle has five steps: input, processing, output, storage and retrieval, and distribution and communication.
- The equipment used in information technology is almost always part of a larger system—a set of related parts that operate together to perform a specific function.
- Information systems, like all other systems, are assembled from parts called components. What you consider to be components or systems depends on the scale you choose to examine. It's an unending spiral of small systems being assembled into larger and larger systems.
- Computers are actually electronic digital computers. Electronic means they use electronic components to process information, digital means they process and store data in the form of the binary digits 0 and 1, and computer means they store and process data based on a set of instructions called a program.
- People who use computers to perform tasks or enhance their performance are called end-users.
- Operating systems, such as Microsoft Windows, make it possible for your computer to run and perform useful work using application programs.
- Application programs, such as Microsoft Word and Excel, or Adobe's Photoshop and PageMaker, are what you use to do word processing, financial planning, photo manipulation, or newsletter layouts.
- Data are the raw materials of information processing. Data include integers, dates, characters, sounds, graphics, movies, animations, and so on.
- Originally computers could only process integers, times, and characters now called simple (or primitive) data. Now computers are powerful and cheap enough to process videoconferencing, phone calls, movies, sounds, and animations called complex data.
- Many of your daily activities, such as making airline reservations, watching a weather forecast, or withdrawing money from an ATM machine are actually interactions with computers that you don't see.
- The Global Positioning System (GPS) lets you easily locate your position anywhere on the face of the earth for the price of a GPS receiver costing as little as a few hundred dollars.
- GPS is used for precision farming, automobile guidance systems, tracking vehicles, scientific research, and the new air traffic control system.
- The GPS system has three basic parts, the 24 satellites in space, five ground stations that monitor them to make sure they are working, and millions of handheld or mounted receivers.
- From almost any point on Earth six of the satellites can be picked up. Each satellite broadcasts very precise signals that a GPS receiver on the ground can use to determine its latitude, longitude, and altitude.

Review Questions

True/False

1. T F The term data, has traditionally been plural and the term datum singular.
2. T F Well-designed hardware works without software.
3. T F The only application for information technology is in business.
4. T F Information technology refers to just hardware devices, and doesn't include the connections between them.
5. T F An operating system makes it possible for you to load application programs.
6. T F Application programs are what you use to do work on your computer. word processing, financial planning, photo manip, newsletter layouts
7. T F Information is created by combining and analyzing facts and details called data.
8. T F One of the major characteristics of a computer is its ability to run a stored program or list of instructions that tell it what to do as events happen.
9. T F A person using the global positioning system (GPS) can locate his or her position anywhere on the Earth within a few hundred miles.
10. T F There are two kinds of software in widespread use: operating system software and application programs.

Fill-In the Blank

1. The phrase Information Technology refers to the creation, gathering, processing, storage, and delivery of information and the processes and devices that make this possible.
2. hardware is any of the physical equipment in a system.
3. Software is a list of instructions that guide the hardware in the performance of its duties.
4. The information processing cycle has these five steps: input, processing, output, storage & retrieval and distribution & communication
5. A system is a set of related parts that operate together to perform a specific function.
6. People who use computers to perform tasks or enhance their performance are called end-users.
7. Operating Systems, such as Microsoft Windows, make it possible for your system to run and perform useful work using application programs.
8. Application Programs such as Microsoft's Word and Excel, or Adobe's Photoshop and PageMaker, are what you use to do word processing, financial planning, photo manipulation, or newsletter layouts.
9. Computer-aided design (CAD) is used to develop products. Computer-aided manufacturing (CAM) is used to product them.
10. The acronym GPS stands for Global Positioning System

Multiple Choice

1. News stories on information technology may be on topics such as ____.
   a. The information superhighway
   b. Multimedia
   c. The Internet
   d. All of the above
2. Information technology can ____.
   a. Process raw data
   b. Recycle processed information and use it as data in another processing step
   c. Package information so it's easier to understand, more attractive, or more useful.
   d. All of the above
3. The five steps, input, processing, output, storage and retrieval, and distribution and communication, are all part of ____.
   a. The information superhighway
   b. The Internet
   c. The information processing cycle
   d. None of the above.
4. Computer data can include ____.
   a. Prices
   b. Flight numbers
   c. Video clips and sounds
   d. All of the above
5. Typical operating systems include Microsoft Windows
   a. Microsoft Word and Excel
   b. Adobe Photoshop and PageMaker
   c. Both a and b
   d. Neither a nor b
6. Computers are used in business to ____.
   a. Process transactions
   b. Allow people to work at home
   c. Do desktop publishing of documents
   d. All of the above.
7. GPS is used to ____.
   a. Determine location
   b. Make weather forecasts
   c. Enhance computer performance
   d. Guide satellites in space

Research Projects

1. Make a list of your day-to-day activities in two columns: those that are influenced by information technology and those that are not. Which list is longer?
2. List all the jobs you can think of in which computers have no direct role. Try to imagine how aspects of these jobs might eventually use computers.
3. Describe a movie or commercial you have seen recently in which a computer played a major role either on-screen or in generating special effects.
4. At the start of the day, what is the first computer that you encounter?
5. Take an ordinary household item and list ways computers may have been used in its creation, manufacturing, or distribution.

CHAPTER

3 THE COMPUTER SYSTEM AND

AN OVERVIEW

Computers have been around now for about a half century. In the old days, their "brains," the central processing units or CPUs, were large, custom-designed, hand-built, and expensive. They threw off so much heat they had to be water-cooled like a car engine so they wouldn't melt. And to keep their large staffs of attendants from roasting, these computers were set off in their own air-conditioned rooms. These large computers were so expensive and complicated that only major corporations used them and only professional staff members had keys to the locked rooms that set them off from the rest of us. Individuals in those firms—but outside of those locked rooms—did little more with the computers than type in data for them to process (their input) and read thick, large printed reports they were programmed to produce (their output).

Then, in 1969, M. E. Hoff, an engineer at the small Intel corporation, successfully reduced the huge custom-built CPU to a fingernail-sized chip that could be reproduced almost like cookies. This was the first microprocessor, and although it was not a general purpose one like those now used in our computers, it led the way and its descendants have changed our world. Microprocessors can now be churned out with assembly-line efficiency. They are cheap, reliable, tiny, and above all powerful. If you took the cover off a personal computer, you could locate one or more if you knew what to look for. But they are now everywhere, and not where you would normally think to look. They all have built-in clocks that determine the speed at which they run. If these clocks ticked like an old watch, there would be a steady ticking background noise around you whose intensity would pick up as you approached the washing machine or toaster or picked up an iron. The noise would become annoying when you started your car because so many overlap and would reach a deafening crescendo as you walked through the office of a Fortune 500 company or the factory floor of a large manufacturing plant. If you wanted to get away from it on a camping trip, you had best leave at home your watch and your camera.

In this chapter we look at the concepts and technology behind the microprocessor and the computer system in which it resides.

OBJECTIVES

After completing this chapter, you will be able to:

- Compare and contrast various types of computers.
- Explain the purpose of the central processing unit and how it works.
- Describe how information is stored in a computer's memory.
- Explain how peripheral equipment, such as a printer or modem, is attached to the computer's ports.
- Explain the components of a computer's architecture.
- Describe how adapter cards can be plugged into the computer to improve its performance.

Computer *n.* 1. an electronic device designed to accept input, process it at high speed, and display the results.

System *n.* 1. An assemblage of things or parts forming a complex whole.

Central processing unit (CPU) *n.* 1. the key component of a computer system capable of interpreting and executing program instructions.

ON THE PACE CD ROM

Central Processing Unit

3.1 Types of Computers: Corporate and Departmental

The computer is at the core of almost all modern information technology systems. The most powerful computers, used by large organizations and departments within organizations, are supercomputers, mainframes, and minicomputers.

Supercomputers

Supercomputers are the most powerful computers available. They are used for many scientific and technical applications, including weather forecasting and automotive design, and are also used to generate the extremely realistic graphics seen in many movie special effects. A recent Intel supercomputer was the first to do over 1 trillion operations a second, three times faster than the fastest previous computer. Whereas most computers have one processor that does calculations one after another, single-file, this supercomputer has over 7,000 processors that do over 7,000 calculations at a time using a procedure called parallel processing. It can calculate in 1 second what it would take all the people in the United States 125 years to calculate using hand calculators.

A graphic display of numerical data can be very computer-intensive and for that reason often requires a supercomputer to process the data. Here a typical supercomputer computation is displayed as a graphic. The analysis is of the airflow over an automobile. Red indicates a high pressure build-up and blue low pressure.

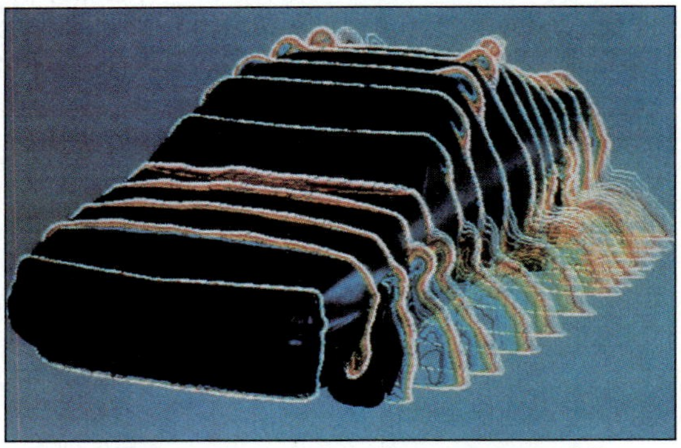

Supercomputer display of air flow courtesy of Cray Research Inc.

Mainframes and servers

Mainframe computers (now called servers) are often the corporate workhorses used for centralized business functions such as accounting and inventory control. They usually occupy an entire room and must be maintained and operated by a highly trained staff of specialists.

Networks

Supercomputers, mainframe computers, and servers are powerful enough to process the data for hundreds or even thousands of simultaneous users. These users may be located in the same building or scattered across the globe. Connecting computers together like this forms networks. There are a variety of devices that people use to connect to these networks.

Minicomputers (now also called servers) are less powerful than mainframe computers and are anywhere from refrigerator size to desktop size. They are frequently used by small companies or by departments within large corporations.

Supercomputer courtesy of Intel

Mainframe computers courtesy of International Business Machines Corporation

Computers

Personal computers (PCs) have the ability to take data from other computers to which they are attached and then process it. For example, a personal computer can add numbers, sort lists, or display the data as graphs. PCs can be connected to other computers but they can also work on their own.

Terminals are much more limited than are personal computers although they look like them.

Servers courtesy of International Business Machines Corporation

Why Are So Many Computers Called Servers?

Until recently, the largest corporate computers were called mainframes and the next largest were called minicomputers. As networks have grown in power and complexity, the role of these large computers has changed and they are now just one computer in a much larger system of computers called a network. However, because of their large size and great processing power, they still occupy a special place. In many cases they are where other computers on the network look for the data they need and they also run the software that controls the communications between all of the other computers. Since they now serve the needs of other computers on the system, they have become known as servers. However desktop computers and workstations are also often used as servers, so confusion reigns. It's fashionable to call almost every powerful computer a server in the hope that it will sell better. As a result, a computer that is called a server may fit on a desktop or in a briefcase, or it may require a room of its own. Until our vocabulary catches up with the marketing department labels, calling a computer a server doesn't tell you much about its size or power.

A network courtesy of courtesy of International Business Machines Corporation

Terminals have only a screen and a keyboard and the electronics that allow them to communicate with the computer to which they are connected and are used only to send information to the computer and receive information from it. Because they lack the ability to process data on their own, they are called dumb terminals. There is a variety of dumb terminal that can perform some limited processing. These are called smart, intelligent, or programmable terminals.

Network computers (NCs) and network PCs (NPCs)—also called managed PCs—are the latest families of computers. Both are crosses between full-featured PCs and the more limited terminals. They are like terminals in that they depend on larger computers for their data and programs. They are like PCs in that they can process the data locally once they have received it. You will learn more about these computers in Chapter 6.

3.2 Types of Computers: Desktop and Personal Computers

Supercomputers and mainframes are custom-designed and so expensive they are sold only in limited numbers. The low-cost mass-produced microprocessor is what has made it possible to put computing on everyone's desktop or in their briefcase. Sales of computers based on microprocessors have been phenomenal with tens of millions sold every year. Their popularity has led to many innovations and the development of many basic types.

Workstation courtesy of Silicon Graphics

Desktop computers and workstations

Desktop computers, those used by most individuals, are designed to be permanently positioned on a desk.

Desktop computer courtesy of Sony

Workstations are small but extremely powerful computers used mainly by scientists, engineers, and people who work with graphics.

Notebook computers

Notebook computers are light-weight and can be easily carried in a brief case. On the road, they can run on rechargeable battery packs. When back home or at the office, many can be slipped into a base unit, called a docking station, that allows you to expand their capabilities to match those of the larger desktop systems.

Notebook computer in docking station courtesy of International Business Machines Corporation

A Shift in Power

In the late 1970s, almost all of the world's computer power was created by mainframe computers with dumb terminals attached. A decade later, these computers generated less than 1% of the world's computer power. The other 99% was created by personal computers.

Computer Language is Fluid

A few years ago, the term workstation referred to any place a person worked at a computer. It was more a location than a thing. When high-powered desktop computers were first introduced, they were called engineering workstations because they were used mainly by scientists and engineers. As other users, such as artists and animators, adopted these powerful machines, their name was shortened to just workstation. Now the word workstation means different things to different people.

Subnotebook computers

In some cases, even notebook computers are too large. For this reason, a number of even smaller subnotebook computers have been developed. Some of these, called organizers, are used to store notes, a calendar, and phone numbers. Other are more powerful.

Handheld computers are the smallest of all computers. They have very small keyboards, so they cannot be easily used for word processing or other applications that require you to enter a lot of data. However, their small size makes them useful in many special applications. For example, salespeople use them to record customers' inventories, and others use them to make calculations, maintain appointment schedules, and store phone numbers and addresses.

Handheld computer courtesy of Hewlett-Packard

Personal digital assistants (PDAs) are among the smallest computers. These devices are designed without a keyboard so they are very small and easy to carry. They range from simple organizers with address books, calculators, and calendars through more powerful units that can send and receive e-mail and even browse the Web.

Subnotebook computer courtesy of U.S. Robotics Palm Computing, Inc.

So What's a PC?

When microcomputers were first introduced, they were referred to as personal computers, or PCs. This was because they were used by individuals as opposed to departments of corporations. When IBM introduced their first personal computer in 1981, they named it the IBM PC. Soon the term PC referred mainly to the machines made by IBM. Over the next few years as more and more companies produced clones of the IBM PC, the term PC began to mean any IBM-like machine. Ironically, the term no longer applies to Apple computers, which were the ones that started the personal computer revolution in the first place.

Micro Ain't What It Used To Be

When the microprocessor came out in 1969, it was first used in desktop computers. Since these were much smaller than the currently smallest minicomputers, they were called microcomputers. Now that microprocessors are used in even the latest and fastest supercomputers, micro no longer means a small computer. For that reason, the term microcomputer is falling into disuse.

3.3 The Anatomy of a Computer

Information systems include a wide variety of computers, fax machines, printers, network connections, and even satellite transmitters. It's not necessary to understand how each of these devices works in detail. However, understanding the principles of digital systems is important even if all you want to do is read articles and buy equipment for the home or office. Although there is a wide variety of devices, the one that is most central to information technology is the computer.

Inside the case

Very few people lift the hoods of their cars to study the parts any more, but in the early days they did. In that era of dirt roads it paid them to know how the car worked in case they needed to fix it or wanted to improve it. In these early days of the computer no one expects you to fix a computer, but you may occasionally be called on to add components to one. These additions might be as simple as plugging in a printer or as complicated (not very) as opening the case and plugging in a fax card. At such times, it helps to know what parts make the computer tick. Here we "lift the hood" of a PC to take a look at some of the major components you'll find inside yours.

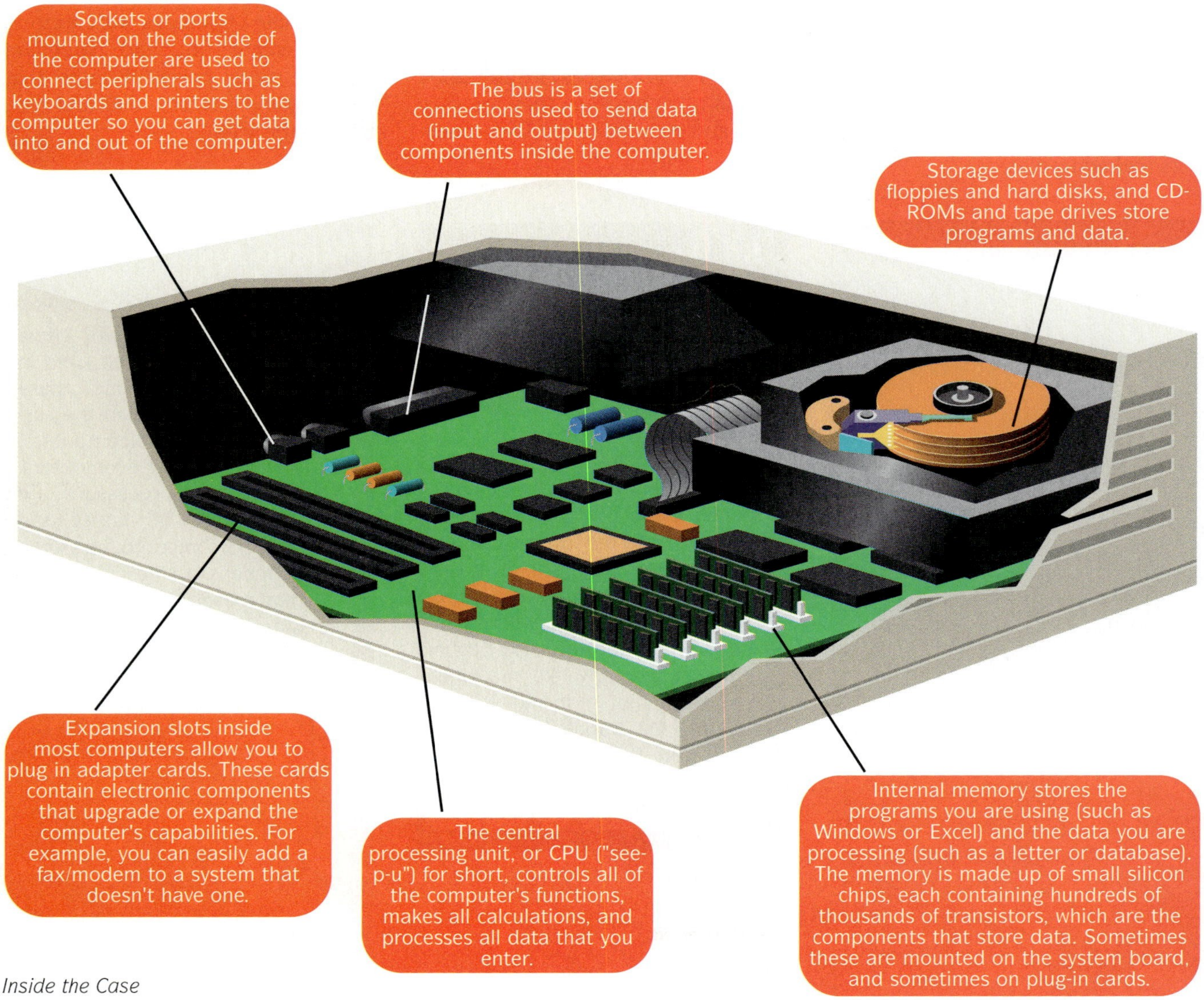

Inside the Case

System board courtesy of Intel

System board

Inside a computer case is the system board, also known as the mother board. This board contains most of the computer's circuits to which the microprocessor, memory, power supply, and other devices are connected.

THE DEVELOPMENT OF THE COMPUTER

The first electronic digital computer built in the United States, ENIAC, was unveiled at the University of Pennsylvania in 1946. It weighed 30 tons, filled the space of a two-car garage, and contained 18,000 vacuum tubes, which failed on average at the rate of one every seven minutes. It cost half a million dollars at 1946 prices.

Today, the same amount of computing power is contained in a pea-sized silicon chip. Almost any home computer costing as little as $100 can outperform ENIAC. Put another way, if the automobile and airplane businesses had developed like the computer business, a Rolls Royce would cost $2.75 and run for 3 million miles on one gallon of gas. And a Boeing 767 would cost just $500 and circle the globe in twenty minutes on five gallons of gas.

Tom Forester, ed., *The Information Technology Revolution* (Cambridge, Mass.: MIT Press, 1985).

REGARDLESS OF WHAT COLOR IT IS, IT'S STILL A BLACK BOX

At times, you may hear the expression "black box." For example, someone may answer a question about how a microprocessor works by replying "Oh, just treat it as a black box." This means that you don't care how it works, just what it does. For example, you may never really understand the electronic theory behind a computer, but you do care about how you input and output data. This means you are treating the computer itself as a black box.

The advent of compact discs (CDs) in the music world and the speed with which they replaced long-playing records (LPs) familiarized us all with the concept of digital processing. Music is stored on compact discs in digital form. Digital processing was first used, however, in computers in the 1940s. What is digital processing? It's the way information, music, or documents, or anything else, is stored in the form of binary digits so that it can be processed and used in modern information technology.

Digital versus analog

Analog signals carry a rich variety of information and look much like waves. We live in an analog world. We are designed to sense and interpret analog light waves. We see and hear not only the highs and lows in these wave signals, but also all of the sights and sounds in between. When you speak or listen, analog waves carry the message. When you listen to a live orchestra, you hear analog signals. Every part of the wave carries information.

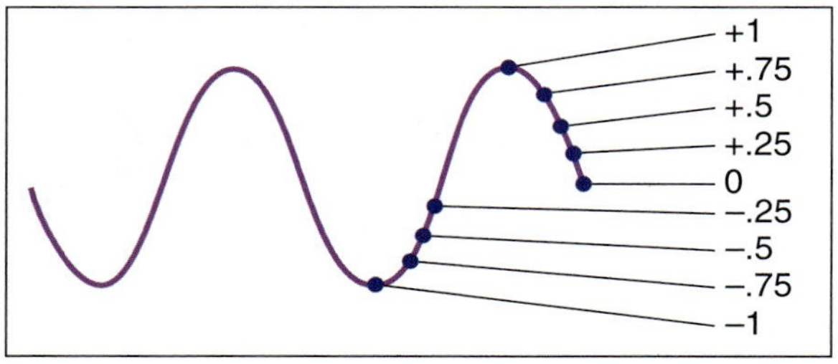

Analog signals

Analog waves are very sensitive to noise distortion. You've experienced this when trying to follow a conversation in a noisy room, when trying to tune in a faint radio station, or when playing an old record on a turntable.

Unlike analog signals, digital signals have only two states, on or off. It's easy for a device to tell these two different states from one another so noise does not affect the signals as much as it does analog signals. Noise is stray information; sound for instance, extraneous to the main message, some of the information in the middle of the wave.

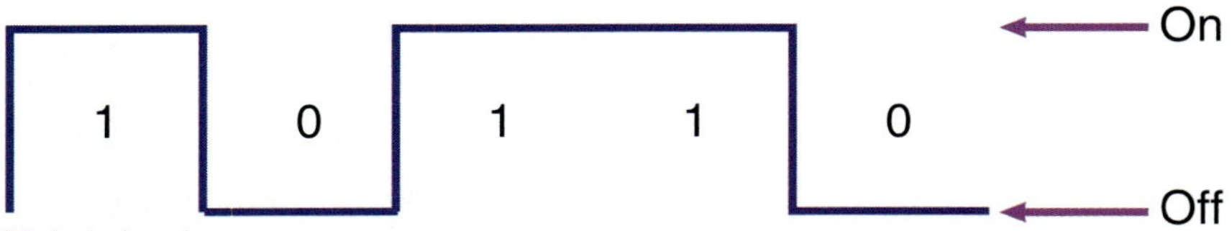

Digital signals

Digital has an advantage over analog in two respects: less noise and finer resolution.

Digital signals can have almost infinite resolution or detail. It's estimated that the human eye can discern 16 million colors. Let's look at just one of them: gray. A good newspaper photograph will have about 256 shades of gray in it, ranging between pure white and pure black. Let's say you wanted to transmit this photograph using light. Imagine how hard it would be to project and discern 256 levels of brightness in a light bulb! Compound the problem with clouds of fog representing noise, sometimes obscuring the bulb, at other times not. Now imagine, instead, eight light bulbs that can be turned on or off. Each of the 256 colors can be assigned a pattern—maybe white when all bulbs are on, middle gray is when the first five are on, and black when all are off and so on. Now it's much easier to transmit the 256 different shades of gray by combinations of on-off bulbs, even when fog partially obscures the bulbs.

Binary numbers

Digital is derived from the word digit, which means a single number. When you write a check or count your change, you use the digits 0 through 9 either alone or in combinations. For example, the digits 1 and 9 can convey $1 or $9, or they can be combined to convey $19, $91, $19.19, and so on. This numbering system, which uses the ten digits from 0 to 9, is called the decimal system. You use this system when you dial the phone, look up pages in the index of a book, address a letter to a specific street address, or count on your fingers.

Computers (and other digital equipment) use a different system the binary system. The binary system uses only two numbers, 0 and 1, to convey all other numbers. Binary numbers are conveyed in an unfamiliar form, so they may look much more complicated than they really are.

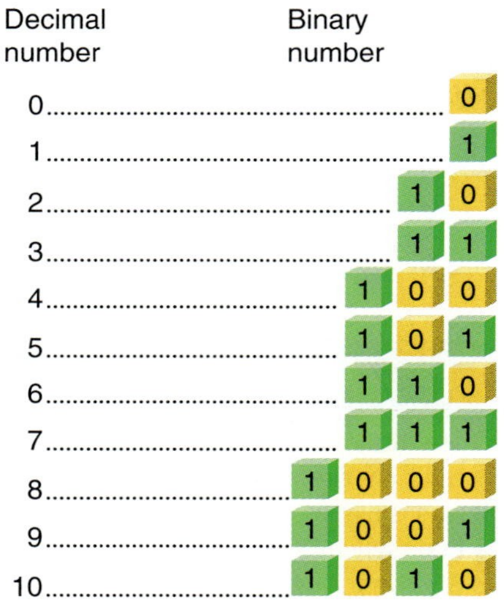

Decimal and binary numbers

Binary Numbers–0s and 1s:

Why digital?

Since the system of binary numbers uses only 0s and 1s, its major advantage is that information represented by the binaries can be processed in several ways with a variety of devices. For example, on/off, high/low, light/dark, north/south, or up/down states or other polarities, can stand for the 1 and the 0 combinations. In fact, all these techniques of paired states are used in microcomputers to store, process, and display information.

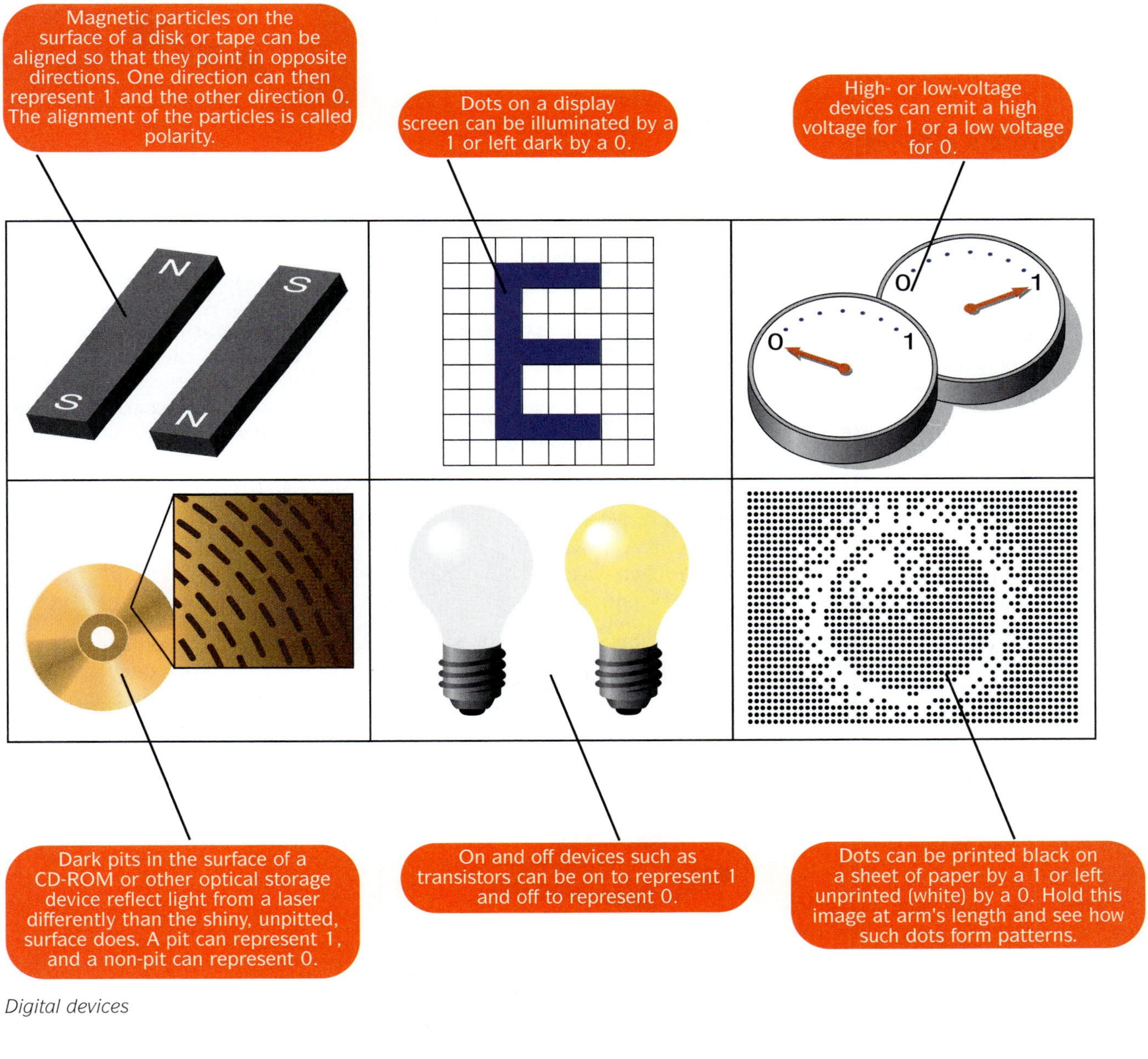

Digital devices

3.5 The Foundations of Modern Information Technology:

As we have seen, there are many ways to represent, store, and display 0s and 1s. However, to give them meaning you have to establish an agreed-on code. Today's digital signals of 0s and 1s are by no means the first signals used to convey information. Over the ages, drums, smoke, flags, semaphores, and other methods have been used to transfer information from one point to another.

Paul Revere's ride—a digital revolution?

When America was a rebellious colony of England, Paul Revere was assigned the job of notifying the Minutemen in the countryside if the British left Boston to attack and by what means they were coming. You may recall Longfellow's poem *Paul Revere's Ride.* Here are a few stanzas:

Listen, my children, and you shall hear
Of the midnight ride of Paul Revere,
On the eighteenth of April, in Seventy-five;
Hardly a man is now alive
Who remembers that famous day and year.
He said to his friend, "If the British march
By land or sea from the town tonight,
Hang a lantern aloft in the belfry arch
Of the North Church as a signal light,
One, if by land, and two, if by sea;
And I on the opposite shore will be,
Ready to ride and spread the alarm
Through every Middlesex village and farm,
For the country folk to be up and to arm.

"One, if by land, and two, if by sea," was a digital message. Revere's friend Robert Newman, the sexton of Old North Church, spied on the British, then lit the lantern and hung it in the belfry arch of the church. Revere, waiting on the other side of the harbor so that he had a head start on the British troops, saw the signal and began his famous ride. (Unfortunately, he was immediately arrested and the news was delivered instead by one William Dawes; so much for legends.) In any case, the forewarned Americans soon fired "the shot heard round the world" at the bridge in Concord.

The two lanterns used by the sexton to signal news of the British could convey three possible scenarios. When both were off (a digital 00) it meant no movement of the British troops. When either was lit (01 or 10) it meant they were moving by land. When both were lit (11) the British were moving by sea.

Lanterns in Old North Church's Steeple

The telegraph—a digital code

Lanterns have their limits when it comes to sending information. It is hard to spell out messages. For example, if the British had been able to take an unexpected route, Paul Revere's prearranged code would not have conveyed the message. This problem was solved by Samuel Morse's invention of the telegraph in the early 1800s.

With the telegraph, a sender taps on a key to send pulses of electricity down a wire to a distant listener. At the listener's end, a device called a sounder clicks when each pulse arrives. Like the lanterns in the tower, this is a digital process—the sounder is on or off. Random clicks, however, must be made to convey information, so Morse developed a code based on short and long pauses between the clicks. (When printed, these were represented as dots and dashes.) An experimental telegraph line was constructed between Baltimore and Washington, and on May 24, 1844, a series of short and long pauses between clicks sent the historic message, "What hath God wrought," down this first telegraph line.

Telegraph dots and dashes communicate information because they follow a code. For example, the well-known SOS (Save Our Ship) is dot-dot-dot, dash-dash-dash, dot-dot-dot.

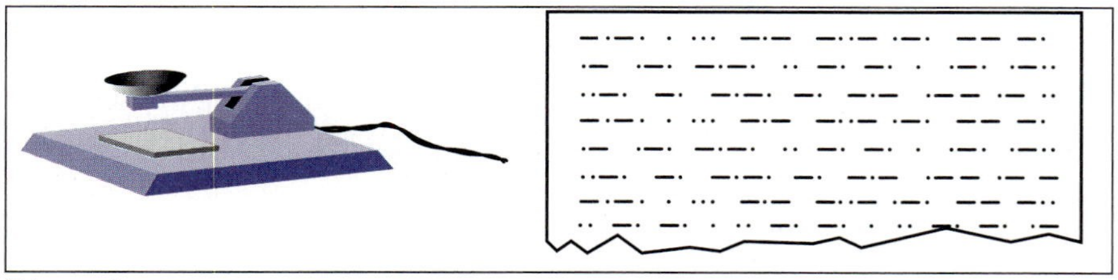
Telegraph

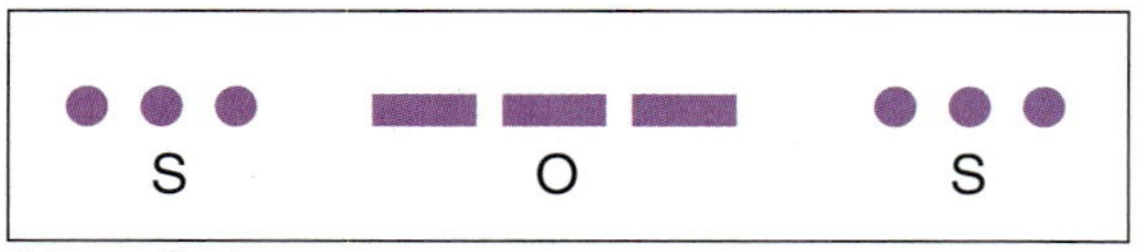

Morse Code

The transistor—the computer's digital device

Like these early message systems, computers need both a device that can send and receive signals and a code that gives the signals meaning. Instead of lanterns or a key to send electrical pulses in a wire, early computers used vacuum tubes, and modern computers use transistors. Like lanterns, transistors have only two possible states: on and off.

Early transistors were packaged one to a container like those in the background of this photo. Today, millions of transistors are created on a silicon wafer. This wafer is then cut apart and the sections are mounted in protective cases like the one shown in the foreground with places to connect wires. These "chips" are the reason modern computers are so small.

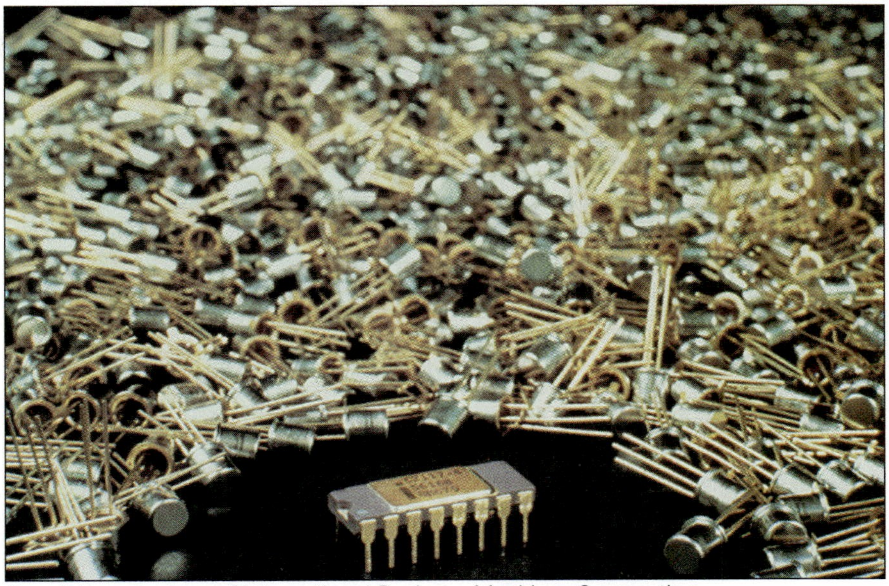

Transistors courtesy of International Business Machines Corporation

Moore's Law

As the ability to put more and more transistors on a chip increases, the cost per unit of computing power falls. In 1965 Gordon Moore, one of the founders of Intel Corporation, predicted that the density of transistors on a chip would double every year and a half. His prediction has turned out to be very accurate. In 25 years, the number of transistors on a chip has increased from 2,300 on the 4004 in 1971 to 7.5 million on the Pentium® II processor. At this rate, Intel chips will contain 50-100 million chips by the year 2000 and will be able to execute 2 billion instructions per second.

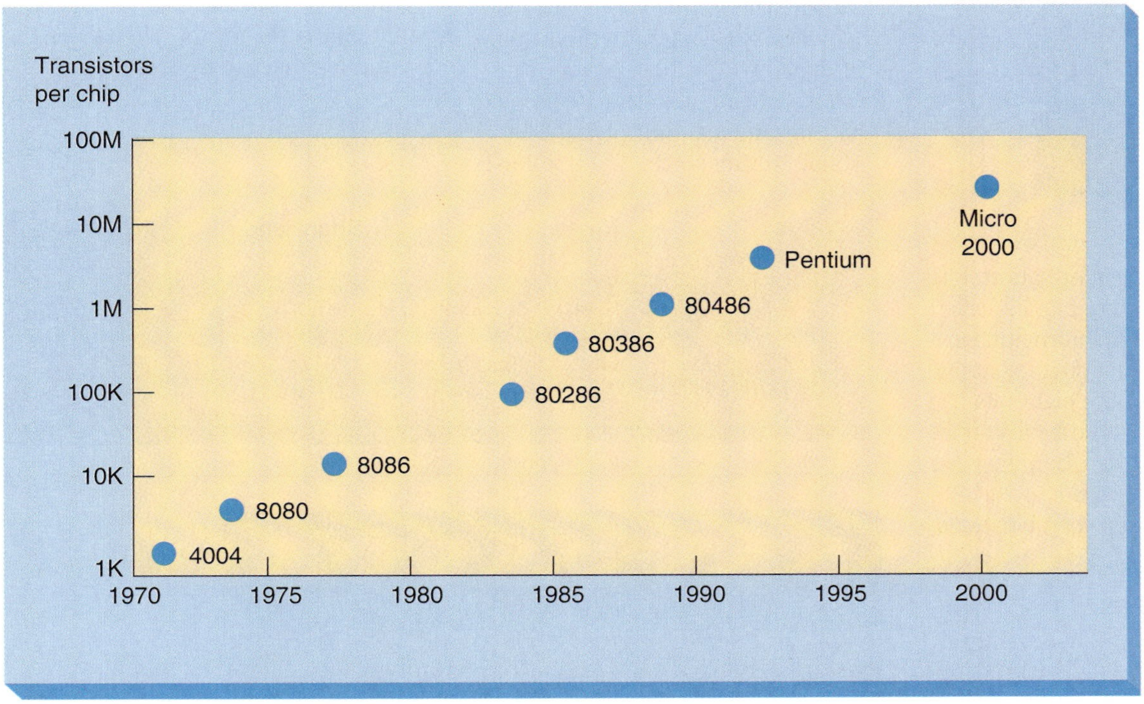

Moore's law

3.6 The Foundations of Modern Information Technology:

Given all that computers and other digital devices can do, it's always surprising to discover that they really perform only a very limited number of procedures. These include adding and subtracting, sorting, and comparing the sizes of numbers. The key to computers is that they perform these few procedures at such blinding speeds that they can carry out an almost infinite variety of complex tasks. To perform its limited repertoire of procedures, a computer needs to convert the information we give it into the digital language it understands, convert our language into bits and bytes, that is, the computer's digital language that stores, communicates, and processes before converting the results back into our language.

Bits and bytes

The smallest unit is the bit, a contraction of the more descriptive phrase binary digit. A bit is a single element in the computer that like a light bulb, has only two possible states, on (indicating 1) or off (indicating 0).

Bits

To convey more information, bits are organized into larger units called bytes, the basic unit of information in a computer system. Each byte contains 8 bits. Since each of the eight bits has two states (on or off), the total amount of information that can be conveyed by a byte is 2^8 (2 raised to the 8th power), or 256 possible combinations.

Groups of bytes

Since each byte can represent only a single character or command, to do anything useful requires a lot of bytes. A memo may require just a few thousand bytes, but an animation may require millions of them. To make it easier to talk about large numbers of bytes, we use a form of shorthand. For example, you would normally say one kilobyte rather than one thousand bytes. As sizes increase, the kilobyte is replaced by the megabyte, which indicates a magnitude of 1,000,000 (1 million). For example, you would say a file's size is 1 megabyte, not 1,000,000 bytes or 1000 kilobytes. At the moment, the term gigabyte (billion) is becoming more common and terabyte (trillion) will be a word you encounter frequently before too long.

- These numbers are often spoken or written using a form of shorthand. For example, the letter K is used for one thousand, an M for one million, a G for one billion, and a T for one trillion. The case of the letter B indicates if the reference is to bits or bytes. For example 10MB is 10 megabytes and 10Mb is 10 megabits.
- These values are calculated by raising the number 2 to various powers. For example, the number 2 raised to the 10th power is 1024 (raising it to the 10th power is the same as multiplying 2 by itself 10 times—$2 \times 2 \times 2 \times 2 \times 2 \times 2 \times 2 \times 2 \times 2 \times 2$). In everyday discussions, the result 1024 is usually rounded off to 1000 or 1KB.

Our language to computer language and back again

As you have seen, computers can process data only in their binary language of zeros and ones. However, we humans read English, Spanish, and other languages and calculate in decimal numbers. To allow us to communicate with the computer, the computer has to translate our input into the binary number language it uses and then has to translate its output back into a language we can read. The way it does this is interesting.

When you type a letter or number on the keyboard, the computer looks it up in a table to find the binary number that has been assigned to represent it. It then uses that binary number during processing. After processing, it reverses the process and looks up each binary number in a table to find the character or other symbol it represents and displays that character for us. The tables the computer uses are called codes.

Value	Name	Shorthand	Power
1	Byte or bit	1	2^0
1,024	Kilobyte or kilobit	1KB or 1Kb	2^{10}
1,048,576	Megabyte or megabit	1MB or 1Mb	2^{20}
1,073,741,824	Gigabyte or gigabit	1GB or 1Gb	2^{30}
1,099,511,627,776	Terabyte or terabit	1TB or 1Tb	2^{40}

The number 2 raised to various powers

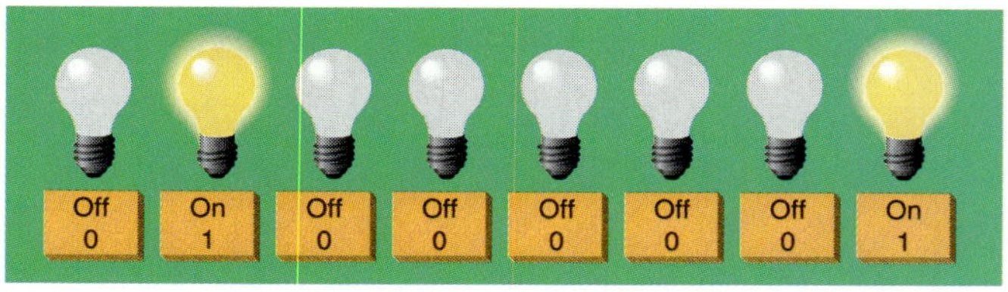

Byte

Bits and Bytes–The Binary Code

There are exactly 256 entries in a computer's code (a few are commands). This is because the eight bits in a byte can convey only 256 possible values—from 0 to 255. Here's why this is so. Each of the eight bits has a value based on its position in the byte. It is the same as in the decimal system where the 2 in 12 represents 2 and the 1 in the next place to the left represents 10. In the case of the byte, however, the values of places or columns are not powers of 10 but powers of 2. The rightmost bit is 1, the one in the place to its left is 2, and next comes 2 to the second power, or 4, and so on through 8, 16, 32, 64, and 128. Using any combination of these bits being turned on or off, you can convey a binary number from 0000 0000 to 1111 1111 or a decimal number from 0 to 255. Each of these 256 decimal numbers can stand for a letter, number, or command.

In the illustration on the right, all bits are on, so the binary value is 1111 1111. The decimal value is 255 = 128+64+32+16+8+4+2+1.

Below only the second and third bits are on, so the binary value is 0000 0110. The decimal value is 6 =4+2.

Bits add up to 6

Codes in use

When you type in characters on your computer keyboard, the binary number assigned to each character depends on the code being used. The computer industry uses several encoding schemes, including the following:

- *ASCII* (pronounced "as-key") is the code used most often on microcomputers. It stands for the American Standard Code for Information Interchange. This code was established by ANSI (pronounced "an-see"), the American National Standards Institute. The ASCII code is shown in the table below right. The 10s are in the left-hand column and the digits across the top row. For example, the @ sign is number 64 and the ® sign is 174. The characters in the shaded cells are in the extended ASCII character set.

Bits add up to 255

- EBCDIC (pronounced "eb-see-dick") is the code used most often on mainframe computers and more powerful servers. It stands for the Extended Binary Coded Decimal Interchange Code.
- ASCII and EBCDIC may be OK for English, but what if you wanted to print French, German, or even Phoenician or Early Hebrew? Programs using UNICODE, such as Windows NT, can support the processing and display of the languages of the modern world and classical and historical languages. Currently, the Unicode standard contains 34,168 characters covering the principal written languages of the Americas, Europe, the Middle East, Africa, India, Asia, and Pacifica.

	0	1	2	3	4	5	6	7	8	9
0										
1										
2										
3				!	"	#	$	%	&	'
4	(	)	*	+	,	-	.	/	0	1
5	2	3	4	5	6	7	8	9	:	;
6	<	=	>	?	@	A	B	C	D	E
7	F	G	H	I	J	K	L	M	N	O
8	P	Q	R	S	T	U	V	W	X	Y
9	Z	[	\	]	^	_	`	a	b	c
10	d	e	f	g	h	i	j	k	l	m
11	n	o	p	q	r	s	t	u	v	w
12	x	y	z	{	|	}	~	•	•	•
13	‚	ƒ	„	…	†	‡	ˆ	‰	$	‹
14	Œ	•	•	•	•	'	'	"	"	•
15	–	—	˜	™	§	›	œ	•	•	Ÿ
16		¡	¢	£	¤	¥	¦	§	¨	©
17	ª	«	¬	-	®	¯	°	±	²	³
18	´	µ	¶	·	¸	¹	º	»	¼	½
19	¾	¿	À	Á	Ä	Ã	Ä	Â	Æ	Ç
20	È	É	Ê	Ë	Ì	Í	Î	Ï	Đ	Ñ
21	Ò	Ó	Ô	Ö	Ö	x	Ø	Ù	Ú	Û
22	Ü	Ÿ	Þ	ß	à	á	â	ã	ä	ä
23	æ	ç	è	é	ê	ë	ì	í	î	ï
24	ō	ñ	ò	ó	ô	õ	ö	÷	ø	ù
25	ú	û	ü	ý	þ	ÿ				

ASCII code

3.7 The Central Processing Unit:

The heart of a computer is the central processing unit (CPU). In most computers, and all desktop and notebook computers, the CPU is a microprocessor, the device that made microcomputers possible in the first place. These CPUs are on small silicon chips, making them easy and inexpensive to manufacture. Each chip contains millions of tiny on/off switches called transistors. Connecting them are microscopic lines of aluminum that act as wires. Together, these transistors and wires create circuits that can manipulate data to make machines do many useful tasks.

The number of transistors on a chip has grown from 2,300 in 1971 to over 7.5 million today. This advance has made today's microprocessors 1,000 times faster than their predecessors.

They keep getting better

Over the years, a number of firms have successfully introduced microprocessors. Since each company usually makes a range of compatible chips, we refer to them as "families" of chips. The most successful family of microprocessors is Intel's, if the number sold is the only criterion. However, other families are manufactured by Apple, Sun, Motorola, Digital, and others. Over the years, the chips in each family have become more and more powerful.

Microprocessor compatibility

The microprocessor is an extremely powerful device. In fact, a single microprocessor is as powerful as mainframe computers used in corporate data processing centers in the mid-1980s.

The differences among the microprocessors made by the same company are significant, but there are far greater differences between Intel and Motorola chips. These differences determine not only the performance of the chip but also whether programs will run on a computer using the chips.

- Programs written to run on the earliest Intel chips used in an IBM PC in 1981—the 8086 or 8088—will still run on the latest Intel chip.
- Programs written for the latest chip may not run well on earlier chips if they take advantage of the later chip's specific improvements.
- Programs written for any Intel chip will not normally run on any Motorola chip; hence IBM programs do not normally run on an Apple computer or vice versa.

(They can be made to run using what is called emulation, additional hardware and software that make them act as if they had the other neccessary microprocessor.)

Microprocessor courtesy of Intel

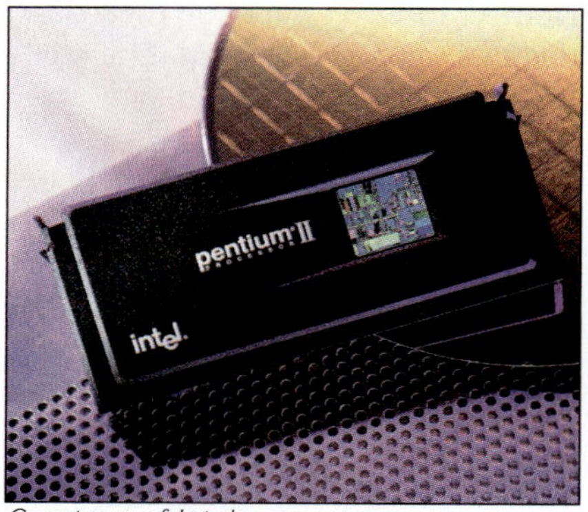

Courtesy of Intel

Name	Date	Speed	Number of transistors	Bus width	Memory
4004	1971	108 KHz	2,300 (10 microns)	4 bits	640 bytes
8008	1972	200 KHz	3,500 (10 microns)	8 bits	16 KB
8080	1974	2 MHz	6,000 (6 microns)	8 bits	64 KB
8086	1978	10 MHz	29,000 (3 microns)	16 bits	1 MB
80286	1982	12 MHz	134,000 (1.5 microns)	16 bits	16 MB
Intel386™	1985	16 MHz	275,000 (1.5 microns)	32 bits	4 GB
Intel486™	1989	25 MHz	1,200,000 (1 micron)	32 bits	4 GB
Pentium® Processor	1993	60 & 66 MHz	3.1 million (.8 micron)	32 bits	4 GB
Pentium® Pro Processor	1995	200 MHz	5.5 million (0.35 micron)	64 bits	64 GB
Pentium® Processor with MMX™	1997	200 MHz	4.5 million (0.35 micron)	32 bits	4 GB
Pentium® II	1997	300 MHz	7.5 million (0.35 micron)	64 bits	64 GB

Intel microprocessor evolution

Co-processors and parallel processors

Because the computer's microprocessor performs many functions, it often causes slowdowns at key points in the computer's operation. To relieve part of its burden, some computers include additional microprocessors, called co-processors, that are dedicated to specific, time-consuming tasks. These co-processors operate under the control of the CPU. For example, co-processors can be used to accelerate the display on the screen or improve the processing of audio and video.

A co-processor is a special case of a parallel processor. In general, two or more processors may equally share the other system resources such as memory. Each processor in the system can operate independently, but the operating system software must coordinate the behavior of the two processors.

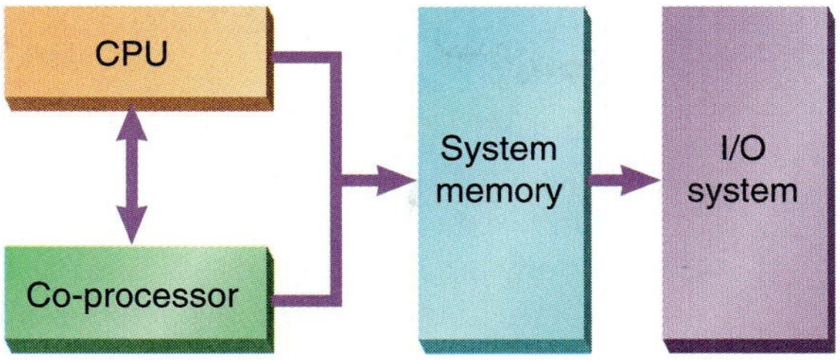

Co-processors

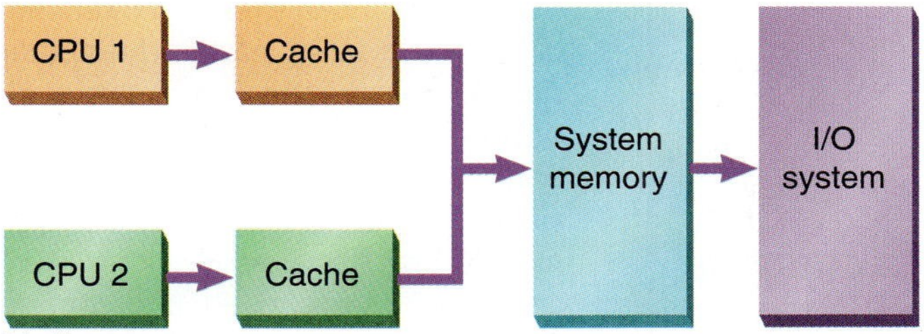

Multiprocessors

Costs of processing data

The introduction of the microprocessor had a dramatic impact on the costs of computing. In 1978, before widespread use of microcomputers, it is estimated that a unit of processing speed cost over $1,000. By 1982 it had fallen to less than $200 and by 1995 it was only 50 cents and it keeps falling.

Embedded microprocessors

Microprocessors are not used just in computers. You'll also find them in your automobile, your telephone, and even your home or office thermostat. It's the microprocessor that lets you redial your phone, makes your thermostat adjusts the temperature, or adjusts fuel flow in your car for maximum mileage. There are even microprocessors embedded in credit-card-sized smart cards that you can use to make phone calls or other purchases.

Embedded microprocessor courtesy of US West

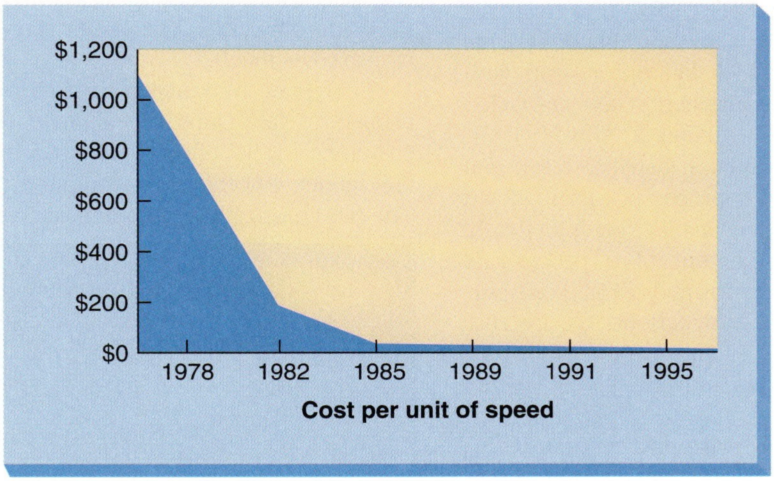

Cost per unit of speed

286, 386, 486,.......Pentium (huh?)

The success of the Intel line of chips led other firms such as Advanced Micro Devices and Cyrix to duplicate, or clone, them. During legal battles over this practice, it became apparent that Intel could not copyright the names 386, 486, and so on that the chips had been known as. To better protect their brand names, Intel did not call the next chip in the series the 586, but instead, called it the Pentium.

3.8 The Central Processing Unit:

When you see ads, read articles, or overhear conversations about computers, you'll encounter phrases such as "It has a fast 300MHz, 32-bit CISC processor." These buzz-words all have meanings that indicate to some extent the speed and power of a microprocessor. There are three basic ways to improve a system's performance: make it carry more data at the same time, make it run faster, or make it more efficient. (You'll find these enhancements at work across the board in computing.)

Improving data capacity

Newer and wider highways can carry more and faster traffic than older and narrower ones. The same is true of computers; the more data they can carry and process, the faster and more powerful they are. The first PCs could process 8 bits at a time. Soon this jumped to 16 bits and then to 32 bits. And the pace continues. Workstations, all larger computers, and even some game machines process 64 bits at a time. (The terms word length or word size are sometimes used when referring to the number of bits that a computer can handle simultaneously.)

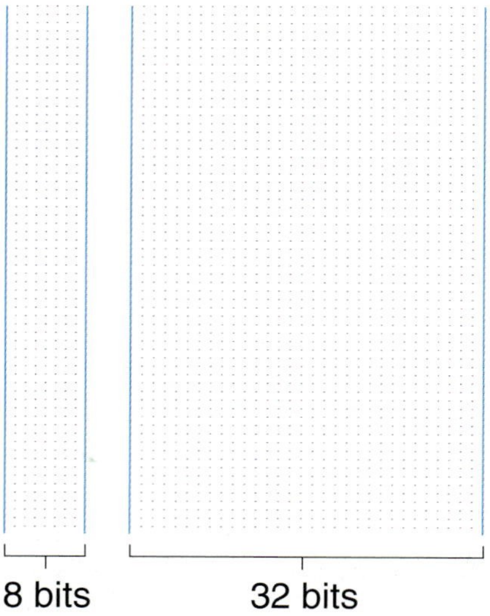

8-bit and 32-bit word lengths

Improving processing speed

Another way to improve performance, is to make a microprocessor run faster. All microprocessors have a built-in clock that like a caller at a square dance sets the pace for all activity. This is normally referred to as a system's clock rate or clock speed, which is specified in megahertz (millions of cycles per second, or MHz). In many cases, the higher the clock rate, the faster the computer. However, microprocessors don't all process instructions in the same number of cycles (ticks of the clock). For this reason, clock rates are only a true speed indicator in the same family of microprocessors. For example, an Intel 300 MHz Pentium II is faster than a 200 MHz Pentium II. However, Motorola microprocessors, like those used in some Apple computers, are just as fast with lower clock speeds.

Improving efficiency

Computers are programmed to perform tasks through a series of simple instructions. The complete set of simple instructions that a microprocessor understands is called its instruction set. Think of it as the microprocessor's vocabulary. The larger the vocabulary, the more sentences you can create. It's the same with the microprocessor. Very large sets of instructions allow it to handle a wide variety of tasks. Microprocessors with these large instruction sets are called complex instruction set chips (CISC). Surprisingly, large instruction sets can cause a microprocessor to slow down in places because it's doing so much. Since 80 percent of a processor's tasks are performed through 20 percent of the instructions, the instruction set can be reduced. Microprocessors using this technique, called reduced instruction set chips (RISC), operate faster than CISC microprocessors in many circumstances. For example, there may be over 300 instructions in a CISC chip's instruction set and less than 200 in a RISC chip's set. In addition RISC microprocessors use special technologies that allow them to process multiple instructions in one processing cycle. They also have substantially fewer elements on the chip so they are cheaper and quicker to design.

Clock rates courtesy of International Business Machines Corporation

CISC microprocessors, such as Intel's Pentium II, are overtaking RISC chips in power and are certainly a lot cheaper since so many more are made. In 1995 it's estimated that the fastest Intel chip was only half as fast as the fastest RISC chip. In 1996 the gap closed so the fastest Intel chip was 90 percent as fast as the fastest RISC chip and the system cost only one-third as much.

In 1993 over 25 million computers using Intel CISC chips were shipped to customers. RISC chips were used in only about 400 thousand computers. The ratio hasn't changed much since.

PowerPC RISC chip courtesy of Sun Microsystems

The Path of Progress

Joy's Law

Comparing computers is like comparing race cars—everyone wants to know which is the fastest. Performance comparisons between machines are complicated because so many factors are involved. However, just as top speed (MPH or KPH) is a guide to race car speeds, instructions per second (IPS) is a guide to computer speeds. And since computers are so fast, the number of instructions per second is in the millions so the raw speed is given in MIPS, millions of instructions per second. In 1984, William Joy, one of the cofounders of Sun Microsystems, predicted that computer performance would increase at a predictable rate. Using the MIPS (millions of instructions per second) as his standard of performance, he developed the formula now known as Joy's Law:

$$MIPS=2^{(year-1984)}$$

For example, in 2000 the number should be 2^{16} or 65,536 MIPS. So far, the performance of chips has been surprisingly close to this forecast. The first microprocessor had a speed of about 6000 instructions per second or .006 MIPS and the Pentium has over 100 million per second or 100 MIPS—over 16,000 times faster.

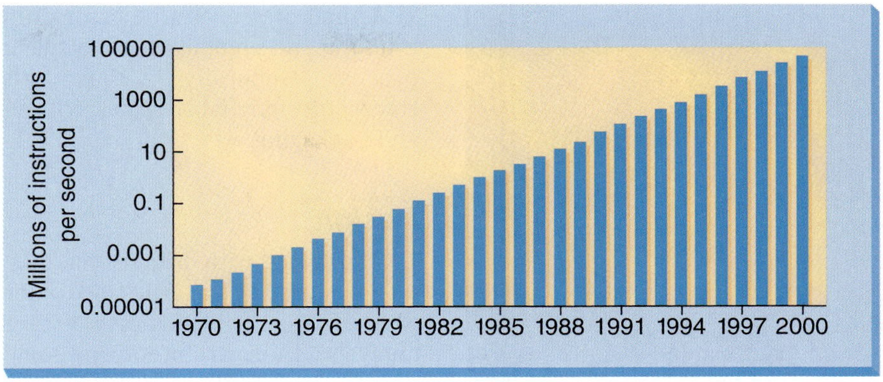

Joy's Law

Benchmarks

Everyone wants to make the fastest computer, and everyone wants to buy the fastest one they can afford. The problem is in determining which is the fastest. Knowing the specifications of the system such as the type of processor it uses is only a very rough guide. Many other variables affect a computer's real-world performance. In an attempt to compare systems, the industry has developed special programs that are run on all machines. These benchmarking programs can be run on many different machines. How fast they run on each should indicate how fast each system is. Unfortunately it doesn't work as well as expected. Computers perform two basic types of calculations: integer processing and floating-point calculations (extensively used in 3D graphics). Microprocessors and systems can be fine-tuned to work better in one of these areas than in the other. Then benchmarking programs can be designed to emphasize one area over the other. The result is that if a marketing manager asks for a better benchmark than a competitor, a combination of system changes and careful selection of a benchmark program may make it happen.

Benchmarks

Design courtesy of International Business Machines Corporation

The birth of a microprocessor chip is a long and complex technological process. Generally, it has four stages: design, fabrication, sorting and packaging.

Design

1. Chips begin with designs that take into account what the customer wants. This step begins with market analysis, then architecture, logic design, and finally laying out the "masks" that will be used to create chips. As you might expect, designs get progressively more complex and more detailed as they go along. The designs are done on sophisticated workstations that will actually simulate how the design will function once it's been manufactured.

Fabrication

2. Masks are created to manufacture the chips. Masks are quartz plates with a stencil-like pattern etched in chrome. To create the chips a photographic process transfers the pattern on these masks to silicon wafers to create circuits. A series of masks is needed because chips actually have a number of layers.

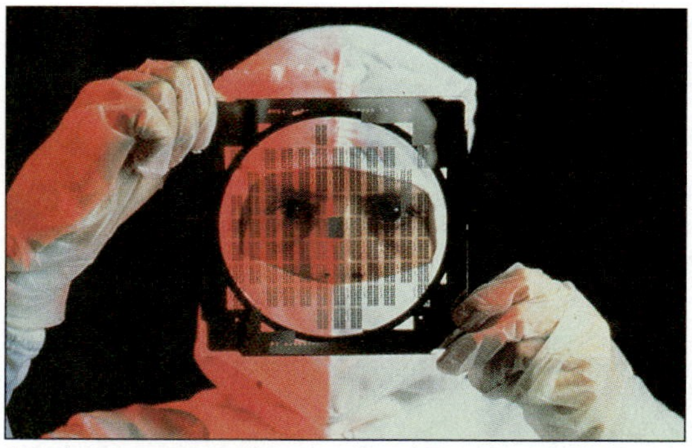

Masks courtesy of International Business Machines Corporation

3. Silicon is manufactured so it is almost pure and formed into long tubelike ingots. These ingots are then sliced into thin round wafers on which the chips are created. These wafers are polished so they have a mirrorlike surface. Silicon, the principal ingredient of beach sand, is the second most common element on earth (oxygen is the most abundant).

4. An insulating layer of silicon dioxide is "grown" on the surface of a polished wafer and then coated with a substance called "photoresist," which becomes soluble when exposed to ultraviolet light. A mask is placed over this layer. When ultraviolet light is shined through the mask's clear spaces, portions of the photoresist are exposed. These exposed portions become soluble and when this layer of photoresist and the silicon dioxide under it is etched away, a pattern of photoresist-covered silicon dioxide remains on the wafer. When that photoresist is removed to expose the remaining silicon dioxide, the first layer of the chip is completed. These and additional steps are repeated to complete the chip.

Photoresist courtesy of Semetech

Sorting

5. The completed wafer contains hundreds of chips, each of which may contain millions of transistors. Each of these transistors must be checked through a process called "wafer sorting." Needlelike probes connect with points on the wafer to perform over 10,000 checks per second. Testing can take from one minute to over an hour depending

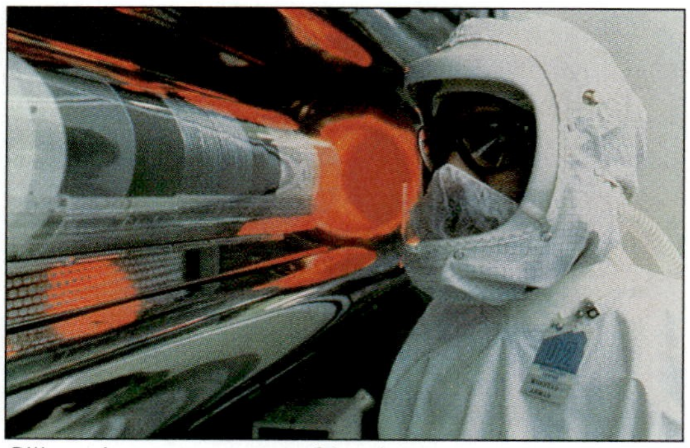

Silicon Ingot courtesy of Intel

Waffer sorting courtesy of International Business Machines Corporation

on the chip's complexity. Any bad chips are marked with dye so they can be spotted later in the process.

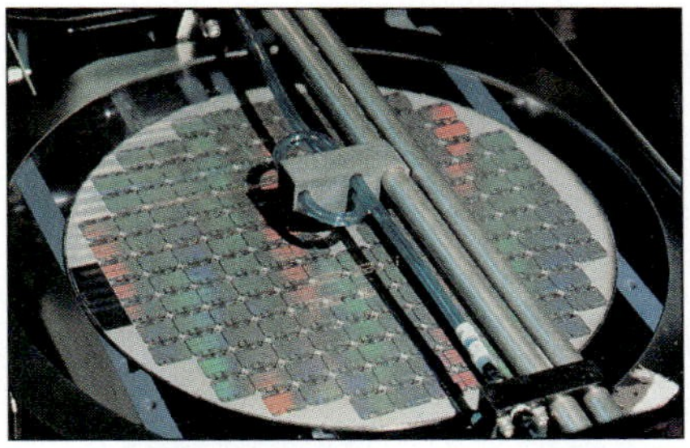

Dies courtesy of International Business Machines Corporation

Packaging

6. After sorting, wafers are cut apart into individual chips using diamond saws. These individual chips are called "dies." Those marked with ink during sorting are discarded.

7. Packaging protects the chip and provides the electrical connections needed for the die to communicate with the circuit board into which it will be mounted.

Packaging courtesy of Intel

How Small Are Chip Circuits?

Chips are so small that the millions of transistors on them must be created with unbelievably thin lines. These are measured in microns (millionths of a meter). A human hair is 100 microns thick and the smallest circuits are now being made with line widths of .4 microns—250 of them would fit in a human hair. The smaller these become, the smaller chips can become. And smaller chips are cheaper and faster.

3.10 Memory: ROM and RAM

For a computer to work, it must contain memory where it can store data and programs until they are needed. In the computer, storage is on memory chips of many kinds which basically, however, fall into two categories: read-only memory (ROM) and random-access memory (RAM). Both are very fast because data is read to and from the chips electronically; they have no moving parts. How fast? The fastest can access data in the time it takes light to travel 2½ feet.

Scrabble—An Analogy

The Scrabble[R] brand crossword game is like a computer's memory. The instruction booklet is like ROM—you can read it, but you cannot change it. The board is like RAM—you can add, remove, or move data to and from, around on it.

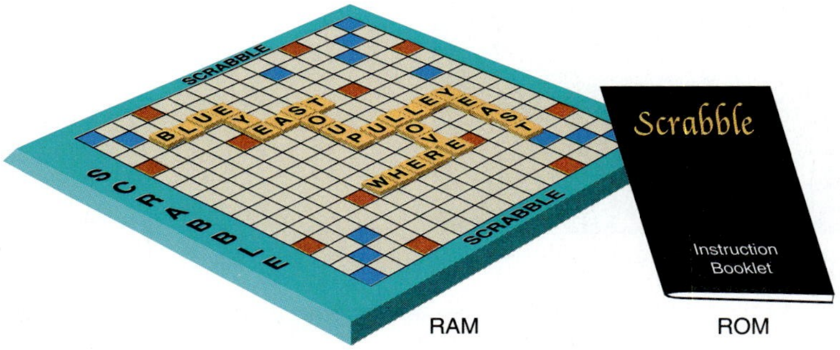

Scrabble[R] Brand game

Read-only memory (ROM)

Read-only memory (ROM) is static and unchanging; as a result it's called nonvolatile memory. The data in ROM is permanently recorded on memory chips by the computer's manufacturer prior to their being sold or shipped and you can't change it. Turning the computer off will not affect it; the data will still be there when you turn it back on. ROM is generally used to store programs and instructions that the computer frequently needs, sometimes called firmware. For example, it contains the instructions the computer follows to start up when you first turn it on and the system's setup program that you use to change settings such as the time and date.

Random-access memory (RAM)

Random-access memory (RAM) is used to store an ever-changing parade of programs and data. When you load a program into the computer or create a word processing document, the data you enter using the keyboard is stored in random-access memory (RAM)—also called main, primary, or user memory. Usually, if you turn off the computer, any programs or data stored in this memory are lost; thus RAM is said to be volatile memory.

The term random comes from the way the data in memory can be located or accessed by the computer. One way to understand random is to think of the differences between a tape cassette and an audio CD disc. To play the third song on a tape cassette, you must first advance the tape past the first two songs. This is called sequential access because you access each song in sequence. With an audio CD disc you can go directly to the track where the third song begins. This is called random access because you can randomly access songs without first advancing through the songs that precede them.

Read-only memory

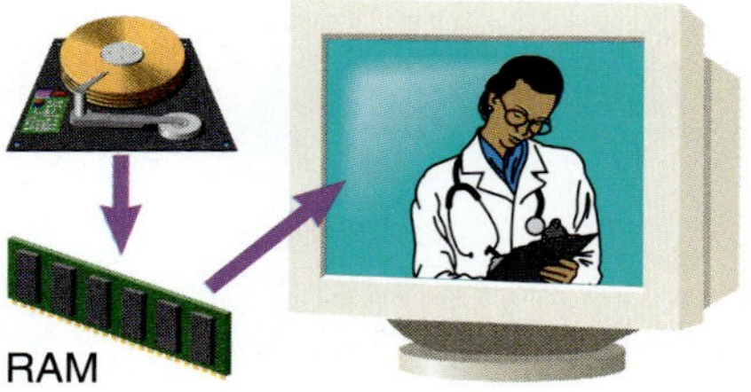

Random-access memory

Types of memory chips

Memory comes in a variety of forms. The computer designer's decision which to use where depends on what their function is to be, and on their speed and cost.

Dynamic RAM (DRAM) is the most common type of main memory. It's dynamic because each memory cell quickly loses its charge so it must be refreshed hundreds of times each second to prevent data from being lost. Here are some of the types of DRAM that have been or will be popular in most desktop systems (listed from oldest to newest):

- Fast Page Mode (FPM) DRAM was used in most computers until EDO RAM came along.
- Extended Data Out (EDO) DRAM is slightly faster than FPM. One variation called burst EDO (BEDO) DRAM assumes that the next data-address to be requested by the CPU follows the current one so it sends that also.
- Synchronous DRAM (SDRAM) can synchronize itself with the clock that controls the CPU. This makes data transfers more reli-

able and faster because timing delays are eliminated. It's anticipated that this form of memory will replace EDO as the most common form of memory.

- Rambus™ DRAM (RDRAM) is the latest design and Intel has announced that all of their future systems will require it. RDRAM is very fast, but the system must be slightly redesigned to use it. RDRAM sends data down a high-bandwidth "channel" 10 times faster than standard DRAM.

Static RAM (SRAM) is like DRAM but it's a lot faster, larger, and more expensive, and consumes more power. It's static because it doesn't need to be continually refreshed. Because of its speed, SRAM is used mainly in a special area of memory called a cache (see Spread 3.11). Flash memory chips are one of the latest storage devices. These chips, a form of static RAM (SRAM) chips, store data much like those used in the computer's primary storage. However, the data stays recorded even when the power is turned off—flash memory is nonvolatile. Since flash memory devices have no moving parts, and are therefore very fast, they may eventually replace slower, mechanical hard disk drives.

Video RAM (VRAM) is used to accelerate the display of graphics on the screen. It does this by using two "ports," one connected to the CPU and the other to the screen. Data flows in one port and out the other very smoothly. A variation of this is Window RAM (WRAM) that supports memory.

Shakespeare to Go Please

In 1976 memory chips could store 16 thousand bits of data. By 1998 they will be able to store 1 billion bits. One of these newest chips can store 10 copies of the complete works of Shakespeare, four hours of compact-disk quality sound, or 15 minutes of video images.

Flash memory chip courtesy of Intel

Memory modules—SIMMs and DIMMs

In most systems you don't add memory by adding individual chips. Instead, memory is plugged into the computer's system board using memory modules. These are circuit boards into which memory chips have been inserted. They in turn are plugged into a socket on the computer's system board. One type is the Single In-line Memory Module (SIMM). Another is the Dual In-line Memory Module (DIMM). These names refer to the package, not to the type of chips they contain. DIMMs are preferred in newer systems because they can be used singly instead of in pairs like the older SIMMs.

When is Enough, Enough?

The first IBM PCs came with 128 kilobytes of memory. Now it's recommended that a system have 16 megabytes—roughly a hundred and twenty-five times more.

DIMM courtesy of Toshiba

Chip Capacity

On PC systems using 32 megabytes, the 4 Meg DRAM isn't widely used. It would take all of the available SIMM memory slots in a typical PC to achieve the 32MB density requirement. At the 32MB memory level, 16 Meg becomes a preference.

3.11 Memory:

In addition to the RAM in your system's memory chips there are other types of memory and other ways to use it. These include ways to store more data, store it so it can be accessed faster, or store it so it can be moved within an application or between applications.

Virtual memory

Very large programs and very large files of data can strain the capacity of even a large computer's memory. To solve this problem, modern operating systems and many application programs store parts of their programs or data outside RAM until needed. This type of storage is called virtual memory. On a system that uses virtual memory, only the parts of the program or data file currently needed are stored in the computer's memory; the rest are stored on a hard disk drive. When the computer needs a part of the file stored on the disk, it moves something in memory to the disk to make memory available. It then moves the program or data from the disk into memory. For example, as you scroll through a long document, only part of it may be in RAM at any one time. The rest remains on the disk until you scroll toward it.

Virtual memory reduces the overall cost of the system because it's cheaper to store data on a hard disk drive than it is to add additional memory chips to the computer. Prices fluctuate a lot, but in 1997 hard disk space cost 9 cents a megabyte. A megabyte of chip memory cost $9 over 100 times as expensive.

Caches

When a computer is operating, it is frequently moving data between the CPU, disk, and memory. To process data, the data must first be moved to the CPU from wherever it is stored. Since this takes time, special techniques have been developed to speed up this operation. The basic technique is to store data in a special area of high-speed memory called a cache that is located between the CPU and main memory. When the processor needs data, it will check in high-speed cache first to see if the data is there. If not, then the processor will retrieve the data from slower main memory.

One way to think about a cache is to compare it to a refrigerator. Every time you want a sandwich (data), you don't make a trip to the store (RAM). Instead, you go to the refrigerator (cache). If you find the sandwich makings there (a cache hit), you save yourself a lot of time. If you find it empty, or storing only moldy cheese (a cache miss), you have to go to the store.

How does the computer know what to store in the refrigerator (cache)? Basically it guesses. When you ask for something that the computer needs to go to RAM or the disk for, it also gets the data that follows it. The assumption is that if you look at the first name in a database, the next one you'll want to look at is the second name. It then moves all of this data into the cache so the CPU can get it from there rather than going to the disk for it. Unfortunately, the computer can't always anticipate correctly what should be in the cache.

Virtually Anything

The term "virtual" means that something does not exist physically but does so logically. For example, RAM in the computer is physical—it is a set of chips. When you design the system so it behaves as if there is more memory than there really is, the new memory is called virtual memory. This concept has caught on in other areas such as virtual reality and the virtual office. In virtual reality, you wear a helmet or goggles and see only computer generated reality. In the virtual office, there isn't a physical building, only people connected together by computer communications. The word "virtual" is both catchy and trendy so expect it to pop up in lots of other places.

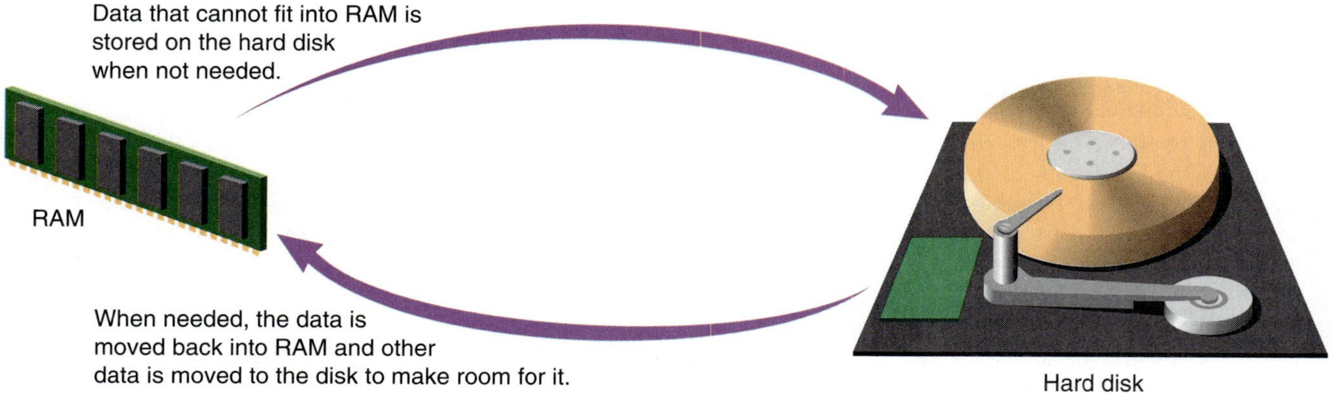

Virtual memory

Other Forms and Uses of Memory

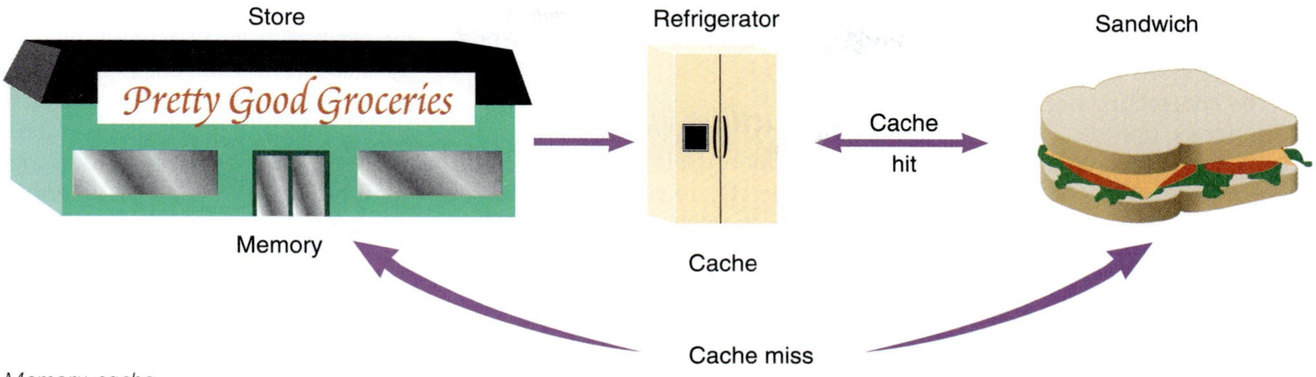

Memory cache

When the CPU finds the right data there, its called a "cache hit." When it doesn't, it's called a "cache miss."

Cache memory uses special chips, often SRAM (Static RAM) chips. On some systems, these chips are four times as fast as regular memory. However the chips cost six times as much. It's this cost that keeps them from being used for all of the system's memory. There are two levels of cache memory:

- Level 1 cache (also called L1, internal, or primary cache) is physically a part of the microprocessor chip. This cache typically ranges up to 256 kilobytes on desktop systems.
- Level 2 cache (also called L2, external, or secondary cache) is in the form of memory chips mounted in special sockets on the system board. This cache is larger than L1, ranging up to 1MB or more.

Buffers

Some programs allocate a small portion of the computer's random-access memory as a buffer. Buffers have several applications. For example, a buffer stores data that you enter from the keyboard until the CPU can accept it. (If the buffer becomes full, the computer beeps, and any keys you press are not stored, so you must reenter them when the CPU empties the buffer.) Another buffer temporarily saves a record of the most recently used commands and deleted text so you can "undo" any mistakes. Still another buffer (sometimes called a clipboard) is used as a storage area when you cut or copy data so that you can later paste it elsewhere. For example, you can create a graph in a spreadsheet program and copy it to the clipboard. You can then open a word processing program and paste the graph into a report.

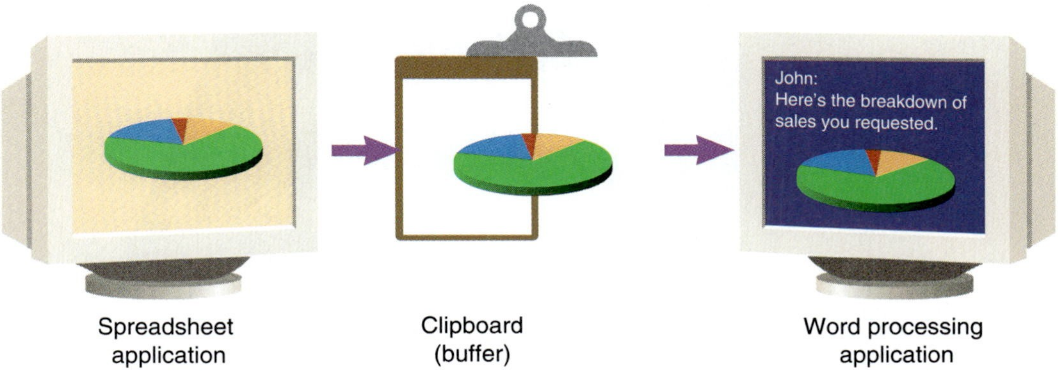

Clipboard

3.12 How the CPU and Memory Work Together

The CPU and memory work together to run programs and process data. The CPU has two main components, the control unit and the arithmetic and logic unit.

The control unit executes the program's instructions, coordinates the activities of the microprocessor, and controls the flow of instructions between the microprocessor and memory.

The arithmetic and logic unit performs arithmetic operations such as add, subtract, divide and multiply. It also performs logical operations to determine how one value compares to another. For example, it can determine if one value is equal to, greater than, or less than another value.

These two units work together with memory in a four-step process to complete a single cycle, called the machine cycle.

The machine cycle

The machine cycle has four steps, fetch, decode, execute, and store. The time it takes to complete the first two steps is called the instruction time (i-time). The time it takes to complete the last two is the execute time (e-time). The time it takes to complete all four steps is the machine cycle.

Registers

When an early microprocessor added two numbers it had a problem. Since it had only one path to memory it could "see" only one number at a time. To allow it to see two numbers, one first had to be moved into a small storage area in the microprocessor itself. This storage area on the chip was called a register. Instructions in the microprocessor then told it where the numbers were to add and where to store the result. Modern microprocessors now have several types of registers. One type may just keep track of which function is now being carried out. Several may be used to store data to be processed. Another may be used to store the results.

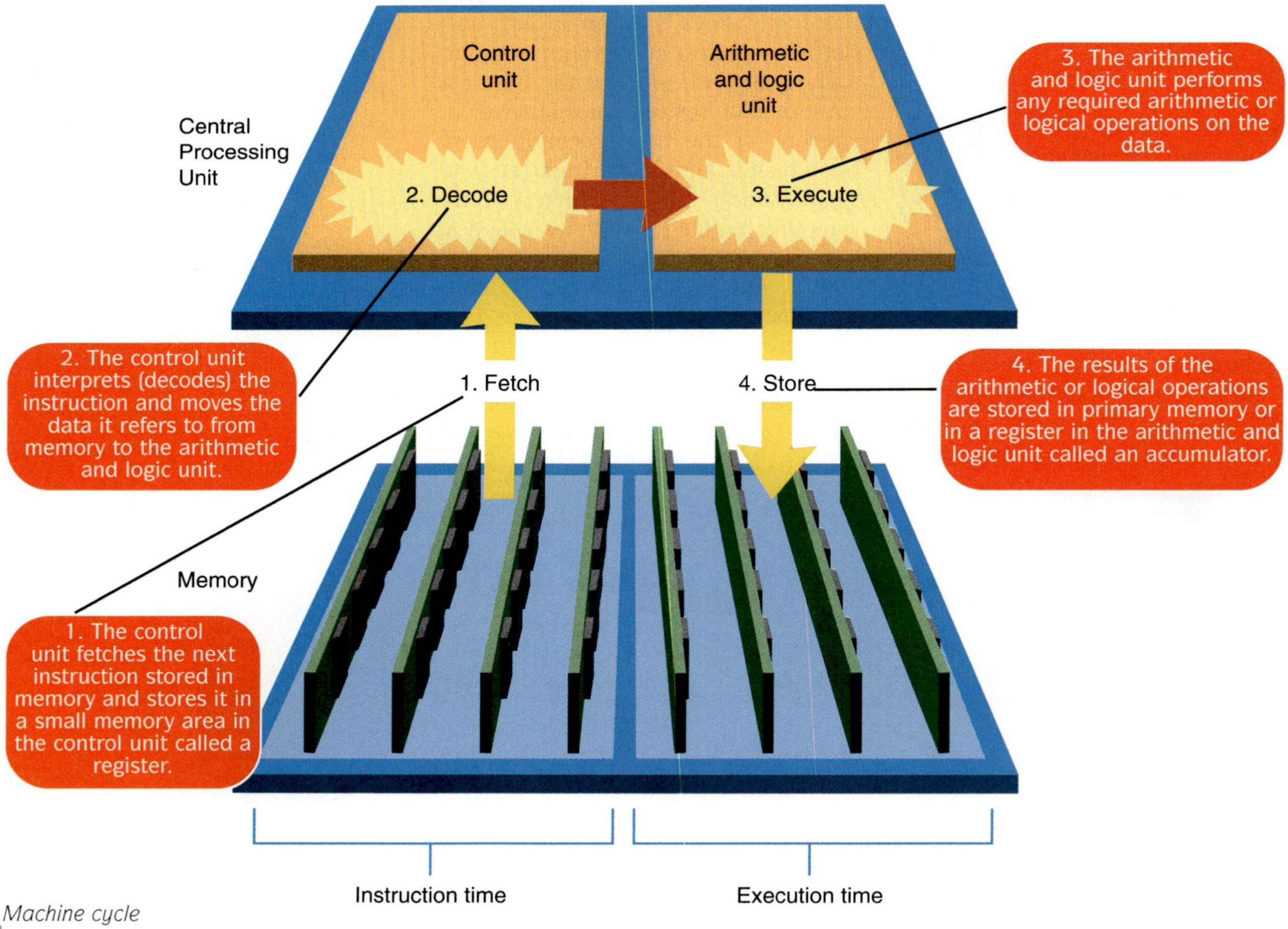

Machine cycle

CPU Hall of Fame

The 4004 was the first microprocessor and was used in the Busicom calculator. This chip contained 2,300 transistors.

The 8008 was twice as powerful as the 4004 and was used by a computer hobbyist to create a device called a "TV typewriter."

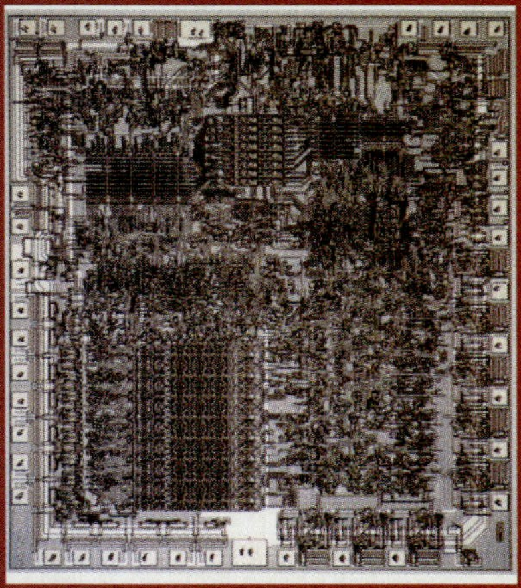

The 8080 was used in the first personal computer—the Altair which was sold in kit form for $395.

The 8088 was the breakthrough chip because it was used in the widely popular first IBM PC.

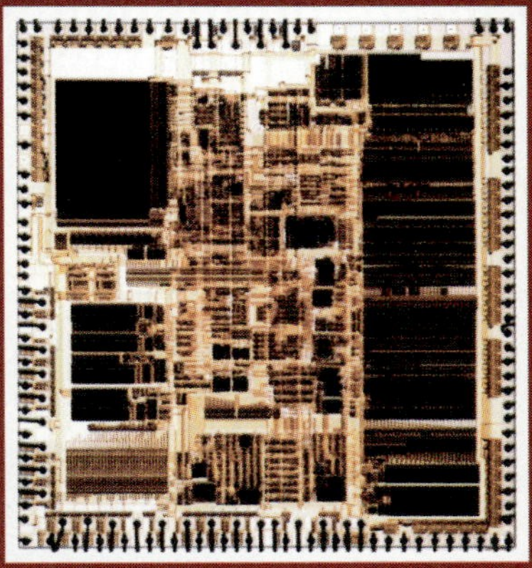

The 286, also known as the 80286, was the next chip in the x86 series and was widely adopted in the industry.

The Intel386TM DX microprocessor followed the 286 and added additional power to the desktop.

The Intel486M DX microprocessor was the first Intel chip powerful enough to make graphic interfaces such as Windows usable.

The Pentium® processor includes two processing units on one chip and contains 3.1 million transistors.

The Pentium® Pro processor, the successor to the Pentium, includes a second speed-enhancing cache memory chip and contains 5.5 million transistors.

Intel chips courtesy of Intel

3.13 Buses for Input and Output:

The computer must have connections, or circuits, along which information travels among all the components. This communication path is called a bus. All communications, whether internal or external, are sent along a bus.

The bus

The bus in a computer is like a highway for the data. A bus is a set of copper connections on the computer's system board. Here you see these connections on a board that has been removed from a system. The concept behind a bus is relatively simple. There are only two ways to connect all the components: Either run wires between each component in the system or connect them all to a common set of wires—a bus. The bus simplifies the design, reduces the number of required circuits, and lowers the cost. A bus also allows new components to be added by simply plugging them into the bus.

Originally, buses were called processor buses because they addressed memory as well as expansion cards. To add memory to these older systems, you could plug memory cards into slots connected to the bus. However, when processor speeds got faster than peripheral devices, memory on newer systems was addressed separately. You can no longer add memory with expansion cards because it needs to be addressed by a faster bus dedicated to that single purpose.

System buses

The system bus is simply a set of connections that connect the CPU to other devices in the computer. For example, any peripheral connected to the bus with an adapter card is connected to the CPU. The system bus includes address lines and data lines. The address lines carry the address of data in memory. The data lines carry the data bits themselves. The number of data lines determines the width of the bus. Think of the data bus as a set of parallel wires, each of which can send one bit at a time. The more wires in the bus, the more bits that can be sent at a time. The number has increased over the years from 8, to 16, and now 32 to keep up with the performance of microprocessors. Some high-end systems are already using the next step bus, one that carries 64 bits.

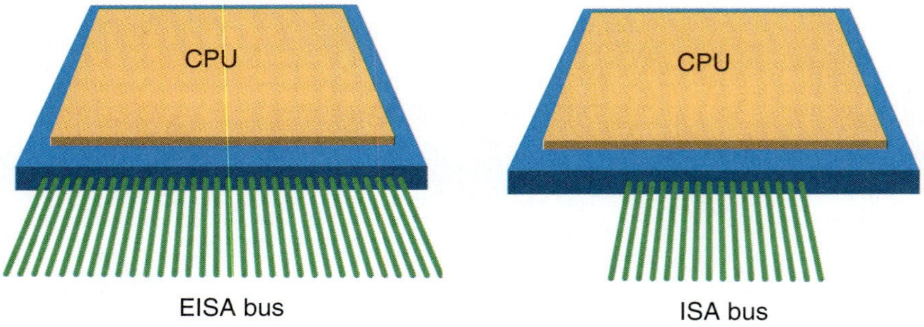

System buses

The bus courtesy of Intel

Local buses

As graphical user interfaces such as Windows have become more popular, parts of the computer system have become bottlenecks to acceptable performance. One of these bottlenecks has been updating the screen display. This is no small task. For example, a high-end display may have 1024 pixels across the screen by 768 down, or a total of almost 800,000 pixels that have to be updated 60 or more times per second. This puts a tremendous load on the system and you notice it when it takes a long time for the screen to be redrawn when you page up or down. To solve the problem, local buses have been added to take peripherals off the I/O bus and connect them, together with the CPU and memory, to a wider data pathway. This speeds up how fast data can be sent from memory through the microprocessor to the screen or other devices.

Almost all new desktop computers use a fast and inexpensive Peripheral Component Interconnect (PCI) bus. PCI was invented by Intel but is now controlled by an industrywide standards committee. Like everything else in computing, PCI is evolving quickly. As microprocessors speed up, it's essential that other components of the system keep up the pace so they aren't a bottleneck. The PCI bus is constantly evolving to meet this challenge. It gets faster in one of two ways: its speed increases or its data path widens. This is like raising the speed limit on a freeway or adding additional lanes. The bus is now fast enough for computers to process multiple video streams and simultaneously support very high-speed networking.

Older computers used first ISA buses (Industry Standard Architecture) and then EISA buses (Extended Industry Standard Architecture). (See opposite page.)

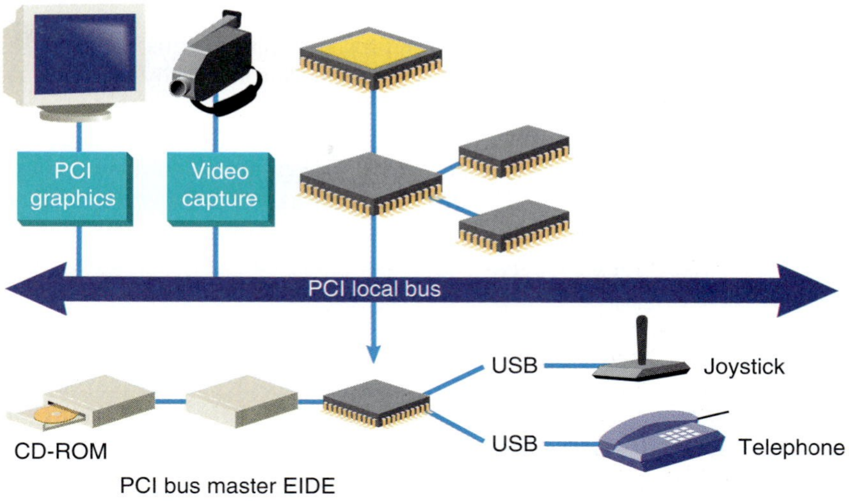

PCI bus courtesy of Intel

The first carried 16 bits at 8MHz and later 32 bits at 10MHz. Both were abandoned as microprocessor speeds increased and they could no longer keep up. For example, where PCI can send up to 256MBps, ISA can send only 5MBps. The local bus uses a new set of connections in line with the normal bus for a direct path to the CPU.

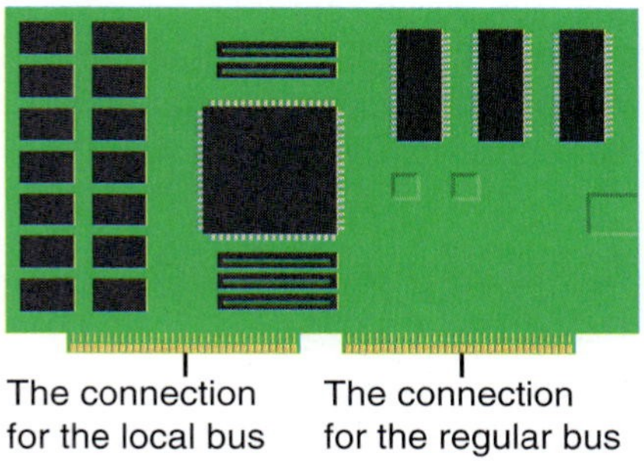

PCI bus connections

PRONUNCATION IS ALWAYS A PROBLEM!

Many people mispronounce words because we learn them from reading, not listening. This is a problem we all have in the computer field. Not only do we read many words before we hear them, but many are not yet in the dictionary so we can't look up the correct pronunciation. Basically, words are pronounced as acronyms, initialisms, or a combination of both.

Acronyms are words where the first letters of each term, or parts of a term, are pronounced as a word. For example, the acronym for random-access memory is spelled RAM and pronounced just the way it is spelled.

RAM

Initialisms are like acronyms but are pronounced a letter at a time. For example, the initialism for central processing unit is spelled CPU and pronounced see-pea-you. The PCI bus is pronounced pea-see-I.

C-P-U

Combinations use both pronunciations. A phrase such as dynamic access memory, is spelled DRAM and pronounced as dee-ram.

D-RAM

3.14 Buses for Input and Output:

Many users like to customize their computers to better serve their needs. To make this possible, most computers have expansion slots inside the cabinet into which you can plug adapter cards (also called add-in boards or cards). These expansion slots are connected directly to the computer's bus, so cards plugged into them perform just as if they were built into the computer. Adapter cards can serve a variety of functions. Some allow the computer to display colors or graphics, send faxes, connect with the Internet, or add sound. Still others connect peripherals or are the peripherals themselves. For example, you can plug in an adapter card that controls a hard disk drive located elsewhere in the system, or you can plug in a card that contains the hard disk drive itself.

Expansion slots and adapter cards

Expansion slots inside the computer allow you to plug in adapter cards that expand the computer's capabilities.

Expansion slot and adapter card courtesy of Compaq

Plug and play

When you want to change equipment on your system, such as plugging a modem into a notebook computer, you often have to first turn it off. If you are adding a new component, such as a fax card, you might even have to configure it. To eliminate these problems, some operating systems support plug and play. Plug and play means the operating system automatically detects new hardware and automatically configures it to run on your system. It does this by loading and unloading device drivers as you connect and disconnect peripherals such as printers, modems, and network cards. When you plug one of these into the computer while it's running, the operating system detects the new device. It then loads the required driver without rebooting the system. Plug and play requires three components that support the technology: an operating system, a BIOS, and devices.

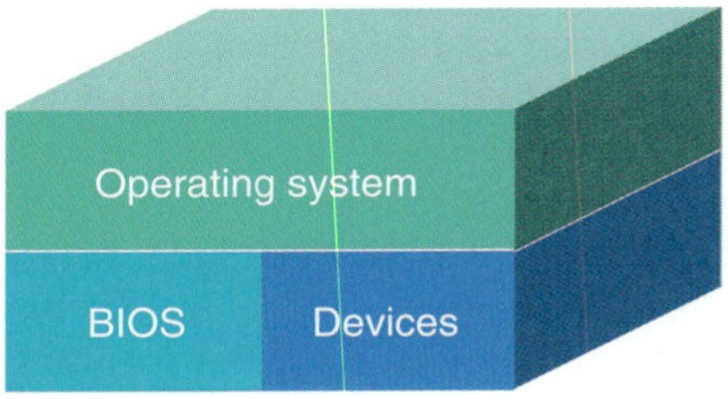

Plug and play

Hot docking

Handheld and laptop computers are often connected to desktop computers, docking stations, or networks. Before plug and play, you had to close all applications and turn the power off before either docking (connecting) or undocking (unconnecting). With plug and play, you can now use warm or hot docking. Both dramatically reduce the time and trouble it takes to dock and undock.

- With warm docking you first press a standard "Suspend" button on the portable.
- With hot docking you don't have to turn the power off or press a suspend key.

Hot docking

Laptop computers

Notebook computers and other small computers do not have much room inside the case for expansion slots and adapter cards. To overcome this problem, PC Card slots are included in some systems. These slots connect slide-in, credit card-sized PC Cards (older versions are called PCMCIA cards) to the computer's bus. Cards are available that allow you to store data, send messages, or connect to networks. The newer PC Card is faster and requires less power than older PCMCIA cards. They are based on a 32-bit bus so they can be used for power intensive applications such as video adapters and network connections.

PC Card courtesy of U.S. Robotics

Multimedia systems

At the current time, one widespread use of expansion slots is to make PCs into multimedia systems capable of displaying high-quality graphics, animations, and sound. These capabilities were originally used for games but are increasingly used for education, business presentations, and demonstrations. To upgrade a PC for multimedia, the system must have added to it a sound card, a CD-ROM drive, and an optional graphics accelerator. All of these components are added using cards that slide into expansion slots in the system's bus.

- Graphics accelerator. Multimedia requires a powerful system capable of showing high-quality illustrations, movies, and animations on the screen. This isn't an easy task because of the amount of information that is sent to the screen to achieve these effects. To speed up the screen display so it isn't a drag on the system, a graphics accelerator card can be inserted into a slot and the display screen is then plugged into that card. These cards have their own processors that take much of the graphics load off the system's CPU.
- CD-ROM drive. Multimedia uses lots of graphics, sound, animation, and movies. All of these take up huge amounts of storage space. To get all of these files onto the same disk, CD-ROM disks are used because they have much more capacity at lower costs than other media. To play these disks, the system must have a CD-ROM drive. To connect the drive to the system, you must plug an adapter card into one of the expansion slots.
- Sound card. PCs, unlike Macintoshes, have a very simple speaker built into them that can do little more than beep like the road-runner. To get high-quality spoken sound from a system, you insert a sound card into one of the slots and then plug speakers into the card. (Note that speakers contain powerful magnets and can harm your system if placed too close to it. Multimedia speakers are shielded to prevent damage to your screen or disks.)

Multimedia system courtesy of International Business Machines Corporation

3.15 Communications with Peripherals

A computer system is like a component stereo system where you use cables to connect a tape deck, turntable, and speakers to the main amplifier. On a computer, the components you plug in are called peripherals. These typically include devices such as printers, display screens, modems, keyboards, mice, scanners, hard drives, and CD-ROM drives. To connect them, you plug their cables into sockets on the computer called ports. Like seaports where ships enter and leave a country, and airports where airplanes enter and leave a city, ports are where information enters and leaves the computer. The number and type of ports on a computer vary, but they usually include serial, parallel, and SCSI (pronounced "scuz-e") ports.

Computer ports

Ports are sockets usually mounted on the back of the computer. You plug cables into these ports to connect peripherals such as printers or modems.

Serial ports (sometimes called RS-232-C ports or asynchronous communications ports) are where you attach modems, devices used to communicate with other computers, and some types of printers. One big advantage of serial ports is that the data is sent and received over only two lines. This makes them ideal for connection to the phone circuits, which also use two data lines.

When data is sent out a serial port, it is sent 1 bit at a time. Since the data is processed inside the computer at up to 64 bits at a time, a serial port is like a narrowing on a highway at a tunnel. Data slows down, just as the highway traffic does, so that it can funnel out of the computer in single file. Serial ports provide slower communications and are therefore not ideal for printer connections.

Parallel ports (sometimes called centronics interfaces) are normally reserved for printers and some types of external storage devices. They carry data 8 bits at a time on parallel paths. Because they can transmit data 8 bits or 1 byte at a time, they are a faster way for the computer to communicate with input and output devices. There is less narrowing than on a serial port, so traffic moves faster.

Parallel ports have one minor disadvantage: their signal does not travel as far as the signal from a serial port. This is important only when you want to connect a printer or other device with a very long cable. The length of a parallel cable is limited to less than 100 feet, whereas a serial cable can be up to 1000 feet long.

Many devices such as scanners, hard drives, and CD-ROMS can be connected to a SCSI port (Small Computer System Interface). One big advantage of this type of port is that more than one device can be connected to the same port. One device is plugged into the port and then another device is plugged into the first device. This process, called "daisy-chaining," reduces the number of slots taken up by all of these devices.

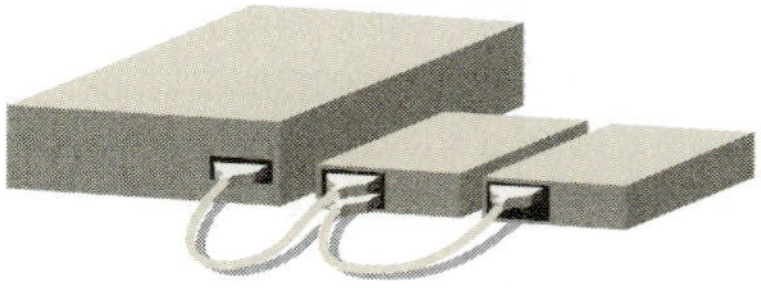

SCSI ports

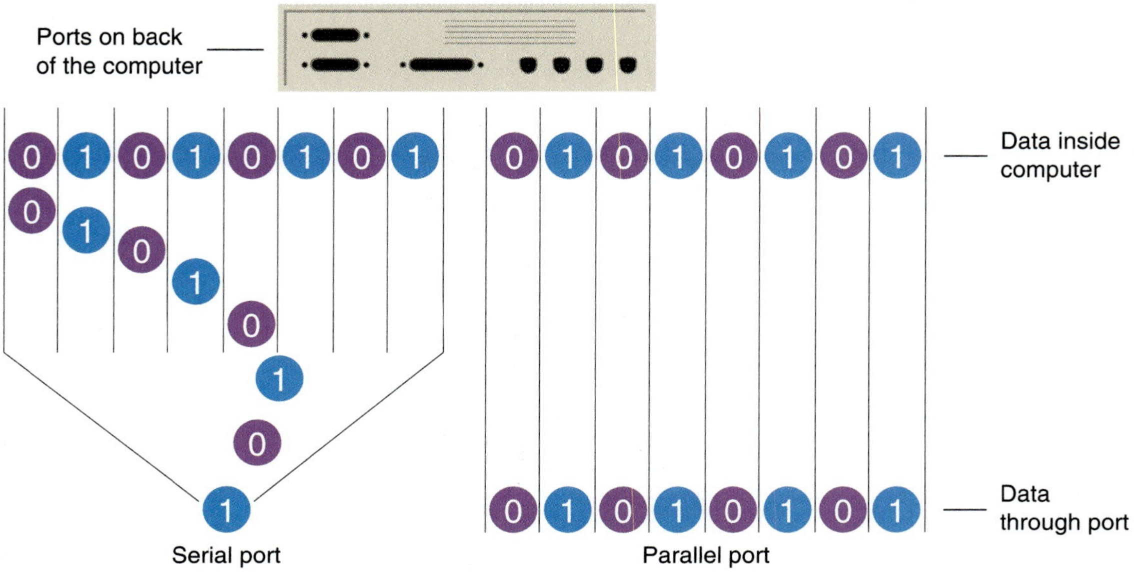

Parallel and serial ports

Universal serial bus (USB) and firewire

As input/output demands have increased, serial and parallel, and even SCSI, ports have become bottlenecks to system performance. Two new but complementary serial ports are now being added to systems to improve this situation. Both of these ports have features in common. They can each:

- ♦ Use thin cables to make connections easier.
- ♦ Allow you to daisy-chain devices so only a single port is needed on the computer.
- ♦ Support plug and play so you don't have to open the case, insert an adapter card, and then run a special program to install the card so the system knows it is there. The computer will automatically recognize the new device.
- ♦ Transfer data much faster than the older serial and parallel ports.
- ♦ Support hot plugging (adding and removing devices with the computer on).
- ♦ Distribute power so low-consumption devices can operate without a separate power cord.

Universal Serial Bus (USB) allows you to plug up to 127 devices into a USB port on the back of the computer, or into any other device already plugged in to that port. For example, you can plug a keyboard into the serial bus port and then plug a mouse into the keyboard. Likely candidates for USB are keyboards, mice, and joysticks, followed by printers, scanners, and external modems. USB is much faster than the older serial port and handles all but the most data-hungry devices such as hard drives, fast CD-ROM drives, and high-end video equipment. One big advantage is that you can easily customize a system. For example, you can have a small mouse for children and a large one

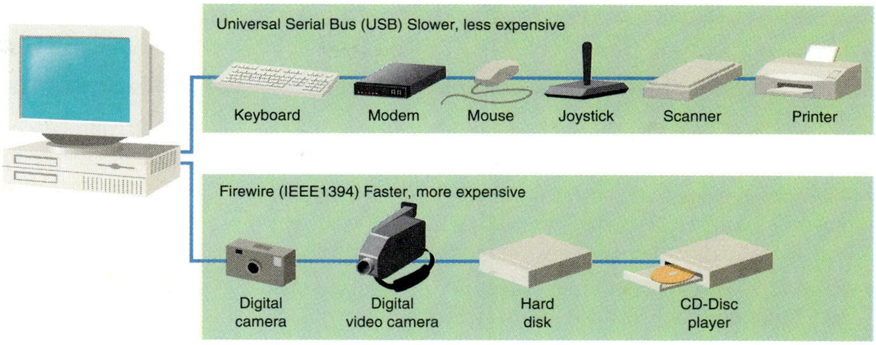

USB and Firewire ports

for adults both active at the same time. USB works at 12 Mbps and is inexpensive.

Firewire was originally conceived by Apple but has since been adopted by the entire computer and consumer electronics industry. Sometimes referred to as IEEE 1394, Firewire is much faster than USB and is designed to connect up to 63 high-bandwidth consumer electronics devices such as digital camcorders, digital cameras, and digital video disc players and also typical PC devices such as CD-ROM drives, printers, scanners, and hard drives. It also enables high-speed Internet connections.

Eventually, many PCs will have both the slower and less expensive USB and the faster and more expensive Firewire connection ports.

Look Ma, No Cables!

The problem with connecting components with cables is it's a hassle. Especially when you want to exchange information between computers, such as a laptop and a desktop. In 1993 Hewlett-Packard became the first computer company to build infrared technology into its computers. Using a beam of infrared light instead of wires, data can be sent from one unit to another. In effect it can "point-and-shoot" files to a device located nearby. The only problem is that the light can't be obstructed and doesn't bend so you can't connect computers through walls or around corners.

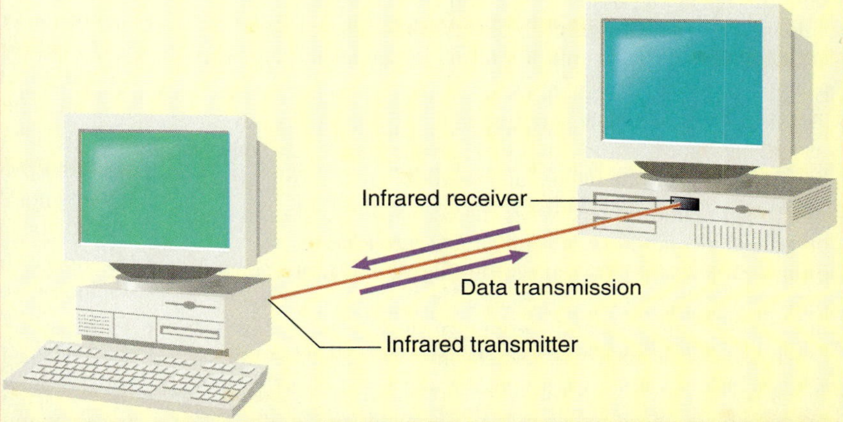

Infrared links

3.16 Enhancing and Testing Your Understanding

Summary

- In 1969, M. E. Hoff, an Intel engineer, created the first microprocessor.
- Supercomputers are used for tasks where great computing power is required. Typical applications include weather forecasting, scientific research, and automotive design.
- Mainframe computers are often used for centralized business functions such as accounting and inventory control.
- Workstations are extremely powerful desktop computers used mainly by scientists, engineers, and people who work with graphics.
- Server is the new name for many mainframes, minicomputers, workstations, and even personal computers.
- Personal computers (PCs) are small enough to stand on a desktop. Smaller versions, called notebook computers can be carried in a briefcase and run on rechargeable battery packs.
- Network Computers (NCs) and network PCs (NPCs) (also called managed PCs) are like terminals in that they depend on larger computers for their data and programs. They are like PCs in that they can process the data locally once they have received it.
- Digital is derived from the word digit, which means a single number.
- Digital processing refers to the way information is stored so that it can be processed and used.
- Analog signals look much like waves and every part of the wave carries information. Digital signals have only two states, on or off.
- The two binary numbers 0 and 1 can be processed by any device that can be set to on/off, high/low, light/dark, up/down, or other polarities.
- In a computer, the device that can store digital signals is the transistor, which has two only states: on and off.
- A bit is a single element in the computer that like a light bulb has only two possible states, on (indicating 1) or off (indicating 0). Eight bits are organized into larger units called bytes, the basic unit of information in a computer system.
- To make it easier to talk about large numbers of bytes, we use kilobyte for one thousand bytes, megabyte for one million, gigabyte for one billion, and terabyte for one trillion.
- ASCII (pronounced "as-key") is the code used most often on personal computers. It stands for the American Standard Code for Information Interchange. EBCDIC (pronounced "eb-see-dick") is the code used most often on mainframe computers and more powerful servers. It stands for the Extended Binary Coded Decimal Interchange Code.
- In many computers, separate microprocessors, called coprocessors, are used to enhance performance in specific areas. In other computers using parallel processing, there is more than one microprocesor used as the CPU.
- Microprocessors used in other products such as automobiles, telephones, and thermostats are called embedded microprocessors.
- The speed of a microprocessor's built-in clock that determines how fast it performs operations is specified in megahertz (millions of cycles per second, or MHz).
- A microprocessor's instruction set is built in. Generally complex instruction set chips (CISC) have a larger instruction set than do reduced instruction set chips (RISC).
- Read-only memory (ROM) is static and unchanging and is therefore nonvolatile. Random-access memory (RAM) is used to store an ever-changing parade of programs and data. If you turn off the computer, RAM contents are lost; thus RAM is volatile.
- When files that won't fit in memory are temporarily moved to the hard disk, the system is using virtual memory.
- When data is stored in memory in anticipation of your needing it, the area it's stored in is called a cache.
- A small portion of random-access memory is used as a buffer so data can be stored until it is processed and so you can undo a mistake.
- The central processing unit, or CPU ("see-p-u"), controls all of the computer's functions, makes all calculations, and processes all data that you enter. In most computers, and all desktop and notebook computers, the CPU is a microprocessor.
- The CPU has two main components, the control unit and the arithmetic and logic unit, that work together with memory in the machine cycle.
- A computer's bus is a set of copper connections used as a highway for data.
- Local buses, such as the Peripheral Component Interconnect (PCI) bus, speed up the system by connecting peripherals directly to the CPU and memory using a wider data pathway.
- To enhance a system, you plug adapter cards into the computer's expansion slots or PC Card slots. These are connected directly to the computer's bus, and cards plugged into them perform just as if they were built into the computer.
- Plug and play means the operating system automatically detects new hardware and automatically configures it to run on your system.
- To connect or disconnect a computer to a network or other computer, you dock or undock it.
- To connect peripherals such as printers and mice, you plug their cables into sockets on the computer called ports.
- Serial ports (sometimes called RS-232-C ports or asynchronous communications ports) are where you attach modems and a few kinds of printers. When data is sent out a serial port, it is sent 1 bit at a time.

Review Questions

True/False

1. T F In 1969, M. E. Hoff, an Intel engineer, created the first microprocessor.
2. T F Dumb terminals are just like personal computers, only with less software.
3. T F The personal computer was made possible by the invention of the micrometer.
4. T F A workstation is a very powerful version of the desktop computer widely used in engineer ing, animation, and video editing.
5. T F Computers process all data as binary 0s and 1s.
6. T F One device that can store and process digital 0s and 1s is the transistor.
7. T F A byte is made up of 2 bits—off and on.
8. T F Which characters are assigned to which combination of on and off bits in a byte is determined by a code such as ASCII or EBCDIC.
9. T F One thousand bytes is called a megabyte.
10. T F A microprocessor is an integrated circuit that can store and manipulate data—it's a computer on a chip.
11. T F In a desktop computer, and many other computers, the microprocessor is used as the central processing unit (CPU)
12. T F Random-access memory (RAM) is where the computer stores the programs and data that you are working on.
13. T F Read-only memory (ROM) is where the computer stores the programs and data that you are working on.
14. T F Virtual memory is used to store data or programs on a disk instead of in RAM.
15. T F To expand a computer's capabilities, you can insert adapter cards in the system's bus.
16. T F A serial port sends data out of the computer one bit at a time and a parallel port sends it one byte at a time.

Fill-In the Blank

1. ______ are used for weather forecasting, automotive design, and movie special effects.
2. ______ computers are often used for centralized business functions such as accounting and inventory control.
3. ______ are small but extremely powerful computers used mainly by scientists, engineers, and people who work with graphics.
4. Memory in the computer such as ROM that doesn't lose its data when you turn the system off is called ______.
5. The prediction that the density of transistors on a chip would double every year and a half is called ______ Law.
6. Each transistor in the computer can store one ______.
7. Eight transistors in a computer can store eight bits or one ______.
8. The code that personal computers use to assign characters to combinations of bits is ______
9. The CPU's control unit and arithmetic and logic unit work together in what is called the ______ cycle.
10. For data to enter or leave the computer it must pass through a ______.

Multiple Choice

1. The smallest computer (in size) is most likely called a ___.
   - **a.** Mainframe computer
   - **b.** Server
   - **c.** Handheld, palm-top, or personal digital assistant
   - **d.** Notebook computer
2. The most powerful computer is most likely called a ___.
   - **a.** Workstation
   - **b.** Minicomputer
   - **c.** Mainframe
   - **d.** Supercomputer
3. A computer advertised as a server might also be called a ___.
   - **a.** Workstation
   - **b.** Mainframe
   - **c.** Desktop computer
   - **d.** Any of the above
4. A personal computer can ___.
   - **a.** Add numbers
   - **b.** Sort lists
   - **c.** Display graphs
   - **d.** All of the above
5. The one device connected to a network that can't process data on its own is the ___.
   - **a.** Terminal
   - **b.** Personal computer (PC)
   - **c.** Network Computer (NC)
   - **d.** Net PC or managed PC
6. The best port to use for video is ___.
   - **a.** Serial
   - **b.** Universal serial bus
   - **c.** Firewire (IE1394)
   - **d.** SCSI

Research Projects

1. Look through ads or visit a computer store and note which processors are currently the least and most expensive. What is each called? What are their clock speeds?
2. Look through the ads and articles in a professional computer magazine and try to determine why some of the computers are called servers.
3. Look at ads or visit a store that sells video cameras to see if any are featuring Firewire connections.
4. Visit a computer store or use magazine ads or Internet sites to put together the computer system you'd like to have. You can add additional components as you move through the chapters of this text. For now just concentrate on the processor, bus, and ports you would like to have. When you find alternatives, such as USB and Firewire, keep track of the cost differences.

CHAPTER

4 INPUT AND OUTPUT

AN OVERVIEW

For an information system to work, it must have input—its food for thought. For you to see what it has done, it must have output—your food for thought. The most familiar input device is the keyboard but there are others that help you enter data more easily. The most familiar output devices are the display screen and printer. Printers have always been a part of the computing scene, but not so display screens.

When the first electronic computers arrived on the scene in the late 1940s, few imagined the day would come when a video screen was standard computer equipment. For one thing, not many people had even seen video screens back then. According to *Variety*, in 1949, there were only 1,082,100 television sets in use in the entire United States, approximately 450,000 in New York City. Nor was it obvious that a computer could have anything to "say" that would require a screen. The need that drove early computer development was how to overcome the difficulty and tedium of calculating tables that told artillery gunners how to aim their big guns under varying conditions. The only kind of output device required for that problem was something that would print numbers.

As computer designs matured during the 50s, 60s and early 70s, the video display started to become commonplace. There were also playful clues during those years that computer output might someday routinely involve more than letters and numbers. Computer printouts in which outline pictures were "drawn" with carefully placed Xs and Os, for instance, adorned many an office and laboratory wall.

In the late 1970s and early 80s screens and graphics moved from the playful edge to the heart of the computer industry action when microcomputers began to be sold in retail outlets. Not only did graphical computer games become a rapidly growing form of home entertainment, but business computing changed dramatically as well. The application given the lion's share of the credit for bringing the PC and into the home office was the electronic spreadsheet VisiCalc, its name derived from the phrase *visible calculator.*

In this chapter we explore the concepts and applications of input and output devices.

OBJECTIVES

After completing this chapter, you will be able to:

- Identify the keys on the computer's keyboard and explain their use.
- Explain how scanners and character recognition work.
- Explain input devices such as bar code scanners and voice.
- Explain how scanners read images rather than text.
- Identify pointing devices such as mice, graphics tablets, joysticks, trackballs, and touch screens.
- Describe fonts and their characteristics.
- Explain how text and graphics are displayed on the screen.
- Compare and contrast the various types of computer display screens.
- Explain how printers form characters and transfer them to paper.

Input *n., v.* 1. to enter data into the computer for processing; the data entered.

Output *n.* 1. to transfer data from the computer to devices that allow you to see, hear, or feel it; the data transferred.

ON THE PACE CD ROM

Spread No.	Title
4-2	Understanding the Keyboard
4-3	Optical Character Recognition
4-7	Understanding Pixels
4-8	Understanding Fonts
4-9	Understanding RGB Color
4-11	Understanding Display Screen Resolutions

4.1 Input and Output Devices:

We now communicate with computers using input and output devices. We use input devices to enter data into the computer so it can be processed. We use output devices to get it out so we can see it or distribute it to others. But input and output devices are not limited to the common display screen and printer. There is a vast range of devices in use and more are being developed every day. One thing to keep in mind is that not all devices do just input or output. Some devices such as modems or fax boards in a computer are two-way in nature, able to both input and output information.

Input devices

There are lots of common types of input devices, almost too many to keep track of. However, the most common are keyboards, pointing devices, and scanners. Coming up fast are speech recognition devices.

- Keyboards are used to enter data by typing it in–a very slow manual process. Unfortunately for those who don't type, almost all data is originally entered using this method.
- Fax modems send and receive faxes.
- Pointing devices are used to move a pointer around on the screen to execute commands or to manipulate the data that has already been entered.
- Scanners are used to enter data into the computer automatically. To use this form of data entry, the data must already exist in a printed form–either as text or graphics. Scanning devices can then read the printed data and convert it into a digital form that the computer can process.
- Speech recognition devices are able to hear your spoken words and then either execute them as commands or enter them as text.

Output devices

Once data has been input and processed you need access to it in a form you can use. The devices you use to do this are called output devices because data is sent or output to them from the computer. The output can be in the form of words, numbers, graphics, sounds, videos, and animations.

- You may want to print your work on paper–called hard copy–so that you can take it with you, share it with others, or file it for later reference. Hard copy can be created with a stunning array of printers that range from small desktop units to units that will paint an image on the wall.
- Output can be displayed on the screen—sometimes called soft copy—when creating, editing, and manipulating data. In this case, the soft copy is an intermediate stage toward producing hard copy. The screen, however, is increasingly the intended final output device for multimedia output.
- Musical output can come through a synthesizer or other musical system.
- Output can be in the form of instructions to another device, such as a robot.

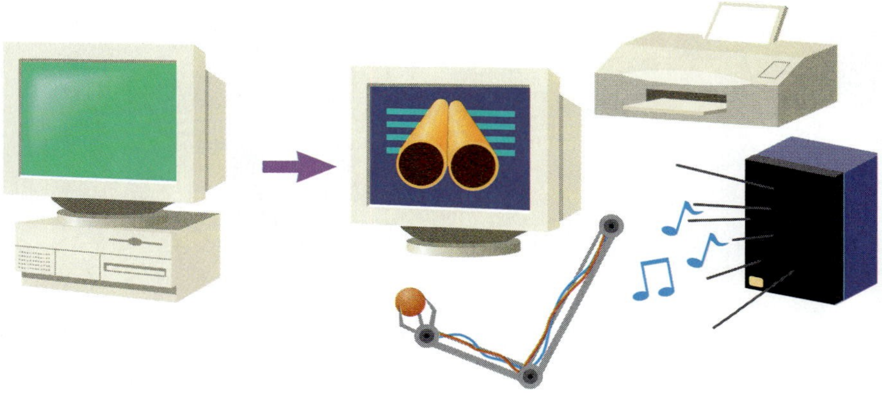

Output devices

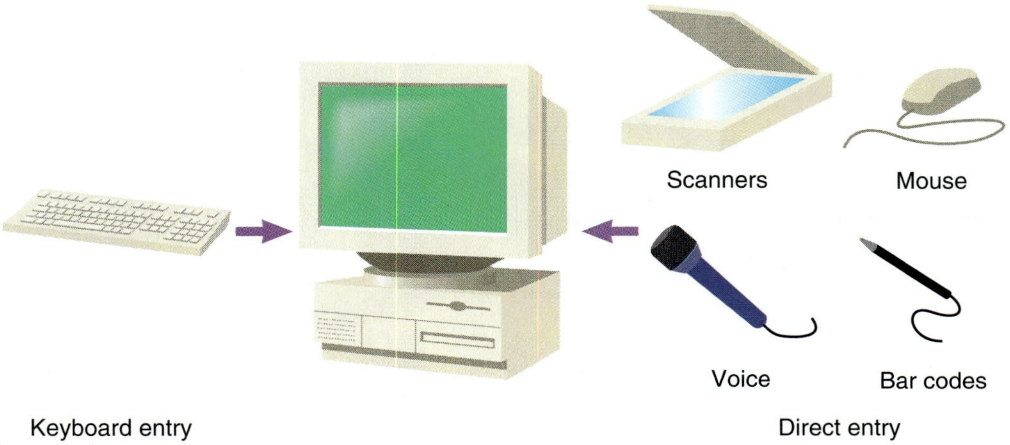

Input devices

Special purpose input and output devices

Special purpose input devices are widely used in information technology. For example, thermometers, barometers, earthquake detectors, atmospheric instruments, and astronomical instruments may be used by scientists. Graphics tablets, digital or video cameras, or even synthesizers may be used by artists and designers. The variety of potential input devices is limited only by the human imagination.

The virtual golf program shown here uses both input and output devices. By swinging the club to hit the ball, the player sends input to the computer. A simulation of the ball's flight and its new position on the course is then displayed (output).

If you like playing the old fashioned pinball machines, you can play them on your own computer although body English doesn't work and tilt isn't a danger.

Virtual golf courtesy of Golftex, Inc.

Pinball keyboard attachment courtesy of Immersion Corporation

Check numbers

When you cash a check on vacation, say at Disney World, it's amazing that it is deducted from your bank account in Chicago or Boston within a day or so. This speed is achieved by devices that read the line of futuristic-looking characters printed on the check using a technology called magnetic-ink character recognition (MICR—pronounced "mi-ker"). The characters on the check are printed with a kind of ink or toner that when magnetized will emit a signal that identifies each character. The checks are fed through reader/sorter machines that magnetize the characters, then read them. These mechanical sorters, first developed in the 1950s, can read, log, sort, and route 2,400 checks a minute as they travel through the machine at 30 miles per hour–processing over 60 billion a year.

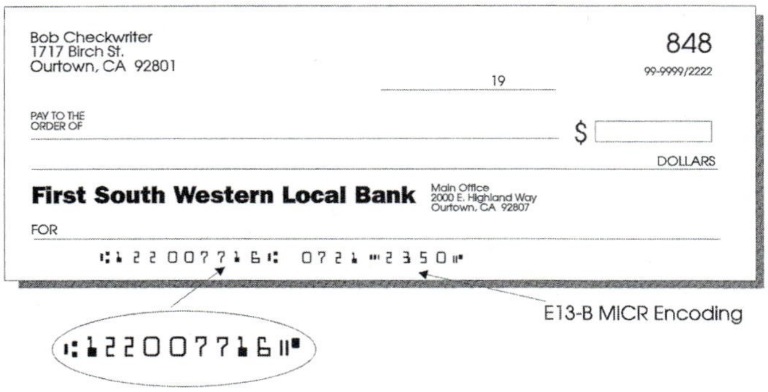

Magnetic-ink character recognition on check courtesy of Troy

Card scanners

Business card scanners are used to scan standard business cards so the person's name, title, address, and phone numbers are automatically entered into a phone book.

Card scanner courtesy of Seiko

4.2 Inputting Text:

Keyboards vary in design and layout from computer to computer, but all have essentially the same types of keys. For example, the keyboard on a desktop computer has the same letter and number keys as the keyboard on a notebook computer. The main differences among various types of keyboards such as these are in the number and location of other or extra keys.

The standard keyboard

The standard computer keyboard matured long before the graphical user interface came into existence. As a result, it contains a number of keys that no longer perform really useful functions unless your mouse breaks and you're forced to use keyboard commands.

- The Escape key is often used to cancel a command in progress.
- Numeric keys located above the alphabetic keys are labeled with both numbers and symbols. When you press these keys, you enter either the indicated numbers or, if you hold down Shift, the indicated symbols.
- Function keys, labeled F1 through F12, perform functions assigned to them by the software such as saving documents or selecting text. Heavily used before the introduction of mice and graphical interfaces such as Windows, they are now used much less often.
- The Backspace key backs the insertion point through the characters in a line of type and usually deletes characters as it does so. This lets you quickly back over and delete characters when you discover a mistake while entering data.
- The Enter (or Return) key is often pressed as the final keystroke of an operation. For example, when you enter data you may have to press Enter to complete the entry or to start a new paragraph.
- Keyboard lights indicate the status of the CapsLock, Numlock, and ScrollLock keys that lock a command ("use capital letters") into place until you strike the key again. Each of these keys toggles between two settings like a wall switch. If it is off when you press it, it turns on. If it is on when you press it, it turns off. When one of these keys is on, the corresponding keyboard indicator lights will be lit.
- The Tab key moves the insertion point to the next tab stop, cell, or space in a form and the Shift+Tab (Backtab) key moves it back to the previous position. The tab and backtab functions are both on the same key which acts as a backtab when you press it while holding down Shift.
- The Shift key has an up arrow on it to indicate that it shifts to enter uppercase letters when held down.
- The Spacebar moves the insertion point one character to the right and enters a space. If there is a character to the right of the insertion point, it may be either pushed to the right or replaced by a blank space depending on how the program is set up.
- Alphanumeric keys are used to enter data. The alphabetic keys are arranged just as they are on a typewriter. When you press these keys, you enter lowercase letters. If you hold down the Shift key when you press them, or if you engage the CapsLock key, you enter uppercase (capital) letters. If you engage CapsLock and then hold down Shift while typing, you enter lowercase letters.
- Arrow keys move the cursor or insertion point in the direction of the arrow you press.
- Numeric keypads have arrow keys that work only when NumLock is not engaged. Many keyboards also have a separate set of arrow keys that work whether NumLock is engaged or not.
- NumLock switches the commands given by the keys on the numeric keypad between entering numbers and moving the cursor or insertion point.

Keyboard

Another Name Change

Older programs refer to a cursor, an underscore character or a box that highlights a character or indicates where the next character you type will appear. Newer programs have changed its shape to a vertical line and its name to insertion point.

Excuse Me, but Which Is the Home Row?

The good news is that the mainland Chinese have simplified their written language so it uses only 5,000 characters. The bad news is that in Taiwan, they use 12,000 characters. Imagine the kitchen-table-sized keyboard that would be required to accommodate this many characters. Keyboards have been built, but many require as many as six separate keystrokes to create a single character from building blocks. Even with 1.2 billion people, computer sales to the Chinese have been understandably slow–less than 1 million in 1995. To improve the market, computer companies are developing new input devices based on the voice or handwriting recognition.

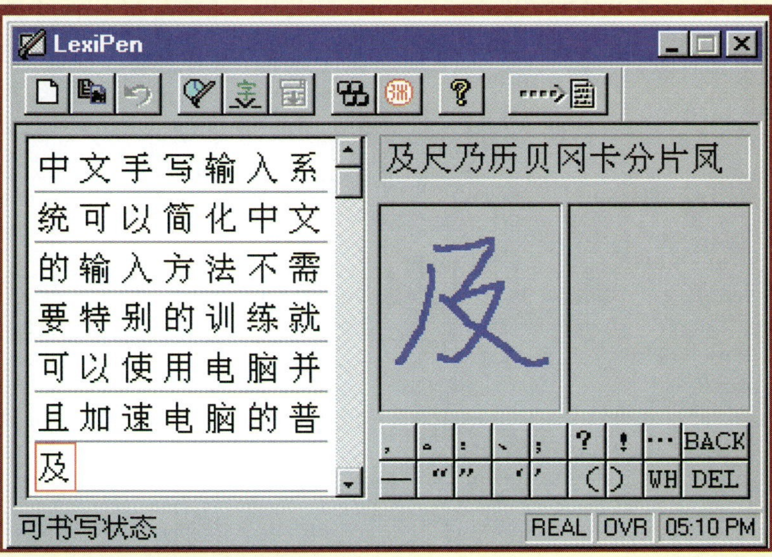

Lexipen. Copyright of Motorola, used by permission

Ergonomic keyboards

The computer revolution has dramatically increased the number of people who use keyboards and thus the incidence of physical stress sometimes caused by using keyboards over a prolonged period. Scientists have made an ongoing study of the problem. Keyboards have been designed to relieve the stress on wrists and arms. The scientific analysis of man-machine interactions is called ergonomics. These new ergonomic designs are intended to reduce repetitive stress injuries.

Ergonomic keyboard courtesy of Workplace Designs

Virtual keyboards

Not all keyboards are hardware. On small handheld computers, the keyboard is displayed right on the computer screen. Called a virtual, soft, or touch screen keyboard, you enter text and numbers by tapping the "keys" with your finger or a penlike stylus.

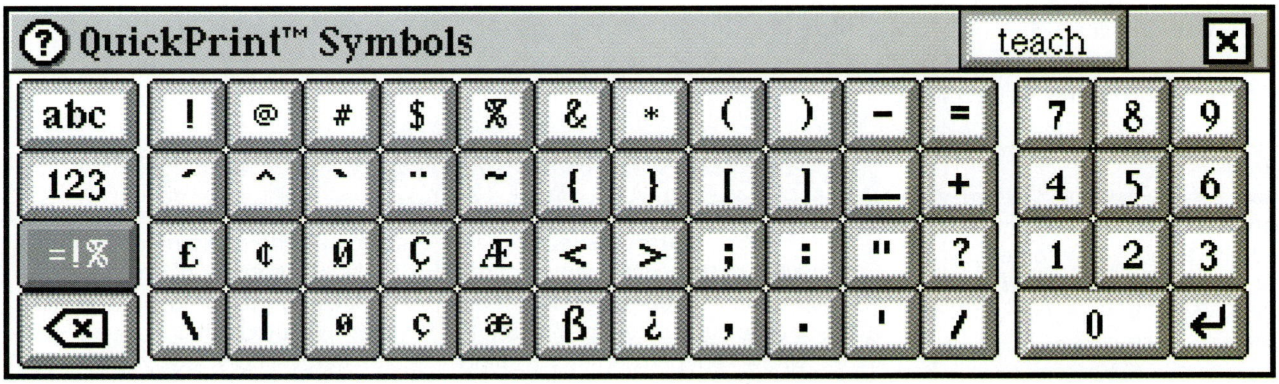

Symbol keyboard. Copyright of Motorola, used by permission

4.3 Inputting Text:

Typing data into a computer can be very laborious and expensive. To speed up data entry, many devices other than the keyboard have been developed. These include optical character recognition, handwriting, and speech recognition, and bar codes.

Optical character recognition

Once data has been printed, you do not have to retype it back into the computer. Optical character recognition (OCR) is like reversing the process of printing. Scanning converts text from a printed form back to an electronic form that you can edit with a word processing program just as if you had entered it through the keyboard.

Optical character recognition is accomplished using a scanner and OCR software as follows:

1. When you scan a document, it is converted to a picture called a bit-mapped image.
2. The OCR software analyzes the light and dark areas on the page, making a guess at how the page is laid out. For example, it is often able to identify graphics and columns.
3. The software looks up each character in its library of character templates trying to find a match for it. The quality of both the original document and the bit-mapped image of it determine the accuracy of this step.
4. The software uses a process called feature extraction to analyze characters more closely. As it makes matches it builds a working alphabet of the characters it has encountered.
5. Characters that can't be identified are displayed using special symbols, or you may be prompted to manually type them in.
6. After the document has been converted, you can save it in the format of the word processing program that you want to use to edit it.

Handwriting recognition

Some new handheld computers replace the keyboard with a touch-sensitive screen on which you write with a stylus. As you write in your own handwriting, a program recognizes your writing, character by character, and converts your written characters into neatly typed text. Handwriting recognition is difficult because there are so many variations, which of course is one of the reasons we rely on signatures as a means of identification. Two approaches are used: cursive recognition and print recognition. In cursive recognition, you write in long-

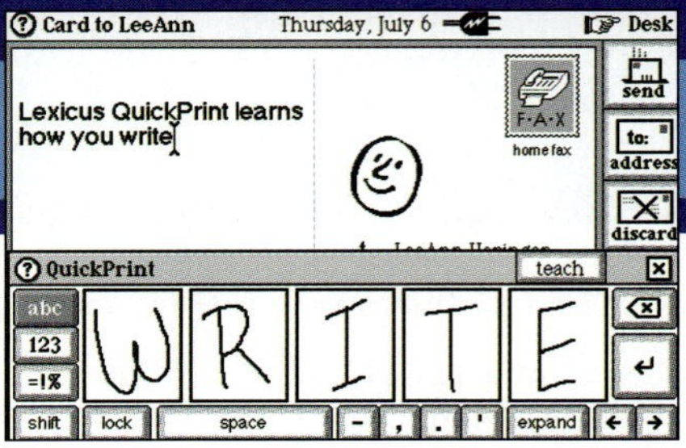

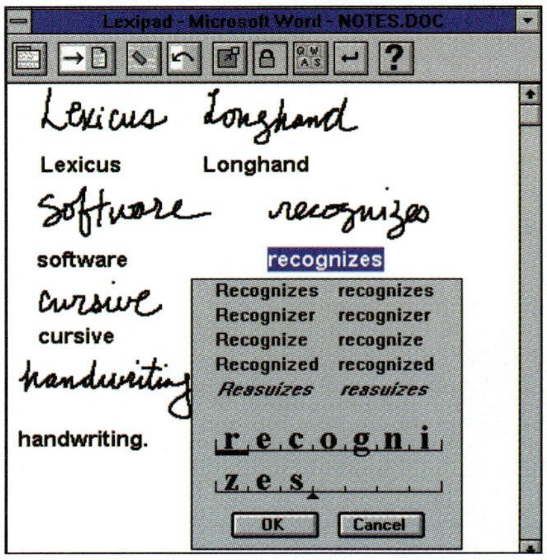

Lexis longhand handwriting recognition software. Copyright of Motorola, used by permission

hand, and in print recognition, you print individual characters in little boxes on the screen. Ideally, a recognizer will work at the same speed at which you write–12 words per minute (wpm) for block printing to 33 wpm for fast longhand.

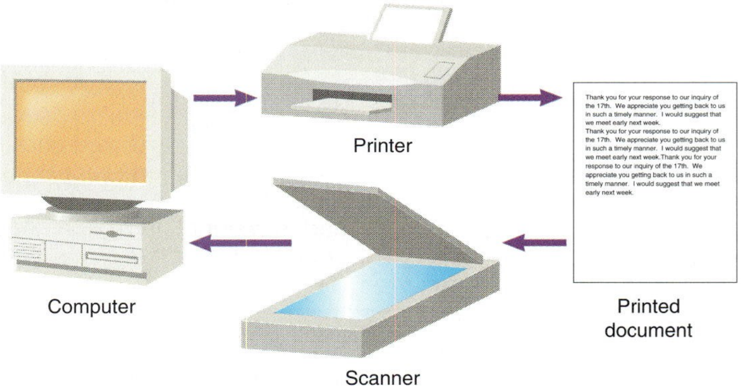

Optical character recognition

Fax and OCR

When a fax arrives, sometimes you'd like to edit it in some way. Not too long ago you would have had to retype it to do so. Now, however, fax software often has a built-in OCR capability so the fax is immediately converted into an editable file.

What's Going On Here?

In 1996, state inspectors in Massachusetts began a survey of bar code scanners at the retail level. Osco drug outlets were discovered to be wrong 76 percent of the time. Lechmere outlets were wrong 35 percent of the time. The companies attributed the problems to errors in downloading price information from headquarters to the outlets. In both cases, two-thirds of the errors were overcharges. Obviously bar code scanners are much more accurate than the people who manage them.

Bar codes and bar code scanners

One of the most widely used direct entry devices is the bar code scanner that reads bar codes. Bar codes are made up of bars of different widths and spacing that convey alphabetic and numeric information about products or addresses. These bar codes can be scanned with either a handheld wand or a built-in scanner that converts the code into an electronic form that can be processed by a computer. There are a variety of bar codes in use including the following:

Bar codes

- ♦UPC (Universal Product Code—EAN outside the United States and Canada) is an eleven digit system used for bar coding general merchandise.
- ♦Code 39 uses nine groups of 3 bars for each character. This technology is popular because it doesn't have to be perfectly printed and it can encode both numbers and letters.
- ♦POSTNET bar code was developed by the United States Postal Service to automate the sorting of mail. It can encode the ZIP code and the first two digits of the street address. It is the most demanding bar code technology because it cannot be reduced or enlarged.

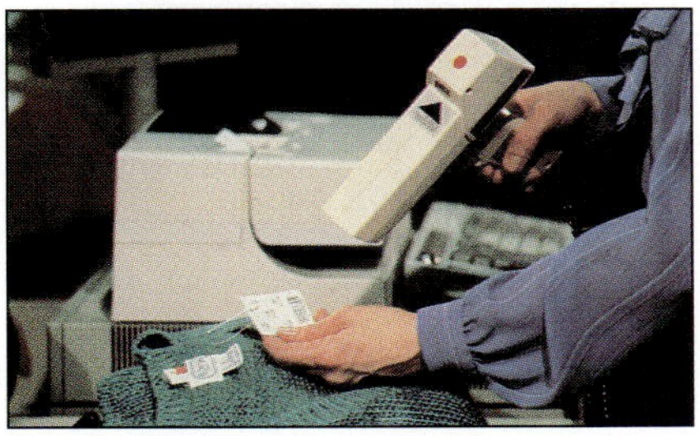

Bar code reader courtesy of International Business Machines

Bar code scanners are accurate, fast, and inexpensive, features that have made them familiar at supermarket checkout counters, where the checkout person uses them to read the bar code labels on cans, boxes, and bags. These supermarket scanners are connected to a computer that contains a complete list of product names and prices for each different bar code in the store. When the scanner reads the bar code on, say, a can of beans, the computer looks up the product number the bar code represents and returns its name and price to the register at the checkout counter.

The information collected by the computer with these devices can also have additional benefits. Since a minute-by-minute record is made of every sale, the store can track inventory and perform marketing analysis in real time. With instant feedback, the managers can know what products are selling, measure the effect of prices and discounts, and compare one product's sales with another's.

There is a variety of barcode scanners:

- ♦A wand is an inexpensive scanner that requires physical contact as it is scanned across a bar code.
- ♦Charge-Coupled Devices (CCD) scanners have a reading head you place over a bar code before you pull the trigger.
- ♦Fixed Focus Optics (FFO) scanners are aimed at a bar code up to 20 inches away.
- ♦Laser scanners use a laser beam to read a barcode when you pull a trigger.

Speech recognition

When you call the phone company for information, you sometimes get a computer that asks you to speak the name of the party you want to call. When you do so, the computer looks up the name and gives you the number, that is, if this speaker-independent system can understand your accent. More commonly, voice systems work only for a single person. They are speaker-dependent. To use one of these systems, you first "train" the computer so it becomes familiar with the way you pronounce each word. To do so, each word in the program's vocabulary–as many as 120,000–is displayed on the screen, and you speak each aloud into a microphone. Your pronunciation is digitized, analyzed, and stored as a voice template.

The next time you speak to the computer, it quickly matches the pattern of your voice against the voice templates stored in its memory. If it finds a match, it displays the word or executes the command. Your speech is analyzed using both an "acoustic model" and a "language model." Using the acoustic model, your speech is compared to speech samples collected from thousands of people. The result is the best acoustic word match and a short list of alternates. Using the language model, statistical analysis is used when words sound alike ("to," "too," and "two") to determine the likelihood that one of them is better than the other in the current context.

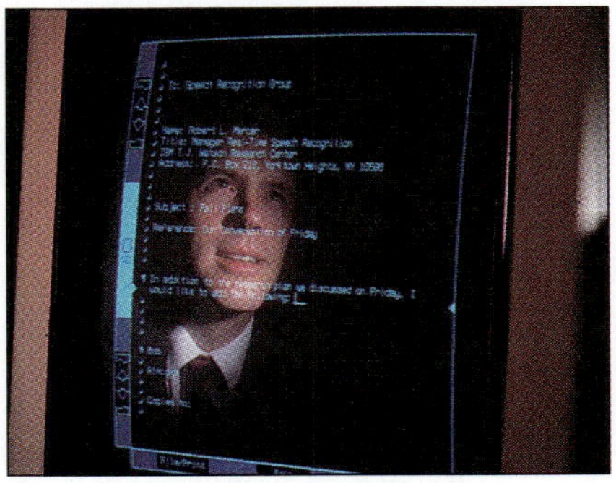

Speech recognition courtesy of International Business Machines

4.4 Inputting Graphics:

Increasingly, graphics such as photographs and drawings are used in documents and multimedia presentations. Drawings created on the computer and photographs taken with digital cameras are already in the digital form needed by the computer. In other cases, however, graphics are created with more traditional tools and must then be converted to a digital form the computer can handle.

Types of graphic scanners

To digitize graphics, you use a scanner, in many cases the same one you use to do OCR scanning. However, when you scan graphics you don't convert text to an editable form. You just take a digital picture of the graphic. Any text in the document is just a part of the picture and cannot be manipulated with a word processor.

Scanners used to scan graphics take many forms. The most common type is the flat bed scanner that holds the paper flat while the scanner moves its scanning optics past it. More expensive, and more accurate, drum scanners keep the scanner's optics fixed and move the paper past them. Inexpensive, handheld scanners are moved across a page, section by section.

How a scanner works

All scanners use a similar approach to scanning a page. To take a digital picture of a document, a flat bed scanner moves a fluorescent bulb over the page. The light is reflected off the page and focused by a lens onto a receptor called a charge-coupled device (CCD). A CCD can read light intensity and since darker areas reflect less light than lighter areas, the device can measure the brightness of every pixel (or tiny square in an imaginary grid) that it scans and assign a value to it. These values are stored as index or palette numbers that identify the brightness of the pixel as closely as possible.

All a CCD can do is measure brightness in a range of grays from pure white to pure black. To measure colors, filters must be used. In a single-pass scanner, CCD light receiving elements are grouped in threes each with a different colored filter to read red, green, or blue colors. In triple-pass scanners, all of the elements use the same filter and three successive passes are made as the filter is changed. Generally single-pass scanners are faster but less accurate.

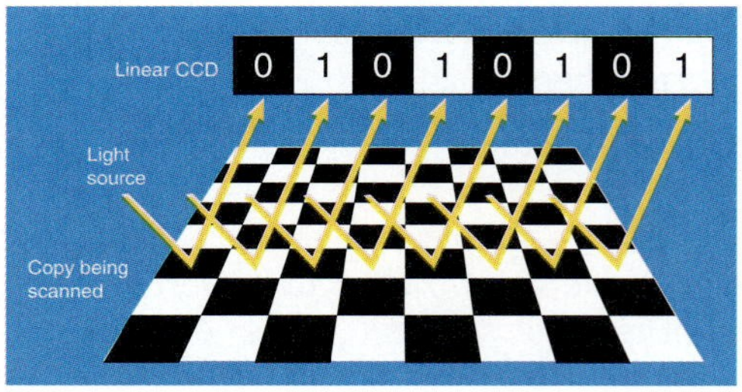

Scanner CCD

When the scanned image is displayed on the screen, the digitizing process is reversed and the numeric value of each pixel in the original image is used to control the brightness and color of its corresponding pixel on the display screen. Once the image has been stored in the computer's memory and displayed on the screen, it can be manipulated by a program designed to work with images of this kind. For example, you can import it into a document or modify it with a paint program.

Resolution

One of the keys to a scanner's quality is its resolution. Scanners are frequently advertised using two resolutions: optical resolution and maximum resolution. For example, a scanner may be marketed as having 600 x 600 optical resolution and 2400 x 2400 maximum resolution.

The optical resolution of a scanner, and the fineness of its scans, is directly proportional to the number of light gathering elements on its CCD. True optical resolution is calculated by dividing the width of a scan by the number of CCD elements being used. For example, a scanner with 3,400 elements scanning an 8.5-inch wide sheet has an optical resolution of 400 dots per inch (dpi) (3400/8.5=400).

Sometimes, manufacturers stress the scanner's maximum resolution (also called interpolated resolution or enhanced resolution). This is the apparent resolution of the image after it has been enhanced with software to make it

Flat bed scanner courtesy of Hewlett-Packard

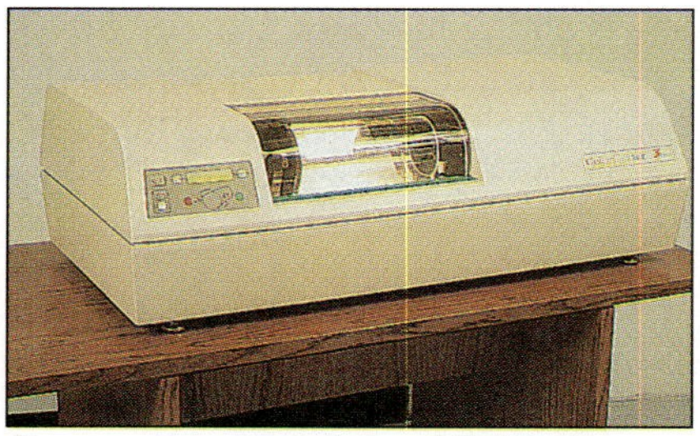

Drum scanner courtesy of Optronics

Sheet-fed scanner courtesy of Visioneer

Handheld scanner courtesy of Logitech

Scanners

look like it has a higher resolution than it actually has. By a process of interpolation, the software adds pixels to the image to increase its resolution. To determine the color of a new pixel, the software evaluates the colors of the pixels surrounding it and uses those colors to guess at the color of the new pixel. The new pixels don't add any new information to the image so they don't improve image detail at all.

Color depth

Color depth refers to the number of colors that a scanner can sense and re-create digitally. It depends entirely on the number of bits assigned to each pixel that is scanned. For example, an 8-bit scanner can sense and store 256 shades of gray or color. (Remember back in our discussion of bits and bytes how 2^8 equals 256?)

A 24-bit scanner uses 8 bits for each color in a pixel–red, green, and blue. When combined, they create 16.7 million colors, called true color because that's the number of colors a human eye can discern. However, because of noise, a scanner must scan using 30 or more bits and then use those to calculate the final 24-bit image. This is why you see scanners promoted with 30, 32, or even 36 bits per pixel. Basically, the more bits per pixel the scanner has to start with, the more accurate will be the final 24-bit image.

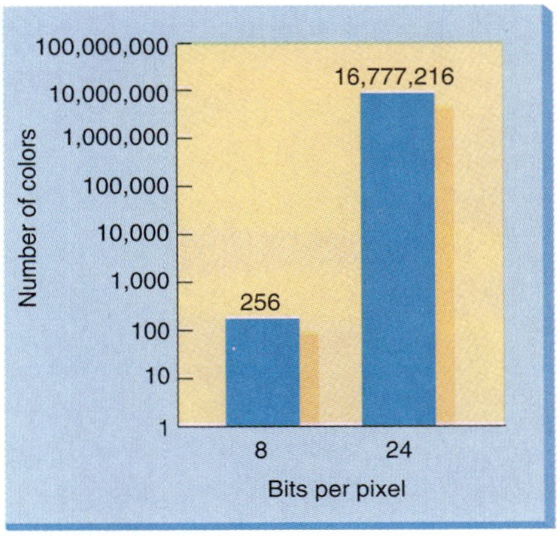

Color depth

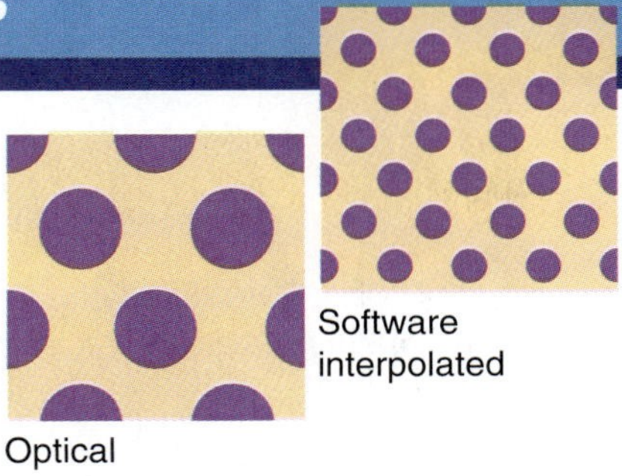

Scanner resolution

Yikes–these files are huge!

The number of bytes required to store a scanned image depends on the type of scanning used. For example, an 8½-by-11-inch image scanned at 300 dots per inch

- ♦ Requires 8 Megabytes when scanned using eight colors.
- ♦ Requires 100 Megabytes when scanned using twenty-four colors.

To store many graphic image files of this size would create serious storage problems. To reduce this problem, scanners can use a special procedure called file compression to store the files in much less space on the disk.

File sizes

Digitizing photos and video

Digital cameras can capture images using the receptors called charge-coupled devices (CCD) instead of film. The images are then stored on a disk or memory in the camera for later transfer to a computer. Once in the computer, the images can be used in a document to be printed or included in a multimedia presentation.

Digital camera courtesy of Casio

Film scanners or recorders are used to digitize slide film and negatives. Frequently, these scanners are owned by service bureaus where customers can take their work to be digitized.

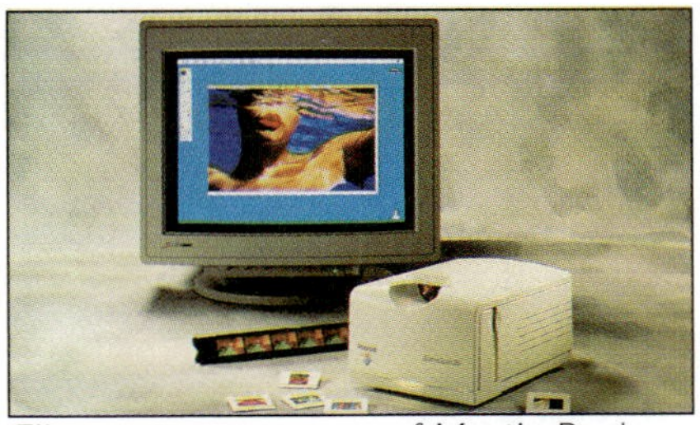

Film scanner courtesy of Martin Paul, photographer

Digital video cameras can be hooked up to a computer to feed images to the screen and to the hard disk. Inexpensive video capture boards allow you to capture individual frames recorded by nondigital video cameras.

Digital video camera courtesy of Hitachi
http://www.hitachi.com/News/Press/news-961113.html

4.5 Picture Essay:

Computer input and output are no longer limited to just text and occasional graphics. Data now include sounds, videos, pictures, animations, and movies. All sorts of devices used to input and output these types of data are rapidly gaining in popularity both in business and with consumers. Here's a peek at some of the hottest.

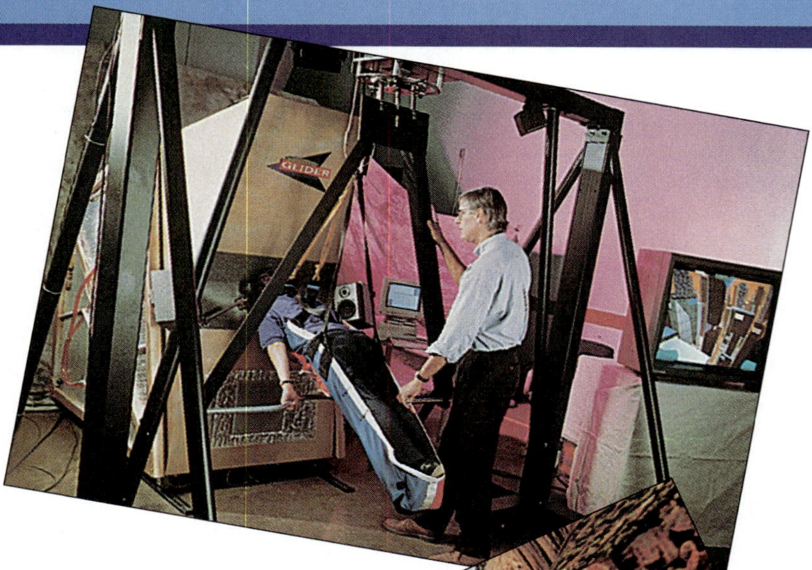

Virtual reality

Virtual reality gives you the feeling that you're experiencing a different space than the one you actually occupy. At the high end of this field are flight simulators used to train pilots. At the lower end are systems that feed images and sounds into a headset combining goggles and speakers. When combined with special gloves, you are able to see, hear, and feel another space. Above on the right, you see a virtual reality apparatus that you climb into to feel the sensations of hang gliding in the Grand Canyon or Manhattan.

Holograms

Computer-generated holograms give the viewer a startlingly realistic 3-D vision. You can even walk around holograms and see an object from different points of view. Below is a photograph of a hologram of a Honda automobile made at the MIT Media Lab.

Hologram courtesy of MIT Media Lab

Virtual reality courtesy of Evans & Sutherland

Beam me up Scotty—3D scanning

At the University of Texas, a laser scans a slowly revolving fossil. The reflected laser light slowly builds a digital 3D image of the object's contours in the computer. This image is then modified using computed tomography, the same technology used in medical CAT scans. Finally, a process called sintering is used to make a 3D copy of the original object. The computer guides a laser so it "carves" the copied shape into a block of nylon or polycarbonate power. This duplicate is so accurate that it can be used by researchers who study in the field. For example, a researcher could measure the wear on a copy of a fossil tooth or study the subtle techniques used to create a pot. The University of Texas is preparing a CD-ROM database that anyone can use to create 3D models of rare artifacts, priceless fossils, and extinct animal skeletons. A scholar or student could even download one of these files and recreate a copy at her own school.

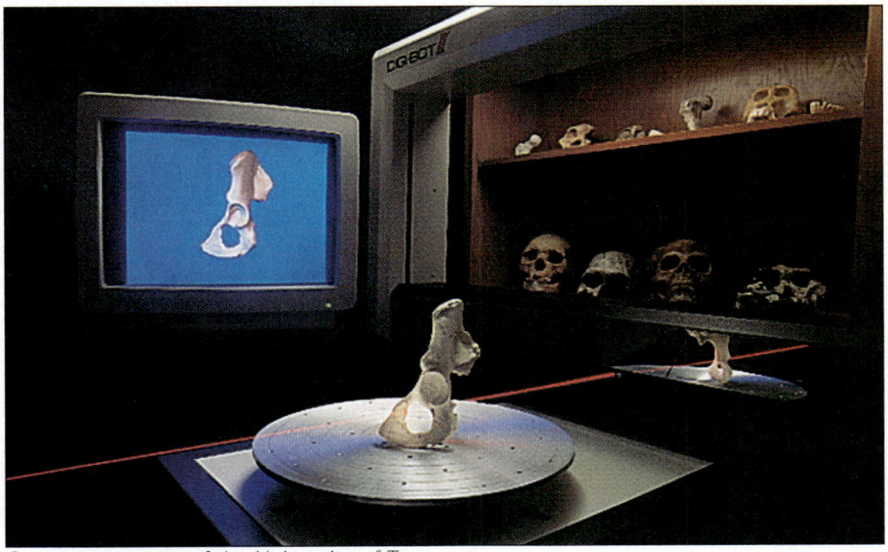

Scanner courtesy of the University of Texas

Body scanning

Cyberware's whole body scanner can scan an entire human body in 17 seconds. The high resolution 3D color model that it creates can be used for perfectly tailored clothes or for special effects in the movies.

A smaller scanner can be used to capture both the shape and color of 3D objects such as this ceramic pot. This is a useful scanner for scientific studies, artistic renderings, and manufacturing.

Whole body scanner courtesy of Cyberware

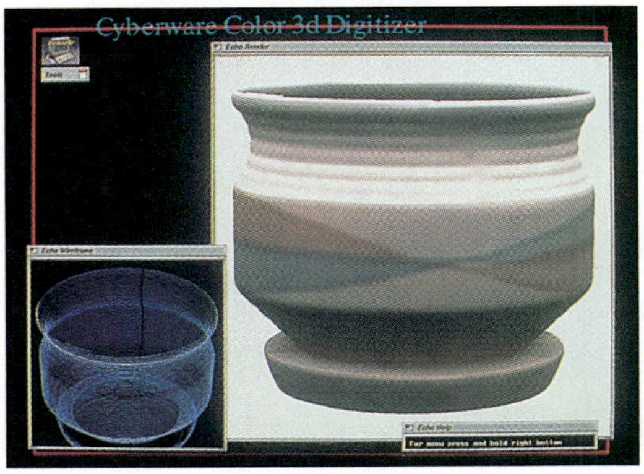

Scanned pot courtesy of Cyberware

4.6 Pointing Devices

Several input devices have been developed to make it easy to execute commands by pointing to, clicking, and dragging things on the screen. Although the mouse is the most common such device, there is a surprising variety available. You can use any of these devices to make menu selections or select text or other objects to be copied, deleted, or moved. You can even drag things on the screen and drop them in new locations

Mice

The most popular pointing device is the mouse, which accounts for about 80 percent of all pointing devices sold. One type of mouse houses a rolling ball and one or more buttons that you press to execute commands. As you move the mouse around on a flat, smooth surface, the ball rolls and feeds electrical signals to the computer to move a mouse pointer on the screen.

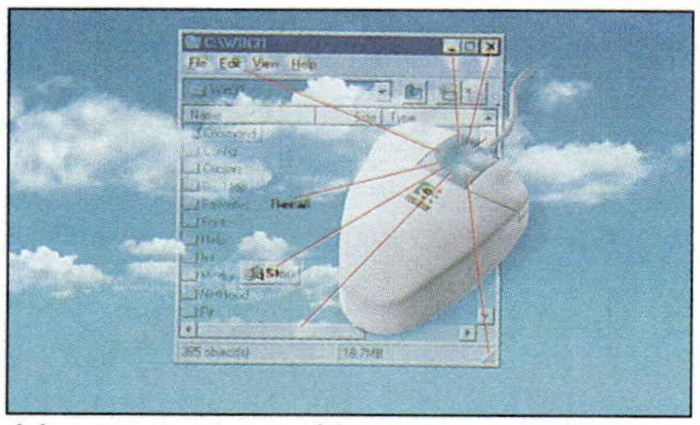

Mouse courtesy of Logitech

Track sticks

Track sticks, often found on notebook computers, are pencil eraser-type pointing devices located in the center of the keyboard.

Trackstick courtesy of courtesy of International Business Machines

Trackballs

Trackballs, also common on notebook computers, are like an upside-down mouse. You spin a ball exposed on their top surface to move the mouse pointer on the screen. The direction you spin the ball determines the direction it moves.

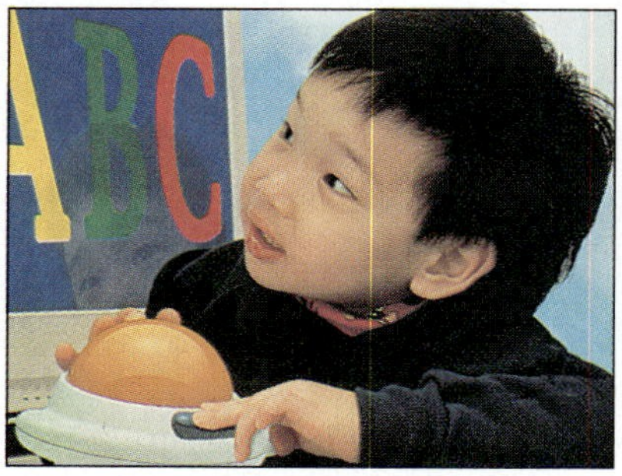

Trackball courtesy of International Business Machines

Fingers

Your finger is the ultimate pointing device. Some computers have touch-sensitive screens. You use your finger to point to a command displayed on the screen, and it is executed. These are mainly used in kiosks, those displays in public places where you point to purchase airline tickets, find directions, or locate stores in malls.

Touch screen courtesy of Casio

Touch pads

Like touch screens, touch pads let your fingers do the pointing. They are flat rectangular pads that sense the movement and pressure of your fingertip to control the mouse pointer. Using finger gestures, you can click, double-click, and drag just as with a mouse.

Touchpad courtesy of Apple

Graphics tablet

Related to the touch pad is the graphics tablet. Instead of using your finger, you use a pencil-like stylus to execute commands and create drawings using the same kind of hand motion you use when sketching or tracing drawings laid on top of the pad.

Graphics tablet courtesy of Wacom

Joysticks

Joysticks are like the controller in an airplane and are most often used with games. Buttons on the stick allow you to fire guns or execute other actions. The Thrustmaster joystick even gives you feedback so it seems like you're using the real thing.

Cordless mice

Mice are fine until you're standing in front of a room full of people giving a computer presentation. At times like this you don't want to have to periodically bend over to use a mouse. The solution is a cordless mouse that you can use to move the mouse pointer on the screen by moving your hand in the direction you want it to move. The mouse senses your hand motion and transmits a signal to the computer to move the mouse pointer in the same direction. Buttons on the cordless mouse allow you to click, double-click, and drag.

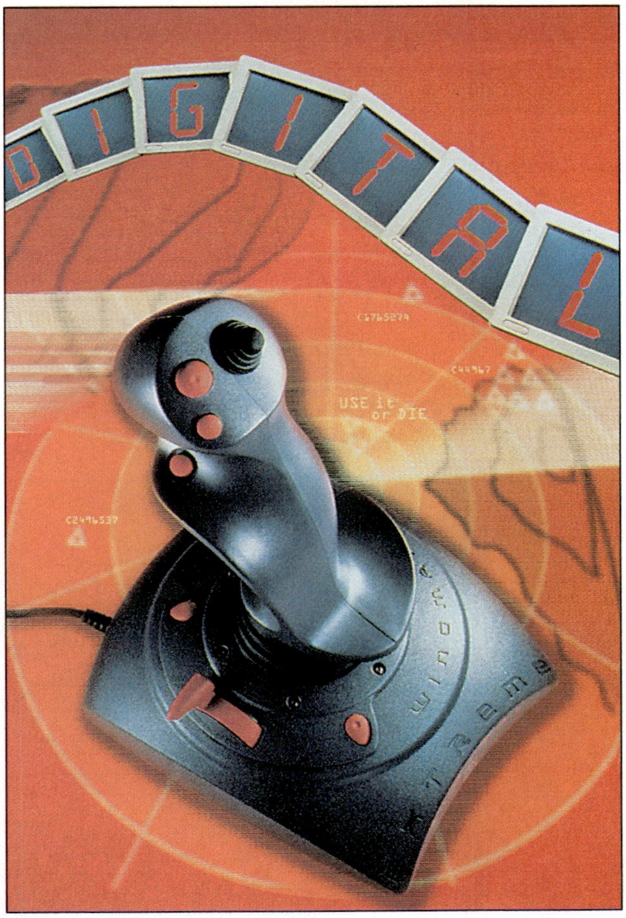

Joystick courtesy of Logitech

Cordless mouse courtesy of Gyration

Mouse Speak

When you use a mouse or other pointing device, here are some basic terms to remember:

- The mouse pointer refers to the arrow or other symbol on the screen that moves when you move the mouse.
- Point means to position the mouse pointer over or on some items on the screen.
- Clicking refers to pressing and quickly releasing the left button on the mouse, right-clicking refers to doing the same thing with the right button.
- Double-clicking refers to pressing one of the buttons on the mouse twice in rapid succession.
- Drag means to hold down one of the mouse buttons while you move the mouse. You do this frequently when you want to highlight a block of text so that you can format it. In other situations, this action drags the highlighted item to a new position on the screen.
- Drag and drop means to drag an item to another position and then release the mouse button to let it go. New programs allow you to move text, copy files, and even copy objects between applications by dragging and dropping them.

4.7 The Foundations of Modern Output:

Turn on your computer and read your e-mail or write a paper. When you need to do some research, jump onto the Internet and browse historic video clips for a history course or art museums and photograph exhibits for an art course assignment. When you're in need of a break, load a flight simulator program and fly through a photo-realistic computer world. Put on 3D glasses and watch as things hurtle out of the screen at you. As different as these experiences may be, they all share one thing in common–you're looking at nothing but dots. Like the impressionist painters who painted wonderful scenes with small dots of paint, your screen, and your printer, create images with small dots.

Pixels–all output is dots

To create an image on the screen or printed page, the screen or page is divided into a grid, creating small squares called picture elements, or pixels. On a typical screen, there may be almost 800,000 pixels. On a printer, the equivalent of a pixel is a dot printed on the page. Each of these pixels has an address so the computer can change any pixel's color and intensity. By specifying colors for each pixel, any kind of image can be created. Controlling, or addressing, individual pixels in this way is called bit mapping. Here you see a reproduction of the famous painting "The Spirit of '76" done in jelly beans. Think of each jelly bean as a pixel and you can understand how dots can form images.

Jelly Bean Spirit of '76 courtesy of Herman Goelitz Inc.

The enlargement of a small portion of a color graphic shows how it too is created from individual pixels.

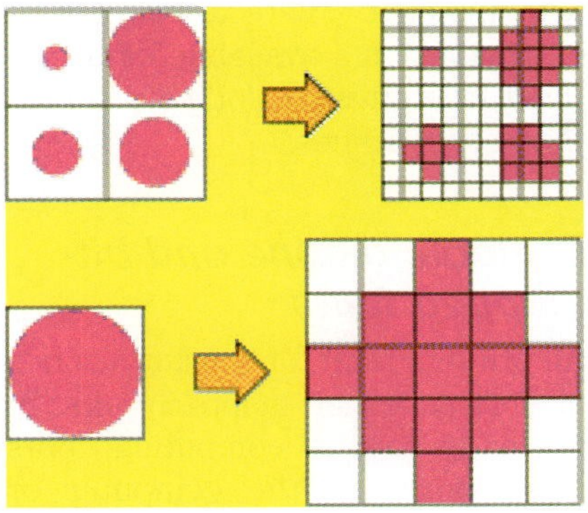

Laser output courtesy of Tektronics

To create shades of gray or color on a laser printer, groups of adjacent pixels are treated as a single unit called a cell. In black and white printing when all of the dots in a cell are on, the cell is black. When all of them are off, the cell is white. The ratio of on and off dots between these two extremes determines how gray the cell is.

Resolution

The quality of displayed or printed text and graphics is called resolution. Resolution is determined by the number of dots used per inch.

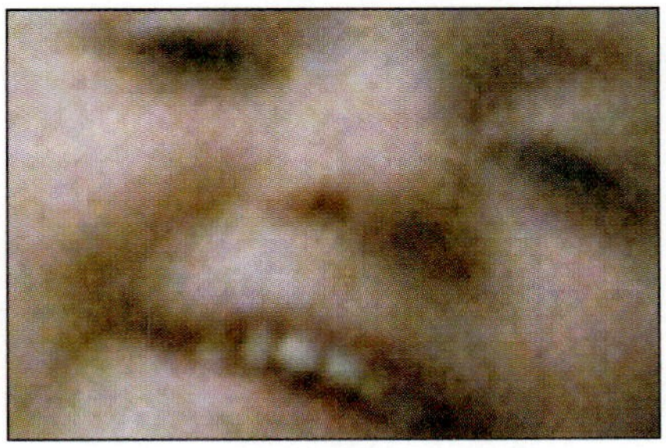

Enlarged graphic showing pixels

More dots per inch makes the dots closer together so text and graphics have more detail and sharper edges.

The resolution of a device is determined by the number of pixels used to form characters and images. Screen resolution is normally specified as the total number of pixels across or down the screen. On resolutions such as 640 x 480 or 800 x 600, the first number is the number of pixels across the screen. The second is the number of pixels down the screen. On printers, resolution is determined by the number of printed dots per inch (dpi). For comparison purposes, monitors use about 50 to 100 dots (pixels) per inch to display text and images, ink-jet and dot-matrix printers print 100 to 200 dots per inch, laser printers 300 to 1200, and commercial typesetting machines 1,000 to 2,400.

Vector Graphics

Although we said all output is dots, it isn't really. In a very few cases it's lines. The image on a CRT display is painted by a moving beam of light. Normally this beam sweeps across the screen in horizontal rows, painting an image dot by dot. However, the computer can make the beam go in any direction. By deflecting it in a controlled way, images can be created by painting lines on the screen, much as images can be created by turning the two knobs on an Etch-a-Sketch game. This approach is used mainly in high-end graphics.

The total number of pixels on the screen depends on the resolution being used. The same is true of a printer. With a resolution of 300 dots per inch (dpi) there are 90,000 dots per square inch. With 600 dpi there are 360,000 dots and at 1200 dpi there are 1,440,000 dots in a square inch.

Resolution

4.8 The Foundations of Modern Output:

A font is a unique family or kind of type with its own look. To display various type styles and type sizes on the screen, the computer must have access to the necessary characters. For example, early computers displayed all text on the screen in the same size and style because that was all they had. Modern computers are usually equipped with a variety of different basic type designs, referred to as type fonts.

Speaking of fonts

Like the early days of the automobile when you could buy any color Ford Model-T as long as it was black, early printers let you use any font, as long as it was Courier.

Courier

Courier

Attractive in its own way, having only Courier to work with certainly limited document design. Today the sky is the limit. You have thousands of fonts from which to choose. Fonts are further subcategorized by their typeface, type style, and type size. For example, you could specify Times Roman, Normal, 18 points.

Helvetica
Times
Peignot light
TektoMM
NewCenturySchlbk
Boulevard, Italic
Courier
Giddyup

Typefaces

You may have noticed in ads and various publications that the design of the type can vary from reserved to wild. For example, Liquid Crystal looks a lot different from Courier. These unique designs are called typefaces and there are thousands of them. The two most common are Helvetica and Times Roman. Helvetica is the classic sans-serif typeface and Times Roman the classic serif typeface. Serifs are the small decorative strokes at the ends of the character's main strokes in Times Roman. You don't find these serifs on Helvetica so it's called a sans-serif typeface, French for "without serifs."

Helvetica Regular
Helvetica Italic
Helvetica Bold
Helvetica Bold, Italic

Type styles

Most but not all typefaces come in a number of variations called type styles. The most common of these are regular, italic, bold, or bold-italic.

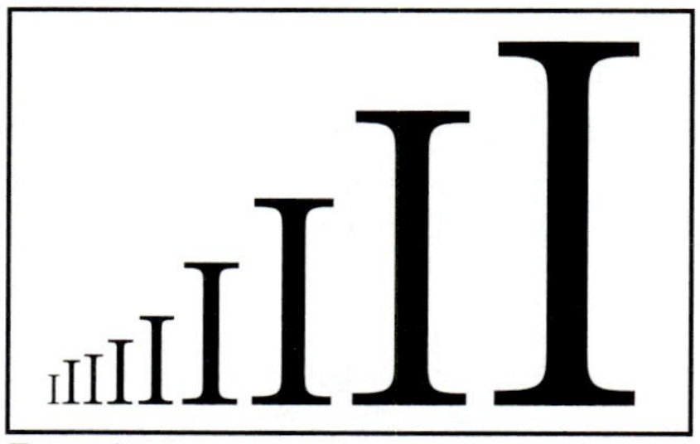

Type sizes

Type size refers to a character's height. This size is specified in points, an old printer's unit of measure. There are 72 points to an inch. Therefore, 72-point type is 1-inch high, and 36-point type is 1/2 inch high. Most documents use 10 or 12-point type for body text.

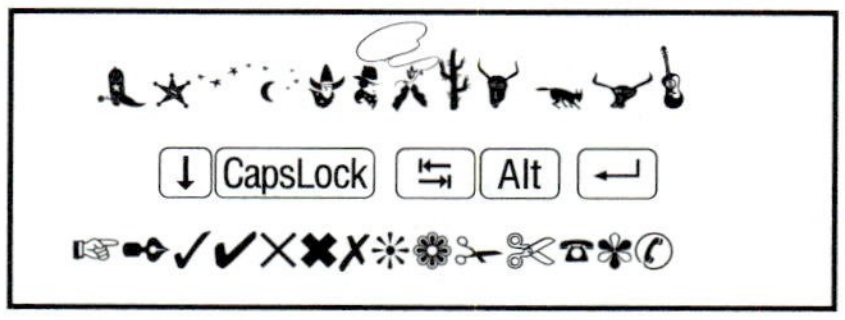

Symbols

A font, then, includes all the sizes and styles available of a certain typeface. Fonts are not just letters and numbers. There are hundreds of symbol fonts available for everything from music to office planning to western scenes.

Scalable outline and bit-mapped fonts

All printers print fonts using a series of dots called bit-mapped fonts. In the early days of computing, fonts were stored in the computer or printer as bit-maps, basically, tiny pictures of each character. The problem with this approach was that the fonts took up a lot of space. To solve this problem scalable fonts (also called outline fonts) were introduced and are now just about the only kind in use. These fonts are stored in the computer not as pictures of each character but as a series of formulas describing their shapes.

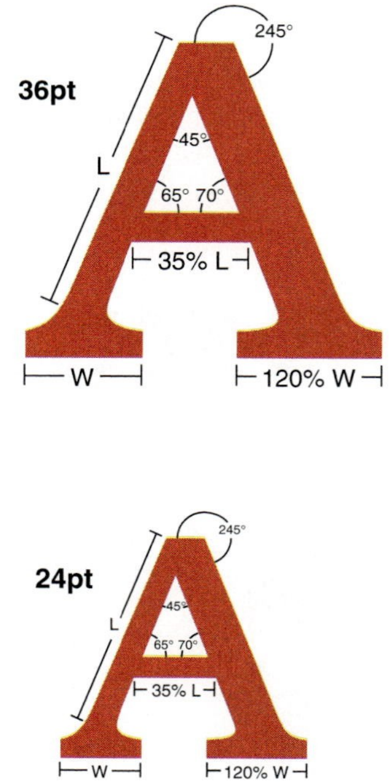

Scalable fonts

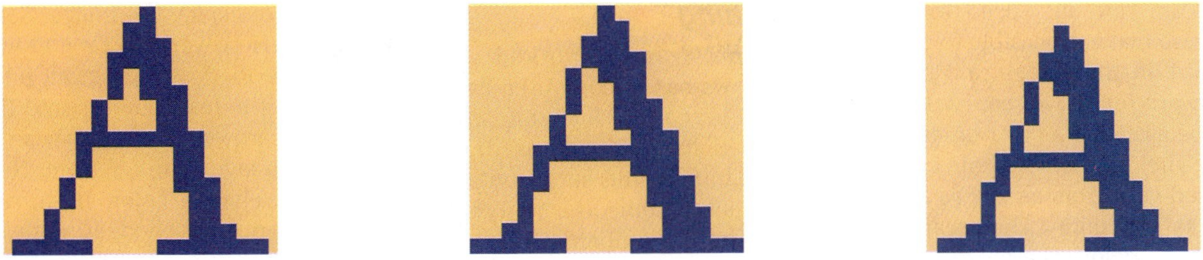

36 pt. medium | 36 pt. bold | 33 pt. medium

Bit-mapped fonts

When a scalable font is to be displayed or printed, an application program called a rasterizer converts it from the formula to a bit-map which can be displayed and printed. Two of the most common rasterizers are Adobe Type Manager that works with PostScript fonts and TrueType, that works with TrueType fonts. These rasterizers reside in the computer so they can process fonts for both the screen and printer. Depending on which fonts you are using, a companion program, either PostScript or TrueImage, resides in the printer. These programs, known as page-description languages, assemble pages for printing. Scalable fonts allow a wide range of sizes while requiring very little space on the disk or in a printer's memory.

WYSIWYG

WYSIWYG, or what you see is what you get, means that the screen display of a document closely matches its printout.

Here the document on the screen looks almost exactly as it will look when printed. To have true WYSIWYG, you need to have matching printer and screen fonts. If you have a printer font that does not have a matching screen font, the document on the screen will not look exactly like the printout. Most scalable fonts come with a matching screen font that is automatically installed on the system when you install the printer font.

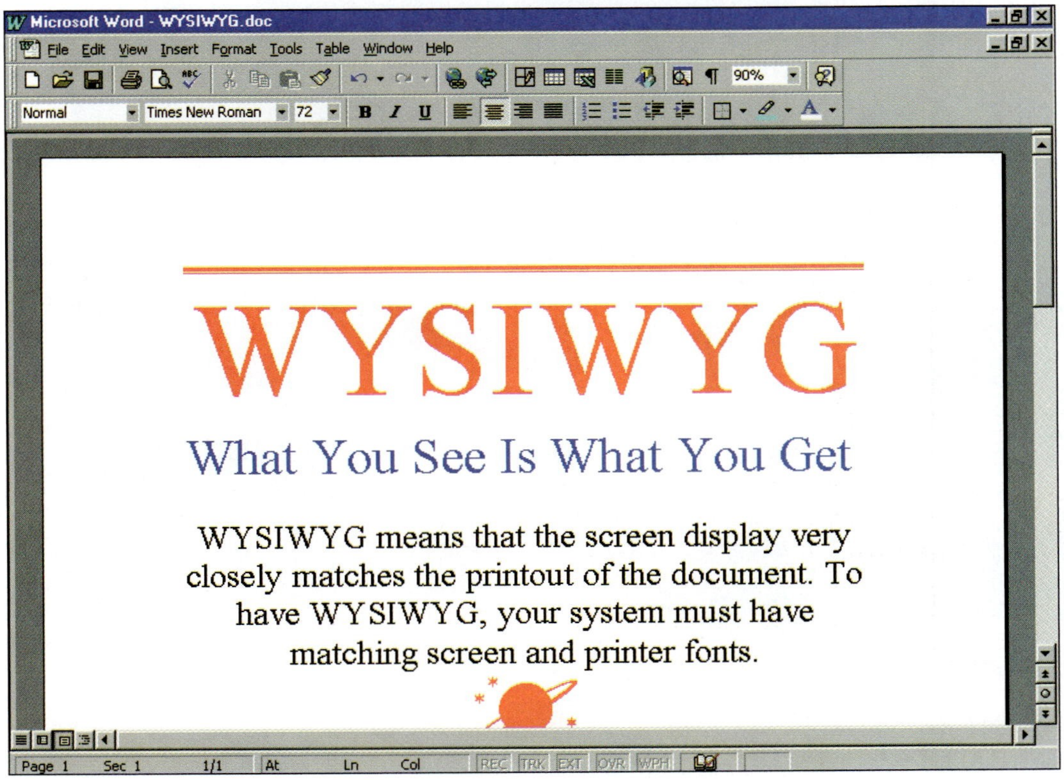

WYSIWYG screen display

4.9 The Foundations of Modern Output:

Pixels are not only used for text. They also make it possible to display graphics on the screen and print it on the printer. To do so, each pixel must be assigned a color or shade of grey. The numbers that can be assigned vary from as low as 2 to as many as 16 million. The greater the number of colors the more realistic the images. Let's look at how this is done.

Palettes

All pixels on a bit-mapped screen are assigned palette or index numbers. These numbers refer to specific colors on the palette being used by the image. By using the palette numbers the computer can display or print the image with the correct colors. For a black and white image the palette contains only two colors, black and white. However, systems can support 16, 256, 65,000, or 16 million colors. The more colors that are used, the more realistic images can look. In many cases, increasing the number of colors improves the image more than the resolution.

Flashing

Anyone who's worked on a Windows-based computer has seen what is called flashing. All bit-mapped images such as drawings, photographs, and such contain pixels. Each pixel is assigned an index or palette number that indicates what its color is. When a program displays the image, it uses those index numbers and a table of colors called the palette, to set the display card to display the image. So far, so good. However, if a second image is then loaded, the program puts that image's index numbers into the display card, overwriting those of the first image. This makes the first image change color, flash, or even take on a psychedelic appearance. In many situations, only one image can be displayed correctly at a time and it's always the one on top.

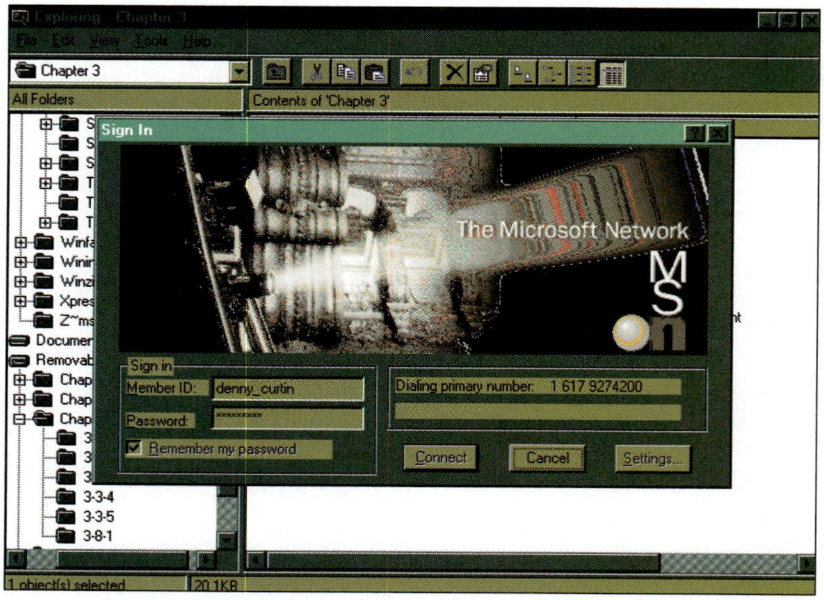

Flashing

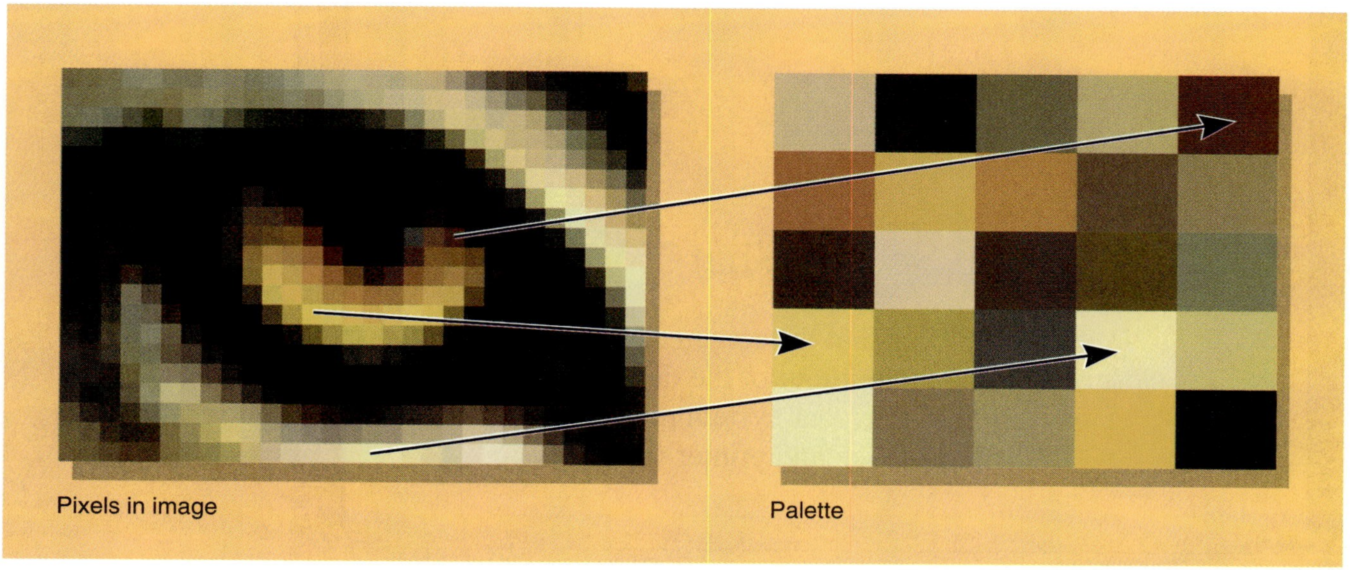

Palettes

The range of colors

The range of colors available called color depth is determined by how many bits are used to store data for each pixel. For example, if only one bit is assigned to each pixel, it can be on or off, black or white. If 8 bits are assigned, it can be 256 colors or shades of gray. With 24 bits it can be over 16 million colors.

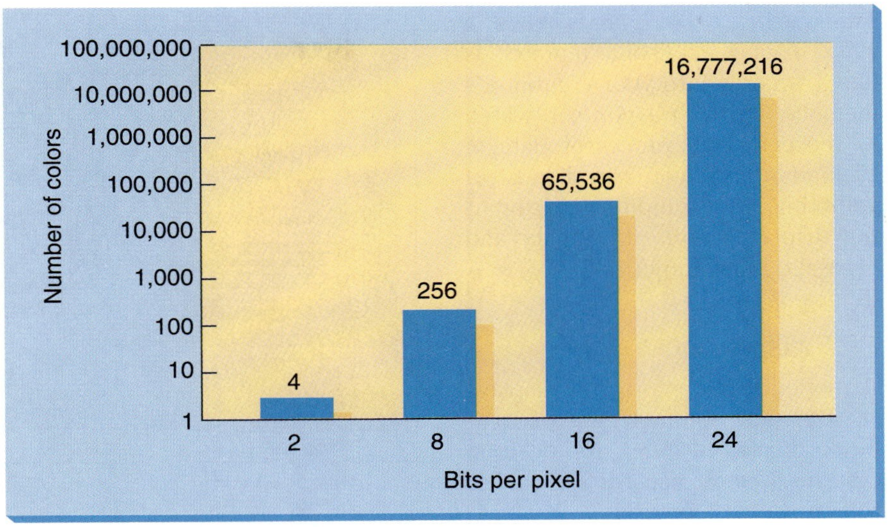

Bits-per-pixel and the number of possible colors

Colors and memory

The number of pixels on a screen, and the number of colors or shades of gray that can be displayed, are limited by the amount of video memory the computer or the graphics card has. For example, a black and white display on a 640 by 480 screen has just over 300 thousand pixels. Since only 1 bit is needed for each pixel, the screen display needs just over 300 thousand bits or 37.5 kilobytes of memory to store the screen information.

At the high end of the scale, a color monitor using 24 bits (true color) at a resolution of 1024 by 768 has almost 800 thousand pixels on the screen. Since each pixel requires 24 bits (or 3 bytes), the screen needs almost 2.5 megabytes of video memory.

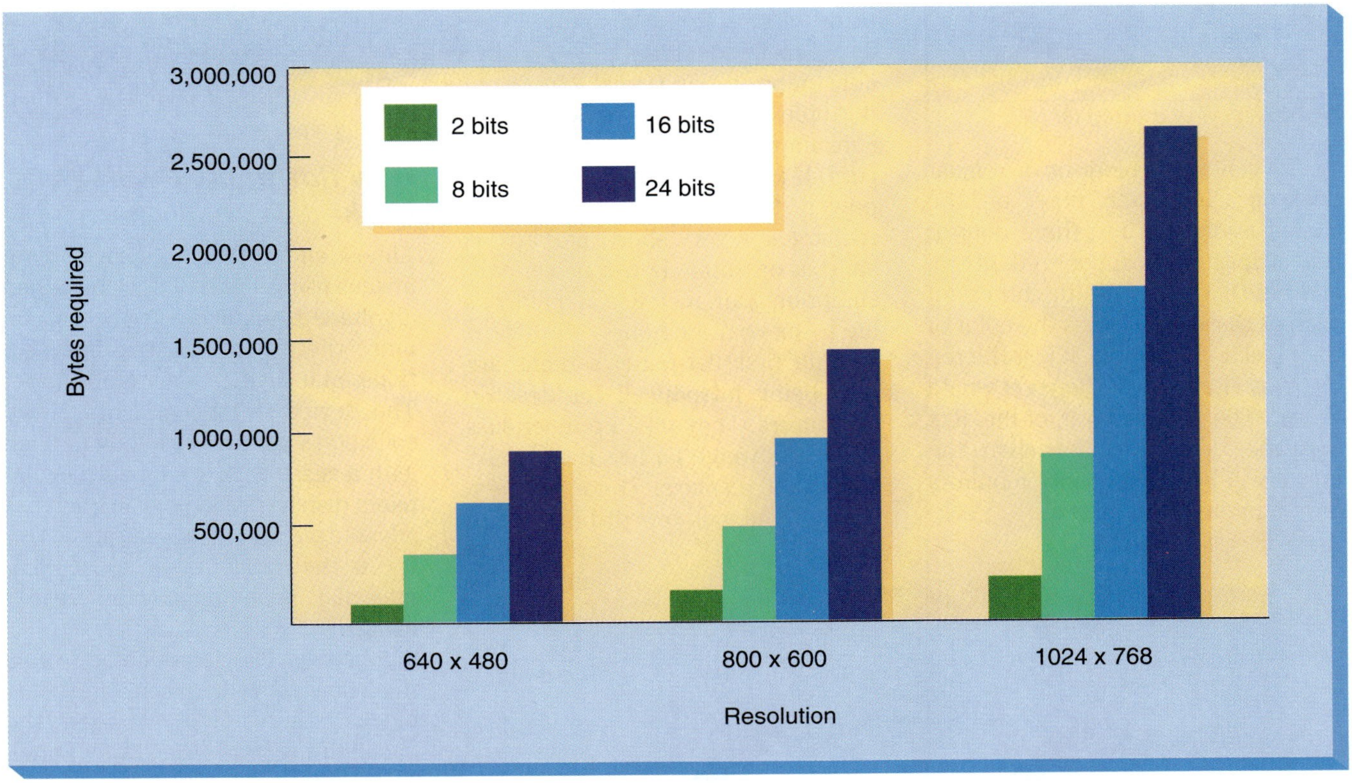

Bits-per-pixel and memory required

4.10 Display Screens:

The display screen, also called a video display or display monitor, is like a window into your computer's memory. Through it you can watch as the computer processes data of all kinds. Since you spend most of your time at a computer looking at the display screen, its quality and capabilities are important.

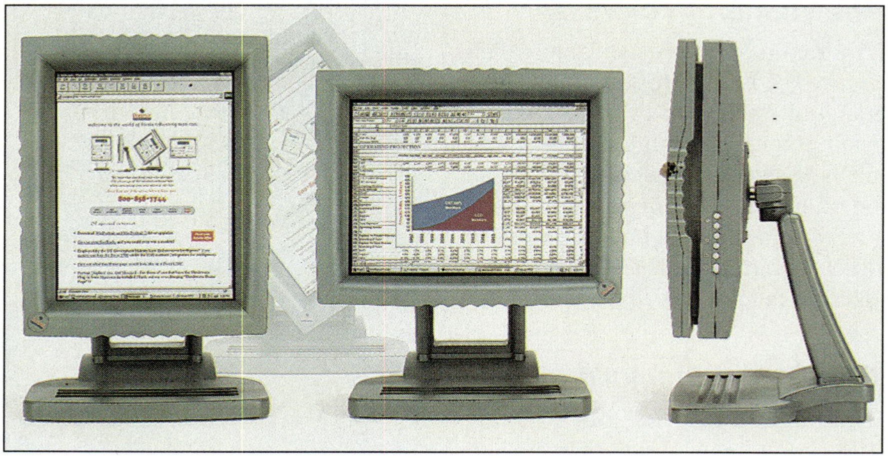

Flat panel desktop monitor courtesy of Portrait Displays

CRT displays

Cathode ray tube (CRT) displays are the most common type of computer display, at least for desktop systems. These displays are similar to your television set, but are capable of displaying much higher resolutions.

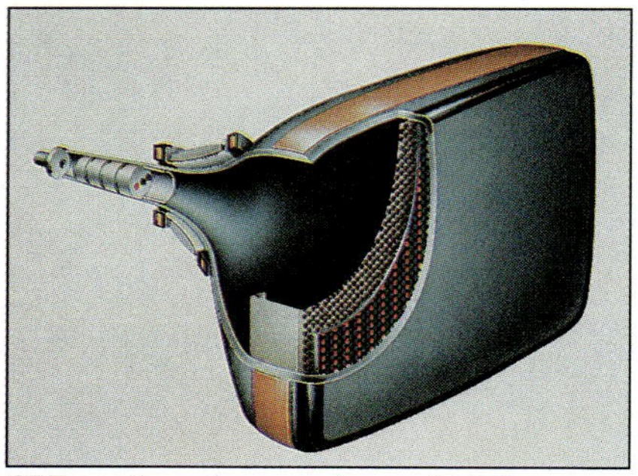

CRT section view courtesy of NEC

To generate colors on a regular desktop CRT, each pixel on the screen is divided into three dots or thin stripes of phosphor (red, green, and blue). Varying the brightness of each of these dots varies the color of the pixel. For example, if just the red one was illuminated, the pixel would be red. The size, or pitch, of the dots or stripes determines how sharp the image will be. High-quality monitors have a pitch of 0.26 or less.

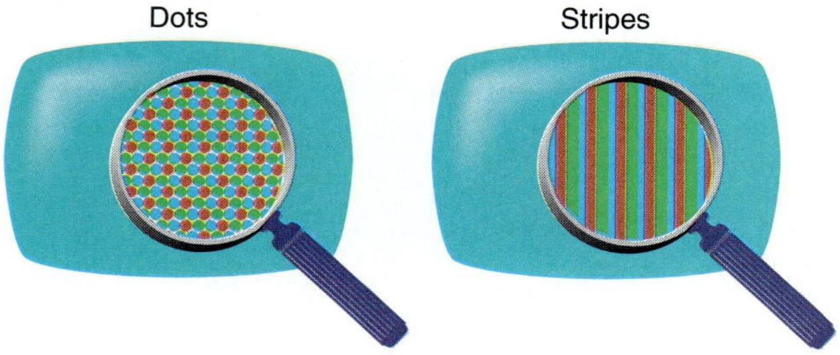

Color screen pitch

Flat panel displays

CRTs have great images but they are bulky and heavy, so portable computers use flat panel displays. These screens are created with a variety of technologies, each of which offers advantages and disadvantages. The trade-offs are usually between readability, power consumption, and cost. In portable computers, power consumption is a major concern. If a display requires too much power, the battery life between recharges is very short, perhaps as short as one hour. Lower power consumption can increase a battery's life to six or more hours.

The first flat-panel screens are now being introduced for desktop computers. They take up much less space and weigh far less than equivalent CRT displays. There will be a time in the not too distant future when large and heavy CRT displays will become history.

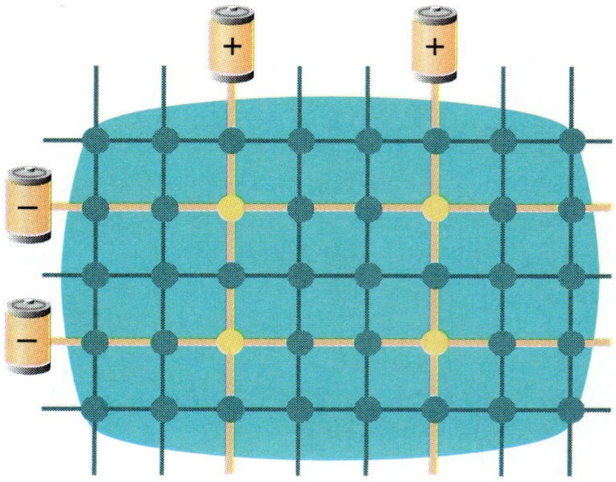

Flat panel display technology

How flat panel displays work

Almost all flat panel displays create images using a grid of devices. When a voltage is applied to a row or column, the devices at the intersections emit light to create an image. The devices in the grid are either solid state diodes or chambers filled with a gas. There are four major flat panel display technologies. Each has advantages and disadvantages.

At the moment, the most common flat panel display is created using liquid crystal display (LCD) technology. The colors come from a thin film of red, green, and blue blocks sandwiched between the backlighting and the LCD panel. There are a variety of LCD types including:

- ♦ Passive-matrix LCDs including twisted nematic LCDs (TN-LCDs) and supertwisted nematic LCDs (STN-LCDs).
- ♦ Active-matrix LCDs including thin-film-transistor LCDs (TFT-LCDs) and active-addressed LCDs (AA-LCDs)–a hybrid of passive- and active-matrix technologies.

These displays are widely produced so they are relatively inexpensive. They also have a very low power consumption, a high contrast ratio, a fast writing speed, and are readable in direct sunlight. Their disadvantages are that they have a narrow viewing angle and defect-free panels are very difficult to manufacture. This keeps them from being produced in larger sizes.

Color plasma display panels (PDP) can be used for very large but thin displays. Screens up to 60" wide and only a few inches thick are already in production. This allows them to be hung on walls, or installed in kiosks and airplanes where space is at a premium. These displays may eventually replace cathode-ray tube (CRT) and rear projection displays. At the moment their cost is very high but they are actually less expensive to make than LCDs. These displays weigh much less than CRT monitors. For example a 35-inch CRT weighs about 240 pounds while a 42-inch PDP weighs about 80 pounds.

Plasma display panels (PDP) use gases contained between two glass panels. These are activated with electrons, and the gases generate ultraviolet rays that stimulate green, red and blue phosphors. PDPs, like CRTs and LCDs before them, will likely first see limited commercial use, then wide distribution in consumer products such as televisions, and then finally migrate to the desktop for computers.

Electroluminescent displays (ELs) are similar to LCDs. The phosphor layer emits light when it is excited by the introduction of electrons between the row and column electrodes. These are the thinnest of all flat panel displays but they are difficult to manufacture and are expensive.

Field emission displays (FEDs) are like thousands of CRTs arranged in a grid, one for each pixel. Electrons are accelerated to strike a phosphor and produce light.

Selecting a Notebook's Screen

Color is now used in most notebook computers. The depth or saturation of the color determines how rich it looks on the screen.

Contrast and brightness determine under what lighting conditions you can see the screen. Contrast of 60 to 1 is considered good.

Response time determines how fast the screen is updated. This affects its ability to display multimedia applications, the amount of flicker you might experience, and whether your mouse pointer lags your mouse movements.

Battery life determines how long you can work unplugged. Some displays consume a lot more power than others.

Sizes smaller than 8 inches (measured diagonally) are too small for long hours of work. A display of 9 or 10 inches is better.

Display modes are not always up to those of desktop computers which frequently run at 800x600 and 1024x768. Keep in mind that high resolutions on small screens are almost unreadable because everything is so small. Most color portables can display 256 colors at 640x480 resolution, and some can display 32,768 and 65,536 colors used for high-quality image editing or multimedia.

42-inch-wide flat panel screen courtesy of Fujitsu

4.11 Display Screens:

To display graphics on the screen, most computers use an adapter card that plugs into an expansion slot to control the video display. Even if the video display is built into the computer, you can use one of these adapter cards to improve it.

Display modes

The number of pixels on a screen is determined by the mode it is in. These modes, or standards, are generally 640 by 480, 800 by 600, or 1024 by 768, although others may be found. Many systems allow you to change the display mode you use. Here a Window's display is shown in the three most commonly used resolutions: 640 x 480, (where x stands for "by") 800 x 600, and 1024 x 768. The lower the resolution, the larger the pixels and hence the elements. These figures illustrate how each of these three resolutions displays the same data. Notice how as the resolution increases, elements become smaller and more of them fit on the screen.

Resolution and display size

640 x 480 resolution (sometimes called video graphics array or VGA) is the lowest common denominator of screen resolutions. For small screens, it's also the only one that's easily readable. Many multimedia programs use this resolution because the publisher knows everyone has a system that can display it.

800 x 600 resolution (sometimes called super VGA) is the most frequently used resolution on 15" and 17" displays.

1024 x 768 resolution (sometimes called extended graphics array or XGA) was first introduced by IBM but XGA never caught on. However, its resolution of 1024 by 768 is widely used on high-end systems with large display monitors.

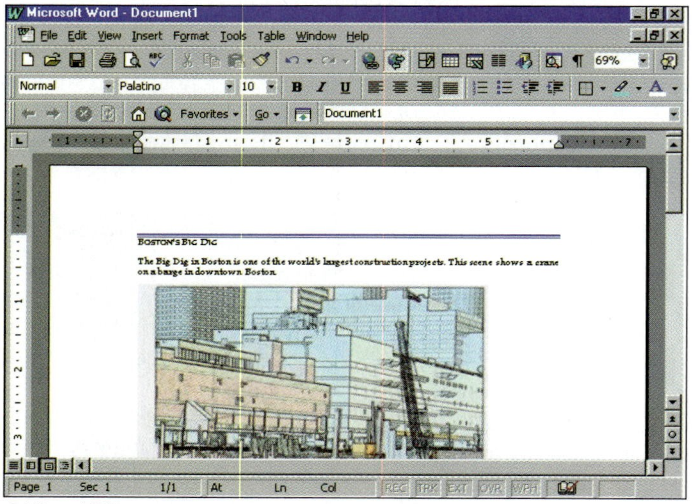

640 x 480

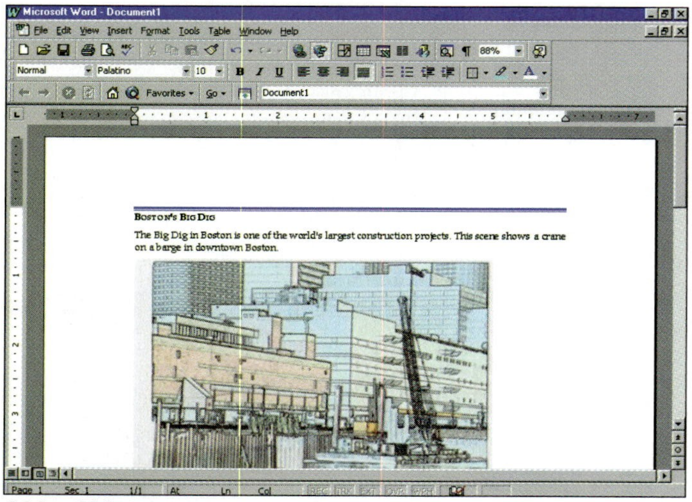

800 x 600

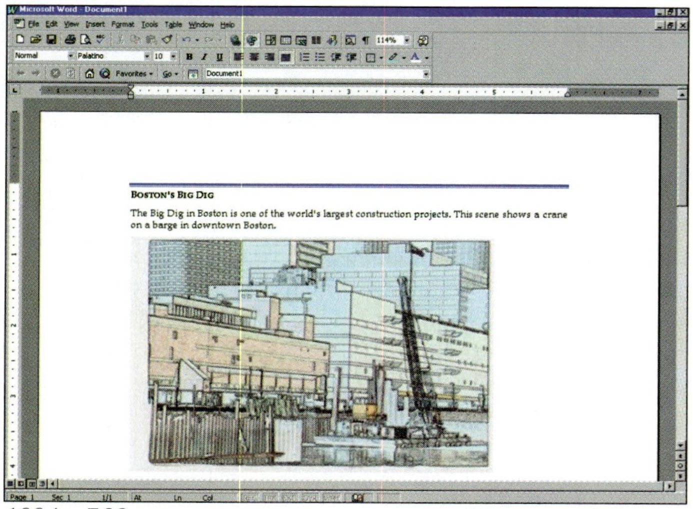

1024 x 768

Multiple frequency display monitors

Inexpensive display monitors are often designed to match only one of the available standard display modes. If so, these fixed-frequency monitors can be used only with that standard. For example, a VGA monitor can be used only with a VGA card. Since display modes are constantly improving, and because many people want to use different modes at different times, the multiple frequency (or multisync) monitor was introduced. These monitors are more expensive than fixed frequency monitors; however, they allow you to change to a higher resolution if your system supports it. They allow the monitor to self-adjust to video signal from a variety of graphics boards. Most multisync monitors can run in their highest resolution and all resolutions below the maximum. For example, a system capable of displaying 1024 x 768 can also display 800 x 600 and 640 x 480. With a fixed frequency monitor, you have to change both the adapter card and the monitor to change resolutions.

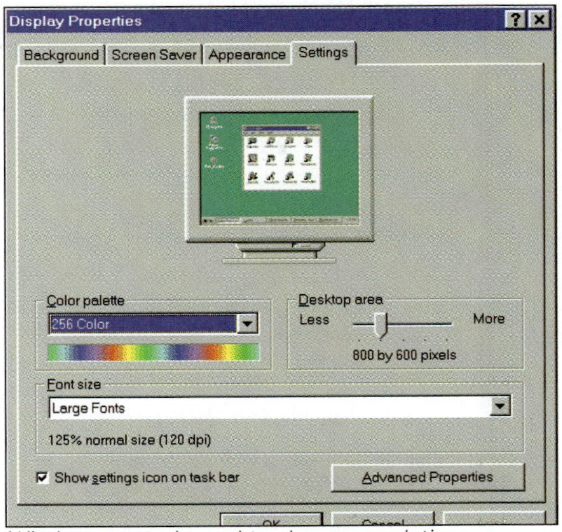

Windows control panel to change resolutions

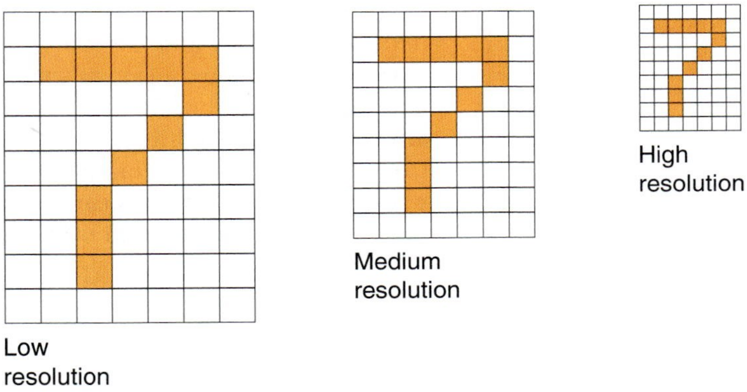

Character matrix

Resolution and size

Changing the resolution of a screen or a printer does not necessarily make text or graphics look better or sharper. The reason is that type and images are assigned only a fixed set of dots, called a matrix. If you increase the resolution, more dots aren't added to the matrix. Each dot just becomes smaller.

As each dot becomes smaller, so does the type or image. For example, a character in a 7 by 9 matrix that is easily readable on a 14-inch display screen can shrink up to 40 percent and become unreadable at a higher resolution. For this reason, using very high resolutions on small monitors makes them hard to read. Normally, 800 by 600 is OK on a 15-inch monitor and great on a 17-inch one and 1024 by 768 is OK on a 17-inch monitor and great on a 20 or 21 inch one. Here's a table to use when deciding what resolution to use on what screen size.

	Screen Size				
Resolution	14	15	17	20	21
640 x 480	•				
800 x 600	•	•			
1024 x 768		•	•	•	
1280 x 1024				•	•
1600 x 1200					•

Resolution and size

4.12 Printers:

Laser printer and output courtesy of Hewlett-Packard

After the display monitor, the second most widely used output device is the printer. Having a printer is essential if the data you process with your computer is to be filed or physically distributed to others. As you have seen, almost all modern output devices create characters and graphics on the page with dots, or pixels. Laser printers are no exception.

Laser printer output

Laser printers are very fast, usually printing eight or more pages per minute, and their cost has fallen to the point where businesses use them widely and even individuals purchase them for home use.

Laser printer output can be both text and graphics and can be very close to professional printing quality. The dots making up the image are so closely spaced that they look like characters typed on a typewriter. Most laser printers can print 600 dots per inch although printers with 1200 and more dots per inch are common.

How a laser printer works

The high quality of laser printouts comes from the image being created with very small dots placed close together. Here is how it's done.

1. As the printer receives digital signals from the computer, a laser beam is quickly turned on and off by the stream of digital 1s and 0s.
2. A rotating mirror deflects the blinking beam in such a way that it "paints" a line across an electrically charged revolving drum. If the printer's resolution is 1200 dots per inch, it can blink on and off 1200 times as it moves one inch along the line. If the beam is on when it passes a point on the drum, it changes the electrical charge leaving a dot with a charge that can attract toner.
3. When the charged dots on the drum revolve past the toner, toner with a charge opposite to the charged dots on the drum adheres to them.
4. The toner is transferred from the drum to the paper under heat and pressure as it is pressed against the revolving drum.

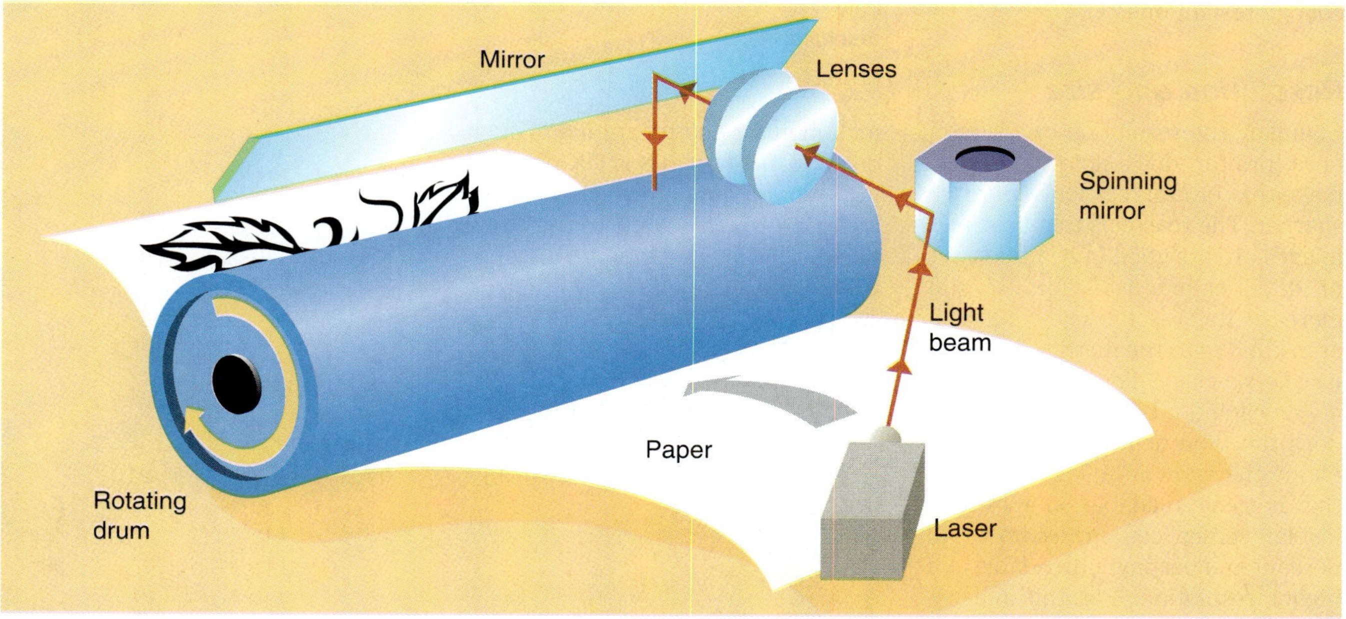

How a laser printer works

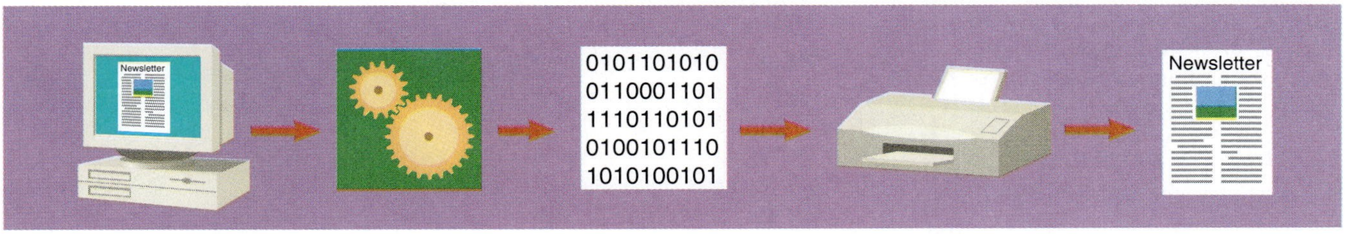

1. With the document on the screen, you select the printer you want to use and then print the document.

2. A printer driver in the computer translates the document for the printer you have selected.

3. The new file describes how all text and graphics in the document are to be handled by the printer.

4. In the printer, a raster image processor (RIP) interprets the file and creates a bit-mapped image of an entire page. It's this bit-mapped image that's printed.

5. The final document matches the format of the one on the screen almost exactly.

Printer control languages

Printer control languages

When you print a document, it goes through a number of steps. The process is controlled by the printer control language that your printer is using. Almost all printers support Hewlett-Packard's PCL 5 language and those used in the graphic arts field also support Adobe's Postscript. These printer control languages are designed to make the format of the printout match the format on the screen as closely as possible. To do so, they specify the size, shape, color, and placement of text and graphics. Each pixel in the document is translated to a pixel on the printed page.

Laser printer features

Even with the best printers, there are differences that affect their use. These include the number of sides the printer prints on, its memory, and its fonts.

Duplex printers print on both sides of a sheet of paper at the same time. This duplex printing is ideal for documents that will be stapled or bound.

Laser printers make up an entire page before printing it. The page is temporarily stored in the printer's memory while it is being processed and printed. If a page contains a graphics image, the memory required for it can be substantial. For example, it takes 1 megabyte to store a full-page black-and-white graphics image that is to be printed with a 300-dpi resolution. To fill the page, the printer has to address over 8 million dots (1 megabyte x 8 bits = 8 million bits). This is obviously a big chore.

All laser printers come with some built-in fonts; however thousands of others can be added. At one time, these were added using plug-in cartridges. Currently they are built-in or distributed on disks and installed onto the system's hard disk drive. From there they are fed to the printer when needed.

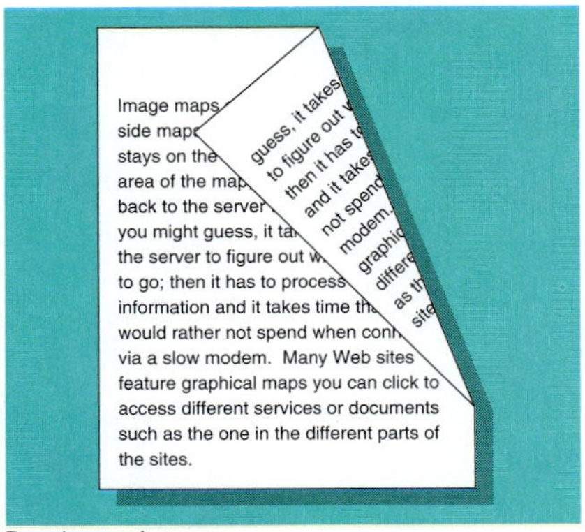

Duplex printer

In addition to lasers, there are a number of other technologies in use to create an image on the page.

Dot-matrix printers

Dot-matrix printers use a printhead containing pins, or wires, arranged in a column to print characters. As the printhead passes across the paper, the computer tells it which pins in the printhead are to be fired to form a particular character. As the pins are fired, they strike an inked ribbon against the paper. The printed dots are arranged in an invisible matrix. The number of pins or wires and dots determines the character's resolution. The latest printers have 18 or 24 wires in their printheads. The printhead on the left below has 9 and the one on the right has 24. Dot-matrix printers have been all but killed off by newer technologies. They are now found mainly in niche markets, especially those where there is a need to print multipart forms.

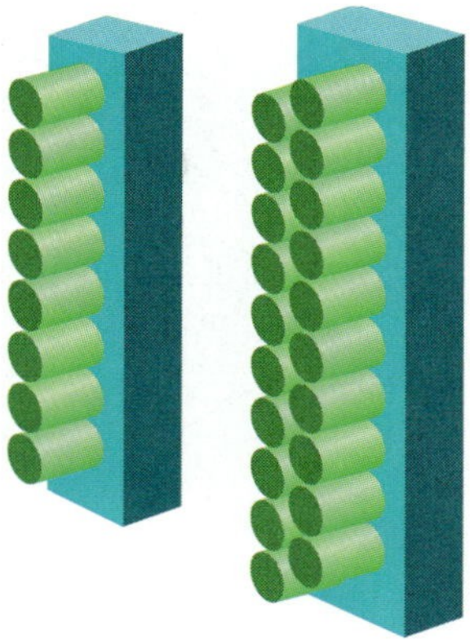

Dot-matrix printhead

Dot-matrix forms printer courtesy of Lexmark

Plotters

Plotters are used mainly for printing large line art such as engineering or architectural drawings. Plotter output can be up to several yards long. Pen plotters (as many as eight colors) are the most common type. The printer stops automatically at certain points so that you can change pens to change colors, or the pens are changed automatically. There are also other kinds of plotters. Inkjet plotters are cheaper but they consume ink rapidly and the ink is smearable until dry. Electrostatic plotters are expensive and require regular maintenance. Thermal plotters are fast but require special paper and can print only two colors.

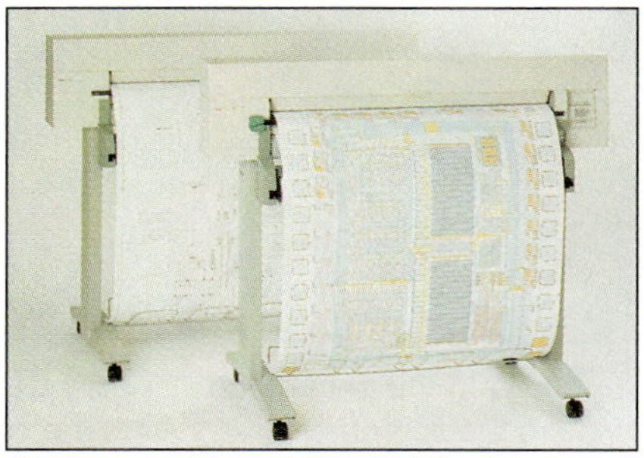

Plotter courtesy of Hewlett-Packard

Label printers

Label printers fill a niche market. Most people hate printing mailing, file folder, or disk labels on their regular printers because of the effort in laying them out. These inexpensive printers are designed specifically to print the occasional label and are very easy to use.

Label printer courtesy of Seiko

Digital presses

When a large number of copies of magazines or books are needed, they are almost always printed using offset presses. Digital offset color printing eliminates the need for much of the preparation, called makeready, that adds to the time and expense of traditional offset printing.

One such digital system, Indigo's Digital Offset Color technology, uses special inks to create a color page on printing plates on-the-fly. These images are transferred from the plate to a blanket, and then from blanket to paper. Since no heat or pressure is used, this technology can print on paper, polyethylene, plastic film, foil, fabrics, metal, and even ceramics.

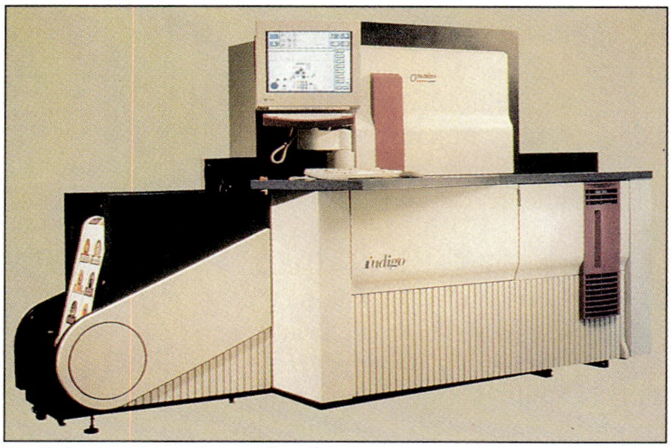

Digital printer courtesy of Indigo

Large color printers

Large color printers generate large format color images of almost photographic quality that are ideal for displays and sales presentations. These devices are available at service bureaus who do the work for you.

Line printers

Found mainly in mainframe departments, heavy-duty line printers are used to print out reports on perforated paper.

Line printer courtesy of Genicom
http://www.genicom.com/printers/linechrt.htm

Large printer courtesy of Hewlett-Packard

Photo printers

Perfect companions for digital cameras, small photo printers print out small photographic quality snapshots.

Photo printer courtesy of Casio

Other Printers

In addition to the printers we've covered, there are many more.

- Electrostatic printers use a dot-matrix printhead to apply electrostatic charges to the surface of the paper. This process is similar to that used in copy machines.
- LED printers have many of the same performance characteristics as laser printers, but instead of using a laser to create the image, they use an array of light-emitting diodes.

4.14 Printers:

A recent survey shows that of color printers used in business, 45 percent are inkjet printers, 35 percent are plotters; 12 percent are thermal-wax transfer; 2 percent are dot-matrix; and 6 percent are other–a diverse assortment that includes dye-sublimation, color laser, and electrostatic printers. As technology advances, expect to see shifts in these market shares. For example, color laser printer usage will skyrocket if the price is brought down.

How solid colors are formed

Color printers use three colors (called subtractive primaries), cyan (blue-green), magenta, and yellow to form all other colors. Often, a fourth color, a solid black, is included so dark blacks are possible. This is known as CMYK, where the last K stands for the extra black.

Colors courtesy of Tektronix

The color printer can print eight solid colors by printing one, two, or three colors on every dot on the page, or by leaving dots blank so they're the color of the paper, usually white. To create the primary colors, most printers overprint two of the subtractive primaries in the same dot to form red, green, and blue. For example, it overprints magenta and cyan on the same dot to create purple. If it overprints all three colors on the same dot, it creates black. For lighter hues, the printer adds in white by leaving some dots unprinted.

How continuous tone colors are formed

Continuous tones

Printing solid colors is fine when printing chart, graphs, or text. But the world is made up of many shades of color. These ranges, which blend into each other in paintings or color photographs, are called continuous tones. A single color such as red may vary slowly and continuously from light red to dark red. To print continuous tones most color printers use a process called halftoning or dithering. (Dye sublimation printers can vary the density of each dot to produce continuous tone images.)

A halftone or dither pattern groups printable dots into groups, called cells, and then uses these larger dots as a single unit to print with. Each cell may be 8 dots wide by 8 high for a total of 64 dots within the larger dot. The three or four primary colors are combined in a pattern of dots in these cells, and the eye perceives them as intermediate hues. This process works best with solid, well-defined colors. However gradients and continuous-tone photographs tend to reveal the dithering patterns that appear on the printout as color bands or splotchiness.

Liquid inkjet

Color inkjet printers use three separate inkjets, one for each of the primary colors (red, green, and blue). Inkjet printers are very quiet and provide laserlike quality at a much lower cost although supplies are relatively expensive. Although you can print on regular paper, better results are obtained when using special paper that doesn't allow the ink to soak in.

Liquid ink courtesy of Tektronix

Liquid inkjet printers use ink cartridges from which they spray ink onto the paper. A cartridge of ink attached to a printhead with 50 or so nozzles, each thinner than a human hair, moves across the paper. The number of nozzles determines the printer's resolution. A digital signal from the computer tells each nozzle when to propel a drop of ink onto the paper. On some printers, this is done with mechanical vibrations.

Solid ink

Solid inkjet printers use solid ink sticks that are melted into a reservoir and sprayed in precisely controlled drops onto the page where the ink immediately hardens. High-pressure rollers flatten and fuse the ink to the paper to prevent smearing. This produces an exceptionally high-quality image with sharp edges and good color reproduction. Solid inkjet printers are also the best for producing low-cost but high-quality transparencies. These printers are sometimes referred to as phase-change printers because the ink moves from a solid to a liquid phase to be printed then back to a solid phase on the page. As a final step, the paper moves between two rollers to cold-fuse the image and improve the surface texture.

Solid ink courtesy of Tektronix

Color laser

Color laser printers use four toner cartridges (CYMK) and all of the other colors can be created by mixing them on the page in the right proportions.

Color laser courtesy of Tektronix

The drum is given a negative charge, and the laser sweeps the drum surface for the first color (yellow). As the drum rotates, yellow toner is applied to the print image. The drum is then recharged, for magenta, cyan, and black passes. Each color builds up the image. When all four colors have been applied, the image is transferred to the paper.

Thermal wax transfer

Thermal wax transfer printers use a roll of wax that is divided into page-sized sections for each of the three subtractive colors (and optionally, black). With this sheet of wax between the paper and the print-head hundreds or thousands of small heating elements in the print-head melt dots of color onto the paper. The paper is a special paper but you can also use transparency film. Thermal wax transfer is one of the most widely used processes in scientific, technical, and business printing.

Thermal wax transfer courtesy of Tektronix

Dye sublimation

At the high end where quality is very important, you'll find thermal-wax transfer and dye sublimation printers. Both use heat to transfer pigment from a plastic ribbon to the paper. The ink ribbon contains sequential panels of pigment in cyan, magenta, yellow, and, optionally, black. (A three-color ribbon produces blacks that are a composite of CMY but they are not as rich.) A pass is made over the paper once for each color. Maintaining accurate registration for each color requires precise paper feeding, which is one reason these machines are costly.

When printing color photographs, there's nothing like dye sublimation printers. These printers are able to produce photo-realistic continuous-tone images that look as if they came from a photo lab. They do so by depositing transparent dyes on the paper with varying intensity to create very subtle gradations from one color to another.

Dye sublimation courtesy of Tektronix

The dye sublimation printer's colors are in a roll of plastic film with consecutive panels of cyan, magenta, yellow and black dye called a transfer roll. The printer's printhead contains thousands of heating elements, each of which can produce 256 different temperatures, allowing the printer to apply varying amounts of pigment. The hotter the temperature, the more dye is transferred. Heat turns the dyes into a gas in a process called sublimation. The gas is then absorbed into a special paper coated with a polyester resin. (Sublimation is the term describing a solid's changing into a gas without going through an intervening liquid phase.) As the dye soaks into the polyester, each puff of dye bleeds slightly, causing the dots to merge. These fuzzy-edged dots contribute to a "dye-sub" printer's continuous-tone talents. Varying the print-head temperature changes the amount of dye evaporated so the density of the color at each point can be controlled. Dye sublimation requires special paper so the cost of paper is higher than with other printer types.

Fiery output

Electronics for Imaging (EFI) was the first to develop a technology that turned a standard digital color copier into a networked color printer that gave good results at an affordable price. Improved versions of that original technology are now used with both copiers and printers. Fiery output devices embedded inside color laser printers and the color copier are used for desktop applications. For commercial printers and corporate, in-house printing departments, more expensive Fiery color servers are used. These systems are widely used in the graphic arts field and are available at most service bureaus listed in the yellow pages of the phone book.

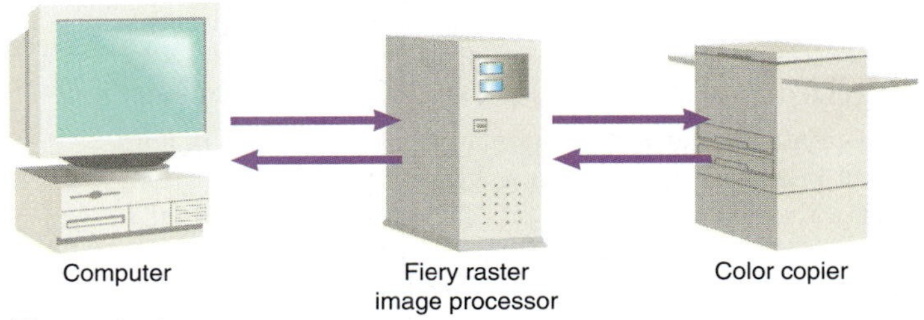

Fiery output

4.15 Enhancing and Testing Your Understanding

Summary

- We use input devices to enter data into the computer so it can be processed.
- Output devices display data in the form of printouts (called hard copy) or on-screen as graphics, sounds such as music, videos, and animations (sometimes called soft copy).
- On small handheld computers virtual, soft, or touch-screen keyboards allow you to enter text and numbers by tapping the "keys" with your finger or a penlike stylus.
- Optical character recognition (OCR) converts documents from printed form to a digital form that you can edit with a word processing program just as if it had been entered through the keyboard.
- Handwriting recognition software converts handwriting on the screen into neatly typed text.
- Bar codes, made up of bars of different widths and spacing, are read with either a handheld wand or a built-in scanner.
- Speech recognition software is either speaker-independent (works for everyone, almost) or speaker-dependent (must be "trained" to recognize your voice).
- The futuristic-looking characters printed on checks are part of a system called magnetic-ink character recognition (MICR–pronounced "mi-ker").
- To digitize graphics you use a scanner such as the one you use to do OCR scanning.
- Scanners and digital cameras (both still and video) capture images using charge-coupled devices (CCD).
- Scanners are frequently advertised using two resolutions: optical resolution and maximum resolution. The optical resolution is the more accurate measurement because it is directly proportional to the number of light gathering elements on the CCD.
- Color depth refers to the number of colors that a scanner can sense and re-create digitally. It depends on the number of bits assigned to each pixel. A 24-bit (or higher) scanner can store 16.7 million colors–called true color.
- Film scanners or recorders digitize slide film and negatives.
- Virtual reality gives you the feeling that you're experiencing a different space than the one you actually occupy.
- Pointing devices include track sticks, trackballs, touch-sensitive screens, touch pads, graphics tablets, and joysticks.
- To create an image, the display screen or printed page is divided into a grid, creating small squares called picture elements, or pixels. The more pixels used to create a screen display or printed page, the higher its resolution.
- To create shades of gray on a laser printer, groups of adjacent pixels are treated as a single unit called a cell. When all of the dots in a cell are on, the cell is black. When all of them are off, the cell is white. The ratio of on/off dots between these two extremes determines how gray the cell is.
- The resolution of a device is determined by the number of pixels used to form characters and images. Screen resolution is normally specified as 640 X 480, 800 X 600, and so on and monitors use about 72 pixels per inch. Printers normally have resolutions up to 1200 dots per inch (dpi), but some have much higher resolution.
- Type fonts are families of type with a unique look subcategorized by their typeface, type style, and type size.
- Type size is specified in points (72 points to an inch).
- Fonts are stored in the computer as a set of equations that describe each character called scalable or outline fonts. A rasterizer converts the font from the formula to a bit-map which can be displayed and printed.
- WYSIWYG, or what you see is what you get, means that the screen display of a document closely matches its printout.
- The range of colors available (called color depth) is determined by how many bits are used to store data for each pixel. With 24 bits it can be over 16 million colors.
- Cathode ray tube (CRT) displays are the most common type of desktop computer display.
- Most portable computers use flat panel displays that create images using a grid of devices. The devices in the grid are either solid state diodes or chambers filled with a gas. The most common is the liquid crystal display (LCD).
- Laser printers are fast and the dots making up the image are so closely spaced (commonly 600-1200 per inch) that they look like characters typed on a typewriter.
- When you print a document, the process is controlled by the printer control language that your printer is using. The two most common are Hewlett-Packard's PCL 5 language and Adobe Postscript.
- Many color printers use cyan (blue-green), magenta, and yellow (called subtractive primaries) to form all other colors. Often, a fourth color, a solid black, is included so dark blacks are possible. This is known as CMYK, where the last K stands for the extra black.
- To print continuous tones, most color printers use a process called halftoning or dithering that groups printable dots into cells and then uses these larger dots as a single unit to print with.
- Color inkjet printers use separate inkjets for each of the primary colors (red, green, and blue). Liquid inkjet printers use ink cartridges from which they spray ink onto the paper. Solid inkjet printers use solid ink sticks that are melted into a reservoir and sprayed in precisely controlled drops onto the page where the ink immediately hardens.
- Thermal wax transfer and dye sublimation printers use heat to transfer pigment from a plastic ribbon to the paper.

Review Questions

True/False

1. T F Inputting data feeds it to the computer's memory where it can be processed by the CPU.
2. T F A typical output device is the keyboard.
3. T F Optical character recognition (OCR) is used to convert printed documents and faxes back into text that can be edited on the computer.
4. T F Digital cameras are used to take photographs in a digital format the computer can read.
5. T F Virtual reality creates a realistic computer-generated 3D environment.
6. T F Pointing devices such as mice are used mainly during presentations to point out things on the screen.
7. T F All visual computer output is created using small dots called *pixels*.
8. T F If your system uses 24 bits to display graphics, you can display over 16 million colors.
9. T F The two most popular types of computer screens use cathode ray tubes or liquid crystal displays.
10. T F The higher the resolution the larger each item is on the screen.

Fill-In the Blank

1. ________ are used to enter data into the computer so it can be processed. ________ are used to get it out so we can see it or distribute it to others.
2. All scanners and digital cameras capture images with a ________ device.
3. Bar codes come in many varieties. One of them is named ________.
4. Check numbers us a technology called ________.
5. To digitize graphics or do OCR scanning, you use a ________.
6. ________ gives you the feeling that you're experiencing a different space than the one you actually occupy.
7. Pointing devices include ________, ________, ________, ________, and ________.
8. The ________ of a device is determined by the number of pixels used to form characters and images.
9. Fonts are categorized by their ________, ________, and ________.
10. The range of colors (called *color depth*) available in a scanner, printer, or display is determined by how many ________ are used to store data for each pixel.

Multiple Choice

1. On the keyboard, the key you press to finalize a command or entry, is ________.
   a. Enter **b.** Control
   c. Escape **d.** All of the above
2. When selecting a scanner, be sure to base your decision on ________.
   a. The number of bits assigned to each pixel
   b. Its optical resolution
   c. Whether it has optical character recognition software included
   d. All of the above
3. The most common computer pointing device is ________.
   a. Your finger **b.** A mouse
   c. A trackball **d.** None of the above
4. Most computers are capable of displaying a resolution of ________.
   a. 640 x 480 **b.** 480 x 600
   c. 256 x 512 **d.** None of the above
5. The overall design of a font is called its ___.
   a. Type style **b.** Typeface
   c. Type size **d.** Serif
6. Fonts are stored in a printer or computer as ________.
   a. Images **b.** Bit-maps
   c. Formulas **d.** Pictures
7. When a screen changes colors unexpectedly, it's called a ________.
   a. Shift **b.** Palette flash
   c. Screen disorder **d.** None of the above
8. Notebook and smaller computers usually use ________.
   a. Liquid crystal displays
   b. Electroluminescent displays
   c. Field emission displays
   d. All of the above
9. Printer control languages include ________.
   a. Postscript **b.** PCL 5
   c. Both a and b **d.** Neither a nor b
10. The best printer for color photographs is ________.
    a. Dot-matrix **b.** Color laser
    c. Dye sublimation **d.** LED

Research Projects

1. Look at the number on one of your checks and then try to locate that same number in the sequence of magnetic ink recognition characters.
2. Look through magazines or visit a computer store and select the best color printer for use both with documents and photographs. Now pick one that is best for photographs. Are they the same printer?
3. Using magazine ads or a trip to the computer store, select the best display screen for use with graphics. Now, pick the best one for under $500.

CHAPTER

5 SECONDARY STORAGE

AN OVERVIEW

Imagine that a rich uncle has died and left you his art collection of hundreds of expensive works that you'd love to hang on your walls. Unfortunately you live in a small apartment and your uncle left you no money for a larger place. The solution is to store the art in a safe place and hang only the pictures that are your favorites at the moment. Periodically, when you tire of a work, you take it to storage, picking up a new picture to display in your apartment. Computers and many other information technology devices work essentially on this basis.

The computer's RAM is the small apartment in our analogy. It can contain only so much at one time. Anything else that you want to use or save must be stored elsewhere, in the case of computers a magnetic or optical disc, a tape, or a chip of some kind. You store this data elsewhere so you can have access to it at some future date in case something happens to your system and you lose the data and need to restore it.

Storing data so it can be read into a machine is not a new concept. Cards punched with holes were used to store data for looms, mechanical calculators, and other machines as early as the mid-1800s. In the first computers in the 1940s, vacuum tubes stored the data, but by the 1950s magnetic tape came into widespread use followed shortly thereafter by magnetic drums. Finally, in 1957 the modern era began when IBM introduced the first hard drive. This early drive used fifty 24-inch disks to store just five megabytes of data. And they weren't cheap. IBM leased them for $35,000 a year or $7,000 per megabyte. Today a 1 gigabyte hard drive, using 2.5-inch platters and costing less than $250, stores data for only $0.25 a megabyte.

Amazing as hard disks are, they aren't the only way to store data today. There are devices that align magnetic particles in different directions as hard disks do but do so on tape or other kinds of disks, and still other devices that burn pits in a reflective surface to store the digital 0s and 1s of the computer language. In this chapter we introduce you to the concepts and applications of secondary storage.

ON THE PACE CD ROM

Spread No.	Title
5-1	Saving and Opening Documents
5-1	Magnetic Storage
5-2	Random and Sequential Access
5-2	Understanding Drive Access Time
5-5	Optical Reading and Writing
5-6	Understanding Data Compression
5-7	Random and Sequential Access

OBJECTIVES

After completing this chapter, you will be able to:

- Describe the basic techniques used to store data.
- Identify the different types of media used to store data.
- Describe floppy disks, hard disks, and optical discs.
- List the uses for magnetic tape.
- List and describe ways to protect and secure your data.

Secondary *adj.* 1. next after the first in order, place, or time.

Storage *n.* 1. the act of storing: state of being stored.

HD
SECTOR 2
SECTOR 3

5.1 The Foundations of Modern Storage:

Your computer's random-access memory (RAM), is a limited resource, yet it must serve many uses. A computer's RAM is never large enough to store all the application programs, documents, and other computer-generated files you work on. For example, a new word processing program requires 24 megabytes of storage, yet most systems today are sold with either 8 or 16 megabytes of RAM to be used for everything. Moreover, most memory is volatile; it will lose its data when you turn the computer off.

For these reasons, secondary storage (sometimes called auxiliary, external, or mass storage) is provided. You use this more permanent storage to store programs and data that you are not using at the moment. Once stored in secondary storage, you can reload them into the computer's memory any time you want to use them.

Storage devices and media

Secondary storage involves both storage devices and storage media (media is the plural, medium is the singular). For example, a floppy disk drive is a storage device and the magnetic disk on which it stores data is the storage medium. The role of the storage device is to read and write the data on the medium.

- ♦ Writing copies data from the computer's memory to the storage media.
- ♦ Reading copies the data from the media back into the computer's memory. The part of the device that writes and reads data is called the read/write head.

The storage medium is the actual material used to store the data. The read/write head reads and writes data to the medium as the medium moves past it. Think of this much as you would think of the storage of music. You can use tape or compact disc players (the devices) to store or play music from tapes or compact discs (the media).

Secondary storage media and devices fall into three main categories; magnetic, optical, and solid state.

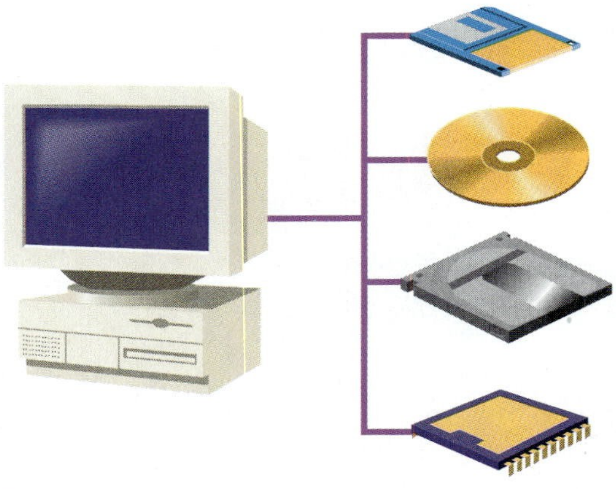

Secondary storage devices and media

Magnetic storage

If you have ever played with two magnets, you know that when held one way, they attract each other. When one of them is reversed, they repel each other. This effect is caused by polarity. Opposite polarities attract, and identical polarities repel. These two magnetic states are used to record data on a disk or tape as follows:

As a disk spins or a tape moves, electrical signals in the drive's read/write head change the polarity of tiny magnetic particles on the medium's magnetic surface to record 0s and 1s. When you open or retrieve a file, the process is reversed. The polarities of the medium immediately under the read/write head induce an electrical current in the read/write head that is transmitted back to the computer in the form of 0s and 1s.

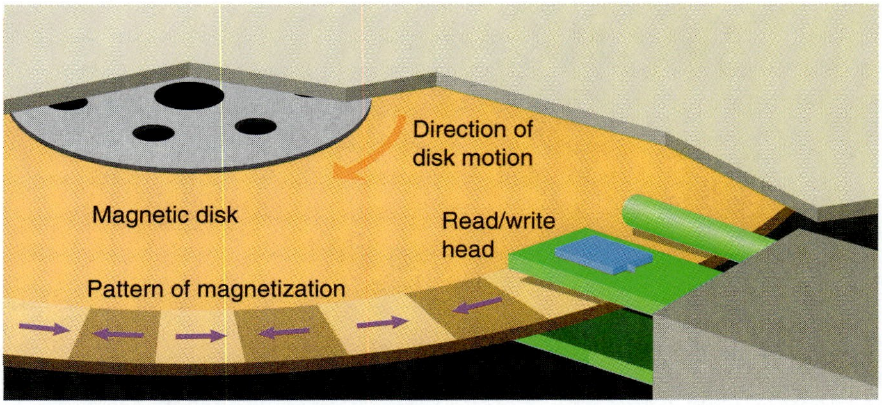

Magnetic disk storage

Optical storage

Optical storage devices use a laser to burn small, dark pits into the surface of a disk. In the case of CDs, CD-ROM, and DVD discs (discussed in Spread 5.5), the pits are created when the disc's surface is forced into a mold. The pits are dark and the places without pits (called lands) remain shiny and smooth. A playback device can read these alternating light and dark spots as 0s and 1s. As the disc spins in the drive, a narrow laser beam is focused on the disk's surface. The amount of light that is reflected back is determined by whether the beam is focused on a pit or a land. Pits reflect less light than the lands do and a device called a photodetector measures the amount of reflected light, and circuits convert its reading into a 0 or 1.

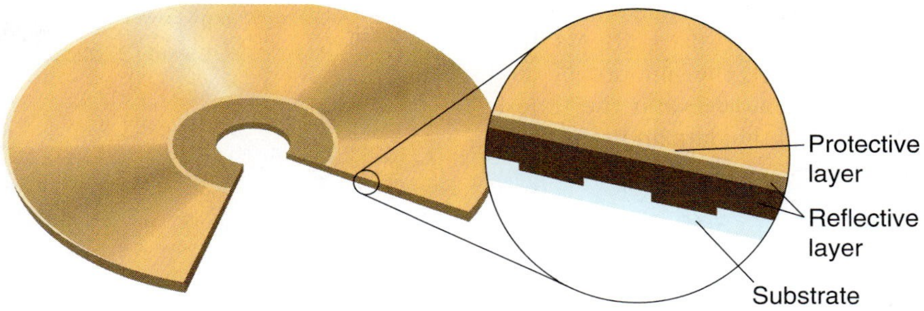

Optical disc

Magneto-optical storage

One of the increasingly popular storage devices is the erasable and reusable magneto-optical (MO) disc-drive. These storage systems offer longevity, removability, high storage capacity, and random access. To record data, the laser in the drive first heats the optical disc's surface. When heated to a specific point, the magnetic orientation of particles can be easily changed by a separate magnetic read/write head. When the area then cools down, the data is hard to erase with other stray magnetic sources so it's more secure than with other media. MO media are available in two formats, rewritable and Write Once Read Many (WORM).

Magneto-optical discs courtesy of International Business Machines

Solid state storage

One of the latest storage devices is called flash memory. This memory uses solid-state chips much like those used in the computer's internal memory (RAM). However, the data in these chips stays recorded even when the power is turned off, that is, memory is nonvolatile. Since flash memory devices have no moving parts they are faster than mechanically operated disks and tapes.

One form of flash memory comes on credit-card-sized PC cards, once called the unpronounceable "PCMCIA cards." These cards plug into slots in the side of notebook computers and take the place of a hard disk drive. They not only perform faster, they also use less energy than a hard disk would. And they are removable—pop one out when it's full and pop in another. Because of their small size, these cards are often used with personal digital assistants (PDAs), organizers, digital cameras, and other handheld devices.

There are three types of PC cards and they vary only in thickness. Type I PC cards are used for solid-state memory. Type III PC cards are used for devices whose components are thicker, such as rotating hard disks.

PC cards for memory applications

Advances in technology keep making drives smaller and smaller. The smaller they become, the smaller the computer can become. The latest advance is the match-book-sized miniature card. This small card isn't just for computers. It is also used in digital cameras, cellular phones, voice recorders, and handheld computers.

Intel memory cards

5.2 The Foundations of Modern Storage:

The kind of secondary storage medium a computer uses affects how data is stored, the amount of data that can be stored, and the time it takes to find the data and retrieve it.

Random versus sequential access

Data is stored randomly or sequentially. This is much like the difference between a song recorded on a compact disc and a song on a cassette tape. The method used determines how you access the data. On the disc you can go directly to any track and play the song, random access. On a cassette tape, you have to advance the tape to the song you want to hear, sequential access. On computers, disks store data randomly and tapes store it sequentially.

Tracks and sectors

For data to be stored on a magnetic disk or tape, it must be formatted. This procedure places electronic marks on the disk's surface so files can be saved and opened in an orderly fashion. On a magnetic disk, formatting divides the surface into circular tracks and pie-shaped sectors, essentially an electronic dart board. Tracks run in narrow concentric bands around the disk. Since tracks can store a great deal of data, the computer divides them into sectors, which makes it easier to find a location on the disk. On older drives these sectors are like pie-shaped wedges that radiate from the center of the disk giving a uniform number of sectors on each track. However, since tracks on the outside of the disk are much longer than those on the inside, this wastes a lot of space. Newer disks use multiple zone recording (also called zone-bit recording), where the number of sectors on a track is based on the length of the track.

Comparison of Storage Devices

Type	Speed	Capacity	Cost	Storage
RAM	Fast	Low	High	Electronic
Floppy disk	Slow	Low	Medium	Magnetic
Hard disk	Fast	High	Medium	Magnetic
CD ROM	Slow	High	Low	Optical
Magneto-optical	Medium	High	High	Magnetic/optical
.25-inch tape	Slow	High	Low	Magnetic
DAT tape	Slow	High	Low	Magnetic

Storage characteristics

Random versus sequential access

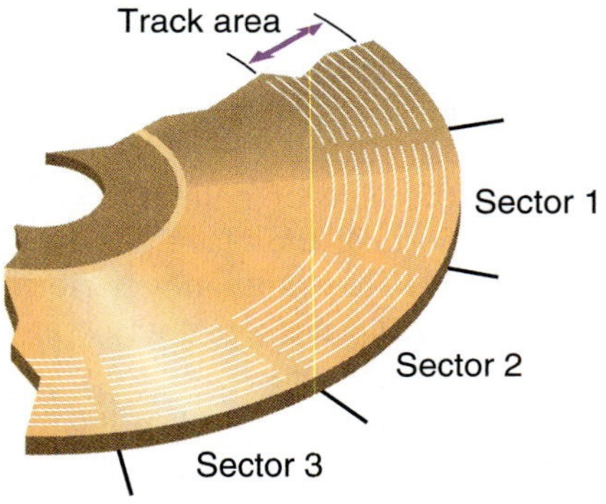

Tracks and sectors

On tapes, there are three different ways of laying down tracks; longitudinal, serpentine, and helical.

- Longitudinal tracks are parallel to the edge of the tape and run its full length.
- Serpentine tracks are also parallel to the edge of the tape. However, after one track is completed, the tape spins in the opposite direction and a second track is laid parallel to the first. This process may repeat many times.
- Helical scans are like those used by your VCR. A rotating read/write head mounted at an angle writes "swipes" at an angle not parallel to the edge of the tape. The tape is moved slightly between swipes so diagonal tracks run parallel to each other. Two or so longitudinal tracks may also be used for fast positioning purposes.

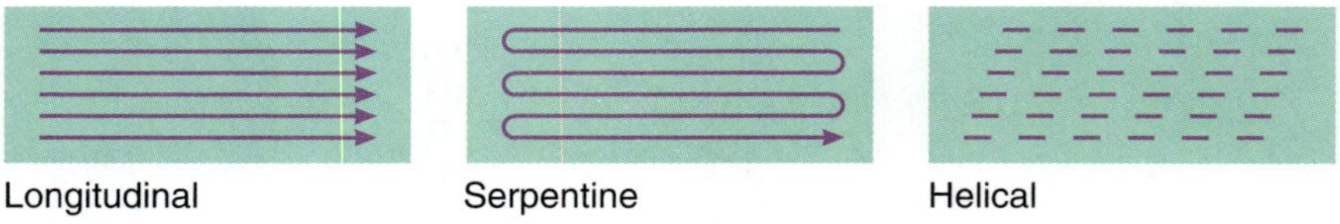

Tape formats

Speed

When you execute a command that requires the computer to find data in secondary storage, it takes time to locate it. There are two very important mechanical features of a drive that affect this: the rate at which the disk spins and the average seek time. The spin rate is the number or revolutions per minute. The seek time is the time it takes the drive to locate a track on which the data is stored. This is expressed in milliseconds (thousandths of a second). Once the drive finds the track, it must then wait for the data to rotate under it. This waiting period is referred to as latency. Seek time plus latency equals access time, the average total time it takes to begin reading data. Access times vary widely among the various storage devices. The fastest access times are found on flash memory devices, the next fastest on hard disks, and the slowest on floppy disk drives and tapes.

Once the computer has located the data in the secondary storage device, it must transfer it to the computer's internal memory. The rate at which data can be transferred is the data transfer rate. Hard disk drives generally have the fastest data transfer rates (other than flash memory), and tapes the slowest; optical and floppy disk drives are somewhere in between. One way to improve the transfer rate is to increase the speed at which the storage medium moves past the read/write head. On circular media, this is called the rotational speed. Some of the fastest hard drives spin at over 7000 RPM.

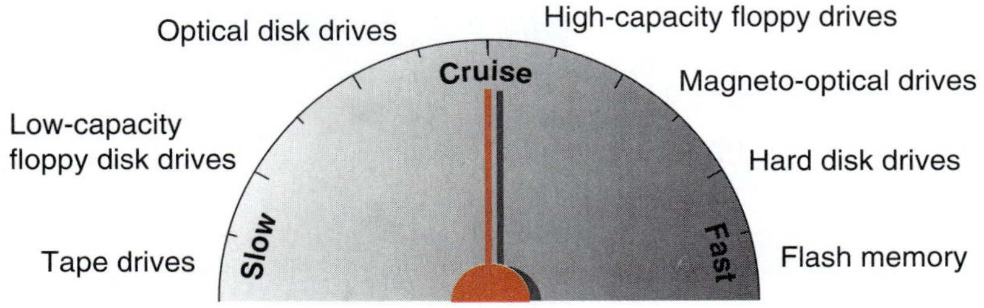

Access times and transfer rates

Storage capacity

How much data can be stored on a particular type of medium, called its storage capacity, depends on several factors. These include density and size or length.

There are two ways to increase the amount of data in a given area, called the areal density and measured in bits per square inch. One is to move the tracks closer together (tracks per inch). The other is to move the bits of data along each track closer together (bits per inch). Think of how many small cars can be parked in the same space as a few large trucks.

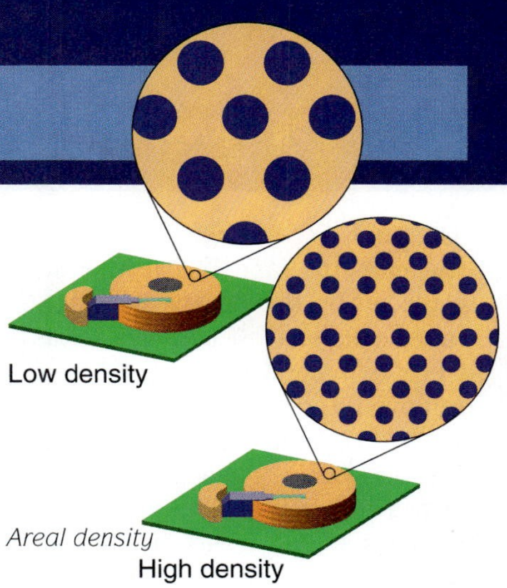

Areal density

Removable media

The typical hard disk drive has both the read/write device and the medium integrated into a single sealed unit. However, many secondary storage devices have removable media. This means that the medium on which you store data can be removed from the device that is used to read and write the data on the medium. Examples of removable media are the common floppy disk, tape, CD-ROM drives, and flash memory cards. There are even hard disk drives with removable media. Removable media give you unlimited storage capacity because you can always insert another disk, tape, or PC card. They also increase the security of your data because you can remove the medium and store it under lock and key or even in another, safer location. Media that can't be removed are only as secure as the device they are physically a part of.

Removable media can be used in two ways, as on-line and off-line storage. On-line storage is used for data that must be instantly available to the computer. Off-line storage is used to archive data that isn't needed at the moment. You might say the book you are reading at the moment is on line while all of those on your shelves are off line. At any time you want, you can put the current book on the shelf (making it off line) and pick up another (making it on line).

On-line and off-line storage

5.3 Storage Media:

The first PC storage medium was the cassette tape but it was soon replaced by the floppy disk (sometimes called a diskette). These disks were so named because when you removed the cover from one, the recording material was a round, flexible piece of plastic. There are now a number of floppy disk technologies in use. The original, now called low-capacity floppy disks, are the familiar fast-fading 5¼-inch and the newer and more popular 3½-inch sizes. It's estimated that by 1998 almost 100 percent of the low-capacity disk market was the 3½-inch disks. Each size works only with drives specifically designed to accept it. Once widely used, these floppy disks are slowly fading in importance as the demands for storage space grow dramatically.

Floppy disk characteristics

The outside appearance of 5¼-inch and 3½-inch disks varies, but both have many features in common.

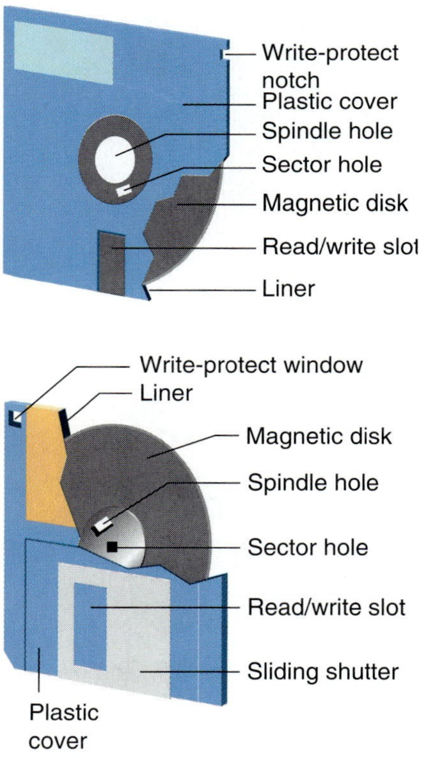

Low-capacity floppy disks

The read/write slot in the plastic cover is where the disk drive's read/write head contacts the surface of the disk. This read/write head stores data on (writes) and retrieves data from (reads) the surface of the magnetic disk as the disk spins inside the drive. On 3½-inch disks, the read/write slot is protected by a sliding metal cover called the shutter. When you insert the disk into the drive, this shutter is automatically slid aside so that the read/write slot is exposed, and the drive can come in contact with the magnetic disk within.

If you were to remove the plastic cover of a floppy disk, you would find a round piece of plastic covered with a metallic oxide, similar to the magnetic recording material used on audio and video tapes. The round disk is sandwiched between two sheets of a soft feltlike material, which is impregnated with a lubricant that protects the disk when it is spinning in the drive.

Write-protecting floppy disks

The disk's write-protect notch or window allows you to write data to a disk when it is not write-protected and prevents you from writing to the disk when it is protected. A switch, or photoelectric circuit, inside the disk drive determines if the disk is write-protected. When it is, the switch disables the drive's ability to write data onto the disk.

- A 5¼-inch disk is write-protected when its write-protect notch is covered by a piece of tape.
- A 3½-inch disk is write-protected when its write-protect window is open.

Floppy disks—the end is near

Over 5 billion 3.5-inch 1.44 MB computer diskettes have been sold since their introduction in 1984. During that same period, hard disk capacities of new PCs have increased from 20 megabytes to 1 gigabyte or more. With such large drives, the old floppy's usefulness is very limited. It would take 700 floppies to hold the same amount of data as a 1 gigabyte drive. There is a race on to replace the floppy with a new device. There are a number of competing, and incompatible, devices being developed and sold, all called high-capacity floppy disks. One of them will probably be the winner. However, things don't always work out as hoped. A few years ago everyone had high hopes for a drive called a floptical. But it flopped. Stay tuned, however, because the limited storage capacity of a floppy disk makes its days numbered.

There are two leading candidates to replace the floppy disk, the 100 megabyte Iomega Zip disk and the 120 megabyte LS-120 diskette.

Write protection

Floppy Disks

The two are not interchangeable so there will be confusion in the market for awhile. Files stored on one disk can't be opened by the other drive.

The LS-120 diskette has the same general shape, weight, and size as the standard 3.5-inch diskette but has 80 times the storage capacity. The drives made for these disks will also accept the common 1.44 MB and will operate it normally, but up to three times faster. If you insert an LS-120 diskette into a 1.44 MB diskette drive, it won't be harmed.

The LS-120 diskette uses magneto-optical technology to enable greater capacity and performance. Named after the laser servo (LS) technology it employs, the drive places optical reference tracks on the diskette that are both written and read by a laser system. The optical sensor in the drive allows the read-write head to be precisely positioned over the magnetic data tracks, enabling track densities of 2,490 data tracks per inch (TPI) versus the 135 TPI for a 1.44 MB diskette.

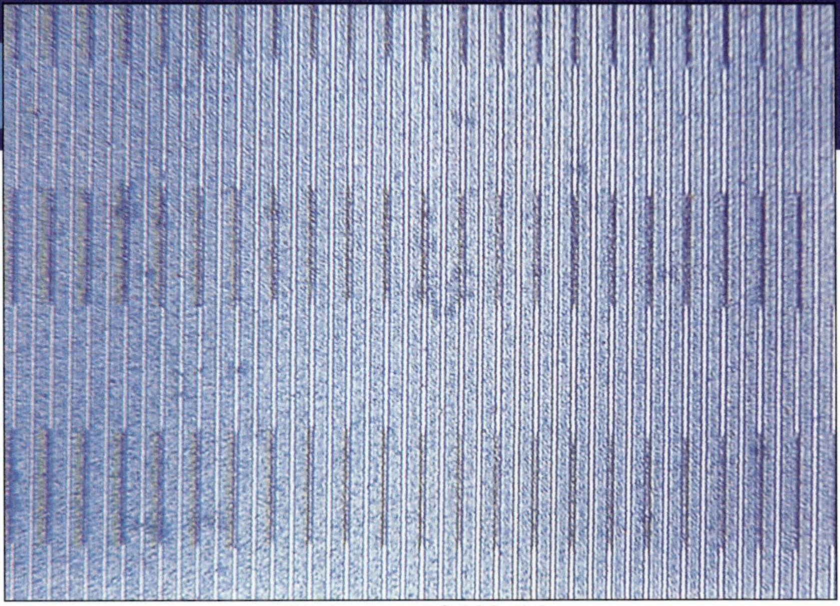
Tracks on an LS-120 disk

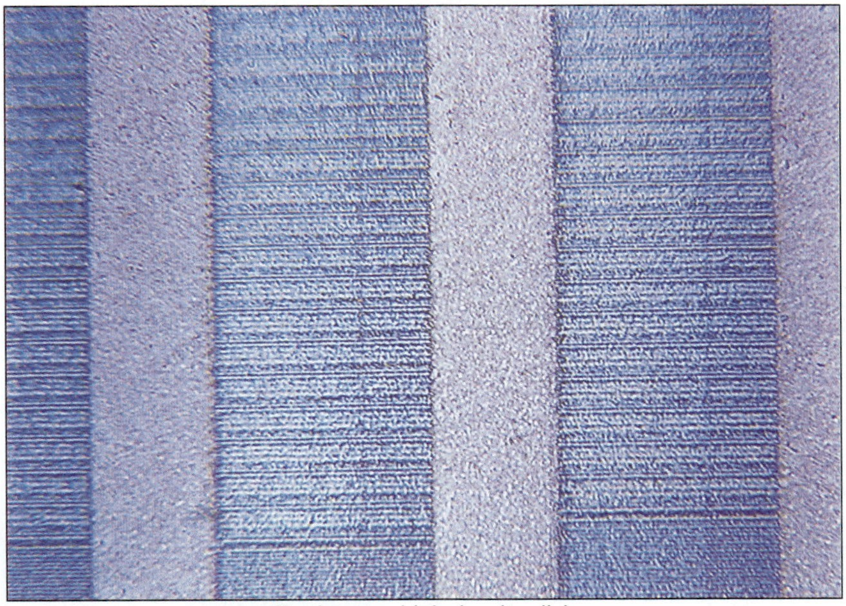
Tracks on a high-density disk

Tracks courtesy of Imation

Memory That Won't Rust

Scientists at Los Alamos National Laboratory have developed a storage technology called high-density read-only memory (HD-ROM). They use an ion beam to etch binary data, letters, or even graphics onto stainless steel pins. A single inch-long pin can store four sets of encyclopedias. The data can last over a thousand years and survive stray magnetic fields, fires, and common chemical accidents.

The Need for More Storage

The need for more secondary storage grows daily. The basic reason for this is an increase in the size of new programs and the size of the files that are created. For example, a few years ago, a CD disc that stored 600 megabytes was thought to be huge. However, without compression (a technique that makes files smaller), one of the CD-ROM discs holds only 30 seconds of video.

5.4 Storage Media:

Hard disk drives, also called hard disks or hard drives, are by far the most popular secondary storage systems. Their combination of reliability, high speed, and low cost is hard to beat. Over the years they have shrunk in size. Today, the most common hard drives are 3.5 inches for desktop models and 2.5 for notebook computers. However, even smaller ones are made.

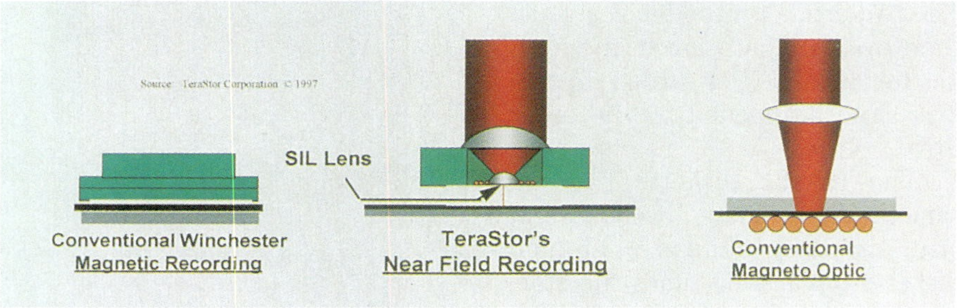

Near field recording courtesy of Terastor

Inside a hard disk

Hard disk are packaged in factory-sealed housings and inside are one or more glass-ceramic or aluminum disks, called platters, that are coated in a thin film of magnetic material similar to that used on audio or video tapes.

Digital data is stored on the platter's surface in concentric circles, called tracks. A read/write head attached to a movable arm reads information from and writes it to these platters. There is a read/write head on each side of the platter since both sides are used. The two heads move in unison and are always opposite each other. The pair of tracks on the top and bottom of the platter, referred to as a cylinder, are recorded as a unit to speed up performance. If the drive has more than one platter, all of the tracks directly above one another are written and read at the same time. If the drive has two platters, the drive's cylinder contains 4 tracks, two on each platter. If the drive has 4 platters, each cylinder has 8 tracks.

Hard disk technologies

To increase the speed and storage capacity in hard drives, a number of new technologies have been developed.

- Magneto-Resistive (MR) heads have made 2 and more gigabyte drives possible. These drive heads change resistance in the presence of a magnetic field (hence their name) and allow a smaller flying height and areal densities of 1 gigabits per square inch are currently being achieved and this should increase to 4 gigabits by the turn of the century.

Side view of platters courtesy of International Business Machines

- A promising new technology, called near field recording, increases areal density by a factor of 10 at a lower cost-per-gigabyte than all existing storage technologies. One of its unique features is a lens (called a solid immersion lens or SIL) in the read/write head. This allows a laser beam to be focused on a very small spot. It's this small spot that allows data to be stored at such a high density.

Hard disk tolerances

On a hard disk drive the read/write heads fly over the disk's surface without making contact except when heads are parked or during drive spin up/down. Flying at 7000 rpm on a cushion of air, the space between the head and the disk is smaller than a piece of dust. To imagine the small tolerances involved, picture a large airplane flying at high speed inches above the ground without making contact. With the high speeds and small spaces involved, even a small particle can cause the read/write head to come into contact with the disk's surface, creating a head crash. With the disk spinning at almost 60 mph, this can cause a lot of damage to the disk and the data stored on it. Top right on the opposite page is shown the distance between the disk and the head compared to some typical items that can cause damage. To prevent these objects from damaging the drive or affecting its performance, hard disks are sealed in an airtight case.

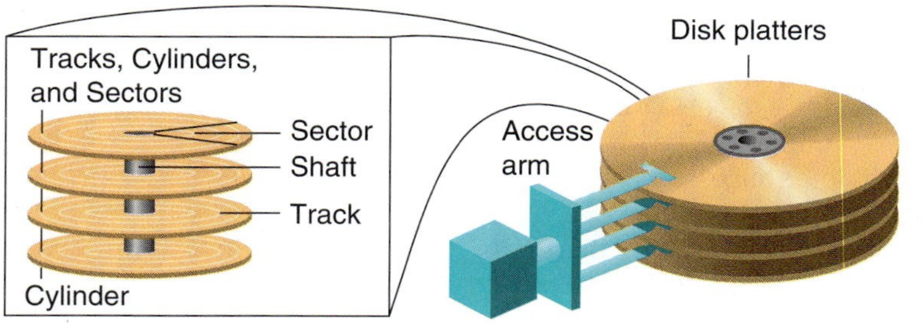

Hard disk cylinders

Although head crashes can be disastrous, it's important to make the head fly closer and closer to the disk's surface. This allows data to be stored more densely. One new technique is to use an IBM technology called predictive failure analysis that constantly monitors head flying height. If there is a change, a warning is issued so you can back up the data. Tests indicate that this can give more than a week's warning of failure.

Hard disk tolerances

Hard disk controllers

For the drive to communicate with the computer, it needs an interface. The computer industry has currently standardized on the IDE (Integrated Drive Electronics) and newer EIDE (Enhanced-IDE) interface. IDE works with only two drives, each of them no larger than 504MB. EIDE works with up to four drives of up to 8 gigabytes and also works with other devices such as CD-ROM and tape drives.

Types of Hard Drive Interfaces

Interface	Megabytes per Second	Drives
IDE	4.1	2
Fast SCSI	10	7
EIDE	16.6	4
Fast/wide SCSI	20	7
Ultra SCSI	40	7

Hard disk controllers

RAID storage devices

Extremely large disk drives, such as those used with mainframe computers, are very expensive. To reduce the cost of secondary storage when large amounts are necessary, Redundant Array of Independent Disks (RAIDs) have been developed. These systems link together a number of inexpensive disk drives, like those used in PCs. By definition, RAID has three attributes:

1. The array of disk drives is viewed by the user as one or more drives.
2. Data is distributed across the set of drives in a defined manner.
3. Data is duplicated or it can be reconstructed in the event of a disk failure.

These systems are not only faster and less expensive, but are also designed to protect data. They do so by storing all data on more than one drive, using disk mirroring or striping. When data is mirrored, it is stored on two drives at the same time. When striped, parts of it are stored on different drives and a record is kept of what is stored where. If one of the drives fails, the data can be reconstructed automatically from the other working drives on which it is stored. In addition, the inoperable disk drive can be replaced without shutting off the system (hot-plugging). Data continues to be stored on the other drives as the broken part is being repaired or replaced.

RAID device courtesy of Clarion

One of the most recent and far-reaching developments in the computer field is the new technology of optical discs. Data is stored on and retrieved from these discs with a laser. These disks currently come in three widely used forms: CD-ROM and DVD-ROM discs, write-once, read-many (WORM) discs, and erasable optical discs. Their main advantage over hard disks is removability and greater density or storage capacity.

Lasers—the optical pen

All optical discs use a laser instead of a magnet to read and write information. The word laser actually stands for "light amplification by stimulated emission of radiation." It is a form of electromagnetic radiation similar to radio and microwaves. In computers, lasers are in the form of solid-state laser diodes. In these diodes, excited electrons give up their excess energy by emitting photons or light. This light is emitted in a very narrow channel with mirrored ends so it bounces back and forth becoming amplified by interactions with other photons. Finally the light is emitted from one end of the diode and focused into a very narrow beam by a lens.

Laser courtesy of International Business Machines

All computers now use infrared lasers to read and write data. However, in the near future you'll be reading about blue lasers. With a much shorter wavelength, these lasers can store four times as much data in the same area. Their beam is only a quarter of the size of one from an infrared laser.

Applications of optical discs

CD ROM and DVD ROM discs have changed the way information is stored, distributed, and accessed. Publishers like using these discs to distribute information and programs because they cannot be illegally copied as easily as floppy disks, they are a lot cheaper to manufacturer, and they don't pass viruses from one user to the next.

Who Said You Can't Make Money In Poetry?

An English publisher has released a CD-ROM disc containing 16,859 poems. Plans are to introduce two more so over 1,350 poets are included covering the years from 600 to 1900. No library anywhere in the world has a printed collection to match this new electronic one. And you don't have to read all of the poems to find what you want. You can search by keyword, title, date, or name. The poets who wrote the collected works may have starved, but the publisher hopes not to. They have priced the disks at $41,000 and immediately over 100 buyers have lined up with money in hand.

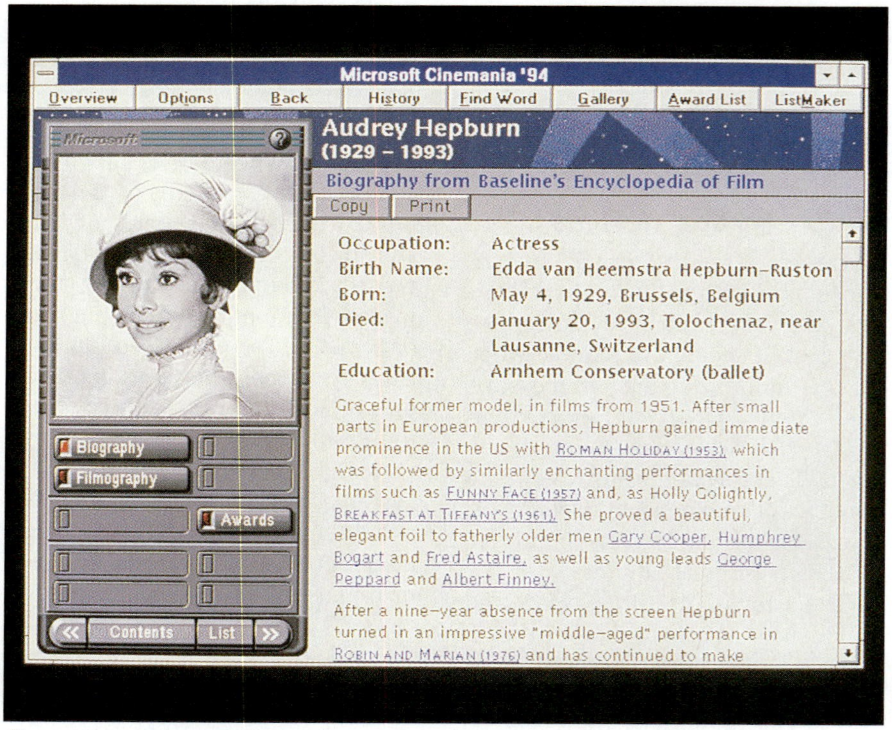

Cinemania courtesy of Microsoft

Types of optical discs

There are so many optical discs on the market that it's easy to get confused. However, it's easier when you organize them into those that can only be read, those that can be recorded on, and those that can be recorded on many times (rewritable). Let's take a look at CD discs and the newer DVD discs.

Optical Discs

CD discs

Types of CD discs

CD-ROM discs are similar in concept to the audio discs (CDs) so popular in the music recording industry. These discs can store up to 660 megabytes of data. Like other media, they are rated by their access times and transfer rates. Since many of their characteristics are fixed by specifications that make them compatible with the millions of drives, performance is boosted by spinning them faster in the drive. The faster they spin the faster are the access times and the higher the transfer rates. The spin rate is designated by the 2x, 4x, 6x, and 16x designations each drive carries. A 16x drive spins 16 times faster than the original drives.

CD-ROM discs courtesy of International Business Machines

Most CD-ROM discs can only be read but there are other versions that you can write to.

- CD-Recordable (CD-R) discs can be written on once. These disks have a thin layer of gold with a layer of green dye below. To record data, the laser forms bumps in the dye layer. When played back, the computer reads a bump as 1 and the absence of a bump as 0. The fact that you can only write to these discs once isn't always a drawback. Many firms need archive copies of data and the fact that the data can't be modified once it's been copied is actually a benefit.
- CD-ReWritable (CD-RW) can be recorded, erased, and reused, just like a hard disk. These discs (and the DVD-RAM discs discussed below) record data by changing a material from a well-structured crystalline state to a less-ordered amorphous state.

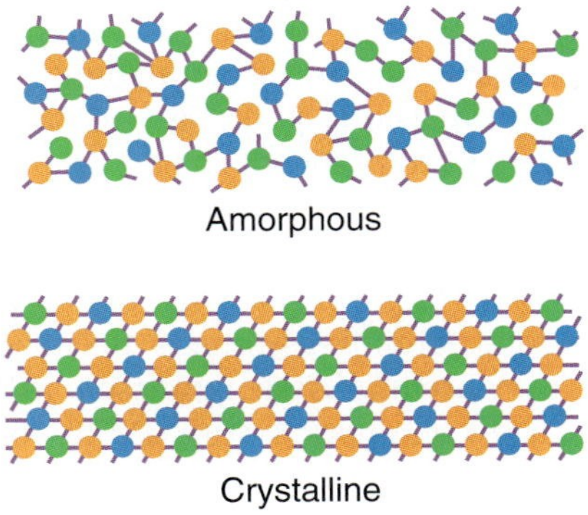

Phase change

DVD discs

This latest generation of optical discs went through so many name changes (digital video disc and digital versatile disc) that only the DVD acronym remains in use. In one massive shift, this new medium is about to replace music CDs, videotapes, 12-inch video laserdiscs, and CD-ROMs. These new (DVD) discs and the computer cousin DVD-ROM discs will initially store 4.7 gigabytes of digital information on a single-sided, single-layer disc the same size as today's CD-ROMs. With compression (discussed in Spread 5.6), that's enough to contain a full-length, full-screen, full-motion feature film, including three channels of CD-quality audio and four channels of subtitles. Future plans include 9.4 gigabyte double-sided or double-layer discs as well as double-sided and double-layer discs that will store about 17 gigabytes. That's nearly 30 times the capacity of today's CD-ROM discs.

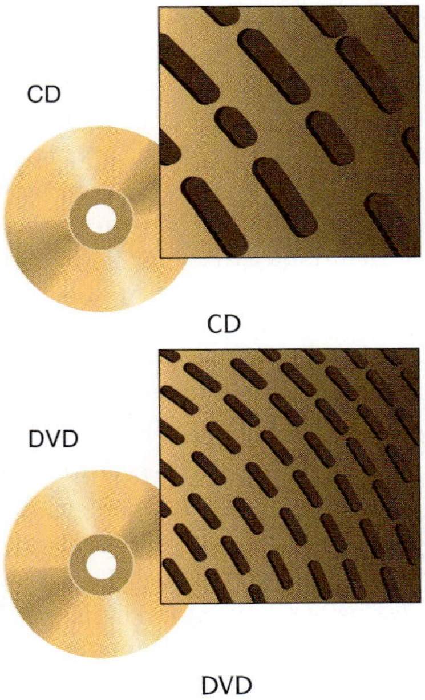

CD versus DVD density

5.6 Increasing Data Storage Capacity

As storage demands have increased, technology has responded with new approaches and new systems. They range from simple, almost manual procedures such as compressing individual files, to elaborate automatic data storage systems.

In the computer industry as in other industries there are economies of scale. This means that if a lot of something is made, each unit of it is cheaper. For this reason, most new secondary storage systems use widely available hardware such as hard disk drives or even Digital Audio Tape. Designing a 100-gigabyte hard drive from scratch is a lot more expensive than putting 20 widely available 5-gigabyte drives in a rack and wiring them together.

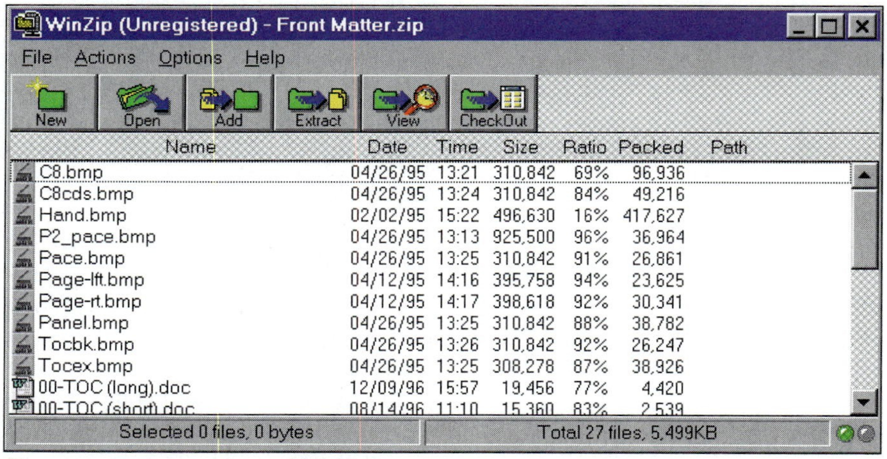

File compression courtesy of WinZip

Compression

It always seems that no matter how much space you have on a disk, you don't have enough. As you add programs and files, you gradually fill the disk until it has less and less free room. When you run out of room, you can no longer save files, and some programs won't run because most programs need room on the disk to store temporary files as you work. Even disks that are not full begin to misbehave or slow down the entire system as the computer has to work harder and harder to find room for the files it needs to operate. Instead of installing a larger hard drive or adding another one to your system, you can use compression to make the files on the disk smaller. There are two forms of compression in use: disk compression and file compression.

- Disk compression compresses an entire disk. Once you run the utility to compress the disk, all subsequent compression is automatic and done "on the fly." That is, when you create a new file, the compression program stores it on the disk in a compressed format. When you open the file, it is then automatically uncompressed.
- File compression is a manual operation that you use to compress selected files. Using a file compression utility program, you can create a single new file, called an archive, that stores one or more other previously separate files in it. As the files are moved into this new file they are automatically compressed. To work with them, you first extract them from the compressed file so they are restored to the disk in the original format. The amount of compression you can expect varies from about 50 percent for word processing documents to 90 percent for bit-map graphics. Some files such as ZIP and GIF don't compress much because they are already compressed. ZIP files compressed with PKZip or WinZip are the most common archive format. Other file compression formats and programs include LZH (LHA program), ARC (ARC, ARCE, PKXARC, and PKUNPAK), and on UNIX systems TAR (Tape Archive program).
- Compressed files don't only save storage space, they also make it easier and faster to send files over networks.
- They are easier to send because files are gathered together into a single archive file.
- They are faster to send because the files are compressed. For example, most audio, video, and graphic files on the Internet are in a compressed format so they can be sent faster.

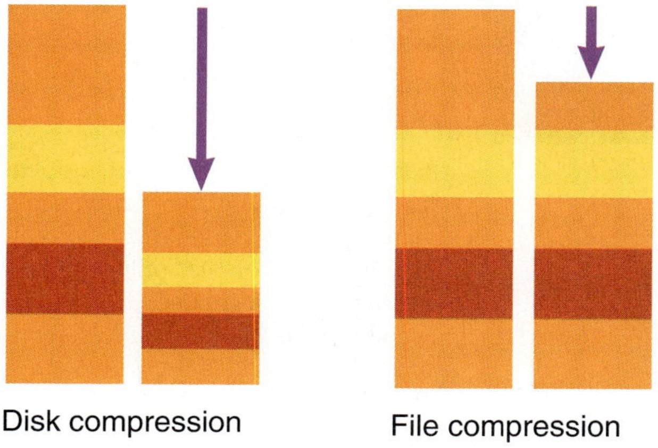

Disk versus file compression

Jukeboxes

The concept of a jukebox, seen in booths at Arnold's diner in reruns of Happy Days, has been reincarnated for use with optical and MO discs. The jukebox holds a number of discs and automatically selects the right disc and plays it for you. With 128 or so discs on line, the amount of information available is tremendous and only a second away.

CD jukebox courtesy of International Business Machines

Hierarchical storage management (HSM)

There are a number of types of storage media and each has its strengths and weaknesses. Two of the most important criteria to judge them by are their access times and their costs. Data that must be instantly accessible, such as the program you are using, is best stored on fast devices even if they are expensive. Data that is just being stored for future use, such as unimportant documents, or files used to restore the system if something goes wrong, can be stored on slower, less expensive media.

As multimedia and graphics become more frequently used in computing, the amount of data that must be stored is turning from a river into a flood. It's estimated that the typical PC LAN network now requires 118 gigabytes of storage space. That is way too much data to store economically on hard disk drives. To solve this problem, a procedure known as hierarchical storage management (HSM) is used. After 30 days, unused files are automatically moved from hard disks to an optical storage system just as with an MO jukebox. After another 60 days, unused files on the optical jukebox are automatically moved to a tape library. Both the optical jukebox and tape library use more than one storage medium but the one with the desired file is autoloaded when needed. As with a jukebox, the right cartridge or tape is inserted at the right time. These systems provide a way to copy or move data automatically, without human intervention, from a more expensive medium to a less expensive one.

To the user, all files appear to be stored on the hard disk. The only drawback is that files on backup media are slower to load. Studies show that if files over 180 days old are moved off the hard disk, it increases storage capacity 50 percent.

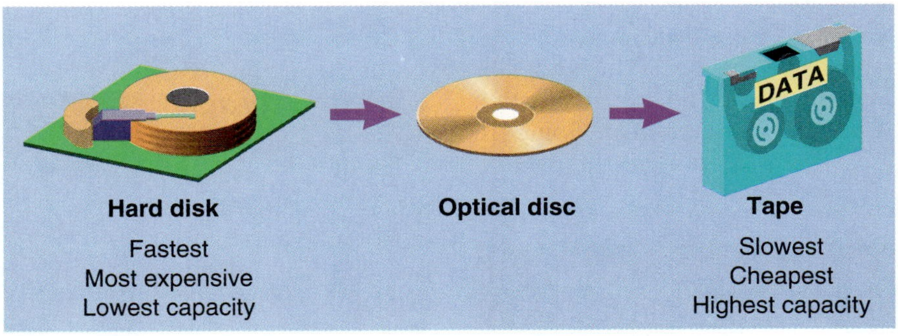

Hierarchical storage management (HSM)

Tape systems for large computers and networks

On mainframe computers and large networks, the tape used for backup can be stored in large tape subsystems called tape libraries. The IBM Magstar uses tapes that can store 10 gigabytes per tape. With multiple tapes being used, the systems can store up to 576 terabytes.

Tape library courtesy of International Business Machines

5.7 Backing Up Your Data

There is nothing more important than backing up your data. The cost of many systems is but a small fraction of the cost of the data they contain. 3M estimates that it costs $17,000 to reconstruct 20 megabytes of sales and marketing data and almost $100,000 for the same amount of engineering data. But backup is also a way to preserve data for future use or to transfer data from one user to another. When backing up your data, you have a lot of choices as to where you store it.

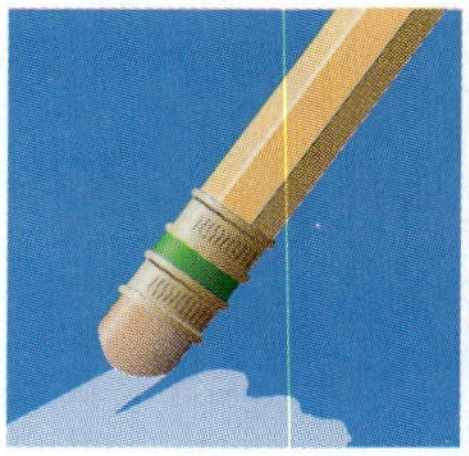

Human errors ranging from mistakes when installing or using programs to dropping a notebook computer can eliminate your data in an instant.

System malfunctions such as a hard disk crash will cause data loss. In some cases, the head of the hard disk comes in contact with the rapidly spinning disk, scraping off magnetic material and the data it contains.

Acts of nature such as fires, earthquakes, and floods can wipe out a system. Even lesser acts such as burst water pipes, power outages, or lightning storms can erase it.

Power failures or brownouts can cause problems with both open files and files on the disk.

Fires in the building or in the computer can destroy all of the data.

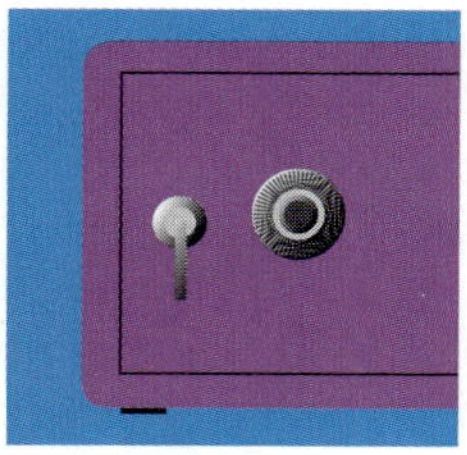

Backed up data is portable data. You can move it to a safe location or you can send it to another site to put on that system.

Why backup?

Why backup?

There are any number of events that can cause your system to lose its data.

- Theft of parts or entire systems can take your data along. It's not hard to misplace a notebook computer or have someone walk off with it, and desktop systems are also frequently stolen.
- Unauthorized users tampering with your system can deliberately or inadvertently lose data.
- Viruses, those malicious programs designed by social misfits, are often transferred to your system without your knowing it. Some are designed to erase all the data on your system.

Flat Earth Society Tries to Round up Members

The home of the president of the Flat Earth Society burned in 1995, and with it went all of the computer records of the society's members. The president, Charles Johnson, says "Since the fire I haven't been able to contact members, so I've been waiting for them to drift in." So far about 400 of the original 3,500 have done so.

Off-site storage

Off-site storage

Make a backup copy and keep it in a place where the same accident can't hurt both the original and the backup. Normally, this procedure is called off-site storage. But how far off-site is important. For example, storing the original and backup copy in the same building is no protection from fire or theft. Storing them both in the same neighborhood is no protection against floods, hurricanes, and earthquakes. The basic rule here is to make sure the same disaster can't happen to both.

Nothing is Forever

Optical storage has a longer life expectancy than tape (up to 15 years or so), but tape should last five years or longer. Eventually, however, tape suffers "print through" where layers above and below wear through affecting data on the tightly wound tape.

Backup media with random access

Many storage media offer random access, just like a hard disk drive. This is a big advantage because you can easily locate and retrieve an individual file or group of files.

- Floppy disks are inexpensive but are slow and have little storage capacity. The newer ZIP, Syquest, and LS-120 disks and drives can store over 100 megabytes and are quickly replacing the older floppy disk drives.
- Removable hard disks are just like your regular hard disk. The difference is that the disk can be removed from the drive and stored in a safe place. A new one can be inserted whenever the current one become full.
- Rewritable magneto-optical discs provide large storage capacity.
- Recordable CD and DVD discs "burn" data onto a CD-ROM disc.

Backup media with sequential access

Tape is still the most widely used backup media because its low cost. While hard disk storage may cost $0.50 a megabyte, tape costs can be as low as $0.0025 per megabyte. Unfortunately, these least expensive media have sequential access. To access a file on the tape, you have to load your backup software, specify the files you want to access, and restore them to the hard disk. This process is slower and less convenient than random access where you slide in a removable disk and use it just like any other disk on your system. There is a real horse race on by manufacturers to increase tape speed and storage capacity. Any comparisons of relative capacities are quickly outdated.

There are many kinds of tapes. Here are just a few of the basic "families":

Backup media with random access courtesy of International Business Machines

- Quarter Inch Committee tape (QIC—pronounced "quick") is currently the most widely used format for backing up PCs. However, tapes from different manufacturers are not always compatible. QIC tapes are available in two sizes, a 3.5-inch minicartridge and a 5.25-inch data cartridge.
- Travan technology dramatically increases the capacity of a tape cartridge by using a tape that is wider and longer than the QIC tape. The Travan cartridge is a bit larger than the older QIC-80 cartridge, and it is somewhat trapezoidal in shape. Early versions can store up to 4 gigabytes uncompressed and 8 gigabytes compressed. More importantly, the drives for these tapes have been standardized so a Travan tape can be used with a Travan drive from any manufacturer.

Tape courtesy of Imation

- Digital Audio Tape (DAT) uses helical scan tracks and achieves a much higher density than QIC tapes.
- Digital Linear Tape (DLT) has been widely used in computer centers but as costs drop it is finding its way into lower-end systems. These tapes have numerous parallel tracks laid down at the same time in the same direction. Current DLT products record two channels simultaneously using two read/write elements in the head, effectively doubling the transfer rate possible at a given drive speed and recording density.

Tape drive courtesy of International Business Machines

Why Backup?

In 1996 it was reported that most of the data gathered by the United Nations on human rights violations in Croatia was stolen. It took four years and numerous investigations to gather the data and one thief and a broken window to lose it. There were no backup copies.

5.8 Picture Essay:

The familiar credit card with the magnetic stripe on its back is about to get a run for its money. Smart cards, widely used in Europe for years, made their first large-scale introduction into the United States during the 1996 Olympic Games in Atlanta. In place of the coin you put into a machine today, or the credit card you use to make small purchases, you may find yourself using a smart card in a few years!

Smart cards

The typical smart card contains a printed image and message, usually an advertisement from the issuer or information about the user, such as a photo and name.

Smart cards courtesy of Gemplus

Embedded in the card is a special type of integrated circuit that stores information in electronic form and controls who uses this information and how it is used. The smart card chip holds about 16 kilobytes of information and that is expected to increase to 32K within a few years. That's enough to store up to 3200 words of text or a digital snapshot of your finger print, palm print, or retinal scan.

Applications

The most common smart card is the prepaid phone card. In France almost all public telephones accept prepaid smart cards. Over 100 million are used annually. As calls are made, their cost is deducted from the card and a display on the telephone indicates how many units are left on the card. When no units are left a new card must be procured. It is expected that smart cards will be used for pay phones in over 100 countries by the end of the century with over 1 billion cards used annually. However, smart cards are also used as cash cards, ID cards, medical record storage, and cellular phone activators.

Phone card courtesy of USWest

In many parts of Europe and Asia, smart phone cards store account and PIN numbers (personal ID number) so that the same cellular phone can be used by different people who simply insert or swipe through their smart card to activate the phone. Airlines and hotel chains are using smart cards to store passenger frequent flyer and frequent guest credits. And smart cards are in wide distribution in the trucking industry where they are used as debit cards for tolls and transit fees, and to keep track of records such as weigh station reports, bills of lading, and state registrations. MasterCard International is committed to the use of smart card technology because this innovation will offer enhanced card security and provide you with faster and safer ways to use your MasterCard to make purchases and payments. Smart cards bring banks as close as your computer. Virtual banking can offer many services over the Internet or over specially equipped phones.

The Magnetic Stripe

On the back of every credit card is a black band called a magnetic stripe. This stripe is made up of magnetic material that stores about one-thousand bits of data–enough for 226 alphanumeric characters. The data is read by swiping the card through a card reader. Widely used for credit cards, these stripes can also be found on hotel room keys and security badges. Despite their popularity, they do not provide enough security for many transactions and fraud with these cards is climbing rapidly.

Magnetic stripe, courtesy of Scott Goodwin Photography

Are They Free?

Hardly, in fact you pay in a number of ways. You pay the face value of the card when you buy it, but the bank then makes money from:

- The "float." You pay cash for the card and they have use of your money till you use all of it on the card.
- Advertising that they sell or use themselves on the face of the card.
- Fees from merchants that accept the card from you.
- Change left on the card when you toss it.

Adding money to a card

Some cards are fixed in value. You purchase them from vending machines, banks, or other outlets in amounts of $1 and up. As you use the card to make purchases, the balance falls. When it's zero, you recycle it or even sell it to a collector. (With billions in use, just throwing them away would create a major environmental problem.) Other cards are more like an electronic purse or wallet that you can spend from and add to. You can insert the card into ATM machines, phones, or card readers next to your PC to have them refilled. Basically, you would just have funds transferred to your card from a credit card or bank account.

Smart card vending machine courtesy of Visa

Electronic wallet courtesy of Hitachi

The retailer's machine

To make a purchase, you hand the retailer the smart card and he inserts it into a machine, much like credit cards today. The big difference is that the machine doesn't have to dial into a central computer to find account information because it's stored right in the card. The retailer's machine deducts the amount of the purchase from the card right in the store. The retailer then collects from the bank or other organization that sold you the card. You are not involved because you have already paid for it. For security, new smart cards are virtually impossible to steal and use because they require the entry of a PIN (personal ID number). The retailer cannot deduct funds from the card unless you first key in a PIN.

Retailer reader courtesy of Gemplus

Balance reader

The smart card has no display on it. To read its contents, you need a balance reader. These devices are so small that some of them have been designed as key rings.

Security

Some smart cards are smarter than others. The simplest cards, such as phone cards, are virtually impossible to copy or falsify, but offer no protection in case of loss. If you lose one, anyone can use it. Other smart cards have one password to restrict its use to one person or machine, and the most sophisticated cards manage several passwords and can use authentication and ciphering techniques to combine total freedom with total security.

The smart card, in association with a well designed security system, has been demonstrated to be an effective weapon against payment fraud. The electronic purse is also an effective protection against counterfeit coins and bank notes. In France pay phone break-ins fell from 44,000 in 1985, before cards were widely used, to zero in 1994. As card-operated public phones ceased to be a target for theft, they were less often out of order. The same benefits can be found in many other applications where coin-operated machines have suffered from low reliability, required regular coin collection, and borne the cost and loss of service caused by vandalism.

Balance readers courtesy of Mondex

5.9 Enhancing and Testing Your Understanding

Summary

- Secondary storage is permanent storage used to store programs and data that you are not using at the moment.
- Secondary storage uses storage devices such as drives and storage media such as disks or tapes.
- A magnetic drive's read/write head changes the polarity of tiny magnetic particles on the medium's magnetic surface to record 0s and 1s. When you retrieve a file, the process is reversed.
- Optical storage devices use a laser to burn pits into the surface of a disc. On commercially recorded discs, the pits are created when the disc's surface is forced into a mold. The pits are dark and the places without pits–called lands–remain shiny and smooth. A playback device can read these alternating light and dark spots as 0s and 1s.
- Magneto-optical (MO) disc drives use a laser to heat the optical disc's surface to a specific point so the magnetic orientation of particles can be easily changed by a separate magnetic read/write head.
- Flash memory uses solid-state chips to store data and the data stays recorded even when the power is turned off.
- PC cards (previously called PCMCIA cards) plug into notebook computers, digital cameras, and other handheld devices, and take the place of a hard disk drive.
- Type I PC cards are used for solid-state memory. Type III PC cards are used for devices whose components are thicker, such as rotating hard disks.
- The match-book sized miniature card is used in digital cameras, cellular phones, voice recorders, and handheld computers.
- On a disk you can go directly to any file in random access. On a tape, you have to first advance the tape through other files to the file you want in sequential access.
- For data to be stored on a disk or tape, the medium must be formatted to divide the surface into circular tracks and pie-shaped sectors. On tapes, tracks are longitudinal, serpentine, or helical.
- A drive's spin rate is the number or revolutions per minute and its seek time is the time it takes the drive to locate a track on which the data is stored. The time the drive then waits for the data to rotate under it is referred to as latency. Seek time plus latency equals access time, the average total time it takes to begin reading data.
- The rate at which data can be transferred from a device to the computer's memory is called the data transfer rate.
- Storage devices with removable media, such as tape and CD ROM drives, give you unlimited storage capacity because you can always insert another medium. They also increase data security because you can remove the medium and store it under lock and key or even in another, safer location.
- New high-capacity floppy disks have been designed to replace the old floppy disks. The two leading ones are the 100-megabyte Iomega Zip disk and the 120-megabyte LS-120 diskette.
- Hard disk drives are by far the most popular secondary storage systems.
- Hard disks contain one or more glass-ceramic or aluminum disks, called platters.
- The pair of tracks on the top and bottom of a platter, called a cylinder, are recorded as a unit to speed up performance. If the drive has more than one platter, all of the tracks directly above one another are written and read at the same time.
- On PCs, most drives communicate with the computer using an IDE (Integrated Drive Electronics) or newer EIDE (Enhanced-IDE) interface.
- Redundant Array of Independent Disks (RAIDs) link together a number of inexpensive disk drives such as those used in microcomputers.
- CD discs can be recorded on once (CD-R and DVD-R), or many times (CD-RW and DVD-RAM).
- A CD-ROM drive's performance is boosted by spinning the disk faster in the drive. The spin rate is designated by the 2x, 4x, 6x, 8x, 12x, and 16x designations each drive carries. A 16x drive spins 16 times faster than the original drives.
- DVD discs initially store 4.7 GB of digital information–enough to contain a feature film. Future plans include 9.4GB double-sided or double-layer discs as well as double-sided and double-layer discs that will store about 17GB.
- Compression is used to make the files on the disk smaller. There are two forms of compression: disk compression (used for the entire disk) and file compression (used for selected files).
- Hierarchical storage management (HSM) systems automatically move unused data from expensive media such as hard disks to less expensive media such as optical discs or tape after a preset number of days.
- Back up your data frequently and keep your backup where the same disaster can't happen to both it and the original data.
- Tape is the most widely used backup medium because of its low cost.
- Smart cards are like credit cards but with embedded circuits that store information in electronic form and control who uses this information and how it is used.
- Stored value, or prepaid, cards contain a fixed amount of cash that declines as purchases are made. They can be used anywhere there is a card reader.

Review Questions

True/False

1. T F Storage medium refers to the material that data is stored on.
2. T F Disks have sequential access and tapes have random access.
3. T F On a disk, data is stored on circular tracks that are divided into sectors.
4. T F Some devices have the media permanently installed and others have removable media.
5. T F RAID storage devices use a number of inexpensive hard disk drives working together.
6. T F On optical discs, the data is stored in pits in a shiny surface.
7. T F To store more data on a disk, the data can be impressed.
8. T F Some storage devices contain a number of tapes or disks to increase their storage capacity.
9. T F The least expensive media for backing up your data are magnetic tapes.
10. T F Smart cards are about the size of a credit card with a microprocessor embedded in them.

Fill-In the Blank

1. Optical storage devices use a laser to burn small, dark pits into the surface of a disc.
2. As a magnetic disc spins or magnetic tape moves, the drive's read/write head changes the ________ of magnetic particles on the medium's magnetic surface to record 0s and 1s.
3. flash memory uses solid-state chips to store data and the data stays recorded even when the power is turned off.
4. Seek time plus latency equals access time, the average total time it takes to begin reading data.
5. Data on a tape can be accessed sequential, while that on a disk can be accessed random.
6. The rate at which data can be transferred is called the data transfer rate
7. For data to be stored on a disk or tape, the medium must first be removed.
8. When a drive's read/write head comes into contact with the disk's surface, it's called a ________.
9. The DVD disc you can write on many times is called CD-Rewriteable
10. Credit cards with microprocessors are called Smart cards.

Multiple Choice

1. The PC card that is used for solid-state memory is a ___.
   - **a.** Type I
   - **b.** Type II
   - **c.** Type III
   - **d.** None of the above
2. Data on a tape is stored so you access it ________.
   - **a.** Randomly
   - **b.** Sequentially
   - **c.** Optically
   - **d.** Manually
3. You can record on this optical disc ________.
   - **a.** DVD-R
   - **b.** DVD-RAM
   - **c.** CD-R and CD-RW
   - **d.** All of the above
4. The speed of a drive depends on its ________.
   - **a.** Access time
   - **b.** Transfer rate
   - **c.** Both a and b
   - **d.** Neither a nor b
5. A hierarchical storage system moves unused data files to ________ after a preset number of days.
   - **a.** Less expensive media
   - **b.** Faster media
   - **c.** Larger media
   - **d.** More convenient media
6. A smart card is a credit-card-sized card that contains ___.
   - **a.** A magnetic stripe
   - **b.** A microprocessor
   - **c.** A modem
   - **d.** A CD-ROM drive
7. The least expensive backup medium is ________.
   - **a.** DVD
   - **b.** CD-ROM
   - **c.** Magnetic tape
   - **d.** RAID drives
8. The ________ optical disc can be written on many times.
   - **a.** DVD-RAM
   - **b.** CD-R
   - **c.** DVD-R
   - **d.** CD-ROM
9. Arrays of inexpensive hard disks linked together are called ________.devices.
   - **a.** IDE
   - **b.** EIDE
   - **c.** RAID
   - **d.** None of the above
10. A storage device small enough to be used in notebook computers and even digital cameras is the ________.
    - **a.** PC card
    - **b.** PCMCIA card
    - **c.** Miniature card
    - **d.** All of the above

Research Projects

Consider the secondary storage components for a new system you are planning to buy. Using the advertisements in a computer magazine, pick out particular examples of each of the following devices and write a brief description of why you would want them and how much they would cost. Keep in mind that many of these components are already part of many systems, so you'll concern yourself with adding them only after the system has been purchased.

- Hard disk drive
- Floppy disk drive
- Floppy disks
- Removable disks
- CD-ROM drive
- DVD drive

CHAPTER

6 SOFTWARE–AN INTRODUCTION

AN OVERVIEW

Computers are just expensive paperweights until they are brought to life with software. It's software that allows the computer to run and allows you to do any useful work. As you are now learning, computers are versatile machines with many abilities. You can change the function they perform just by changing the program that you use. Computers have become so widely used that you may already be somewhat familiar with the software equivalent of the hit parade. You may have used or read about programs such as Windows, Windows NT, DOS, and UNIX. You might even have used a word processing, spreadsheet, database, or graphics program in your work. But as popular and useful as these mass market programs are, they are by no means the only kind of programs that are available. Visit a computer superstore or thumb through a software mail order catalog and you'll find an amazing selection. There are programs to organize your family tree, design a flower garden, edit or design book pages, draw cartoons, and even help you write your own programs or develop your own multimedia shows.

Until the development of the personal computer, most programs were developed by the company that was using them or by the firm that sold or serviced their computers. There were so few computers that it was not possible to develop programs with mass markets. For example, in 1965 there were only about 10,000 computers in the United States. Even the best program might sell only a few hundred copies at a very high price.

When smaller and less expensive personal computers became popular in the 1980s, they sold by the millions. This opened up a vast market for companies that wrote and marketed programs. As the size of the potential market grew dramatically, prices fell significantly.

In this chapter we look at the most common types of programs including operating systems, utilities, and application programs.

ON THE PACE CD ROM

Spread No.	Title
6-4	Understanding Multitasking
6-6	Drive, Folder, and File
6-7	Understanding Drive Fragmentation
6-9	Understanding Drivers

OBJECTIVES

After completing this chapter, you will be able to:

- Describe the basic types of software that are available.
- Compare and contrast various user interfaces and operating systems.
- Explain the function of and uses for an operating system.
- Describe document-centric computing and its importance.
- Discuss important software-related issues.

Operating system *n.* 1. the software that allows a computer to function by automatically managing and controlling its resources.

Application program *n.* 1. the software that you use to perform useful work on a computer.

6.1 Software:

Computers can't operate without instructions—step by step procedures that tell them what to do and when to do it. These instructions, called programs or software, are written by specialists called programmers. Distributed on disks or over the Internet, these programs are then used by the rest of us. There are basically two types of software, systems software and applications programs.

Operating systems

Systems software includes programming languages and operating systems. Programming languages are used to create all other types of programs and are discussed in Chapter 11. Operating systems are what make the computer work. For any program to run on a computer, the operating system must first be running because it coordinates activity between you and the computer. Through it you tell the computer to do such things as start your word processing program, save a document, or print a file. Because the operating system is so important, it is loaded automatically when you turn on the system. Once loaded, it manages many aspects of your system without your involvement or awareness. In this respect, it is like your body's respiratory system, which keeps you breathing even though you are hardly aware of it.

Application programs

The computer is like an actor, and a software program is like a script. When an actor changes scripts, he or she performs a different role. By changing programs, you can make your computer perform different functions. Many tasks that you work on with a computer are called applications and the programs you use to perform them are called application programs. For example, an application is writing a letter, preparing a budget, or creating a mailing list. The application programs you use for these applications are word-processors, spreadsheets, and database managers. The development and wide distribution of these inexpensive application programs is what has made the computer a truly useful tool for everyone from advertisers to zoologists. The application program you use depends on the task you want to perform.

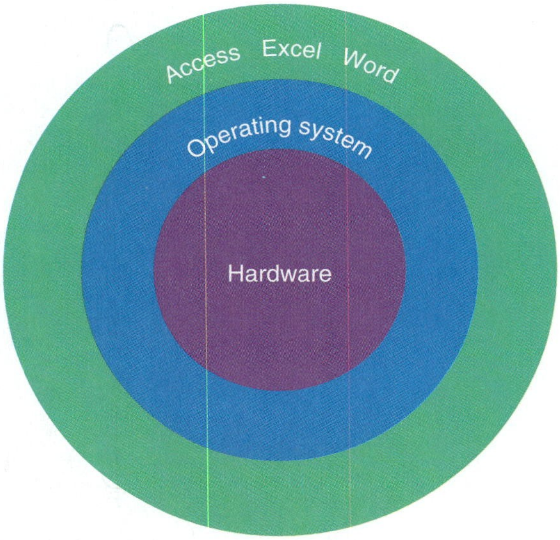

Operating system and application

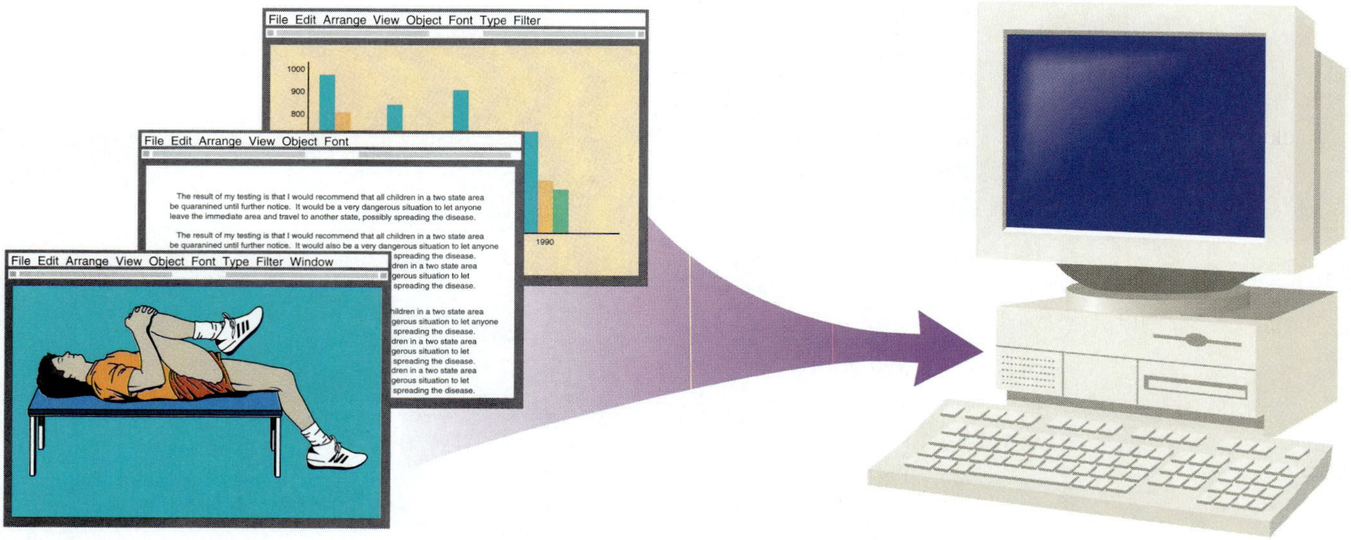

Application programs

Other programs

Application programs aren't the only popular programs. There are programs for entertainment, education, and reference. There are also many programs that perform very specific tasks on your computer called utility programs. Some of these are closely related to the operating system and others to application programs. For example, a utility program may be used to compress the files on a disk, an operating system chore. Another might be used to graph the percentage of microprocessor capacity in use at any given moment. A different utility program might be used to view documents in a variety of formats, an application task. You'll find many of these special purpose programs throughout the field of computing:

- Antivirus utilities let you protect your system from viruses.
- File view utilities let you see the contents of a wide variety of documents even when you don't have the application on your system.
- Diagnostic utilities let you find and fix problems on your system.
- Uninstall utilities allow you to remove applications and files you no longer need.
- Performance enhancement utilities let you speed up your system or increase storage space.
- Backup utilities let you protect your files by making copies of them on tapes or disks.

Progress

If there is one thing you can count on in computing, it's change. For many people, that's what makes the field so exciting. There seem to be more powerful and useful systems available almost every day. However, change doesn't happen overnight. It takes time for improvements to ripple through the system. It's like waves that ripple first through hardware, then through operating systems, then on to applications. Applications cannot be dramatically improved until the first two phases have been completed.

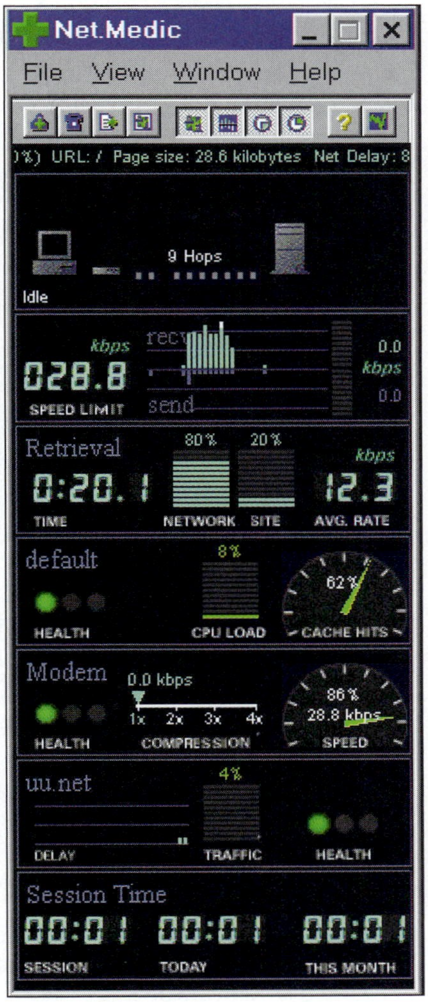

Utility program courtesy of VitalSigns

Waves of progress in computing

Your Mom May Have Been an Operating System

It might surprise you to know that the first computer operating systems were humans. During the 1950s, programs were fed into the computer from a stack of punched cards. Each time the program was to be changed, the operator fed in a new stack. During this era, one key figure in the development of UNIX (still a major operating system) said they knew they needed an operating system. "We just couldn't take the time to get them (programs) on and off the machine manually. We needed an operating system to sequence jobs through and control machine resources." Operating systems have expanded their functions beyond the basic role of executing programs. Most are now actually large collections of related programs that work together to help you both operate and manage your system.

6.2 User Interfaces

When you first start your computer, the display that appears on the computer's screen is called the interface. It's called this because it is where you and the machine interact. On the earliest computers, the only user interface was the printer and occasionally a bank of blinking lights. However, as computers became more interactive so did the interface.

Windows 98 active desktop

Interfaces and operating systems

The interface is very closely related to the operating system. In fact, every operating system has an interface built in so you can communicate with it. However, the interface is also somewhat separate because the same operating system can sometimes have more than one interface. The chances are that in this course you are using what is known as a graphical user interface that you interact with by clicking menus and buttons with a mouse. However, that isn't the only kind of interface in use. If you look around the computer lab or your school's offices, you're sure to encounter one of the older character-based interfaces. These interfaces were created years ago, work fine, and won't be replaced until the entire system is updated. However very few, if any, new ones are being created. Almost all software publishing companies now develop operating systems and application programs with graphical user interfaces. Programs with character-based interfaces are rapidly receding in history's rear-view mirror.

Graphical user interfaces (GUIs)

Graphical user interfaces (*GUI*–pronounced "goo-ee") were developed at Xerox PARC in the 70s and then first introduced in 1980 on a computer called the Xerox Star. There are now many competing GUI inter-

Character-Based Interfaces

When computers were first developed, all programs used what is known as a character-based interface. These programs displayed just a fixed set of characters–the letters A through Z and a through z, the numbers 0 through 9, and a very limited set of other characters such as , ©, fi, and Ä. Altogether, less than 256 characters, called the character set, can be displayed by these programs. Since the underlying operating system doesn't support graphics, each programmer has to devise his or her own way to define commands. Character-based interfaces are faster and require less memory than graphical interfaces but they are considered harder to learn and use.

The prize for the worst user interface ever developed is shared by dBASE's infamous dot prompt (a white period on a black screen) and DOS's equally dreadful command prompt (A:\>). In dBASE you had to type commands such as SORT ON FIRST_NAME TO NEWFILE. In DOS you typed such equally easily forgettable commands as COPY A:*.TXT C:\WORD\NEW.

```
C:\>DIR *.BAK

Volume in drive C is PROGRAMS
Volume Serial Number is D845-2F2F
Directory of C:\WINDOWS

SYSTEM    BAK        2,052   04-15-97    1:57p   SYSTEM.BAK
WIN       BAK        8,637   04-15-97   12:55p   WIN.BAK
WININIT   BAK           45   04-19-97    8:16a   WININIT.BAK
ACTIVE-1  BAK        9,015   04-19-97    5:27a   Active Setup Log.BAK
          4 file(s)         19,749 bytes
          0 dir(s)     434,470,912 bytes free
C:\>
```

faces in the marketplace but the biggest seller is Microsoft's Windows. All GUIs have a number of features in common:

- They display overlapping windows on the screen. Each window can contain an application program or a document. This allows you to quickly switch back and forth between tasks.
- You operate them by pointing and clicking on a digital "desktop." You execute commands by pointing to a command on the screen so you don't have to remember how to execute it.
- They have a WYSIWYG (What You See Is What You Get) display that shows a document on the screen much like it will look when it is printed.
- Commands are consistent from program to program. For example, the way you delete something from a document is always the same whether it's a word, drawing, or database record that's being deleted. This makes it easier to learn new programs because many of your existing skills are transferable.

Graphical user interface courtesy of RandomNoise
http://www.randomnoise.com/helix/productframe.html

Pen-based interfaces

The drawback of most computers is that you have to type data into them. The size of the keyboard imposes a limit to how much the size of the computer can be reduced. If you want a computer that fits in your pocket, a different operating system and user interface is needed. On most new handheld systems, the interface is touch-sensitive. You use a stylus to write on it or to point to commands and the text or command is read off the screen. The screen can sense the position of the stylus and either execute commands or display handwriting on the screen. Here is the Cassiopeia that uses the Windows CE operating system.

Cassiopeia pen-based computing courtesy of Casio

Touchscreen interfaces

You'll find lots of kiosks in airports, museums, and other public places that are operated by pointing to pictures or icons on the screen. These systems are so simple to use that no instructions are necessary.

Kiosk courtesy of International Business Machines

Conversational interfaces

It seems unlikely that computing will always be primarily a process of clicking and dragging items on a desktop. For computers to be as useful as possible, they will eventually have to respond to spoken commands. Progress has been slow in this area but programs are improving and you can now both operate your applications and enter data using voice recognition software.

Natural Language courtesy of Dragon Dictate

6.3 Application Programs

As you've seen, you can change a computer's function just by loading a different program. There are thousands of application programs from which to choose—from the commonplace to the exotic.

Horizontal market applications

There are certain tools that are useful to almost anyone in any job. These include word processing and spreadsheet applications that make it easy to work with text and numbers. Since these applications are used to perform basic and general tasks, they can be used by almost everyone regardless of the job or situation. These are called horizontal market applications and include most of the best-selling programs.

Most horizontal market programs are sold in stores in shrink-wrapped boxes. For this reason, they have been called shrink-wrapped software. Sometimes a group of these applications is bundled together in what's called a suite and sold at a discounted price.

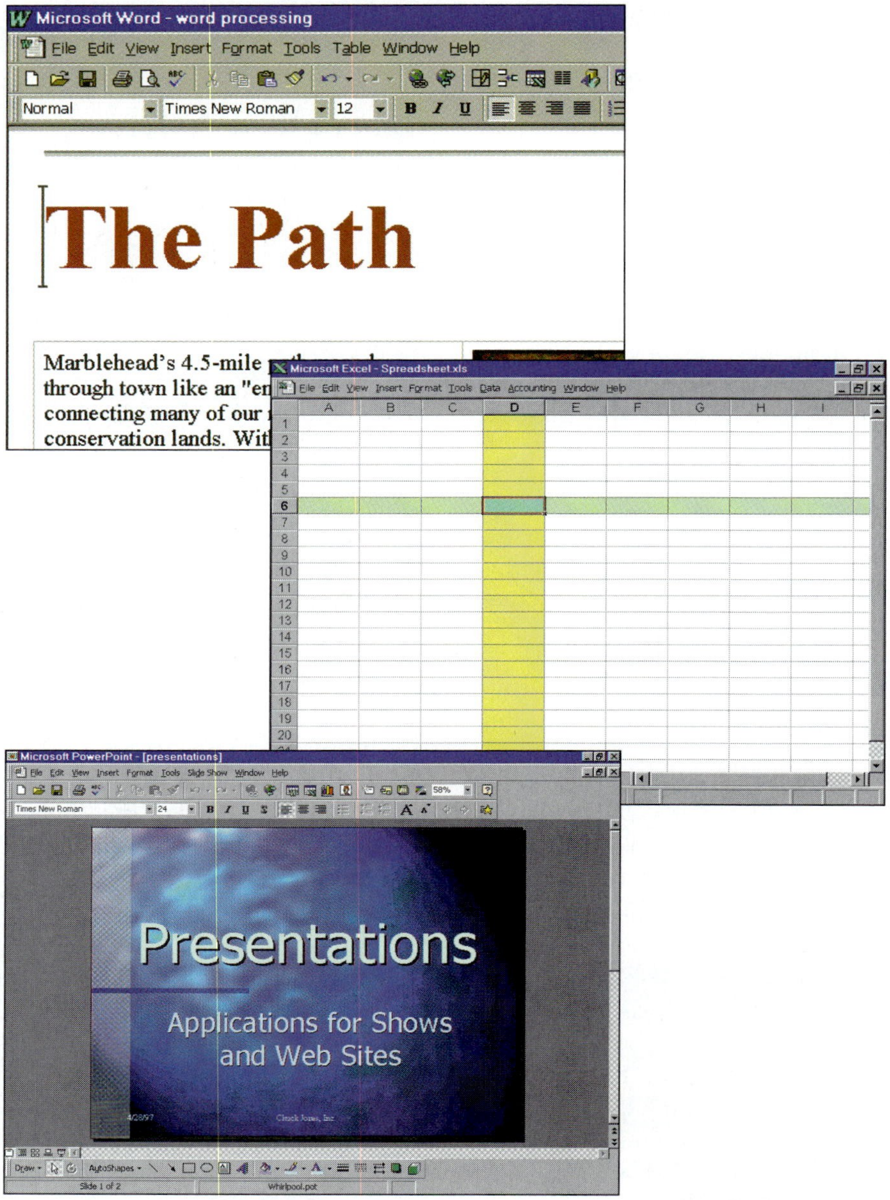

Suite courtesy of Microsoft

Vertical market applications

There are many applications that are specific to a single industry or a single task. For example, the process of estimating building costs is confined primarily to the construction industry, but in that industry, every company does it. The same is true of selling tickets in the airline industry or tracking output from oil wells in the oil industry. The programs developed to computerize these industry-specific applications are called vertical market applications.

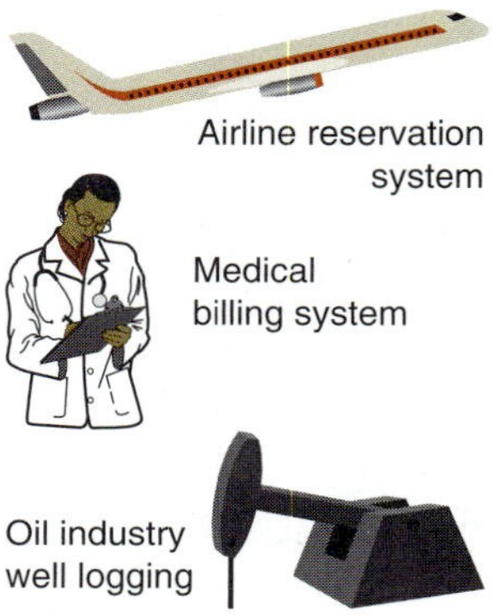

Vertical applications

Custom applications

The problem with both horizontal and vertical applications is that they take a "one size fits all" approach. For this reason, a company may decide to write its own applications, creating what's called custom software. This approach is expensive, but sometimes the higher cost is justified because the software is tailored to the company's operation. At other times the higher cost can't be avoided, because no software exists for the task the company envisions. For example, when Federal Express Corporation decided to computerize its system so it and its customers could know where any package was at any time, it couldn't buy the software anywhere, at any price. It had no choice but to write its own.

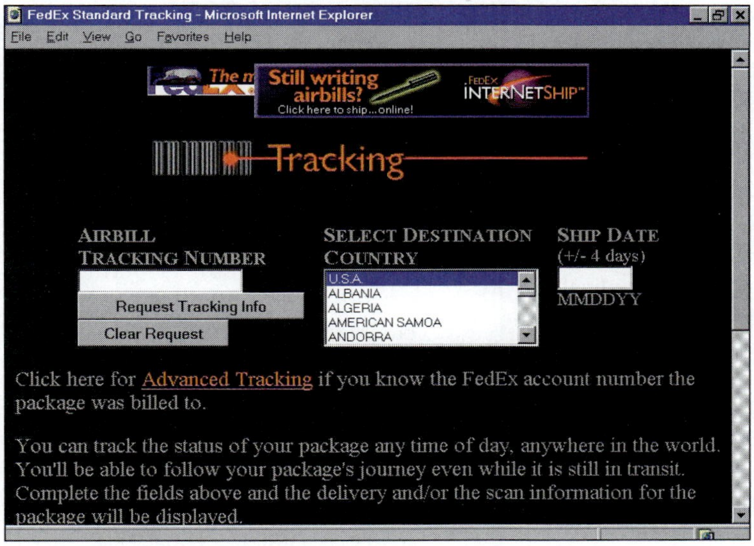

Custom application courtesy of Fedex

Shareware and public domain software

Many companies, both large and small, distribute software that they encourage you to copy and distribute to others. This is a form of marketing because they hope people will try it and continue using it. Until recently, most of these programs—called shareware or freeware—were developed by small companies or individuals However, with the competitive race going on over Internet software, there are now many free programs available from large companies such as Microsoft. These free programs are copyrighted and the rights that you are granted are spelled out in the documentation or displayed on the screen when you start the program. In some cases, a shareware publisher will ask for a small payment or registration fee if you try the software and then find that you use it ("try before you buy"). To encourage you to register the program and pay the fee, they usually offer printed documentation and notification of updates. Usually the fees are so small, you should pay them without hesitation unless you delete the program from your computer.

In a few cases, program developers or publishers go past giving their software away; they also give away their rights to it. The program then moves into the public domain. There are then no restrictions on what you can do with such public domain software.

Shareware Web site courtesy of Tucows

6.4 Operating Systems:

Although you do your work with application programs, it's the operating system that makes them run. Operating systems have grown and keep expanding their roles. They have become more and more complex as new tasks have been added. Normally, new tasks such as playing videos or connecting to networks are performed by new application programs. However, as soon as one of these applications becomes popular, its role is absorbed into the operating system. This way, it becomes part of the "platform" that application developers can assume everyone has when they write their programs. Let's take a look at the modern operating system and the kinds of tasks it performs.

Controlling input and output

One of the primary functions of an operating system is to control all the aspects of the computer's resources, making things go faster and smoother just as roads with signs and stoplights work more efficiently than those without. While performing traffic control functions within the computer, the operating system decides where programs and data are stored in the computer's memory. It handles communication among the computer's components such as the printer and display screen. And it handles communications between you and your application programs.

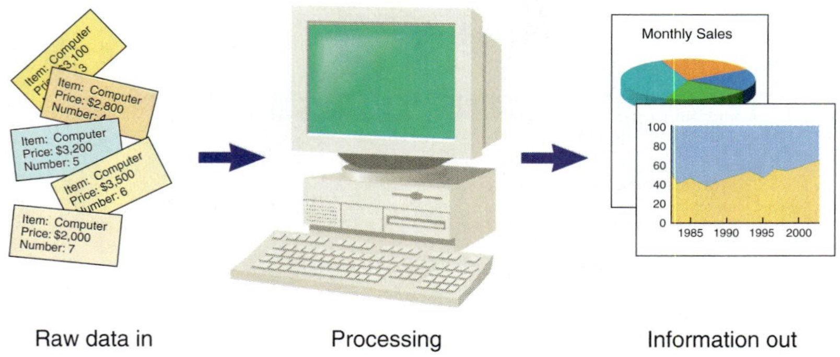

Controlling input and output

The role of BIOS

When you first start your system it has no idea what drives it has so it can't even load its operating system. To solve this problem, a computer has a Basic Input/Output System (BIOS) that it looks for as soon as you turn it on. It can find it because this small program is permanently stored on a read-only memory (ROM) chip. Since it's a small software program embedded in a chip, it occupies a middle ground between the software and hardware. For this reason it's often called firmware. BIOS performs a number of important functions. It interprets keystrokes, displays characters on the screen, handles communication through the computer's ports, and even tests the system every time you turn it on. The purpose of this system is to give software a link to the hardware. When you ask an application program to print a document, the request is first passed to the BIOS and then sent on to the printer. This system isolates the software from the hardware. That way, if a system's hardware is changed radically, all you need to change is the BIOS. This gives hardware designers the freedom to improve systems without worrying that they will make all previous software obsolete.

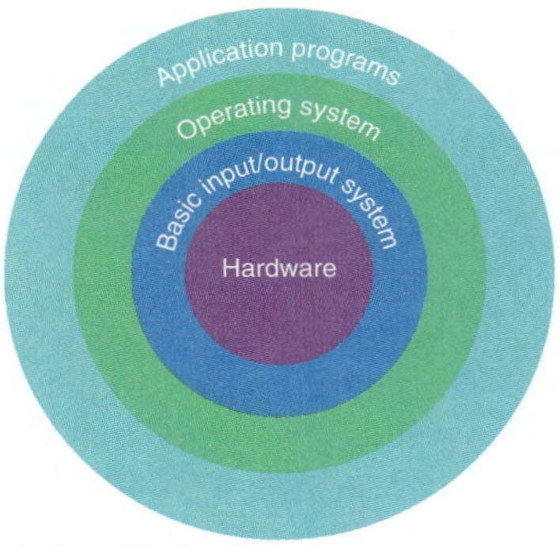

Basic input/output system

Processing commands

The command processor portion of the operating system interprets what you enter from the keyboard. In this respect, it is rather like an interpreter. If you spoke only English and tried to carry on a discussion with someone who spoke only Spanish, the two of you would need an interpreter to translate, as in the box below.

User command:	Save this file please.
Translation:	Favor de guardar este archivo.
Message to user:	Lo guardo en el disco.
Translation:	I'll save it on the disk.
Message to user:	Bien. Está archivado.
Translation:	There, it's saved.

Processing commands

The same is true of a computer. When you use an application program, the program's commands are interpreted by the operating system for the hardware. For example, you might open a document by clicking a button on the program's toolbar. At another time you might do so by dragging the file onto the application's icon and dropping it. The operating system interprets these commands and copies the document on the disk into the computer's internal memory.

Introduction

Multitasking

Modern operating systems allow you to multitask, that is, perform multiple tasks at the same time with different programs. For example, you could be downloading a large file from the Internet with one program, while editing a document with another. Older operating systems could run only one program at a time. Since most systems have only one microprocessor, they allow multiple programs to run by quickly switching back and forth among them. Although only one program is actually active at a time, the processor switches so fast that they all appear to be active. This process is called time-slicing or task-switching because it slices up the CPU's available time as it switches back and forth among the running applications. Today's systems use a form of multitasking called preemptive multitasking. This just means that access to the microproccesor is controlled so one application can't seize it and hold onto it for long periods. One application can "preempt" another application to get a fair share of the processor's time.

Multithreading

Most applications process data and commands sequentially. Only when one task is finished do they begin another. The application therefore follows a single thread from the beginning of a session to the end and individual operations are strung along it like beads on a necklace. A multithreaded operating system on the other hand lets application programs start and run two or more threads simultaneously. It's similar to multitasking but takes place within a single program. For example, one thread in a word processing program can be reading the keys you press while a second thread displays data on the screen and a third thread prints the document.

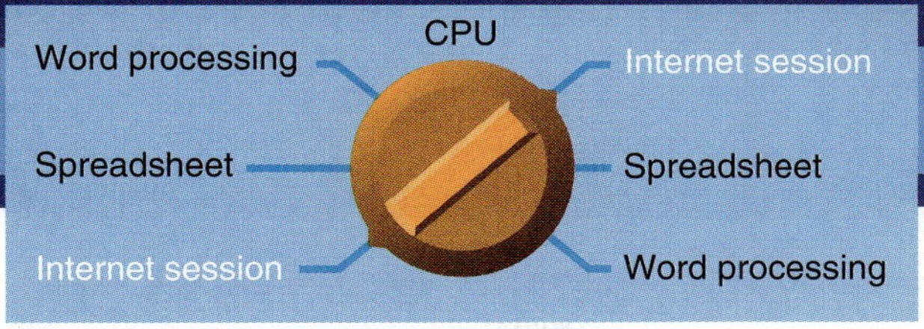

Switching between tasks

Multitasking

Multiuser

Some operating systems are designed so that many users can be connected to the system at the same time. This multiuser capability is found on operating systems used with mini, mainframe, and supercomputers.

Multiuser courtesy of International Business Machines

Multiprocessor support

Some applications need as much processing power as possible. For example, anyone doing forecasting, modeling, simulation, or computer-aided design never has enough power. Some operating systems support multiple processors–in some cases hundreds.

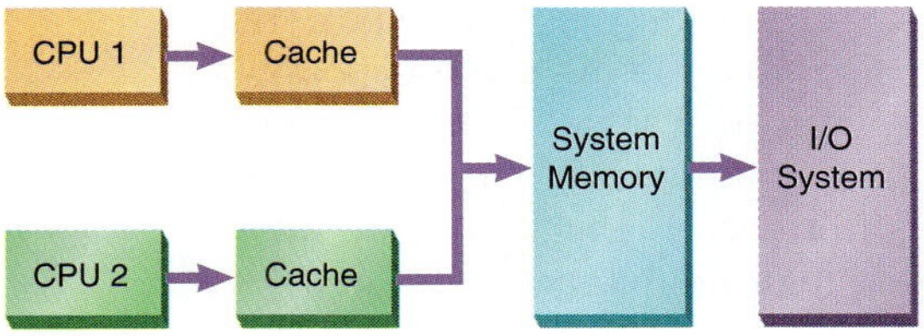

Multiprocessor

Miscellaneous tasks

In addition to the tasks we've just discussed, the operating system also performs these tasks:

- ♦ The operating system continually monitors your system and if it detects something wrong, it notifies you with an error message.
- ♦ The operating system runs each program in its own protected space so that a problem with one program will not affect any others that are running.

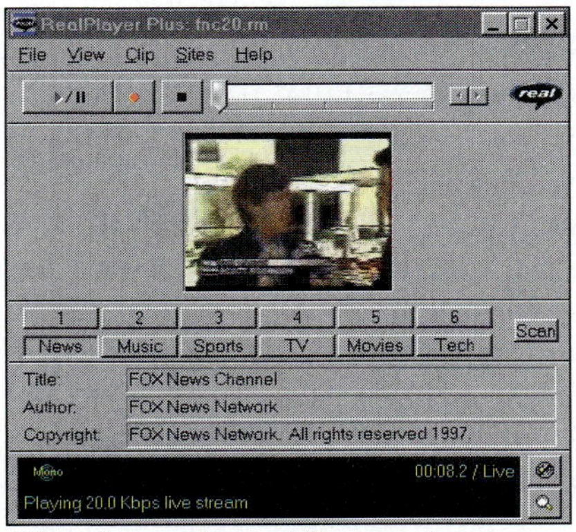

PC radio courtesy of Progressive Networks

- ♦ To conserve power, power management cuts power at those times when it isn't needed.
- ♦ Now that computer systems can display video and animations, play sounds, and even display virtual reality, operating systems have been adapted to support these applications.

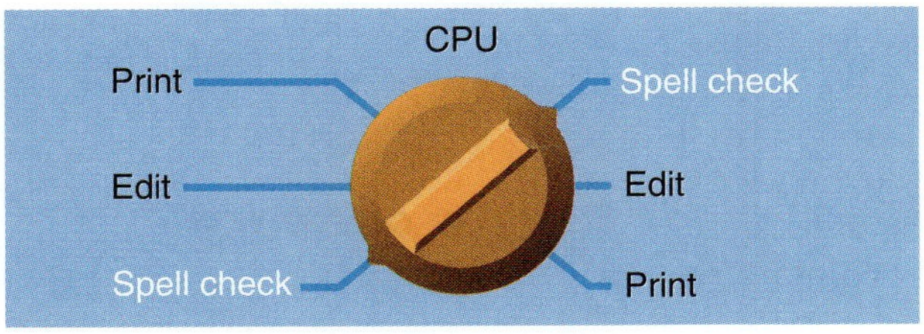

Switching between threads

Multithreading

6.5 Operating Systems:

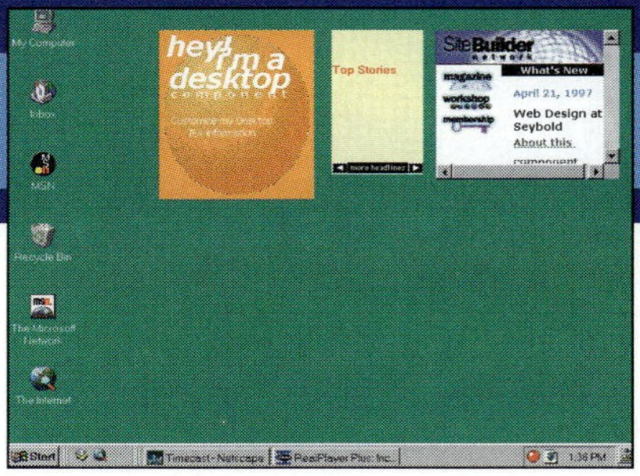

Windows 98 active desktop

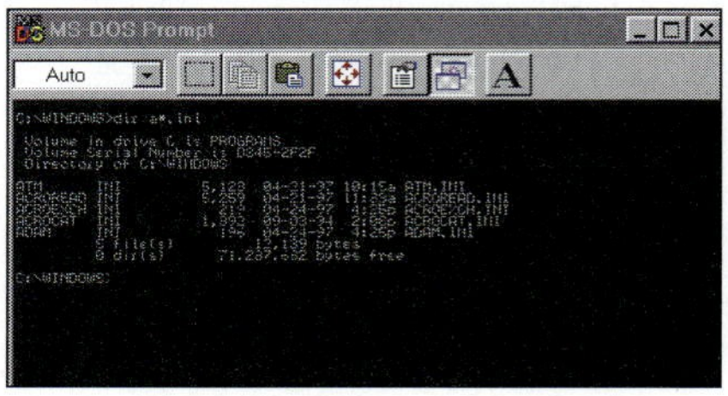

DOS

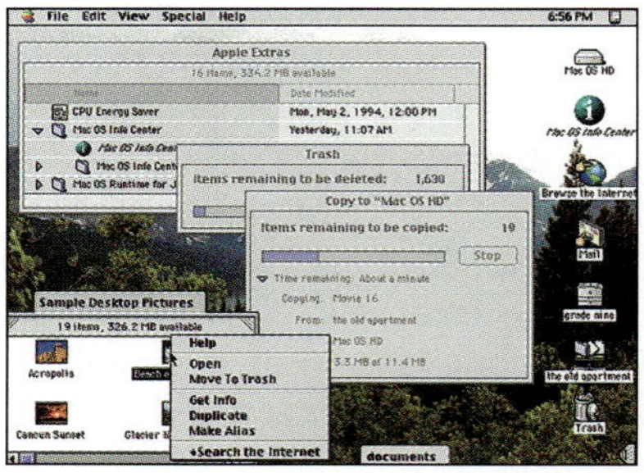

Mac OS 8.0

From the fastest supercomputer and largest mainframe, right down to the smallest embedded microprocessor in your car or watch, every computer uses an operating system. Over the years, a variety of operating systems have been developed and many remain in use. When the IBM PC set the standard for microcomputers, DOS became the most widely used microcomputer operating system. Today, DOS has been replaced on many computers by more powerful operating systems such as Windows, UNIX, Windows NT, and OS/2. These more powerful operating systems make it possible to run tasks on less expensive microcomputers that were once performed on expensive mainframe and minicomputers.

Tasks and operating systems

Operating systems come in lots of flavors. Each has been designed with specific tasks in mind. Many companies use large mainframe, mini, or supercomputers, that require operating systems designed to handle the tasks the computer performs. For example, a mainframe computer may have thousands of other computers connected to it and may be processing huge databases of information. The operating system has to be designed to handle all these transactions. On the other hand, a handheld computer may be used by a single user for only a few tasks. The operating system could be a lot more limited and still handle this role very well. In between these two extremes are the networked computers that are now the most common making connections with computers elsewhere on the network and encountering not only text but also multimedia applications. These networked computers require operating systems that can handle a wide assortment of tasks.

Operating system characteristics

There are a variety of criteria, some of which you are already familiar with, that you can use to compare operating systems.

- Single tasking or multitasking?
- Single threading or multithreading?
- Character-based or graphic user interface?
- Weak or strong security?
- 8, 16, 32, and 64 bits processed at a time?
- Portable or not? (A portable operating system is not dependent on a specific microprocessor.)
- Proprietary or open? (Proprietary operating systems work only with one type of computer. Open operating systems run on a variety of machines.)

Types of operating system

Desktop operating systems

Operating systems that run on desktop computers are the least powerful and least secure operating systems. They are also the most common. Generally, you find three types: Windows, Apple's System 8, or the rapidly fading DOS.

Windows in its many versions (3.1, 95, 98) is currently the leading desktop operating system, running on over 90 percent of all new systems sold.

Macintosh's System 8 runs on the Apple Macintosh and PowerPC and was the first widely used graphical interface.

DOS was first introduced in 1980 with IBM's original IBM PC. This rapidly dying 8-bit operating system is at the low end of the scale, with character-based interface, single tasking, and no security.

Server operating systems

Modern organizations' computers in networks are connected to one another not directly but through powerful computers called servers that provide security to the networks and route traffic from one network to another, complicated tasks requiring special operating systems. These powerful operating systems are also used for tasks such as engineering design, order processing, and payroll critical to a company's continued existence, called mission critical applications, that were previously run only on larger mainframe computers. These powerful 32- or 64- bit operating systems are secure, multitasking, multithreading, and open. All have recently had graphical user interfaces developed for them. All but OS/2 are portable in that they run on more than one type of microprocessor.

Windows NT (NT stands for New Technology) is the fastest-growing server operating system.

Operating System/2 (OS/2) competes with Windows and is a powerful operating system but has had trouble catching on.

UNIX was originally developed at AT&T's Bell Labs in 1973. Unfortunately, a number of versions have been developed that are based on, but slightly different from, the original and from each other. Applications written for one variant of UNIX will not usually run on another. This is one of the reasons UNIX runs on only 1 percent of microcomputers. To help solve this problem a consortium consisting of Sun, HP, IBM, Digital, AT&T Bell Labs, Novell, and SCO all agreed on a single Common Operating Software Environment (COSE) and a Common Desktop Environment (CDE).

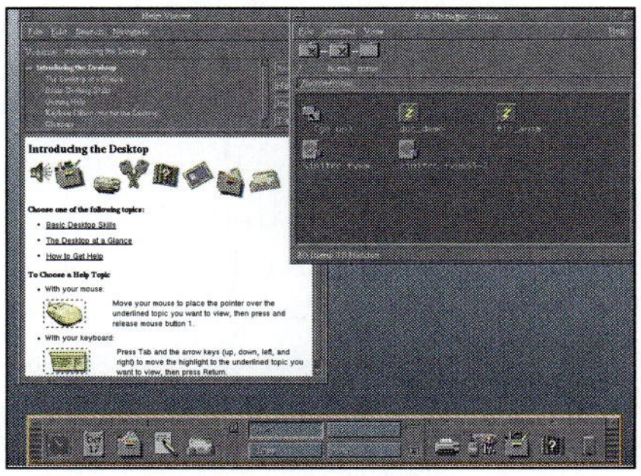

Common desktop environment courtesy of Xi Graphics
http://www.linuxmall.com/xinside/clue/CDE-top.html

Mainframe operating systems

In the days when mainframe and minicomputers dominated the computing world, each computer company developed its own operating system. For example, some IBM mainframe computers use an operating system called open MVS and Digital Equipment Corporation minicomputers use one called VMS. These companies developed not just their own operating systems but also the applications that ran on top of them. These are called proprietary systems because they are all owned by a single proprietor. Because there were so many competing operating systems, it was hard to make computers talk to one another. Although costly, these operating systems are both powerful and secure—capable of handling all of the tasks that define a modern operating system.

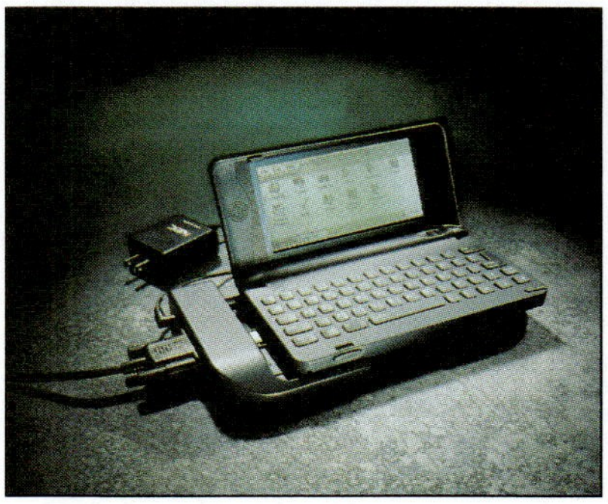

Handheld computer courtesy of NEC

Handheld operating systems

Windows CE, visually similar to Windows 95, uses a small keyboard and a touch-sensitive screen.

Embedded operating systems

When a microprocessor is used inside a small device such as a watch or toaster, it still needs an operating system. One such operating system is a version of DOS called embedded DOS. Embedded DOS is stored on a memory chip instead of a hard drive and turns on instantly when the device is turned on. When the power fails, and every appliance's clock in your house blinks that dreaded digital 00:00, you are seeing a system crash. You then have to use DOS and its clock button interface to reset the time. The fact that you may have to use different procedures to set the time on each appliance makes you realize the value of standard interfaces.

Embedded operating system

Hard disks can contain thousands of files and the operating system is used to manage them. You must understand three things: the name of the file, the folder it's in, and the drive it's on.

Filenames

When files are saved, they are assigned filenames so you can identify them later. On most systems, filenames have two parts: a name and an extension. Think of them as first and last names.

The name is something you choose so you can identify the file later. On DOS you are limited to only 8 characters for the name but on newer operating systems, you can use long, descriptive filenames.

The extension is separated from the name by a period. Its purpose is to identify the file format or the application that created it. For example, a .bmp extension means the file is a graphic and .doc often means it's a word processing document.

On Windows systems, extensions play an important role. They allow programs to identify which applications created which files. Being able to identify a file's format can be important. For example, if you display the name of a file on the disk and then double-click it, Windows will first open the application that created the file and then that application opens the file. Also, if you use a program such as Word to open a document, the dialog box that appears normally lists only those files with the .doc extension, on the assumption that you are usually interested only in word processing documents. (You can see other file types, but it requires an extra step to do so.)

Folders

Imagine working in an office where you might be told to get all the correspondence on next year's sales campaign only to discover everything thrown together in one box. You have to pick through everything to gather together what you want. Contrast this with an office that uses file cabinets to store files. A well-organized file cabinet uses hanging folders to group related documents together. If a further breakdown is needed, manila folders are inserted into any of the hanging folders. It is easy to locate and pull out the documents you need. The same is true of hard drives. To master computing, you need to understand the concept of folders and how they are used to group together related files. For example, on your system you might find a folder named Windows. This folder contains the Windows operating system. If you were to open that folder, you'd find other files and folders holding parts of the Windows operating system.

Newyork.bmp
DOS 8.3 Filename

New York Skyline.bmp
Windows 95 long filename

Filenames

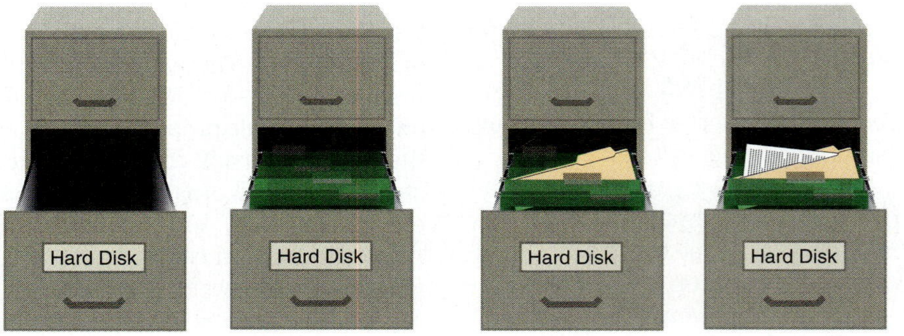

A new hard disk, like an empty file drawer, has no organization.

Dividing a hard disk into directories or folders is like dividing a file drawer with hanging folders.

Subdividing directories into subdirectories or subfolders is like putting manila file folders into the hanging folders.

Files can be stored in any of the directories or folders.

Folders

Drives

Many systems have more than one drive. To tell them apart, drives are assigned letters or names. For example, a drive into which you can insert a floppy disk may be drive A or B. The hard drive the computer looks to first when you turn it on is C. Additional drives might be D and E. Since the number and type of drives vary from system to system, so does the letter or name of each.

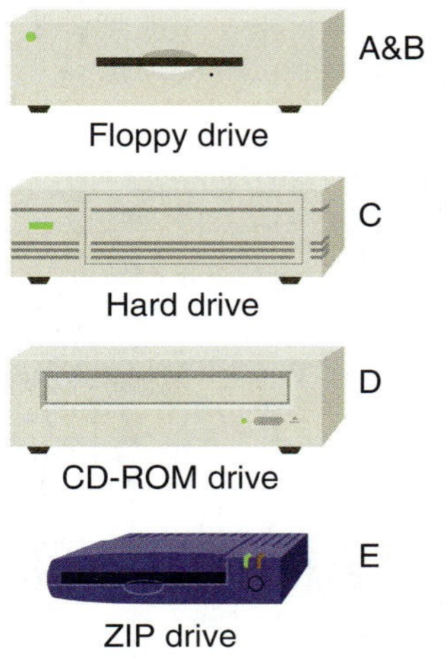

Drives

Trees

One way to illustrate the organization of folders on a drive is using a tree. In this view, all folders branch off from the drive. If any of these folders contain other folders, those folders are shown as a second branch from the first.

When using a tree, you can expand and collapse the entire tree or any branch. This allows you to alternate between a summary of the drive's contents, and details of each file. On the right, on Windows tree the plus signs indicate that a branch has been collapsed and it contains hidden folders. The minus signs indicate that the branch has been expanded.

Paths

When you have files stored in folders on a disk, you have to follow a "path" to get to them. For example, if a file named *John.doc* is in a folder named *Letters* on drive C, the path to that folder is *C:\Letters\John.doc*. If *John.doc* is in a folder named *Memos*, the path is *C:\Memos\John.doc*. The drive specification in the path is C: and the folder's name is separated from it by a backslash.

C:\Letters\John.doc

Path to file in a folder

The backslash is also used when you have folders within folders. If the *Letters* folder contained a folder named *Vendors*, the path to it would then be *C:\Letters\Vendors\John.doc*.

C:\Letters\Vendors\John.doc

Path to file in a subfolder

In most cases, you don't have to type in these paths. Most new programs and operating systems let you use a mouse to open folders until you find the file you are looking for.

File managers

Operating systems include a separate program that you use to explore the drives, folders, and files on your system. There are a variety of these but they all allow you to display the folders on a drive arranged like a tree. Clicking any of the folders displays a list of its contents.

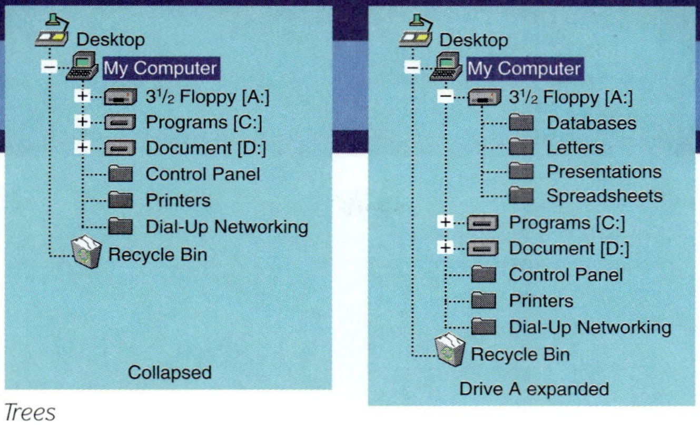

Trees

When browsers and search engines were first developed for the Web, people soon discovered they could locate and get to a document anywhere in the world more easily than they could locate and get to one on their own system. As a result, browser technology is now being put to use in file management. Microsoft's Active Internet Platform (API) technology allows you to browse your own documents as well as the Web. In fact, a document on your local hard drive looks the same as a page anywhere on the Web.

Search engines on the Web keep track of millions of documents by searching them out and listing words they contain in an index. When you search a word, the search engine looks it up in the index and lists the name and address of every document in which it can be found. You can go to the document just by clicking its name. These search engines made looking for documents so easy that personal versions have now been published for use on your own system.

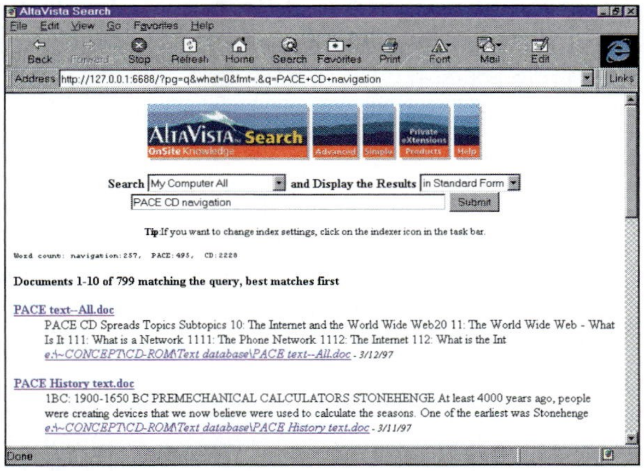

AltaVista Personal Edition courtesy of Digital

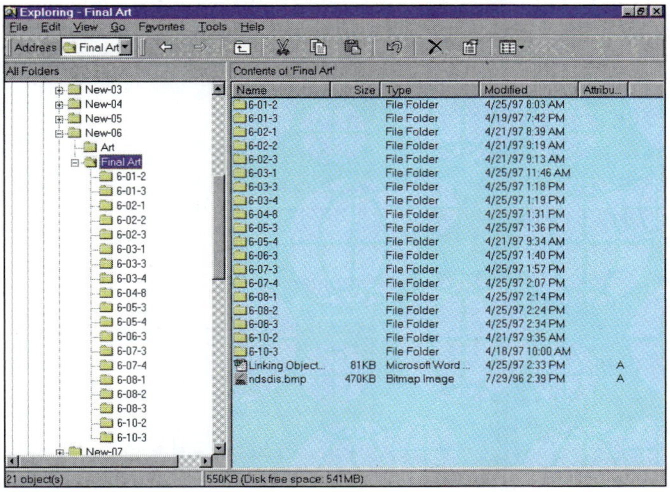

Windows Explorer

6.7 Operating Systems:

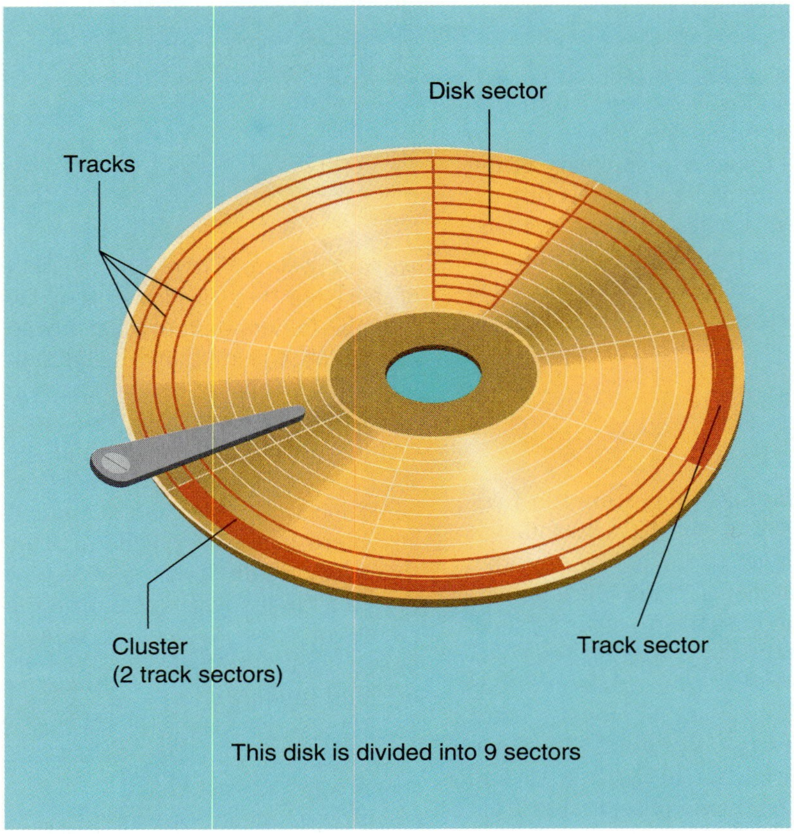

Clusters

In addition to a file manager, operating systems also include utility programs that you use to manage your disk and files. The list of such utility programs is almost endless, but here we discuss the ones you should be aware of.

Formatting

One utility program is used to format disks so they can store data (see Spread 5.2). Formatting also creates a directory of the locations of each file called a file allocation table (FAT). When you save a file, the operating system stores it in groups of sectors, called clusters, the smallest storage unit the computer can address. To do so, it looks in the file allocation table for empty clusters and then stores the file in one of those locations. The address of the cluster where the file begins and the one where it ends are then listed in the file allocation table. When you open the file, the operating system uses those addresses to locate the clusters and open the file stored in them.

Fragmenting

If a group of friends go to a concert, they can reserve seats early and all sit together in the same row. If they wait till later, the chances are they'll have to take whatever seats are still available scattered about the auditorium. It's like this with disks. When you first use a disk, data is laid down in a linear fashion. Each part of a file is stored in adjacent clusters, much as one seat in a row is next to another. However, as you begin to delete old files and add new ones, things begin to become less orderly because fragments of files are scattered in clusters located in different areas on the disk. This file fragmentation slows the computer down because it takes longer for the drive to locate, save, and retrieve the fragmented files. To fix this problem, you need to regularly defragment or defrag the disk. This procedure moves data around on the disk, so file fragments are again joined together on the disk's tracks. This procedure is often overlooked by computer users, who then wonder why their system gets slower and slower as time goes by. In many cases, the system will even begin to misbehave. Programs crash or files don't open. It's amazing how often these problems can be fixed just by defragging the disk.

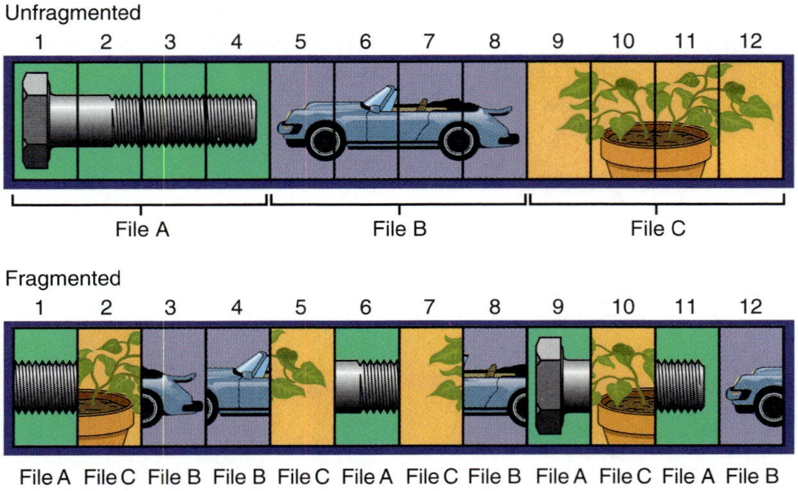

Disk fragmentation

Disk scanning

When a disk is manufactured it isn't always perfect. Some areas of the disk may not be usable. The manufacturer scans the disk and electronically marks bad areas as unusable so no data will be stored there. As you use the disk, other areas may become bad. For this reason, a utility program is used to scan the disk at regular intervals to locate and mark any bad sectors. If you don't do this, the operating system may store parts of a file in them and then you won't be able to retrieve that part of the file. In addition, scanning finds and fixes problems with files. For example, when systems crash, parts of files may be left scattered on the disk and become lost. The disk scanning program locates these lost clusters and stores them together in a separate file. In some cases, you can open these files and recover lost work.

File deletion and recycle bins

Many of the files you create on a computer eventually become outdated and no longer needed. To remove these files from the disk, you delete them. On many newer operating systems, this procedure doesn't actually delete them from the disk. Instead, it moves them to a separate area of the disk called a recycle bin or trash can. If you decide later that you want to recover the file, you open the recycle bin and restore it to the disk. When absolutely certain that you'll never need the files in the recycle bin, you empty it. This procedure deletes the files from the disk and you can no longer recover them. However, if you ever delete a really important file, don't do anything without seeking expert help. There are programs that can recover deleted files, provided any subsequent commands didn't place new files in the place on the disk where they are stored.

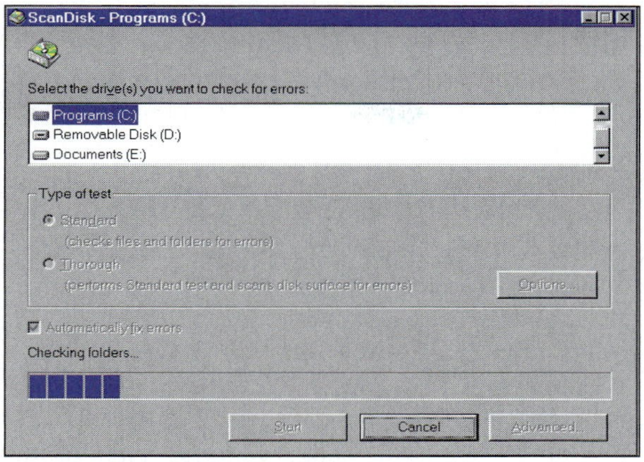

Windows ScanDisk utility

Multimedia Utilities

Many people don't know that you can play audio CDs on a computer equipped for multimedia. All you need is CD player software that comes with the operating system or with the CD drive. The CD player software works much like a real CD player. You click buttons to start, stop, or change tracks.

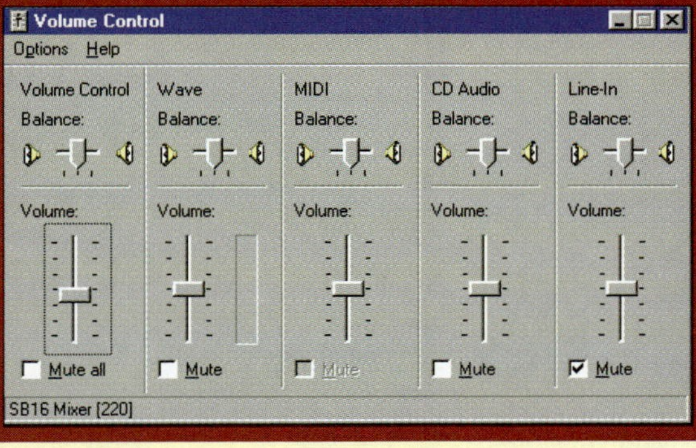

Windows volume control

Recycle bin

6.8 Document-Centric Computing

Until very recently, the emphasis in the computer field was so much on application programs that word processors, spreadsheets, and databases all stood alone. It was hard to move data among them. For example, a table created with a spreadsheet was difficult to move into a word processing document. The first step in improving this situation was to make programs work better together when it came to exchanging data. The current stage is to change the focus from the programs to the document itself. The applications become supporting players to the elements in the document. Word processors for words, spreadsheets for tables, graphics program for illustrations are all available from within the document. You're no longer moving data from one program to another, you're calling up applications within the document. This new approach is called document-centric computing.

Object linking and embedding (OLE)

Not too long ago, a document created with a word processing program contained only text. Today, it can also contain graphics, spreadsheet data, database data, sound, video, and animations. Each of these files is linked to the program used to create it. Called a compound document, this new type of document is created with pieces from various programs using a technology called object linking and embedding (OLE—sometimes pronounced "olé," as if you were a bullfighter) or a similar technology called OpenDoc.

Object linking and embedding lets you work with complete or partial files called objects, created by other applications. An object can be a complete file on the disk (called a source document) or a part of a file that you copied or cut out of another source document. For example, if you want to place an illustration created on one program into a document created on another, the illustration is the object. The document into which the object is placed is the compound document. There are two ways to place an object into a compound document. You can embed it or link it.

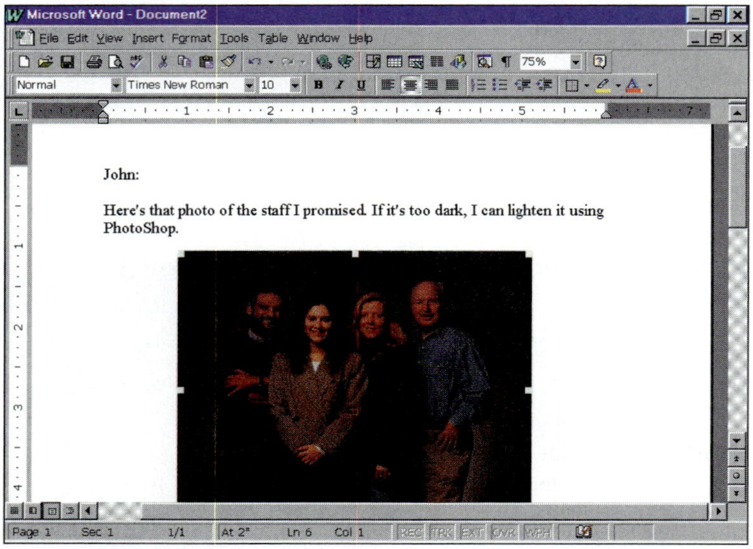

Compound document

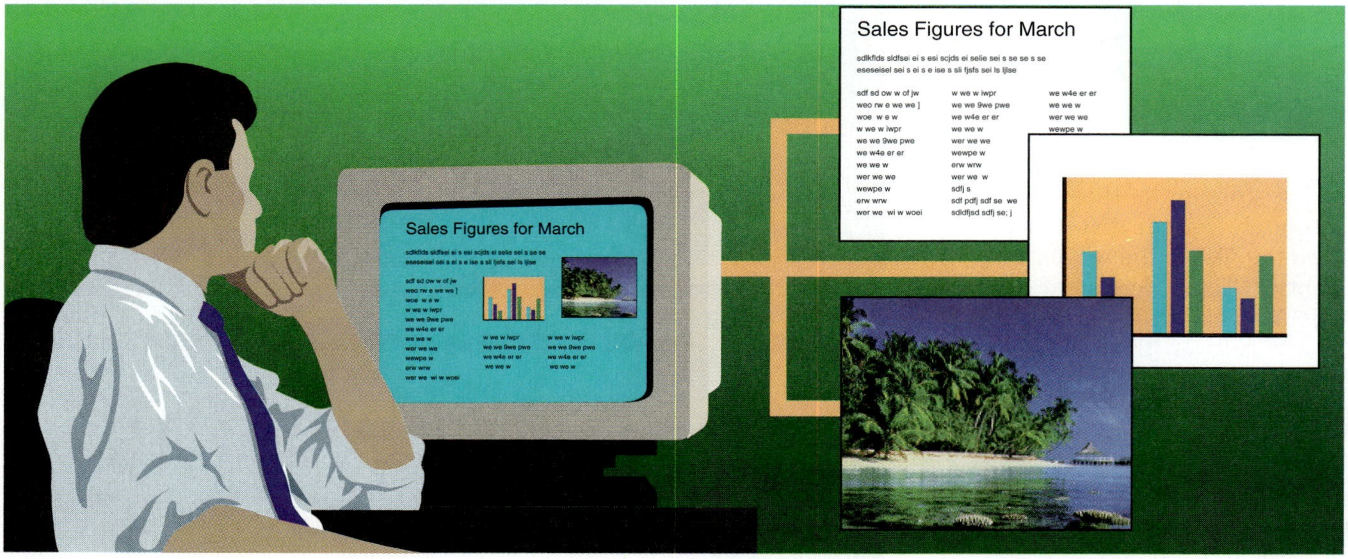

Object linking and embedding

Embedding data

When you embed an object, the data in the source document is copied to the compound document. There is no link between the compound document and the object's source file on the disk. Changing the object in one place doesn't change it in the other or any others.

Double-clicking an embedded object changes the menus and buttons on the application you're working with to those found on the application that created the object. Any changes you make now will appear only in the embedded object. The original source document on the disk remains unchanged. On the right, an Excel chart has been embedded in a Word document. Double-clicking it changes the menu and buttons to those of the Excel application that created it. You can now edit it for your purposes within the Word document only.

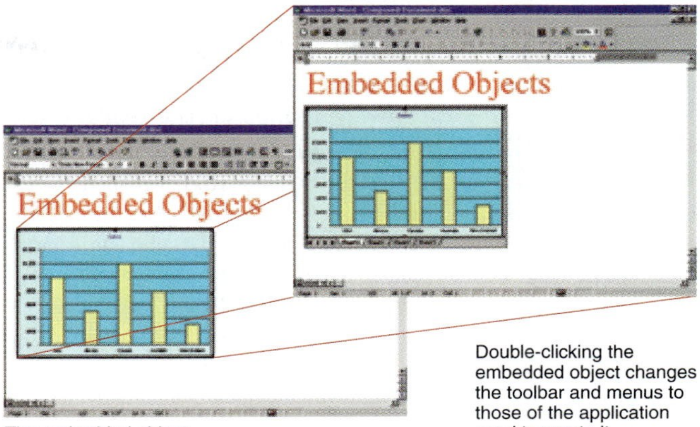

The embedded object

Embedded data

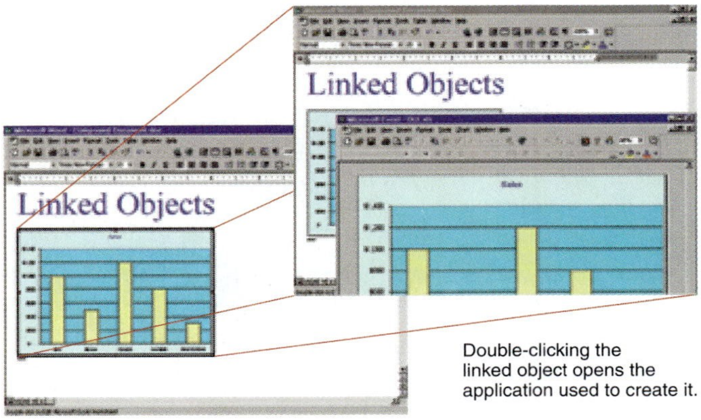

The linked object

Linked data

Linking data

Linking is similar to embedding with significant differences. When you link an object, it isn't copied into the compound document. Instead, a link is established between that document and the object's source document on the disk. The link allows an image of the object to be displayed in the compound document without actually being there. Linking files can keep the destination document's size smaller because you can specify that the linked file not be stored in the document.

Double-clicking a linked object opens the application that created it. Any changes you make affect both the linked object *and* the original source document on the disk. Above right, an Excel chart has been linked to a Word document. The image has then been double-clicked to open Excel so you can edit the chart in the graphics application you originally used to create it.

Choosing Between Embedding and Linking

In many ways, linking and embedding are very similar. After all, they both place an object into another document and allow you to edit it. However, there are times when you should choose one over the other.

You should link when using the same object in more than one compound document. This way, when you edit the object, the changes are immediately reflected in all of the compound documents to which it is linked. For example, if you prepared a budget in Excel, you could link it to different memos to your boss and your team members. Should you have to update the budget, you would only have to do it once. The changes would be automatically reflected in all the memos.

On the other hand, you use embedding when you want to:

- Edit the object right in the document in which it's embedded. (Linked objects must be edited with the separate application that created them.)
- Make changes in the object that won't affect the original file the object is taken from. For example, if you embed an Excel budget in a Word memo, you can edit the copy in the memo without affecting the original copy created by Excel.
- Send the document to others so they can edit both the compound document and its embedded objects without changing any source files.

6.9 Major Software Issues

After you understand how to use operating system and applications programs, you should know or at least be aware of how the programs are initially started up, some of the major causes of problems and failure, and what you can and can't do about it when things don't work.

Installing and uninstalling programs

Before you actually use a new application program, you must install it by running an installation program (also called a setup program). The installation process copies the program's files to your hard disk and customizes the program for your system's hardware.

When you install an application on your system, many separate files are copied to your hard disk. When you decide you no longer need the application, you use an uninstall program. In theory this removes all the files. In reality, lots of files are often left on the disk. Separate programs have been developed to locate and remove them.

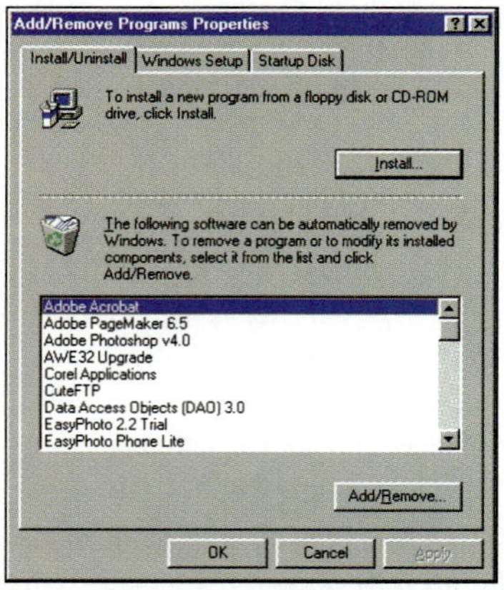

The Windows install and uninstall utility

Drivers

Upon receiving the information you supply about your screen, printer, and other devices when you install a program, the program knows what *device drivers* to use. Drivers are small programs that translate the program's generic instructions into instructions for a specific piece of hardware. When a new piece of hardware comes on the market, the programmers of an operating system just write a driver for it; they don't have to revise the program itself. Operating systems generally have a library of device drivers, one for each specific hardware item. If you have a piece of hardware that the program does not include a driver for, you may be unable to use the hardware. Using a printer or display screen without the correct driver can give totally unexpected results.

Reprinted from INFOSYSTEMS, May, 1985. Copyright Hitchcock Publishing Company.

Drivers

Program updates

Companies that publish application programs and operating systems generally update them every year or so. Program updates (also called upgrades) generally include corrected old features as well as new features that improve the program. When faced with a new version, find out what features the new program has. If it does not have any that you need, you probably should not buy the new version.

Version numbers are used to indicate a programs release. Generally these numbers have a decimal point. A change in the whole number (6.0 to 7.0) indicates a major revision. A change in a decimal (7.1 to 7.2) indicates a minor revision. However these rules are not adhered to in a couple of respects:

- Marketing departments change version numbers to keep up with the competition.
- Changes, especially bug fixes, are made without changing the version number. This is called slipstreaming and causes end users all kinds of problems because copies of programs with the same version number may be slightly different.

New features are always the lure, but there are problems associated with updating software or changing systems. One of the biggest problems in computing is called compatibility or more accurately, incompatibility. This problem arises on a number of levels.

- If you change from one system to another, such as from Apple's to Microsoft's, you have to get all new software.

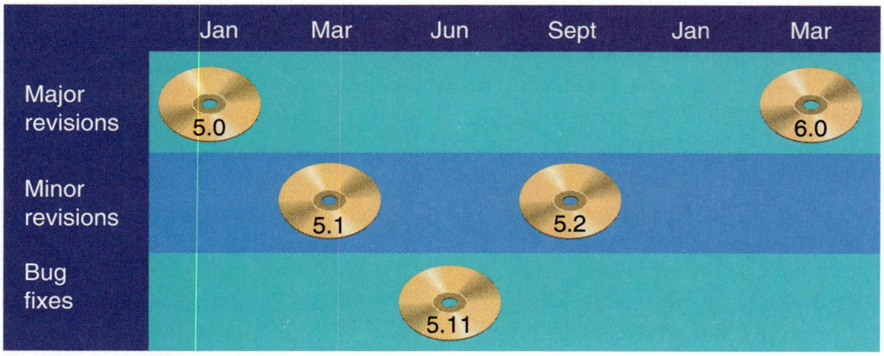

Program upgrades

- New bugs may be introduced by updating.
- When operating systems are upgraded, some applications may not work. Also, some hardware won't work because there aren't drivers for it.
- There may be incompatibilities with documents created with previous versions.

Program distribution

Programs are increasingly distributed on CD-ROM discs. But newer forms of distribution are emerging and it's increasingly common to transfer software to your system over the Internet. This is especially true of upgrades and such accessory programs as drivers and filters for file conversions. See the illustration above right.

Technical support

The typical computer contains dozens of devices and programs, many from different companies. The complexity is overwhelming. Products such as First Aid 97 have been developed that reduce this problem. Called call avoidance software, these programs diagnose a system and even make fixes on their own. They are also connected to the Internet so, if they can't figure out how to fix a problem, they can dial into a database and look up the most current information.

Bugs

There is no doubt that over an extended period of using your computer, inexplicable things will happen to you. Suddenly a message appears that tells you an error has occurred or your keyboard freezes so you can't type or operate the program any more. This is almost always an error on the part of the programmer called a bug.

Internet distribution courtesy of Software Net
www.software.net

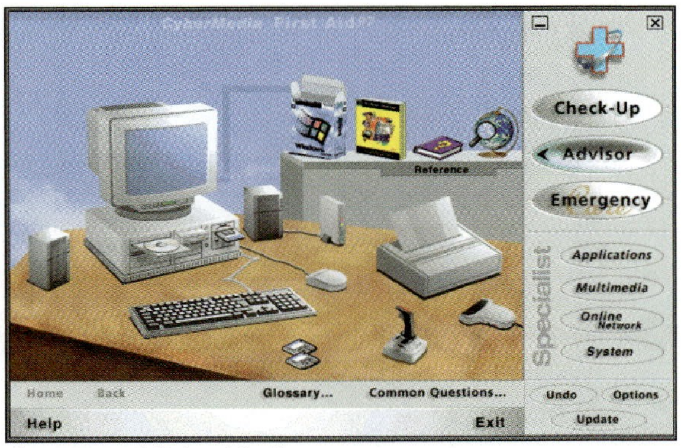

Courtesy of CyberMedia

Disclaimers

Disclaimers that come with software are designed to limit the publisher's liability. Usually incomprehensible to anyone but a lawyer, here is a refreshing change.

> "If EasyFlow doesn't work, tough. If you lose millions because it messes up, it's you that's out millions, not us. If you don't like this disclaimer, tough. We reserve the right to do the absolute minimum provided by law, up to and including nothing. This is basically the same disclaimer that comes with all software, but ours is in plain English and theirs is in legalese. We really didn't want to include any disclaimer at all, but our lawyers insisted."

Disclaimer courtesy of EasyFlow

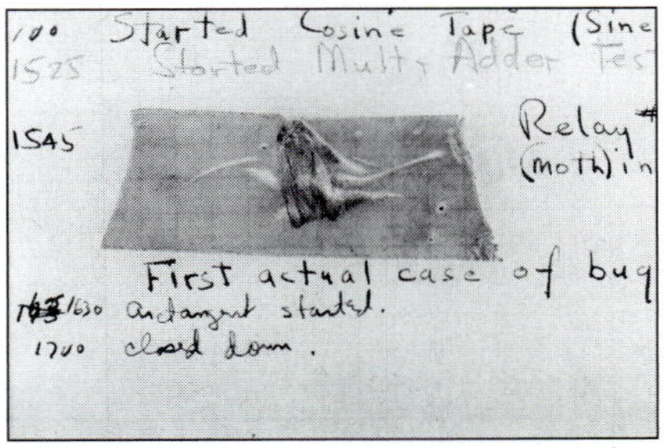

Bug photo courtesy of Naval Surface Warfare Center, Dahlgren Division
Dahlgren, Virginia

Were They Looking for Bugs?

In Gouldsboro, Maine, a man went to do some work on his computer, and found two 3-foot-long milk snakes curled up on the warm hard disk drive. The snakes were removed by a game warden on his first high-tech service call.

6.10 Picture Essay:

The rapid growth of the Internet has suggested to people that huge full-featured applications are not the only way to compute. An alternative approach is to keep applications on a computer that you connect to over the Internet or other network and download them when you want to run them on your computer. Since the application has to be sent over a communication link, it has to be small, hence the name applet for some of these applications. In addition, the applications should run on any system, or be platform-independent, allowing you to run the same application on an Apple Macintosh, IBM PC, or Sun workstation.

Network computers (NC) courtesy of Network Computer, Inc.

The computer

The small inexpensive computer used in network computing is called a network computer (NC). It has no built-in disk storage and plugs right into a company's local area network, where with a browser it can access the Internet or company intranet. There are advantages to this kind of computing model:

- It's easier to maintain. The applications reside on a server and not the NC so they need to be installed only once not hundreds or thousands of times on PCs throughout an enterprise.
- They're lower-cost. IBM expects that long-term cost of ownership should be only one-fourth to one-half that of a PC.
- There's no need to back up data. It's done automatically on the server.
- Security is increased because a company's data is not scattered across desktops throughout the enterprise. However, it's available for any network computer although there is no disk storage for it. You can't take it with you.

The software

On a high-speed network like those found in many offices, regular applications can be run on network computers. In the home, or over the Internet, new technologies are being developed to make it possible to distribute programs on demand. The two leaders in this area are Microsoft's ActiveX controls and Sun's Java. Both of these technologies are used to create small software components that are then embedded in Web pages or other applications. They can be run with your browser over a network such as one in your office or school or the Internet. Both ActiveX controls and Java Applets are stored on a central computer, a server. Other comput-

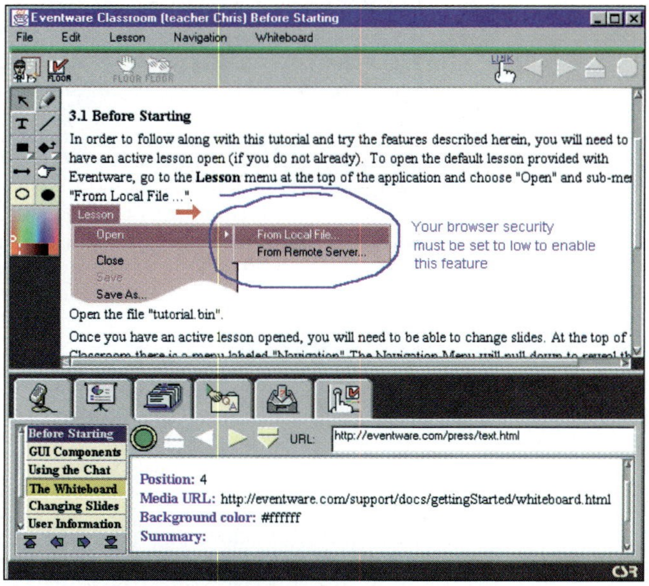

Java image courtesy of CSR,Inc.

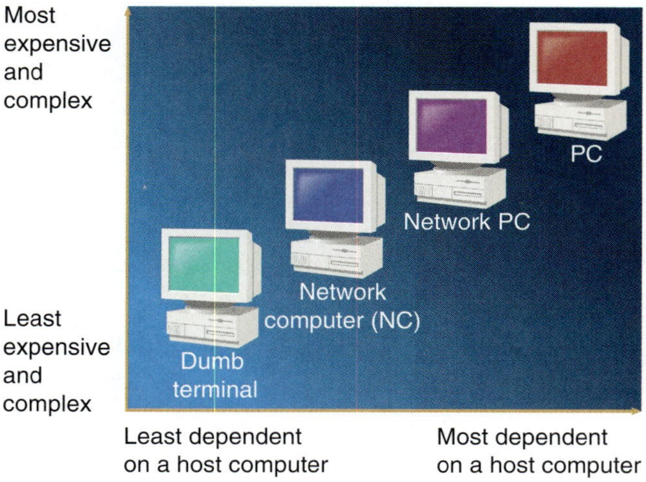

ers on the network can then execute them. When they do so, the control or Applet is downloaded to the computer and run there. When the job is done, the control or Applet is closed, removing the copy from the computer's memory but leaving the original file on the server where it can be run again later. In some models of network computing, even the data files are saved on the server's hard drive.

Component software

Both object linking and embedding (OLE) and OpenDoc allow applications to exchange information and data. This means that prebuilt software elements can now be mixed and matched. These programs can be designed as reusable building blocks that can be easily connected together. Each part is an independent program that manipulates and displays a particular kind of data. For example, any program you are working with can bring up your favorite spelling checker, grammar checker, or graphics program, allowing you in theory to build the ideal application program by choosing from a wide variety of components created by any number of publishers. Instead of the application program being the center of activities, the document becomes the center and applications are called up only as needed. This new approach to using computing software is called component software.

The Managed PC

When enthusiasm for the network computer (NC) began to spread in the business world, Intel and Microsoft became very concerned. Many business people were put off by the complexity and cost of the personal computer on which their businesses were based. The network computer promised a simpler, less expensive vision of computing and a surprising number of people liked the idea. If these machines found wide acceptance, sales of the Intel-based PC running Microsoft Windows might suffer. To stop the groundswell of enthusiasm for the network computer, Intel and Microsoft jointly developed their own vision, the NetPC or Managed PC. Basically, these machines are smaller versions of the standard PC with a lot fewer options. They are sealed so users can't insert adapter cards and other devices selected from a bewildering array of choices. Users also can't install their own software. It is the wide variation of hardware and software on PCs that drives up support costs in a large organization and that made a simpler form of computer desirable. Like network computers, NetPCs are designed to be managed from a central place on the network. This brings down the costs of installing, maintaining, and trouble-shooting PC software and hardware. Software installation and updates, BIOS updates, and even shutting computers on and off are managed remotely from the server.

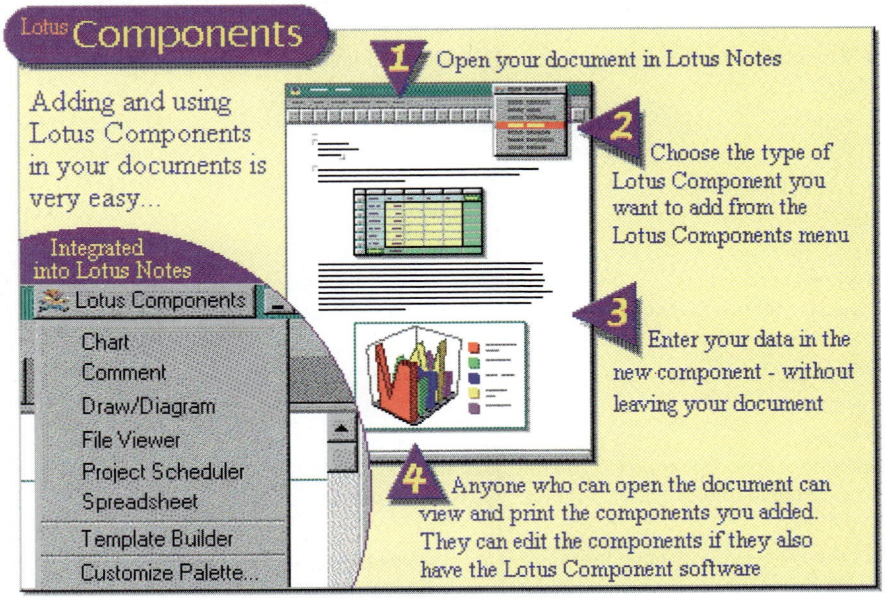

Component software courtesy of Lotus

6.11 Enhancing and Testing Your Understanding

Summary

- Systems software include programming languages and operating systems. Programming languages are used to create all other types of programs. Operating systems are what make the computer work.
- Many tasks that you perform with a computer are called applications and the programs you use to perform them are called application programs.
- When you first start your computer, the display that appears on the computer's screen is called the interface because it is where you and the machine interact. Older computers use character-based interfaces and newer ones use graphical user interfaces.
- A program that is distributed free in the hope that you will like it and pay for it is called shareware or freeware. These programs are copyrighted and protected.
- Software that has been donated to the public with all rights given away is called public domain software.
- The Basic Input/Output System (BIOS) isolates the software from the hardware. That way, if a system's hardware is changed radically, all you need to change is the BIOS.
- Multitasking means the computer can perform multiple tasks at the same time with different programs.
- Multithreading lets an application program start and run two or more threads (activities) simultaneously.
- Proprietary operating systems are supplied with a computer manufacturer's systems such as IBM's MVS and Digital's VMS. Generally, these systems work only with one type of computer, and it's very difficult for the user to change to a different operating system.
- Windows in its many versions is currently the leading desktop operating system.
- Windows NT and UNIX are two leading operating systems for servers.
- When a microprocessor is used inside a small device such as a watch or toaster, it uses an operating system such as embedded DOS.
- Files are assigned filenames so you can identify them. On most systems, filenames have two parts: a name and an extension.
- A filename extension is separated from the name by a period and identifies the file's format or the application that created it.
- Folders on a disk are used to group together related files. If you open a folder that isn't empty, you'll find other files and folders.
- Disk drives are assigned letters or names to identify them.
- Folders on a drive are arranged in a tree. You can expand and collapse the entire tree or any branch to alternate between a summary of the drive's contents, and details of each file.
- When you have files stored in folders on a disk, you have to follow a "path" to get to them. For example, if a file named *John.doc* is in a folder named *Letters* on drive C, the path to that folder is *C:\Letters\John.doc*.
- Operating systems include a separate file manager program that you use to explore the drives, folders, and files on your system.
- A utility program is used for format disks so they can store data. Formatting also creates a directory of the locations of each file called a file allocation table (FAT).
- A utility program should be used periodically to defragment or defrag the disk. This moves data around on the disk, so file fragments are again joined together on the disk's tracks.
- A utility program should be used to scan the disk at regular intervals to locate and mark any bad sectors and fix problems with files.
- On newer operating systems, deleting a file moves it to a separate area of the disk called a recycle bin or trash can. If you decide later that you want to recover the file, you open the recycle bin and restore it.
- Document-centric computing puts the emphasis on documents and the ability to call up the application you need to create or edit them.
- A document containing graphics, spreadsheet data, database data, sound, video, and animations created by other programs is called a compound document.
- An object in a compound documentcan be a complete file or a part of a file that you copied or cut out of another document.
- You should link when using the same object in more than one compound document so when you edit the object, the changes are immediately reflected in all of the compound documents to which it is linked.
- Normally, you use embedding when you want to edit the object right in the document in which it's embedded, make changes in the object that won't affect the original file the object is taken from, or send the document to others so they can edit both the compound document and its embedded objects without affecting the original.
- Before you actually use a new application program, you must install it by running an installation program (also called a setup program).
- Drivers translate a program's generic instructions into instructions for a specific piece of hardware.
- Program updates (also called upgrades) generally include corrected old features as well as new features that improve the program.
- Version numbers are used to indicate a release and are important when asking questions about your program.
- An error caused by a computer's hardware or software is called a bug.
- Disclaimers that come with software are designed to limit the publisher's liability.

Review Questions

True/False

1. **T F** The two largest categories of software are system software and applications.
2. **T F** System software includes the operating system that manages your system.
3. **T F** Applications software includes all of the programs that you use to complete tasks that enhance your skills and performance.
4. **T F** When you turn on a computer, it automatically loads its operating system so you can then load the application programs you'll want to use.
5. **T F** Graphical user interfaces (GUIs—pronounced "gooies") use icons, buttons, and pull-down menus to execute commands.
6. **T F** When a computer runs two or more programs at the same time it's called multitasking.
7. **T F** To save a document, you have to specify three things: the drive to save it on, the folder to save it in, and the name of the file.
8. **T F** On a fragmented disk, parts of the files are scattered, or fragmented. There are utility programs that will unfragment the disk for you.
9. **T F** Once you delete a file from the disk, it cannot be recovered.
10. **T F** Documents created with pieces from other programs are called compound documents.

Fill-In the Blank

1. __________ means the computer can run more than one program at the same time.
2. __________ means an application program can start and run two or more tasks simultaneously.
3. Systems software includes __________ and __________.
4. __________ gives software a link to the hardware and isolates them from each other.
5. On Windows systems, __________ allow programs to identify which applications created which files.
6. Folders on a disk are used to group together related files. If you were to open one folder, you'd find __________ and __________.
7. When you have files stored in folders on a disk, you have to follow a __________ to get to them.
8. When you __________ an object, changing the object in one place doesn't change it in others.
9. When you __________ an object, changing the object in the compound documents also changes the original copy.
10. Before you actually use a new application program, you must __________ it by running a special program.

Multiple Choice

1. The operating system determines if a computer can be ___.
   a. Single tasking or multitasking
   b. Single threading or multithreading
   c. Character-based or graphic
   d. All of the above
2. The software that must be loaded into the computer before you load a word processing program is __________.
   a. A programming language
   b. The operating system
   c. A utility program
   d. All of the above
3. When an operating system runs two programs at the same time it is __________.
   a. Multitasking **b.** Multithreading
   c. Multiprocessing **d.** Multiuser
4. The software that has no restrictions regarding its use is __________.
   a. Freeware **b.** Shareware
   c. Public domain **d.** All of the above
5. The most widely used operating system is __________.
   a. UNIX **b.** DOS
   c. Windows **d.** Windows NT
6. An operating system owned by a single company is called __________.
   a. Public **b.** Portable
   c. Proprietary **d.** Multiuser
7. To keep related files together you __________.
   a. Give them the same name
   b. Store them in the same folder
   c. Use the same extension
   d. All of the above
8. The path to a file named january in a folder named budgets on drive D is __________.
   a. D:\budgets\january **b.** D:\january\budgets
   c. D:/budgets/january **d.** D:/january/budgets
9. Editing a __________ object changes both the original and the copy in the document you are working on.
   a. Linked
   b. Embedded
   c. Both linked and embedded
   d. Neither linked nor embedded
10. To keep your system running better you should periodically __________.
    a. Delete unused files **b.** Defrag the disk
    c. Scan the disk **d.** All of the above

Research Projects

The new computer you are going to purchase comes with a choice of Windows or Windows 95. Using computer magazines or the Internet, try to find out the pluses and minuses of each. Based on your analysis explain which you chose and why you did so.

CHAPTER

7 WORD PROCESSING &

AN OVERVIEW

Imagine having typed a 20-page research paper on a typewriter, only to discover that you want to add a paragraph on page 2. You might face the choice between abandoning your new paragraph or retyping 19 pages. If this has not happened to you, it has happened to millions of others in the not very distant past when typewriters were the principal instrument for creating personal and professional documents. This is one of the reasons word processing programs took off so fast when they were introduced on PCs in the late 1970s.

What is so unique about word processing programs is the way they separate the process of entering and editing text from the process of printing it. With a typewriter, every time you type a character it is more or less permanently imprinted on the paper. With a word processing program, the text has a more malleable existence on the computer screen. It's easy to change an electronic page. Text can be quickly copied, moved, deleted, or typed over. If you insert new text, any text below it moves down automatically. When people first did word processing, it seemed like magic. The blessing to students, for instance, released from the drudgery of typing and retyping, is perhaps hard to imagine today. From that day forward, typewriters were dead.

But progress didn't stop there. Visionaries also had their eyes on killing a large part of the printing business and enabling individuals to create their own complex documents. Within a decade, desktop publishing was developed. Up until then, getting a professional-looking brochure, price list, newsletter, or even manual was an expensive and time-consuming process. The text was written and illustrations gathered. These went to a designer who laid them out, then to a compositor who set the type for the printer who put the text and illustrations in place on negatives and then made printing plates used to print the final product. Now all of this can be done electronically by an individual using desktop publishing programs and even some of the more advanced word processing programs. The printer is left with making negatives and printing them on a press.

Now we're in a new phase—getting rid of the printing press and just displaying the material on the screen on a Web site that anyone can visit at any time. Instead of having to request a company's catalog, you can just browse their Web site. It's often faster and easier—especially when you need to search for a specific product. With electronic publishing over the Internet, paper, printing, and even distribution are taken out of the process. Now anyone can be a worldwide publisher.

In this chapter we look at some of the application programs that make all this possible. We'll look at still others as you progress through the text.

OBJECTIVES

After completing this chapter, you will be able to:

- Describe the basics of entering and editing text in a word processing application.
- Describe basic document formats that can be changed.
- Explain the desktop publishing process and describe some of its main features.
- Describe the new field of desktop publishing for the screen.
- Identify other popular features of word processing and desktop publishing applications.

Word processing *n.* 1. the process of using a computer to enter, edit, and format text.

Desktop publishing *n.* 1. the process of using a desktop computer to lay out pages and add graphics for printed documents or the screen.

ON THE PACE CD ROM

Spread No.	Title
7-1	Thesaurus
7-2	Find and Replace
7-2	Outlines
7-2	Merge-Printing
7-2	Footnotes and Endnotes
7-4	Graphic Images
7-4	Table of Contents
7-4	Columns
7-5	Hypertext Links

Desktop Publishing

7.1 Entering and Editing Documents

Word processing is by far the most widely used computer application because word processing is used for communication, our most common activity. Word processing is used to write, edit, and format memos, letters, reports, manuscripts, contracts, and every imaginable type of document. No matter what the information is, or what form it takes, the chances are it was initially composed and written using a word processing program.

Word wrap

As you enter text into a document, you do not have to press Enter at the end of each line in order to move to a new line. The word processing program automatically does this for you. Each document has preset margins and when the end of a line is reached, the program calculates whether the word being entered fits on the line. If it won't fit without crossing the right margin, the program automatically moves the entire word to the beginning of the next line. This function, called word wrap, is common to all word processing programs.

Editing

When editing a document to correct mistakes, you can move the insertion point where you want to enter new text and then just type it in. To delete characters, you press Backspace or Delete. Pressing Backspace deletes characters to the left of the insertion point and pressing Delete deletes those to the right. You can also drag the mouse to highlight any section of the text and then copy it to another file, move it to some other place in your document, give it a new format, or delete it all at once.

Spelling checkers

Spelling checkers compare all words in a document with a list of words in the program's dictionary. Any words not found in the dictionary are highlighted and you can then decide whether to change them, leave them as is, or add them to the dictionary. If you decide to change them, you can do so by selecting another word from a list of suggestions that is displayed when the word is highlighted. It's important to note that a

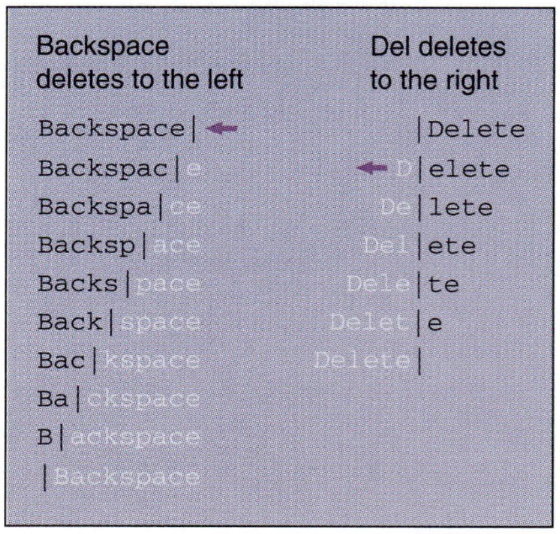

Editing

highlighted word isn't necessarily misspelled. It just means the word isn't in the dictionary. You'll find many names and industry-specific words highlighted even when spelled correctly. If you add each of these words to the dictionary as you encounter them, they won't be highlighted in any subsequent spell-checks. Here a misspelled word has been right-clicked and a suggested replacement word is listed on a pop-up menu.

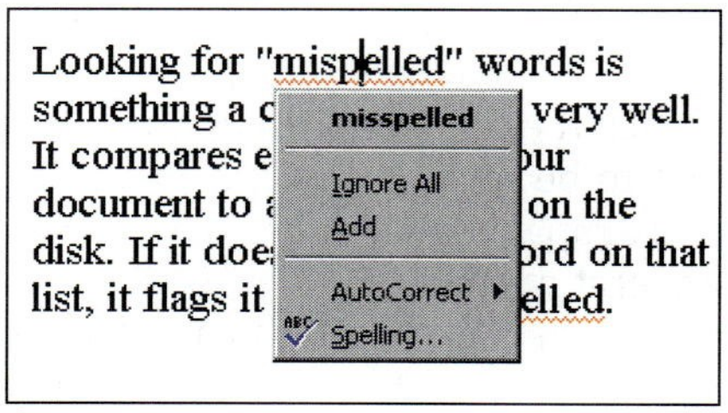

Spell checking

Programs that have an autocorrect feature highlight words that aren't in the dictionary as you type them. This makes it easy to correct misspellings as you go along.

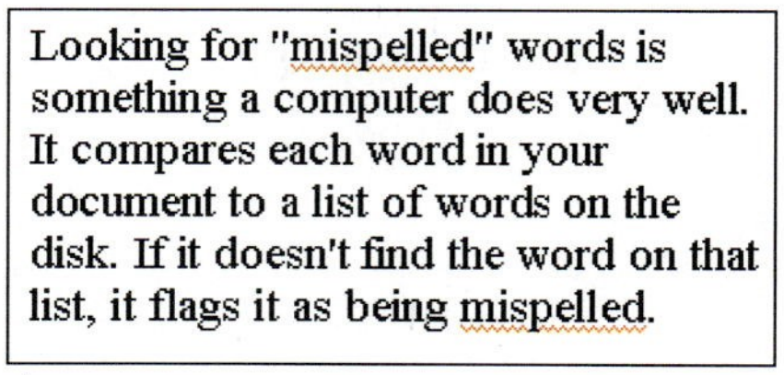

Autocorrect

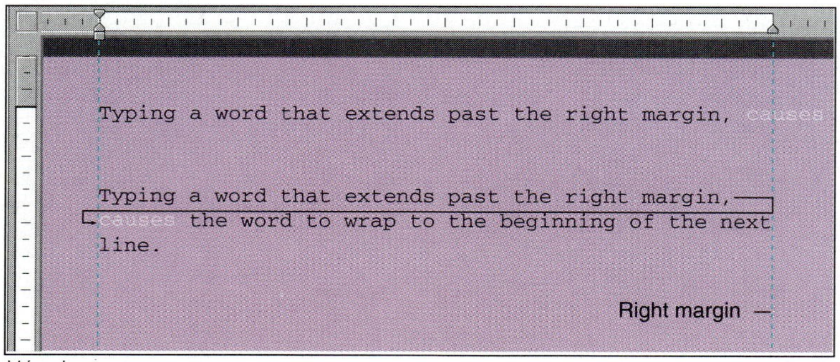

Word wrap

Be Careful with That Spelling Checker

A spell-checking program changed "biotech" to "batik" in an entire chapter of the book *The World of 2044*.

A spell-checker at a Boston-area magazine substituted ACLJ for ACLU in an April 1994 article. The ACLJ is the American Center for Law and Justice, which is affiliated with the Rev. Pat Robertson, and politically far apart from the American Civil Liberties Union (ACLU).

Source: *Computerworld,* January 8, 1996, p. 2.

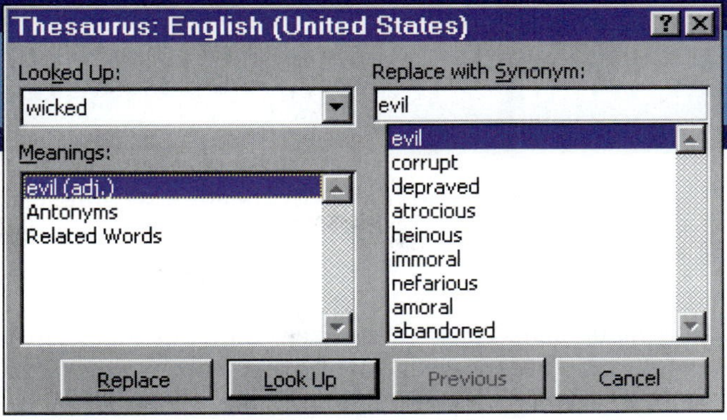

Thesaurus courtesy of Microsoft

A word of caution! Spelling checkers are nice, but you can't solely rely on them. They check only for spelling, not for usage. For example, spelling checkers would find no problems in the sentence, *Eye wood like two except you invitation, butt can knot, unfortunately, their are another things i half too due,* or in Hamlet's "too bee oar knot too bee."

Grammar checkers

Grammer checkers are programs that check the grammar in your documents as you go along. Checking grammar is certainly a good thing to do, as you can improve your writing while you write. A grammar checker highlights grammar or usage problems such as double negatives, jargon words, and punctuation errors, and highlights possible style problems such as wordy expressions, clichés, weak modifiers, split infinitives, and consecutive nouns. However, a word of caution is appropriate regarding grammar checkers. They make suggestions; it's up to you to accept or reject them. Grammar checkers are not to be relied on too heavily. They are simply not sophisticated enough, at least at this point. Good writing is a matter of judgment and taste, something you have to input in the computer, not vice versa. As *The Economist* put it, "Until computers can make more sense of the vagaries of language, grammar checkers are products up with which we will not put."

Thesaurus

When using a thesaurus, you highlight a word and request the thesaurus to display a list of synonyms (words with similar meanings) and antonyms (words with opposite meanings). For example, when the word *wicked* is highlighted, the thesaurus may display the synonyms *sinful*, *erring*, *nefarious*, *wayward*, *dissolute*, *vile*, and *vicious* or the antonyms *godly*, *innocent*, *good*, or *honorable*. You can then select one of the suggested words to replace the highlighted word in the document, look up one of the words or another word, or quit the thesaurus and return to the document. Since the fact that a thesaurus (meaning "treasury" in Greek) is merely suggesting to you alternative word choices, a thesaurus is a very useful program to have.

Reference sources

When you are writing, there are many reference materials available on CD-ROM discs and on the Web. For example, you can refer to atlases, dictionaries, encyclopedias, quotation dictionaries, almanacs, and thesauruses. You can search for information you want and even cut and paste it into your own document, properly referencing or attributing it of course to avoid plagiarism (assuming you don't violate someone's copyright protections). Here is the Web site for the Purdue On-line Writing Laboratory (OWL) where you can get useful information about grammar and style.

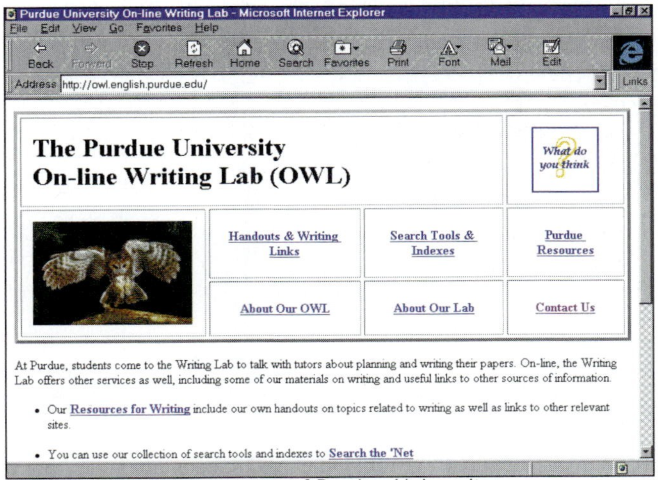

Reference sources courtesy of Purdue University
http://owl.english.purdue.edu/

Grammar checking courtesy of Microsoft

7.2 Other Word Processing Features

The most powerful word processing programs have so many features that no one but the most workaholic of users understands them all. However, there are many features that are very useful to almost everyone. Here are just a few of them.

Find and replace

To locate words or phrases in a document, you use the Find command. If the word or phrase you specify is found, the program highlights it. To substitute one word or phrase for another, you use the Replace command specifying what word or phrase you want to find and what you want to replace it with. If it's found, the program highlights it and offers you the opportunity to replace it or leave it unchanged and look for the next occurrence. Both the Find and Replace commands can also be used to find and replace formats as well as text. This allows you to do such things as easily change some or all boldfacing in a document to italics, and so forth.

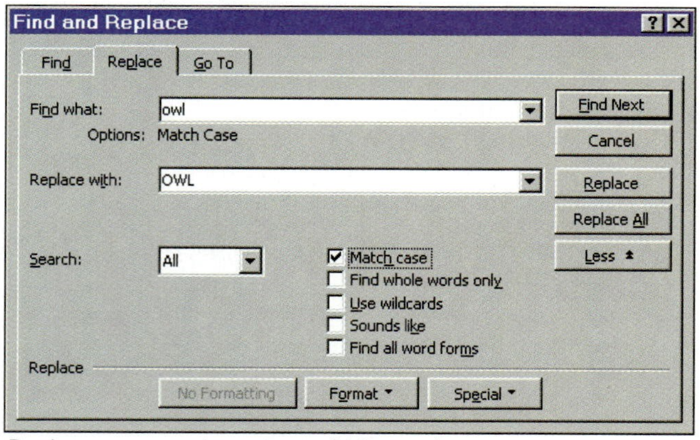

Replace command courtesy of Microsoft

Outlines

The Outline command allows you to switch between two views of the same document. In one view you see it as you normally do, but in the outline view you see just the headings. When the document has more than one level of headings, you can expand or collapse the outline to see various levels of detail. This gives you a great overview of the document's structure and organization. And when the document is displayed in its outline view, you can move, copy, or delete the headings and this automatically moves, copies, or deletes the text under those headings.

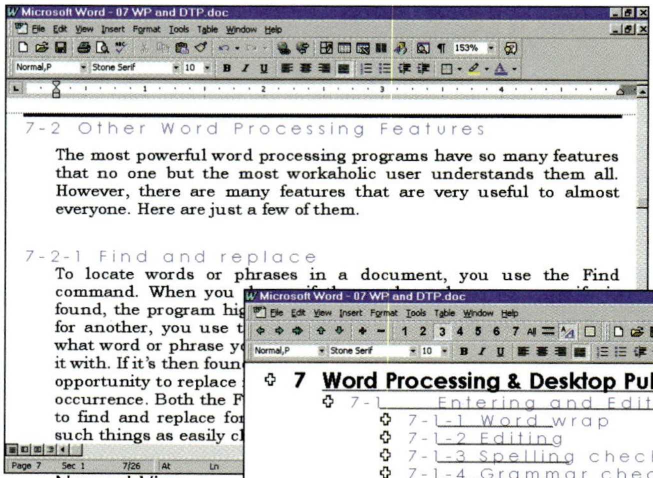

Normal View

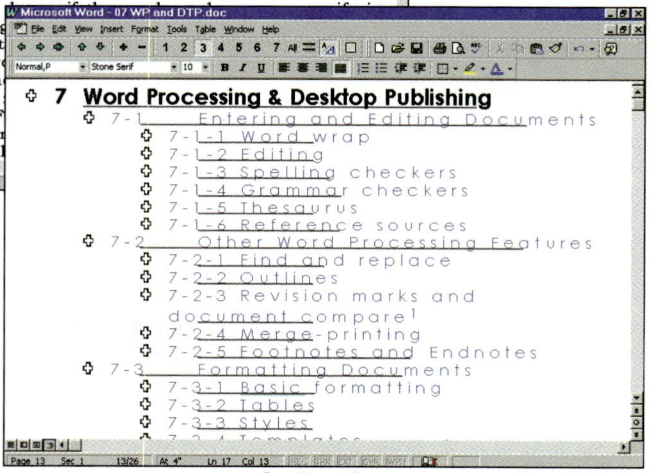

Outline View

Revision marks and document compare

When more than one person is involved in the creation of a document, opinions about what to add or what to cut

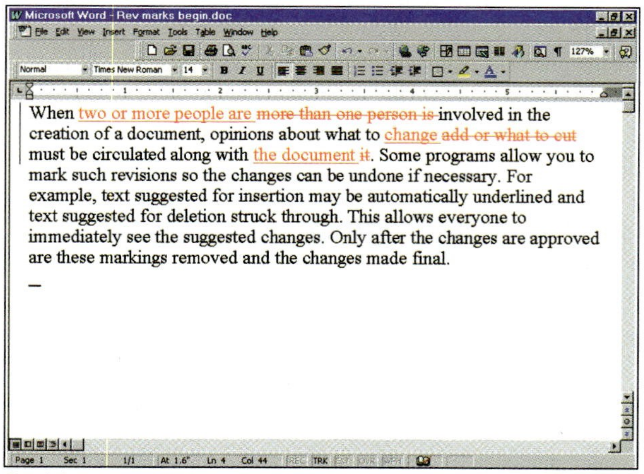

Revision marks

must be circulated along with the document. Some programs allow you to mark such revisions so the changes can be undone if necessary. For example, text suggested for insertion may be automatically underlined and text suggested for deletion struck through. This allows everyone to immediately see the suggested changes. Only after the changes are approved are these markings removed and the changes made final.

Documents sometimes go through many revisions before the final version is printed and distributed. All changes are not necessarily good ones, but it is hard to keep track of changes from version to version. A document compare feature compares two versions of a document and highlights the differences between them.

Merge-printing

One advantage of word processing programs is the way they allow you to automate your work. Instead of individually entering and editing tens, hundreds, or thousands of letters, envelopes, mailing labels, forms, or other documents, you can merge-print them.

To merge-print you need two files: a data source and a main document. The data source is a document containing the data to be inserted during merge-printing. It might be a table of names and addresses, paragraphs for contracts, or descriptions of products. The main document contains the general form of the text that is to appear in every copy. The main document also contains merge codes that specify where data is to be inserted and where in the data source it is to come from. For example, the salutation in the main document may read **Dear <gender> <last name>**. When you merge-print the merge codes are replaced by data drawn from a data source. Since different data is inserted into each copy, multiple customized copies are printed.

Footnotes and endnotes

Footnotes are used to add comments to a document without interrupting the flow of the narrative. Only a small reference number appears in the body text; the footnote itself is placed at the bottom of the same page. Endnotes are identical to footnotes except they are printed at the end of a section or at the end of the document. On the computer, all of the details of numbering and printing the notes are handled automatically. If you insert or delete notes above existing ones, all of the following notes are automatically renumbered to reflect the change.

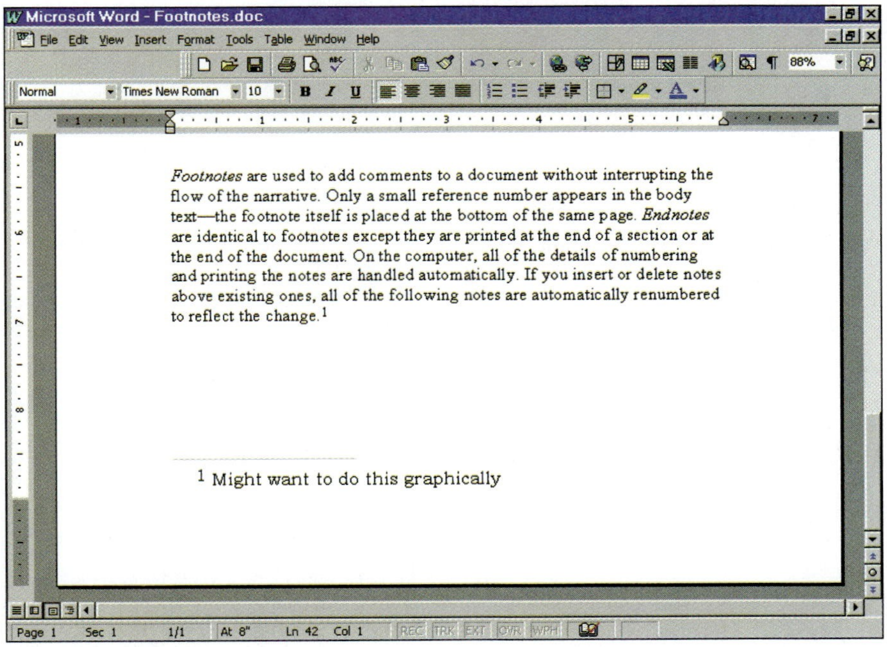

Footnotes

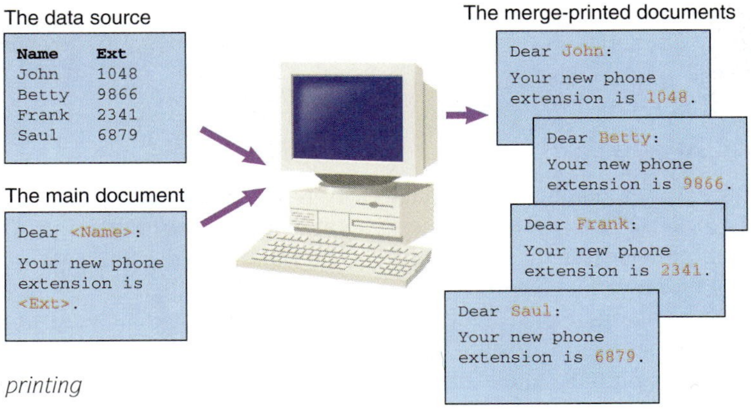

Merge printing

7.3 Formatting Documents

When you want to make a document both more attractive and easier to read, you use formats. All word processing programs have built-in format settings called defaults, which are designed so you can easily override them.

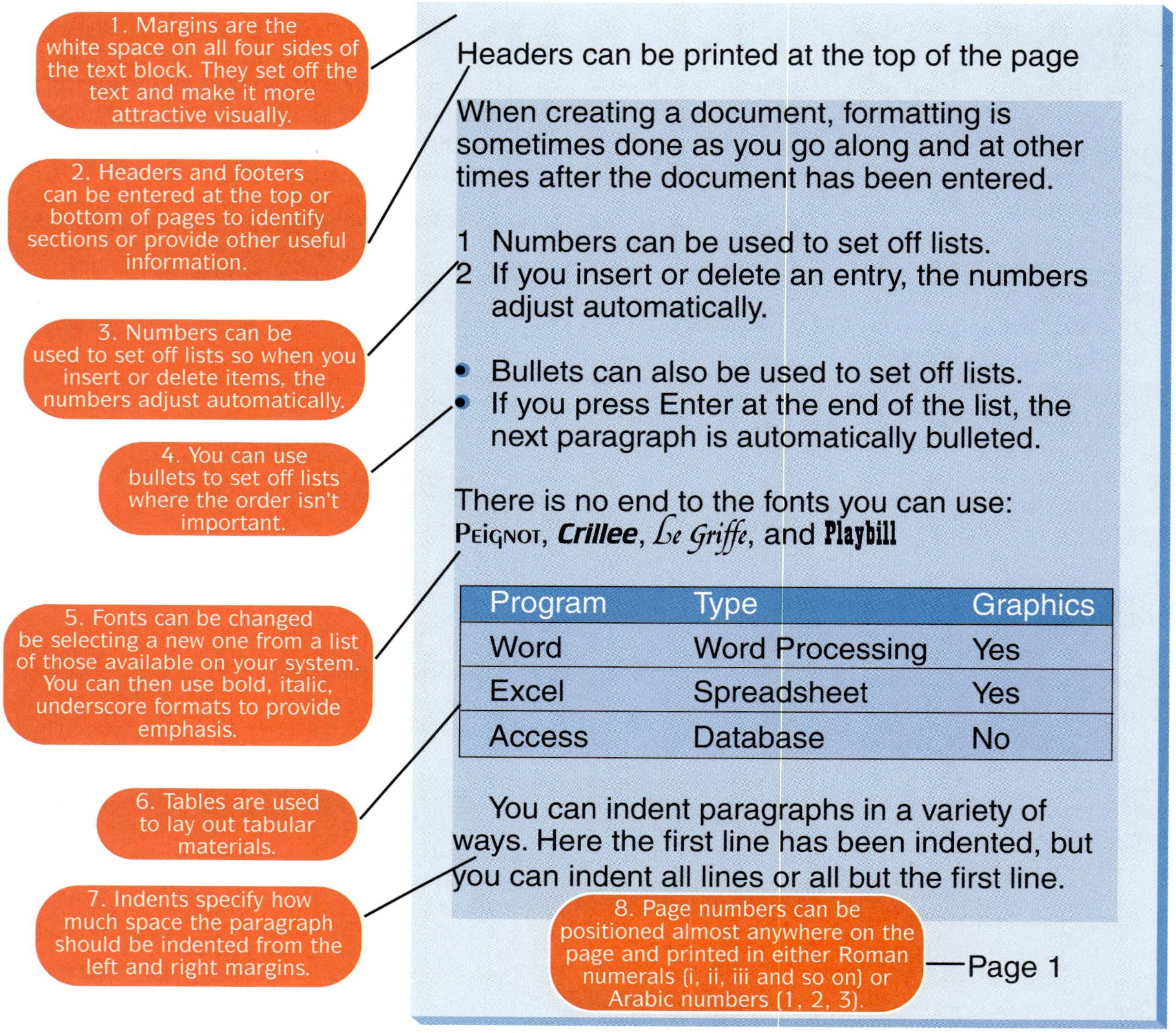

Formats

Basic formatting

When creating a document, formatting is usually a separate stage–often completed after the document has been entered. The ease of applying and changing format lets you play with a document's design. Here are just a few of the formats that are available for you to work with.

Tables

It used to be that you entered a table using tab stops that divided the table into columns. However, it takes a great deal of skill to lay out and edit a table this way, and even with great skill, certain tables are still very difficult to lay out in this manner. The table feature now included in most programs allows you to create a blank table by specifying the number of rows and columns it should contain. The intersections of the rows and columns create cells. As you type data into a cell, the text wraps within the cell and the cell's depth adjusts automatically. You can easily adjust column widths, format entire rows or columns, and insert and delete rows and columns. You can even enter numbers in some cells and formulas in others to make calculations, for example, to total a column of numbers.

Table 1. Major U.S. Dams and Reservoirs

Order	Dam Name	River	State	Height	Year
1	Oroville	Feather	California	754	1968
2	Hoover	Colorado	Nevada	725	1936
3	Dworshak	N Fork Clearwater	Idaho	718	1973
4	Glen Canyon	Colorado	Arizona	708	1966
5	New Bullards Bar	North Yuba	California	636	1970
6	New Melones	Stanislaus	California	626	1979
7	Swift	Lewis	Washington	610	1958
8	Mossyrock	Cowilitz	Washington	607	1968
9	Shasta	Sacramento	California	600	1945
10	Hungry Horse	S Fork Flathead	Montana	564	1953
11	Grand Coulee	Columbia	Washington	551	1942
12	Ross	Skagit	Washington	541	1949

Tables

Styles

When formatting documents, you frequently find yourself applying the same formats over and over again. You can save yourself a lot of time by using styles—formats that you have saved and named. For example, you can create a style that specifies text be uppercase and boldfaced. When you select text and then specify this style from a list of available styles, the selected text becomes uppercase and boldfaced.

Styles also make revisions a snap. Assume you have formatted a hundred headings and decide that you want to change the format from boldfaced to underlined. Revising the format associated with the style automatically changes all the headings formatted with the style. In addition, specifying styles is necessary when you want to generate an outline view, a table of contents, or an index.

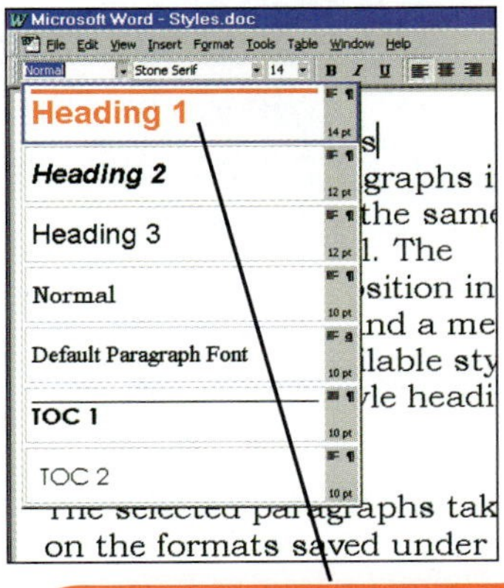

Here, all of the paragraphs in the document have the same style, named normal. The insertion point is positioned in the top line of text and a menu listing all of the available styles is displayed. The style *Heading 1* is selected.

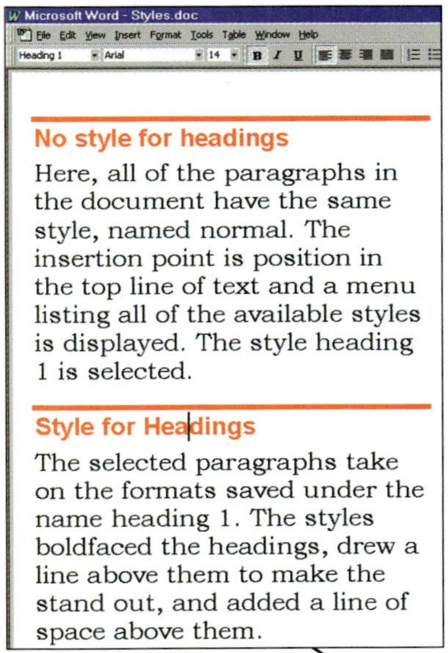

The selected paragraphs take on the formats saved under the name *heading 1*. The style boldfaced the headings and made them red, drew a red line above them to make them stand out, and added a line of space above them to separate them from the previous paragraph.

Templates

It's not unusual to be working with a variety of documents such as memos, letters, and reports. Each document type may have its own distinct formats, and the styles that you use for each can be stored together in a special file called a template. Templates also store text and page layout settings specific to the type of document that you are working on. When you create a new document, you specify which template you want to base it on and all of the styles and other formatting tools stored in the template become available.

Many programs (not just word processors) come with templates already prepared for your use. Below is shown a template for an invoice. All you have to do is replace the existing text with your own and you have a fully formatted document.

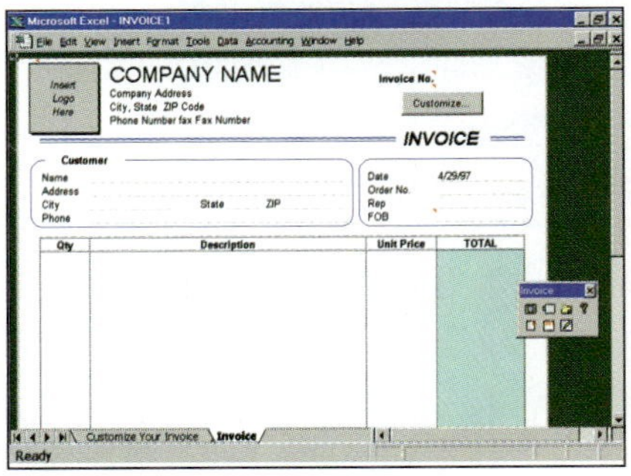

Typical template

Wizards and helpers

Some procedures are so detailed that it's hard to remember the exact steps to follow. In these cases, many programs now come complete with wizards or helpers that guide you through the process step by step. These wizards are interactive. They ask you questions, and take action based on the answers you provide. Below is the first screen in Word's fax wizard that creates a fax cover sheet for you.

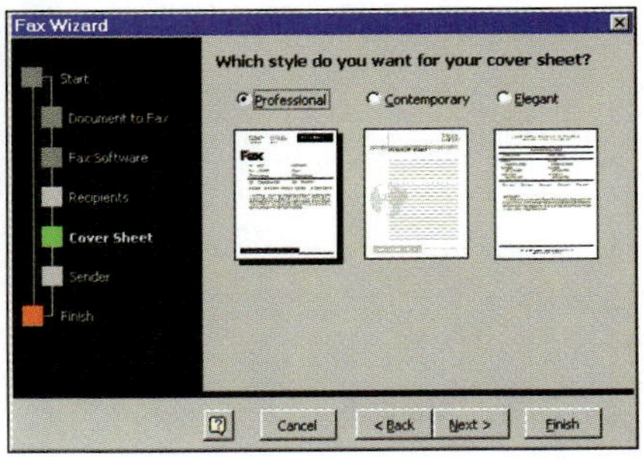

Typical wizard

7.4 Desktop Publishing for Print

We all take it for granted when we receive reports, mailers, newsletters, brochures, and other documents in color, with graphics, different fonts, multiple column layouts, and even tables of contents and indexes. At one time these had to be prepared by professional services, but now they can be done by you or me on the desktop. This is what is implied by the phrase desktop publishing.

Page layout

One of the primary functions of a desktop publishing program is to lay out pages or do page layout, a function so critical to the process that you often hear these programs referred to as page layout programs. Computerized page layout allows you to easily and accurately place text in columns and insert graphics. By dragging guide lines to specify where text and graphics belong, page elements can be placed with great precision. Layout programs also have master pages. Any text or graphics placed on these pages appears on all pages in the document.

Graphics program

Graphic images

It's often necessary or desirable to include graphics in a document. To do so, you must first obtain the image. There are four ways to obtain images:

- You can buy "clip-art" files that have been specially created for use in desktop publishing.
- You can scan the image into the computer.
- You can create the image on the screen with a graphics program or modify clip-art to better meet your needs.
- You can use a program that takes a snapshot of, or captures, the screen display, and saves it as a graphic file on the disk.

Special characters

Many programs allow you to enter special characters that are not on the computer's keyboard. These characters include Greek letters, foreign currency symbols, and foreign language accents, mathmatics and other special symbols. To enter such characters you can select the character from a list or palette. On some programs you can also enter special characters by turning on Num Lock, holding down the Alt key, and typing the character's ASCII number on the numeric keypad. For example, typing Alt-0189 enters the symbol fi.

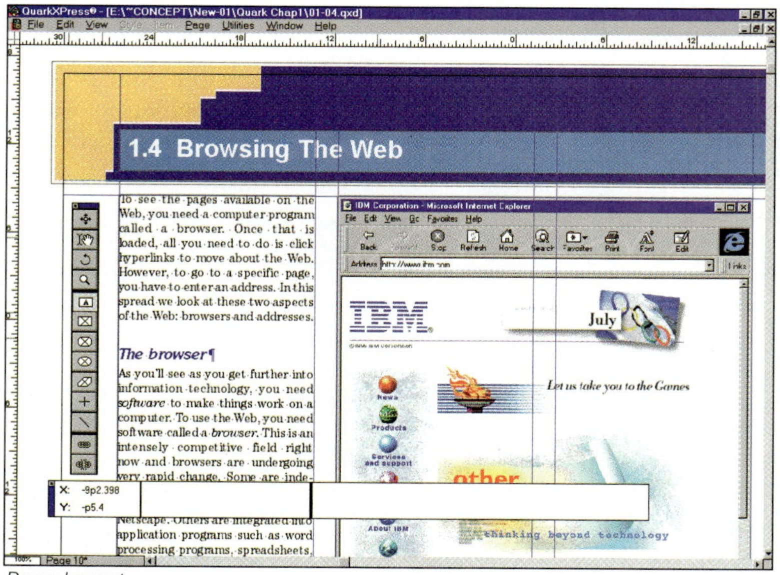

Page layout

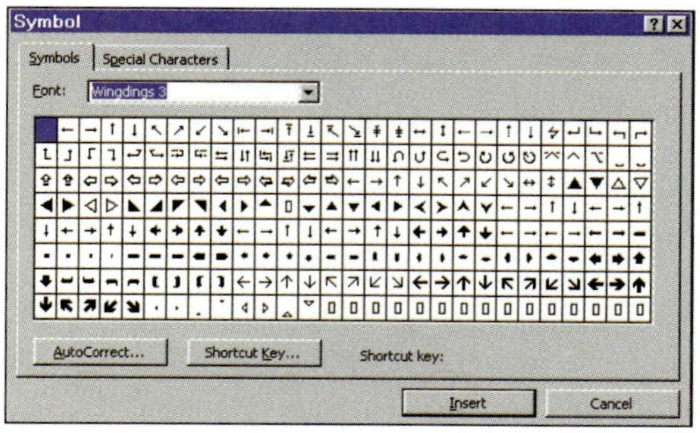

Symbols and special characters

Tables of contents and indexes

When working on a long document with many topics and sections, you often need to prepare a table of contents or an index which list headings or subjects in the document and provide page number references for them to help readers find the information they need. To automatically create one of these lists you follow three steps: format the items to be listed, specify the position of the list, and generate the list.

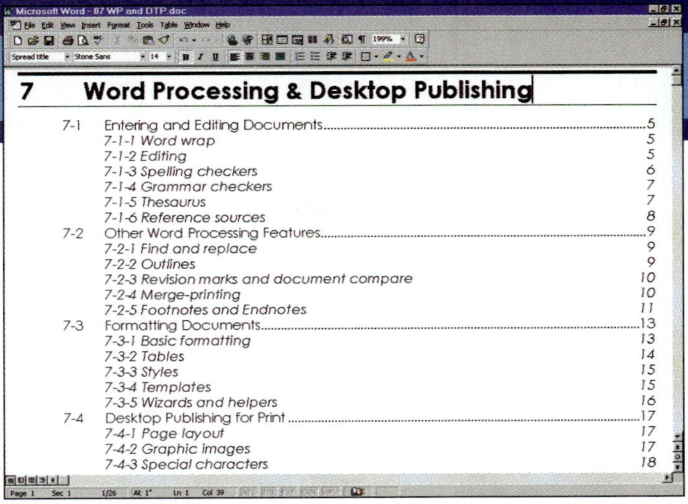

Table of contents

Columns

You can print text in two or more newspaper-style columns so text flows from one column to the next. As you enter text, it gradually fills the first column. When that column is full, text flows into the next column. When the last column on the page is full, text starts to fill the first column on the next page. If you add text to or delete text from any of the columns, the remaining text adjusts within the columns.

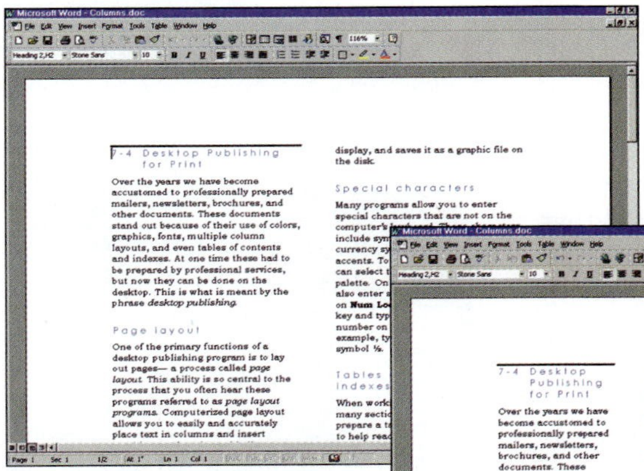

Document in two columns

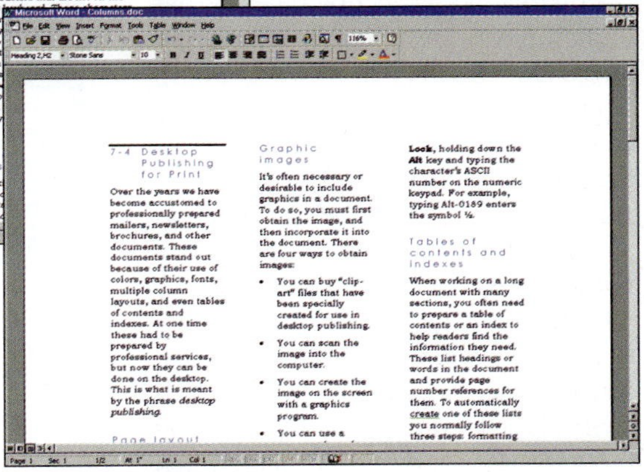

Document in three columns

Desktop publishing versus word processing

Desktop publishing programs were introduced because until very recently, word processing programs were better at editing than formatting. However, many desktop publishing features have been incorporated into word processing programs. Today word processing and desktop publishing programs overlap quite a bit. For many documents, you no longer need to create the document on a word processing program and then transfer it to a separate desktop publishing program for page layout. Using only a word processing program, you can now create and lay out very sophisticated documents such as forms, newsletters, manuals, charts, brochures, letterheads, logos, catalogs, reports, and even books.

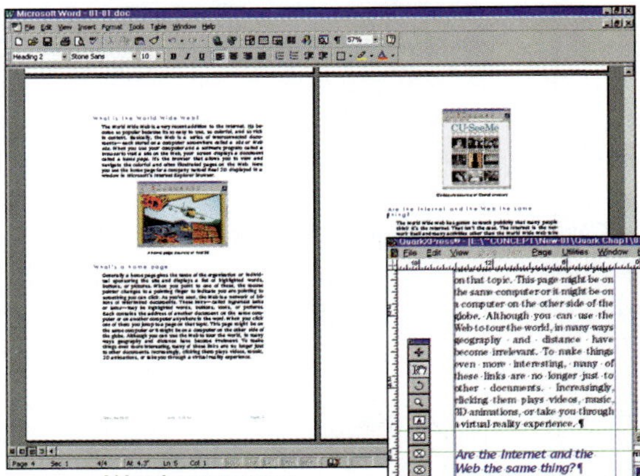

Word processor

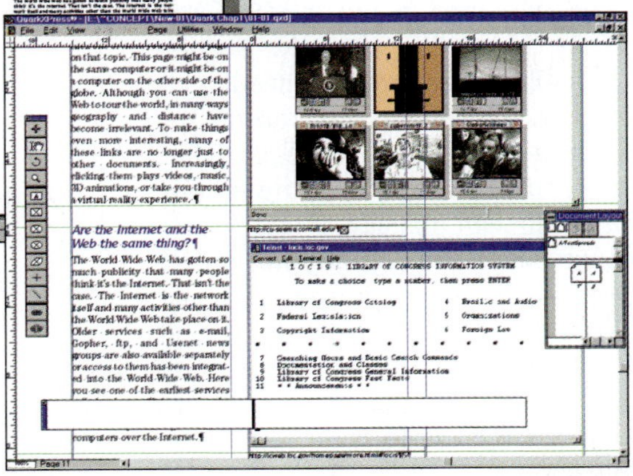

Desktop publisher

Desktop publishing versus word processing

7.5 Desktop Publishing for the Screen

Until very recently, desktop publishing meant preparing print materials. However, with the explosive growth of the Web and multimedia, desktop publishing is increasingly for the screen. One thing about this form of output, it saves paper, printing, binding, and distribution costs. The person who views the pages bears the cost of accessing and printing them.

Hypertext markup language

Pages published on the Web need to be not only eye-catching and attractive but also functional, which requires formatting and linking to other pages, done by inserting into a document hidden codes or tags that communicate in a special formatting language called hypertext markup language, or HTML. This is a subset of a much larger standard language called standardized generalized markup language (SGML). The reason for the popularity of these formatting languages is they are not specific to any one program. If you format a document in Microsoft Word, the formats are specific to that program. The document can't be read by other programs or on other systems without some form of conversion. A Web page obviously aspires to being read, understood, and linked to as universally as possible.

HTML tags are text so they can be read by any program. For example, when formatting your Web page, you add a tag *<H1><CENTER>* to specify that the section that follows is a centered heading. A similar but slightly different tag such as *</CENTER></H1>* specifies the end of the format. Any editing program can display HTML documents and their tags and many programs can interpret the tags and format text accordingly. Most browsers also have a Source command that lets you view the tags that created the formats you see on the screen.

Hypertext links

When designing pages that will be displayed on the screen, you are not limited to a linear approach. You can format text or graphics so that when you click them you jump elsewhere in the document. These clickable "hot spots" are called hyperlinks. When you click on one of them it takes you to another place on the same page, an entirely different page, or even a page on another computer. Clicking them allows you to quickly jump around the Internet following any clues on any path you choose. HTML tags activate these links by specifying a page to jump; or a graphic, sound, video, or animation to display or play.

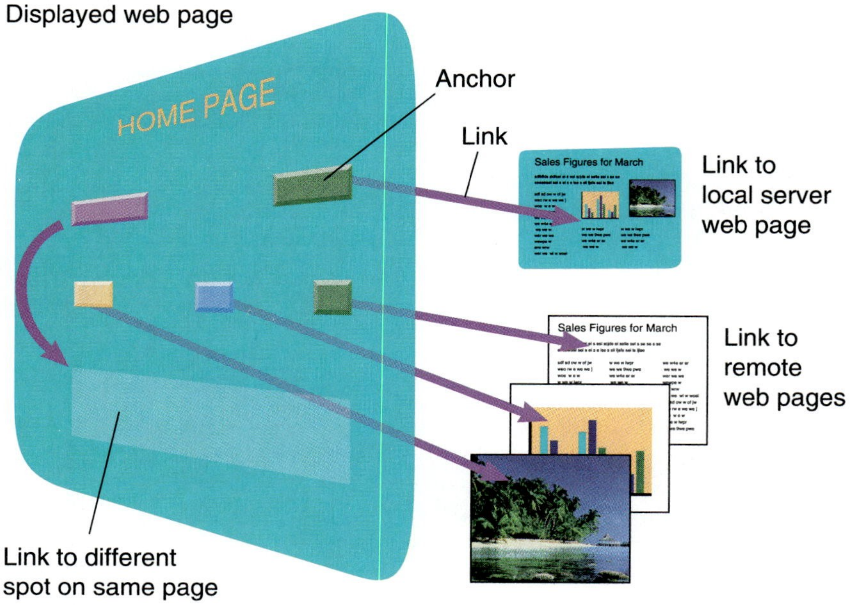

Hyperlinks

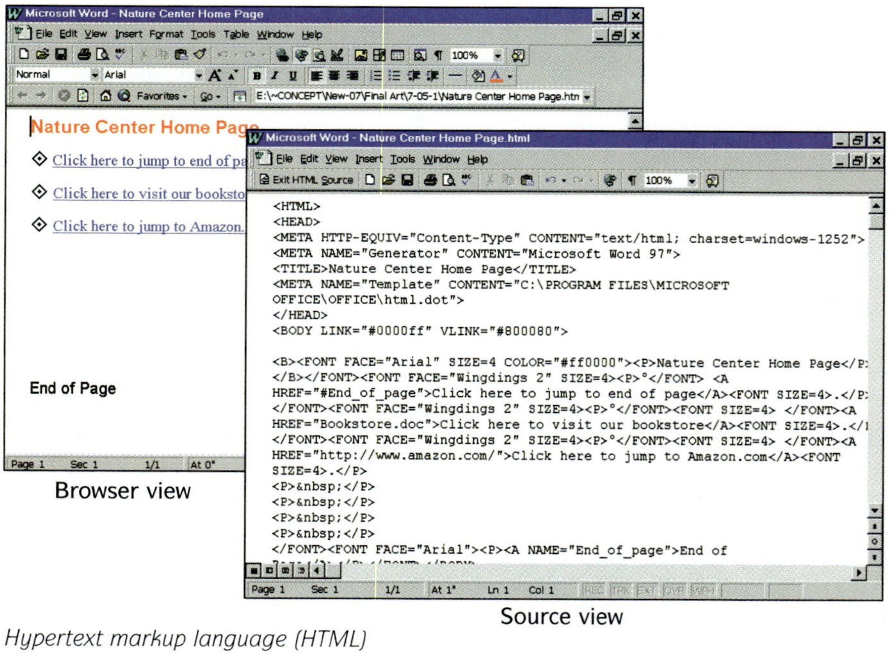

Hypertext markup language (HTML)

Internet enabled applications

With the increased use of the Internet and internal intranets, more people are creating and distributing documents using HTML formats. Standard application programs such as word processors now include the tools you need to format such pages; that is, they apply HTML styles to various elements. The application program does the rest of the work for you. You can even insert hyperlinks into regular documents. Above right, you see a page being edited and formatted using Microsoft Word. Clicking any of the highlighted text, the hyperlinks, jumps you to specific pages on the Web.

Internet page layout programs

Although you can use standard application programs to create Web pages, some sites are too complex for this approach. Special programs have been developed to desktop publish pages for these sites.

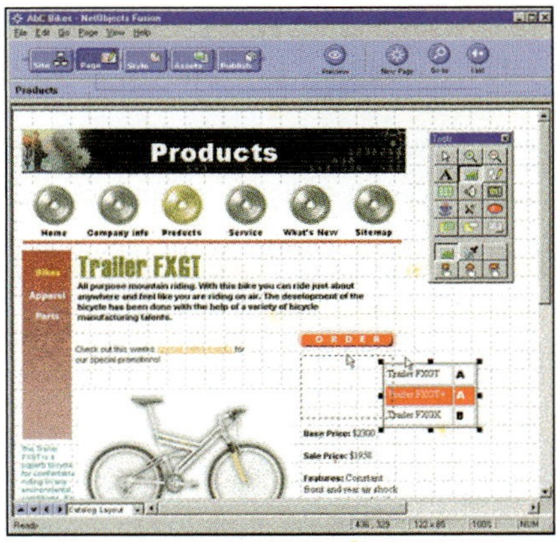

Courtesy of NetObjects
http://www.netobjects.com/html/pagedraw.html

These special programs do more than just let you lay out and format the pages. They also help you manage the site. These tools can make anyone a Web publisher. For example, Fusion's Site Builder is an application that lets you organize pages

Word 97 with an HTML document open

on the site by just dragging and dropping them as shown below.

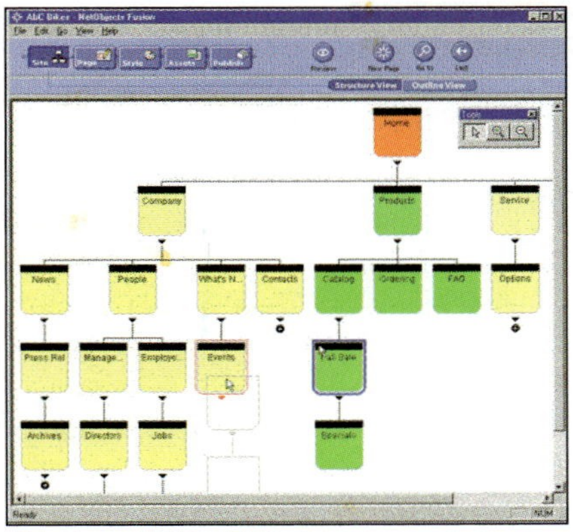

Courtesy of NetObjects
http://www.netobjects.com/html/sitestructure.html

Document conversions

Today, when someone prepares a document, they can't always be sure how it will be distributed. It could be sent to a printer or posted on the Web to be viewed with a browser. And when the plan calls for distributing it both ways, people want to be sure the job doesn't have to be done twice—once for a printer and again for display on the screen. To prevent duplication of effort, application programs include file conversion filters. These filters allow you to save a document in various formats or open documents created in another format. For example, you might save a document in the application's native format so the file can be used by a printer and also save the file in HTML format so it can be posted on the Web.

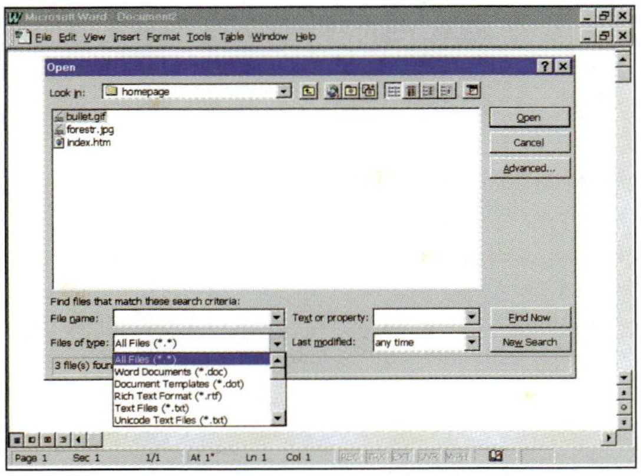

Filters that open documents in other formats

Portable document formats

HTML has its limits, especially when you want to view or print a full-color document. Acrobat is a program, that allows you to create visually rich documents in a portable document format (PDF) that can be viewed and printed on all kinds of computers.

To create a PDF file, you just print a document to a PDF file on the disk rather than to the printer. PDF is a universal electronic file format so virtually anyone can view and print a PDF file using the free Acrobat Reader.

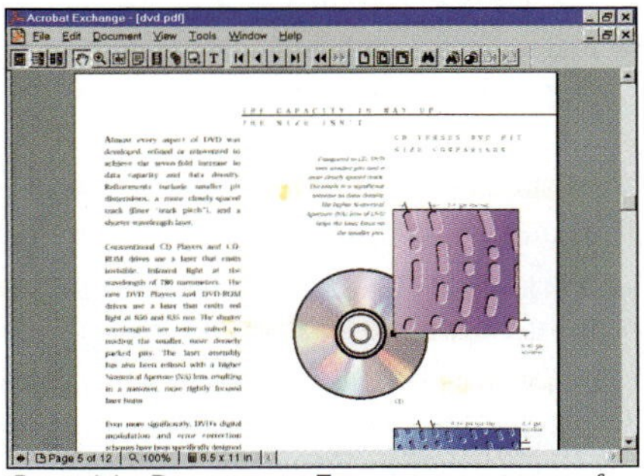

Portable Document Format courtesy of Sony

7.6 Enhancing and Testing Your Understanding

Summary

- Word processing is by far the most widely used computer application.
- As you enter text into a document, if a word won't fit without crossing the right margin, the program automatically moves the entire word to the beginning of the next line.
- Pressing Backspace deletes characters to the left of the insertion point and pressing Delete deletes those to the right. You can also drag the mouse to highlight a section of text and then copy, move, format, or delete it all at once.
- Spelling checkers compare all words in a document with the words in the program's dictionary.
- An auto correct feature highlights words that aren't in the dictionary as you type them so you can correct misspellings as you go along.
- Spelling checkers check only for spelling, not usage, so beware. Grammar checkers are useful if you're aware of their limitations.
- A thesaurus is used to look up synonyms (words with similar meanings) and antonyms (words with opposite meanings).
- To locate words or phrases in a document, you use the Find command. To replace them, you use the Replace command.
- The Outline command allows you to switch between normal and outline view where you see just the headings.
- Some programs allow you to mark revisions to help you remember where they are so the changes can be undone if necessary.
- A document compare feature compares two versions of a document and highlights the differences between them.
- Merge-printing takes the data from a data source and inserts it into a main document where specified by merge codes.
- Footnotes add comments to a document without interrupting the flow of the narrative. A small reference number appears in the body text. The footnote is placed at the bottom of the same page. Endnotes are identical to footnotes except they are printed at the end of a section or at the end of the document.
- To make a document both more attractive and easier to read, you use various formats. All word processing programs have built-in format settings, called defaults, designed to be easily overridden if you wish.
- Headers and footers can be entered at the top or bottom of pages to identify sections or provide other useful information.
- A table feature allows you to create a table using the intersections of rows and columns that form cells. As you type data into a cell, the text wraps within the cell and the cell's depth adjusts automatically.
- Styles are formats that have been saved and named. When you select text and then specify a style from a list of available styles, the selected text becomes formatted by that style. If you change the format of a style, all elements formatted with that style will automatically reflect the change.
- Styles can be stored together in a template along with text and page layout settings for specific types of documents that you may work on.
- Wizards or helpers guide you through detailed procedures step by step.
- Desktop publishing is used to professionally prepare mailers, newsletters, brochures, and other documents using colors, graphics, different fonts, multiple column layouts, and even tables of contents and indexes.
- Page layout involves accurately placing text in columns and inserting graphics.
- There are four ways to obtain images for use in documents: buy clip-art, scan images, create them with a graphics program, or take a snapshot of a screen display.
- Many programs allow you to enter special characters or symbols that are not on the computer's standard keyboard.
- You can format headings for a table of contents or subjects for an index and then generate such lists automatically.
- Text in desktop publishing newspaper-style columns flows from one column to the next. When a column is full, text flows into the next column. When the last column on the page is full, text starts to fill the first column on the next page.
- An increasing amount of desktop publishing is screen-oriented for the creation of Web pages and multimedia.
- Web pages are formatted by inserting tags into a document that use a special formatting language called hypertext markup language, or HTML, a subset of a much larger standard language called standardized generalized markup language (SGML).
- Most browsers have a Source command that lets you view the tags that created the formats you see on the screen.
- You can format text or images so that clicking them jumps you elsewhere in the document or to another document or file. These clickable "hot spots" are called hypertext links. HTML tags are used to create these links by specifying a page to jump to or a graphic, sound, video, or animation to display or play.
- Standard application programs such as word processors now include the tools you need to format HTML documents by applying HTML styles to various elements.
- Special Web site development tools make it easier to create and manage large sites. They let you lay out pages and organize the site.
- Filters in many application programs allow you to save a document in various formats or open documents created in another format. This lets you exchange files among programs.
- Acrobat is a program that allows you to create visually rich documents in a portable document format that can be viewed and printed on Apple as well as IBM PC and other types of computers.

Review Questions

True/False

1. T F To start a new paragraph in a document you have to press the Enter key.
2. T F You can delete characters or words with the Backspace and Delete keys.
3. T F Some word processing programs highlight words that aren't in their dictionary when you press Spacebar to end the word.
4. T F All of the words that are highlighted during a spell check are spelled incorrectly and must be changed.
5. T F When you merge-print a document, data from a data source such as a database is inserted in the document at places indicated with merge codes.
6. T F Styles are saved formats that you can apply to other elements in a document just by selecting their names from a menu.
7. T F If you apply styles to a number of elements in a document, and then change the definition of the style, all elements with that style change automatically.
8. T F Word processing and desktop publishing programs will automatically generate a table of contents for a document that lists both the heads and the numbers of the pages on which they fall.
9. T F In a document formatted with newspaper-style columns, text wraps from the bottom of one column to the top of the next.
10. T F Documents to be placed on the Web where they can be viewed with a browser are formatted using the hypertext markup language.
11. T F A thesaurus looks up synonyms and antonyms.
12. T F The Find command is used to automatically replace all occurrences in a document of a specified word with a substitute word.
13. T F Outline view is used to see just the headings in a document so you can see its overall structure.
14. T F Merge-printing is used to generate multiple copies of the same document with each copy having personalized information.
15. T F Templates are used to create different types of document formats.
16. T F To precisely format documents you use a page layout or desktop publishing program.

Fill-In the Blank

1. As you enter text into a document, when a word automatically moves to the beginning of the next line, it is called ______
2. There are four ways to obtain images for use in documents: ______, ______, ______ or ______
3. Spelling checkers compare all words in a document with the words in the program's ______
4. Programs that have an ______ feature highlight words that aren't in the dictionary as you type them.
5. The ______ command allows you to switch between normal view and a view where you see just the document's headings.
6. Merge-printing takes the data from a ______ and inserts it into a ______ where specified by ______

Multiple Choice

1. To look up a synonym, you use a ______.
   - **a.** Spelling checker
   - **b.** Grammar checker
   - **c.** Thesaurus
   - **d.** Any of the above
2. Merge-printing requires ______.
   - **a.** A source document
   - **b.** A main document
   - **c.** Merge codes
   - **d.** All of the above
3. ______ guide you through detailed procedures step by step.
   - **a.** Macros
   - **b.** Styles
   - **c.** Wizards
   - **d.** Templates
4. To print text at the bottom of every page, you use ______.
   - **a.** Footnotes
   - **b.** Endnotes
   - **c.** Footers
   - **d.** Headers
5. A template can save ______.
   - **a.** Styles
   - **b.** Macros
   - **c.** Page layouts
   - **d.** All of the above
6. Acrobat is a program that allows you to ______.
   - **a.** Create documents that can be displayed on any system
   - **b.** Make documents more colorful
   - **c.** Create visually rich documents
   - **d.** Format documents more precisely
7. Outline view lets you ______.
   - **a.** Display all of the document
   - **b.** Display just headings
   - **c.** Expand and collapse levels of headings
   - **d.** All of the above
8. When you format a document, you ______.
   - **a.** Edit its content
   - **b.** Add new material
   - **c.** Change its appearance
   - **d.** None of the above

Research projects

1. Now that your system has been completed, it's time to select some applications software. Using computer magazines or the Web, do the following:
   - **a.** Find out what are the latest versions of Microsoft Word and Corel Wordperfect. Are there any features you like that one has and the other doesn't?
   - **b.** Locate programs that allow you to create and edit pages to be published on the Web. Do you find any features that sound attractive?

CHAPTER

8 SPREADSHEET & DATABASE

AN OVERVIEW

Spreadsheets and database management applications are the primary tools of analysis. Each is unique in its own way.

Spreadsheets were the first "killer" applications that made personal computers almost indispensable in business. When VisiCalc was introduced for the Apple in the late 1970s, and later, when 1-2-3 was released for the IBM PC, each created a sensation. For the first time, complex calculation and analysis were easy to perform. Spreadsheets are still among the most popular programs and it isn't their mere ability to calculate numbers that is the reason for this. It is how they make it easy to explore a range of possible outcomes. Changing one number on a spreadsheet can cause other changes to ripple throughout. For example, on a spreadsheet mortgage calculator, changing the principle or term of the loan immediately displays a new monthly payment.

If spreadsheets are the tools for analysis, database management applications are the tools for data storage and retrieval. These programs allow you to store massive amounts of data in a highly organized fashion and make it easy for you to zero in on just the specific data that you need. That is, database management applications store large collections of data that can be viewed in ways that turn the data into useful information. For example, you can store details about every sale your business makes. Later, you can count the number of hammers you sold last month, or look up the names of the people who bought them. Increasingly, corporations are finding great and new value in the databases they have built in the normal course of business. An entire new industry is growing up around the prospect that all these old records can be mined for useful information. It's like panning for gold at Sutter's Mill—a second time. The gold rush of 1849 brought out all the gold that could be profitably retrieved at the time, but today new technologies may find a lot more. Using the new information technologies, managers can find relationships in data that were never before obvious.

In this chapter we look at some of the features and applications of these tools.

OBJECTIVES

After completing this chapter, you will be able to:

- Compare and contrast spreadsheets and databases.
- Explain the value of using charts, graphs, and maps to display data.
- Describe the basic procedures you use to work with spreadsheets and databases.
- Identify some applications of spreadsheets and databases.
- Explain the value of Internet connectivity.

Spreadsheet *n.* 1. application program into which you enter labels, numbers, or formulas, basic elements that can be combined to solve almost any kind of numeric problem.

Database *n.* 1. large amounts of data stored in a highly structured way so it can be easily accessed using questions called queries.

Database management application *n.* 1. application used to create, manage, and query a database.

ON THE PACE CD ROM

Spread No.	Title
8-1	The Spreadsheet—What It Is
8-1	The Spreadsheet Screen Display
8-1	Spreadsheet Models
8-2	The Spreadsheet—How It Works
8-2	Entering and Formatting Data
8-3	Chart Types
8-3	Graphs as Analysis Tools
8-6	Forms
8-6	Reports
8-7	Exploring Queries
8-7	Simple Queries
8-7	Complex Queries
8-8	Spreadsheets—Online
8-8	Databases—Online

APPLICATIONS

8.1 Spreadsheet Applications: Introduction

Spreadsheet programs have taken the drudgery out of working with numbers. They not only allow you to quickly calculate and analyze numbers, they also let you quickly explore a variety of possible outcomes.

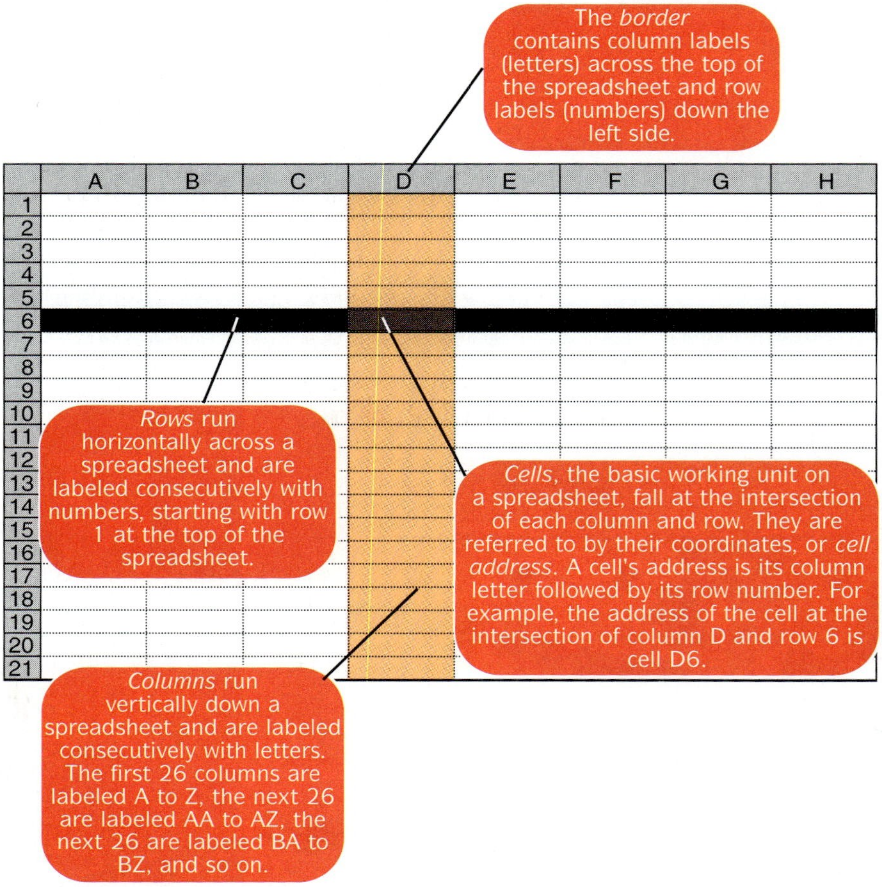

The spreadsheet

The spreadsheet screen display

All spreadsheets (sometimes called worksheets) have a similar look. Basically a spreadsheet is the arrangement of rows and columns that appears on the screen when you first load the program. Shown here are some of the elements you can expect to see.

The spreadsheet window

The display screen is just a small window on a large spreadsheet, but you can scroll around the underlying spreadsheet with the scroll bars or keyboard keys. This is much like using a small magnifying glass to examine a large newspaper, section by section. This display window is tiny compared to the underlying spreadsheet. For example, Excel and 1-2-3 have over 4-million cells. If printed so each cell was 1 inch wide and / inch tall, the spreadsheet would cover an area 21 feet wide by 341 feet long.

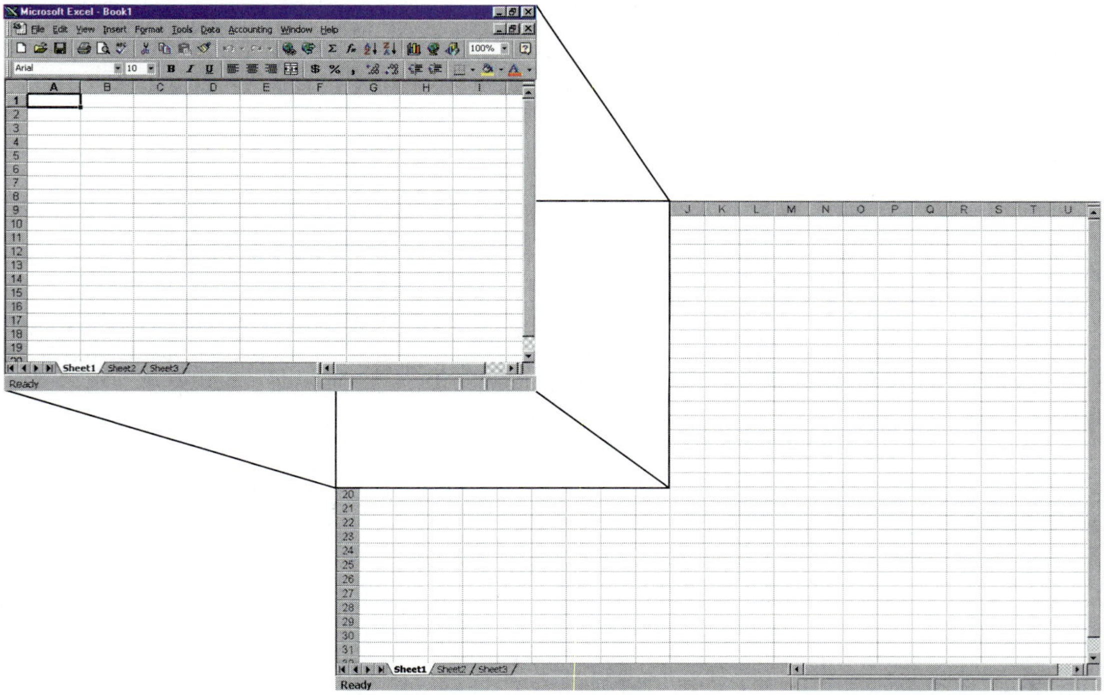

The spreadsheet on your screen is a window to the larger spreadsheet

Spreadsheet models

A spreadsheet is useful when you're working with numbers or when you want to display numeric data graphically. In business, spreadsheets are used to analyze or project the performance of products, salespeople, or dealers. Spreadsheets compare costs, prices, and gross margins of individual products in a product line. They also analyze sales, calculate prices, forecast budgets, and make cash-flow projections. To analyze data or make predictions or projections with a spreadsheet, you create a model of the situation by entering numbers to be calculated, formulas to do the calculations, and labels that identify the elements used in the model. You use models to simulate real-world situations. Just as a plastic scale-model of an airplane represents, or simulates, a real plane that might be built, a spreadsheet model simulates a financial or other numeric situation, of your own or an entire industry's.

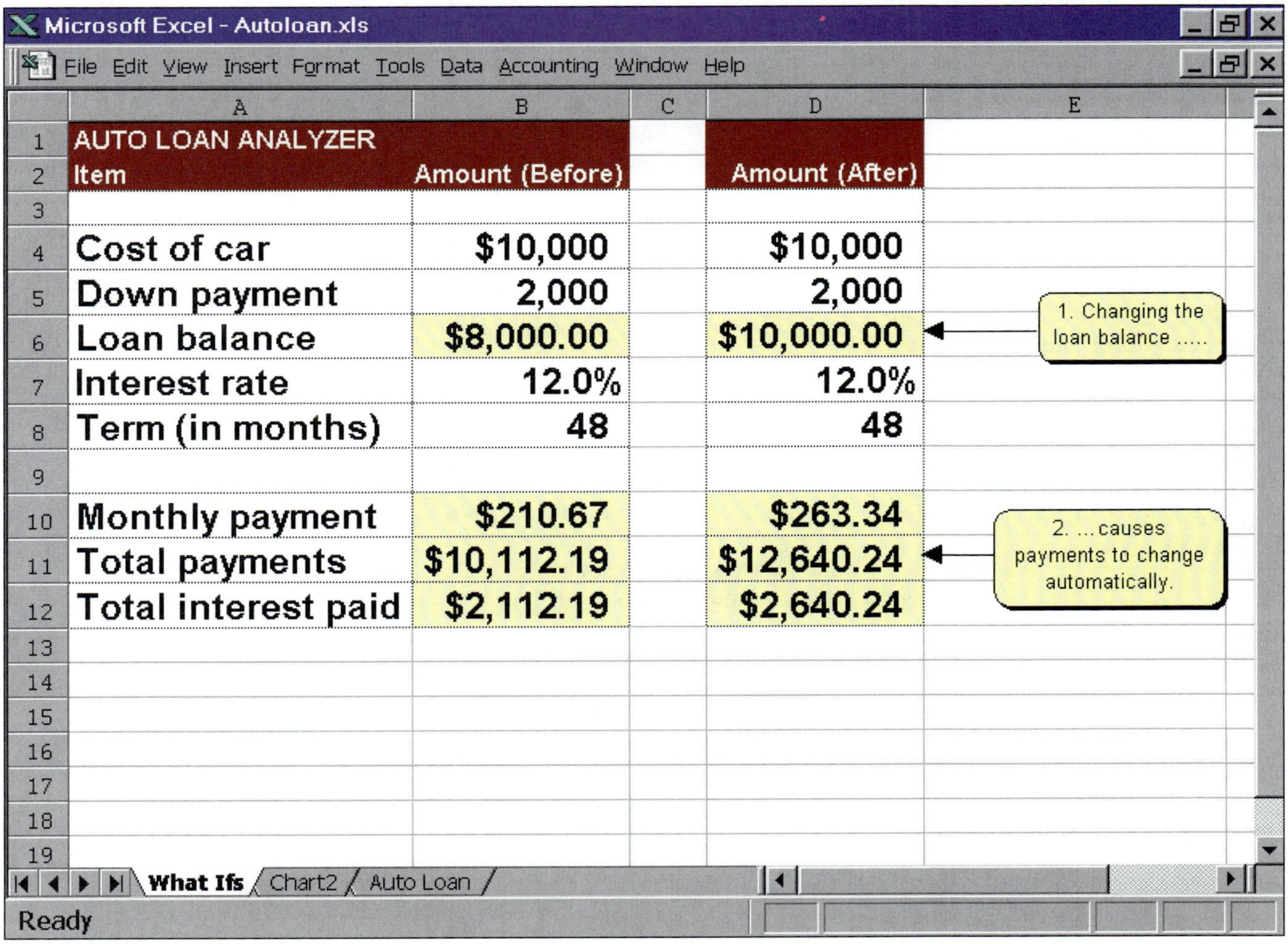

A spreadsheet model

Spreadsheets are much more structured than word processing applications. For example, on a word processing application you can enter any data anywhere on the page. With a spreadsheet program, you can enter data only into cells. The data aren't always typed in, but rather are copied from the organization's mainframe or network server to a user's desktop computer (called downloading). This saves time and eliminates the possibility of introducing errors.

Entering data

To enter data of any kind into a spreadsheet, you click one of the cells or use the keyboard keys to select a cell. The selected cell is then the active cell—the only one into which you can type data. For some procedures such as formatting, or cutting and pasting, you can extend the selection to highlight and select a block of cells. There are only certain things you can enter into the active cell: labels, numbers, formulas, functions (a type of formula), and formats.

Formulas, cell references, and what-ifs

Spreadsheets wouldn't be among the top-selling programs if it weren't for their ability to explore what ifs—called sensitivity analysis. For example, when doing a home loan analysis, you can change the amount borrowed, the interest rate, or the period of the loan to see how changes in these three variables affect your monthly payment.

Spreadsheets allow you to explore what-ifs because of the way formulas and functions can refer to other cells. The formulas contain cell references—the addresses of the cells where the numbers to be calculated are entered. The formula calculates any numbers in the cells that it refers to just as if those numbers were in the formula. In the example shown at the top on the right, original sales are in cell B1 and costs in cell B2. The formula in cell B3 is =B1 minus B2. It subtracts the 90 in cell B2 from the 100 in cell B1. If you now change the number in B1 (sales) or B2 (costs), the formula will calculate a new profit. This immediate recalculation gives you the ability to easily change numbers and see how the change affects the outcome.

	A	B
1	Sales	$100
2	Costs	90
3	Profits	$10

Original

	A	B
1	Sales	$110
2	Costs	90
3	Profits	$20

Sales changed

	A	B
1	Sales	$100
2	Costs	95
3	Profits	$5

Costs changed

Formulas

	A	B
1	Monthly Payment	
2	Calculator	
3	Cost of car	$ 20,000
4	Down payment	$ 2,000
5		
6	Loan required	$ 18,000
7	Interest rate	12%
8	Term (in months)	48
9		
10	Monthly payment	$474.01

Labels (green cells on the illustration) identify the model and its parts.

Numbers (blue cells on the illustration) are calculated by formulas entered into other cells.

Formulas (yellow cells on the illustration) perform calculations such as addition, subtraction, multiplication, and division.

Functions (red cells on the illustration) are like complicated formulas that have been prepackaged for you.

Cell entries

Formats

Formats (all cells containing data in the illustration to the right) control the way numbers are displayed on the screen and the way labels are aligned in their cells. These are used to make screen displays and printed reports more readable and attractive. One thing to be aware of is that the same number can be displayed in a variety of ways, just by changing its format. In the illustration shown here, all of the numbers are the same, 0.100099 rounded off only for display purposes.

	A	B
1	Numbers	Labels
2	0.100099	Left
3	0.10010	Center
4	0.1001	Right
5	0.100	Color
6	0.10	Color Background
7	10%	
8	$ 0.10	

Cell formats

Functions

Many formulas are complex or time consuming to enter. In these cases functions have been built into the program to perform many of these calculations for you. Functions calculate such things as monthly payments on a loan, averages, totals, and standard deviations. The organization of a function is called its syntax. The values on which a function performs operations are called its arguments and these can be numbers and cell references. Parentheses tell the program where arguments begin and end. In the display in the illustration labeled "Functions" to the right, there is a section that lists sales by region (green cells). There is then a section of functions that analyze the sales (orange cells). Each of the functions begins with an equal sign followed by a name that describes its function. All of the functions have the same argument; that is, they apply to the range of cells between B2 and B6.

	A	B	
1	Region	Sales	
2	Eastern	10,000	
3	Western	5,000	
4	Central	12,000	
5	Southern	7,000	
6	New England	5,000	
7	Sum	39,000	=SUM(B2:B6)
8	Average	7,800	=AVERAGE(B2:B6)
9	Minimum	5,000	=MIN(B2:B6)
10	Maximum	12,000	=MAX(B2:B6)
11	Standard deviation	3,114.48	=STDEV(B2:B6)

Functions

Templates

It's rare that a person completely understands both a spreadsheet and the nature of a problem to be solved. When persons have masteries of each area, they can develop models that can then be used by other people. For example, they could create an expense form or a price quote. To do so, they first build and test a model using real numbers. Then they delete all of the numbers and distribute the model as a template which is designed to be used over and over again. Because the template still retains all the labels, formulas, and functions, anyone with minimal experience can enter new numbers and the formulas calculate an answer. Templates are so helpful that many application publishers design a variety of them and include them with their programs. Below is a template for an invoice that comes with Microsoft Excel.

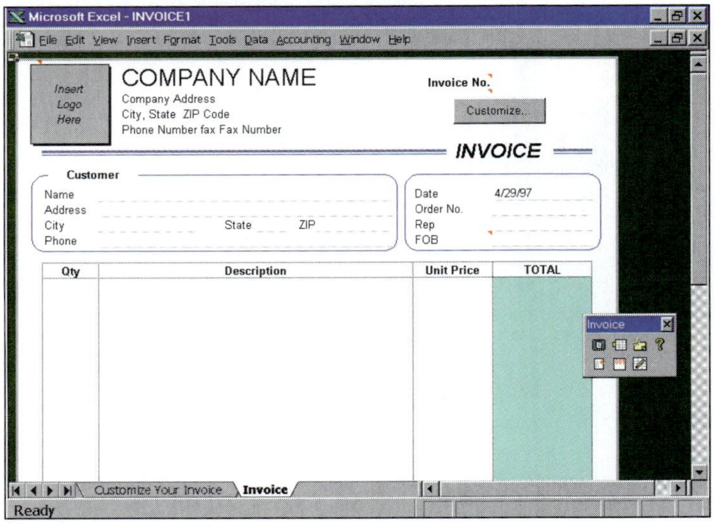

Templates

8.3 Spreadsheet Applications:

Using the graphics capabilities built into a spreadsheet, you can create charts and graphs to analyze numeric data. For example, you can use graphs to find trends and relationships between sets of numbers such as sales, expenses, and profits over a period of time. Once you've created graphs you can use them to explore what-ifs, print them for distribution to others, or incorporate them into your documents and presentations.

Charts as analysis tools

Graphs are powerful analytical tools. Because the chart is linked to the data on the worksheet, it changes when the data changes. This allows you to see graphically how changes affect a problem. Graphs can show trends and relationships between series of numbers that would otherwise be missed. A spreadsheet might show you that sales, costs, and profits are all rising but still, it's hard to tell the relationships among the numbers. The relative rates of change are much more obvious on a graph. Here you can quickly see that although profits are rising, they aren't rising as a percentage of sales.

Chart types

Graphs are important tools in business because managers and analysts often need to find or illustrate patterns in sets of numbers. Choosing the right type of graph for your data is one of the most important decisions you'll have to make. Excel has fifteen basic chart types and many subtypes. The choice you make depends on the kind of data you're plotting. Normally you will be charting one of two types of data: discrete or continuous.

Discrete data are a series of values, such as sales or profits, measured at selected intervals. Only the measured points are meaningful. If sales are $100 million in 1998 and $144 million in 2000, you can't use the chart to estimate that 1999 sales were $122 million. Charts of this kind are frequently called time-series charts and are used in business to plot daily, weekly, quarterly, or annual sales, profits, or inventory. The best chart types to use for discrete data are bar and column charts. See below.

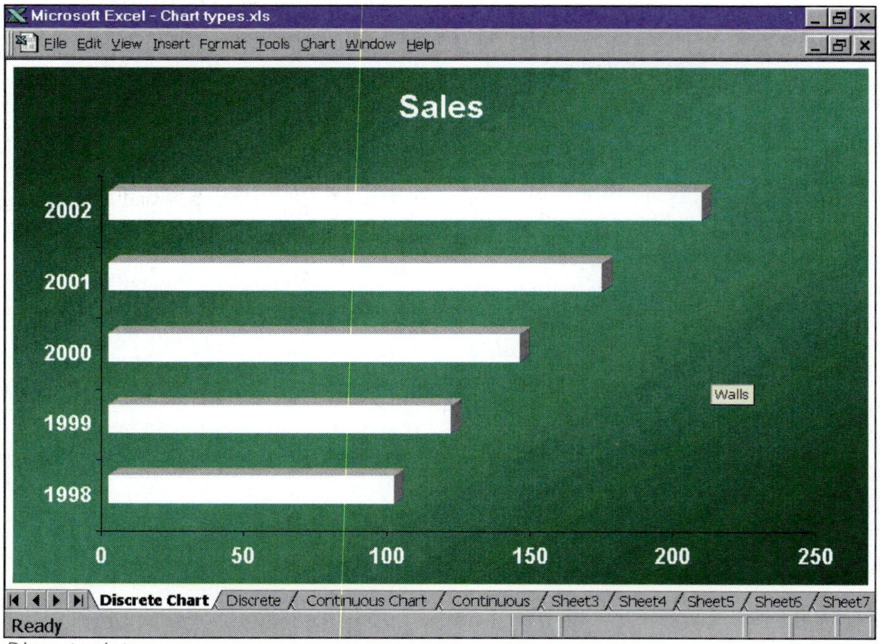

Discrete data

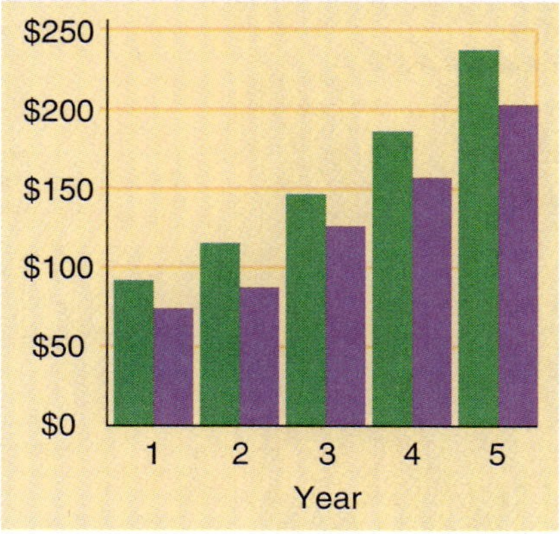

	A	B	C	D	E	F
1	Item	Year 1	Year 2	Year 3	Year 4	Year 5
2	Sales	$ 100	$ 125	$ 156	$ 195	$ 244
3	Costs	80	100	130	165	213
4	Profits	$ 20	$ 25	$ 26	$ 30	$ 31

Worksheet and chart

Continuous data are also series of measurements at specified intervals but the measurements at key points indicate an uninterrupted trend. Although each data point is a discrete value, values between the measured data points can be estimated from the chart through interpolation. Imagine a balloon rising through the atmosphere taking a temperature reading every 1000 feet. If the temperature charted was 17 degrees at 10,000 feet and 8 degrees at 20,000, you could estimate from the chart that it was 12 degrees at 15,000 feet. The best chart types to use for this kind of data include line and area charts.

Here are just some of the graph types available on the Microsoft Excel spreadsheet program. The best ones for charting discrete data are bar, column, and line charts. The best for continuous data are area and line charts.

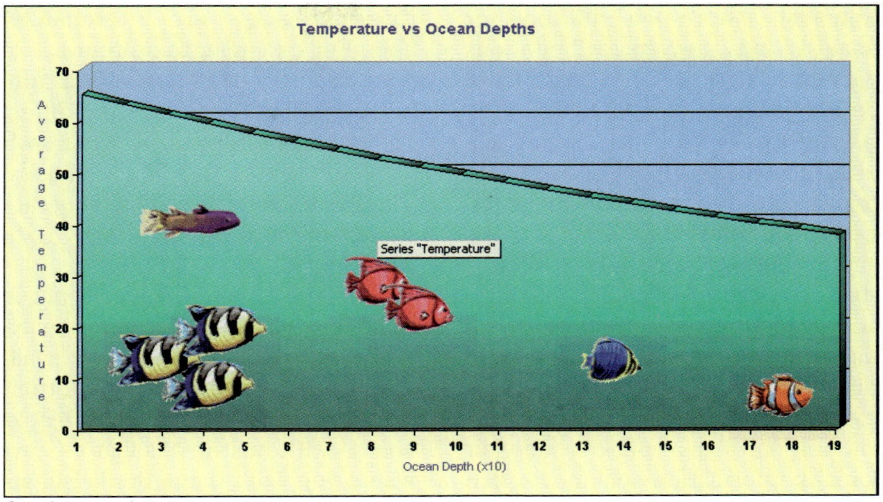

Continuous data

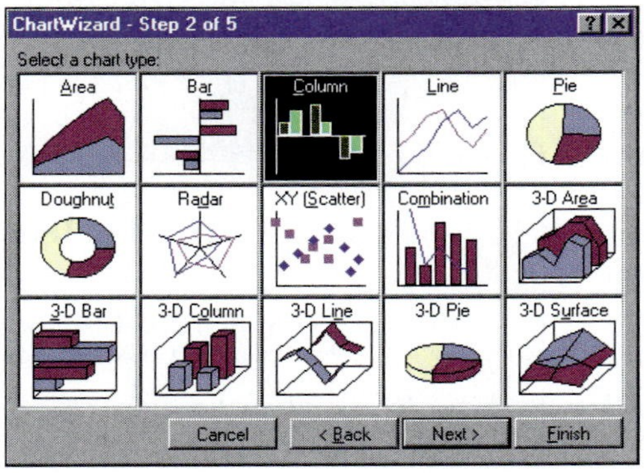

Excel chart types

Maps

Maps can be linked to data to illustrate situations or reveal relationships. Location is often an important part of the decision-making process. For example, an insurance company could analyze its exposure to flood damage claims by listing all policy holders living within a specified flood plain. A story illustrates this particularly well. In 1856, John Snow, a doctor in London, plotted on a map all the cases of cholera he could find. The map clearly showed they were all clustered around a single public well. Once the relationship between contaminated well water and cholera was seen on the map, the epidemic was quickly stopped by removing the pump handle.

Computer programs that make such analysis possible on a large scale are called Geographical Information Systems (GIS). Small-scale versions of this technology are available in spreadsheet programs.

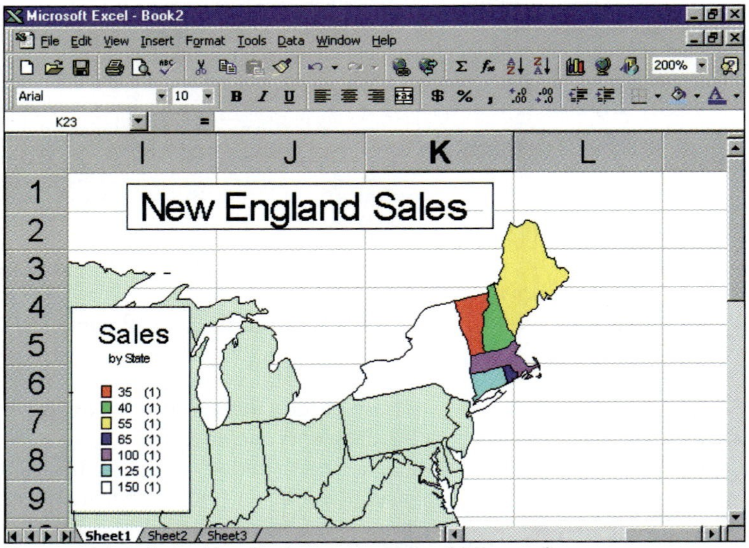

Geographic Information Systems courtesy of Microsoft

For example, Excel allows you to link data to a map and then use colors or shadings to indicate ranges of values. The procedures you use to create the map are much like those you use to create a chart.

8.4 Database Applications:

Spreadsheets are powerful tools for analysis but they have limitations when dealing with large amounts of data. For these kinds of tasks, database management applications are used. The management of databases is one of the most important applications of computers. A database is simply one or more tables of data that are organized and stored in a very structured way. Databases are used in an amazing number of places. When you order something by mail or phone, place airline reservations, enroll in a college course, or look up information on a movie on a CD disc, you are interacting with a database.

What are databases?

In one respect, databases are nothing but collections of plain old facts: facts about stocks and facts about flights, facts about employees and facts about customers. But, when enough facts are gathered together they become very valuable and even fascinating. *Scientific American* has described databases as "the foundries of the information revolution." They have become so important to the functioning of a business that they are one of its major assets. Imagine L.L. Bean or any other mail order company without their databases of millions of customers, or American Airlines without its database of flight information and seat assignments. Computers allow you to store and manipulate this powerful data and computers allow you to gather it in the first place.

Databases versus spreadsheets

Many people find it difficult to understand the difference between spreadsheets and databases. This is understandable because both store data in tables, that is, in rows and columns. For some simple tasks, there isn't much difference and these programs are interchangeable. For example, to store a list of your record collection, either tool might suffice. However, their differences become apparent when you want to tackle other kinds of jobs. There are two criteria that separate them: analytic ability and data capacity.

A spreadsheet has many built-in functions that you can use for analysis. If the right function isn't available, you can create your own formulas. Spreadsheets are like blackboards with built-in calculators anywhere you want them. Spreadsheets provide charts or graphs of your data so you can see relationships graphically. They are ideal tools for analyzing sales, profits, loans, and performance. If you worked on Wall Street, you might use a spreadsheet to analyze a company's stock to see how it had performed over the past decade.

A database is more like a data warehouse. Its primary function is to handle enormous amounts of data, such as details on every stock listed on the New York Stock Exchange. Imagine hundreds of companies, each with its stock price changing minute by minute as mil-

Database courtesy of American Airlines

Terminology Problems

As in so many other areas of the fast-moving computer field, there are certain inconsistencies in vocabulary and spelling use.

When reading about databases, you will often find the term spelled as database or data base. There is no difference between the two terms; the spelling just hasn't been standardized.

Until recently, it was considered grammatically correct to use datum when referring to a singular and data when referring to a plural. For example, you would say, "I have a single datum, but many data." Now it is becoming acceptable to use data in both situations. For example, here is the headline for an advertisement from Hewlett-Packard. "It's amazing what data can do if you arrange it properly."

lions of people buy and sell shares simultaneously. There isn't a spreadsheet anywhere in the world that could store this vast amount of fluctuating data.

Beyond a database application's impressive storage capacity are the tools databases give you to search for data. You can ask and get answers to simple or extremely complex questions called queries. You might ask a database to list only those stocks that have fallen more than 10 percent last year, have a price more than 20 times earnings, and company sales of over $1 billion. Instantly you'll have a list of the stocks that match all those criteria.

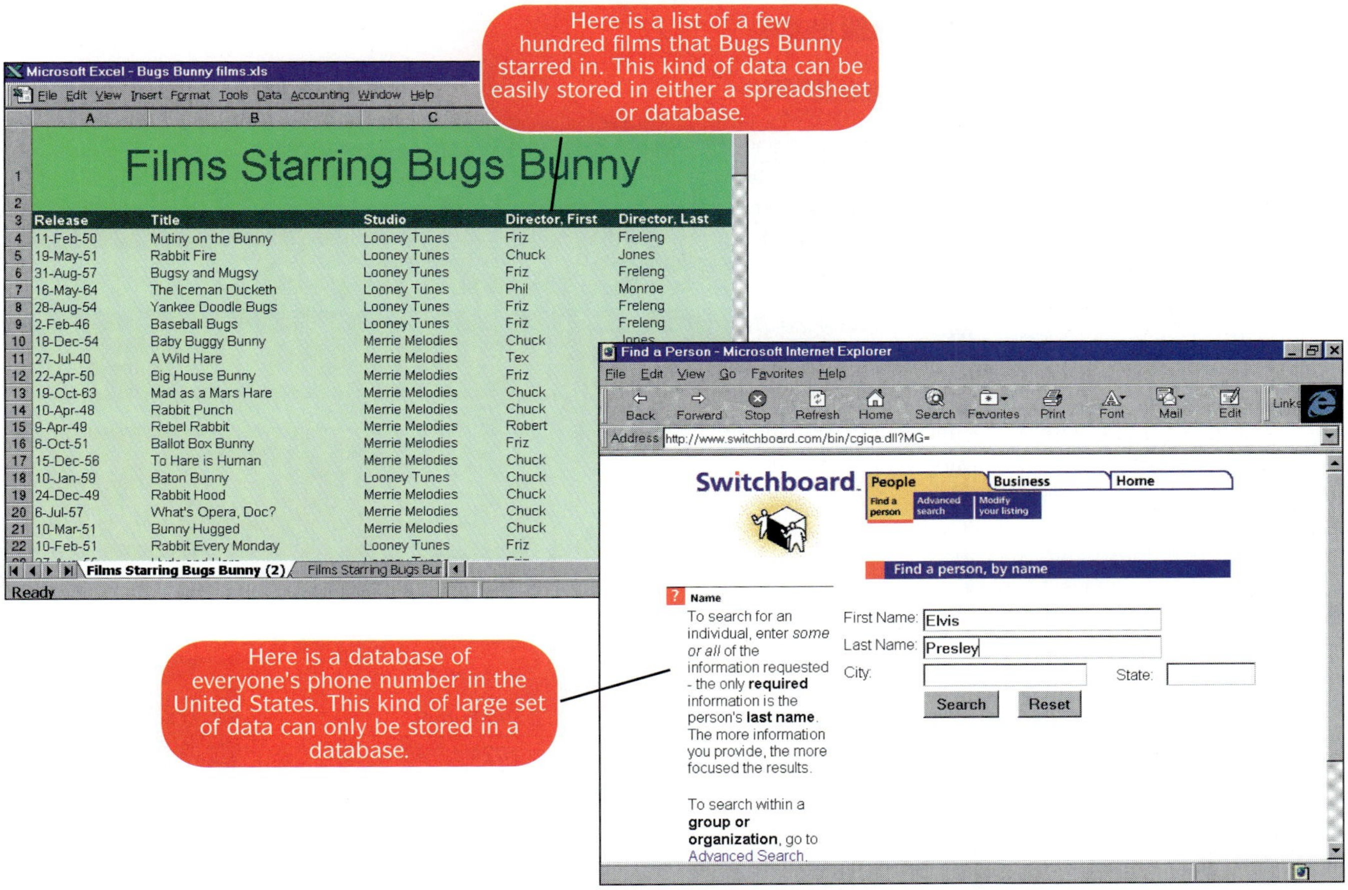

Spreadsheets vs. databases courtesy of Switchboard

HOW BIG CAN THEY GET?

It's common to use the analogy of set of index cards when explaining a database. But that diminishes the scale of information being stored. Many large companies such as UPS and Wal-Mart have enormous databases over the 1 terabyte limit. This is one thousand billion bytes of data. It staggers the imagination. Wal-Mart's was over 4terabytes in 1995. One company in the field estimates that you would have to cut down 42,000 trees to make the paper used to print a terabyte of data.

In databases this big, access must be limited and queries must be prioritized so the process doesn't slow down too much to be usable.

8.5 Database Applications:

The data in database tables is not stored randomly; it's stored in a highly organized way so that the program can find it later. To work with databases, you have to understand a few principles about how data is stored.

Database organization

In a database, data is stored in a very structured way using tables. As you type data you are entering fields. A set of fields related to the same item is a record.

Creating databases

To use a database, you must first create the tables that it contains. Many of us build small databases but really critical ones are designed by experts and we only work with their end product. The first step in creating a database table is to describe each field by specifying its name, length, and the type of data to be stored. During the design phase, you have to consider what questions you'll want the database to answer. You then use this information to plan the fields in each table. Each record contains information about a subject, for example, a customer. To describe the subject, say, a specific customer, you must decide what facts describe her or him and differentiate her or him from all other subjects. These facts are called attributes and are used as the database's fields. Attributes for a customer could be the customer's ID, last name, first name, street address, city, ZIP code, area code, and phone number. The attributes you select determine what fields each record in the database will contain.

1. As you enter data, you type it in from the keyboard. The first level of organization is the numbers and letters you type.

2. Combinations of characters create data that is stored in *fields*. A field is a piece of the information about a person or item. For example, fields can be used to store a person's name, an address, a phone number, or a price. Fields can be numbers (101), names (June), names and numbers (100 Elm Street), or formulas (100*3).

3. Related fields are stored together as *records*. A record is like an index card: it contains all the information about a product, person, or other item. For example, it might contain a person's ID, last name, first name, street, city, state, ZIP code, area code, and phone number.

4. Related records are stored together as *tables*, for example, a list of customers.

5. Related tables are stored together as a *database*. Since the tables can be combined any time you want to there is no need to store duplicate data.

1

ID
1

2

ID
1001

3

ID	Last Name	First Name	Street	City	Phone
1001	Jones	Frank	100 Elm	Oakland	555-1789

4

ID	Last Name	First Name	Street	City	Phone
1001	Jones	Frank	100 Elm	Oakland	555-1789
1002	Smith	Susan	200 Main	Sarasota	555-1902
1003	Ashley	Bill	100 Woods	San Jose	555-0232

5

ID	Last Name	First Name	Street	City	Phone
1001	Jones	Frank	100 Elm	Oakland	555-1789
1002	Smith	Susan	200 Main	Sarasota	555-1902
1003	Ashley	Bill	100 Woods	San Jose	555-0232

ID	Date	Amount
1001	1/10/99	10.00
1002	1/11/99	15.00
1003	1/12/99	20.00

Record 2

Microprocessor	Pentium II
Screen resolution	1024 x 768
Hard disk capacity	2 gigabytes
RAM	16 megabytes
CD-ROM drive	Yes

Record 1

Microprocessor	
Screen resolution	
Hard disk capacity	
RAM	
CD-ROM drive	

Attributes

Relational databases

The expressions database and database management program are often used very loosely. In fact, there are two types of programs used to manage tables of highly structured data: record management programs and database management programs.

Both spreadsheets and word processing programs have simple database functions. They can each be used to create lists and then these lists can be sorted. However, these programs limit your data to a single table and are referred to as record management, file management, or flat-file database programs. Using single tables has its limitations. You have to store the data for different applications in separate tables but the tables can't be combined. To change an item that appears in both tables, you must change it separately in each table. Let's say you wanted to store customer purchases. To do so, you'd have to use only one file and if the same customer made more than one purchase as Susan Smith did below, you'd have to duplicate a lot of data each time.

As the amount of data being processed increases, the record management method of using separate files to store data becomes cumbersome because a lot of the data must be duplicated. An employee's name might appear in several different tables, for example, payrolls, vacation, time records, and expense accounts. There are some serious disadvantages to this duplication:

- ♦ It increases the amount of data entry.
- ♦ It increases the risk of errors in the information.
- ♦ It requires more storage space.

Using a relational database eliminates these problems related to duplication. Each piece of information need be stored only once in a database, because the database management application can combine the data stored in two or more tables. This is a major advantage since many applications require more than one table. For example, an accounting system requires separate tables for the general ledger, accounts receivable, and accounts payable.

To combine, or "relate" tables, each table should have a key field containing attributes that uniquely identify each record. There are many kinds of attributes that can be used in key fields. If you open your wallet, you'll probably find a lot of them: Social Security number, driver's license number, charge card number. Such keys allow the database to bring the same data to bear on different tasks or accounts.

ID	Last Name	First Name	Street	City	Phone	Date	Amount
1001	Jones	Frank	100 Elm	Oakland	555-1789	1/10/99	10.00
1002	Smith	Susan	200 Main	Sarasota	555-1902	1/11/99	15.00
1003	Smith	Susan	201 Main	Sarasota	555-1903	1/12/99	20.00
1004	Ashley	Bill	100 Woods	San Jose	555-0232		

Record management

The original tables can be linked on a common field

ID	Last Name	First Name	Street	City	Phone
1001	Jones	Frank	100 Elm	Oakland	555-1789
1002	Smith	Susan	200 Main	Sarasota	555-1902
1003	Ashley	Bill	100 Woods	San Jose	555-0232

ID	Date	Amount
1001	1/10/99	10.00
1002	1/11/99	15.00
1002	1/12/99	20.00

ID	Last Name	First Name	Street	City	Phone	ID	Date	Amount
1001	Jones	Frank	100 Elm	Oakland	555-1789	1001	1/10/99	10.00
1002	Smith	Susan	200 Main	Sarasota	555-1902	1002	1/11/99	15.00
1003	Smith	Susan	201 Main	Sarasota	555-1903	1002	1/12/99	20.00

A new table can then be created that contains any or all fields from the related tables.

Relational database

Over time, more and more data is added to the database, and it can be used over and over again for different applications. We might use the same database to locate or update various information, to analyze projects and plans, or to merge-print form letters or other documents.

Forms

Database tables are not very interesting to look at all day, looking as they do much like a spreadsheet. To make a database more user-friendly, forms are created and displayed on the screen. People then type data into these various forms and it is automatically entered into the database. Once the data has been entered, the form can also be used to view, edit, or delete it.

More than one form is created for the same database, giving users different views of the data. A payroll accountant looking at a payroll database might see the salaries of every employee while a tax accountant might see just the withholding information.

Entering data-validity checks

Databases are frequently designed by experts but used by anyone who knows how to type. All a user has to do is enter data into a form on the screen. No one expects users to understand the complexities of the database. To reduce the number of errors entered into the database, the designers can specify certain rules for what can be entered into each field. For example, you can be prevented from typing text into a price field or typing too few characters in a ZIP code field. These are called validity checks because the database checks that the data are valid before accepting them.

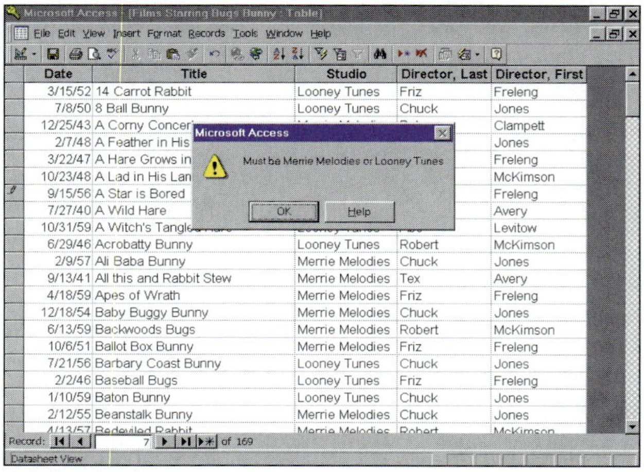

Validity check

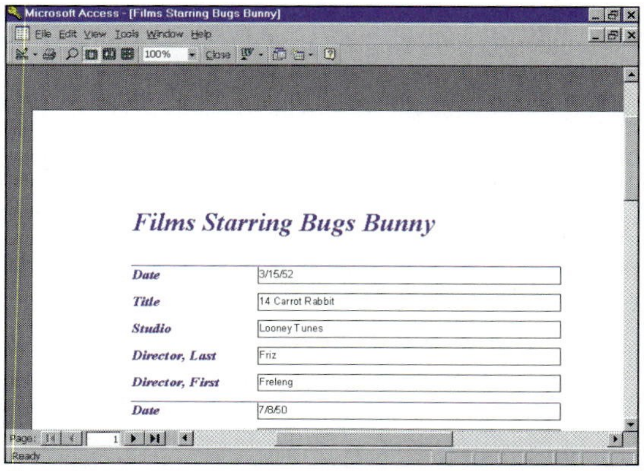

Report

Form courtesy of Microsoft
http://www.microsoft.com/msaccess/internet/JobForum/A_V_Cust.htm

Printing reports

Databases contain vast amounts of information, more than most individuals need, especially in large organizations. Most people don't actually use a database itself. Generally, they look through reports containing just the information they are interested in. Many such reports can be created from the same database. Using the same database of employees, you might create a report that references just names and addresses or a report showing salaries and benefits. Above is a typical report containing selected, relevant data from each record on a famous rabbit.

Exporting to a spreadsheet

Databases are great for storing data but not as powerful as spreadsheets when it comes to analyzing it, so data from the database is frequently exported to a spreadsheet, in most cases just the set of records appropriate to the problem being looked at. For example, in a sales database, you might download to a spreadsheet January's sales in California to see how they compare to last year's or another state's sales.

Exporting to a word processor

It's common to use a query to isolate appropriate database information and then export that data or link it, usually in the form of a table, to a document you're creating on a word processor. It's even more common to use the database in conjunction with a word processing program to mail-merge documents. The word processing program is used to create the form letter or other document containing merge codes that refer to fields in the database from which the data are retrieved when the document is merge-printed.

Media databases

Databases have been developed that store not just text but also sounds, images, movie clips, and animations. Such applications allow you to catalog, categorize, and retrieve media assets, regardless of their format, physical location, or quantity. Cumulus automatically organizes and catalogs your media and graphics files into a browsable on-line library, accessible over your network, the Internet, or removable media. It retrieves files on command, using a visual table of contents.

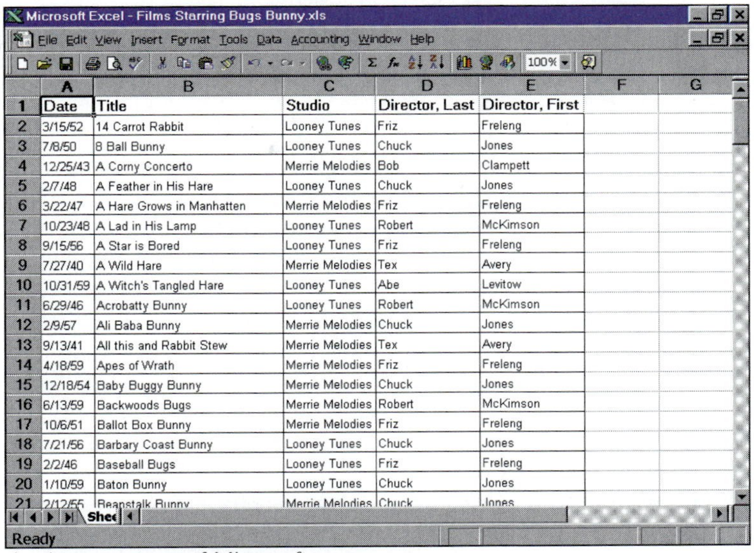

Analyze courtesy of Microsoft

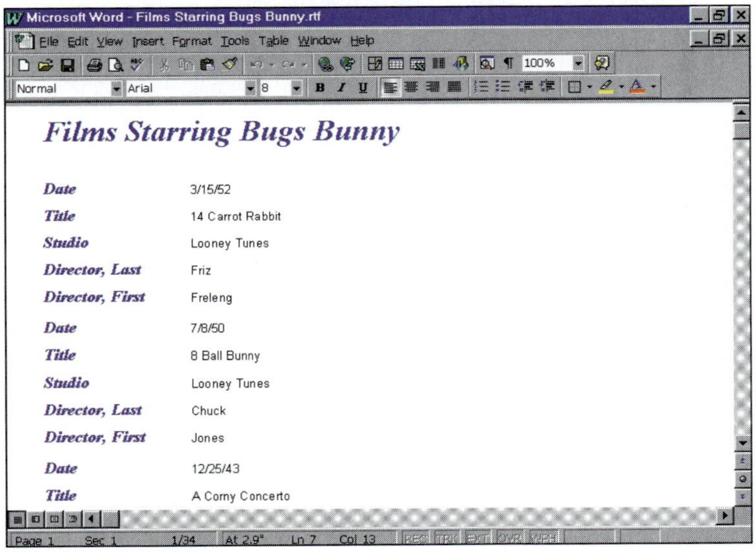

Merge

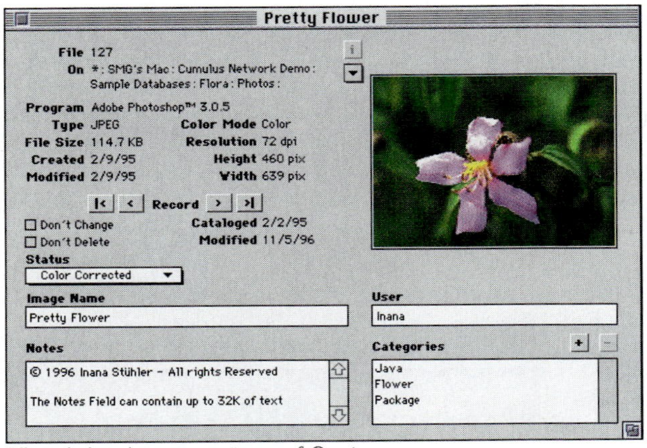

Visual database courtesy of Canto
http://www.canto-software.com

8.7 Queries-The Essence of Computing

To locate information in a database, you ask questions called queries. Querying a database may sound like something strange and exotic, but it's actually an everyday experience for many people, like you. When you sit down at the computerized card catalog in the library, or use a home computer to look up information on the Internet, or look up a customer's account at your job, you are querying a database.

What are queries?

Databases can contain thousands of fields and millions of records. However, we usually are interested in only a part, or subset, of this data. Queries allow us to create a new table that contains only those fields and records in which we are interested. Review again Spread 8.5 on the meaning in databases of fields, records, and tables. For example, if you have two tables, one with customer name and address information, and another with charge account information, you can create a query to extract from them just the information you want. If you want to call late payers, you can create a new table that lists just the name, phone, and date and amount of the charge. This new table, called a dynaset, contains only some of the fields from each table and contains only those records where payment was past due.

You can use queries to update or delete groups of records. The dynaset can be used as the basis for a report. Most reports begin by first using a query to gather just the data you want the report to list.

Creating queries

The ways you create queries vary from program to program, but there are essentially two: a query-by-example form or a query language.

Using a query-by-example (QBE) fill-in form, you first select the fields you want to include and then specify what records are to be listed. You don't want all of the records, just the ones that interest you. To narrow the list, you use criteria that specify a field to look in and a value to look for. The value can be text, numbers, or dates. After specifying the fields to be included and the criteria to be used, the program creates the new table, the dynaset. This new table contains only those records that match the criteria you specified.

Here a query is created. The criterion is the "Jones" in the "Director, Last" field. It specifies that only films by Chuck Jones should be listed.

When the query is executed or run, only those records that match the specified criteria are listed in the dynaset. See below.

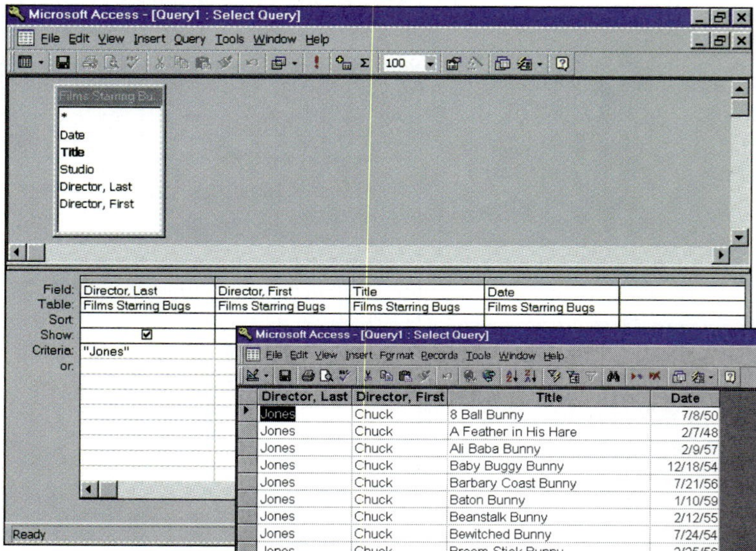

Query by example

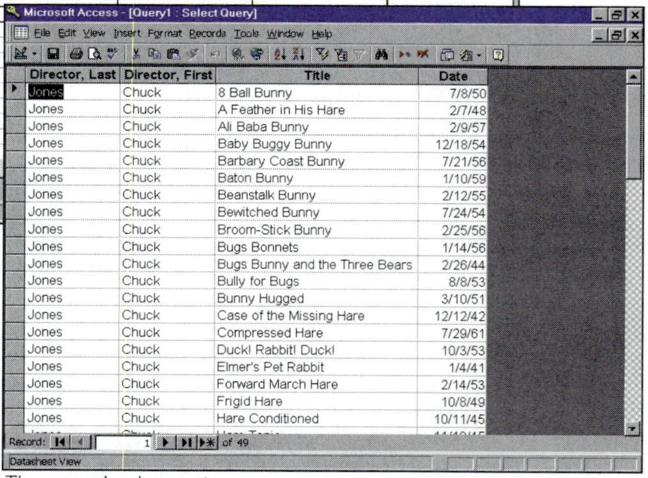

The query's dynaset

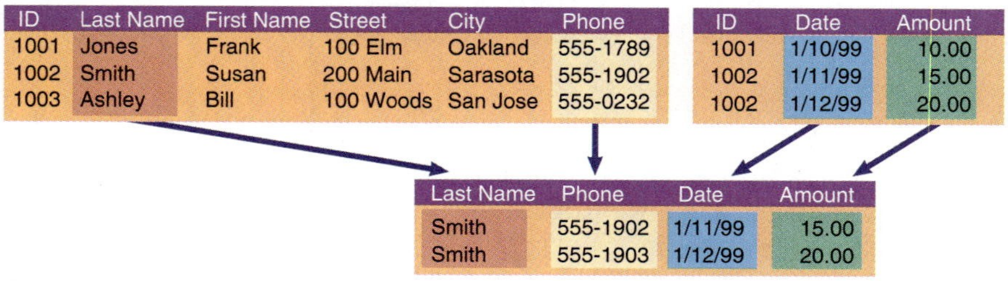

A query

```
SELECT DISTINCTROW
(Customer List).(Last Name),
(Customer Charges).Date,
(Customer Charges).Amount,
(Customer Charges).Phone

FROM
(Customer List) INNER JOIN
(Customer Charges) ON
(Customer List).ID= (Customer
Charges).ID

WHERE(((Customer List).
(Last Name))="Sen"));
```

Structured query language

In addition to query-by-example (QBE) fill-in forms, queries can be written out, much like a programming language. The most popular query language is structured query language (SQL). On the right is the same query we used in the query by example, but written out in SQL. As you can see, this is a very detailed way to specify queries. For that reason, the details are usually hidden from you and you create the query in a more intuitive way, perhaps by filling in a form.

Using relational operators

If you search for a word, number, or phrase, you are actually looking for exact matches. For example, searching for 100 will find only that number. In many situations, that's not enough; you want to see a range of records. You can widen the scope of your search using the relational operators "less than," "greater than," "equal to," and "not equal to." Below, you see a number of original lists each with a different relational operator at work. For each operator, you see its name, the way it's expressed, and the results it generates. For example, the "greater than" operator expressed as >120 lists only those numbers from the original list that are greater than 120.

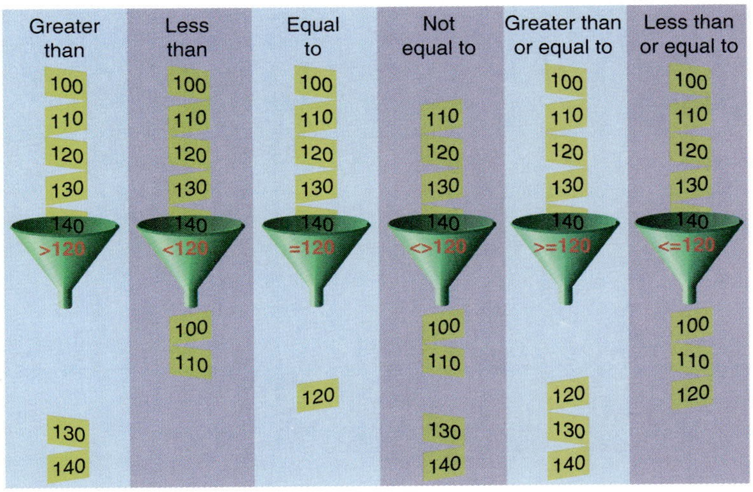

Relational operators

- > (greater than) looks for matches where the field contains data greater than the criterion.
- < (less than) looks for matches where the field contains data less than the criterion.
- = (equal to) looks for matches where the field contains data equal to the criterion.
- <> (not equal to) looks for matches where the field doesn't contain the data in your criterion.

You can also use these operators in combinations. For example, >= (greater than or equal to) or <= (less than or equal to).

Using logical operators

Sometimes, you want to find a record or a group of records that meet more than one criterion. To do so, you use two or more criteria connected by the logical operators AND, OR, and NOT.

- AND operators require that all conditions be met. In the example below, the number must be greater than 120 and less than 140.
- OR operators require that one condition be met. In the example below, the number must be greater than 120 or less than 110.
- NOT operators require that a condition not be met. In this example, there must be less than 120 but not 110.

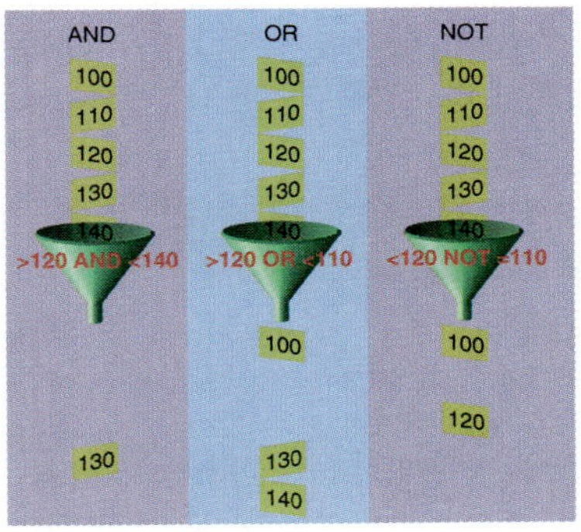

Logical operators

In compound statements, AND and OR statements can be combined. In the following example, there must be a CA OR a MA in the *State field* and *100* in the *Amount field*.

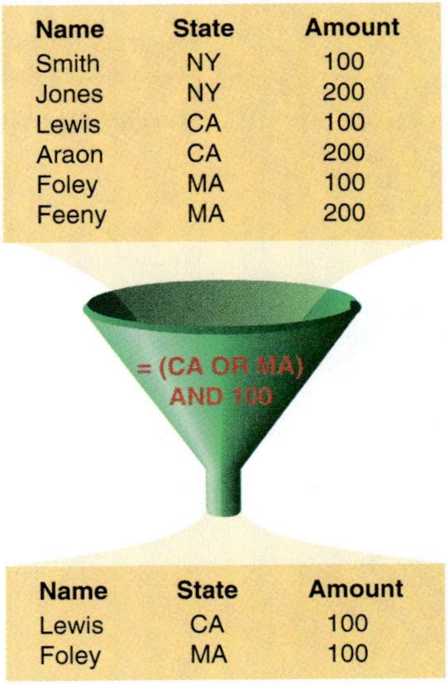

Compound statement

8.8 Internet Connectivity

Web browsers provide an increasingly familiar way to look at data stored in databases on the Web or on company intranets. To make reading and presenting data easier, both spreadsheets and databases are now designed to work well with Web applications. Most people use these enhanced application programs to develop content for Web pages. However, businesses are also using large database applications to create very dynamic pages and to enable transactions over the Internet.

Dynamically updated on-line databases

There are some databases that store constantly changing data. Typical of these are databases used for stock market prices and sports scores. When you view one of these databases on-screen, fields change value as you watch. The pages are being updated dynamically.

Querying on-line databases

Until the Web came along, most people never directly encountered databases. If we called information to find someone's phone number, ordered by mail, or made reservations, someone else took down the information and entered it into their database for us. With the Web, we are now face-to-face with databases almost every time we visit sites. However, we don't see the databases; we see their forms. In some cases, the form is for you to use to enter a query. For example, you might use a search engine to locate information. Or you might use a form to search for a package at Fedex or a book at Amazon.com. In these situations, we are directly querying someone else's database.

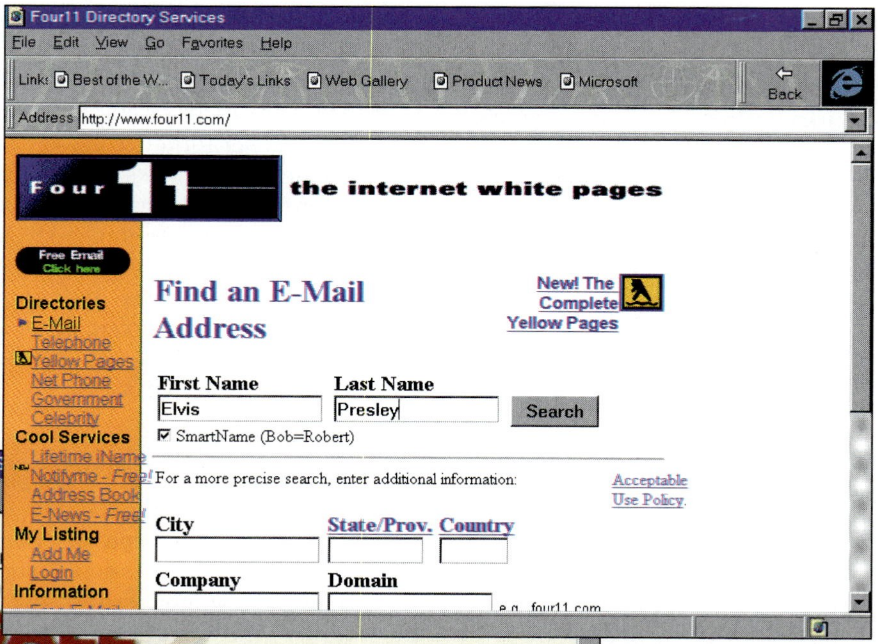

On-line database courtesy of Four11
http://www.four11.com

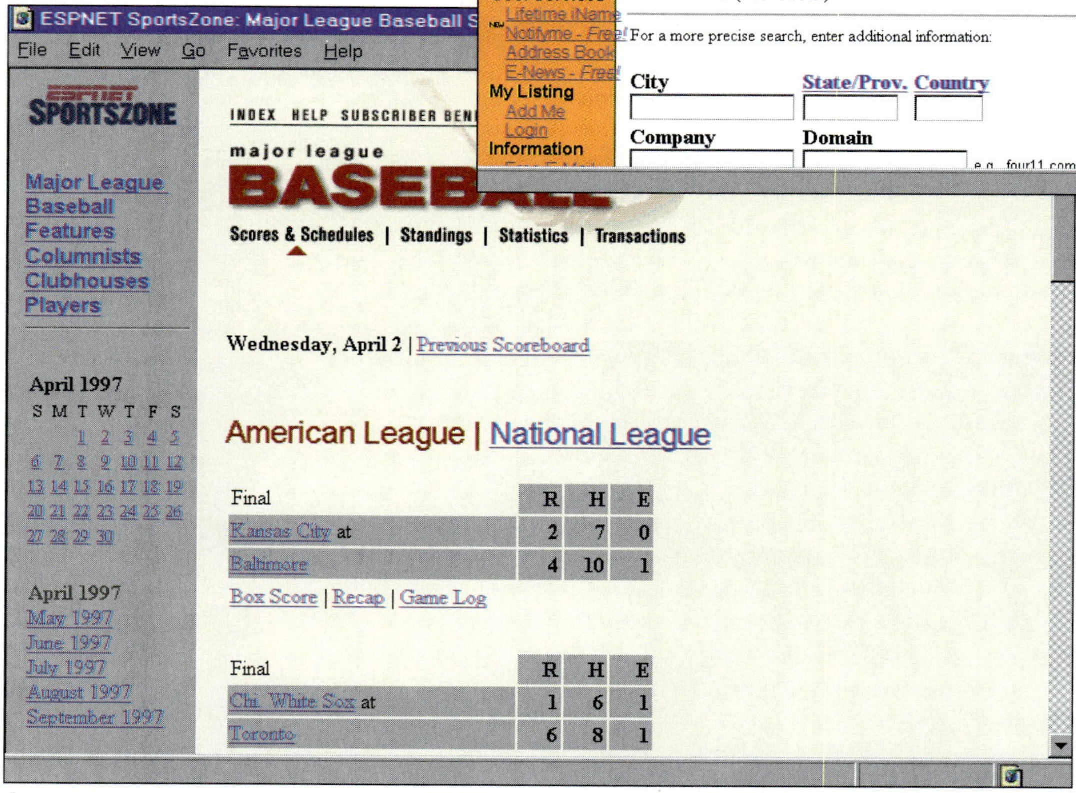

Sports scores courtesy of Starwave
http://espnet.sportszone.com/ncw/today/sco.top25.html

Entering data into on-line databases

Many databases are set up so you can enter data into them using a form displayed on the screen. When you fill out one of these forms, whether to give an opinion, register for a service, or purchase an item, you are directly entering data into someone's database. Databases are at the very heart of what's called electronic commerce. They allow companies to create electronic "storefronts" that are entertaining and simple to use. Examples of electronic commerce applications include home shopping and banking applications on the Web and video on-demand applications for interactive television.

Web page development tools

With the increased demand for complex electronic document sharing via the Internet or an organizations' intranet, it has become critical to be able to easily create, edit, and convert files for these two important media. Spreadsheets and databases can create documents that are then posted on the Web or on an intranet. Spreadsheet models can be displayed as fixed or interactive tables. Databases can be used to create forms into which people type information that is then added to the database. They can use similar forms to locate information in the database so it's displayed on the screen. These documents can be posted in their own native format and viewed through special viewers. For example, you can post Word and Excel documents in Word and Excel formats. Since browsers can't normally read these formats, you use special Word or Excel viewers that work just like other browser plug-ins. They can also be converted to HTML documents and posted so they can be viewed by anyone with a standard browser.

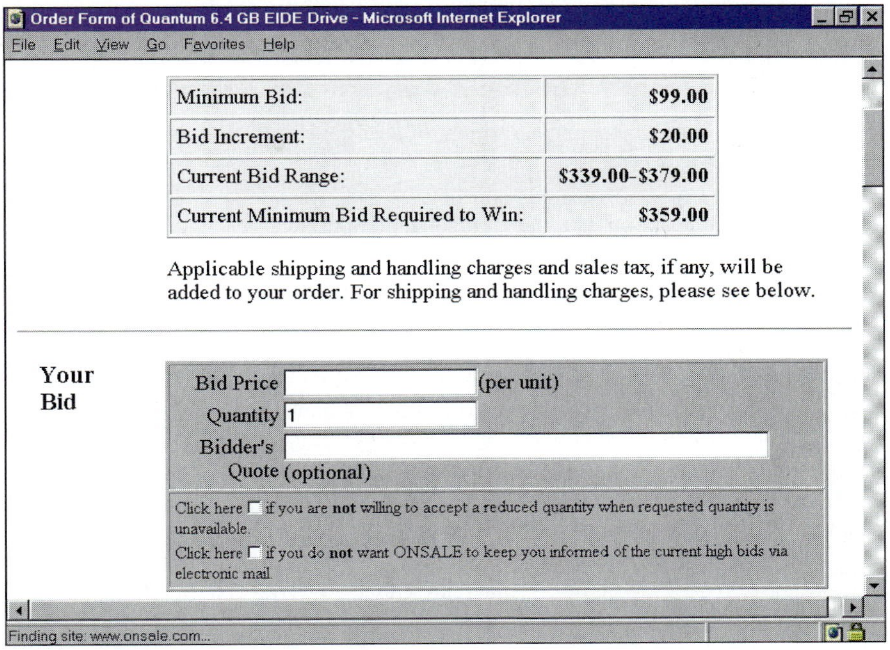

On-line database courtesy of OnSale
https://www.onsale.com/category/bid/00063091.htm

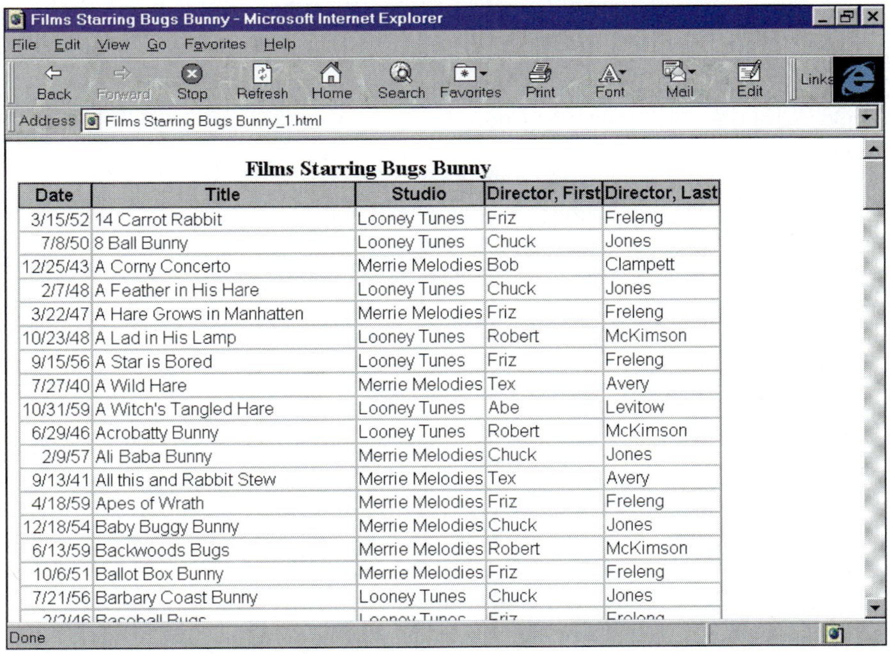

Films Starring Bugs Bunny

Date	Title	Studio	Director, First	Director, Last
3/15/52	14 Carrot Rabbit	Looney Tunes	Friz	Freleng
7/8/50	8 Ball Bunny	Looney Tunes	Chuck	Jones
12/25/43	A Corny Concerto	Merrie Melodies	Bob	Clampett
2/7/48	A Feather in His Hare	Looney Tunes	Chuck	Jones
3/22/47	A Hare Grows in Manhatten	Merrie Melodies	Friz	Freleng
10/23/48	A Lad in His Lamp	Looney Tunes	Robert	McKimson
9/15/56	A Star is Bored	Looney Tunes	Friz	Freleng
7/27/40	A Wild Hare	Merrie Melodies	Tex	Avery
10/31/59	A Witch's Tangled Hare	Looney Tunes	Abe	Levitow
6/29/46	Acrobatty Bunny	Looney Tunes	Robert	McKimson
2/9/57	Ali Baba Bunny	Merrie Melodies	Chuck	Jones
9/13/41	All this and Rabbit Stew	Merrie Melodies	Tex	Avery
4/18/59	Apes of Wrath	Merrie Melodies	Friz	Freleng
12/18/54	Baby Buggy Bunny	Merrie Melodies	Chuck	Jones
6/13/59	Backwoods Bugs	Merrie Melodies	Robert	McKimson
10/6/51	Ballot Box Bunny	Merrie Melodies	Friz	Freleng
7/21/56	Barbary Coast Bunny	Looney Tunes	Chuck	Jones

Web database created with Access

8.9 Enhancing and Testing Your Understanding

Summary

- Spreadsheets and database management applications are the primary tools of analysis.
- Spreadsheets, especially VisiCalc and Lotus 1-2-3, were the first "killer" applications that made personal computers almost indispensable in business.
- Database management applications are the tools for data storage and retrieval. These programs allow you to store massive amounts of data in a highly organized fashion so it can be viewed in ways that turn it into useful information.
- A spreadsheet is the arrangement of rows and columns that appears on the screen when you first load the program.
- The border contains column labels (letters) across the top of the spreadsheet and row labels (numbers) down the left side.
- Rows run horizontally across a spreadsheet and are labeled consecutively with numbers, starting with row 1 at the top of the spreadsheet.
- Columns run vertically down a spreadsheet and are labeled consecutively with letters. The first 26 columns are labeled A to Z, the next 26 are labeled AA to AZ, the next 26 are labeled BA to BZ, and so on.
- Cells, the basic working unit on a spreadsheet, fall at the intersection of each column and row. They are referred to by their coordinates, or cell address. A cell's address is its column letter followed by its row number. For example, the address of the cell at the intersection of column D and row 6 is cell D6.
- The display screen is just a small window on a large spreadsheet, but you can scroll around the underlying spreadsheet with the scroll bars or keyboard keys.
- In business, spreadsheets are used to analyze the performance of products, salespeople, or dealers. They compare costs, prices, and gross margins of individual products in a product line. They also analyze sales, calculate prices, forecast budgets, and make cash-flow projections.
- To analyze data with a spreadsheet, you create a model of the situation by entering numbers to be calculated, formulas to do the calculations, and labels that identify the elements used in the model. You use models to simulate real-world situations. Just as a plastic model of an airplane represents, or simulates, a real plane, a spreadsheet model simulates a financial or other numeric situation.
- Spreadsheets are much more structured than word processing applications. For example, on a word processing application you can enter any data anywhere on the page. With a spreadsheet program, you can only enter data into cells. The data aren't always typed in. Often they're copied from the organization's mainframe or network server to a user's desktop computer (called downloading). This saves time and eliminates the possibility of introducing errors.
- To enter data of any kind into a spreadsheet, you click one of the cells or use the keyboard keys to select it. This selected cell is then the active cell—the only one into which you can type data.
- For some procedures such as formatting, or cutting and pasting, you can extend the selection to highlight and select a block of cells. There are only certain things you can enter into the active cell: labels, numbers, formulas, functions (a type of formula), and formats.
- Spreadsheets make it easy to explore a range of possible outcomes because changing one number on a spreadsheet can cause other changes to ripple throughout. This ability to explore what ifs, called sensitivity analysis, is possible because of this ability of formulas and functions to refer to other cells.
- Formulas contain cell references, which are the addresses of the cells in which the numbers to be calculated are entered. The formula calculates any numbers in the cells that it refers to just as if that number were in the formula.
- Functions are built into spreadsheets to calculate values such as monthly payments on a loan, averages, totals, and standard deviations. The organization of a function is called its syntax. The values on which a function performs operations are called its arguments and these can be numbers and cell references text.
- A spreadsheet model with the numbers removed is a template that can be used repeatedly because it retains all of its labels, formulas, and functions. Entering new numbers calculates a new answer.
- Using the graphics capabilities built into a spreadsheet, you can create charts and graphs to analyze numeric data.
- Because charts are linked to the data on the worksheet, they change when the data changes. This allows you to see graphically how changes affect a problem.
- Discrete data are a series of values, such as sales or profits, measured at selected intervals. Only the measured points are meaningful. The best chart types to use for this kind of data include bar and column charts.
- Continuous data are a series of measurements at specified intervals where the data points indicate an uninterrupted trend. Although each data point is a discrete value, values between the measured data points can be estimated from the chart, which is called interpolation. The best chart types to use for this kind of data include line and area charts.
- Maps can also be linked to data to illustrate situations or reveal relationships that would otherwise go undiscovered. Computer programs that make such analysis possible on a large scale are called Geographical Information Systems (GIS). However, small scale versions of this technology are available in spreadsheet programs.
- A database is one or more tables of data organized and stored in a very structured way.

Review Questions

True/False

1. T F Spreadsheets contain rows and columns. At the intersection of each is a cell into which you can enter data.
2. T F When you enter labels, numbers, and formulas to solve a financial problem, you are creating a model.
3. T F A formula in any cell can refer to other cells so numbers in those cells are calculated by the formula.
4. T F A function is the result that has been calculated by a formula.
5. T F Charts based on data on a worksheet automatically change if you change the worksheet data.
6. T F Continuous data are for selected intervals and there is no relationship between the values.
7. T F In a database table the rows are fields and the columns are records.
8. T F Database forms are used to enter, view, and edit data in a database.
9. T F Both spreadsheets and databases can be used to create interactive components to Web pages.
10. T F Logical operators are used to determine if one number is larger or smaller than another.

Fill-In the Blank

1. The arrangement of rows and columns on the screen is called a spreadsheet or a __________.
2. The active cell is the only one in which you can enter data.
3. A __________ is a type of formula that makes complex calculations easy.
4. A spreadsheet __________ is a model from which all of the numbers have been removed but which retains all of the labels and formulas so you can enter your own data.
5. Discrete data is data sampled at selected intervals to determine the pattern in the data so data can be estimated between the measured points.
6. __________ can contain two or more tables that can be linked using a field common to two or more tables.
7. Relational operators include ___>___, ___<___, and ___=___.
8. Logical operators include ___and___, ___or___, and ___not___.
9. __________ are like questions that you use to locate records in a database.
10. __________ are used to print out all or some of the data stored in a database.

Multiple Choice

1. When you analyze a numeric situation with a spreadsheet, you first create a ___.
   - **a.** Database
   - **b.** Model
   - **c.** Template
   - **d.** All of the above
2. When working with a spreadsheet you can only enter ___
   - **a.** Numbers and formulas
   - **b.** Numbers, formulas, and functions
   - **c.** Labels, numbers, formulas, functions, and formats
   - **d.** All of the above.
3. To plot profit and loss over a five year period, it would be best to use a ___ chart.
   - **a.** Pie
   - **b.** Line
   - **c.** Bar
   - **d.** Area
4. Geographic information systems are used to ___.
   - **a.** Locate yourself anywhere on the face of the earth
   - **b.** Relate data to locations
   - **c.** Distribute data to various locations
   - **d.** None of the above
5. Spreadsheets and databases are similar in that they both ___.
   - **a.** Store data in rows and columns
   - **b.** Let you sort data
   - **c.** Let you find data
   - **d.** All of the above
6. Spreadsheets and databases are different in these respects ___.
   - **a.** Spreadsheets have many built-in functions and data bases don't
   - **b.** Spreadsheets provide charts or graphs of your data and databases don't
   - **c.** Databases can manage much more information
   - **d.** All of the above
7. A major problem with record management programs is that they ___.
   - **a.** Cost more than relational databases
   - **b.** Force you to duplicate data
   - **c.** Are no longer made
   - **d.** Are integrated into application programs
8. The smallest unit of data in a database is a ___.
   - **a.** Table
   - **b.** Record
   - **c.** Field
   - **d.** None of the above.
9. To make data entry easier in a database, you can create a ___.
   - **a.** Report
   - **b.** Form
   - **c.** Query
   - **d.** Operator
10. To locate information in a database, you can use ___.
    - **a.** Relational operators
    - **b.** Logical operators
    - **c.** Queries
    - **d.** All of the above

Research projects

1. Using the Internet or computer magazines, look up information on Microsoft Excel. List any features you find. List which of these features appeal to you and describe why they do.
2. Think about daily activities that might bring you into contact with a database either directly or indirectly. Make a list of the activities and write a brief description of what data the databases might contain.
3. Think through the courses you are taking or any jobs you may have and try to list places where charts and graphs might make relationships clearer. Describe what relationships you might want to show on the chart or graph and why you would want to show them.

CHAPTER

9 COMMUNICATIONS - THE

AN OVERVIEW

OBJECTIVES

After completing this chapter, you will be able to:

- Identify how information technology devices enhance the public telephone network.
- List some typical methods that individuals and groups use to communicate with each other.
- Describe two basic types of files and explain how they are transferred over networks.
- Describe bandwidth and explain its importance.
- Explain how computers are connected together into local, metropolitan, and wide area networks and how these differ from one another.
- List the kinds of media and other hardware you need to communicate between computers.
- Describe intranets and explain their growing popularity.
- Describe how networks are linked to one another to form the Internet and how they communicate.
- Describe current and future dial-up connections to networks.

Communication *n.* 1. act of imparting knowledge of; making known. 2. giving to another; imparting; transmitting.

Networks *n.* 1. a netlike combination of lines, veins, passages. 2. a group of devices linked by wire or broadcast so information can be sent to one or all.

Originally all computers and other information processing devices stood alone and their information was available only to those who had direct connections to them. Since the value of data increases dramatically when it's easier to collect and distribute, computers and other information processing devices are now connected to one another in networks.

Information flows through such networks everywhere. In some places, the signs of its flow are evident. Cables run every which way on telephone poles, dishes are mounted on the sides of buildings, and large antennas occupy the high ground. But in most places the signs are hidden. Cables run underground and invisible broadcast signals fill the air. You walk through a thick soup of data that flows from point to point. Some of the information being sent is familiar, for example, telephone conversations and radio and television broadcasts. Much of it is not public. It may be

- Signals from an ATM machine while someone makes a withdrawal.
- A credit card authorization when someone makes a charge at the local hardware store.
- A query from a high school student to the Library of Congress over the Internet.
- A divisional report being sent from a local office to corporate headquarters.

Whatever the information is and wherever and however it is flowing, it is being communicated with modern information technology and computers are involved at many points in the process.

And we're just at the beginning. Work is going on right now to build the information superhighway. We'll be able to watch European or Japanese or Latin American TV stations or browse through libraries located anywhere in the world, bank and shop for groceries over the phone, and buy just about anything from "virtual" malls. This is all just around the corner.

A recent U.S. government report stated, "All Americans have a stake in the construction of an advanced National Information Infrastructure (NII), a seamless web of communications networks, computers, databases, and consumer electronics that will put vast amounts of information at users' fingertips. Development of the NII can help unleash an information revolution that will change forever the way people live, work, and interact with each other."

In this chapter we explore the foundations and applications of the communications technology that will make all of these things possible.

ON THE PACE CD ROM

Spread No.	Title
9-5	Understanding Communication Bandwidth
9-12	Understanding Analog Modems
9-12	Understanding Parity

ELECTRONIC WEB

9.1 Network Applications:

You've already read about and probably used the Internet, the largest of all networks. Most of the sites on the Web are actually connected over the same telephone lines we use for phone calls. Since you are already so familiar with this phone network, it's a good place to start a discussion of networks. Let's look at a few of the services that run on the worldwide phone network.

Fax

A facsimile machine is a telephone copy machine. You insert the original document into your machine and a copy comes out on another facsimile machine anywhere else in the world all at the cost of a short phone call. In 1994, 40 percent of a typical Fortune 500 company's phone bill was for fax calls. U.S. West estimated that in 1994 25 percent of the traffic over their lines was fax.

With a fax/modem adapter card installed in your computer connected to the phone line, you are in the fax send-and-receive business. You can use the system to send faxes directly from the screen or from a file on your disk. Faxing directly from your computer eliminates the time it takes to print out a document and walk to the fax machine to send it. When you send a fax, the fax machine or fax/modem card converts it from text you can edit into a digital picture format. It's this picture that is sent over the phone lines. Some fax software can convert the text in a received fax back into an editable form. This optical character recognition (OCR) software makes it possible to edit, format, or revise a fax that someone sends you.

Fax-back services

Many companies now have what is called a fax-back service. You dial their number, answer a few questions by pressing numbers on your phone, and hang up. The company's fax machine then automatically sends you a fax of the information you requested.

Fax-back service

Fax Was First

It surprises many people to learn that fax machines predated telephones. The fax process was invented in 1842 by Alexander Bain, a Scottish clock-maker. His invention used a pendulum that swung back and forth over raised metal letters. Each time it touched the metal, it sent a electrical charge down a telegraph wire to "paint" the letter's picture at the other end of the line.

PC facsimile

Beep, Beep!

A story in *America's Network* magazine describes a Texas rancher who has equipped some of his cows with beepers. The cows are trained to associate the beep with feeding, so when he wants them to come to the barn, the rancher just dials the pager number. The beeper-equipped cows start heading home, and the others—cows being cows—just follow the leaders. That's right, you can even drive cattle on the information highway!

Voice mail

One of the big problems in business is "phone-tag," where you call someone, discover he or she isn't there, and then leave a message for the person to return your call. When the person does call back, you aren't there, so he or she leaves a message for you. A computer-based solution to this problem, called voice mail, automates phone answering and messaging. When you are connected to a person's extension, if they don't pick up the phone, the voice mail system answers and asks you to leave a message. Sophisticated systems have an automated attendant that routes you to the right person when you press the keys of a touch-tone phone. For example, the attendant may tell you to press 1 to reach marketing, 2 to reach service, or 3 to place an order. The voice mail system then routes the call to the appropriate department. If no one answers, a digitized voice asks you to leave a message. Now, it's even possible to leave video voice mail.

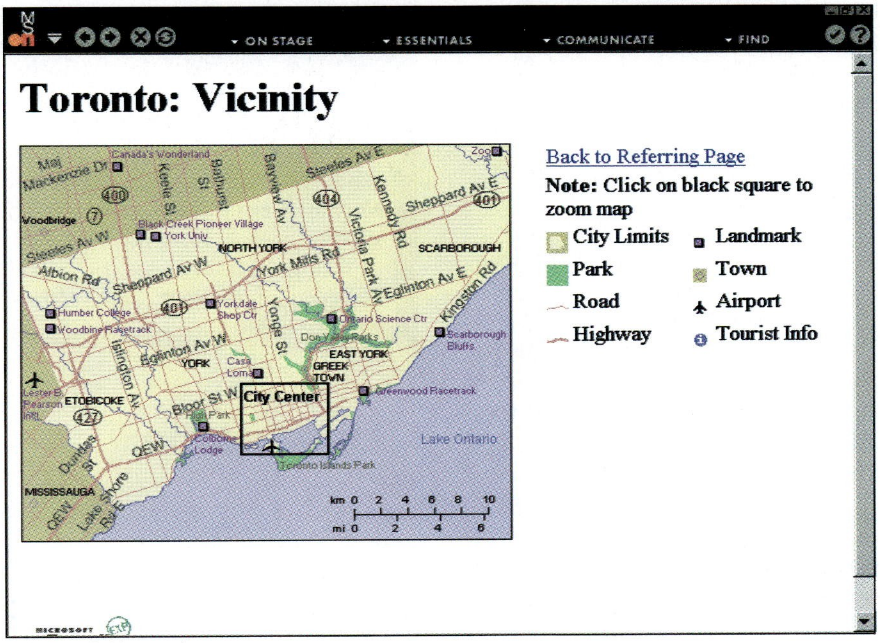

Microsoft Network

Video voice mail courtesy of Intel
http://www.intel.com/comm-net/proshare/prod/VS200DS.htm

On-line services

Until a few years ago, users encountered large computer networks only at work or school. Networks were introduced at home through the large commercial information services such as CompuServe, America On-line (AOL), and Microsoft Network. These companies typically use their own private networks to deliver information and services to their paying members. You can use their services to locate important information or to exchange electronic mail with other subscribers. You can post messages to other members on message forums. Other users read these and post their responses—creating a thread that can then be followed by others interested in the subject. These services allow users to type messages back and forth in real time in what is called chat mode. The latest versions of these services are now tightly integrated with the World Wide Web. You can use a browser to view the service's pages and follow links between the service and pages located elsewhere on the Web.

To lower your connection costs, these services establish hundreds of phone numbers around the county. To connect with the service you dial one of these numbers called a point-of-presence (POP). Usually, this is a local phone call so you don't have to pay long distance charges.

Although these first large on-line services remain quite popular they have been eclipsed almost overnight by the success of the Internet's World Wide Web.

One of the key benefits of networks is that they put you in touch with other people. Much of this communication is person-to-person in the form of electronic mail.

Warning!

Don't ever assume your e-mail is private. It can almost certainly be read by the mail supervisor and others in the organization. Networks are rarely secure and you should always assume that what you send can be seen by others. Even if the network administrator can't see the contents of messages, others on the network may try to gain access. With enough time, computational resources, and experience, they may be able to. The only way to protect your privacy is to use encryption, which is discussed in Chapter 13.

Electronic mail

Many people have access to campus- or company wide electronic mail (called e-mail), making it possible to have almost instantaneous communication. The cost of sending an e-mail message is lower than other forms of communication and for many people e-mail is more convenient.

To send e-mail to someone, you just need their address, which has two parts, the user's name and the name of the computer his or her mail is stored on called a domain name. These two parts are separated by an "at" sign (@). A typical e-mail address might read dcurtin@interserv.com.

E-mail address

Store and forward

When you send a message, it is stored on a computer somewhere until the addressee reads it. This process is called store and forward because the message is stored until the addressee signs on to the network or accesses her electronic mail service. When she does so, the message is transferred (forwarded) to her computer where it can be read. Once a message has been read, it can be printed, replied to, saved, or deleted.

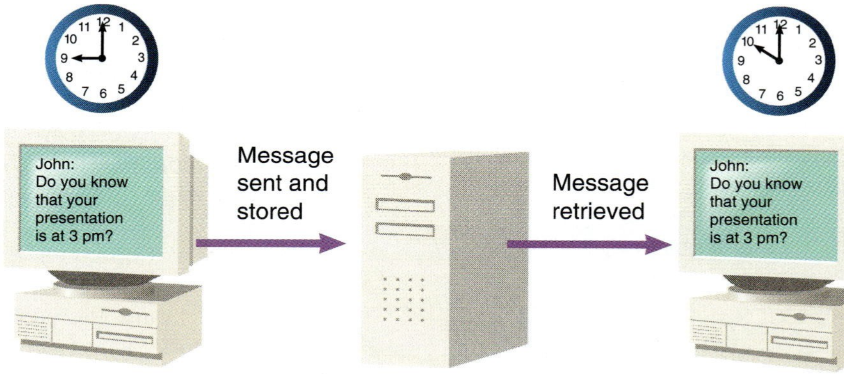

Store and forward

E-mail software

To send or receive e-mail, you need e-mail software that allows you to write, read, and file messages. If you save messages, you can then use special search commands to locate specific messages by looking for keywords, names, or message dates.

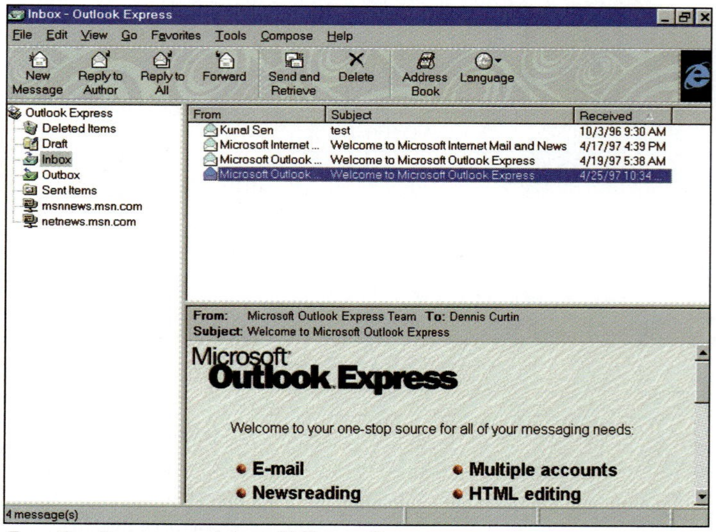

E-mail software courtesy of Microsoft

Stop and think

E-mail is not like regular mail sent through the post office (called snail mail). It is instant and impulsive. You can dash off a note and it's in the recipient's mail box instantly. This is a two-edged sword. Unlike with a word processed message, you don't take the time to carefully edit your ideas, address an envelope, carry it to the mail box, activities that provide a cooling off period. Using e-mail, all of us have posted messages we wished we hadn't sent, and received some we're sure the sender would like to take back. To avoid problems, try to establish some guidelines. Some of the widely accepted rules—called e-mail etiquette—include the following:

- Don't ever write and send nasty notes impulsively. If you have something to get off your chest, always say it in person rather than in e-mail.
- Don't ever refer to third parties in an unflattering way. Copies of e-mail can be forwarded to them at the click of a button.
- Be careful of inflections, nuances, and sarcasm. Things said one way may be taken in another. If the message is important, take the same time to write it carefully and edit it as you would take with a written letter.
- Don't ever use your company's name in personal postings outside the company. It can cause the company, and you, legal problems and embarrassment.
- Try to act as civilized as possible—and do unto others as you would have them do unto you.

E-Mail Filters

E-mail is so easy to write and send that many people are inundated by it. To control this flood of incoming mail, filters are becoming increasingly popular. These programs screen the mail, sort it by importance, and even delete any that meets certain conditions. Such a program can automatically place mail from your boss at the top of the list and delete any e-mail sent from specified addresses.

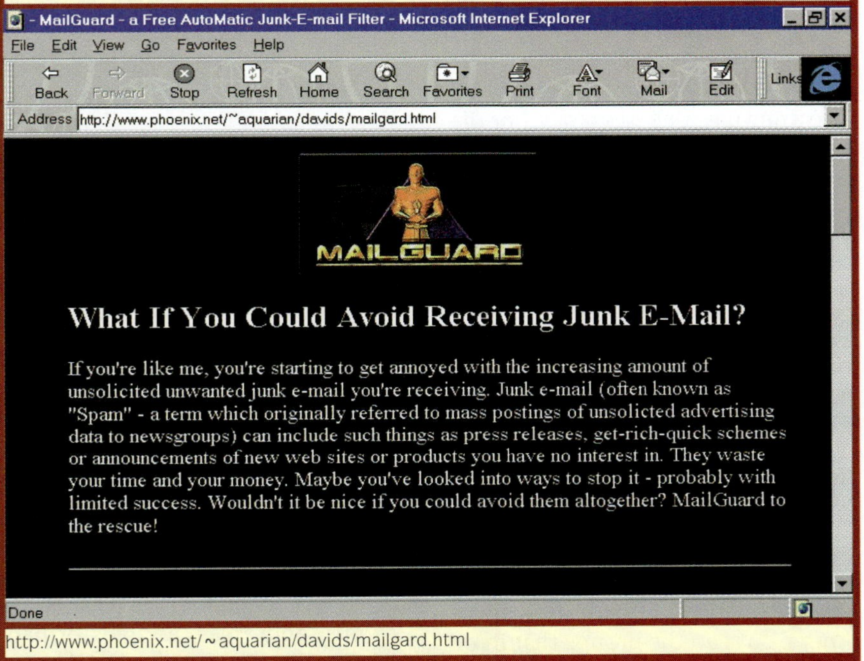

See-I'm Smiling!

When people exchange e-mail, it's not like talking face to face. The body language and voice intonations we use to convey inflections are missing. Imagine saying to someone, "I hate you," but doing it with a smile rather than a glare. When sending e-mail, it has become common to add inflections with symbols—called emoticons. For example:

- The symbol :-) looks like a sideways happy face and means "I'm smiling." It's created by typing a colon, a hyphen, and then a right-parentheses. Other people use <s> or <g> to indicate a smile or grin.
- The symbol :-(looks like a sad face and means "I'm sad or unhappy."
- The symbol ;-) looks like a winking face and means "I'm saying this in jest."

A few of these work, but sometimes, people go too far. Try to figure out what these mean (the key follows):

:*) :-& ;-/ :-\ :-| |-o

(clowning, tongue tied, skeptical, undecided, ambivalent, and bored)

Another technique is to use all uppercase letters WHEN YOU WANT TO SHOUT.

9.3 Network Applications:

In addition to one-on-one communication, there are many group discussions or activities going on over networks.

Newsgroups

Usenet (Users Network) is a collection of thousands of ongoing topical discussions called newsgroups. Each newsgroup covers a specific topic such as alternative living or zoology. Also known as bulletin boards or discussion groups, newsgroups are used by people to share common interests. Usenet is not a part of the Internet, or even a network of any kind. It is a system for carrying on discussions that can be delivered in a number of ways, the Internet being just one of them.

Newsgroups are ever-changing bulletin boards where you can post messages, called articles, for everyone else to read and respond to with public postings of their own or by private e-mail. Some news groups are moderated so a person reads each message before it is made available to others. To read the groups that interest you, you use a newsreader program or your Web browser.

All newsgroups are organized into seven categories, each with its own name. Newsgroups within these categories often have multipart names, listed in increasingly narrower order from left to right and separated by periods. For example, rec.music.folk is one of many groups in recreation and folk is one of many groups in music.

Mailing lists

Mailing lists use e-mail to keep groups informed on topics or events they wish to know about such as when a particular Web site has been updated. Listserv and Major Domo are popular mailing list software programs. When placed on a server, they allow you to automatically subscribe to a mailing list. To do so, you send e-mail to the list's administrative address and say something like subscribe Dilbert_List your name in the body or subject of the message. The mailing list software interprets your message and adds your address to the appropriate mailing list. To unsubscribe, you'd send the message unsubscribe Dilbert_List your name. Mail reflectors are similar to mailing lists. An e-mail message sent to a mail reflector might contain the message Send update. The mail reflector would then automatically reply to the request and attach the requested file.

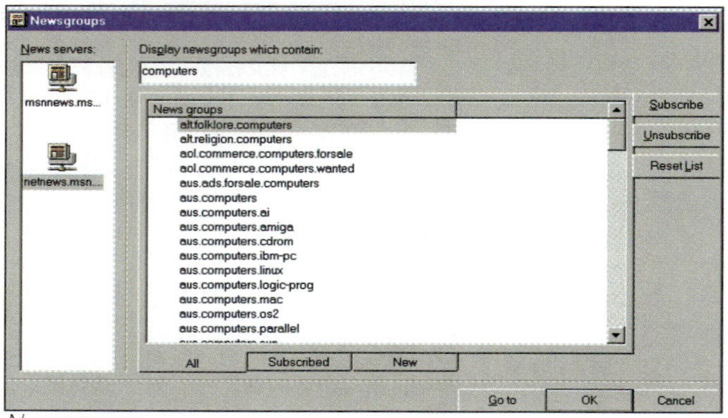

Newsgroups

Keep Your Eyes Open, You May Be Spammed!

As you get more involved with the Internet, you may find yourself the recipient of a mass-mailing called a spam. They are called spams because they reminded some wit of a routine in Monty Python's Flying Circus that goes:

"*Well there's egg and bacon; egg, sausage and bacon; egg and spam; bacon and spam; egg, bacon, sausage and spam; spam, bacon, sausage and spam;* and so on."

The spammer gets a list of the e-mail addresses, perhaps of people using Usenet newsgroups and then sends the same message to everyone on the list. People on the Internet are not happy about these mailings. There is always a temptation to return such a message to where it came from in the hopes that if everyone does the same thing you'll flood their system. Unfortunately this usually does no good because spammers are hit and run artists. All you'll do is cause harm to another innocent party who was used by the spammer.

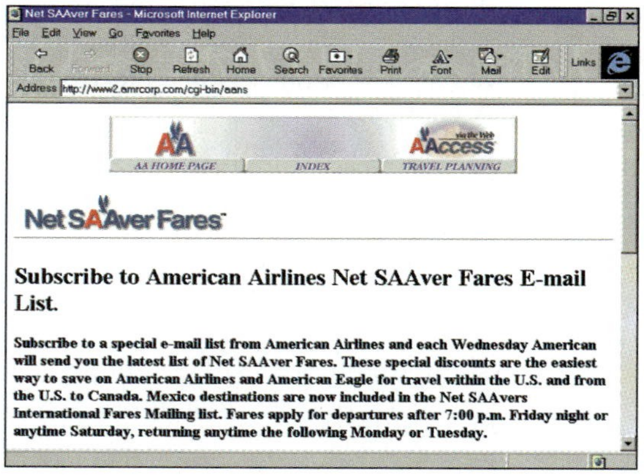

Mailing list

Group Communications

Microsoft's Comic Chat

Flame Wars

When someone says something insulting to others or is misunderstood on the Internet, other people get angry and begin to send in heated responses. In a very short time charges and insinuations are flying fast and furiously back and forth. These colorful exchanges are referred to as flame wars. If you're at the receiving end, you've been flamed. In other cases, people use ALL CAPS to show that they are shouting at you.

Usenet Newsgroup Categories

Name	Description
comp	computer subjects
sci	scientific subjects
soc	social and cultural issues
rec	recreational topics such as hobbies, music, art, and sports
talk	current events, debates, controversial issues
news	newsgroup topics dealing with the Usenet system
misc	other topics

Internet relay chat

If e-mail isn't fast enough, Internet relay chat (IRC) allows you to chat with other users in real-time. As soon as you type your message, everyone else can see it. Any user with IRC software can go to an IRC computer called an IRC server, create a channel on some topic, and invite others to join in. A variant on this theme is Microsoft's Comic Chat. Here, you select a character called an avatar to represent you on the screen. What you type is then displayed in a balloon over your cartoon character.

Network games

Multiplayer games are one of the hot attractions on the Internet. The first popular games were text-based. The most popular are MUDs (multiuser dialogue) and their variants such as MOOs—object-oriented MOOs.

With more and more multimedia being made available, graphical games are becoming more popular. For example, The Gaming Zone Web site offers many games including the Chess game shown here. You can play against another person located anywhere in the world. If you'd rather not play, or if you are just learning, you can watch others play or you can play against the computer.

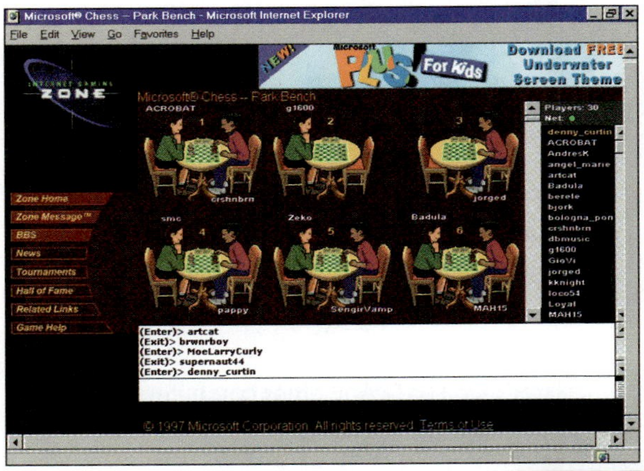

Chess game courtesy of Microsoft
http://igz2.microsoft.com/

Video conferencing

Business travel is time-consuming and expensive. People do it, however, because there is no substitute for a face-to-face meeting with a customer, client, or other members on the same corporate team. Nothing builds relationships the way personal meetings do. However, to reduce travel to a minimum, many companies are now using video conferencing. Cameras at more than one location (they can be continents apart) transmit videos of the participants to the other locations. Not quite a personal visit, but a lot more personal than a letter.

Initially, video conferencing equipment was expensive. Now, it has been reduced to adding an inexpensive video camera to a multimedia PC connected to the Web. The software then compresses the signal and sends the sound and picture to the other meeting locations.

Video conferencing courtesy of C-Phone

9.4 Network Applications:

One of the most common uses of networks is exchanging files. Let's say you want to share a spreadsheet or report with friends or coworkers. To do so, you need to get a copy of the file to them so they can open it on their own machines. There are many ways to transfer files other than copying them to disks and mailing them. Let's look at the most popular methods.

Uploading and downloading

When you transfer files between computers, you are uploading and downloading them. These terms simply refer to the direction of transfer. Uploading means you are sending the file to another system. Downloading means you are transferring a file from another computer to yours.

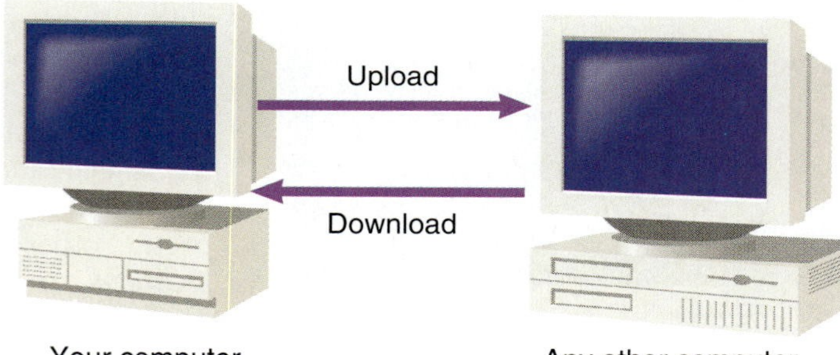

Uploading and downloading

ASCII and binary files

There are two basic types of files: ASCII and binary. ASCII files contain only a limited set of characters and have almost no formatting. Because of their simplicity, they are easy to transfer. Binary files on the other hand have lots of formatting and much of it is specific to the program that created the file. A picture, a video, a word processing document, a spreadsheet, a database, or an animation vary so widely they don't transfer easily between networks that use different protocols, and files must be converted as they move from one network to another, always a messy process. However, as you'll see, there are solutions to this problem.

Shared disks

On local area networks (LANs), there are no serious problems with transferring files. It's as easy as moving or copying a file to a public folder. Friends or coworkers can then move it from there to one of their own folders.

Shared disks on LAN courtesy of International Business Machines

FTP on the Internet

One of the wonderful things about the Web is how easy it is to transfer files. Files are routinely downloaded to your computer as you browse the Web. These files—one or more for every page you view—are temporarily stored on your hard disk so if you click the browser's Back button or visit the same site again, the computer can get them off your hard drive faster than it can get them from the original site.

You can also exchange files with friends or coworkers or download them (transfer them to your computer) from other computers on the network. If you look around, you can find free programs to download along with thousands of books, papers, satellite images, and even movies. The Internet tool used to transfer files from one machine to another is ftp (file transfer protocol). When files are made available on the Web, all you have to do is click the hyperlink that initiates the download process and ftp works invisibly in the background to transfer these files to your own computer. On older systems, you can log onto another computer and "browse" through its files looking for those you might be interested in. Normally you would need a password to log onto the system. However, using anonymous ftp, you can browse through computers that allow you to do so by using the name anonymous to log on. You can then use any password, although it's common practice to use your e-mail address as a courtesy.

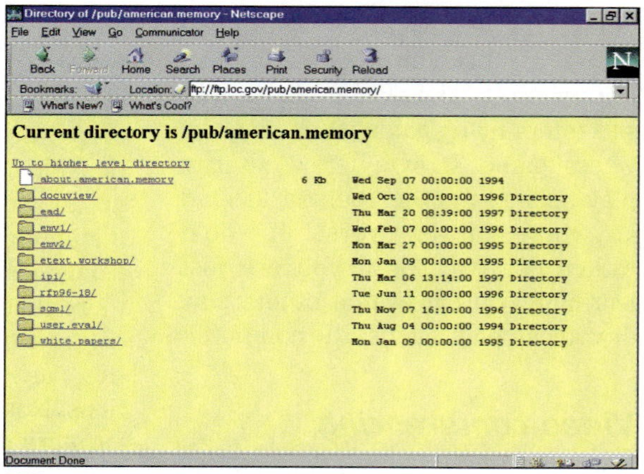

FTP
ftp://ftp.loc.gov/pub/american.memory/

Binary files as e-mail attachments

One of the most convenient ways to transfer files is as attachments to e-mail messages. How you use e-mail to send binary files depends on whom you are sending them to.

If the person you are sending the file to is on the same network, you just attach the file to an e-mail message and send it. The recipient can then easily open it at the other end. If you are sending it across the Internet to a different network, the message will pass through other computers called gateways that may not be compatible. Sending a binary attachment to e-mail through these gateways often gives the recipient a very corrupt file. Then you first need to use a program to convert the binary file to an ASCII text file. This is called encoding. The recipient must use a similar program to convert it from ASCII back to binary, decoding, so the file in its original file format can be opened and manipulated on the recipient's system just as it was on yours.

Some programs have this conversion capability built in, but with others you have to use a separate program such as Wincode that performs this task for you. There are currently two dominant encoding schemes in use:

- ♦ UUcoding (binary to ASCII) and UUdecoding (ACII back to binary) were originally developed for UNIX-to-UNIX e-mailing, hence the UU in their names.
- ♦ MIME (multipurpose Internet Mail Extension) uses a form of encoding called "Base64" which has been better designed to allow messages to pass through a network's various e-mail gateways.

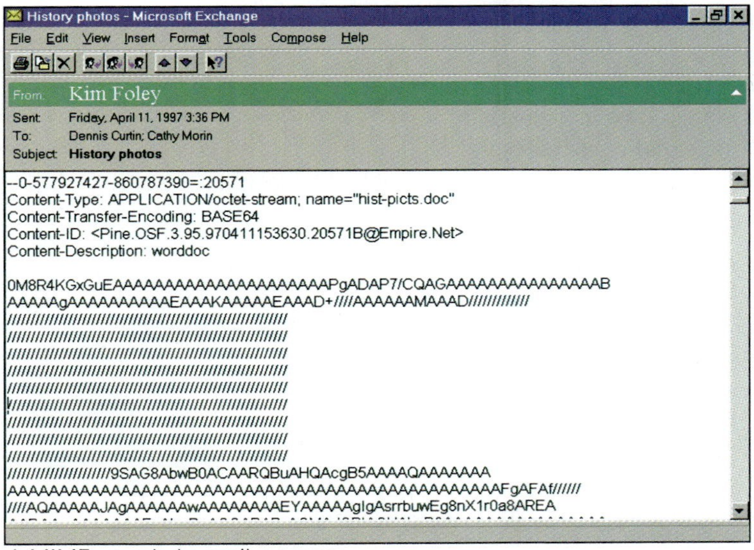

A MIME encoded e-mail message

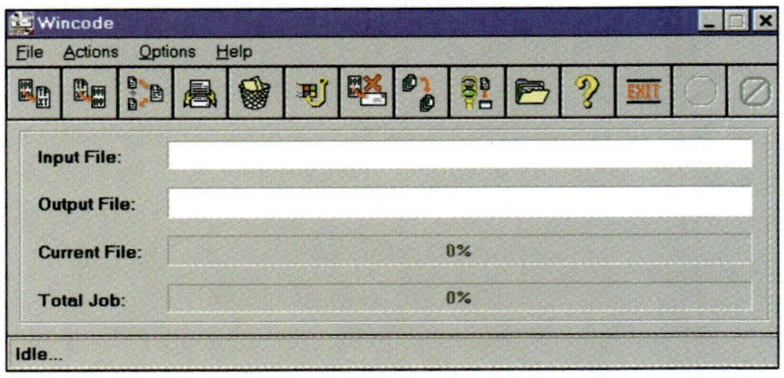

Wincode courtesy of Snappy

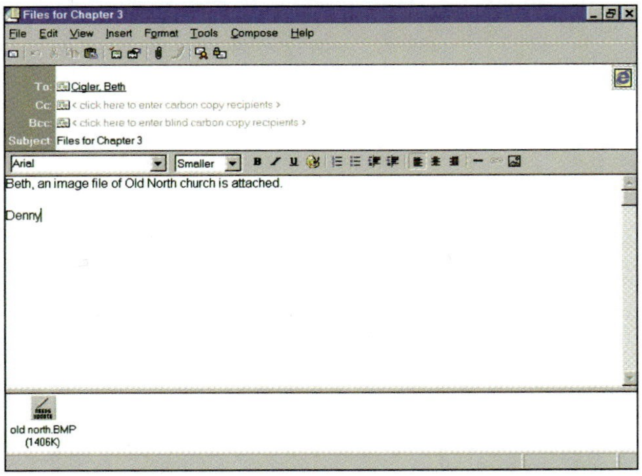

E-mail attachment

Virus Scanners

There are immature, antisocial misfits who get kicks out of making your life miserable. They do so in the computer world by writing viruses designed to alarm you or cause you real harm by deleting files or damaging your system. Since programs and even document files can contain viruses, your system should be protected when you download files. A virus scanner—a software program—detects and deletes viruses from your computer. These are discussed in Chapter 13.

9.5 The Foundations of Modern Networks:

Connections to the Internet and other networks are often referred to as pipes by people in the computer field. The analogy is to water pipes or traffic lanes. Each determines how much "flow" there is of water or traffic. Imagine trying to put out a major house fire with a garden hose or commuting to a major city center on a one lane road. In communications, this is referred to as a "bandwidth problem." Bandwidth simply refers to the amount of data that any channel can carry.

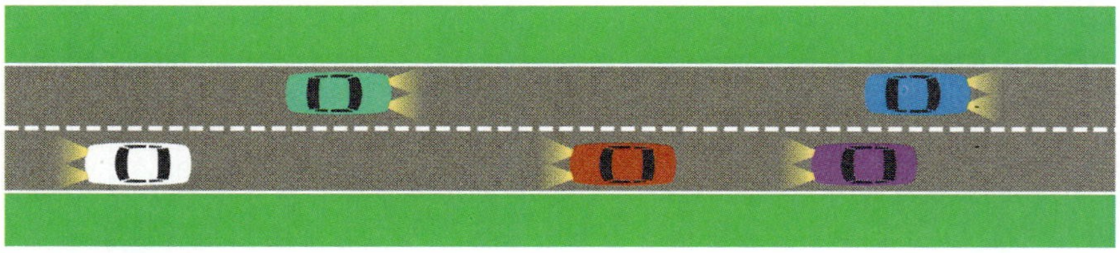

Low bandwidth

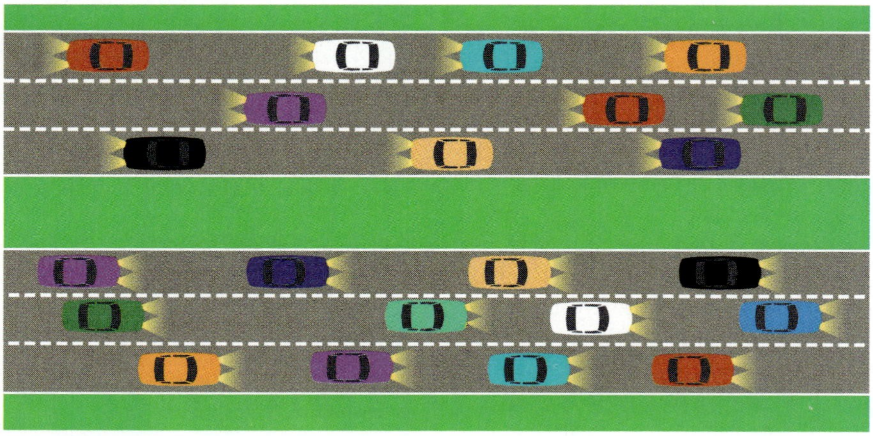

High bandwidth

bandwidth

How big is your pipe?

When it comes to bandwidth more is always better because it's faster, but more bandwidth usually costs more money. For that reason, there is a wide range of available bandwidths. Which you pay for depends on what you're sending and receiving. Text and even voice don't require a great deal of bandwidth. However, a wide bandwidth is required for video and systems where many people are all using the network at the same time.

Just as traffic engineers measure highway capacities in vehicles per hour, we measure computer transmission speeds in bits per second (bps). The following terms are used:

- Bits per second (bps).
- Kilobits per second (Kbps)—thousands of bits per second.
- Megabits per second (Mbps)—millions of bits per second.
- Gigabits per second (Gbps)—billions of bits per second.

Bandwidth and frequency

Technically, bandwidth is the difference between the highest and lowest frequencies the media can handle. These frequencies are measured in Hertz (Hz), which means how often the signal changes from one state to another. For example, a voice-grade phone line can transmit a range of frequencies between 300 and 3000 for a bandwidth of 2700, sufficient for an intelligible voice conversation. The human voice has a range of 20 to 20,000 Hz so it would require a bandwidth of 19980 (20,000 minus 20) to transmit it with full fidelity. (This explains why your phone doesn't sound as good as your stereo.) If data is transmitted at 2700 Hz over a phone line, the signal changes state from one frequency to another 2700 times each second. Each of these changes of state normally can carry a single bit, although other technologies allow more than one bit to be piled on each change. The more changes of state that can be carried in a given period of time, the more bits can be communicated.

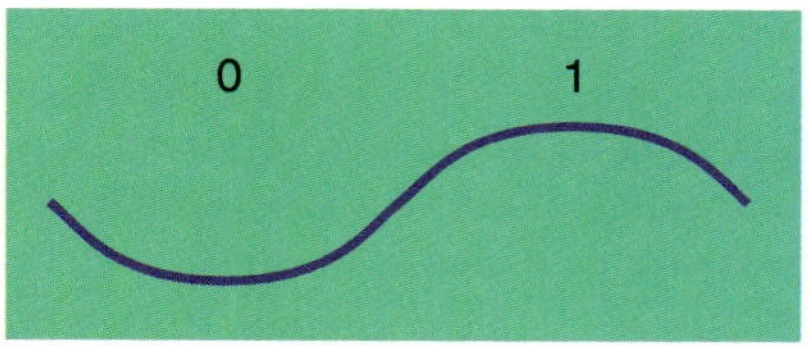

Low frequency
Narrow bandwidth

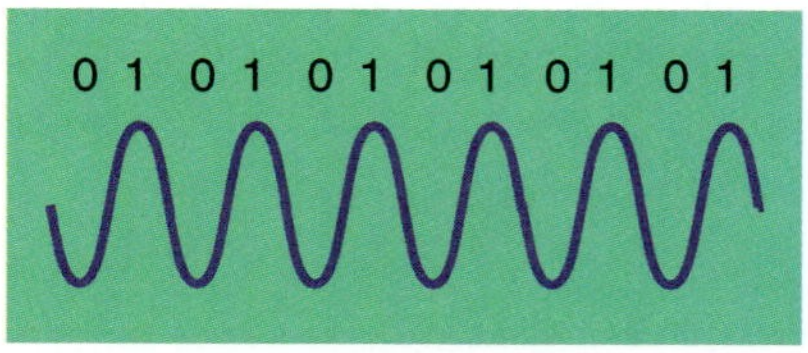

High frequency
Wide bandwidth

Frequency

Bandwidth and data

The bandwidth determines how fast data can be sent in a given period of time, measured as you've seen in bits per second (bps). Obviously, the bigger the file or the faster data must be sent, the more bandwidth you need. When sending just unformatted text, a page contains only about 5,000 bytes or 40,000 bits (5,000 × 8 bits), so it can be transmitted fairly quickly. Graphic files can be much larger, millions of bytes in size. These take much longer to transmit over a given connection than text. The largest consumer of bandwidth is video. To obtain television-quality video on your computer's screen, video has to be displayed in 640 × 480 resolution—meaning there are 307,200 pixels on the screen. Using 8 bits per pixel to display 256 colors would require 2,457,600 pixels on the screen to create a frame. That's almost 2.5 megabits. But things get worse: To convey the illusion of motion, a movie displays 30 frames per second. That's a grand total of 73,728,000 or 73 megabits per second. That's clearly not possible. Luckily, compression techniques for video allow a video signal to be sent at only 1.5 Megabits per second, still much faster then most dial-up lines.

Element	Number
Pixels per screen (640 x 480)	307,200
Bytes per pixel	8
Total bits per screen	2,457,600
Frames per second	30
Total bits per second	73,728,000

Video transmission times

Multiple calls on same wire

Influences on bandwidth

All data in computing and communications is sent using part of the electromagnetic spectrum, electricity, radio, or light. Regardless of how it's sent, there are always limitations, some physical and some social or business limitations. Each medium has a physical limit. Fiber-optic wires that use light to send signals have a much higher physical limit than do copper wires used for the connection to your phone line. Then other considerations come into play. Television and radio use part of the available broadcast bandwidth; each station is allowed only a tiny fraction so that other stations can use the medium. Along their wires or cables, the phone companies can't make money with only one call on a line. They need to squeeze as many transmissions as they can onto the same wires to increase traffic. To increase bandwidth, they can add more wires to the line or change the way the signals are sent and received. When it comes to squeezing more bandwidth out of existing lines, it's a never-ending pursuit.

ATM

In most networks, users compete for a piece of the same bandwidth. In an ATM-based network you are guaranteed a specific transmission rate. When sending video, this is especially important. On other networks, if the user can't get enough bandwidth the video will either be of poor quality or won't be transmitted at all. On an ATM network, the required bandwidth is always available.

Bandwidth And the Internet-The Diamond Lane

The National Science Foundation connects a number of university supercomputer centers with a very high performance Backbone Network System (vBNS). Recently upgraded to carry 622 megabits per second, it is much faster than the 45 megabits per second on the Internet.

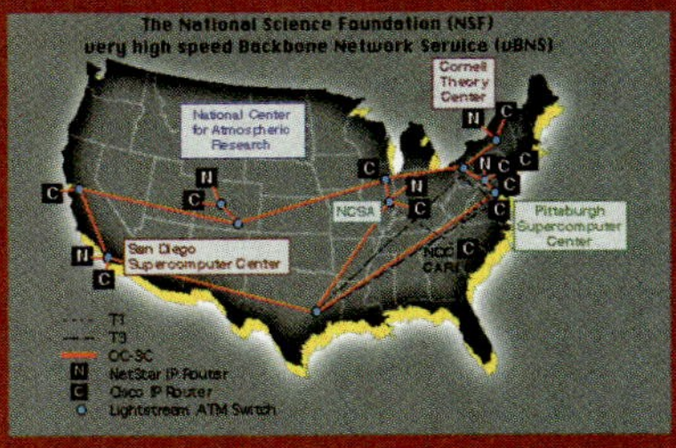

http://uadis.bpa.arizona.edu/byang/a2/vbns.html

9.6 Local Area Networks:

Up till now, we've talked mainly about network services such as the Internet that are available over the phone system. However, not all computers are connected to the phone system, at least not directly. Most of them are connected by their own systems of wires running through office buildings and campuses. These networks of computers within a small area are called local area networks or LANs.

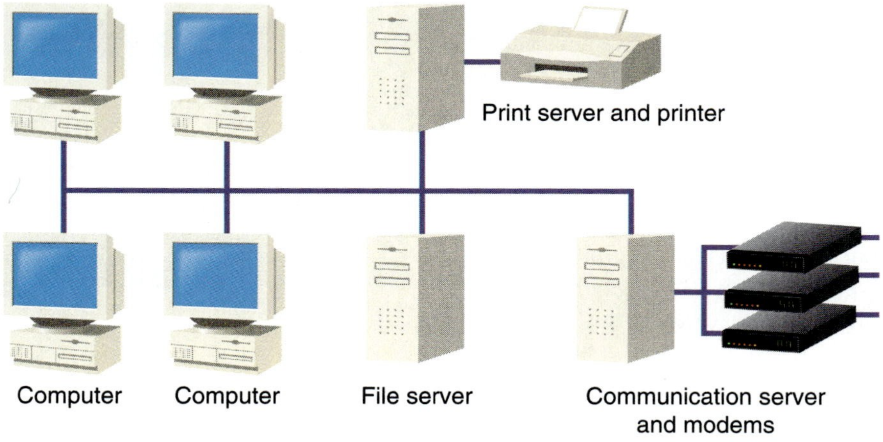

Local area network

Network resources

The old saying that "the whole is greater than the sum of its parts" is true of computers and other information processing devices. When connected to other computers, a computer becomes a gateway to immense amounts of local or international resources. Computers are connected to networks for a variety of reasons.

E-mail. One the most popular network applications is e-mail, the sending of messages to others on the network.

Sharing peripherals. Networked computers can share expensive peripherals such as plotters, laser printers, and hard disk drives.

Sharing files. When computers are linked, you can easily share or exchange files with other users on the network.

Groupware. Many computer activities involve more than one person. For example, an advertising campaign may be conceived by one person, written and illustrated by others, and approved by still others. Application programs, commonly called groupware, have been developed to make team or group activity easier. A document can be made available on the network to all members of the group so they can add suggestions or make modifications instead of using the interoffice mail. A typical groupware application is a common calendar on which anyone can make entries that others can see. Another is a document anyone can add to or change while others can see who is making the changes.

Network applications are one new development in computing. In this model, the application rests on a computer somewhere on the network, not on your own machine. When you want to use it, you transfer it to your system. The advantage of network applications is that a company has to fix or upgrade only one copy on the network. Under the current model, they have to fix or upgrade every copy on every machine. Network applications designed for the Internet are often written in languages such as Java or ActiveX.

Network users

To use a network, you first log on with an ID and a password. The ID is assigned by the network administrator. The password is selected by you and can (and should) be changed frequently to improve security. Because network software can be customized, what you see when you log on depends on the system's design. Normally you'll find printers, hard disks, and other shared assets listed on your system's dialog boxes even though they are located elsewhere on the network.

LAN users courtesy of courtesy of International Business Machines

Network administrators

Systems organized into a network are supervised by a network manager or administrator. This person can be a member of either the department the network is located in or the corporate computing department. The network manager is responsible for setting up or enforcing network procedures. He or she adds and removes users and assigns IDs and levels of access. For example, one user may be authorized access to correspondence files but denied access to financial analysis files. Some users can be given just read-only access, whereas others can be allowed to enter and update the files. This security prevents unauthorized users from altering files. The network administrator is responsible for troubleshooting problems should they arise and assisting both new and experienced users with problems.

Passwords

Many systems provide a high level of security by letting you assign passwords. Without a password, you can't use the system. If you do have a password but forget it, you can't use the system, so be sure to use passwords that you will remember.

- Don't share your password with anyone.
- Choose a password that is hard to guess. Mix letters with numbers, or select a famous saying and choose every fourth letter.
- Don't use a password that is your address, pet's name, nickname, spouse's name, telephone number, or one that is obvious such as sequential numbers or letters.
- Use longer passwords because they are more secure; six to eight characters is realistic.
- Be sure that your password is not visible on the computer screen when you enter it.
- Be sure that your password does not appear on printouts.
- Don't tape passwords to desks, walls, or terminals. Commit yours to memory.

LAN administrator courtesy of International Business Machines

9.7 Local Area Networks:

Although it's not necessary to know how networks work to use them, understanding them helps when you select a service, set up your system, or use services such as e-mail. Computers and other devices can be connected to form a local area network in several ways. These connections are the network's architecture or topology. A network's architecture is the way the data flows within the network, not to the way its parts are physically arranged in an office.

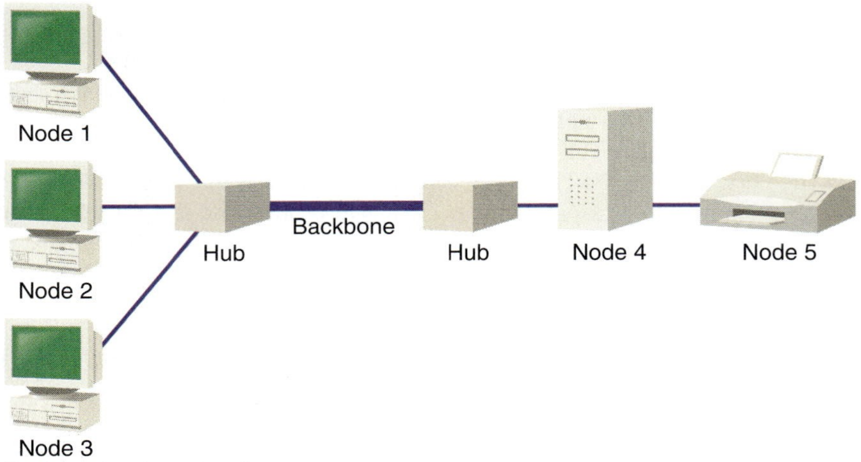

Basic parts of a network

Basic network architecture

The basic building blocks of a network are nodes, hubs, and backbones.

- A node is any piece of hardware on the system that can be addressed by a message from another node, that is, a computer, printer, fax, modem, or CD-ROM drive.
- Nodes are connected to a hub, also known as a concentrator, whose purpose is to simplify the wiring of the nodes to each other and to route signals between the nodes.
- A backbone is a high-capacity link to which many nodes or hubs can be connected. It's designed to carry lots of traffic.

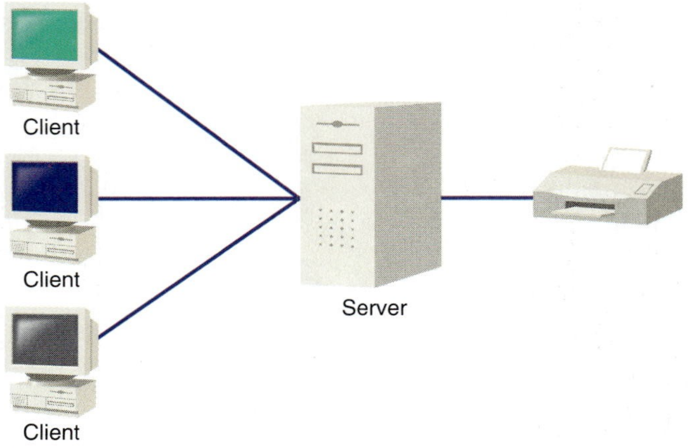

Server

Servers

A server on a LAN is any computer that can be shared by other computers working on the LAN. In many cases, the server has to be the most powerful computer on the network, because it is shared among so many users, or clients, so-called because these computers depend on the server for programs and data, or connections to other computers and devices. Let's look at some common types of servers.

- A file server stores data files and some application programs. It has large amounts of secondary storage in the form of hard disks, CD-ROM drives, tape drives, and other storage devices.
- A print server stores print jobs on a hard disk until the printer is ready to handle them.
- A communication server can be a fax or modem over which data from any other node can be sent. It can also be used as a gateway to the Internet.

Ring architecture

Ring architecture arranges the nodes on the network in a circle. When one of the computers on the network sends a signal, it passes it to the next node on the network. If it is not addressed to that node, it is retransmitted to the next node and so on around the circle until it reaches the node it is addressed to. The connections between computers are not direct; instead, each computer attaches to a hub and the ring itself resides inside the hub.

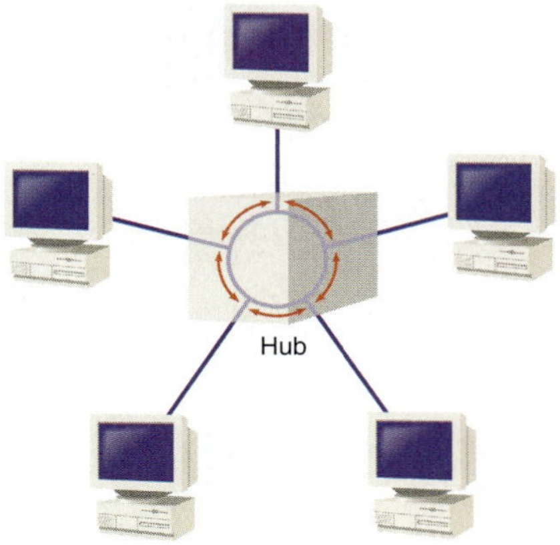

Ring topology

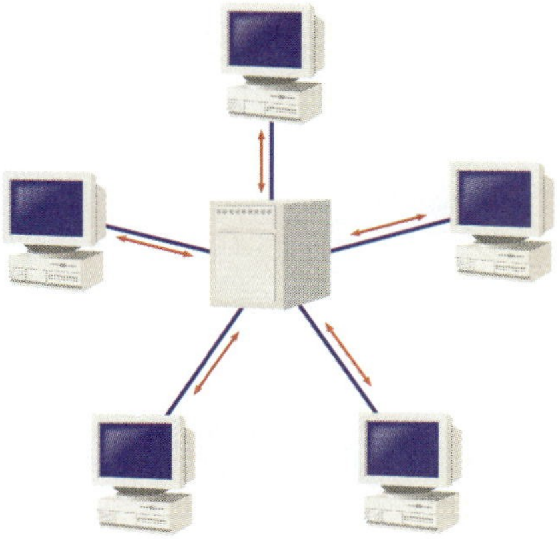

Star topology

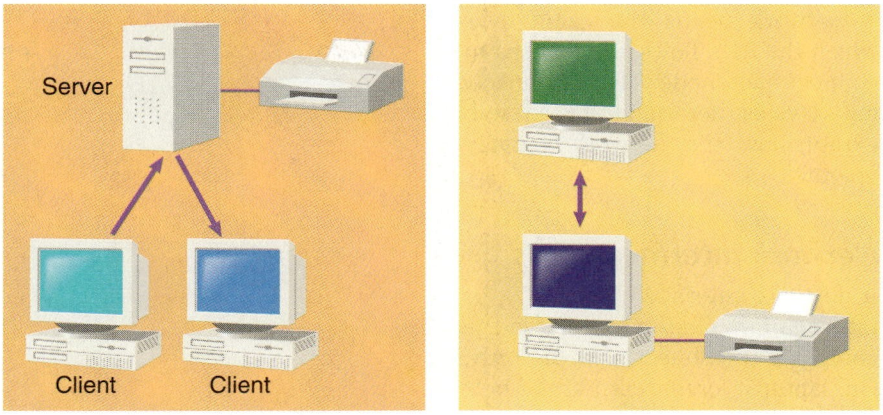

Client/server network

Peer-to-peer network

Client/server vs. peer-to-peer networks

Star architecture

Star architecture has the nodes connected to a central, or host, computer. When one of the computers on the network sends a signal, the host routes it to the node it's addressed to. There are no direct connections between the nodes on the network except through the host computer.

Bus architecture

Bus, or linear, architecture connects all nodes to a single bus, much as the components are organized within the computer. A signal addressed to another node is sent to the bus. All other nodes on the network examine the signal to see if it is addressed to one of them. Typically, wires connect each node to the network's backbone, which is a fixed length of cable with terminators at both ends to stop reflections when signals hit the end.

Peer-to-peer networks

The main problem with most networks is that they are difficult and expensive to set up and administer. To make things easier and less expensive, a peer-to-peer network is available. These networks are set up and run by the users, rather than by the corporate computing department. In these networks all the computers are equals. Unlike a client/server network, data do not pass through a server. You could be working on a spreadsheet on your computer while it was also routing print jobs from all of the other computers to your laser printer.

Wireless network connection courtesy of U.S. Robotics

Wireless LANs

Like radio or broadcast TV, wireless local area networks are connected by signals through the air instead of by wires. The base station connected to the network broadcasts to individual computers. Wireless LANs allow you to carry a laptop anywhere in a building to make a presentation. They eliminate the need to run cabling through an old building.

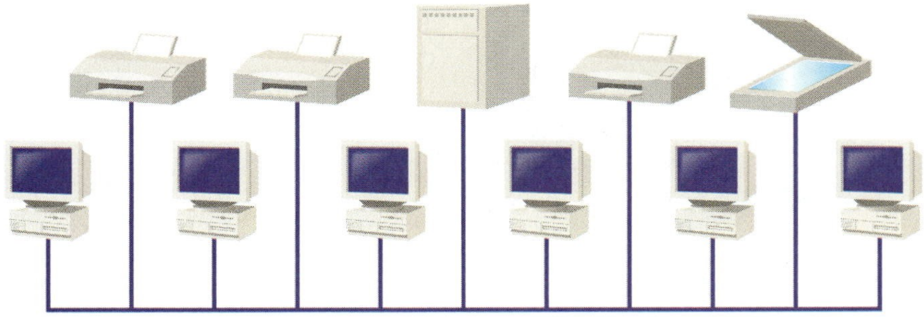

Bus topology

A network needs the cable over which the data flows and devices to connect each node. These connecting devices determine to a large extent how the network actually operates.

Fiber-optic wires courtesy of Corning Incorporated

Network interface cards

A network interface card (NIC), or LAN adapter, plugs into a slot in the computer to connect it to the LAN. On laptops, credit-card-sized network interface cards slip into bus slots on the machines. The network interface card serves a number of purposes:

- It makes the physical connection or bridge between the computer and the network.
- It converts the parallel data on the computer's bus into serial data for the network.
- It boosts or amplifies the signal's strength so it can flow through the cables.

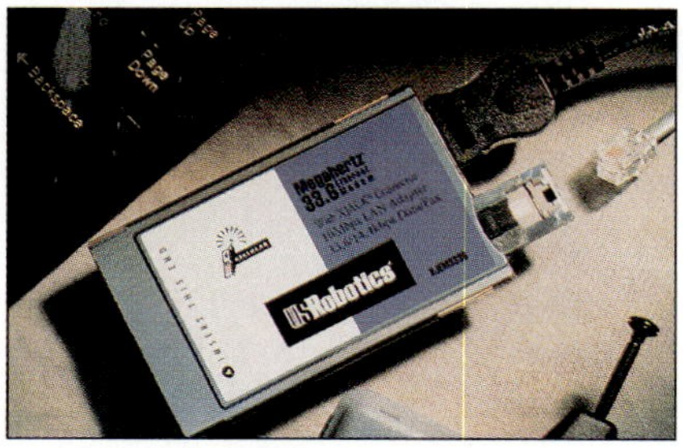

Network interface card courtesy of U.S. Robotics

Physical links between devices

When signals are sent through a hand-wired network, they are sent along a common set of wires or cables, the network's circulation system. Three types of cables are used to connect the devices: twisted pair, coaxial, and fiber optic.

Twisted-pair wires are similar to the wires used to connect your telephone. They are the least expensive way to connect computers because the wire is cheap and easy to install. Their disadvantages are that they are relatively slow and have a tendency to pick up noise that can cause high error rates.

Coaxial cables like those in your cable TV system are layered with an inner wire surrounded by an insulating material that is, in turn, surrounded by a braided wire. This braided wire shields the inner wire from any noise in the environment that can affect the quality of the transmission. Coaxial cables are reliable and have a wide bandwidth, so they can transmit data much faster than twisted-pair wires.

Fiber-optic cables are made of plastic or glass fibers the thickness of a human hair and covered with an opaque sheath that keeps light from entering or escaping. The digital signals from a computer are used to code pulses of a light beam that carry information read at the receiving end. Fiber-optic cables are fast and reliable, as well as small and light. They have an extremely wide bandwidth, so a large number of signals can be sent simultaneously. Their only drawback is that they are more difficult to install.

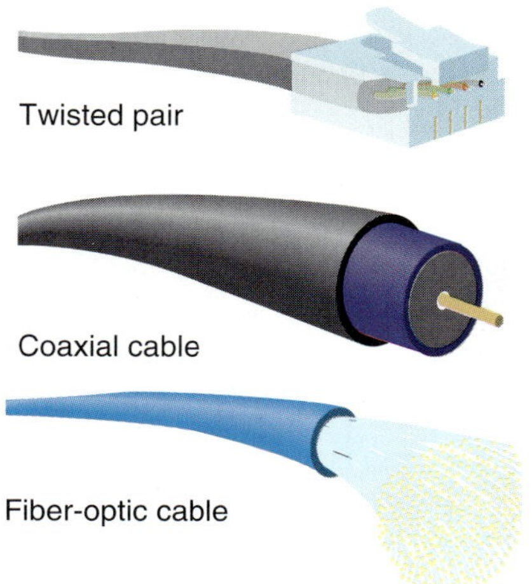

Wires

Media access control

The cabling in a network can carry signals from only one node at a time or signals would interfere with one another. For this reason, a LAN needs a media-access control (MAC) scheme to prevent any overlapping signals. In a classroom where everyone spoke at once there would be chaos. The classroom media-access scheme is raising your hand and waiting to be called on so everyone has a chance to speak with everyone else's undivided attention. The network interface card determines the access method used by the network. The two most popular access methods are Ethernet and token-ring.

Ethernet

The first network access system, called Ethernet, was developed by Xerox in the 1970s to link computers to laser printers. Ethernet employs Carrier Sense Multiple Access/Collision Detection (CSMA/CD), using all nodes which listen to the traffic on the network and try to send data only when it's quiet. It's much like a group of people trying to have a polite conversation. If two nodes transmit at the same time, they detect the collision, and all nodes go quiet for a short, random period before attempting to resend the data. Since the periods are random, one node will send first and gain control of the network.

The three most popular implementations of Ethernet are called 10Base-5, 10Base-2, and 10Base-T. The number 10 indicates the speed in megahertz, "Base" indicates that it's based on Ethernet, and the last number indicates the cable used to connect the node, for example, 5 for 0.5-inch thick coaxial cable, 0.2 for .2-inch thick coaxial cable, and T for twisted pair.

Ethernet can use any of the network architectures, star, bus, or ring. 10Base-5 and 10Base-2 use a bus architecture and 10Base-T uses a star architecture.

Like other systems, Ethernet is constantly improved to move more data. The latest version, Gigabit Ethernet, delivers data at gigabit speeds making it possible to deliver multimedia applications over the network. At the moment, Fast Ethernet operating at 100 megahertz is being widely installed.

Media access control courtesy of International Business Machines

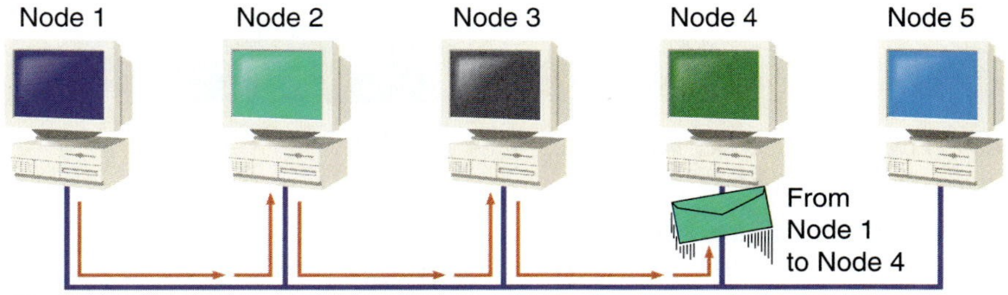

Ethernet

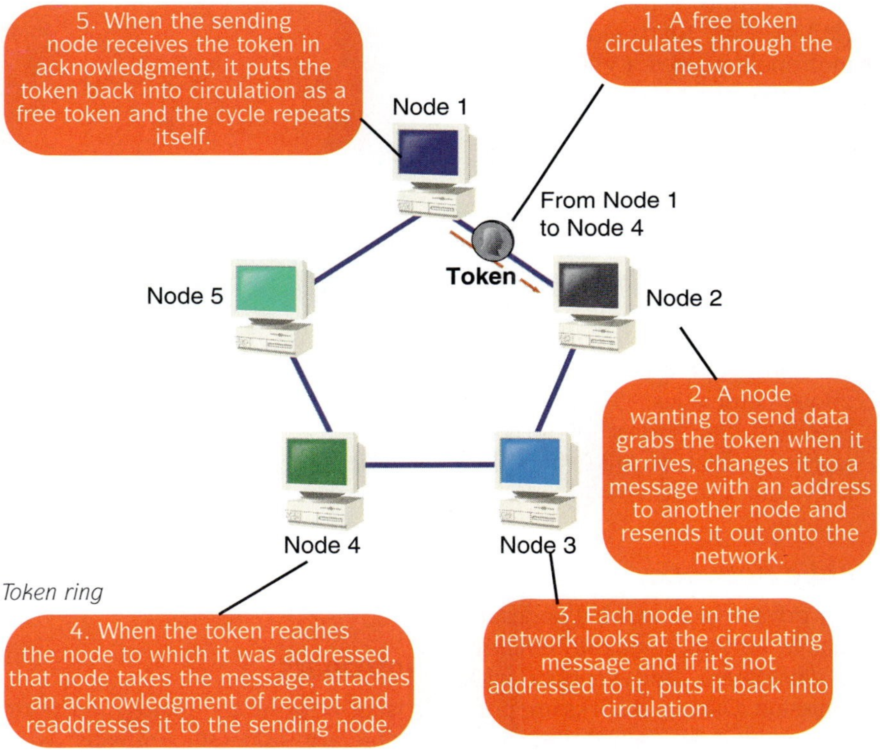

Token ring

Token ring

Token ring is the major alternative to Ethernet. Unlike Ethernet, where nodes battle for the network, token-ring networks are more orderly. Nodes cannot address the network without first obtaining permission in the form of an electronic token that circulates around the network. Because the token must circulate to all machines, token-ring networks use a ring architecture. These networks use shielded or unshielded twisted-pair wiring.

Token ring has a number of advantages. First, the sending node always gets confirmation that its data was received. Second, it always guarantees that the next node on the network gets access when a transmission is complete.

9.9 Wide Area Networks:

Local area networks usually work only in a single building or on a campus where computers are closely grouped. To connect facilities scattered all over the city, country, or world local area networks need to be connected to each other in wider networks.

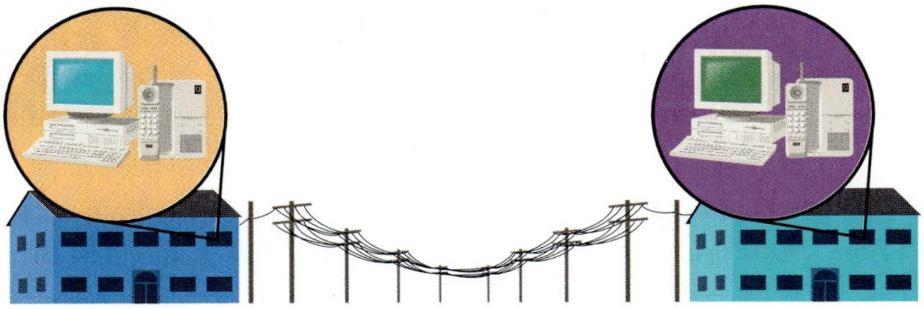

Public telephone network

Metropolitan and wide area networks

Depending on the area covered by the expanded network, it is called a metropolitan or wide area network.

- Metropolitan area networks (MANs) are scattered around a metropolitan area. Cellular phone networks are a good example of such networks.
- Wide area networks (WANs) have elements scattered over a larger geographic region. Parts of the network may be connected by cables and other parts by microwave or satellite transmissions. Typical wide area networks are those operated by the telephone companies. The Internet is probably the widest of all networks in that it links not only LANs but also other WANs.

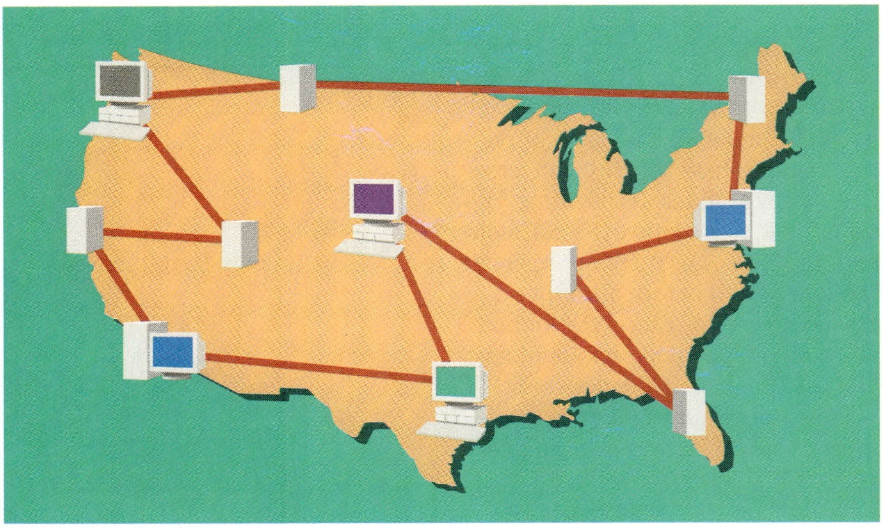

Internet

Public networks

Many private wide area networks are available only to corporate employees, customers, and vendors with permission. Other networks are public in that anyone can use them for a fee. Given the high cost of setting up a private wide area network, very few organizations own their own outright. In almost all cases, the physical parts of a network larger than a local area network travel over the public networks owned by phone companies and other service providers called commercial carriers. In some cases, companies lease lines so they have a specified capacity available at all times and the right to put a certain amount of traffic over these circuits without delays. Traffic from other customers of the public carrier may be going over the same physical lines at the same time.

Intranets

Using Internet technology, corporations are building company wide intranets accessible only to their employees and other invited users. Intranets are used not only for posting documents within an organization, but also for linking software, databases, and hardware into a universal network.

These private intranets share the same software and hardware as the Internet and speak the same language, but are fenced off from others on the Internet by defensive barriers called firewalls (see next page).

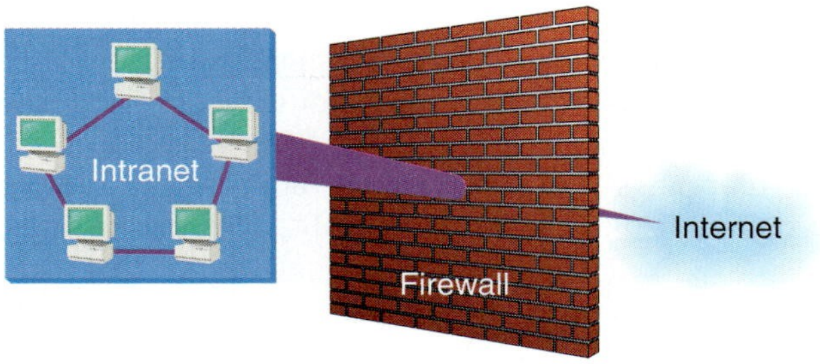

Intranet

Introduction

Ford Motor Company uses its intranet to link design centers around the world so engineers can collaborate on the design of new cars. Sun employees use their intranet for e-mail, expense reports, benefit changes, travel authorizations, and as an information resource for marketing, product, and corporate information.

Intranets are popular for a variety of reasons.

- The resources on the intranet are accessible to anyone, anywhere as long as they have a computer, a modem, and a password.
- Complex data and applications can be used over the intranet with ease.
- Learning to use an intranet is simple. If you know how to use the Web, you know how to use an intranet.
- Costs are lower because so much software and so many connections are available from so many sources.

Firewalls

The metal between an automobile's passenger area and engine compartment is called a firewall because it's designed to prevent an engine fire from spreading into the passenger compartment. The same idea is used in networking to prevent unauthorized users on the Internet from reaching the files and programs on the local area network. When a computer connected to the outside Internet is also connected to an inside local area network, a firewall is installed between the Internet and the local network.

Users behind the firewall can access Internet services but can't provide them or intranet services to others outside the firewall. If a company wants to provide interactive services, it puts a file server outside the firewall. Since outsiders can't get past the firewall, any files that you want them to access are put on that server. E-mail, mailing lists, and news services are store-and-forward services where the outsider does not have interactive access to computers inside the firewall.

Why firewalls?

One of the reasons firewalls are necessary is the number of attacks that can be launched against a network connected to the Internet. Here are just some of them:

Data driven attacks are encoded in normal data, for example, in a word processing document's macros. Since it's assumed to be data, a data driven attack may penetrate a firewall and then launch an attack against a system behind the firewall.

Trojan horse is when a program that appears to do something normal actually contains a trapdoor or attack program.

DNS spoofing is having a computer assume the domain name of another system. IP spoofing is when a system impersonates another system by using its network address.

IP splicing/hijacking or session stealing is an attack in which an active session is intercepted after an authentication has been made, allowing the attacker to assume the role of an authorized user and gain access information.

Social engineering is the name for an attack based on deceiving users or administrators at the target site. One way it's done is to telephone a user or operator and pretend to be an authorized user.

Viruses are self-replicating code segments that may contain attack programs or trapdoors, secret entry points that let users get to your data without you knowing it.

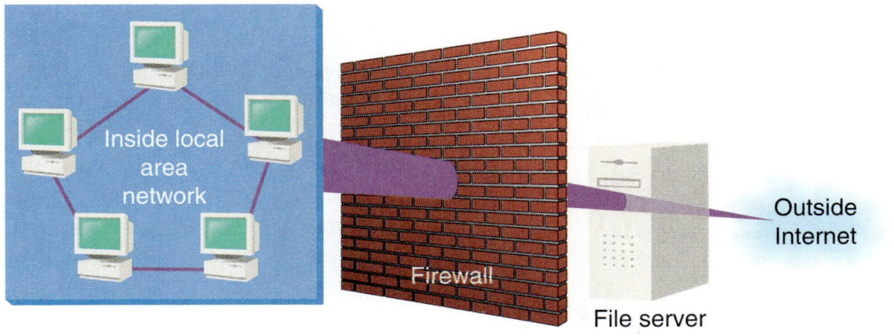

Firewall

9.10 Links between Networks:

When you send data over wires or cable or broadcast it through the air, you are sending it over transmission media. Media with a narrow bandwidth, such as the wires running from your phone, can carry voice and data but can't carry the large amounts of data required by video. Other media, such as coaxial cable used to connect your TV to a cable system, have a much wider bandwidth and can easily carry video signals. The fastest of all media are fiber-optic links.

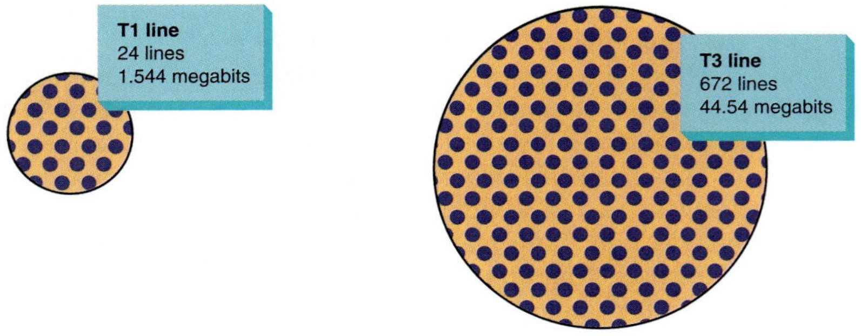

Type	Kilobits per line	Number of lines	Total Bandwidth
T1	64 kilobits	24	1.54 megabits
T3	64 kilobits	672	44.54 megabits

T1 and T3 connections

Network devices

When signals are sent through a network, they must be sent in the right direction, and they must also sometimes be amplified so they travel farther or converted so they can be transferred to a different network. These are the roles of a series of hardware devices called repeaters, bridges, routers, and gateways.

- Repeaters, also known as physical relays, connect segments of a network, and since signals get weaker and less distinct with distance, these small devices refresh and enhance them before sending them along. Their job is to extend the network as far as possible, perhaps to another building.
- Bridges, also known as data link relays, connect networks which use different physical links. For example, a network running on twisted-pair wires is connected to one using coaxial cable with a bridge.
- Routers control where messages are sent on networks. The router keeps the addresses of other nodes in a table. If the address of a message sent though the router is on the network, the message is forwarded. If the address is not on the network, the router forwards the message to another network by sending it to a gateway.
- Gateways are used to connect different types of networks. Since two networks may not share a common protocol these devices translate each network's protocol so the other network can understand the data.

Wired links between networks

When networks are connected, it usually means there is heavy traffic between them. To accommodate the need for high bandwidth connection, the phone companies have added special wires to some of their services, the equivalent of adding more lanes to a highway. One of the most common is called a T1 line. Since a phone line can carry only 64 kilobits per second, a T1 line uses 24 of these lines running in parallel and can therefore carry 24 phone conversations, for a total bandwidth of 1.544 megabits per second. If more capacity is needed, a T3 line is used. These lines are equivalent to 672 voice-grade telephone lines and have a bandwidth of 44.54 megabits per second. This is fast enough for the most bandwidth-hungry applications such as high-quality video conferencing, collaborative computer-aided design work, and work with very large databases over a busy network. A T3 line is typically installed as a major networking artery for large corporations and universities with high volume network traffic. For example, the backbones of the major Internet service providers are T3 lines.

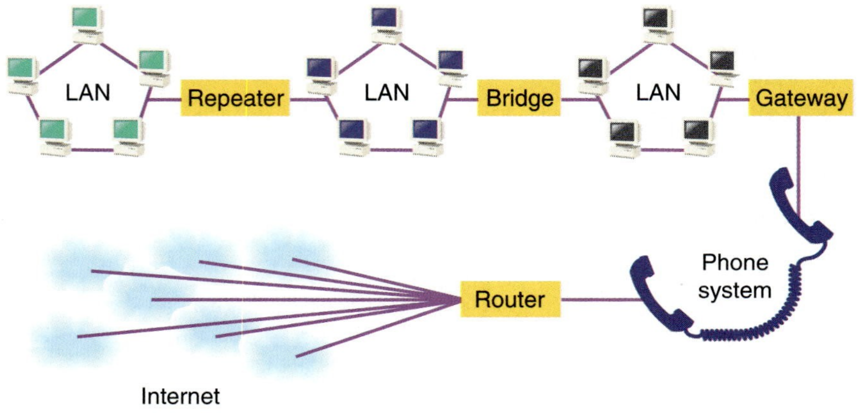

Net hardware

Broadcast links between networks

Having parts of the network scattered over a large geographic area presents connection problems. These networks must be connected over cables that are privately owned or else leased from companies such as the phone company. The cables may be shared with other users or dedicated to just a single user. In places where cables are not economical, other forms of connections based on radio waves are used. Over short distances, high-frequency microwaves send the signal. Over longer distances, satellites can be used.

Microwaves are sent and received using small dish antennas. You frequently see these small dishes mounted on high buildings or towers. They are useful only for sending short distances since the beam cannot be blocked. These line of sight transmissions must avoid other buildings or mountains and can't follow the curvature of the earth.

Satellites are used for extremely long-range transmissions. Signals are sent (uplinked) to the satellite from a ground-based dish antenna. The satellite then retransmits the signal (downlinks it) to another station. You may have seen mobile ground stations mounted on large trucks near the site of a major sporting event. Television networks use satellites to transmit their signals from the site of the event to their broadcast center, perhaps a continent or more away.

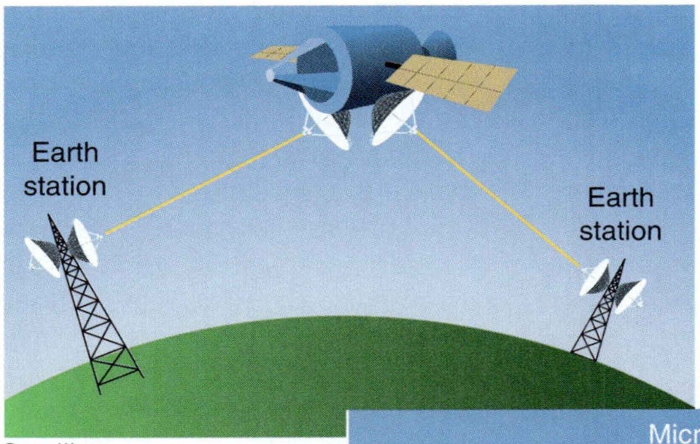

Satellites

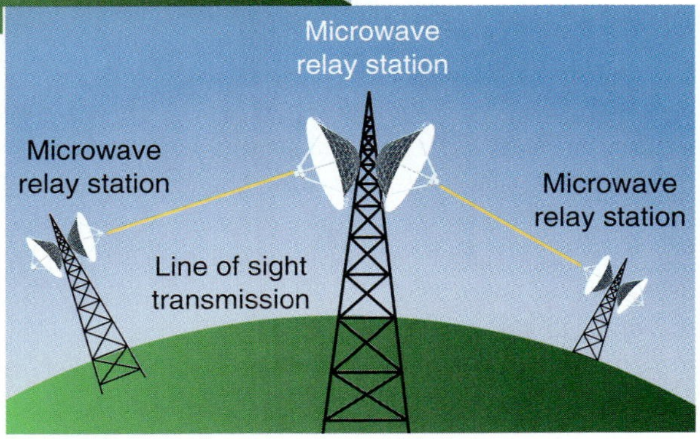

Microwaves

Systems

Physical media such as cables and broadcast media such as radio waves may be combined. When you are connected to a WAN such as the Internet, your data may go through wires to a certain point, then be broadcast to a satellite where it's rebroadcast to another point where it resumes its trip by wire. Since there are various types of connections being made, the speed and quality of the signal are determined by the speed and quality of the worst link.

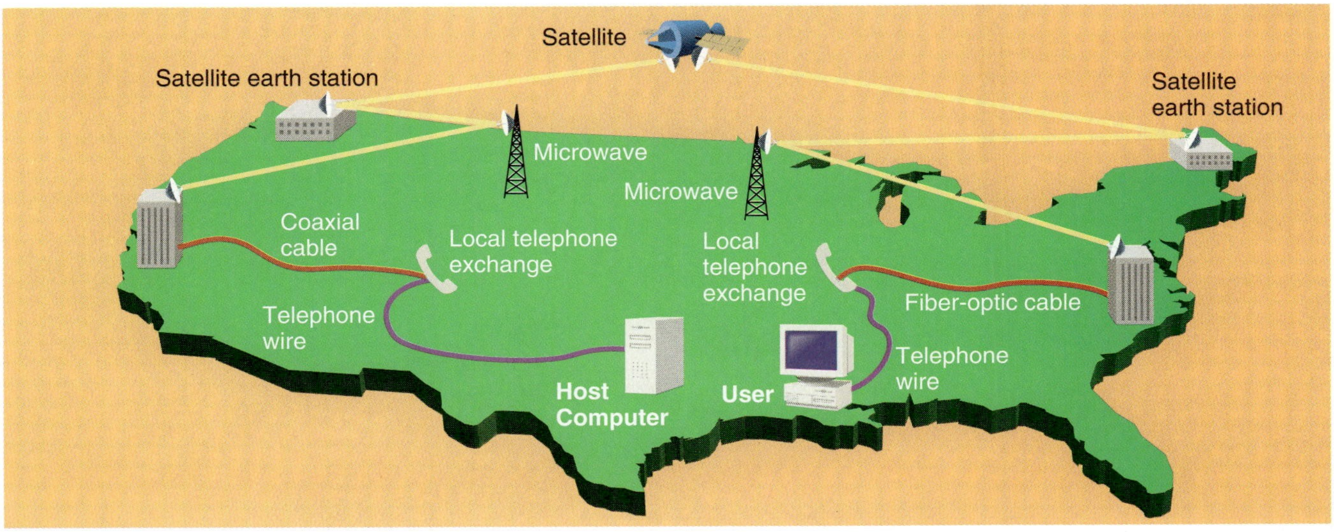

System

9.11 Links between Networks:

When you think of networks like the Internet, it's natural to think of the telephone network as an analogy. Partly this is because a lot of the Internet's traffic flows over the same phone system that delivers your phone call. There is a big difference however in the ways these two networks organize their information flows.

Circuit-switched networks

The phone network is a circuit-switched network. When you pick up a phone in New York and dial a number in California, switches along the line route the call and reserve a circuit for you straight through to your destination. This circuit is dedicated to your call and only your call. It's as if a single wire were strung between you and the person you are talking to.

Packet-switched networks

Circuit-switched networks are OK for phone calls but they really aren't efficient when lots of data must be sent between two points. In these situations, it's better if the connection worked more like the postal service. In this analogy, you write a message and put it into an envelope. You then drop the envelope into a post office box. The post office sorts it and sends it mixed up with a lot of other mail to a regional post office where it is again sorted. From there, some of the mail is taken by carriers to local addresses but a lot of it is passed on to the next center closer to its destination. Your letter may pass though a number of these sorting centers before it is eventually delivered to the recipient. As the sender, you don't have to know how the post office gets the letter there. You're responsible only for getting the address right. The post office will do the rest.

On the Internet, as with the post office, all you have to do is get the address right and Internet will do the rest. And like the post office, it doesn't send data directly from one point to another. Instead, it sends it to another computer called a router. Routers look at the data's address and pass it on to the next router closer to the destination. Eventually the data arrives at the address to which it was sent.

How the data is sent is what makes the Internet possible. When you send or receive data, the Internet doesn't open up a dedicated line for you like the phone company does. If it did, the line would be doing nothing much of the time and would be withheld from other users until it was relinquished. This would be too wasteful of precious resources. Instead, the Internet breaks everyone's data into small sections called packets, intermingles packets from any and all users, and then reassembles them at their various destinations. It's as if you wanted to write a long letter but had only post cards to write on. You could begin the letter on post card 1 and finish it on post card 10. As long as you then addressed them to the same place, and assigned each a sequential number, the recipient could reassemble them and read them in order even if they arrived out of order and at different times. This is how the Internet works and why it's called a packet-switched network. Data is broken up into pieces, addressed and numbered, and directed by routers to its destination. To make this work, all computers must be following the same rules, called protocols.

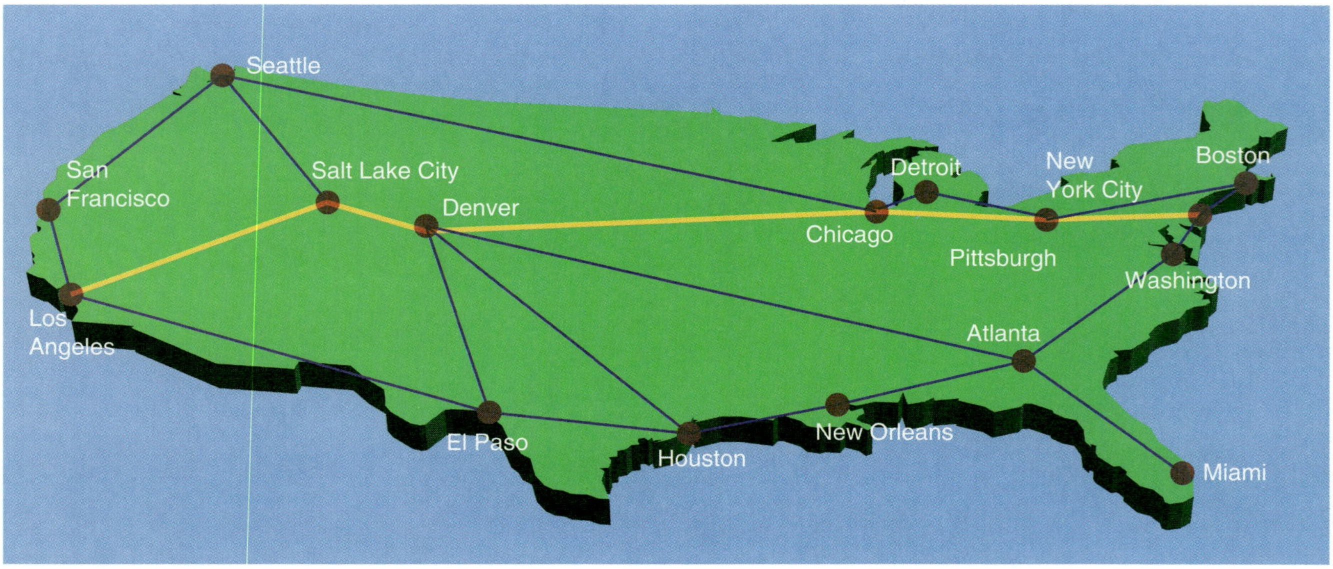

Circuit-switched network

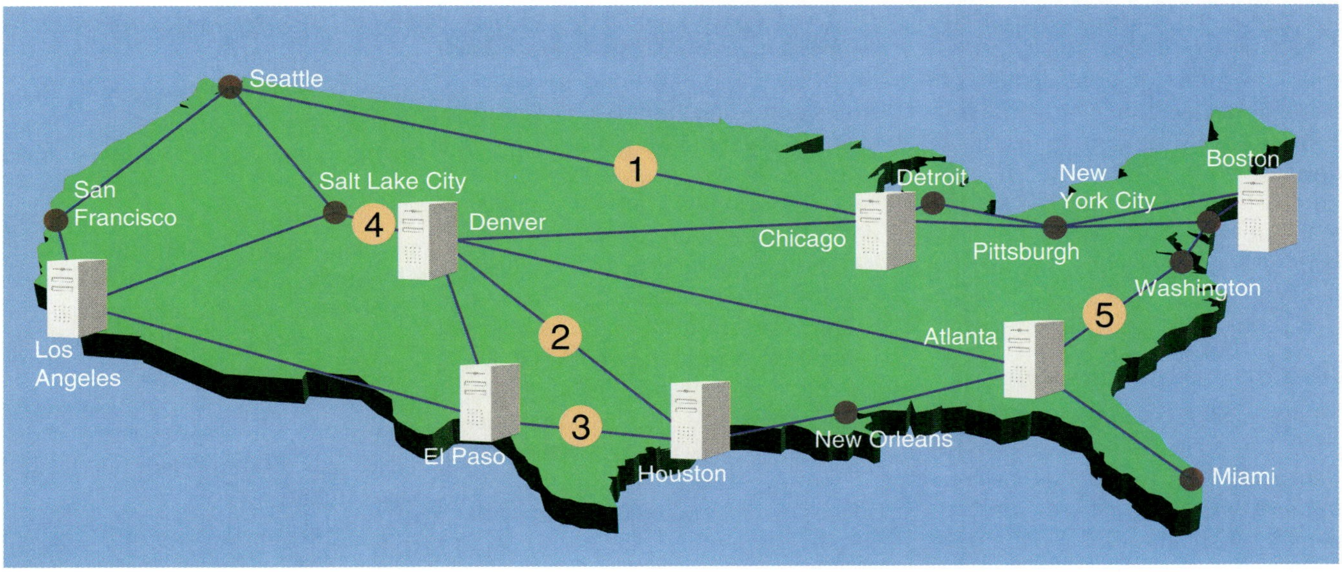

Packet-switched network

The language of the Internet

On the Internet there are two sets of basic rules, the Internet Protocol (IP) and the Transmission Control Protocol (TCP), Internet-speak for "If your computer speaks the same language as the other computers on the Web, they can talk to each other."

Internet Protocol (IP). The first step in getting data to the right place is to get the address right and in a form that can be read by everyone that handles the message along the line. A letter sent through the post office to an address handwritten in Chinese won't get to a recipient as quickly as one typed in English, because each time it is handled, there will be problems reading the address. On the Internet the Internet Protocol (IP) governs the way data is addressed and routed along the Internet. To get a message from one user to another, the message is put into an Internet/Protocol "envelope" and addressed to the recipient. Routers then move it through the system to the user with that address.

Transmission Control Protocol (TCP). If you sent a huge graphic file to someone else on the network, it could tie up other people's work as they waited for your transfer to be finished. To eliminate this problem, another protocol, called Transmission Control Protocol (TCP), breaks your message up into packets, each containing between one and 1500 characters. It numbers each of the units, puts each into an IP packet (envelope), and sends them. Each packet may travel a different route and take a different time to arrive at its destination. Some may even get lost or damaged in transit. At the recipient's end TCP extracts the data from each envelope, checks each for accuracy, and reassembles them into their original order. If it finds that any data are lost or damaged, it requests that those packets be retransmitted.

TCP/IP protocols

9.12 Networks:

When you are not physically part of a network, you can still access it over the public telephone network using a device that connects your computer to that network. The device you use depends on what kind of link you need. At the moment, the most commonly used connecting device is an analog modem.

Analog phone modems

In essence, an analog modem lets your computer use the telephone. Using a Web browser or other communications program, you can then connect with any similarly equipped computer or network.

There are two main types of analog modems. One is an adapter card or PC card that plugs into an expansion slot in the computer. The other is an external modem that connects to the computer's serial port with a cable. Both types are then connected to the telephone's wall jack with a standard phone cable.

Currently many modems operate under the international standard called V.34. This standard allows analog modems (and faxes) to communicate at rates as high as 115.2 kilobits per second but over the telephone lines they operate at top speeds up to 33.6 kilobits per second.

How analog modems work

Analog modems are needed to connect computers to phone lines because the computer generates digital signals but telephone lines carry analog signals. A modem at the sending end converts the computer's digital signals into analog signals (modulation). The modem at the receiving end then converts the analog signals back into digital signals (demodulation) so that they can be used by the computer. The name modem derives from these two procedures: **mo**dulate and **dem**odulate.

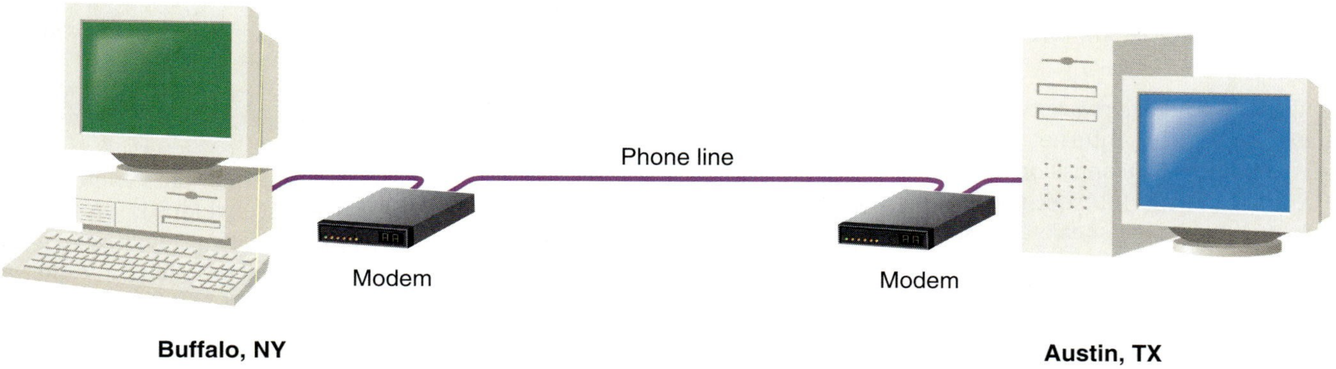

Modems

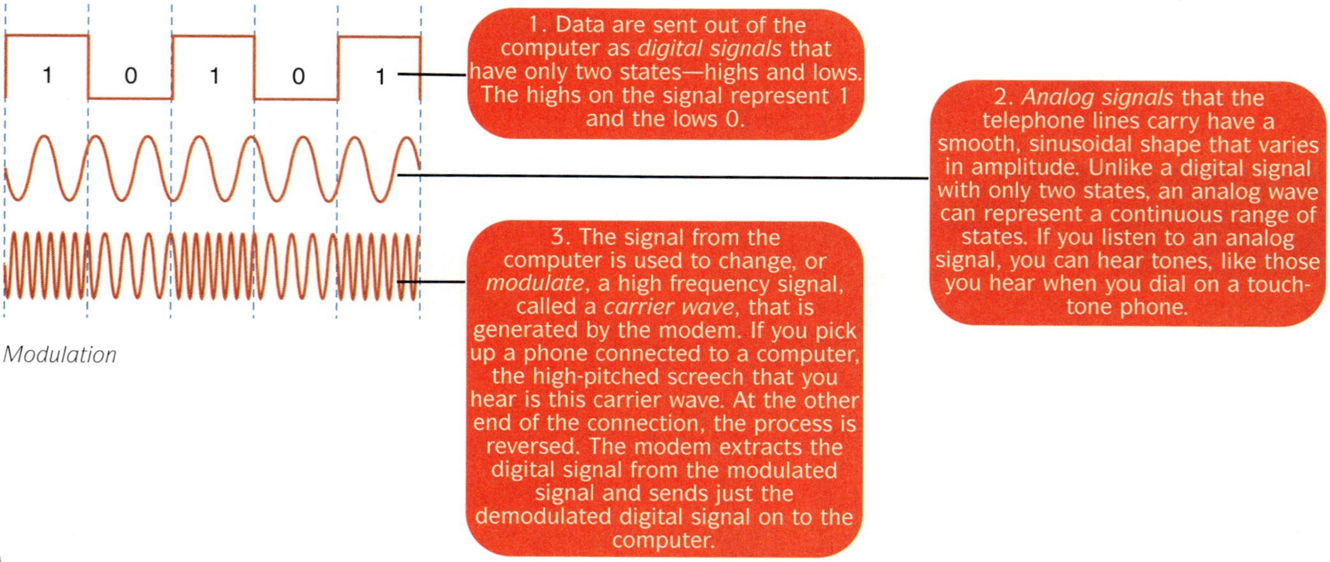

Modulation

56.6 K modems

The latest 56.6K modems assume that your company or service provider has a digital connection to the phone network. This allows their system to send data to you (downstream) at 56 kilobits per second because that data isn't modulated. However, because you have to modulate signals to send them back (upstream), you are limited to 33.6 kilobits per second in that direction.

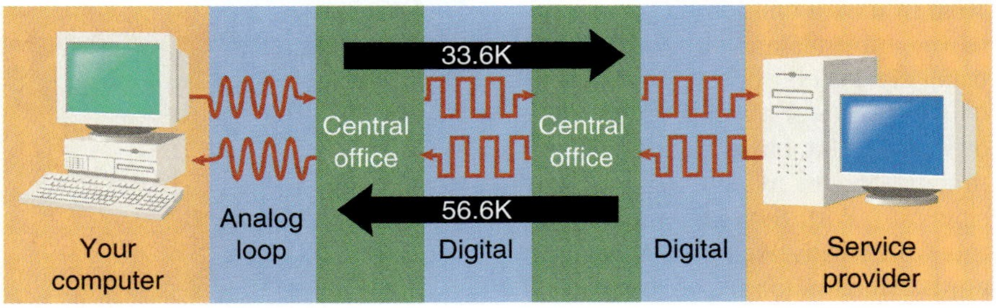

56.6K modems

Simultaneous voice and data

Normally you have to choose whether to use voice or send data when you make a call. However, new technologies such as VoiceView and Digital Simultaneous Voice and Data allow you to do both on the same call.

A VoiceView modem lets you alternate between voice and bursts of data on a single phone call. During a conversation, you can send faxes or data back and forth by clicking on the send icon. During data transmission, there is a temporary suspension of verbal communication, but it resumes automatically after the data has been sent.

Digital Simultaneous Voice and Data (DSVD) is another technology that allows you to exchange data or fax transmissions as you talk. Unlike VoiceView, it allows you to do so simultaneously. You can discuss and even manipulate documents, graphs, or spreadsheets during a telephone call. It allows interactive game players to speak to their off-site opponents as they are playing the game!

Voice and data at the same time

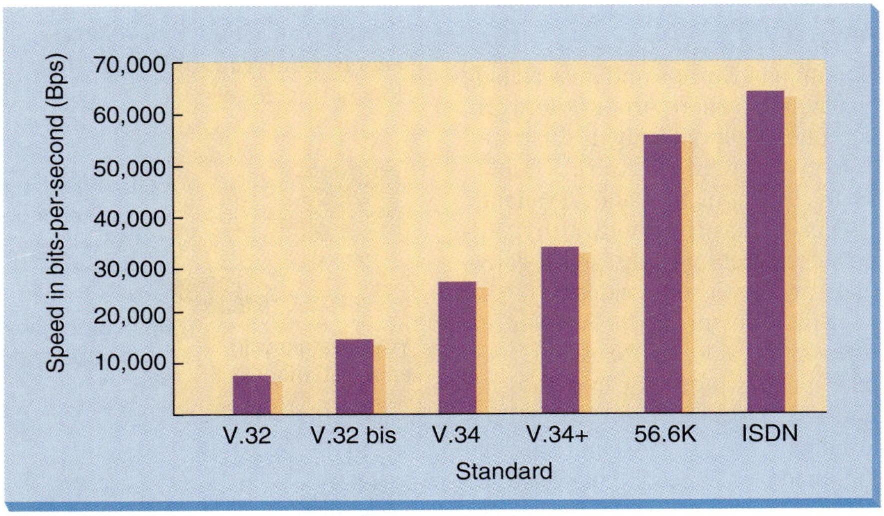

Standards

Telephone Network Traffic

Less than a decade ago, only 20 percent of the traffic sent over a telephone was data (the rest was voice). Today, 50 percent of the traffic is data and some estimate that by the end of the century data will comprise 80% of telephone traffic.

Most of us are still forced to connect to the Internet and other networks using slow-speed phone lines. These connections work well when sending or viewing text, but graphics and multimedia trickle in at a frustratingly slow rate. With the new emphasis on the World Wide Web and networked applications such as ActiveX and Java, much faster connections are needed. Don't despair, there are faster connections on the horizon, and many of these are already available in selected areas or being tested right now. Over the next decade, the use of these higher-speed connections will be available to more people as the services are expanded around the world.

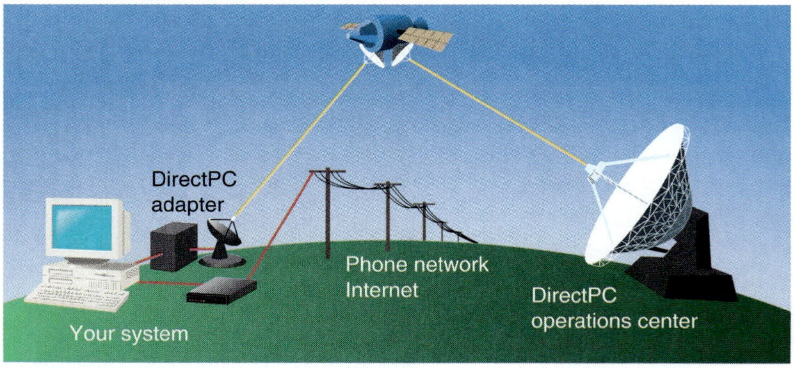

DirectPC

DirectPC

DirectPC uses satellites to download information to your computer at 400 kilobits per second. You send commands and data back over a phone line at the speed of your modem connection.

Integrated services digital network (ISDN)

Common in Europe and increasingly available in other parts of the world is a phone service called Integrated Services Digital Network (ISDN). ISDN is popular, where available, because it has the bandwidth needed to simultaneously send voice, data, and even some video.

Unlike even faster coaxial or fiber-optic cable, ISDN can be used over the existing phone lines into you house or business. Since ISDN lines are digital, they don't require an analog modem. Instead, you need an ISDN terminal adapter, sometimes called an ISDN modem or digital modem. This service provides three channels: one for ringing signals and two for data and voice communications at 64 kilobits per second each. These two channels allow you to talk on the phone and transmit data over the same line. If you bond the two channels together, you can send data at between 115.2 and 128 kilobits per second versus about a maximum of 56.6 kilobits for an analog modem.

Asymmetrical digital subscriber line (ADSL)

Like ISDN, Asymmetrical Digital Subscriber Line (ADSL) is a technology used to deliver video and other high-bandwidth data streams over a standard pair of copper telephone wires. ADSL is capable of sending data at a speed of 9 megabits per second from the other computer to you (downstream) and 800 kilobits per second from you back (upstream). How is this done?

When you make a phone call, you are actually using less than 5 percent of the line's capacity. ADSL uses the other 95 percent. Research has shown that although telephone lines are swamped with noise, there are parts of the line that are almost always clear. With ADSL, the line is broken up into 255 channels, called "bins." One of these bins is reserved for voice and the other 254 for the data. At any given moment, some of these bins are noisy while others are clear and which are clear and which are noisy changes from second to second. Modems using special chips called digital signal processors continually monitor each bin and rush data down the clear ones, avoiding the noisy ones.

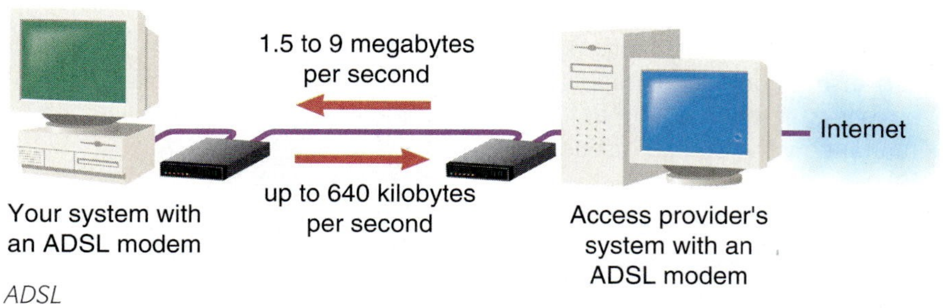

ADSL

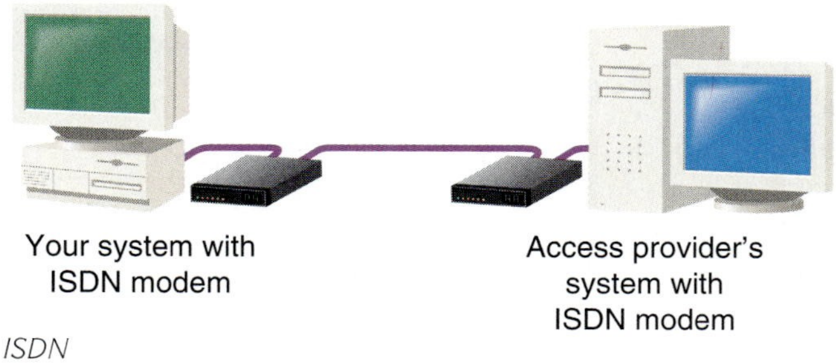

ISDN

Cable modems

The coaxial cable that comes into your home from the cable company can carry data much faster than a telephone line and analog modem. However, when these cable systems were built, they were designed to send video to your home (downstream). Like a tree, the data flows from the cable station out a wide bandwidth trunk that then branches off to individual homes. No one anticipated that you would want to send anything back (called upstream). These one-way systems are slowly being converted to two-way systems. By 2001 it's expected that these upgraded lines will be accessible by 85 percent of American homes. To connect to an upgraded cable line, you use a two-way cable modem. The first cable systems were sending data to you (downstream) at 1.5 megabits per second and allowing you to send it back (upstream) at 300 kilobits per second.

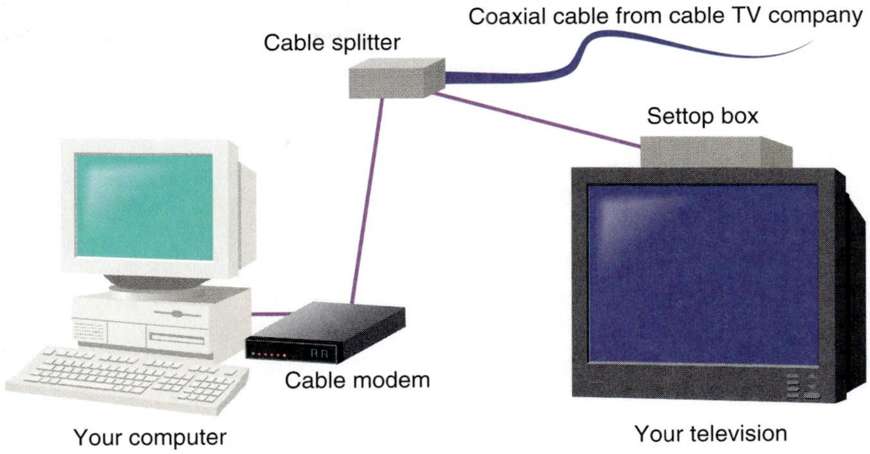

Cable connection to the Internet

Wireless connections

The ultimate network connection is a wireless one that allows you to connect from anywhere at any time. These are already available to those who use a modem to connect a laptop computer to a cellular phone. Like phone connections, these offer only 33.4 kilobit per second connections. Packet radio, like cellular-telephone systems, consists of a network of two-way radios. These radios are in turn connected to the phone system and Internet. They are less expensive than cellular connections but operate at the same slow speeds. The best choice in the short term seems to be wireless cable networks. These systems use powerful transmitters to broadcast signals (usually cable TV signals) over a relatively small area. For network access, these have very high capacity but it must be shared by all of the users. Although it can send almost 30 megabits per second, each subscriber will have to be limited to 1 megabit per second or less, perhaps as little as 128,000 bps.

In the long run, the best network access will be through direct satellite links. With these systems, you can be canoeing in the wilderness and check into the office or check the weather on the Web. Two networks for this kind of access are being developed: Iridium and Teledesic.

Iridium plans a network of 66 satellites for full global coverage and Teledesic plans to launch 840. The satellites talk not just to ground stations but also to each other, allowing them to pass on connections to other satellites as they orbit out of range. These networks are designed to offer videoconferencing and interactive multimedia. In the diagram of the Iridium satellite network shown below. Each satellite flies overhead and looks down for signals in its coverage area.

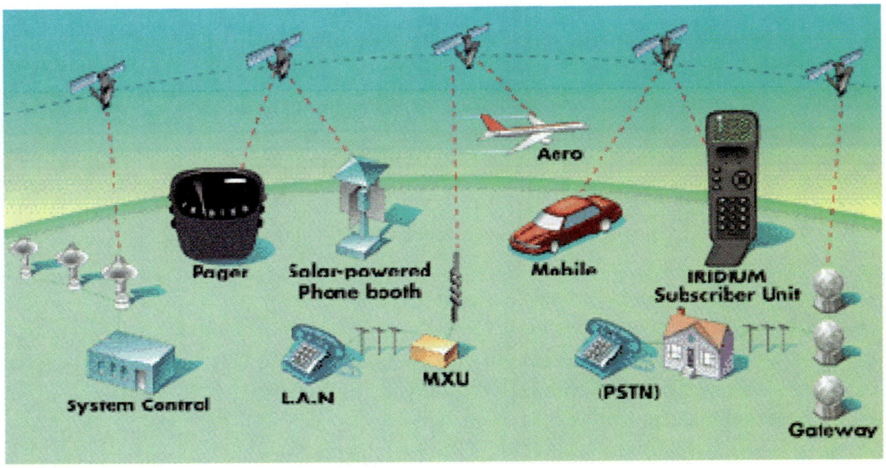

Satellite modems courtesy of Iridium
http://www.iridium.com/systm/systm.html

9.14 Enhancing and Testing Your Understanding

Summary

- A facsimile machine is like a copy machine where you insert the original document into your machine and a copy comes out on another facsimile machine anywhere else in the world using the phone lines.
- A computer with a fax/modem adapter card installed can send and receive faxes over the phone line.
- To connect with a commercial service you dial one of their numbers, called a point-of-presence (POP).
- An e-mail address has two parts: the user's name and the name of the computer the user's mail is stored on called a domain name. An "at" sign (@) separates these two parts.
- Usenet (Users Network) is a collection of thousands of ongoing topical discussions called newsgroups.
- Sending an insulting or abusive e-mail message or newsgroup posting is called a flame. An exchange of such messages is called a flame war.
- Mass unwanted e-mailings are called spams because they reminded someone of a routine in Monty Python's Flying Circus.
- Mailing lists use e-mail to keep groups informed. Listservs and Majordomo are the most popular mailing list software packages.
- Video conferencing uses cameras at two or more locations to transmit pictures of the participants to the other location.
- Uploading means you are sending the file to another system. Downloading means you are transferring a file from another computer to yours.
- ASCII files contain only a limited set of characters and have almost no formatting so they are easy to transfer.
- Binary files have lots of formatting, much of it specific to the program that created them. Because these files vary so widely they don't transfer easily between networks.
- Ftp (file transfer protocol) is the Internet tool used to transfer files from one machine to another.
- One of the most convenient ways to transfer files is as attachments to e-mail messages.
- Just as you measure highway capacities in vehicles per hour, you measure bandwidth in bits per second (bps).
- Computers connected together within an office building or on a campus form local area networks or LANs.
- Wireless local area networks are connected by radio signals instead of by wires.
- Groupware allows people to share a common calendar or collaborate on a project over a network.
- Network applications rest on a computer somewhere on the network, not on your own machine. When you want to use one, you open it, transferring it to your system.
- The network manager or administrator is responsible for setting up or enforcing network procedures.
- The way data flows within a network is called the network's architecture or topology.
- A node is any piece of hardware on the system that can be addressed by a message from another node.
- A hub, also known as a concentrator, is what nodes are connected to. It simplifies the wiring of the nodes to each other.
- A backbone is a link designed to carry lots of traffic to which many nodes or hubs can be connected.
- A server is any network computer that can be accessed by others to receive files, send print jobs, or connect to the Internet. The computers that are connected to the server are called clients because they depend on the server for programs, data, or connections to other computers and devices.
- A network interface card (NIC), also called a LAN adapter, plugs into a slot in the computer and allows it to be connected to the LAN.
- Twisted-pair wires, similar to the wires used to connect your telephone, are the least expensive way to connect computers. Their are relatively slow and have a tendency to pick up noise that can cause high error rates.
- On an Ethernet network all nodes listen to the traffic on the network and try to send data only when it's quiet.
- Token-ring nodes can only send signals onto the network when they have possession of an electronic token that circulates around the network.
- When a network is larger than a single building or campus, it is called a metropolitan or wide area network.
- Intranets use the technology on which the Internet is based, but access is limited to a company's employees and other invited users.
- Firewalls are defensive barriers that fence off a private network from the Internet.
- The phone network is a circuit-switched network. When you dial a number, switches along the line route the call and reserve a line for you straight through to your destination.
- Packet-switched networks break data into pieces called packets, then address and number it. When the packets reach their destination, they are reassembled.
- Internet Protocol (IP) governs the way data is addressed and routed along the Internet.
- Transmission Control Protocol (TCP) breaks your message up into packets, each containing between one and 1500 characters. It numbers each of the units, puts each into an IP packet (envelope), and sends them.
- Analog modems at the sender's end convert the computer's digital signals into analog signals (modulation). Another modem at the receiver's end then converts the analog signals back into digital signals (demodulation).

Review Questions

True/False

1. T F To fax a document from a computer, you first make a printout.
2. T F An e-mail address contains the user name and the name of the computer where his or her mail box is stored, the domain name.
3. T F Many newsgroups form threads, a series of messages that begin when someone starts a new topic, and then others post their own responses.
4. T F Mailing list programs such as listserv and Majordomo are used to print mailing labels and manage marketing programs.
5. T F Groupware lets people work together on projects over the Internet or other network.
6. T F When a file is being transferred to your computer, it's being uploaded to you.
7. T F When you use a network to send data, the data can move only at a certain speed and has only a certain carrying capacity called bandwidth.
8. T F A wide area network (WAN) covers an entire building.
9. T F On a network, a server is used to store applications and data, often databases.
10. T F On an Ethernet network all nodes listen to the traffic on the network and try to send data only when it's quiet.

Fill-In the Blank

1. An e-mail address has two parts: the __________ and the __________ separated by an "at" sign (@).
2. __________ is a collection of thousands of ongoing topical discussions called newsgroups.
3. Sending an insulting or abusive e-mail message or news group posting is called a __________.
4. Mass unwanted e-mailings are called __________.
5. __________ files contain only text, use only a limited set of characters, and have almost no formatting so they are easy to transfer.
6. __________ files have lots of formatting, much of it specific to the program that created them.
7. __________ control where messages are sent on networks.
8. The phone network is a __________-switched network; the Internet is a __________-switched network.
9. Computers connected together within an office building or on a campus form local area networks or LANs.
10. On a(n) __________ network all nodes listen to the traffic on the network and try to send data only when it's quiet.

Multiple Choice

1. The connections that give the highest possible bandwidth are ___.
   a. Twisted-pair wires　　b. Coaxial cable
   c. Fiber-optic cable　　d. T1 lines
2. Local area networks are commonly used for ___.
   a. E-mail　　b. Sharing printers
   c. Sharing files　　d. All of the above
3. To make the data on your system available to anyone who wants it, ___.
   a. Tape your password to your computer
   b. Use your middle name, or better yet, your last name for your password
   c. Leave your computer running overnight
   d. Any of the above
4. A network node is ___.
   a. Any addressable piece of hardware on the system
   b. The device to which hardware is connected
   c. The high-speed link through which signals are sent
   d. Any of the above
5. Local area networks connect computers in the same ___.
   a. Building　　b. City
   c. Region　　d. All of the above
6. When you transfer a file from another computer to your own, it's called ___.
   a. Importing　　b. Downloading
   c. Moving　　d. None of the above
7. The easiest file to transfer because it contains so little formatting is a(n) ___.
   a. Binary file　　b. ASCII file
   c. Word processing file　　d. Spreadsheet file
8. Only a ___ network has all of the computers connected to a central computer.
   a. Ring　　b. Bus
   c. Star　　d. Peer-to-peer
9. Groups of people can interact over the Internet using ___.
   a. Newsgroups　　b. Mailing lists
   c. Groupware　　d. All of the above
10. Files attached to e-mail are sent as ___.
    a. Binary files　　b. ASCII text files
    c. Either a or b　　d. Neither a nor b

Research Projects

1. Research Internet connections available in your local area.
   - Call your phone company and ask about the cost and availability of ISDN or ADSL.
   - Call your cable TV company and ask about the cost and availability of a cable connection.
   - Check with your public library to see what connection speeds they have.
   - Use the Internet to check on the cost and availability of DirectPC.
2. Find out if the computer you use at school or work is connected to a network. If so, what kind of network is it? Describe it in as much detail as possible.

CHAPTER

10 MULTIMEDIA

AN OVERVIEW

It began with games and now it's become dynamic Web pages, interactive courses, and catalogs with sound and video. It's multimedia—one of the fastest growing and most exciting areas in the information technology field. Like electronic French chefs, hundreds of thousands of people are stirring together the ingredients of text, pictures, animations, movies, and sound, following almost as many recipes. The results range from simple slide shows to dazzling, inspiring, interactive presentations. Not too long ago the term "multimedia" referred to a room full of slide projectors, tape decks, and movie projectors. Multimedia presentations were hard to put together and even harder to run. Many of them took weeks of preparation and they were then shown only once, perhaps at a corporate sales meeting. The computer has changed all of that. Now multimedia is moving to the center of things. It's easier to stitch together the various elements and, once finished, the multimedia presentation is available to be shown over and over again

Multimedia is widely used in the entertainment and education fields. For entertainment, you can play computer games that seem almost alive with sound and motion. In education, interactive multimedia programs allow you to study and progress at your own pace and branch into areas of interest when you want to. You can even be a multimedia developer of sorts using traditional office applications. You can embed sound or video in spreadsheet or word processor documents so when recipients click an image or icon they get an explanation of key points.

Multimedia has entered the mainstream because it's so attention-holding and effective. It's used everywhere from business presentations to museum exhibits. Holiday Inn uses it to train employees. When they click on topics the system "talks" to them. It has reduced training time on a new property management system from 14 days to 6 days.

OBJECTIVES

After completing this chapter, you will be able to:

- Identify applications of multimedia.
- Compare and contrast bit-map and vector images.
- Describe some common graphic effects and techniques.
- Explain how computers process sounds and videos.
- Describe how multimedia elements are assembled into a presentation.
- List the common multimedia presentation devices.
- Explain how multimedia is used on the Web.

Media *n.* 1. the means of communication. 2. plural of medium.

Multimedia *n.* 1. the combined use of several media, such as motion-pictures, slides, and music.

SOLD

10.1 Multimedia:

Down through history, and over recent years, various media have been developed that inform or entertain: paintings, books, magazines, newspapers, movies, radio, photography. Using computers, multimedia fuses two or more of these media together on the premise that the combination is better then any of the individual components. Multimedia can be used for entertainment, corporate presentations, sales presentations, education, training, simulations, kiosks, digital publications, electronic reference materials, museum exhibits and more.

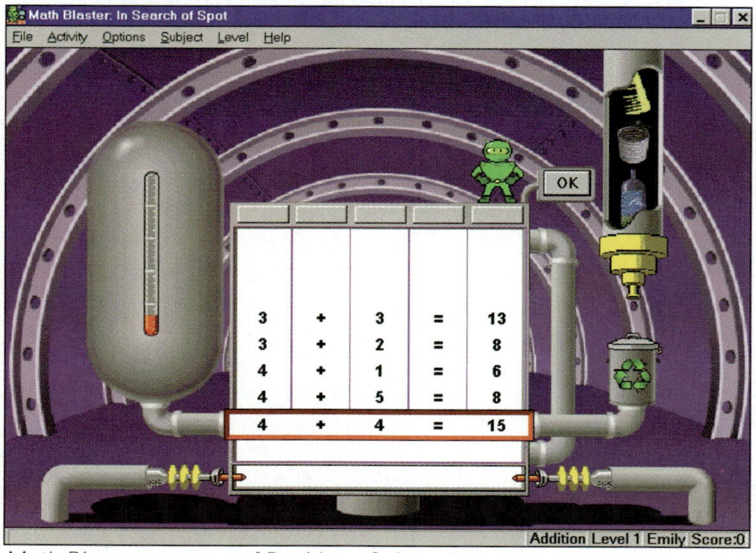

Math Blaster courtesy of Davidson & Associates

Multimedia in entertainment

One of the earliest applications of multimedia was for games, and many people thought that was what multimedia was really useful for. There is no question that multimedia can improve the quality of games, and it is that very game-like quality that can enhance a learning experience. Parents watching their children play innovative games see how powerful multimedia is at teaching them how to read or solve math problems even though the children perceive the experience as just a game. Building on the power of this perception innovators have increasingly used multimedia to support all kinds of activities that are not just games.

Multimedia in software training

As computer applications programs become more complex, software publishers are building multimedia presentations into their programs to introduce new features and walk the user through them. In companies, this form of presentation will take a big load off the overworked technical support staff. For individuals at home or in small businesses, it will make programs easier to learn and use.

Multimedia in education and training

Multimedia is extensively used for education and training in schools, businesses, and the home. Multimedia education allows you to proceed at your own pace. It brings presentations alive with sounds, movies, animations, and interactivity.

PACE program that accompanies this text

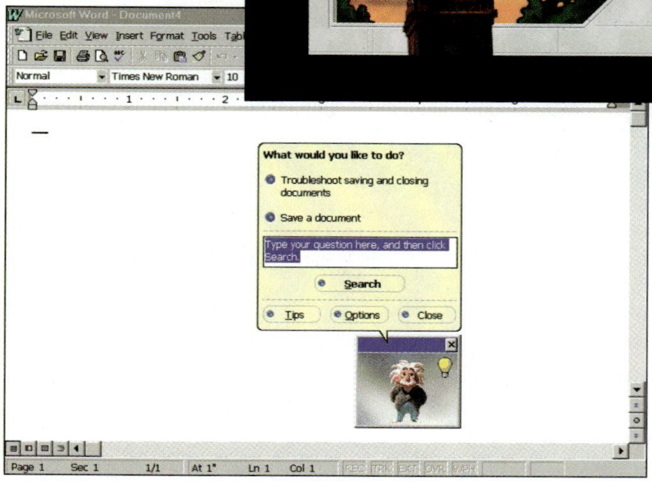

The Office 97 animated help character

Multimedia on the Web

When the Web was introduced, it was all text. Soon graphics were added and opened up new possibilities. Photographs and drawings could be used to illustrate and explain products and accessories, to demonstrate the workings of technology and nature, or just to make pages more attractive. Multimedia was introduced using tools such as Java and Shockwave. Now Web pages display animations, play sound, and allow you to interact with them. It's possible to experience full multimedia over the Internet or intranets.

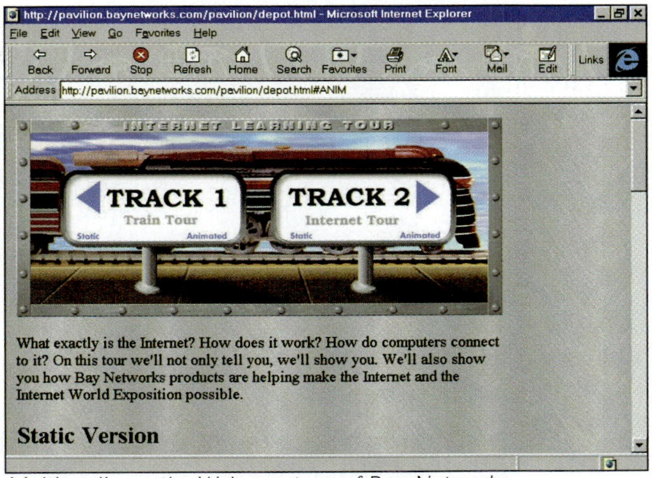

Multimedia on the Web courtesy of Bay Networks
http://pavilion.baynetworks.com/pavilion/index.html

Multimedia in office work

Multimedia isn't just for expensive commercial productions. It can be used to enhance ordinary communications. Using technology such as Microsoft's OLE and ActiveX or OpenDoc, you can insert sound and movie objects into other applications such as word processing or spreadsheet documents. Double-clicking on the embedded icon in the document runs the media clip or plays the sound.

Windows Media Player controls multimedia-hardware devices and plays media sequences, such as video clips, animations, and sounds. Media Player can be embedded in a document belonging to another application. It lets you start, pause, and stop the sound or movie or drag a slider bar to quickly move to a specific spot.

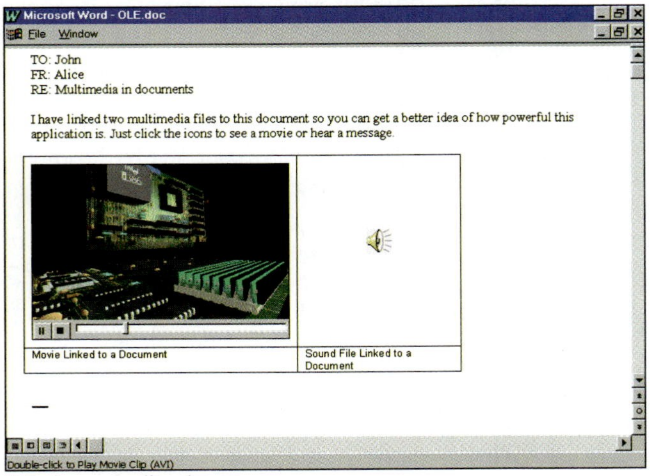

Windows media player

Multimedia servers and databases

Databases called universal servers are now able to store the elements that are displayed on the screen. Fields are used to store images, text, sound files, and videos. The multimedia program draws on these stored elements to create the show. These powerful databases, accessed over networks, are the new organizational libraries.

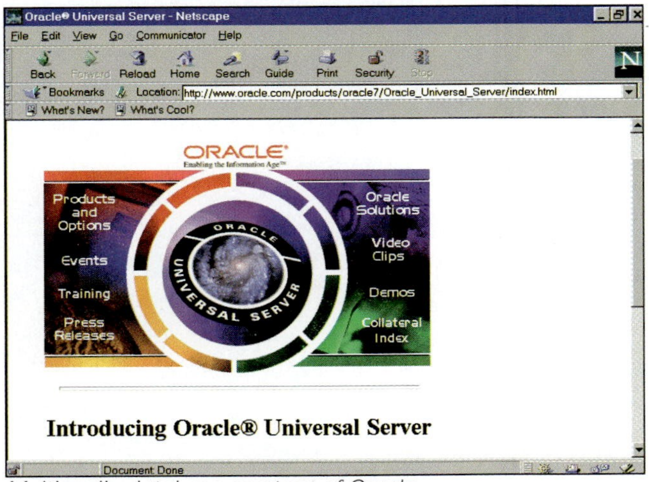

Multimedia database courtesy of Oracle
http://www.oracle.com/st/products/uds

10.2 The Tools of Multimedia:

The still images you see in multimedia programs (and many that you see in print) have been created or manipulated on a computer in a digital format. There are two basic forms of computer graphics: bitmaps and vector graphics.

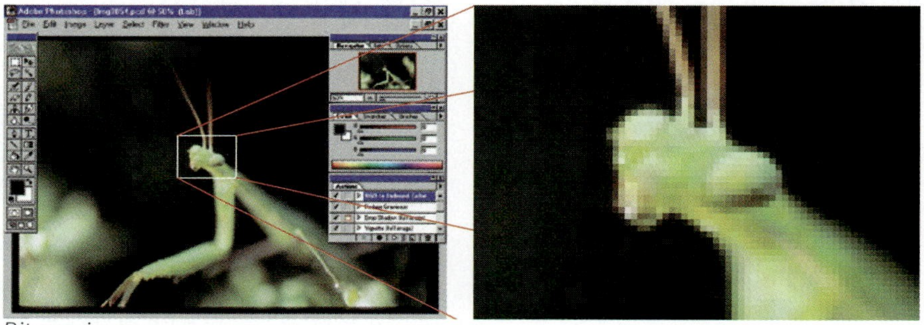

Bitmap image

Bitmap images

Bitmap images are formed from a matrix of pixels with different colors. Bitmap images are defined by their dimensions in pixels as well as by the number of colors they represent. For example, a 640 × 480 image contains 640 pixels and 480 pixels horizontally and vertically. If you enlarge a small area of a bitmap image, you can clearly see the pixels that are used to create it. When viewed normally, the small pixels merge into continuous tones much as newspaper photographs do. Each of the small pixels can be a shade of gray or a color. Using 24-bit color, each pixel can be set to any one of 16 million colors.

All photographs and paintings are bitmapped and any kind of image can be saved or exported into a bitmap format. When you print any kind of image on a laser or inkjet printer, it is first converted by the computer or printer into a bitmap form so it can be printed with the dots the printer uses. To edit or modify these bitmap images you use a paint program.

Bitmap images are widely used but they suffer from a few unavoidable problems. They must be printed or displayed at a size determined by the number of pixels in the image. Printing or displaying one at any other size can create unwanted patterns in the image. Bitmap images have large file sizes that are determined by the image's dimensions in pixels and color depth. To reduce this problem, some graphic formats such as GIF and JPEG store the images in compressed format.

Bitmap File Formats

- BMP is a standard uncompressed format for Microsoft Windows and IBM OS/2. It has a maximum of 16.7 million colors (24 bits per pixel) .
- PCX is a ZSoft format and is used widely for paint and desktop publishing programs. It has a maximum of 16.7 million colors (24 bits per pixel).
- GIF (pronounced "jif" and standing for Graphic Interchange Format) supports up to 256 colors (8 bits per pixel). It is a compressed format that keeps file sizes smaller. This format is widely used on the Web since files can be sent faster than many other formats. Files in this format have the extension .gif.
- JPEG (pronounced "jay peg" and standing for Joint Picture Experts Group) supports 16.7 million colors (24 bits per pixel). The images are also compressed so file sizes are even smaller than GIF files. Files in this format have the extension .jpg.
- TIFF (Tagged Image File Format) provides the highest quality but has large file sizes. This format supports 16.7 million colors (24 bits per pixel) and files have the extension .tif.

Bitmap editing courtesy of Dennis Curtin

Vector graphics

Vector graphics are really just a set of graphical objects such as lines, rectangles, ellipses, arcs, or curves, called primitives that the program stores as numerical coordinates and mathematical formulas specifying their shape and position in the image. Draw programs, also called vector graphics programs, are a format widely used by computer-aided design programs to create detailed engineering and design drawings, and have become popular in multimedia for 3D animation.

Draw programs have a number of advantages over paint programs:

- Precise control over lines and colors.
- Ability to skew and rotate objects to see them from different angles or add perspective.
- Ability to scale objects to any size to fit the available space. Vector graphics always print at the best resolution of the printer no matter what size you make them.
- Color blends and shadings can be easily changed.
- Ability to wrap text around objects.

When working with a draw program, you can display the image in two views: wire frame view or shaded. In wire frame view, you see just the underlying lines in a skeletal view of the image. The image is displayed this way because it can be manipulated on the screen a lot faster. To see what the finished model looks like, you apply colors to the wire frame and display it with the wire frame covered by shaded surfaces.

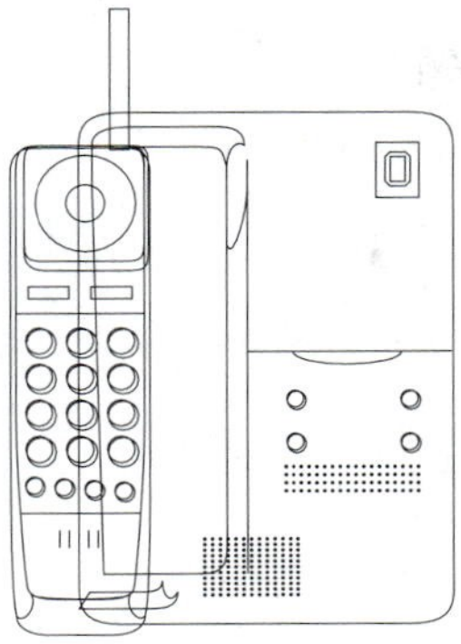

Wireframe view

Shaded 3D graphic

Vector graphics

Digital Modeler

To convert an existing 3D object into a 3D object on the screen, you can use a digital modeler. As you trace the object with the modeler, it translates the points on the actual object into positions on the screen which are stored in the computer. These digital points are used to create a wire frame view of the object.

3D Modeler courtesy of Immersion Corporation

Various techniques are used to make images more realistic or interesting, and even put them in motion.

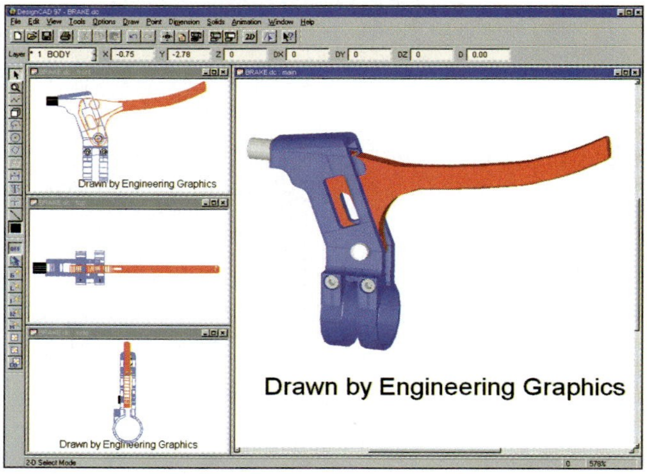

3D image courtesy ViaGrafix

3D graphics programs

Vector graphics come in two basic forms, 2D and 3D. 2D graphics show only length and width and 3D graphics have depth. 3D graphic programs are an extension of draw programs. You can create 3D models using a wire frame view called modeling. In a 3D image, each shape is created using a framework of polygons. To give the framework a surface or solid appearance, shading is added. In some cases, the shading is just a flat, even color. In other cases sophisticated techniques are used to create a color gradient, texture, or highlights.

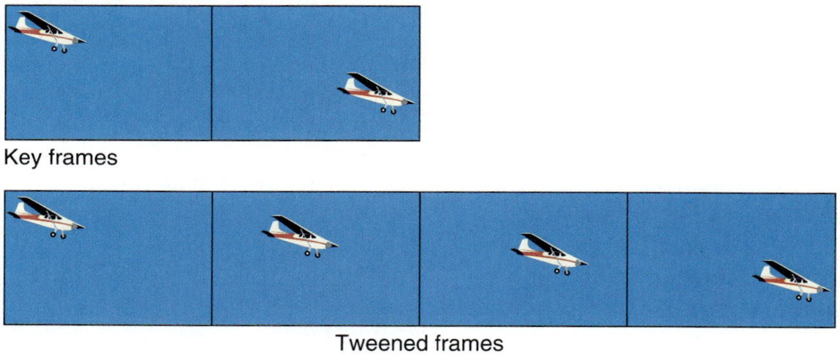

In-betweening series of images

Animation

The effect of action and motion in a Bugs Bunny cartoon is created by projecting still pictures, called cells, one after another at a rate of 30 per second. When the cells are projected fast enough, the illusion is of smooth motion.

Computer animation is also done by projecting a series of still images, called frames. Using animation software, you create a beginning and ending frame for an action, and after specifying these as the key frames, the computer uses a process called in-betweening (or tweening) to create the intermediate frames. This saves a great deal of work since older cell-animation required every frame to be drawn by hand.

For computers to calculate animated motion, the wireframe model is designed with joints. The animator then adjusts each joint in the structure to put it in the desired position. The science of motion called kinematics is the foundation for calculating movements, especially where there is more than one joint, as in an arm or leg. Forward kinematics calculates the positions of the elements step by step until the animation arrives at a final position. This is a well understood process but should the final frame put a character's hand into his chest instead of into his pocket inverse kinematics can be brought to bear. Here you specify the final position and calculate backward.

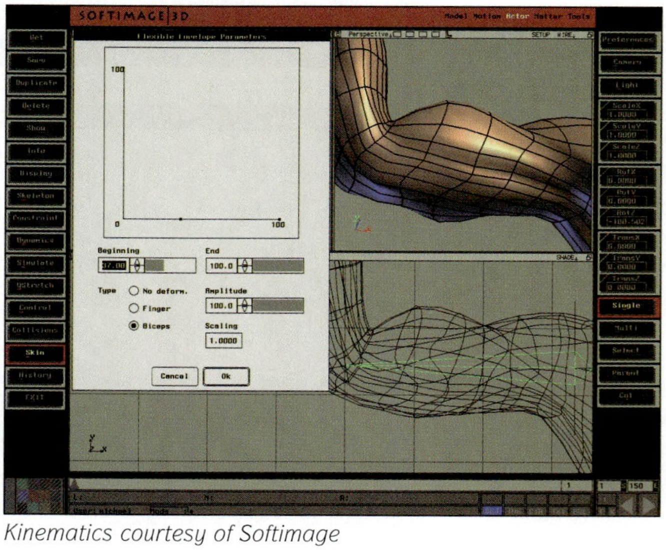

Kinematics courtesy of Softimage

Shading

After 2D or 3D vector graphics are created in wire frame view, the next step is to add a surface to the wire frame to give the image body and solidity. The programs used to do this are called shaders. Shaders can not only add color fills but also simulate a variety of other surfaces such as walls, metal, fabric, glass, wood, sky, and fur. A process called texture mapping can apply a bitmapped image over a surface to give it a more realistic appearance like putting wallpaper on a wall.

One form of shading is called ray tracing. Just as on a stage or movie set, you arrange light sources to illuminate the object and position your "camera." The ray tracer calculates the light rays and figures out where there should be highlights and reflections on the model.

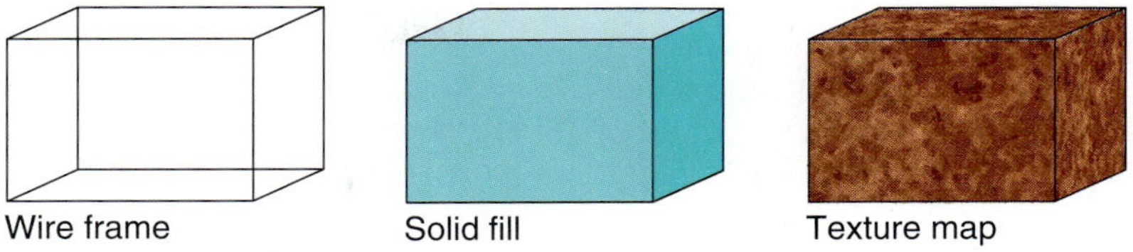

Texture map

Ray tracing courtesy of http://overlord.nrl.navy.mil/page1.html
email to doyle@overlord.nrl.mavy.mil

Anti-aliasing

The edge pixels may give an image displayed on the screen ragged edges. Anti-aliasing smooths the edges of the image by altering the contrast and colors of its edge pixels, making the contours of the image appear truer and easier to see.

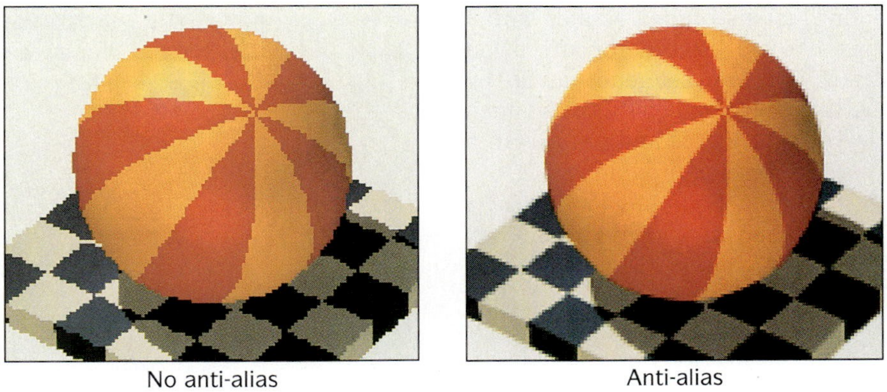

Anti-aliasing courtesy of Ray Dream

Morphing

Morphing blends two images to create a third. Starting with photographs of a young girl and an elderly woman, the morphed image shows someone with characteristics of both. When done as a series of steps, an animation shows the young girl growing old. To make morphing realistic, certain areas of the image, such as the eyes, must be overlapped on the first and last images and locked in place. This way, other parts of the image seem to transform around these fixed points.

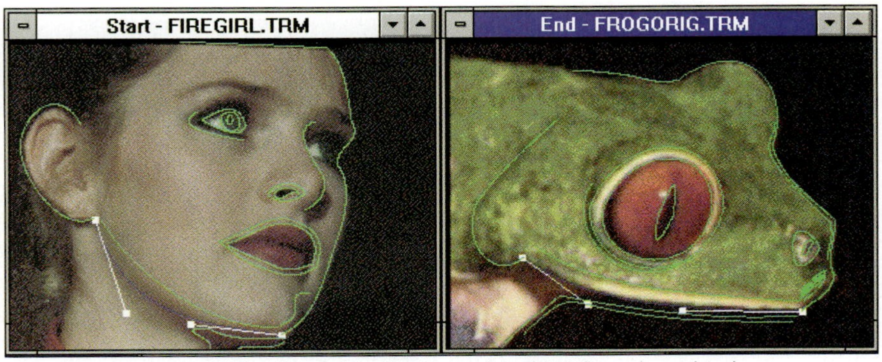

Morphing courtesy of http://www.blackbelt.com/blackbelt/bx_wi_mo.html

10.4 The Tools of Multimedia:

There is nothing like sound and music to make a multimedia presentation more interesting and effective. There are two basic kinds of sounds you can include in a multimedia presentation; sound data and live synthesized sound.

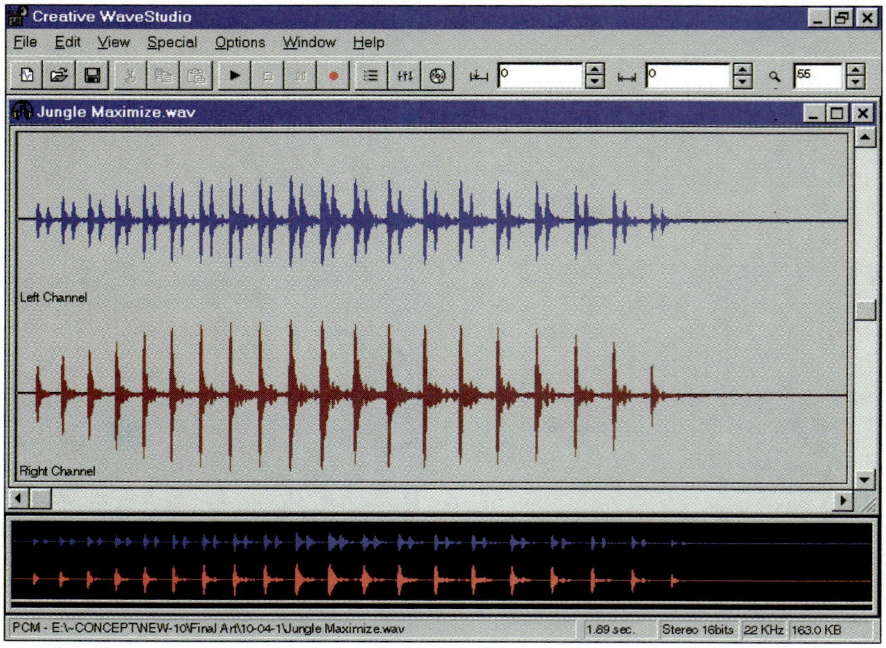

Sound editing

Digital sound data

The sounds that you hear in the world around you are in the form of analog signals, but can be easily digitized and stored on disks just like other data. The analog waves are sampled at evenly spaced points and the sound at those points is measured and stored as digital values called sound data. When this digital data is played back, your sound card and speakers use the digital values to re-create the original analog waves.

Various software programs record, play, and edit digitized sounds. Editing programs adjust the individual instrument sounds with a mixer to get the tone or affect you want. You can sequence audio by cutting and pasting sections much as you edit words and phrases in a word processing program.

Window's Sound Recorder plays, records, and edits sound files. It will add echoes, insert, delete, and soften sounds.

WAVE files are the most common file format for Windows sounds. These files take up a lot of space–approximately 1 megabyte for each minute of playing time. These files have the extension .wav.

Sound recorder

So Where Do I Get The Sounds?

On some systems, you can speak into a microphone attached to the sound card and your voice is digitized and stored on the disk for playback. You can buy disks with prerecorded sounds. These can be special effects sounds or music. Music, like other creative works, is often copyrighted so you have to be careful about what you use. Some collections that you can purchase are royalty-free but even with those you have to be careful. The rights to use them may not include the rights to incorporate them into multimedia presentations that are sold.

MIDI

Not all computer-generated music is created by playing back stored data. Music is actually made using a synthesizer, an electronic musical instrument with attached keyboard that creates sounds that mimic any instrument in an orchestra or creates sounds that would otherwise be difficult or impossible to make. Some commercial music is a blend of actual or traditional musicians and sound engineers, creating effects on synthesizers. There are synthesizers that make the strings of a guitar sound like the tones of a trumpet.

To standardize communications among computers and electronic musical instruments such as synthesizers, MIDI (Musical Instrument Digital Interface) devices are used. If you connect two MIDI keyboards with a cable, the notes you play on one keyboard (the master) are mimicked on the other (the slave). When MIDI instruments are connected to a computer loaded with the right software, you can store, compose, arrange, record, edit, play back, and even print your music.

Unlike WAVE files, MIDI files do not store actual sounds. Instead they store the commands that are sent to MIDI devices to reproduce the desired sounds. As a result, the file sizes are much smaller than WAVE files. These files have the extension .mid.

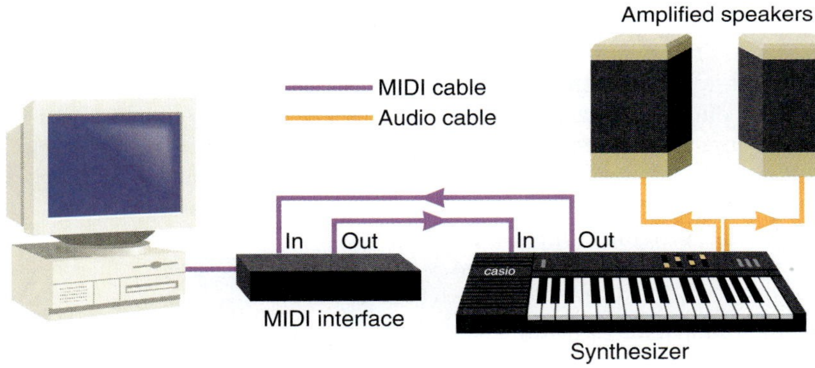

MIDI music system

3D sound

The latest audio cards are designed to simulate the theater experience of surround-sound but using only 2 speakers. Called 3D sound, these cards require speakers that support SRS (Sound Retrieval System). SRS is a sound recording and playback technology that gives sounds acoustical effects as if they are reflecting off walls in a real concert hall.

3D sound courtesy of Intel
http://developer.intel.com/ial/rsx/index.htm

10.5 The Tools of Multimedia:

Video is ever more widely used in multimedia in spite of computer images tending to be small, grainy, and even jerky because of large file sizes and the time it takes to transmit or play back these files. Progress is being made fast in these areas and it won't be long before computer video is as good as, or better than, broadcast television.

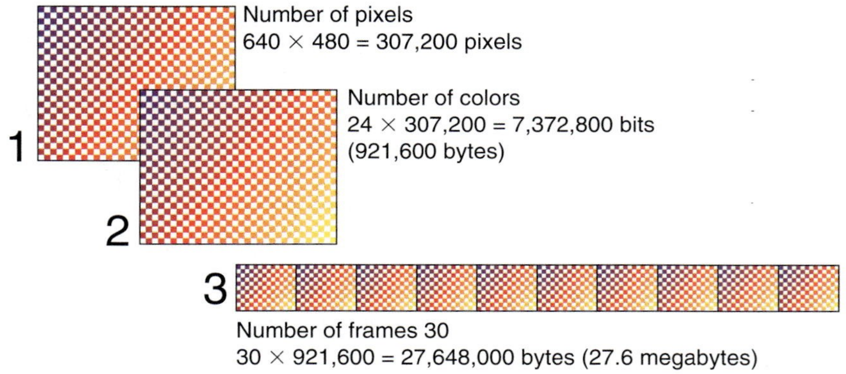

File sizes

File sizes

To display movies or videos on a computer, they must first be digitized, and resulting file sizes are enormous. A digitized feature-length film can take up 100 gigabytes of disk space. The figure above shows how much data is required for just *one second* of video displayed on a 640 x 480 screen at 30 frames per second:

With 307,200 pixels, each using 24 bits for true color, it takes over 221 megabytes of data to place one second of video on your screen. A CD-ROM disk with over 600 megabytes of storage would hold less than 3 seconds of video. And worse, it would take up to 70 minutes to transmit that 30 second to another device. Now that would be VERY slow motion.

Compression

To make it possible to store video and play it back at a usable rate, files are heavily compressed using a video **co**mpressor-**dec**ompressor (a codec). During this process, data that is duplicated or which has no value is eliminated or saved in a shorter form, greatly reducing a file's size. There are two basic types of compression, lossless and lossy.

Lossless compression (also called reversible compression) uncompresses the video when it's played back so its quality matches the original source. Although lossless compression sounds ideal, it doesn't allow much compression. Generally, compressed files are still a third the size of the original file, not small enough to make much difference in most situations. For this reason, lossless compression is used mainly where detail is extremely important as in x-rays and satellite imagery.

Lossy (rhymes with bossy) compression does not uncompress video to the same quality as the original, and some data is always lost. It allows for great compression, up to 200:1, and is largely used in satellite television broadcasts, some computer multimedia programs, and "real-time" applications such as video conferencing where speed is more important than quality. When done well, lossy compression compresses the file but plays back the video so it's visually lossless and the image quality appears normal, even if some data are lost.

How compression works

Compression is a technology that removes data from video images to reduce the size of the files. The trick is to remove data that isn't obvious to the viewer. There are two approaches, both used by all compression programs: interframe and intraframe.

- Interframe compression (also called spatial compression) removes duplicate data that appears within a single frame. For example, if large areas of the sky are the same shade of blue, only the value for one pixel needs to be saved along with the locations of where the other identical pixels appear in the frame.

Interframe compression

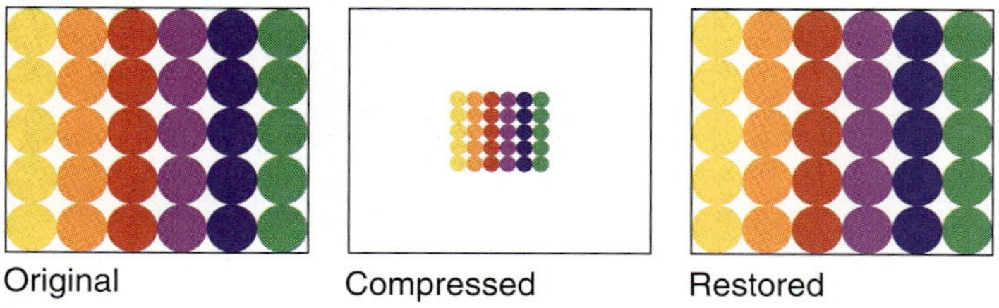

Compression

- Intraframe compression (also called temporal compression) looks for duplicate information in frames that follow one another. For example, in a scene with a flying bumblebee, the background may not change much or at all between frames. In this case, all of the data in the first frame is stored. In the next frame, only the data that has changed is stored and the rest thrown away. In a scene with a bouncing ball, the data is saved once and then played back in different positions. The system displays the first frame, then updates it with just the changes stored for the next frame. MPEG leaves uncompressed frames (called key frames) every half second but compresses those in between. If you were able to slice through a compressed video stream, all the intermediate frames would contain only parts of the image that had changed since the last frame, perhaps a winking eye or a moving object.

Compression

Image sizes and quality

On many multimedia programs, the video window is quite small because many desktop computer systems are not able to send video data to the screen fast enough to make the image larger. On more expensive systems, full-screen video is possible. To allow a program to run on slower systems, video is commonly displayed in 256 colors with a resolution of about 320 × 240 or 360 × 240 (called SIF, or Standard Image Format). This is only one-quarter the size of a 640 × 480 VGA display. However, this isn't as bad as you might think. TV sets show only 240 lines per vertical inch so the 320 × 240 image on the screen has the same resolution although it's much smaller in size.

Video editing courtesy of ImMix

Video editing

Video editing begins when an analog video tape is digitized. This is done by connecting a VCR to a computer's video capture card. The card converts each frame of the video to a digital format that can be manipulated in the computer. It also routes the sound to the system's sound card so it can be digitized. Programs such as Windows' VidEdit or Adobe Premier allow you to edit the stored data. You can copy, move, or delete frames and add special effects such as dissolves and wipes between scenes. When finished, these programs also compress the video. To get the edited video back onto a tape, you use a scan converter or an RGB-to-NTSC converter. These devices convert the digital signal back into an analog one.

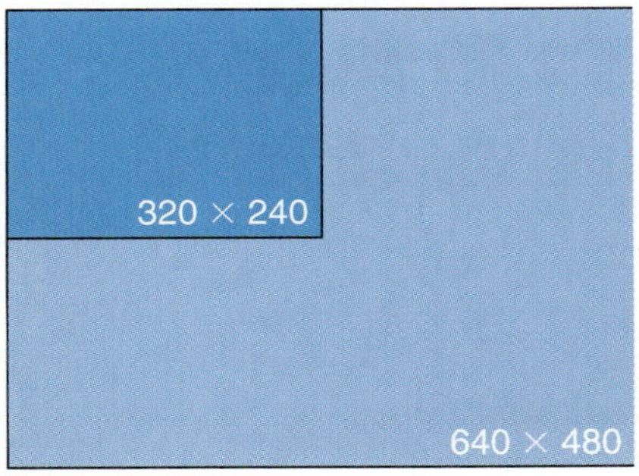

Image sizes

10.6 The Tools of Multimedia:

Once you have assembled your text, graphics, sounds, animations, and movies for a multimedia presentation, you blend or stitch them together with a program that allows you to import file formats from many applications and control such external hardware as videodiscs, CD-ROM or DVD drives, videotape players, and special effects cards. There is an amazing variety of software available for this task, ranging from very simple slide-show programs to very complex professional packages that can be programmed for special effects.

Presentation that allows you to choose level of interaction courtesy of Ray Dream

Types of presentations

There are two basic types of multimedia presentations, noninteractive and interactive. The type you choose affects the tools you select to create the presentation.

Noninteractive or linear presentations are like movies. They look the same each time you run them. In automatic mode everything appears on the screen for the time determined by the developer. There is no provision for user input, or your interaction is limited to clicking a Forward or Done button. These shows are typically used for presentations at sales meetings or conventions.

At a minimal level interactive presentations require that you click hyperlink buttons or graphics to continue. However, they can be much more complex and allow viewers to take multiple paths through the material. Interaction is used for games, entertainment, and education. To engage and hold the viewer's interest and attention, the program allows her to select topics, affect actions, or navigate in her own way through the material.

Presentation graphics programs

Easy-to-use presentation graphics programs allow typical end-users to put together multimedia shows for presentations on their own. Originally designed to create overhead transparencies, they originally allowed you to add text, create outlines and bulleted lists, and illustrate key points using charts and graphs. Current versions have been greatly enhanced and you can sequence files from draw, paint, and animation programs and digitized movies and sound. The final show can be a self-running screen show, or a series of slides or overheads. If a screen show, you can control how long each slide is on the screen, specify when sound or video plays, and use transitional effects between slides such as screen wipes, zooms, and dissolves. The latest versions allow you to create animations by sequencing together frames of still graphics. When played back, these frames create the appearance of motion like a movie or cartoon.

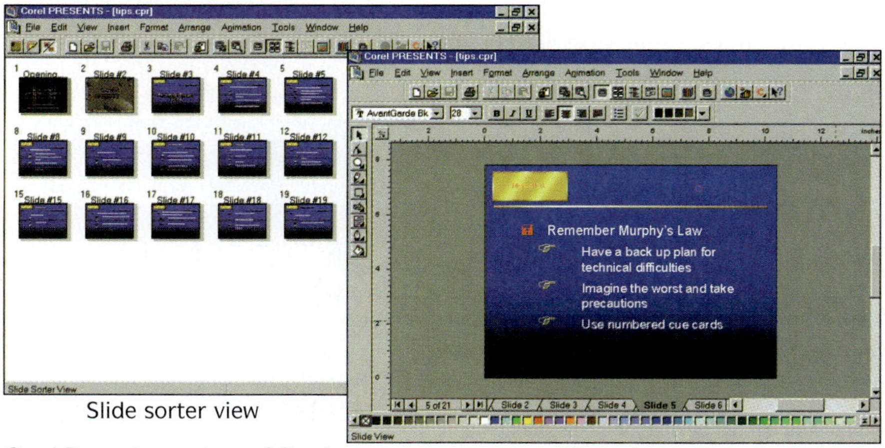

Slide sorter view

Slide view

Corel Presents courtesy of Corel

Professional development tools

Professional multimedia development programs called authoring software give you total control over an interactive presentation. In addition to allowing you to give the viewer interactive control over the sequence and timing of sounds, videos, graphics, and animations, they provide a scripting language (also called a programming, macro, or authoring language) in which you write programs to control the action. Director's scripting language is called Lingo.

The development team

Multimedia productions can be expensive. Their preparation requires a team of people, each with a mastery of a special set of skills. Whether some people fill more than one role or one person fills them all, the kinds of skills that are required are listed below.

- ♦ Instructional designers bring expertise on how people learn and how materials should be structured.
- ♦ Producers coordinate the development process.
- ♦ Subject matter experts bring their knowledge of the subject to the project.
- ♦ Interface designers create the on-screen navigational system for the program
- ♦ Writers work on scripts, any text that appears on screen, and the documentation.
- ♦ Designers work on the program's graphics, overall look and feel, and the interface design.
- ♦ Artists create any graphics that appear on-screen.
- ♦ Programmers stitch the elements together using the development software that has been selected for the task.

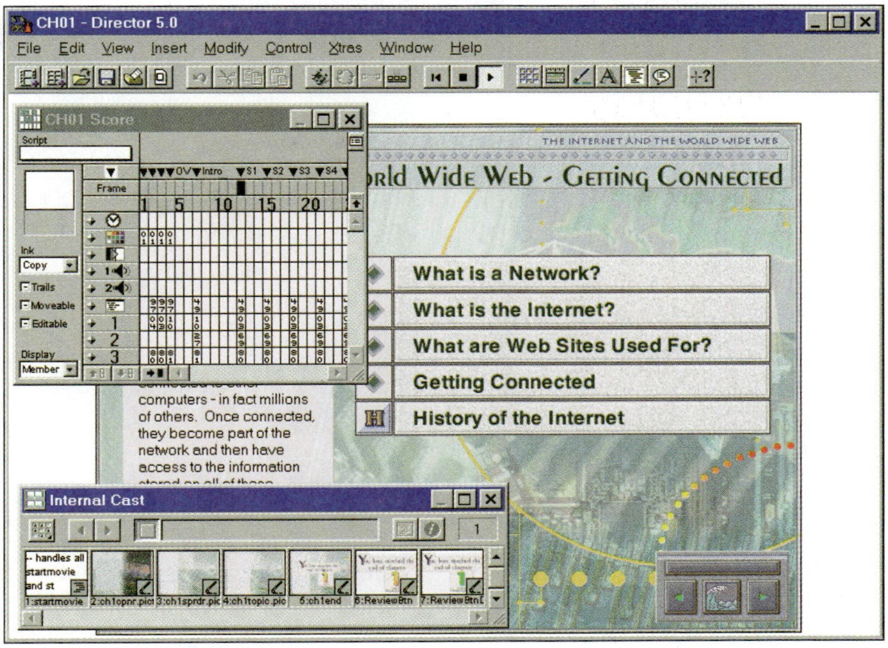

Director courtesy of Macromedia

The Team

10.7 Delivering Multimedia:

Once your multimedia presentation has been assembled it's show-time! If the show is designed for a single viewer, the desktop computer screen is the "theater." If the presentation is shown to a group, the computer becomes part of the "projection system."

Projector courtesy of In Focus Systems, Inc.

The multimedia computer

Using a local CD-ROM drive or a network connections, multimedia is often displayed right on the desktop. If more than one person is watching, you can connect the computer to a projector to get a larger image on a screen or the wall that can be seen by a room full of people.

Another device you can use to project the computer image is an LCD panel placed on top of an overhead projector. When the panel is connected to an outlet on the computer, the computer's image is projected onto a wall or screen.

Overhead projector panel courtesy of Panelight Display Systems, Inc.

Kiosk courtesy of International Business Machines

Kiosks

Kiosks are often used for multimedia shows. You find these in museums and other public spaces where anyone can operate them by touching areas of the screen and choosing items from menus.

Presentation Devices

Television screens

Since large computer screens are very expensive, less expensive television screens are often used for large displays. Television uses a different signal, so the computer must have an adapter card, called a scan-converter, that converts the computer's digital signal to the analog signal needed as input by the TV. These screens are not good for displaying text, especially when it's small, but are fine for color and motion.

TV screen courtesy of International Business Machines

Slide projectors

Slide projectors, such as Kodak's new Ektapro, can be controlled by software running on a computer and the slides can be generated by computers. This gives you the ability to display a multimedia show to a very large audience. Using the serial port on your computer, you can connect up to 16 projectors.

Slide Projector courtesy of Kodak

Cordless mouse

A handheld cordless mouse contains a gyroscope so the mouse pointer can be moved about the screen with subtle hand movements instead of having to roll the mouse on a flat surface. This is ideal when you want to walk about the room during the presentation.

Cordless mouse courtesy of Gyration

As you've seen, when the Web first started, it displayed just text and a few images. Pages were informational, but not much more. With improvements in browsers and HTML, and with the addition of plug-ins, multimedia has gradually crept onto the Web. First came movies and sounds that you could download to your system and play from there. Then came animations and interactivity that worked much the same way. We are still in the very early stages of this dramatic change in what's available on the Web. Major problems have to be solved to make real Web multimedia convenient and widespread. As you might expect, the biggest problem is bandwidth. Once this problem is solved you'll be able to take interactive courses at home, try out product simulations from your home, interact with television programming, and even make video phone calls. Let's take a look at some of the first Web multimedia applications that have become popular.

Helper Applications and Plug-Ins

Generally speaking, helper applications are programs that expand the number of file types you can view on the Web. For example, they can allow you to view movies and sound clips. They can be launched from the browser but are not a part of it. They display their files in separate windows. Plug-ins and ActiveX controls, on the other hand, make the file appear as though it's a part of the page you are viewing. Typical plug-in applications are virtual reality displays and animations.

Audio and video

Both audio and video have a major bandwidth problem. Their files are huge and yet they must be played back at a constant, uninterrupted speed. If there are any delays, the sound is bad and the pictures worse. Currently, the way to ensure quality is to send the entire audio or video file over the network to the hard disk on the user's machine. It can then be played back from there if people are willing to wait that long. To overcome this waiting problem, compression and streaming are used.

Compressing the data, you might say, like car-pooling, can help by squeezing more data into the same space. When an audio or video signal is compressed, useless data is dropped completely. Duplicate data is also dropped but codes tell the computer "this data is just like that earlier data, so copy that data here." For example, if two people are talking on a video, the background remains mostly unchanged from frame to frame so all of the frames but the first can be dropped and reconstructed at the receiver's end from the first frame.

Since the computer can often play back audio and video faster than it can be sent over the network, the streaming process is a way to give the playback a headstart. The computer quietly receives and stores enough of a broadcast so it can keep up, and then begins playing that part back while the rest of the data is received in the background.

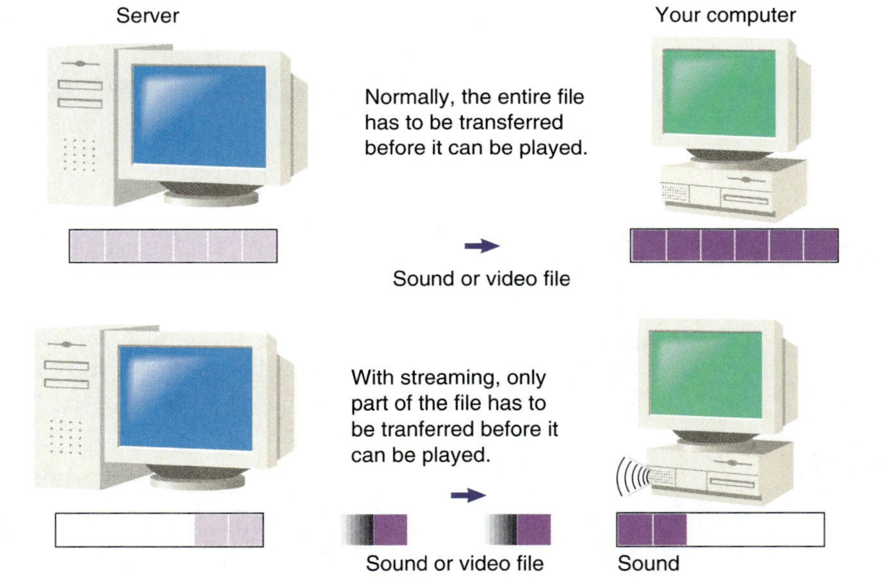

Streaming

Virtual reality modeling language (VRML)

2D pages aren't enough when you want to "walk through" a 3D architectural model, or shop in a mall that you can walk through looking at various shops on your way, or experience a flight simulator or an arcade-style game. The 3D model is sent over the Internet using the Virtual Reality Modeling Language (VRML), the language used to describe textures, lights, and camera angles. The 3D model can be sent over the Internet as fast as ordinary text and reconstructed at your end. To view the model when it arrives, you need a viewer that re-creates (renders) the original 3D model on your system. You can then navigate through the 3D scene using buttons supplied on the viewer. You can move the scene in relation to your point of view (imagining yourself turning around) or move your point of view in relation to the scene (as if you were walking or flying from room to room).

VRML isn't only for games or entertainment; it has serious business applications. Research shows that users find a 3D world easier to understand and navigate than a 2D world. Here is a virtual reality scene of the Microsoft campus that you can navigate with your mouse. In the scene at the very bottom we have "flown" up to look at the scene from above.

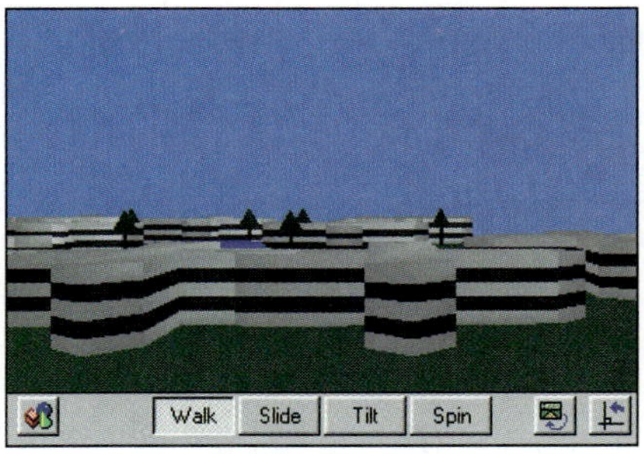

Original scene

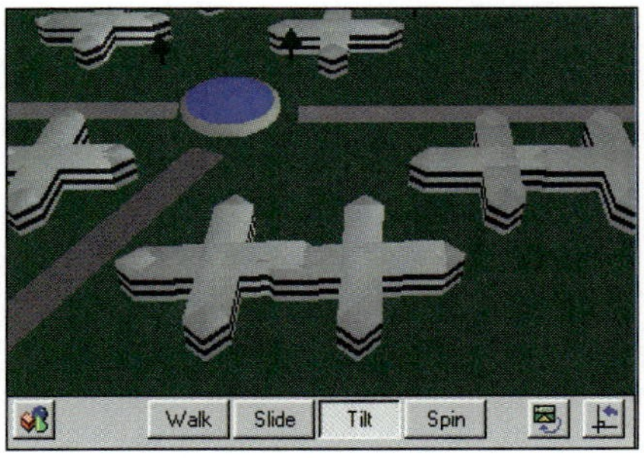

Tilted scene

VRML courtesy of Microsoft

Dynamic HTML

Dynamic HTML is an extension of the hypertext markup language (HTML) designed to add rich animation, sound, and interactivity to the World Wide Web. This means that a page can respond immediately to user actions, such as a mouse click, without having to retrieve an entire new page from the server.

Until recently, the entire Web was based on a single standard, HTML. Any information presented in HTML format is available to everyone, regardless of which browser they are using. Adding multimedia to pages was beyond the ability of HTML. To fill the gap, a slew of new technologies such as Java and Shockwave were introduced. However, these technologies have two big problems. One is that most users haven't installed the separate programs, called plug-ins, needed to display the multimedia effects on their system. Another is that these technologies are slow. Your system and the server are continually exchanging requests and files—a very slow process.

To make all pages viewable by all users and to speed things up, proposals are being considered to extend the range of things HTML can do. This new dynamic HTML builds interactive multimedia effects right into the page so they are all there on your system all of the time. In its first version, dynamic HTML supports the following multimedia effects without the page being updated from the server:

- Dynamic styles change the color, size, or style of the text on a page. A heading may cycle through a series of colors to draw attention to it or just pointing to a heading may cause it to change size or color.
- Dynamic content changes the words, pictures, or multimedia on a page. A logo may change from an image into a name or text may move as music plays.
- Positioning lets a Web developer precisely position pictures, text, and objects on a page. This allows them to make Web pages as attractive as pages seen in books and magazines.
- Layering allows text to be placed over an image or vice versa. In addition to being good for design purposes, this also improves interactivity. Just pointing to an item on a list of contents can display a description of what that item contains. Layered objects can also move around on the screen, rotate, and change colors.

One of the best things about dynamic HTML is that you don't have to be a rocket scientist to use it. The popularity of the Web has been based on the fact that you don't have to be a programmer to create great Web sites. HTML brings this same ease of use to creating dynamic content.

Video over the Internet is one of the fastest-growing applications. However, it has problems. When you go to the theater, the film is projected at 30 frames per second. That quality is available over the Internet only in a few situations where high bandwidth is available. To send video over low bandwidth phone lines, three things are done: the video is compressed, its size is reduced, and the number of frames received drops as low as 1 or 2 per second. The result is a small, fuzzy, jerky movie. This is only a temporary growing pain. As high bandwidth connections become more available, video will get better and more popular.

Intel Intercast courtesy of Intel
http://www.intel.com/iaweb/intercast/demo0.htm#graphic

Types of broadcasts

For the broadcasting of video (and audio), there are two approaches: live and on-demand feeds. Each presents its own problems.

- A "live" feed is a real-time continuous broadcast. (Real-time means the broadcast is seen or heard as it's happening. It hasn't been taped or recorded and then rebroadcast.) When viewing or listening to a live broadcast over the Internet, you would see and hear the same thing as someone viewing or listening in the originating city, with perhaps a few seconds delay.
- An "on-demand" feed is the playback of a previously recorded session. The viewer or listener can fast-forward, back up, or pause this kind of transmission—as if he were using a tape player.

Web TV

Imagine television in the 1940s. There was almost no programming, the pictures were small and fuzzy, and black and white, almost no one was broadcasting, and no one receiving. By the late 50s all of those problems had been solved. The Internet today is like television in the 40s. Before too long, it will be richer and more useful then television could ever be. That's because it's cheaper, allowing many more people to get involved. Television, whether its broadcast or cable, has a small handful of "gatekeepers," people who decide what you'll see and when you'll see it. They charge you or advertisers to recover the heavy investments they make in programming and in the system that delivers it to you including all of that over-

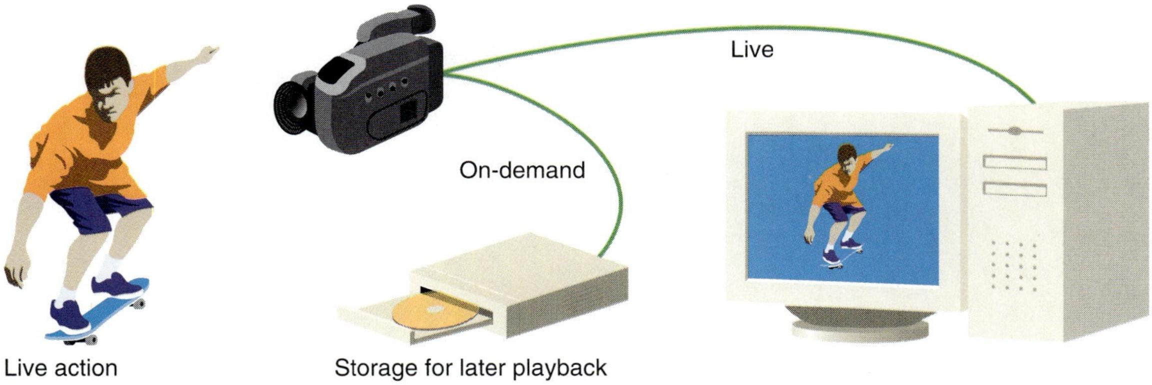

Live vs. on-demand video

head for offices and staffs. On the Internet anyone can open a TV studio at home and put videos on a hard disk or feed live broadcasts to the network through a computer. Anyone who points a browser at the "station's" Web address can watch the broadcast. As this technology matures, schools, clubs, churches, and entrepreneurs can all become broadcasters at a small fraction of what it costs today. Web TV is not only cheap, it requires no license, and it can be accessed by anyone, anywhere in the world.

Once quality video is possible on a large scale over Web TV, the costs will be so much lower than they are today that the number of "broadcasters" will rise dramatically. You'll be able to tune into college courses from around the country, watch narrow special interest programming that cannot be supported on more expensive broadcast or cable TV. Companies can offer inexpensive training to remote employees or those in the home office.

For companies with high-speed internal networks or expensive connections between offices, video transmission is here and now. For the rest of us, most of whom are connected over phone lines, video over the Internet still has limited use. It will take more readily available high bandwidth connections from the phone company (ISDN), the cable company (cable modems), or others to make it a reality. It's just a matter of time.

Intel's Intercast technology shows one possible future for television. It brings together broadcast TV and the Internet. As you change channels, background information can be fed from an Internet site and displayed on the screen along with the program. Here is a brief description of the numbered parts in the illustration at the top of the opposite page.

1. Program Window displays the televised broadcasts. The size of the window can be varied from small to full-screen. Smaller window sizes provide progressively more room for viewing accompanying Web pages.
2. Intel Intercast Viewer displays both broadcast and Internet HTML pages. Hypertext links on broadcasted pages guide you to the appropriate sites on the Internet's World Wide Web.
3. HTML Index is an index of all the downloaded HTML pages. Pages are saved on your hard disk as they are received and arranged in folders you open by clicking on the appropriate icon.
4. Browser Navigation Buttons navigate the World Wide Web, bookmark favorite sites and print Web pages. There's even a Location window to key in URLs. Intel Intercast technology includes the pictured browser, but other vendors may also develop browsers that are compatible.
5. Program Buttons, similar to those you'd find on a TV, enable you to change channels, raise or lower the volume, and view closed captioning. Use the snapshot button to capture video images right off the screen.

Now It's on Cable!

The Internet is now available in some homes though a subscription with the local cable TV company. These connections can be hundreds of times faster than a phone line and a modem. Using one of these connections requires a special device called a cable modem. With a cable connection, multimedia and video are displayed as big, bright, fast moving pictures.

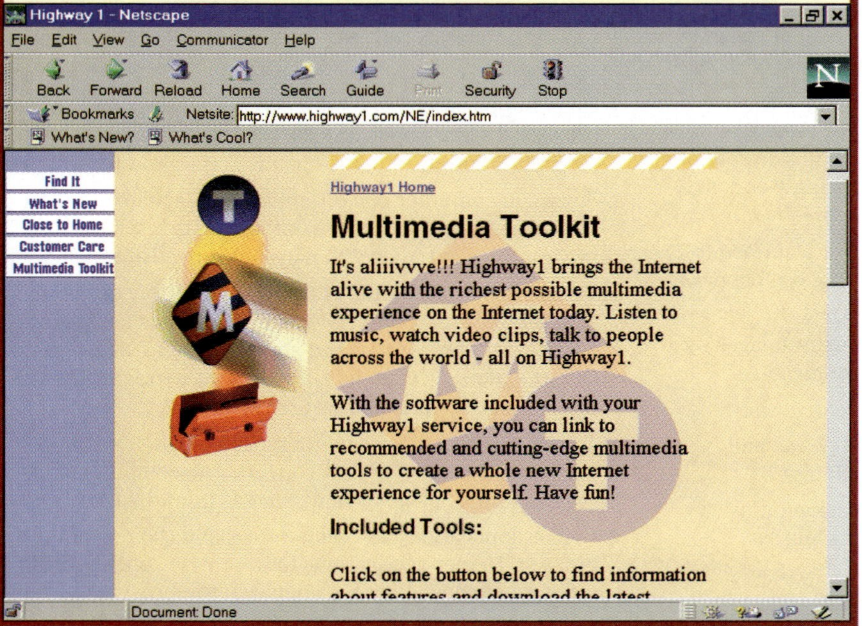

Cable TV connection courtesy of MediaOne

10.10 Enhancing and Testing Your Understanding

Summary

- Multimedia uses text, sound, images, animations, and video to inform or entertain.
- Using Microsoft's OLE and ActiveX or OpenDoc, you can insert sound and movie objects into other applications such as word processing or spreadsheet documents.
- Many databases are now able to store images, text, sound files, and videos. The multimedia program then draws on these stored elements to create a multimedia program.
- Bitmap images are formed from a matrix of pixels with different colors. Each pixel can be a shade of gray or a color. Using 24-bit color, each pixel can be set to any one of 16 million colors.
- To edit or modify bitmap images you use a paint program.
- Vector graphics are really just a list of graphical objects such as lines, rectangles, ellipses, arcs, or curves, called primitives, and stored as a set of numerical coordinates and mathematical formulas that specify their shape and position in the image.
- Draw programs are used to create and edit vector graphics.
- A draw program can display an image in wire frame view where you see just the underlying lines and in shaded view where you see the wire frame covered by shaded surfaces.
- 2D graphics show length and width and 3D graphics have depth. You can create 3D models using wire frame view called modeling.
- In a 3D image, each shape is created using a framework of polygons.
- Computer animation is done by projecting a series of still images, called frames.
- For the computer to calculate an action, a model of a character is designed with joints. The animator then adjusts each joint in the structure to put it in the desired position.
- To add body to a 2D or 3D vector graphic wire frame, you use a shader that can add color fills or simulate a variety of other surfaces such as walls, metal, fabric, glass, wood, sky, and fur.
- Texture mapping applies a bitmap image over a surface to give it a more realistic appearance like putting wallpaper on a wall.
- Anti-aliasing smooths the edges of characters or images by altering the contrast and colors of their edge pixels.
- Morphing blends two different images to create a third.
- When sounds are sampled at evenly spaced points and stored as digital values they are called sound data.
- Music stored in the computer and played back on musical instruments such as synthesizers uses MIDI (Musical Instrument Digital Interface).
- To store video and play it back at a usable rate, files are heavily compressed using a video compressor-decompressor (a codec).
- Lossless compression (also called reversible compression) uncompresses the video when it's played back so its quality matches the original source.
- Lossy (rhymes with bossy) compression does not uncompress video to the same quality as the original source and some data is always lost.
- There are ways to compress video. Interframe compression removes duplicate data that appears within a single frame. Intraframe compression looks for duplicate information in frames that follow one another.
- Once you have assembled all of the text, graphics, sounds, animations, and movies, you have to stitch them together to make a multimedia presentation. To do so, you use a program that allows you to import file formats from many other applications and control such external hardware as videodisks, CD-ROM players, videotape players, and special effects cards.
- Interactive presentations allow you to interact with the presentation and even select different paths through the material.
- Presentation graphics programs are used to put together multimedia shows for presentations.
- Authoring software is used to put together complex interactive presentations.
- Using a local CD-ROM drive or a network connections, multimedia is often displayed right on the desktop. If more than one person is watching, you can connect the computer to a projector or LCD panel on top of an overhead projector to get a larger image on the wall that can be seen by a roomful of people.
- To use a regular television for a presentation, you must have a scan-converter that converts the computer's digital signal to the analog signal needed as input by the TV.
- Helper applications and plug-ins expand the power of a browser. Helper applications for a browser open a file in a separate window. Plug-ins open it in the browser window.
- Since the computer can often play back audio and video faster than it can be sent over the network, a streaming process is used to give the playback a headstart.
- Virtual Reality Modeling Language (VRML) is used to send an interactive 3D model over the Internet as fast as ordinary text and reconstructed at your end. To view and navigate the model, you need a viewer that recreates (renders) the original 3D model on your system.
- To use a regular television for a presentation, you must have a scan-converter that converts the computer's digital signal to the analog signal needed as input by the TV.
- Helper applications and plug-ins expand the power of a browser. Helper applications for a browser open a file in a separate window. Plug-ins open it in the browser window.
- Since the computer can often play back audio and video faster than it can be sent over the network, a streaming process is used to give the playback a headstart.

Review Questions

True/False

1. T F Multimedia fuses two or more media together.
2. T F You can not yet insert multimedia elements such as sounds, illustrations, or even movies, into a word processed document.
3. T F Bitmap images such as photographs and reproductions of paintings are created from very small dots called pixels.
4. T F 2D but not 3D graphics can be animated.
5. T F To remove the ragged edges from text in an image you use anti-aliasing to smooth the edges of the characters by altering the contrast of its edge pixels.
6. T F Morphing merges one image into another to create a series of images showing steps in the transformation.
7. T F A keyboard can be plugged into the computer and music and sound effects can be created using a protocol called Musical Instrument Digital Interface (MIDI).
8. T F To store video and play it back at a usable rate, files are compressed using a video compressor-decompressor, called a codec.
9. T F Interactive presentations allow you to make or change the path through the program.
10. T F To use a television screen for a computer presentation, all you need is a cable to connect the two since both use the same signals.

Fill-In the Blank

1. There are two basic forms of computer graphics: __________ and __________.
2. __________ images are formed from a matrix of __________ with different colors.
3. To edit or modify __________ images you use a paint program.
4. To edit or modify __________ images you use a draw program.
5. A draw program can display an image in two views: __________ and __________.
6. __________ applies a bitmap image over a surface to give it a more realistic appearance like putting wallpaper on a wall.
7. __________ compression uncompresses video when it's played back so its quality matches the original source.
8. __________ compression does not uncompress video to the same quality as the original source.
9. Professional multimedia development programs called ________ give you total control over an interactive presentation.
10. An interactive 3D model can be sent over the Internet using __________ and then reconstructed at your end so you can navigate through it.

Multiple Choice

1. Multimedia programs contain ___.
   - **a.** Text and graphics **b.** Sounds
   - **c.** Animations and movies **d.** All of the above
2. A graphic image formed from dots is called a ___.
   - **a.** Vector graphic **b.** Bitmap graphic
   - **c.** 2D graphic **d.** All of the above
3. To edit vector graphics, you can use a ___.
   - **a.** Shader program **b.** 3D program
   - **c.** Draw program **d.** All of the above
4. To preserve the most detail in an image or video, you use ___ compression.
   - **a.** Interframe **b.** Lossless
   - **c.** Intraframe **d.** Lossy
5. You can insert sound and graphics into a ___.
   - **a.** Document **b.** Spreadsheet
   - **c.** Database **d.** All of the above
6. Automatically generating animation frames between two key frames is called ___.
   - **a.** Cell animation **b.** Frame animation
   - **c.** In-betweening **d.** 3D animation
7. To add color and body to a 3D graphic, you use ___.
   - **a.** Shading **b.** Texture mapping
   - **c.** Ray tracing **d.** All of the above
8. Blending two images into one to create a new image is called ___.
   - **a.** Compression **b.** Animation
   - **c.** Morphing **d.** All of the above
9. To play prerecorded sounds (sound data) you need ___.
   - **a.** A MIDI card **b.** A sound card
   - **c.** A synthesizer **d.** All of the above
10. Anti-aliasing is used to ___.
    - **a.** Remove duplicate images
    - **b.** Avoid duplicate filenames
    - **c.** Smooth the edges of text and graphics
    - **d.** All of the above

Research Projects

1. Play a computer game and try to determine if the characters have been created with a 2D or 3D animation program. Can you identify any areas where texture mapping was used?
2. Using computer magazines, the Internet, or a visit to a computer store, determine what features the latest and most expensive sound card has. Which of these features are not in the least expensive versions?
3. Assume that you want to compose music on the computer and record your own works. Determine what kind of equipment will you need? Make a shopping list.
4. Assume you want to edit photographs and make montages of them. Find out what software packages are most often used for this and which brand is the most popular.

CHAPTER

11 INFORMATION TECHNOLOGY

AN OVERVIEW

Corporate employees are increasingly mobile and more and more are working at home, telecommuting. Back at the office, layers of bureaucratic management are being compressed to make the corporation more responsive to the market and to speed decision making. All this is made possible by improved information flow. Not too many years ago rooms full of people did nothing all day but type letters (the typing pool), other roomfuls entered data into the computer system (data entry clerks), and rooms full of folks analyzed the data. By the time the information reached management it was already out of date so decisions were made looking backward in the rearview mirror instead of forward through the windshield.

Information is the lifeblood of the modern business organization. It is used to make decisions, convey needed actions, evaluate results, and exchange ideas. Information is not raw numbers or facts. To be useful, information must be *created* by processing raw data available to the organization as quickly as possible and then immediately distributing it to those who want or need it. Computers used for this purpose are engaged in information processing (or the more dated term data processing).

Improvements in information processing for management are in a way the least surprising. What's more exciting is the way information technology can bring creative people together to develop new products and services expeditously. Instead of being just the scorekeepers as computers once were, they are now the tools of creativity and profit making.

The increased computerization of the workplace has led to major change in the way almost all jobs are performed and has also created new jobs in the computer industry itself—the specialists.

In this chapter you'll explore the role of computers in modern business. As an employee, an entrepreneur, a manager, or a consumer, you are sure to interact with computers.

OBJECTIVES

After completing this chapter, you will be able to:

- Describe the role that computers play at the corporate level.
- Identify transaction processing and the various computer systems used to handle it.
- Describe how computers are used by managers to make decisions.
- Compare and contrast how computers are used in marketing, advertising, and sales.
- Compare and contrast how computers are used in design, production, and manufacturing.
- Explain why the Internet is important to business and describe how it is being used for business purposes.

Information *n.* 1. data acquired by informing or being informed: communicated knowledge. 2. knowledge derived from study, experience, or instruction.

Technology *n.* 1. the application of science, especially to industrial or commercial objectives.

Business *n.* 1. an occupation, profession, or trade. 2. the purchase or sale of goods to make a profit. 3. a person or corporation engaged in commerce, manufacturing, or a service.

IN BUSINESS

11.1 Corporate Computing:

There is so much information today that without information technology, companies would be swamped. Much of the information flows into a company from outside sources during the normal course of business. For example, a customer places an order and information is collected and matched with records about prices, discounts, and inventory. Or a vendor bids on services the company needs and new information comes in.

Other information comes from internal sources. The advertising department is given a budget for this year's advertising, sales people submit travel and expense vouchers, new employees are added to payroll, and engineers design new products. In some cases, information is the company's product. For example, it may sell financial reports or business statistics.

As information flows into and through the company, it is collected, analyzed, and acted on. The way this is done is one of the most interesting and also one of the fastest-changing areas in computing.

The origins of information processing

Originally, all corporate information was stored on paper forms and it wasn't unusual for a large business to have thousands of different forms and thousands of people to process them. The forms were endless. One form would be used to record an employee's salary, another to record vacation days owed and taken, still other forms for sick days, benefits, and on and on.

Early computer courtesy of International Business Machines

With the development of computers in the 1950s, centralized computer centers called data processing departments were created to process some of the data that flowed into the organization. Large mainframe computers automated some of the preexisting manual processes. The mainframe was much like a large electronic filing cabinet storing all of the forms electronically.

Gradually new approaches were introduced and information processing became both more flexible and more powerful. One of the big steps was the introduction of the corporate database that made it possible to eliminate duplicate data and use queries to locate information. The mainframe changed from being just a large storage device into a tool that allowed people to have much more information on which to base their decisions. Before computers, a large firm might not know what its sales were until months after the fact. This was much too late to take corrective action early enough to substantially affect outcomes. After computers, sales could be known on a daily or even hourly basis, making management much more knowledgeable about its business.

The problem with this early approach was that these mainframe computers were so expensive to own and operate they could be used only for corporatewide tasks. Large computers in organizations are still used mostly for this purpose. They process payrolls and keep track of inventory and sales, tasks that require the computer to process highly structured data. The computer calculates numbers, sorts entries into a specified order, and finds a specific record when needed. Programmers write programs for each task. Often these programs display a form on the screen that is filled in by an operator to feed information into the computer. If the form does not have a space to enter a comment, you cannot enter one. In many cases, these systems have been so important to the company for so long that they are referred to as legacy systems.

Buzzwords

Just when you think you've got a handle on language, you run across something like this: "For starters, SSGA (State Street Banks Global Advisors, Inc.) is one of those companies whose names are bandied about when people talk about the 'bleeding edge.' In fact, name a technology or business buzzword and State Street Bank is involved with it. The company is globalizing its mission-critical applications. It is downsizing to open systems architectures."

Source: LAN Times, August 23, 1993, p. 57.

Modern information processing

Because large mainframe computers are so expensive to buy and maintain, they are used only for data that is essential to the firm's survival, so-called mission-critical applications. With the widespread adoption of low-cost PCs, information process-

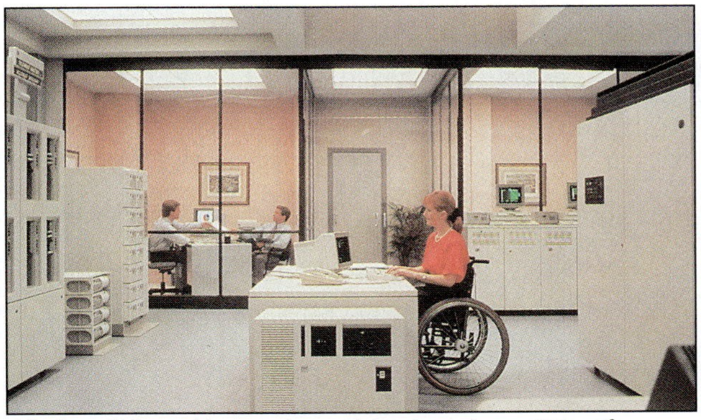

Modern information systems department courtesy of International Business Machines

ing has changed dramatically, much of it moving to the employee's desktop. In the 1980s, standalone desktop computers, those not tied into a larger system, began to appear throughout the corporation. As technology improved, these standalone computers began to be connected into networks. As a result, their overall computational power increased dramatically.

Companies are increasingly using these powerful new networks to process data that is essential to the firm's existence. Mission-critical chores such as order processing, payroll, and inventory control are moving from the mainframe computers in a process called downsizing because costs are reduced.

Computers' new influence doesn't stop there. They are increasingly being used for new tasks ranging from analysis to design, production, and manufacturing.

As the role of computers in the organization has changed dramatically, so has the role of the people responsible for their first adoption and use. The old data processing department has evolved into an entirely new one—the information systems or information technology department. Information systems departments are operated by a specialized staff and perform or support information processing for other departments throughout the firm.

Information processing leadership

Modern information systems don't just happen. They are assembled, managed, and maintained by a staff in the corporate computer center, sometimes called the information center. The chief information officer (CIO), also called the information systems manager and a variety of other names, manages this department and guides the organization's information technology decisions. Because of the terrific rate of change in the underlying technology, this is not a very secure job at the moment. Recent surveys indicate that the average tenure in this job is five years and that one-third of the people who leave are asked to do so. As we all go through this unprecedented transition, the business world is very turbulent. Companies are trying to reduce costs by implementing new technology that is not tested and proven. Managers have to make educated guesses about which technologies to use. If they guess wrong on some of the larger issues, they may find themselves in trouble.

Do You Need Incentive?

Workers who use computers, but who are similar in every other respect to workers who do not use them, earn a fat bonus of 10 to 15 percent for their knack with these machines.

Source: *The New York Times,* February 14, 1992. D2, referring to a study by Alan B. Kruger of Princeton University.

Information processing leadership courtesy of International Business Machines

Change

Many of the people in upper management today started their careers in the 1960s. The change in their lifetime has been amazing. They have seen career opportunities in agriculture shrink dramatically while jobs in services and information have grown just as dramatically. You may experience as much change in your own lifetime.

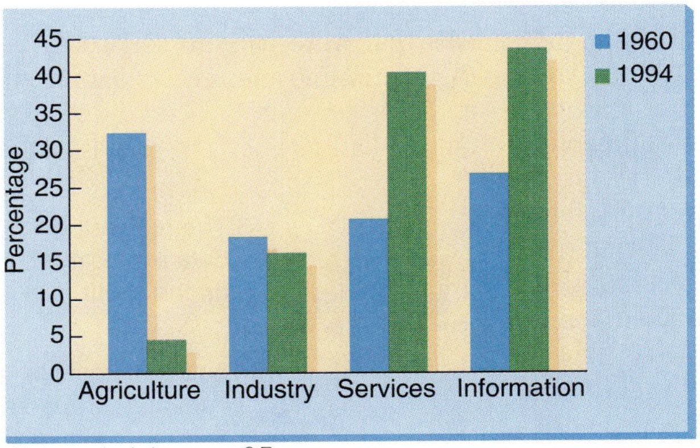

Change in jobs over 25 years

11.2 Transaction Processing

Most organizations interact with the outside world. They take orders or reservations and they buy products and services from suppliers. Each of these contacts is a transaction. One of the key functions of the computer is to record and manage transactions. To do so, a procedure called on-line transaction processing (OLTP) is used to enter and find data in real time.

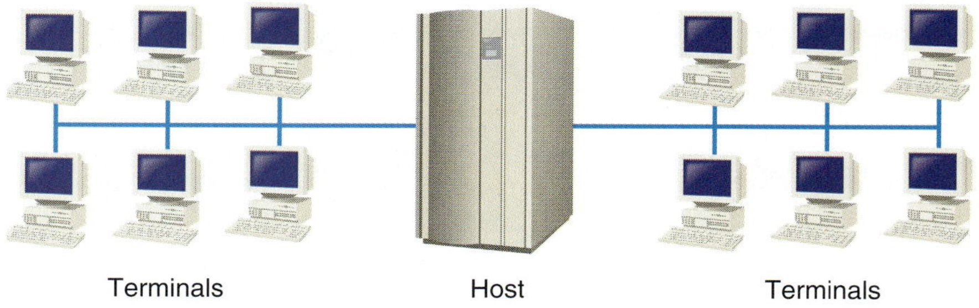

Host-terminal computing

Transaction processing courtesy of International Business Machines

What is transaction processing?

Once you are aware of transaction processing, you suddenly see it everywhere. Buy something from a catalog, make a credit card charge, enroll in a college course, and you encounter these systems. Let's take a look at just one common transaction, placing an airline reservation and the chain of events set off by a simple phone call. You pick up the phone and call the airline. The reservations agent who answers your call is sitting in front of a computer. When you inquire about a flight, the agent enters a query into his computer, which displays all the details about available flights. If you decide to fly, you are asked for a credit card number that when entered into the computer automatically connects with your credit card issuer to check that it's valid. Another query is used to display the seating on the chosen flight. Because many other agents are working simultaneously, some of the seats may suddenly be taken while they are looking at the screen. The agent selects an available seat and that information is logged into the computer. All of your data is fed from the reservation agent's computer back into a system where it is accessible to people throughout the corporation. When you check in at the airport, the people there issue you a boarding pass based on the information. Back at headquarters, the same information is being used to make decisions about prices on the seats still remaining on the flight.

Centralized transaction processing

The traditional information processing system was centralized around a mainframe computer. The mainframe was the only computer in the system. Connected to it were terminals that were used to send data to the mainframe and receive data from it. These terminals, called dumb terminals, had no ability to process data on their own. This form of computing is called host-terminal computing because the terminals are all connected to a mainframe host.

Client-server systems

The development of low-cost PCs and networks made it possible to replace the more costly mainframe through a new form of computing called client-server computing. Since an organization's mission-critical applications are as large and as important as ever and more, having all the computers on an equal footing isn't practical. For security, ease of management, and overall performance, many small computers are now connected to a larger and more powerful computer much as terminals have long been connected to mainframe computers. This central computer generally holds the majority of the data and the programs that manage it. The smaller computers then access the data and perform additional computations on it. The large computer in such a system is the server and can be a PC, workstation, or even a mainframe. The smaller computers are the clients.

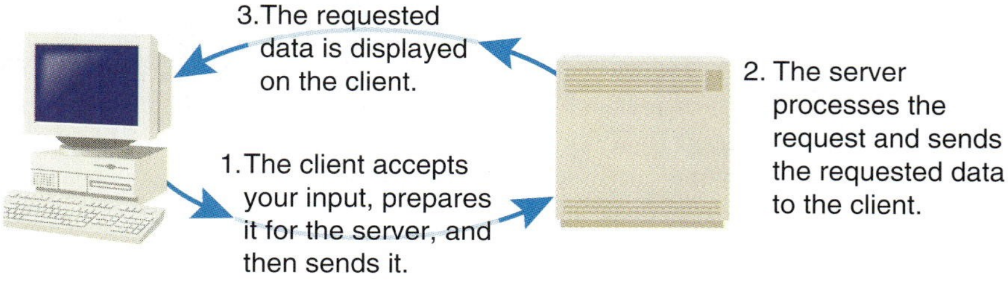

Client-server system

Client-server software

Client-server applications are split into a front end and a back end. The front end is the client component and it works just like any other application where you enter data. The front end prepares data for the server and sends it there. The back end is a powerful computer, perhaps even a mainframe. The back end waits for requests from the clients. When it receives one, it processes the request and returns the result to the client. The client then presents the processed data to the end-user.

The back end of the program can be complex and powerful because the end-user does not see it or have to interact with it. Users work on the front end of the program that can be very easy to use, hiding all of the program's complexity behind pull-down menus and a graphical user interface. One big advantage of this division is that various front-end components can be used with the same back-end system. For example, a reservation agent sees a different view of the data from that seen by the accounting department although they are both using the same back end.

Distributed computing and replication

On a client-server system, the data is maintained on the server but is manipulated by the client. Many systems, however, cover large geographic areas. You can make a reservation on American Airlines from anywhere in the world. It would be very slow and very expensive to have only one server handle all clients. Thus there may be many servers on the network, each with its own group of clients. Computing is now distributed and the software must be also. A database that must be accessed from anywhere in the

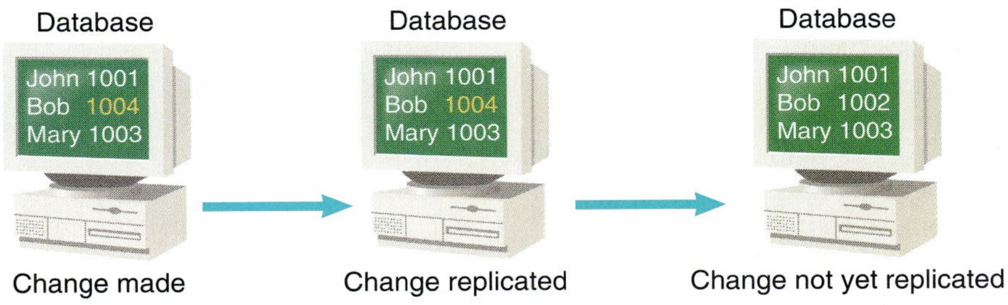

Replicated database

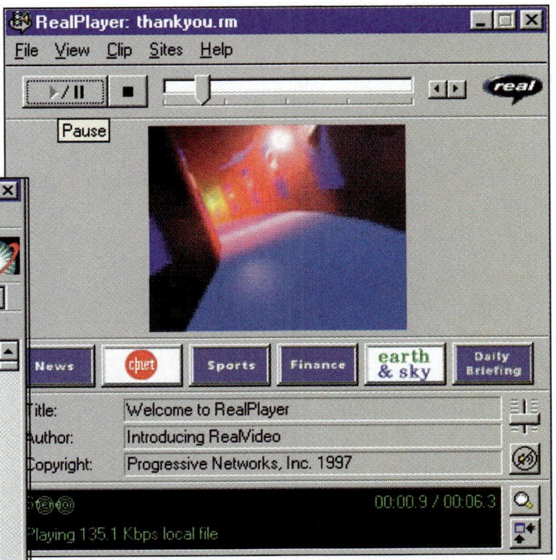

Video clients to view video fed from a Web server over the Internet courtesy of Progressive Networks

Courtesy of VXtreme, Inc.

The amount of information stored in the corporate database is often so vast as to be meaningless to managers. Just imagine the amount of data entered into computers each day by a major airline, information on hundreds of aircraft, thousands of employees, and tens of thousands of passengers. To make this information useful, it must be digested or summarized so it can be used by managers and employees to analyze, direct, and plan their activities.

Decision support systems—an introduction

Not all information that a manager needs is provided on a routine basis in a structured way. Occasionally new information must be gathered and analyzed, especially when a big decision must be made. The programs developed to help a manager integrate and analyze unstructured data from many sources are called decision support systems (DSS). For example, economic forecasts on inflation might be used to modify sales and expense forecasts over a 10-year period. The population growth projection for a metropolitan area might be used to adjust forecasted sales for a new store. The spreadsheet is a common decision support tool since changing numbers lets you ask "what if" questions. As decision support systems have evolved, a variety of tools have become available. In this spread, we'll look at a few of the more promising types. Keep in mind that many organizations use more than one approach and more than one tool.

Executive information systems

Executive information systems (EIS) provide up-to-date information to support decision making by managers. Their emphasis is on interactive graphical displays and an easy-to-use interface that presents information from the corporate database. An executive information system has a number of unique advantages over printed reports.

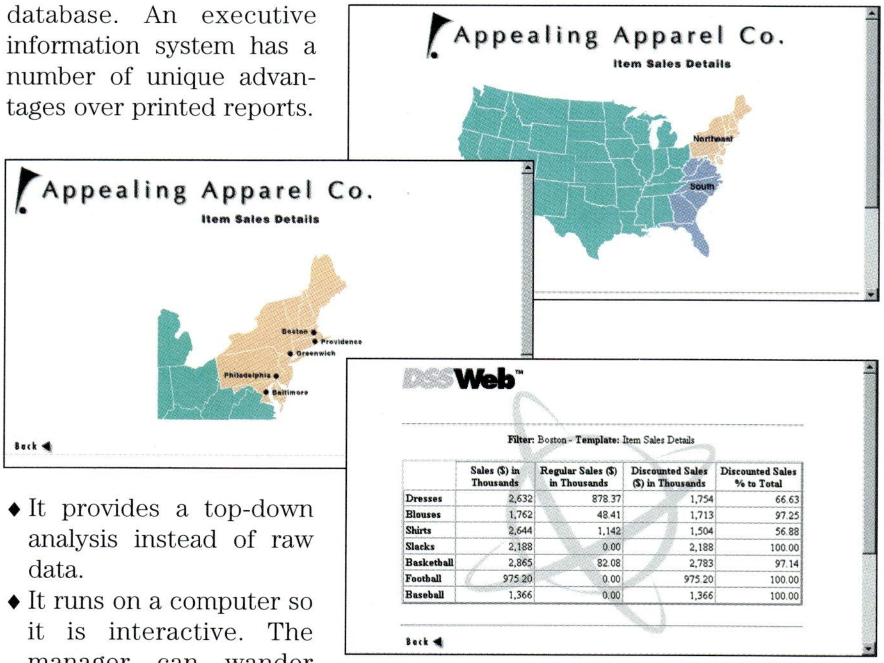

	Sales ($) in Thousands	Regular Sales ($) in Thousands	Discounted Sales ($) in Thousands	Discounted Sales % to Total
Dresses	2,632	878.37	1,754	66.63
Blouses	1,762	48.41	1,713	97.25
Shirts	2,644	1,142	1,504	56.88
Slacks	2,188	0.00	2,188	100.00
Basketball	2,865	82.08	2,783	97.14
Football	975.20	0.00	975.20	100.00
Baseball	1,366	0.00	1,366	100.00

Decision support system courtesy of MicroStrategy
http://dssweb.strategy.com/projects/gis/home.html

- ♦ It provides a top-down analysis instead of raw data.
- ♦ It runs on a computer so it is interactive. The manager can wander through it at his or her own pace looking for useful information.
- ♦ It presents data graphically as well as numerically, making it easier for the user to spot trends and relationships.

Geographical information systems

Many types of data are easier to analyze presented graphically. A geographical information system (GIS) relates data to maps. National sales shown by county, state, or region using colors for various ranges of sales, making it easy to spot where sales are high and low. Management then has knowledge of where sales are lower than expected. Without a GIS system this kind of analysis is so time consuming that is isn't done on a regular basis. Problems areas remain undiscovered, and actions delayed, for months or even years. After the Northridge earthquake of January 17, 1994, the City of Los Angeles, used GIS to immediately analyze damage to the city's sewers. Please see the GIS map on following page.

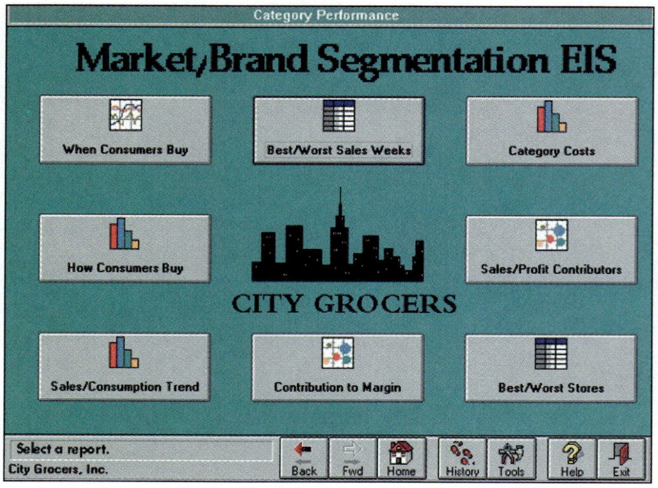

EIS courtesy of MicroStrategy
http://www.strategy.com/olap/img_eis.htm

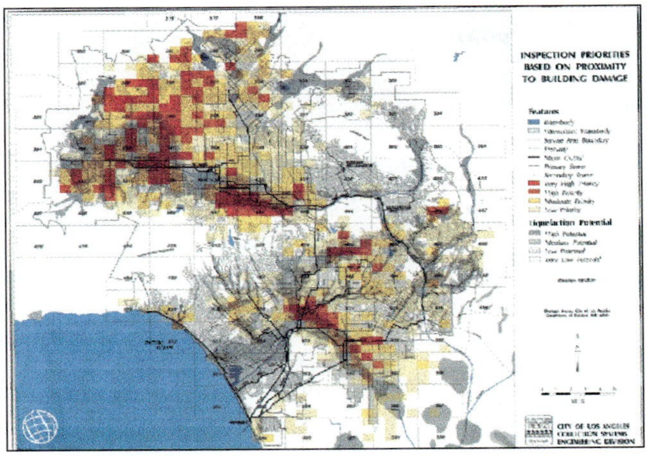

GIS courtesy of Bureau of Engineering, City of Los Angeles
http://www.esri.com/free/map_book/vol_10/htmls/quake_la.html

On-line analytical processing

On-line analytical processing (OLAP) allows users to view graphic and tabular presentations of their organization's data. Many people in organizations use their computers to enter basic queries and generate simple reports. A much smaller group called decision support specialists use much more complicated queries to answer more complicated questions. The smallest group of all uses the costly executive information systems (EIS) to analyze the database. All of these people work in discovery mode. This means that they are data explorers. Finding the answer to one question often leads to another question.

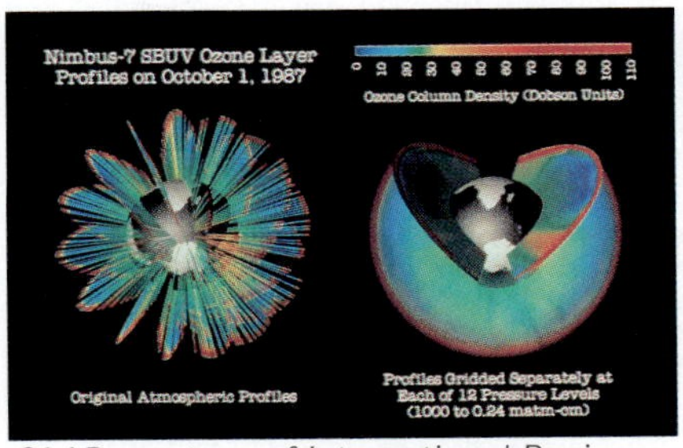

OLAP courtesy of International Business Machines
www.almaden.ibm.com/dx/samples/Samples.html

Data warehousing

Since on-line transaction processing involves real-time transactions, data that is 6, 12, or 24 months old may not be needed and so can be stored elsewhere. Recently, it has been recognized that this data, combined with current data, contains an enormous amount of information from which one can discover trends that would never be seen on a day-to-day or month-to-month basis. To make this data more useful, it is now being stored in a separate database called a data warehouse.

The database in a data warehouse is not the same as the database used for transaction processing. Databases used for transaction processing are designed to update thousands of records per second but are not designed for sophisticated querying. Data warehouse databases are designed to analyze terabytes of data and billions of records. They are organized to better allow analysis using special techniques.

Data-mining

Once data warehouses are created, the data stored there is "mined." When you are data-mining (also called "information discovery"), you don't pose questions. Instead, you have the system look for past patterns that may predict future behavior. This approach can result in valuable previously unknown facts. By contrast, on-line analytical processing (OLAP) and decision support systems (DSS) both depend on your asking specific questions, which limits what you may find to what you think it's worthwhile looking for.

When data-mining, you process more general requests. For example, instead of asking how many people in each state bought a Ford Explorer last year, you look for characteristics of the people who buy Ford Explorers. The results may reveal things you hadn't even intended to look for. Perhaps you'll find that the majority of buyers are women and most of them have young children.

The lines between the OLAP, DSS, and data-mining categories are blurring, however, as attractive data-mining features are being incorporated across the board.

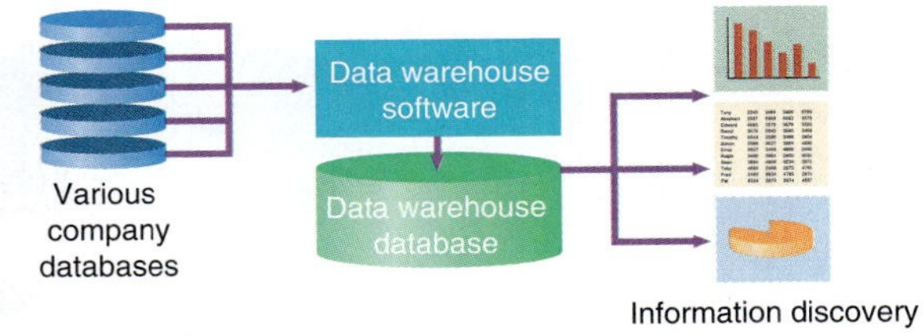

Data warehouse

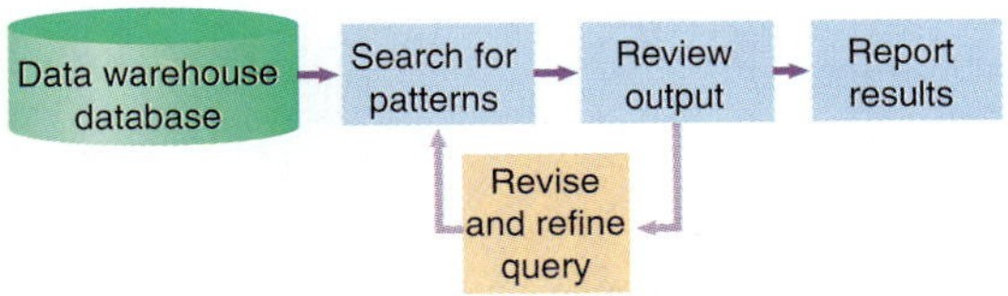

Data-mining

11.4 Marketing, Advertising, and Sales

Marketing departments are responsible for supporting sales by planning promotions, analyzing markets for new product opportunities, and developing marketing campaigns. They analyze markets, compare their results with those of other firms, look for seasonable patterns, and analyze discounts, promotions, and profits.

Advertising departments create ads and other promotional materials and ad campaigns.

Sales departments are directly responsible for selling the organization's products or services. They must analyze sales to compare actual results with forecasts.

The new wave of information technology has many time-saving benefits and creative new tools for people in marketing, advertising, and sales.

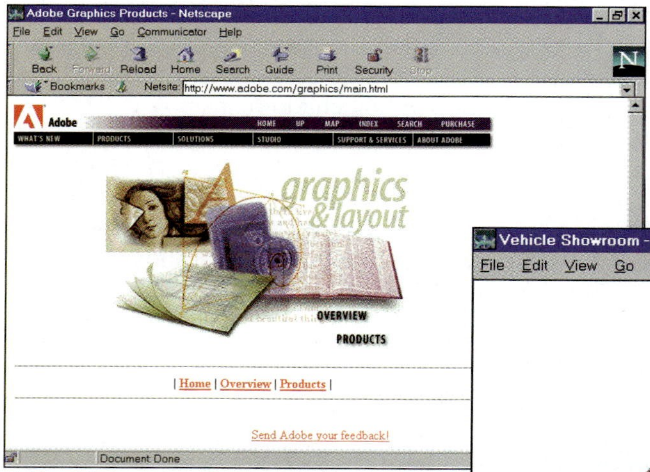

Advertising courtesy of Adobe
http://www.adobe.com/graphics/main.html

Digital printing

Desktop publishing and graphic applications are used extensively in marketing, advertising, and sales departments to put together ads, catalogs, brochures, and Web pages

When the advertising department needs a full-color brochure in a hurry, they can now run the job on direct digital printing presses. These new digital presses eliminate the need for printing plates and conventional inks and accept page layout data directly from the computer. Direct digital presses will revolutionize the way widely distributed information is printed. Using traditional offset printing, you would lay out the brochure in a page layout program like Quark Xpress or PageMaker and deliver the files to a service bureau, which would use those files to print the pages on photographic film. This film would then be sent to a printer who would use it to make printing plates to be mounted on the cylinders of a printing press to transfer ink to paper. With digital presses all the steps between layout page and printing are eliminated.

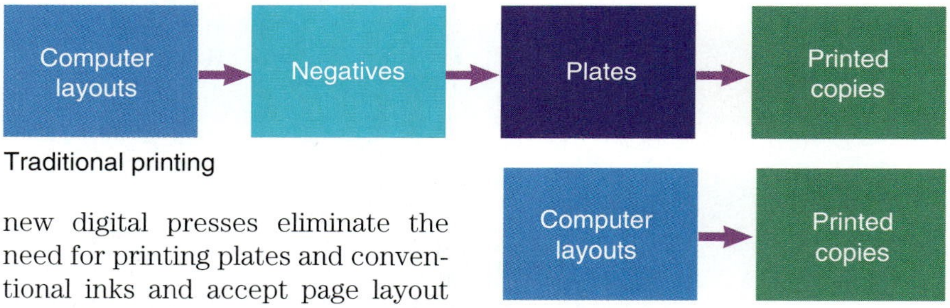

Traditional vs. digital printing

There's no film, no plates, and no ink.

What are the advantages of digital printing?

- Speed because of the number of steps that have been dropped.
- Flexibility because data can be inserted into the document as it prints just like mail-merging with a word-processing program.
- Convenience because you can print documents only when and where you need them for just-in-time printing.
- Customization because you can do finely targeted printing.

What are the disadvantages?

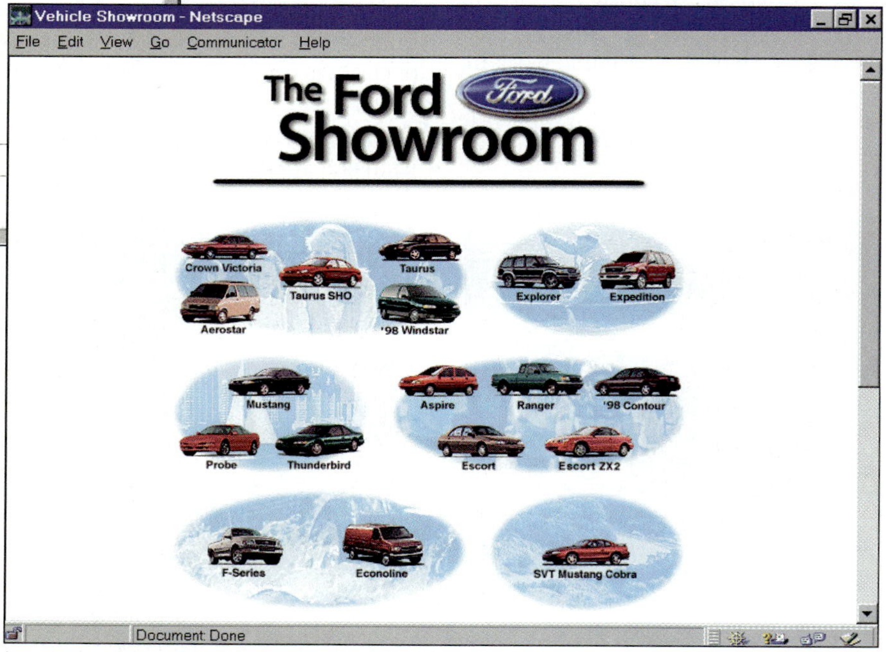

Internet advertising courtesy of Ford
http://www.ford.com/showrooms/

- Quality is poorer than offset printing but this is expected to change.
- Costs are much higher than offset printing.
- Job losses in the graphic-arts industry already hard hit by the widespread use of Mac and PostScript systems.

Internet advertising

Organizations trying to get exposure for their products and services are starting to use the Internet.

Customer lists

We are all familiar with direct mail brochures addressed to us by name with bold lines such as "Mr. Lewis, you'll be the first on your block to own the jet dirigible." But that's primitive. It won't be long before you start receiving direct mail pieces that refer to your specific interests, your credit rating, your income, your health, and whatever other kinds of information are being collected. Direct mail will start sounding like "Now that you have been promoted to vice president and have passed your annual physical, isn't it time to reevaluate your life insurance policy? This is especially important now that your daughter Nancy is about to graduate from high school and you've taken up white-water rafting." The software tools available for analyzing mailing lists are getting more and more powerful.

Presentations

Everybody in corporations attends presentations but sales and marketing people depend on presentations most. The nature of their work requires that they present to customers, to each other, and to other members of the organization. Application programs have been developed to make presentations. To begin, you create a series of frames much as you would organize slides for a slide show. You can use templates to format the text, add graphics, and bring in animations. As you polish the show, you can change the sequence of images, add special effects such as having one frame dissolve into the next, and specify how long each frame is displayed so the show works automatically.

Demos

A close relative of the presentation is a demo—short for demonstration—programs that you can run on your own system to get an idea of what a product is like. Widely used to promote computer software, demos are increasingly used in other product categories. The worst of these are just slide shows of one frame displayed after another. The best are entertaining and almost gamelike in their feel. Special programs have been developed to create these demos; many are created using one of the popular multimedia programs. New technologies such as Shockwave and Java are making it easier to run these demos over the Internet, but they are usually large so don't play well over a dial-up connection.

Presentation courtesy of International Business Machines

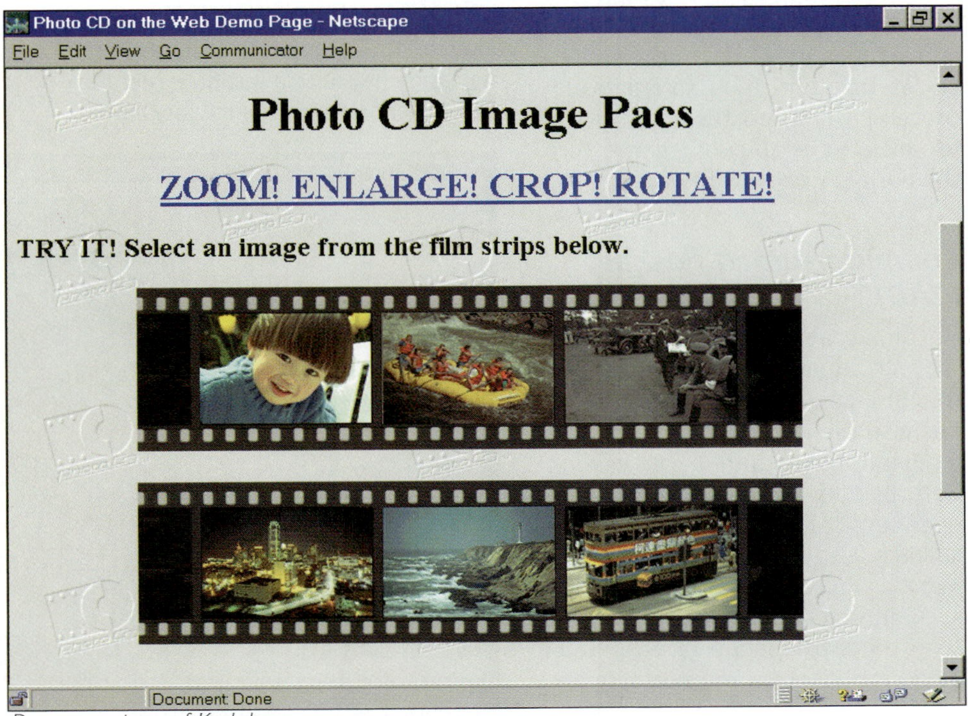

Demo courtesy of Kodak

11.5 Design, Production, and Manufacturing

In the global economy, it is absolutely necessary for the firm to keep costs as low as possible to remain competitive. Since design, production, and manufacturing consume so much of a manufacturing company's budget, great saving are being made by automating these procedures as much as possible.

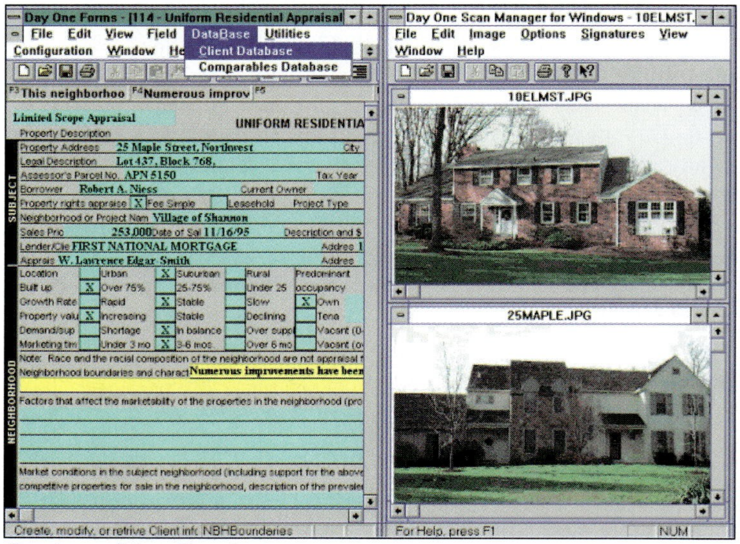

Courtesy of Day One, Inc.
http://www.day1.com/bgwksdmo.htm

Electronic data interchange (EDI)

Electronic Data Interchange (EDI) is the computer-to-computer exchange of business documents in a standard format. These formats look much like standard forms and are highly structured. One widely used format is for purchase orders and consists of an outer digital "envelope" with the addresses of both the sender and receiver. Inside the digital envelope a series of standard codes define the part number, cost, tax information, shipment methods, bill-to-location, ship-to-location, and contacts to call. This EDI purchase order can be automatically generated by the buyer when inventory falls below a certain point and sent via networks to the supplier. At that end it is automatically processed and creates a list of the products to be shipped even before the normal work day begins.

Computer-aided design (CAD)

Not long ago all products went through an initial phase in which rough engineering drawings were taken to the drafting department to be hand-drawn in ink on vellum. Returned to the designer or engineer, any changes required their going back to the drafting department again. There wasn't anything at all interactive about the process. With the introduction of computer-aided design software, not only are drawings easier to create and store, they are much easier to revise, no small advantage since revisions are the main activity in product design. One of the latest innovations is to automatically convert drawings into VRML files so the designer can "fly-through" the product seeing how the components fit together inside the model.

Feature prototyping

One of the problems with product design is getting an intimate feel for the appearance and behavior potential of a product. New software generates computer prototypes, which can be distributed and tested by actual customers. Usage data from these tests is collected automatically and used to refine product specifications until they precisely meet customers' needs. This process helps ensure new product market success before costly and time-consuming investments in engineering and manufacturing are made.

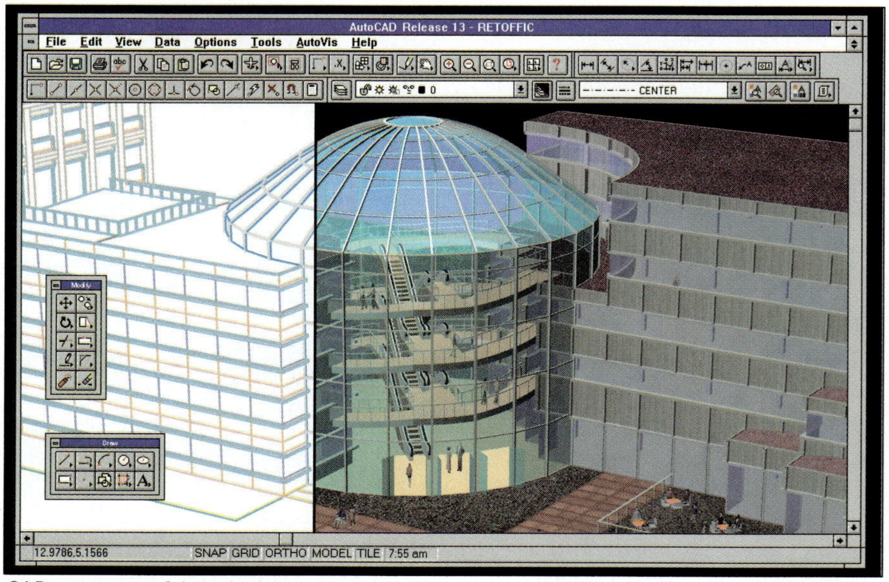

CAD courtesy of Autodesk

Better than communicating with customers using written specifications, static drawings, flip charts, or multi-media authoring tools, Altia Design allows customers to actually try proposed product features using fully functional prototypes, providing accurate and valuable feedback to the firm based on customers' experience that can make the difference between a resounding market winner and an embarrassing product failure.

Feature prototyping courtesy of Altia

Computer-aided manufacturing (CAM)

Computer-aided manufacturing (CAM) refers to industrial automation using computer-controlled machines and processes. Some CAM software can take a CAD drawing and create the code for programming a Computer Numerical Control (CNC) machine such as a laser or lathe.

Drawings can be used to program robots, the much more versatile machines that are used to assemble, weld, and paint products. Not all uses of robots are in heavy industry. Igor Cronsioe of Living Design uses robot-assisted manufacturing (RAM) for the industrial production of decorative fabrics and leather. The input is a combination of design ideas and special programming functions that merge during manufacturing to create output with continuous variation. The goal is to eliminate the mass-produced look while keeping the products affordable.

Project management

When projects from marketing campaigns to construction projects are undertaken, keeping track of all the tasks is a big job and that's what project management programs have been developed to do. One concept they use is the critical path, the series of tasks that must follow one another in order and can't be overlapped or begun until the previous one is completed. For example, a roof can't be put on a house until the walls are up, and the walls can't be built until the foundation is completed. When these dependent tasks are laid out end to end, they form the project's critical path. Any delays in the tasks on this path delay the entire project. Tasks not on the critical path like paving the driveway do not affect the project's completion date. Speeding up a project, called crashing the schedule, can be done only by changing the dates on the critical path, but changing some dates on the existing critical path may result in another path's becoming critical. Since this process is so interactive, it lends itself to computerization. Graphics are often used to show the complicated relationships in the timing and sequence of a project.

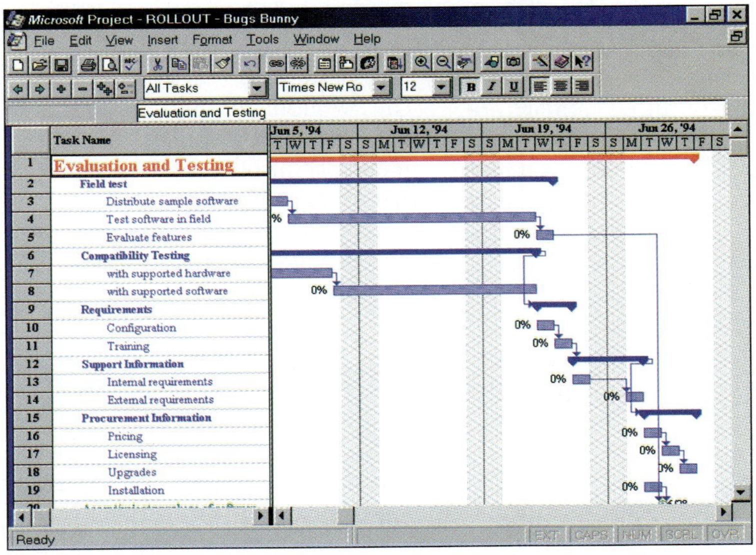

Project management courtesy of Microsoft

CAM courtesy of Igor Cronsioe
http://www.archaid.se/elmo/

11.6 Business on the Internet

The new wave of popularity of the World Wide Web has turned attention to its possibilities for commerce. And this means not only promoting products or services, but also selling them and getting payment via the Web.

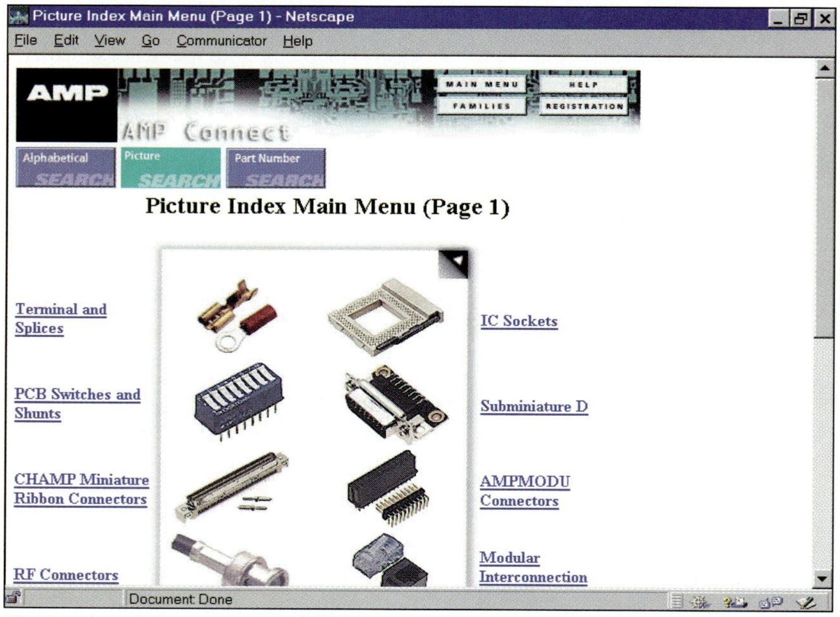

Electronic catalog courtesy of AMP
http://connect.ampincorporated.com/AMP/bin/AMP.Menu?M=MENU&ID=10111

Electronic catalogs

Companies' Web home pages that educate the public about their products and services are beginning to replace printed product catalogs that are expensive to produce and distribute and are soon out of date. Business-to-business electronic catalogs are a rapidly growing business. One electronic parts manufacturer, AMP, that spends up to $10 million to publish 400 catalogs a year expects to save enormous amounts of money once electronic catalogs replace the printed ones. Customers benefit because printed catalogs are hard to file and search through for the right product. Search engines built into electronic catalogs allow potential buyers to search an entire product line using various keywords or other characteristics. If you are interested in 6 amp fuses, you can just do a search for "6 amp fuses" and find every kind the company offers.

Web advertising

As you browse the Web, you find many pages adorned with companies names, medallions, and icons. These companies have paid the Web sites to put these elements on their pages, and the hope is that someone visiting the page will click one of the ornaments to visit the advertiser's Web site. To help advertisers measure the effectiveness of their ads and to develop leads to follow, software has been created that lets the companies know who is clicking and what they are viewing. This raises some serious privacy issues and a lot of people object to this capturing of information about their behavior. The wonderful thing about the world of computers is that creative minds are also developing software that conceals your identity from these advertisers. These programs will become popular defenses as Web users start getting phone calls around dinner time that begin "Hi, my name is Steve. We understand that you have recently shown interest in advanced CD-ROM drives. I'd like to introduce you to our high speed version at only $19.95 a month."

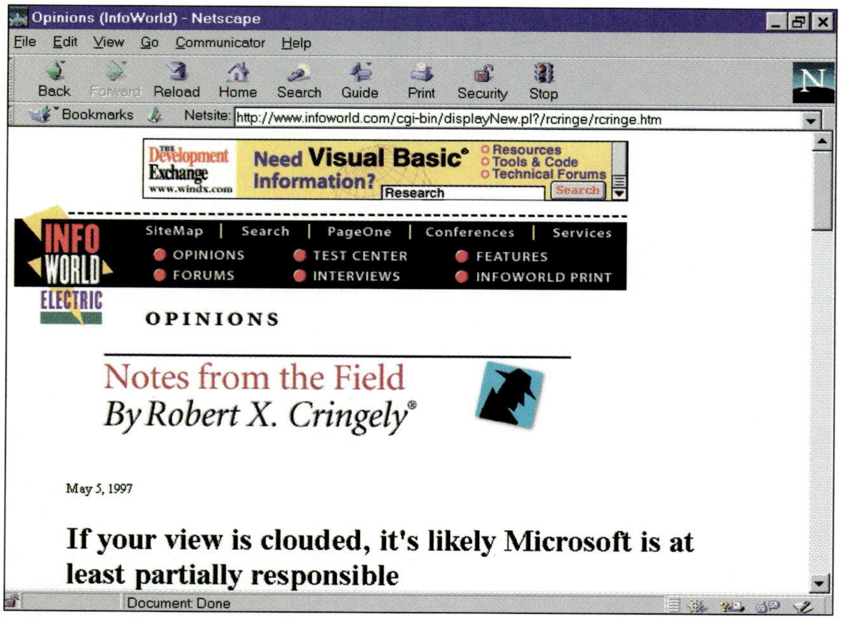

Web ad courtesy of Infoworld
http://www.infoworld.com/

Secure transactions

One the early struggles with the Internet was finding a way to safely buy and sell goods or transfer funds over it. But eventually this has been achieved. Since messages go though so many computers between a buyer and seller, no transaction was secure. Credit card numbers and other sensitive information could easily be captured. The goal was to enable electronic commerce by providing a safe, convenient, and immediate payment system on the Internet for transactions between consumers, merchants and their banks as well as between individuals by processing them in real time and passing authorization codes back to merchants. Here is how one of these secure payment systems works.

1. You visit the merchant's Web site and select items to be purchased and enter shipping instructions. The merchant's server then returns to you a summary of the item, price, and transaction ID.
2. You click the Pay button which launches the CyberCash wallet. You choose a credit card from your wallet and click OK to forward the order and encrypted payment information to the merchant.
3. The merchant receives the packet, strips off the order, and forwards the encrypted payment information digitally signed and encrypted with his private key to the CyberCash server. The merchant cannot see the consumer's credit card information.
4. The CyberCash server receives the packet, takes the transaction behind its firewall and off the Internet, unwraps data within a hardware-based crypto box (the same ones the banks use to handle PINs as they are shipped from ATM network to ATM network), reformats the transaction, and forwards it to the merchant's bank over dedicated lines.
5. The merchant's bank forwards the authorization request to the issuing bank via the card associations or directly to American Express or Discover for instance. The approval or denial code is sent back to CyberCash.
6. CyberCash returns the Approval or Denial code to the merchant who passes it on to you. From step 1 to step 6 takes 15 or 20 seconds.

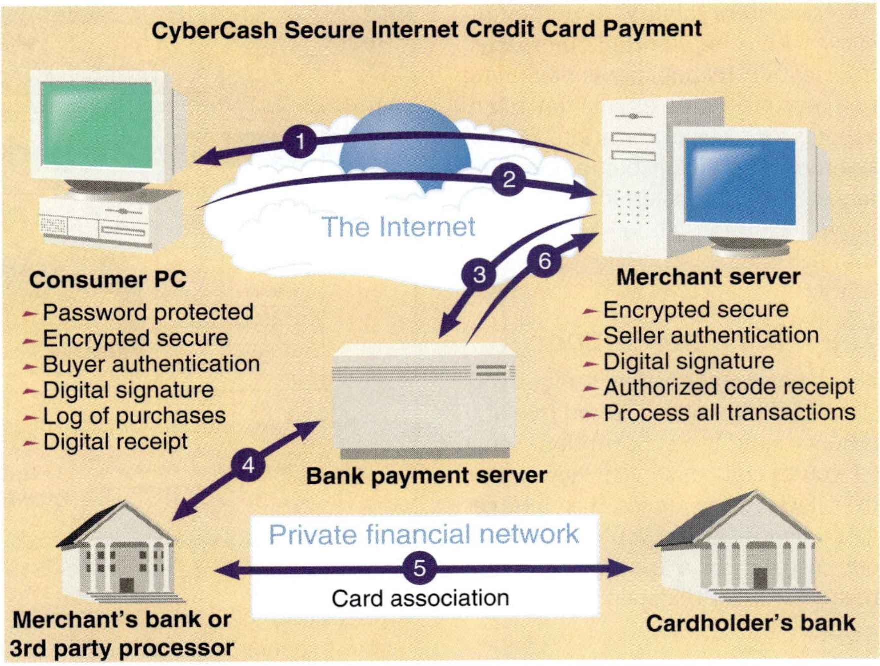

How Internet payment systems work, courtesy of Cybercash
http://www.cybercash.com

Micropayments

Imagine you were able to go to a magazine stand, browse through various magazines, and tear out and pay for only the pages you wanted. What if each time you read an ad, the advertiser paid you? This kind of commerce is all now possible on the Internet. Until recently, very small charges on the order of fractions of a cent could not be handled economically. It was like trying to pay for a gumball with a credit card. Very inexpensive microcommerce transactions are important to online publishers that want to sell newspapers by the article, cartoons by the strip, or music by the song. Micropayment systems, such as Digital's MillicentTM system, are making this possible. Using this system, you sign up for a "wallet," and then buy a few dollars worth of script using a credit card or other form of payment. When you visit a site offering the service you can look at detailed information that would normally be available only to subscribers, for only pennies per page. By visisting those sites where advertisers give you script to visit their site, you can probably keep your browsing free with the offsetting payments.

Courtesy of Digital
http://www.digital.com/flash/126/

11.7 Life Outside the Office

As computers' ability to communicate with one another increases, information technology is beginning to have profound effects on many aspects of the organization, one of the most significant being how they make it much easier for people to move around while keeping in touch.

The mobile newspaper courtesy of the New York Times

The mobile newspaper

Many newspapers offer on-line versions of their editions, some free and others requiring a subscription. Some let you to customize your newspaper by selecting the topics that interest you the most. When you're mobile, or out of town on a trip, you can still read your favorite paper.

Telecommuting

It's estimated that over 11 million Americans are employed in part or full time telecommuting programs. Millions more work from home informally or operate home-based businesses. This is seen by many as being more productive and also better for the environment. In certain circumstances, telecommuting may even be required.

California's Silicon Valley has been one of the first regions in the nation to respond to the federal air-quality law requiring companies of 100 or more employees to establish telecommuting projects. A survey of Silicon Valley companies that have established telecommuting projects to meet the air-quality regulations shows that there are still many technological hurdles to overcome before workers can have the same functionality at home that they do in the office.

- Desktop videoconferencing is at this point harder to do with people not at central locations; it adds so much to interpersonal business communications that it has become almost a necessity.
- Telephone-to-PC integration technology needs to be simplified and improved.
- ISDN services are sometimes not available and are always too complex and too costly. One large company found that it costs the company $10,000 or more per year for leased lines and 8 cents per minute for the ISDN service.
- Telecommuters must have access to the proper tools. For example, they might need whiteboard collaborative tools (see below).
- Security must be improved perhaps with dial-back services to ensure it's really an employee logging in and not just someone who stole or guessed a password.

There are also some problems with telecommuting to be addressed on the personal side as well as the technical side.

- Telecommuters must be 10 to 15 percent more productive because of the high cost of equipment.
- It is difficult for managers to measure productivity and performance and they need to see a gain. New developments brought about by information technology of course can't be productivity-neutral for them. Bosses may view telecommuting as losing control over their employees

Telecommuting courtesy of Apple

White boards

White boards are multimedia tools that allow cooperation among geographically dispersed people over a network or the Internet. White boards allow a document or an image to be viewed simultaneously by all participants in a conference so they can share ideas interactively by voice or by drawing comments or sketches that everyone can see. It's the electronic equivalent of the physical white board. Why are they called white boards? The chalk dust associated with blackboards or chalkboards was a problem in the electronics industry. It contaminat-

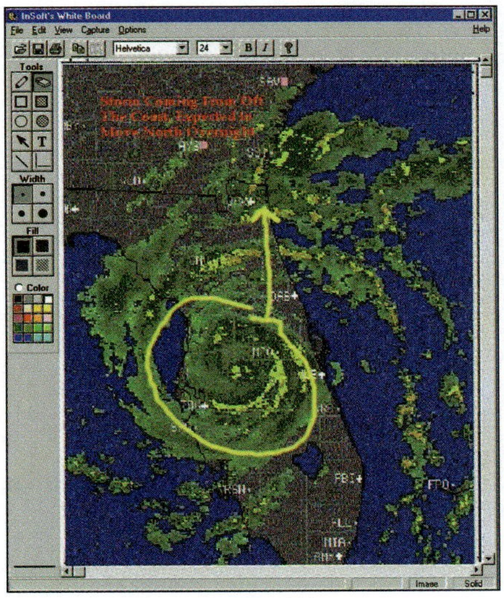

White board courtesy of Netscape
http://home.netscape.com/eng/mozilla/3.0/relnotes/cooltalk/images/Whiteboard-screen.jpeg

ed equipment. The solution was the "white board" a surface on which people could write or draw using erasable marking pens. The name has been carried over to the digital version.

Wireless mobile computing

Computers are making it increasingly easy for workers to roam outside the office while remaining in constant touch through e-mail, file transfer, or some form of conferencing.

With a radio modem, a roaming employee can use radio frequency (RF) communications in most major U.S. cities to send and receive e-mail without searching for a phone jack. Cellular Digital Packet Data (CDPD) which will soon be available nationwide on the same radio frequency used by cellular telephones transmits digital data as packets as well as voice. Pricing will be based on file size rather than connect time, and CDPD communication will be more expensive than traditional means for some time. Price Waterhouse plans to equip virtually all of their 7,000 to 10,000 staff members with CDPD modems. These tax and management consultants and auditors who work in the field will then have access to the company's networked computers and data from wherever they are just as if they were at their desks in the office.

CDPD is not alone and has to compete with other services such as Ardis, jointly owned by IBM and Motorola, and the RAM Mobile Data network, a venture backed by BellSouth Corp. Unlike those services, CDPD devices will be able to interoperate with one another. The RAM and Ardis networks use a different part of the radio spectrum, and each has different spacing. If users today want to communicate with users on the other services, they have to buy a radio modem for each one.

Wireless computing courtesy of International Business Machines

Virtual corporations

With the growth of networks and easy connections, a new virtual corporation is possible. The company-in-a-box is a dream of many engineers and planners who envision businesses operating in cyberspace to coordinate employees and provide services on-line.

Who knows, at some point in the future it may seem quaint to bring people together at the same place to work or be educated. Many of these groupings will take place electronically, with everyone home or wherever they want to be. And it may not be as far in the future as you imagine. Pacific Bell, a major telephone company, is exploring the concept of the virtual office. The virtual office can be anywhere, the den, the kitchen table, the car, a customer's conference room, or wherever people's jobs take them. It can mean office sharing or "hoteling," having two or more people assigned to an office normally used by one person, the people there on different days, or in the case of hoteling, people reserving space ahead of time.

The virtual office set up can be at low cost. It will allow managers and others to spend more time with customers; improve employee satisfaction and productivity working with fewer interruptions; alleviate traffic congestion; improve air quality; and greatly reduce real estate costs. It will reduce or eliminate commuting so there is more time after hours for family and friends.

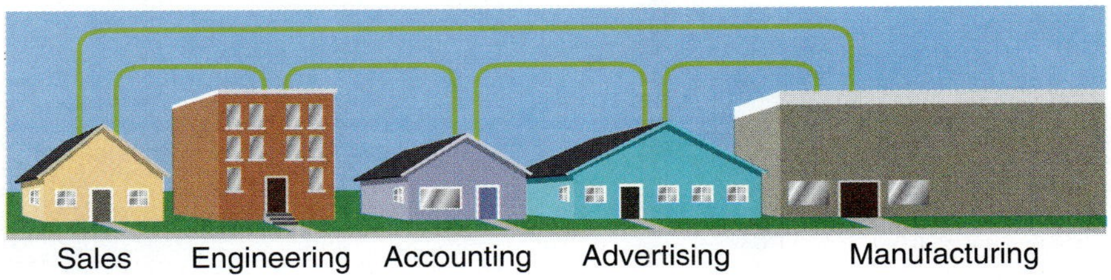

Virtual corporation

11.8 Careers

When it comes to computers at work, you can run but you can't hide. No matter what firm you might work for, or what your position might be in the firm, the chances are that a computer will be involved in some aspect of your work. Regardless of where you are in the corporate hierarchy, you will be expected to know how to perform a core of activities with computers. If you can't do this common core, you'll not be able to do your job.

We are all end-users

Since computers are so widely used in business, most jobs require computer skills specific to a field and an understanding of the computer tools used to enhance performance. In these jobs, the computer is not absolutely essential but central and very useful. For example, managers use computers to draft memos, letters, and reports; to prepare financial plans and forecasts; and to evaluate data stored in the company's computers. Designers, engineers, and scientists use computers to run experiments, analyze structures and designs, and prepare working drawings for production.

Computer-related positions

For other jobs the computer is everything. At the moment, there are an amazing number of positions open in the fast-growing computer field. These positions use the computer as the essential tool for the job. Typical positions are:

- Data entry operators enter data into computers. For example, they enter the prices and stock numbers of items in inventory, sales and shipments, and employee records.
- Word processing operators prepare finished documents based on what others prepare. Some of these positions are secretarial. The operator works for a person directly and prepares only his or her work. Others work in centralized departments that prepare work from people in one or more divisions in the company.
- Desktop publishers prepare documents such as booklets, magazines, newspapers, and books for printing so they can be distributed to others.

Computer-related positions courtesy of International Business Machines

- Editors edit and proofread reports, advertising materials, articles, and books.
- Illustrators prepare line drawings for use as illustrations in books, magazines, and newspapers.
- Animators prepare animated art for use in movies or multimedia productions.

Computer science positions

All of the computer services within an organization are supported and maintained by a highly trained staff. Here are just some of the people who orchestrate services for management and other end-users.

- Computer operators operate large computers. They load programs and data, back up files, run jobs, and print reports.
- Computer librarians maintain files and when appropriate company databases of data, and provide employees with access to company and public databases of information. They maintain corporate data, keep records, and determine which files can be deleted.
- Programmers write programs that are used to process the company's information.
- System analysts analyze, evaluate, and design company information

End-users courtesy of International Business Machines

systems ensuring that information systems meet the needs of both management and employees. Once they determine the needs to be met, they design a system, and consult with the developers who write the programs.

- Information systems managers manage all of a company's information systems and resources. Generally they report to high-level officers and manage a staff of people in the information processing, or data processing, department who perform the tasks required to implement the company's systems.
- Trainers teach people how to use computer systems. Some trainers work in-house for companies; others work for firms that provide training to companies on a contract basis.
- Microcomputer specialists train and assist computer users so users get the most benefit from their computers.
- Technical support people answer questions from people who use computers. Many of these people work for companies that supply computer equipment to firms.
- Technical writers write descriptions of programs and computer systems so that others can understand and use them.
- Consultants fulfill several roles, from designing systems to installing them to training users how to operate them.
- The microcomputer manager is in charge of the microcomputers scattered through the organization. This manager's job is to ensure that employees are trained, problems are solved, and needs are met.
- Webmasters manage an organization's Web site and coordinate the development of the text, graphics, and multimedia elements that are to be displayed on Web pages.

Finding a position

Now that you know how to use computers, why not use one to find a position? The World Wide Web is full of employment services and company listings of job openings. (See Monster Board below.) You can search for specific company listings, openings in specific fields, listings in specific geographic areas, or general listings. There are even Web sites that offer advice on how to approach prospective employers and prepare resumes:

Search for "career."

Newsgroups such as us.jobs.misc, triangle.jobs, bionet.jobs.

Remember that if you e-mail a contact, a first impression makes all the difference just as it does in person or by letter. One recruiter says he puts the most weight on the first paragraph. Also, he thinks that people who send just resumes and not cover letter e-mails aren't communicators and feels that says a lot.

Computer scientists courtesy of International Business Machines

Career paths

Almost all positions have career paths that allow you to move up the career ladder to positions with more responsibility and higher pay. Secretaries can become supervisors, programmers can become department managers, and salespeople can become marketing or sales managers. Some employees who gain extensive experience within a large firm become entrepreneurs and start their own businesses. Many word processing operators have started small firms that do word processing for professionals and other people who do not have their own full-time staffs to do work of this kind.

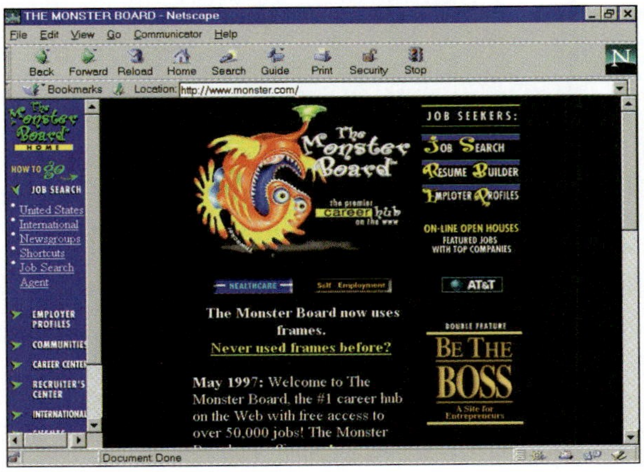

Courtesy of The Monster Board

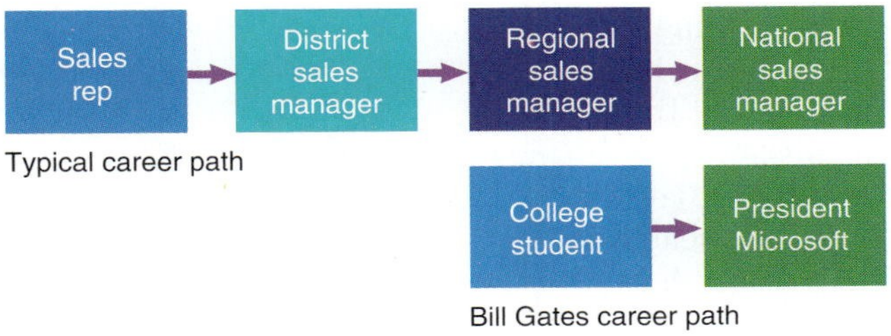

Typical and not so typical career paths

11.9 Keeping Up-to-Date

Many people think that education is something you undergo only during one stage of your life. After college, you work but no longer have to learn. This is not only wrong, it is foolhardy. Technology is changing so rapidly that what you know today will be outdated in a few short years. A consultant was quoted in the *New York Times* as saying, "Too many people won't give up until they see their industry die. People in publishing are a perfect example. They will not take a step to retrain themselves to do something different until they are told they don't have a job anymore."

Another consultant said, "Most companies are not looking for someone to manage people. They are looking for someone to make a contribution. No one today is paid to simply manage the activities of others. Companies cannot afford to do that."

The gist of both quotes is that you need to posses a body of skills, and you need to keep them up-to-date and learn a new set of skills before your old ones are outdated. As technology continues to advance, things will be done differently, if not better, then faster. Keeping ahead of the changes requires effort. People do it by joining associations such as user groups or professional organizations. Many do it by reading periodicals in their field or taking classes so they stay informed of new trends and new opportunities.

The Internet

When it comes to information about computing, the Internet has it all. There is more information on computers than you could ever possibly digest. The great thing about the Web is that you can use it to keep in touch with changes in the field and groups that make these changes happen. For example, you can keep up with the latest research in computing at IBM's research site.

User groups

Almost every large urban area has an organization of computer users called a user group. For example, in Boston, the Boston Computer Society has over 10,000 members organized into special interest groups (SIGs), each devoted to a special area of computing. You can join a SIG on a specific application program, a specific programming language, or a more general topic such as desktop publishing. These groups hold periodic meetings where new products are demonstrated and members can learn from specialists in the industry and from each other. They offer classes for introductory and advanced topics. A side benefit is you get to know people who share interests and help each other advance their careers.

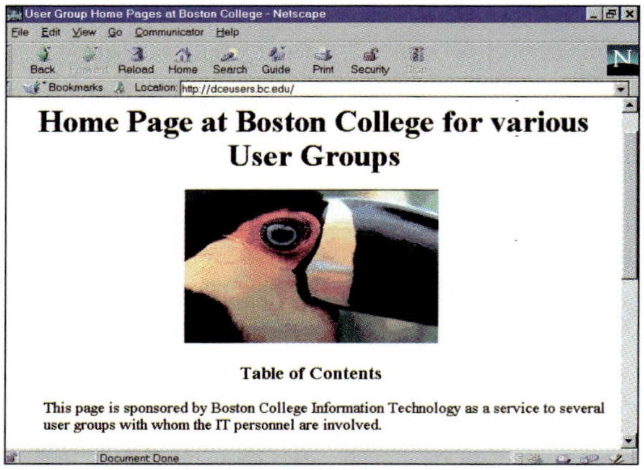

User groups courtesy of Boston College
http://dceusers.bc.edu/

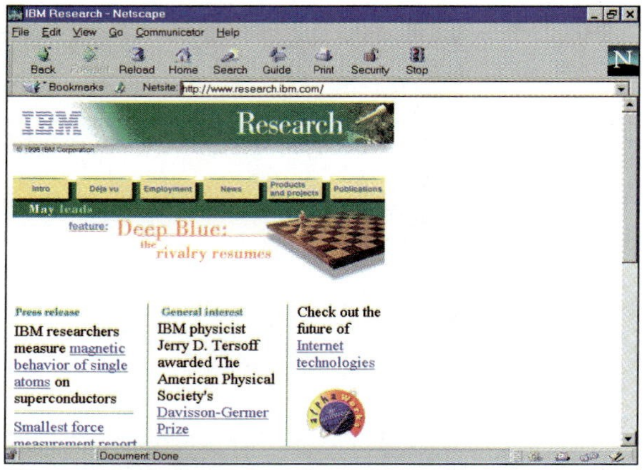

IBM research courtesy of International Business Machines

Professional organizations

Professional organizations are generally open to all interested parties. As a member, you receive the organization's publications and invitations to local and national meetings where meeting members present papers on topics of interest. Many firms that supply hardware, software, or services exhibit their newest products at such meetings and have professionals on hand to answer questions. Some of the professional organizations in the computer field are listed in the orange boxes below and at the right of the next page.

- Educom is a nonprofit consortium of higher education institutions that facilitates the introduction, use, and access to and management of information resources in teaching, learning, scholarship, and research. Available on the web at http://www.educom.edu.
- The Data Processing Management Association (DPMA) represents information systems (IS) professionals. With nearly 12,000 members and 5,000 student members throughout the U.S. and Canada, DPMA's mission is to promote the effective, responsible management of information technology to the benefit of its members, their employers, and society. Their address is 505 Busse Highway, Park Ridge, IL., 60068. Available on the Web at http://www.dpma.org.

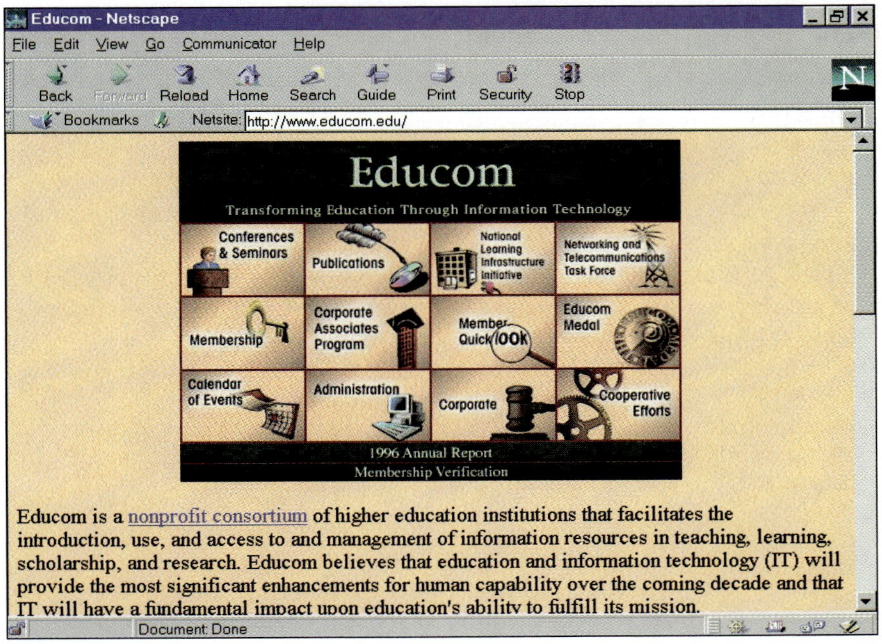

Professional organization courtesy of Educom
WWW.educom.edu

Publications

Newspapers, magazines, and books are a common way to learn about new areas in your field and keep up-to-date. Publications published daily, weekly, or monthly are periodicals. Those aimed at people in a specific field are called trade papers. Once you locate a periodical that addresses the things that interest you, you can pay their subscription fee. In some cases, the periodical is a controlled-circulation publication. This means that advertising covers the entire cost and it is sent free to qualified professionals. These publications are hard for unqualified people to get without paying the subscription fee because most have a very narrow definition of what it means to be qualified. In one way or another, however, the definition determines whether or not you are in a position of authority and have money to spend on things that their advertisers have to sell. One way to preview these publications is to visit the electronic versions on the Web. Most offer enough free information on these sites for you to get a feel for their interests and level.

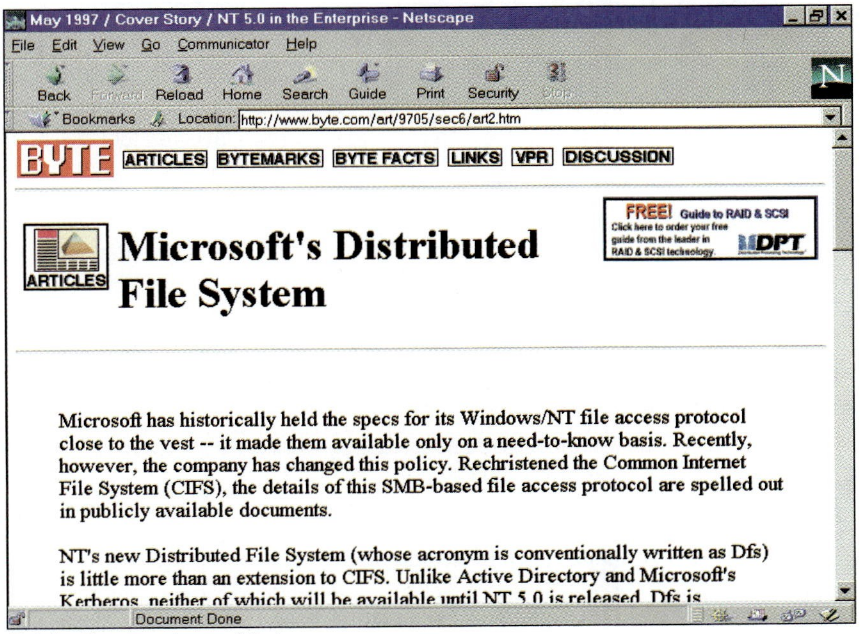

Publication courtesy of Byte
www.byte.com

- *InfoWorld*, the voice of personal computing in the enterprise, emphasizes microcomputers and their place in the corporate information system. It has sections on software, hardware and networking news; enterprise computing, reviews, and columns by industry pundits and even humorists such as Robert X. Cringely who invites readers to call him with industry secrets.

  http://www.infoworld.com

- *Computerworld*, the newspaper of information systems management, is published weekly and contains articles that are of interest to computer professionals that work in information or data processing centers. It has sections on such topics as advanced news, technology, desktop computing, workgroup computing, applications development, management, and careers.

  www.computerworld.com

11.10 Enhancing and Testing Your Understanding

Summary

- Much information flows into a company from outside sources during its normal course of business. Other information comes from internal sources. In a few cases, information is actually the company's product.
- Mission-critical chores are moving from the mainframe computers to networks in a process called downsizing.
- When organizations take orders or reservations and they buy products and services from suppliers they are involved in transactions. A procedure called on-line transaction processing (OLTP) is used to enter and find data in real time.
- The traditional information processing system was centralized around a mainframe computer. Connected to it were dumb-terminals that were used only to send data to and receive data from the mainframe.
- A new form of computing is called client-server computing. The large computer in such a system is the server. The smaller computers are the clients.
- Programs that help a manager analyze unstructured data are decision support systems (DSS).
- Executive Information Systems (EIS) provide interactive up-to-date information to support decision making by managers.
- Geographical information systems (GIS) relate data to maps.
- On-line analytical processing (OLAP) allows users to view graphic and tabular presentations of their organization's data.
- To make older data more useful, it is stored in a separate database called a data warehouse.
- Once data warehouses are created, the data is "mined."
- Desktop publishing and graphic applications are used extensively in marketing, advertising, and sales departments.
- When the advertising department needs a full color brochure in a hurry, they can now run the job on a direct digital printing press.
- Electronic Data Interchange (EDI) is the computer-to-computer exchange of business documents in a standard format.
- Computer-aided design (CAD) software makes engineering drawings easier to create and store and much easier to revise.
- Computer-aided manufacturing (CAM) refers to industrial automation using computer-controlled machines and processes.
- Project management programs keep track of all of the tasks in a project.
- Electronic catalogs are cheaper to produce than printed catalogs and much easier for the customer to search for products.
- One problem with electronic commerce has been ensuring the security of transactions.
- Micropayment systems make possible small transactions on the Web such as selling newspapers by the article, cartoons by the strip, or music by the song.
- It's estimated that over 11 million Americans are employed in formal telecommuting programs.
- White boards allow a document or an image to be viewed simultaneously by all the participants in a conference so they can share ideas interactively by voice or by drawing comments or sketches that everyone can see.
- Webmasters manage an organization's web site and coordinate the development of the text, graphics, and multimedia elements that are to be displayed.
- Almost all positions have career paths that allow you to move up the career ladder to positions with more responsibility and higher pay.
- Almost every large urban area has an organization of computer users called a user group or Special Interest Group (SIGs).
- Publications such as newspapers, magazines, and books are a common way to learn about new areas in all computer fields and keep up-to-date. Those that are published daily, weekly, or monthly are called periodicals. Those that are aimed at people in a specific field are called trade papers. Once you locate a periodical that addresses the things that interest you, you can pay their subscription fee to receive the publication. In some cases, the periodical is called a controlled-circulation publication. This means that advertising covers the entire cost and it is sent free to qualified professionals.

Review Questions

True/False

1. T F In a centralized computer system, all end-users are connected to a central computer and often use dumb-terminals.

2. T F The new network computing model is a centralized one so it's much like the old terminals connected to a mainframe arrangement.

3. T F Step up to the ATM machine, insert a credit card in a cash station's fuel pump, order a product over the Internet, and you're engaging in a transaction.

4. T F At the heart of a transaction processing system is a database that displays information and stores new data.

5. T F Client-server computing uses a lot of inexpensive desktop computers connected to each other without a central computer.
6. T F Geographical information systems (GIS) are used to analyze rocks, deserts, and other geological formations.
7. T F On-line analytical processing (OLAP) displays data using graphs or tables so you can see relationships you might otherwise miss.
8. T F A data warehouse is a fire-proof building in which old computer tapes and disks are stored in case they are needed again.
9. T F Electronic Data Interchange (EDI) refers to the computer-to-computer exchange of business documents in a standard format without human intervention.
10. T F Computer-aided design programs are used to create drawings that show an object's parts and how they are to be assembled.

Fill-In the Blank

1. The introduction of the __________ made it possible to eliminate duplicate data and use queries to locate information.
2. When organizations take orders or reservations and they buy products and services from suppliers they are involved in __________.
3. Client-server applications are split into a __________ and a __________.
4. To make older data more useful, it is stored in a separate database called a __________.
5. Once data warehouses are created, the data is __________.
6. When the advertising department needs a full-color brochure in a hurry, they can now run the job on a __________.
7. __________ is the computer-to-computer exchange of business documents in a standard format.
8. __________ refers to industrial automation using computer controlled machines and processes.
9. Project management programs locate the __________ which is the series of tasks that must follow one another in order and can't be overlapped.
10. __________ manage an organization's web site and coordinate the development of the text, graphics, and multimedia elements that are to be displayed.

Multiple Choice

1. An organization engages in transactions when it ___.
   - **a.** Orders supplies **b.** Sells goods or services
   - **c.** Takes reservations **d.** All of the above
2. In a client-server system, data is usually stored on the ___.
   - **a.** Client **b.** Server
   - **c.** Network **d.** None of the above
3. To analyze a business, managers use
   - **a.** Decision support systems (DSS)
   - **b.** Executive Information Systems (EIS)
   - **c.** On-line analytical processing (OLAP)
   - **d.** All of the above
4. Data mining is used to ___.
   - **a.** Discover unexpected relationships
   - **b.** Find a specific piece of data in a huge mass of data
   - **c.** Remove old data from a database
   - **d.** None of the above
5. Electronic data interchange is used to ___.
   - **a.** Exchange business documents in a standard format
   - **b.** Exchange e-mail
   - **c.** Send databases back and forth
   - **d.** Make corrections in other databases
6. Maufacturers use ___ to improve their products.
   - **a.** Computer-aided design
   - **b.** Computer aided manufacturing
   - **c.** Prototyping
   - **d.** All of the above
7. Micropayment systems make it possible to ___ on line.
   - **a.** Have small transactions
   - **b.** Buy microprocessor systems
   - **c.** Arrange computer loans
   - **d.** All of the above
8. Special interest groups primarily ___.
   - **a.** Offer training and meetings on specific aspects of computing
   - **b.** Lobby manufacturers for better products
   - **c.** Lobby government officials for consumer protection
   - **d.** None of the above
9. Centralized computers in large organizations have been managed by ___.
   - **a.** Information systems departments
   - **b.** Data processing departments
   - **c.** Information technology departments
   - **d.** all of the above
10. Multiple copies of the same database are kept up to date using ____.
    - **a.** Data warehousing **b.** Replication
    - **c.** Downsizing **d.** None of the above

Research Projects

1. Use magazines or the Internet to search for any information you can on data-mining. What applications has it been used for? What problems do users encounter?
2. Use an Internet search engine to search for "data pro cessing department," "information systems department," and "information technology department." Which term gives you the most hits? Check out some of the sites and see if you can learn more about what these departments do.
3. Use magazines or the Internet to explore client-server computing. Can you find any negatives about this approach? What are the positives? How popular is it?
4. Go though the Sunday edition help-wanted ads in a large metropolitan newspaper and make a list of the computer-related jobs you find. Make sure you explore all job categories to see what jobs require computer-related skills.

CHAPTER

12 PROGRAMMING AND SYSTEM

AN OVERVIEW

Modern information technology combines glass, plastic, and metal into computers that, when an electric current is run through them, perform useful work by the addition of a series of step-by-step instructions called programs. Programs give meaning to the process. All the software described in this book is made up of many ingenious instruction sets. Walk through a modern corporation's computer center, a large computer store, or a state-of-the-art factory, and the amount of software you'll encounter is staggering. And that's only the programming you can see. The chances are your automobile, your camera, your watch, and many of your household appliances contain programs that make them work.

Programs, or software or code, are created by people who use word processors or editing programs to write them out just as you would write out a highly detailed and structured outline or report. The programs are put through some additional procedures (the subject of this chapter), and presto! the programmer has made a piece of hardware do his or her bidding.

There are thousands of programmers writing programs on a full-time basis. Corporations spend billions every year developing programs. Why all this investment of time and money? Because programs are essential to the operation and competitiveness of a modern corporation. They perform the crucial tasks of monitoring transactions, keeping track of inventory and payroll, and making production machinery function. That's only a part of programming. Programs are created to educate, amuse, entertain, and challenge you. The consumer side of the business is vast and growing larger all the time. There are fortunes to be made (and lost) on this new frontier and everyone wants a piece of the action.

In this chapter we look at the concepts and procedures involved in developing all kinds of programs, be they accounting programs for a Fortune 500 company or electronic games for your computer.

OBJECTIVES

After completing this chapter, you will be able to:

- Explain why programs are needed and describe who creates them.
- Identify the differences between programing language levels and generations and give some examples of each.
- Explain how procedural languages differ from earlier languages and describe how they are created.
- Describe various programming methodologies and explain why they were developed.
- List the steps used in developing programs and systems and explain why these steps are necessary.
- Describe a few basic programming techniques.

Programming *n.* 1. the act or process of planning or writing a program.

Development *n.* 1. the act or process of developing; growth; progress.

ON THE PACE CD ROM

Spread No.	Title
12-6	Adding Two Numbers
12-6	Input and Output
12-7	Branching
12-7	Looping
12-8	Functions
12-8	Program Decomposition

DEVELOPMENT

12.1 Programs:

When you use an operating system or application, you are depending on a program that was written by someone, or some group of people telling the computer exactly what to do in every foreseeable situation within a certain range of possibilities. Some instructions control the way the program looks to you on the screen. Others prescibe the menus to display and actions to take when you select a menu choice. Still others save and retrieve files from the disk, boldface words, add numbers, and perform all the other tasks that you ask your computer to do.

John von Neumann courtesy of Princeton University
http://ei.cs.vt.edu/~history/VonNeumann.html

The stored program concept

A computer is a piece of complex electronics just like your TV or stereo. There is a crucial difference, however. Most other machines are designed for a specific purpose and their functionality is achieved by the parts that are used in them and the way these parts are interconnected. Computers are designed to be general purpose machines. You can use the same computer to write letters, manage your checkbook, play chess, organize your schedule and of course lots of other things. A computer's behavior can be changed without changing its actual physical parts. These machines contain a "memory" device (RAM) in which you can store and execute specific instructions to do particular tasks.

This wasn't always the case. In early computers, programs weren't stored in the computer's memory. Memory was so precious, only data was stored there. The programming instructions were added by changing wires on the machine or by using toggle switches on a panel. John von Neumann proposed that if the program was also stored in memory, computers could be even more powerful. One big reason was that program instructions could be easily changed just by loading a new program. As the program executed, it could easily change the instructions in memory.

The program ladder

A computer can't do anything without a software program residing in its memory (RAM). However, most computer memories are volatile– they forget everything once the power is turned off. Let's review the types of programs required to put your computer to work. Each of these programs must be written and distributed before you can use your system.

1. All computers have a built-in basic input/output system (BIOS) program that is in a nonvolatile part of the system's memory (ROM). This program is executed the moment you turn on the computer.
2. Once the BIOS is loaded, it allows the computer to read the next piece of software, the operating system, from some permanent medium such as a hard disk. The operating system is software that is used to do all the housekeeping necessary to use the machine.
3. The combination of the hardware and the operating system software brings the machine to life but is still quite useless as the computer can't do anything for you yet. At this point you have to add one or more application programs to make the computer do what you want—play chess or write a report. Application programs are stored on floppy disks, hard disk drives, CD-ROM discs, or even ROM chips which retain their content without power (like audio and video tapes).

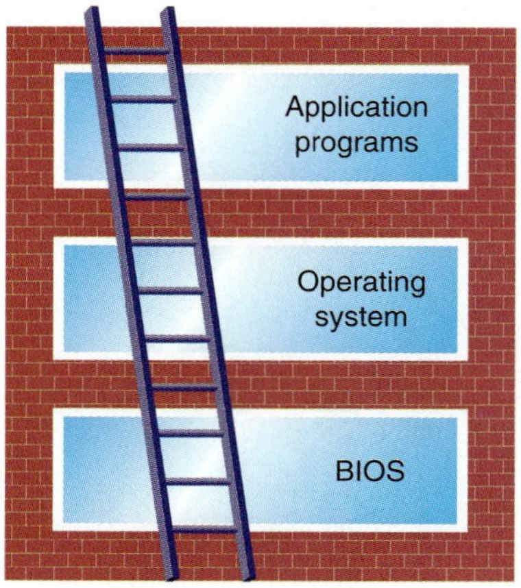

The program ladder

Programmers

Computer programmers write programs. They convert specifications (precise descriptions) of business or scientific problems into sequences of detailed instructions to solve the problems by computer. The programmer describes how data is to be structured in the computer and specifies the precise steps and processing logic which cause the program to produce the desired results.

The process of writing programs combines both science and art and is one of the most detail-oriented tasks that one can engage in. A program must direct the computer through a process one step at a time. If the steps are not complete, or if they are out of order, the program doesn't work. The program also doesn't work if one set of steps conflicts with another set of steps in the program. Sounds simple until you consider that the 4.3 million lines of instructions in the Windows NT operating system program would fill more than 75,000 pages if typed single-spaced on 8½ by 11 paper. Just as in simpler technology, a single faulty part can bring the entire machine down. In terms of pure numbers of things that could be wrong, computer programs are by far the most complex product of the human imagination.

Programmers don't just write programs; they test and correct them and also prepare instructions for those who will use their finished programs. They modify programs to increase their operating efficiency or to respond to changes in work processes and maintain records that document the programs development and revisions.

In large organizations, programmers tend to be clustered together in the computer center. Although they report to the management of that center, their real clients are the end-users throughout the corporation who rely on them to write the programs needed to do their own jobs better. In software companies that specialize in writing computer software, programmers are the computer equivalent of writers, authors, and film producers. Using nothing more than a keyboard, they create programs that pull together text, graphics, sounds, movies, and animations that perform useful work, inform, educate, entertain or that are the tools used in turn to create other such programs.

Programmers courtesy of International Business Machines

You can also be a programmer

All the software programs that you purchase have been created by professional programmers. But programming isn't limited to professionals. Increasingly, end-users are taking on some programming responsibility. Many of the macro and query languages built into application programs are easy to learn and use. They allow you to complete small programming tasks on your own without the help of professional programmers. Microsoft Office applications allow you to turn on a macro recorder, execute commands or enter data, and then turn off recording. You can save the recorded activities in a file and play them back again later. If you look at the macro, you'll find that it's a program automatically written for you in a language called BASIC Application Edition.

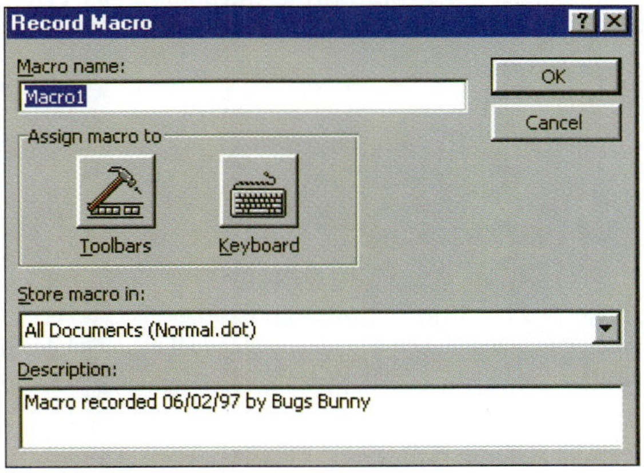

Macro

12.2 Programming Languages-First and Second Generation

When a programmer writes (codes) a program, he or she uses a programming language. Hundreds of programming languages have been written but only a small handful have found widespread use. Here we'll take a look at how languages have developed over the years.

Generations and levels

When you hear people talk about programming languages, you usually hear references to generations and levels, two sides of the same coin.

- Languages are grouped into generations based on when they were first conceived. It is generally accepted that there are four such generations.
- Languages are grouped by level based on how much they are like or unlike the language the computer itself uses, called machine language. The levels include low-level, high-level, and very high-level languages. The lower the level of the language, the closer it is to the language the computer uses.

As programming languages advanced from one generation to the next, they opened new opportunities and became easier to use. The trend has been to make them more Englishlike. The first programming languages were just a series of 0s and 1s. The latest languages are more readable, at least to someone familiar with the language.

The instruction set

Every computer processor (CPU) is designed to "understand" and interpret a fixed set of instructions called the instruction set. These are very simple instructions such as "load a number from memory," "add these two numbers together," or "skip the next instruction." The number of instructions in the instruction set of a typical processor is rather small, a few hundred at most in a RISC chip and 300 or more in a CISC chip. However, these small sets of instructions can be assembled in an almost infinite number of ways to produce an almost infinite variety of programs. This is like a composer using a piano's 88 notes to create an unending variety of musical pieces by combining and sequencing them in various ways.

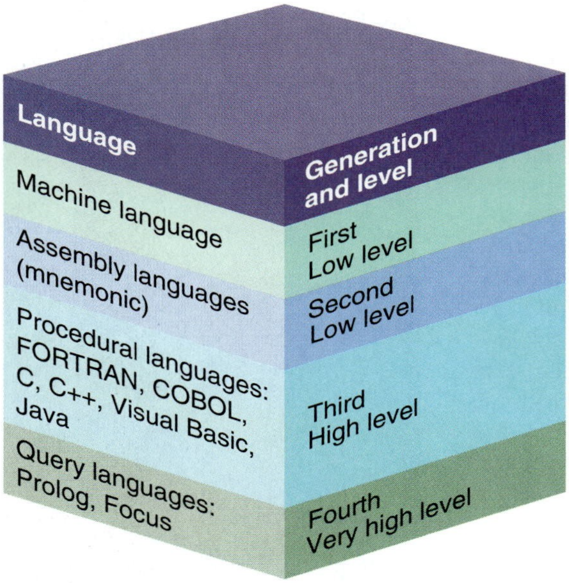

Program generations

Each type of processor has its own specific instruction set. The instructions understood by a CISC Pentium II processor inside an IBM PC are different from those understood by a RISC PowerPC inside a Macintosh. This is why programs written for IBM PCs won't usually run on Macintoshes and vice versa.

Mnemonic	Description
ADD	Add
AND	Logical AND
CLC	Clear Carry
CMP	Compare
CMPS	Compare memory at SI and DI
DIV	Divide
IN	Input
INC	Increment
INT	Interrupt
LABEL	Label
LOOP	Loop CX times
NOT	Logical NOT
OUT	Output
WAIT	Wait

Example instructions from Intel 8086 instruction set

Machine language—the first generation

Processors' instruction sets, in conjunction with some rules about how the instructions can be combined, constitute what are known as machine languages. They are called languages because, like regular spoken languages, they have a fixed set of words (the instructions) and a syntax that specifies how these words can be combined to form sentences. You can think of a program as an essay written using the words that are allowed in a given language following the rules of grammar or syntax of that language. The syntax of any programming language is much simpler than a natural language's but the rules are much stricter. We expect computers to do things exactly and correctly every time. Therefore it is essential that computer languages don't have the ambiguity of natural languages.

Since most computers are designed to handle numbers, each instruction in the instruction set is represented internally by a number. For example, the instruction "load into accumulator" may be represented by the number "28" and a memory location by the number 1000. Therefore, if you look at a machine language program, all you will see is an array of numbers. The processor picks up these numeric instructions one at a time, interprets them, and does whatever needs to be done. The simple machine language program below would add together numbers found in two memory locations and store the sum in a third location.

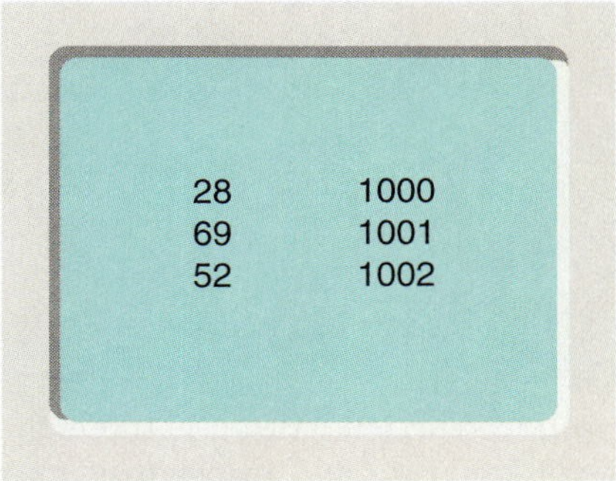

Machine language

Although no one writes programs in machine languages any more, these are still the only languages that computers can understand. Programming languages have improved dramatically, but at some stage in the development process, programs must be translated into machine language so the computer can understand it.

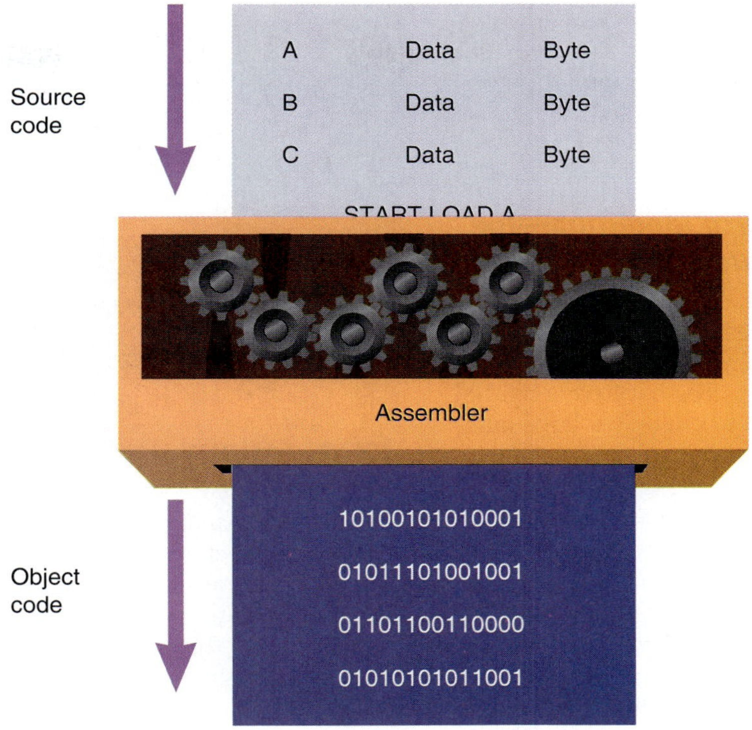

Assembler

Assembly language—the second generation

Writing machine language programs can be very tedious and susceptible to error since you have to use numbers to represent both commands and memory locations. Also, machine language programs are hard to edit or revise because all memory addresses refer to specific physical areas of memory. To make programming easier, assembly languages were developed. In these languages, each numeric instruction is assigned a short name (called a mnemonic) that is easier to remember than a number. The instruction 28 that loads a number into the accumulator might be given the name "LOAD." Assembly language also lets you assign names to memory locations instead of referring to them by number. To retrieve the salary of an employee, you needn't use the address 1000 (which would mean nothing to a person reading the program), but can use the word "SALARY." If someone looks at the code years later, they will know immediately what this address means. The processor (CPU) can't understand assembly language. Therefore, a program called an assembler is used to translate assembly language into machine language. The assembler reads in each mnemonic instruction (called the source code) and using an internal chart converts each to its corresponding machine language numeric code. The resulting machine language program saved in a separate file is referred to as object code.

Although assembly languages were developed early in the history of computing, they are still widely used in some situations, especially where execution times are critical. They are also used in situations where more advanced languages are not available for the work at hand. Like machine languages, assembly languages are specific to each type of processor.

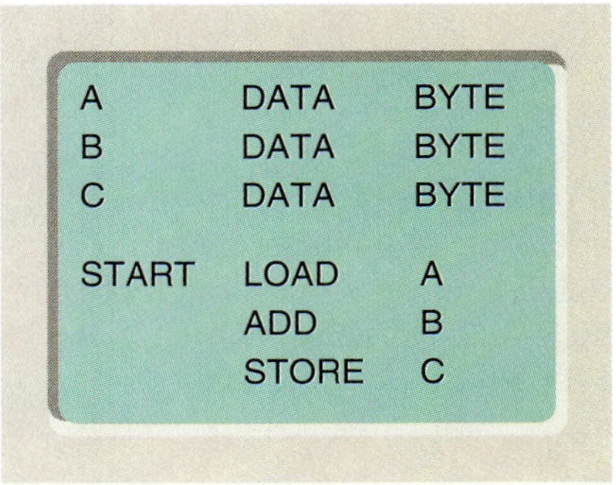

Assembly language program

12.3 Programming Languages-Procedural Languages

Assembly language was an improvement over machine language, but for large complex programs, it was not the ideal tool, and had to be improved in its turn.

Language	Year	Primary Application
FORTRAN	1954	Science and engineering
COBOL	1959	Business
BASIC	1965	Education
Pascal	1971	Education
C	1972	General
Visual Basic	1992	General
Java	1996	General

Procedural language—the third generation

The vocabulary of assembly language is just the small instruction set of the processor. For example, if a processor does not have a built-in instruction to multiply a large number by another, but only the ability to multiply single digits together, to use such a processor to multiply large numbers, you would have to write a tedious program for long-multiplication. In a procedural language, there is a word for long multiplication. When writing the program, the programmer uses that word. Later in the process, a separate program called a translator handles all the details of specifying how long-multiplication is done. Even though the vocabulary has been enriched, the programmer still has to specify each procedure in painstaking detail. It's for that reason that this generation of language is known as procedural language.

Procedural languages were the first programming languages that were independent of the hardware on which their programs ran. You can use procedural languages to write programs for many kinds of computers. Some of the most popular procedural languages, past and present, include FORTRAN, COBOL, BASIC, Pascal, C, C++, and Java.

Translators

Since typical procedural language has a richer vocabulary and a more complex syntax that allows programmers to write their instructions in a more abstract and succinct manner, a translator is needed to explain this language to the machine. A translator program analyzes the program (the source code) and writes an equivalent machine language program (the object code). There are two kinds of translators: compilers and interpreters. The kind used depends on two things: the programming language the program was created with and the processor it is being translated for.

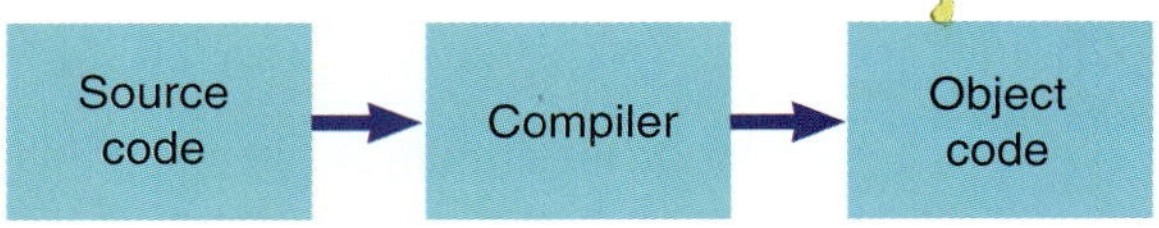

Compile

Compilers are translators used before a program is run to produce a complete machine language program that is stored on the disk so it can be executed later.

Interpreters are used to do the translation on the fly. They read each instruction written in the high-level language and translate it into instructions that the processor immediately executes. Once one task is done, the interpreter fetches the next instruction and translates that one. Since the translation is done on the fly, interpreted programs often run slower than compiled code. No object code is created in the process so no executable program file is stored on the disk for later use. To use a program written in an interpreted language, you must have the interpreter program present on your computer. Programs written in the new Java language can run on any kind of system because interpreters have been developed for each of the different types of systems.

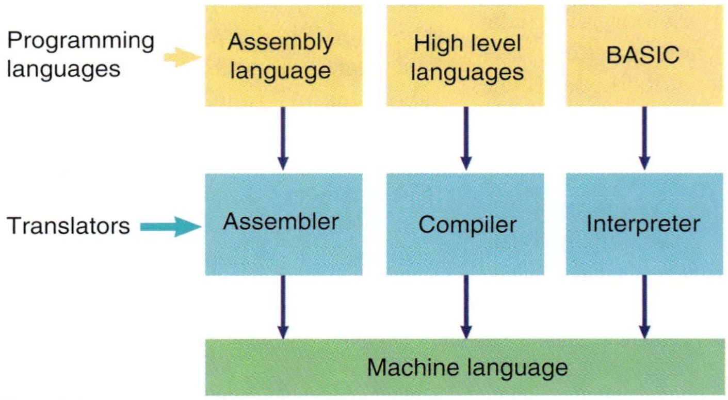

Translate

Interpret

Compilers are used with such programming languages as Cobol, C, and C++. Interpreters are used for programs written in most versions of BASIC and the new Internet language called Java.

P-codes

Interpreting a high-level language can slow down the execution speed, because the interpreter for a complex language can itself be a fairly large program which must sit in your computer's memory while it is interpreting. An alternative approach between compilers and interpreters is known as p-code.

1. First the compiler translates the program to the intermediate p-code. This language is between assembly language and the source high-level language in complexity and is still machine independent.

2. P-code interpreters are written for each target machine. P-code being a simple language, the interpreters are easy to write and small. When the P-code is run, the interpreter executes it a line at a time fairly swiftly.

The advantage of p-code is the speed gained by keeping the program independent of the machine it will run on till the very last moment. Many of today's popular languages (like Visual Basic) use this middle approach.

Procedural languages—Java

Java is a new procedural language that has gained great popularity. An ideal language for programs that run on networks such as the Internet, Java programs, called applets, are typically stored on a server. When you execute the program it is transferred from the server to your computer. As it is transferred it is interpreted by a translator called Java virtual machine on your computer. This allows the same program to be run on almost any computer, PC, Macintosh, or even a mainframe. All you need is an interpreter that can translate the program for the computer.

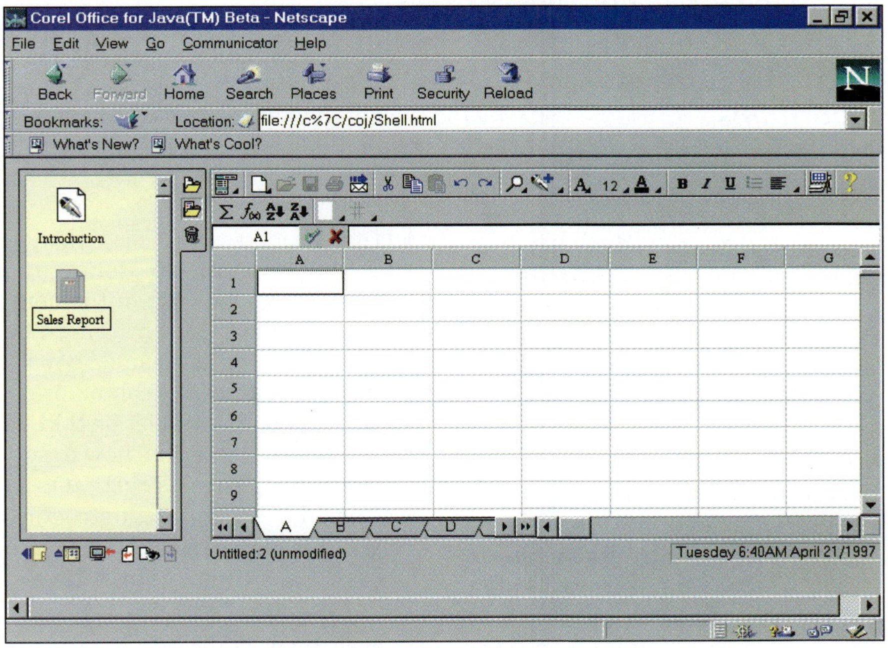

A Java Applet courtesy of Sun Microsystems
http://www.sun.com/javastation/images/browserlarge.gif

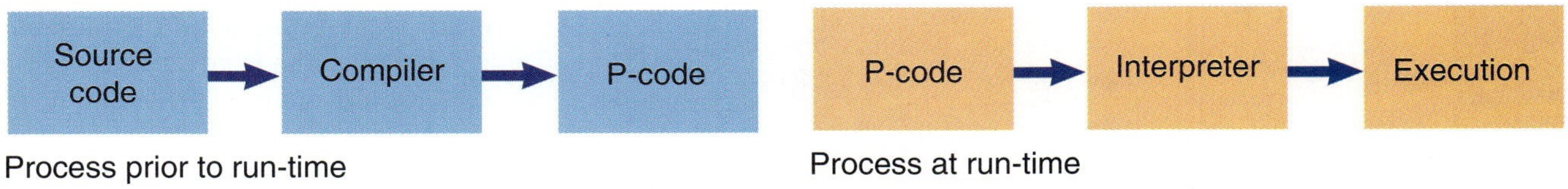

P-code

12.4 Programming Methods

As we've seen, some programs have millions of lines of code. Building complex programs requires a disciplined approach. Most modern programs are too big for one person to write. When a group of people work together on a program and break it into separate parts that can be worked on independently, it's essential that everyone follow the same rules or programming methodologies. Over the years, there have been numerous attempts to develop methodologies that make programming more a science than art.

> **So It's Only Goo After All**
>
> Bill Gates, the cofounder of Microsoft and one of the computer industry's leading magicians, knows how to keep things in perspective. During an interview with a reporter for *Computerworld*, he was quoted as saying "For example, we're closing all our warehouses in Europe to move to a single warehouse. It's very complicated because of currency requirements and such. So we're writing this new application, and no one is saying, 'Oh, this is so easy—it's object oriented. No problem.' What a bunch of BS. Hey, 90% of the application has to do with the complexity of the issues you're dealing with and not some goo."
>
> Source: "Bill Gates: Face to Face," *Computerworld,* May 24, 1993, p 127.

Data structure and algorithms

The first step in programming methodology was to realize that every program deals with two distinct things, data structure and algorithms, that need to be treated separately.

- Most programs deal with aspects of real life entities such as sales, expenses, or employees. Each of these entities must be represented in the program in the aspects we're interested in, or abstractly. That is, in a company's employee database we would abstract out of the whole picture and keep only those pieces of information that are relevant to the task (age, salary, address, and so on and not information such as blue is his favorite color). Moreover, this abstract representation of the real world may have important complex interrelationships that must be captured. This abstract representation of the real word inside a computer is called the data structure.

- Data structures are manipulated by the program to derive the desired output. A list of the company's employees may have to be sorted by their last name so mailing labels for checks can be printed. The computer must be told, in a step-by-step fashion, how to sort the records. This instruction is an algorithm. A good data structure design leads to simpler and more reliable algorithms. For example, in the illustrations below, the following steps would occur:

1. Go through Stack 1 and pull out the record with the minimum salary.
2. Put the selected record in Stack 2.
3. If Stack 1 is not empty, then go back to Step 1.

This is an algorithm.

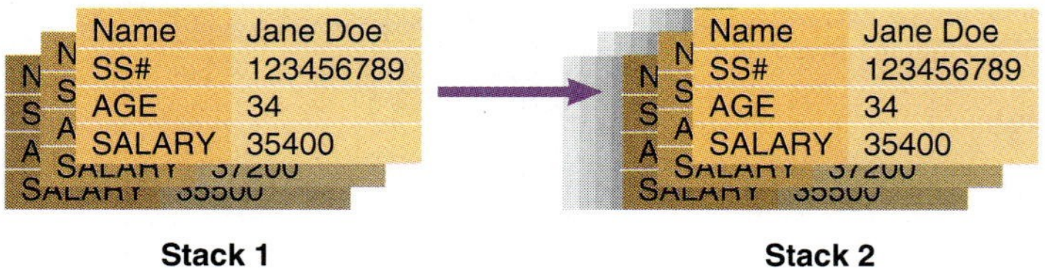

Algorithm

Block structured programming

The next advance in programming method was the introduction of block structured programming. In older style codes, programmers would often use a word called "GOTO" to jump to another part of the program. While reading such a program, each time you came across a GOTO statement, you had to flip through the code to reach the section where the program went to next and remember where you came from and why. Soon you would come across another GOTO statement and do the same. Very soon there would be too many things that you had to remember

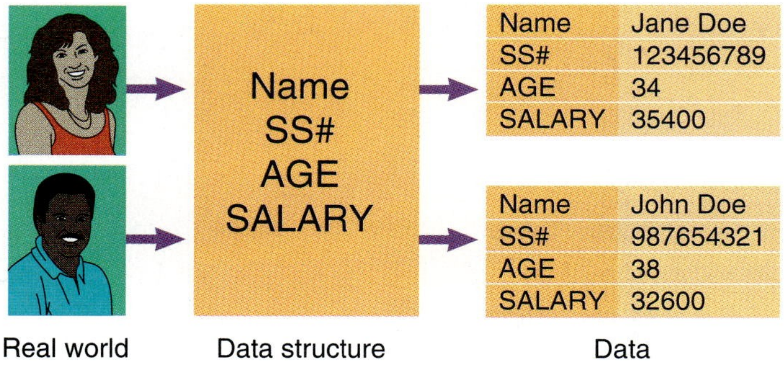

Data structure

and you start to lose the context. In block structured programming, the GOTO statement is virtually unused. The recommended style is to have reasonably small blocks of code, usually less than a page, where the only entry point into the section is from the top and the only way to exit out is through the bottom. As a result, someone reading the code need not remember any details of what happened inside a block once she is done with that block.

Modular programming

Block structured programming led to another evolution, known as modular programming. Many programming projects involve subgroups of programmers working independently on different parts or modules of the program. To make it easy to assemble the finished modules, each module hides all details of its implementation and only exposes those details which other parts of the program need to access or use that module. Other parts of the program can't "see" inside the module. This allows the programmers of each module to make internal changes without informing or involving the rest of the group, as long as the external interface is not changed. This separation and deliberate information hiding is not only useful for large programming groups but may be helpful even when a single programmer is writing all the modules.

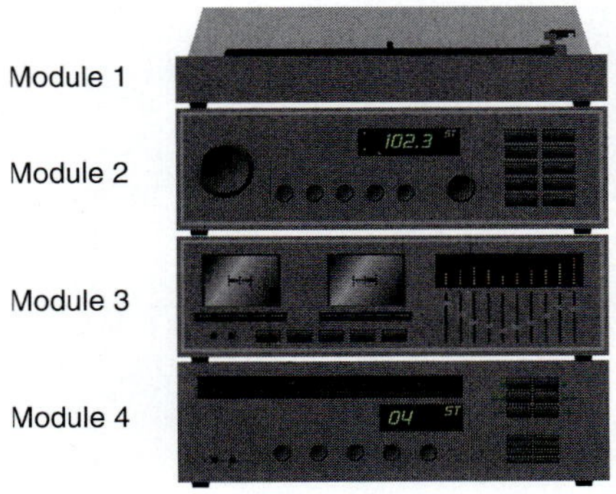

Modular program

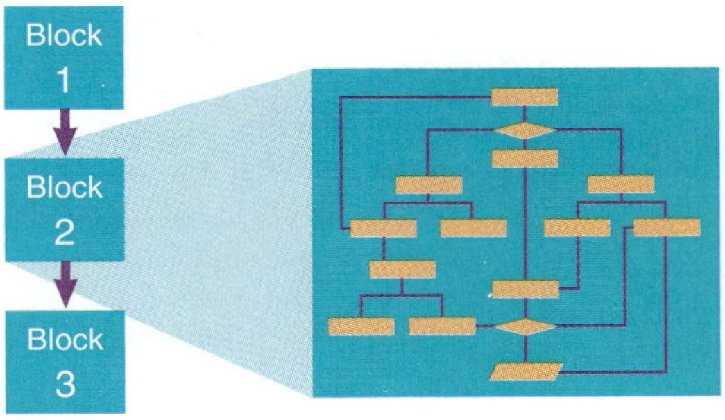

Block structured program

This is because he or she can forget all the implementation details of a finished module and think of it as a prefabricated part. Think of this as being like a component stereo system. The internal details of each component are not exposed but the external controls needed to operate each unit are, as are the outlets needed to connect them with cables.

Object oriented programming

A recent trend in programming methodology is object oriented programming (OOP) where the real world is represented by objects. An object is a combination of data structures and procedures that operate upon or extract information from these data structures. For example, there could be an object called "Date."

- The internal data structure of the date object will hold the day of the month, the month, and the year. How these three quantities are represented is entirely up to the designer of the object. The month could be represented by a number between 1 and 12, or by three-letter codes such as JAN, FEB, and so on.
- The date object will also have a number of procedures associated with it. There could be a procedure called "GetMonth," whose task is to get the month number from the data structure. A user of the Date object will use this procedure to get the month, instead of directly touching the data structure. As a result, one can change the internal representation of the month from a number to a three-letter code and make the corresponding change in the GetMonth procedure, and this would not affect anyone who uses this object. To them it will appear that nothing has changed. To a user, the date object behaves like an intelligent entity that can answer questions and take care of itself.

The main advantage of object oriented programs is their reliability and manageability, especially in situations where many programmers work on the same project. Object oriented programs are usually written in the general purpose C++ language or a special SmallTalk language designed specifically for object oriented programming.

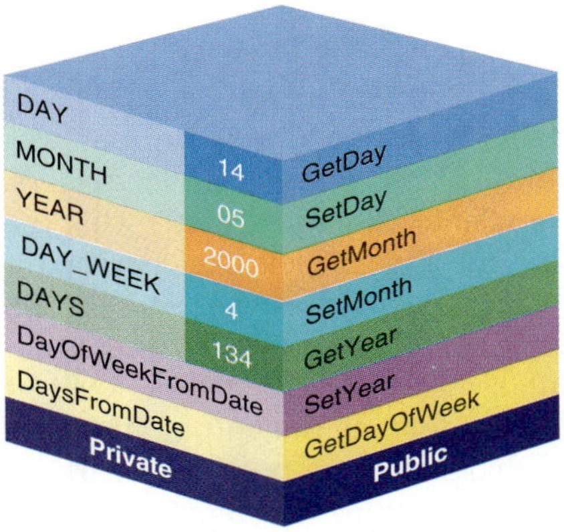

Object oriented programming

12.5 How Programs Are Developed

During the development stage of a new system, a decision is made as to whether to buy commercially available software or write new programs in-house. If the decision is made to write it in-house, or to modify commercially available software, a series of 5 steps is begun, the first two of which lead up to a defined solution to a business problem, and are closely related to the business and the people in it. The last three steps those cover the actual writing and testing of the program and are related to a specific programming language.

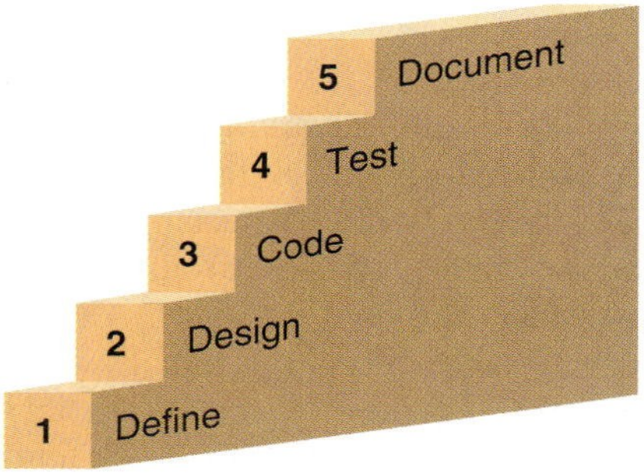

Program steps

Step 1 Defining the problem

The first step in creating a new program is to define exactly what problem it is intended to solve. One way to do this is to have the end-users, or clients, describe exactly what the output should look like. Perhaps it should be a report that shows sales by region or an invoice listing products ordered. Whatever form it takes, defining the output automatically establishes two other parts of the definition: the required inputs and processing. If an invoice is the desired output, then the program needs input from the database listing company products and prices and a customer list of names and addresses.

Step 2 Designing the solution

The parties affected by a proposed program or change in a program usually have a shopping list of things they want to see happen. There is almost never such a thing as the "ideal" design. During the design phase, programmers sort through the various possibilities and attempt to come up with the most elegant solution. This process isn't done in their heads. Designers, like the rest of us, need to keep notes and have a way to describe their designs to others. There are many techniques used at this stage, including flowcharts and pseudocode.

Flowcharts

A flowchart is a graphical way of illustrating the steps in a process. It uses symbols connected by flowlines to represent processes and the direction of flow within the program. Some of the key symbols used include:

- The termination symbol (the oval) indicates the start and stop of every algorithm.
- The decision symbol (the diamond) indicates that a decision is to be made by an IF-THEN-ELSE statement. The program takes one direction when the condition is true and another direction when the condition is false.
- The process symbol (the rectangle) indicates a calculation required by the algorithm.
- The input/output symbol (the parallelogram) indicates that information is to be entered or output.
- The connector symbol (the circle) brings together two branches of the program.

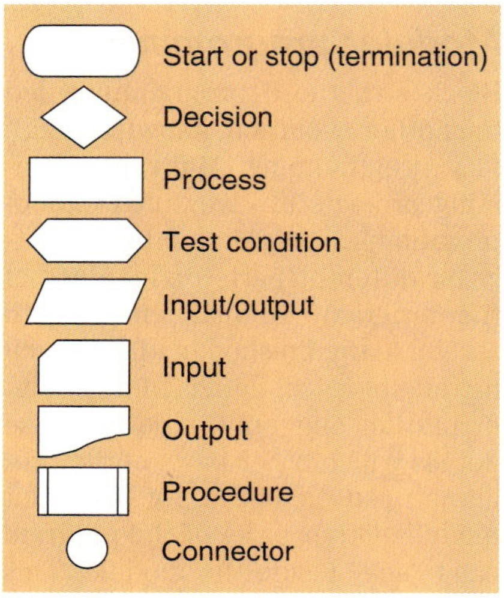

Flowchart symbols

Defining the problem courtesy of International Business Machines

Pseudocode

Pseudocode is simply an English-language-like way of writing programming code. In many ways it is like an annotated outline that you might prepare for a report. It is much more precise than a written description of a process and much less precise than the actual code that follows. Each step in the program is described with almost the same level of detail that will be used in the final program. However, unlike the final code, pseudocode doesn't require exact syntax so the programmer is able to focus more on the bigger picture.

```
Calculate monthly bonus:
Repeat for all employees
   Set S to Total Sales
   Set E to Total Expenses
   Net Sales is S–E
   If Net Sales less than
         Bonus is 0
   Else
         Bonus is 5% of Net Sales
End Repeat
```

Pseudocode

Step 3 Coding the program

Once the design phase is finished, code is written so the program provides the solutions defined during the design phase. At this point a programming language such as BASIC, COBOL, C++, or Java must be chosen. You'll learn more about this stage later in this chapter.

```
Sub CalcBonus
For I=1 to NumOfEmployees
   S = Emp(I).Sales
   E = Emp(I).Expenses
   NetSales = S – E
   If NetSales < 10000 then
         Emp(I).Bonus = 0
   Else
         Emp(I).Bonus = NetSales / 20
   End if
Next I

End CalcBonus
```

Real coding in BASIC

Bugs–Who Made The Mistake?

Every program has flaws called bugs–some have thousands of them. So when something goes wrong, don't automatically assume it's your fault. The term bug is often credited to Grace Hopper, a U.S. Navy programmer. She used it to describe a problem caused when a moth flew into the contacts of an early computer, the Mark II. Actually, the term was used before by Thomas Edison. Here is an extract from a letter he wrote that clearly uses the term in its modern computer context.

"I have the right principle and am on the right track, but time, hard work, and some good luck are necessary too. It has been just so in all of my inventions. The first step is an intuition, and comes with a burst, then difficulties arise—this thing gives out and then—'Bugs'—as such little faults and difficulties are called—show themselves and months of intense watching, study, and labor are requisite before commercial—success–or—failure–is certainly reached."

Source: Letter from Thomas Edison to Theodore Puskas, November 13, 1878.

Testing

Step 4 Testing the results

After all the analysis, design, and programming, the chances are the program won't work the way it was intended to. This is normal and expected because there are too many places where problems might be overlooked or mistakes introduced. During the testing and debugging phase, testers and selected end-users look for bugs, or things that make a program fail. This can be a massive task. As Windows NT was nearing completion, Microsoft fixed over 1,000 bugs in a single week. As they were doing so, another 700 were discovered. Fixing one bug can create new ones somewhere else in the program.

Step 5 Documenting the finished product

When writing a new program or modifying an existing one, it's important to keep a permanent record of what was done. This writing a description of a program or a change is called documenting the program. Programs need to be documented for three separate groups.

- End-users need documentation telling them how to operate the program. For this group, documentation might be a manual or the on-line help system.
- Technical support people need documentation that helps them set up the program, find errors, and fix problems.
- Programmers need documentation so they can revise or update the program later. This documentation includes a description of the program, both written and in the program itself, flowcharts and other tools used in its creation, and notes about changes.

12.6 Programming Techniques-Introduction

To write a program, you use a word processing program or a text editor to write lines of code, much as you would write out a list of steps in any procedure. Although many programs are typed in on a program like the one you use to write memos or letters, some developmental systems include the equivalent of spelling and grammar checkers. These programming tools help catch some of the simpler mistakes a programmer might make. Let's take a look at how a few simple programs might be written.

Adding two numbers

One of the simplest programs that you can write is one that adds two numbers together. The program takes the numbers from two different memory locations, adds them, and then stores the results in a third memory location. The flowchart for this program would look like the diagram above right.

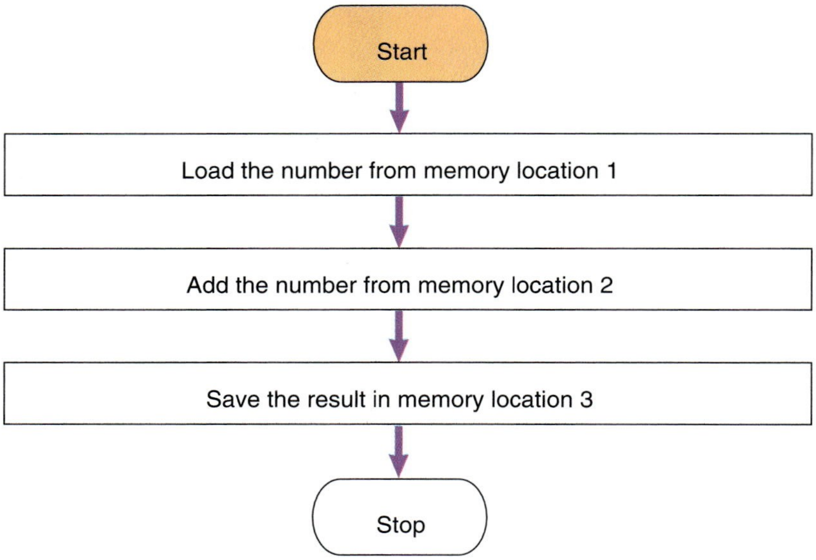

Adding numbers

The actual program code you write to implement this program depends on the programming language you are using. Below is what this same program looks like in typical representations of machine language, assembly language, and BASIC.

Now take a look at how these three simple programs work.

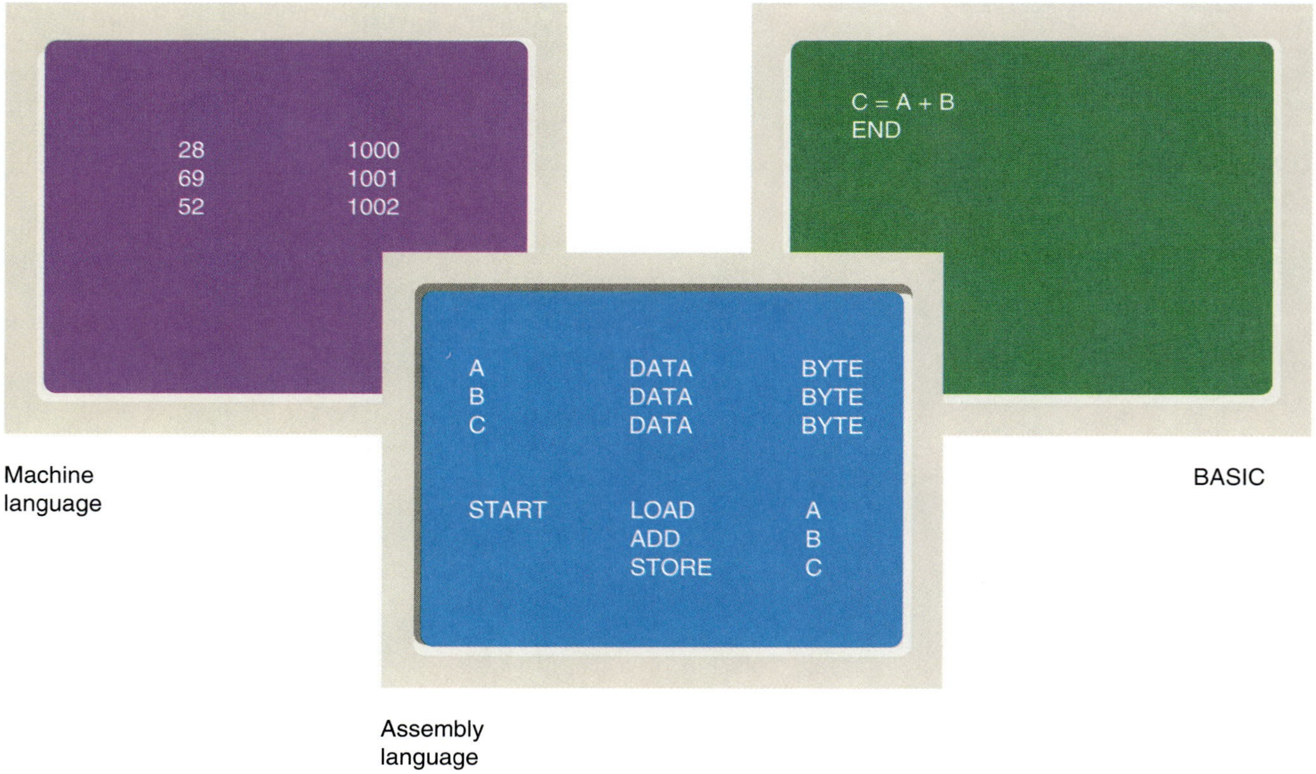

Adding numbers programs

- In the machine language program, the command 28 loads a number from storage location 1000 into the CPU's accumulator. The command 69 adds the number in memory location 1001 to the number already in the accumulator. The command 52 stores the resulting number in the accumulator in memory location 1002.
- In the assembly language program, the first three lines define three memory locations and name them A, B, and C. In the next three lines the program loads the number in memory location A into the accumulator, adds the number in location B to the one in the accumulator, and finally stores the result in memory location C.
- The BASIC program just says the number in memory location C should be the sum of the numbers in memory locations A and B.

Input and output

Adding and storing numbers is usually just part of a longer program. At some point, you'll want to be able to enter new data (input) and see the results displayed on the screen (output). Below is a flowchart for a greeting program that asks you to enter first your name and then your age and displays the results on the screen, and is the greeting program as it would be written in the BASIC language. The colors in this figure relate parts of the program to the matching colors in the flowchart.

1. **CLS** clears the screen.
2. **PRINT "What is your name?"** prompts you to enter your name by displaying "What is your name?" on the screen.
3. **INPUT name** reads the user input and stores your name in an area of memory that will be referred to as *name*.
4. **PRINT "and your age?"** prompts you to enter your age.
5. **INPUT age** stores your age in an area of memory named *age*.
6. **greet1 = "Hello" + name** stores the word Hello followed by a space and then the contents of memory area *name* in a new area of memory named *greet1*.
7. **greet2 = "so you are" + age + "years old"** stores the phrase *so you are* followed by a space and then the contents of memory area *age* followed by a space and the word *years* in a new area of memory named *greet2*.
8. **PRINT** prints a blank line of the screen.
9. **PRINT greet1** prints the contents of memory area *greet1* to the screen.
10. **PRINT** prints a blank line of the screen.
11. **PRINT greet2** prints the contents of memory area *greet2* to the screen.
12. **END** ends the program.

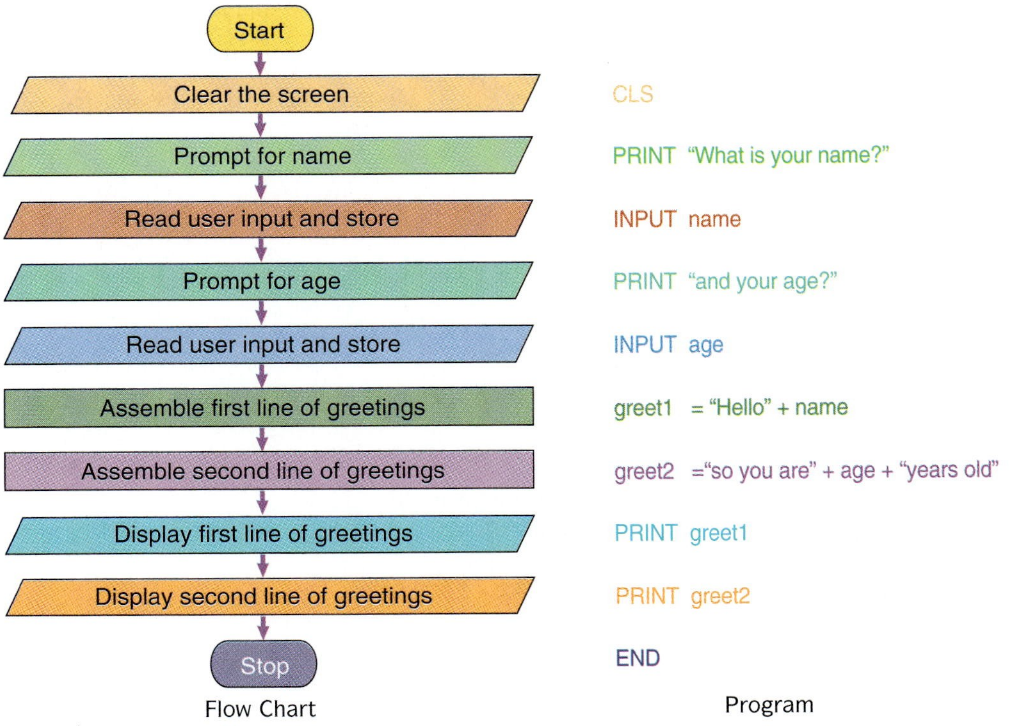

Input and output

12.7 Programming Techniques-Branching and Looping

The last two programs you have looked at are linear; they start at one point and proceed step by step to the end. Most programs are more complicated than this however, and have to branch or loop.

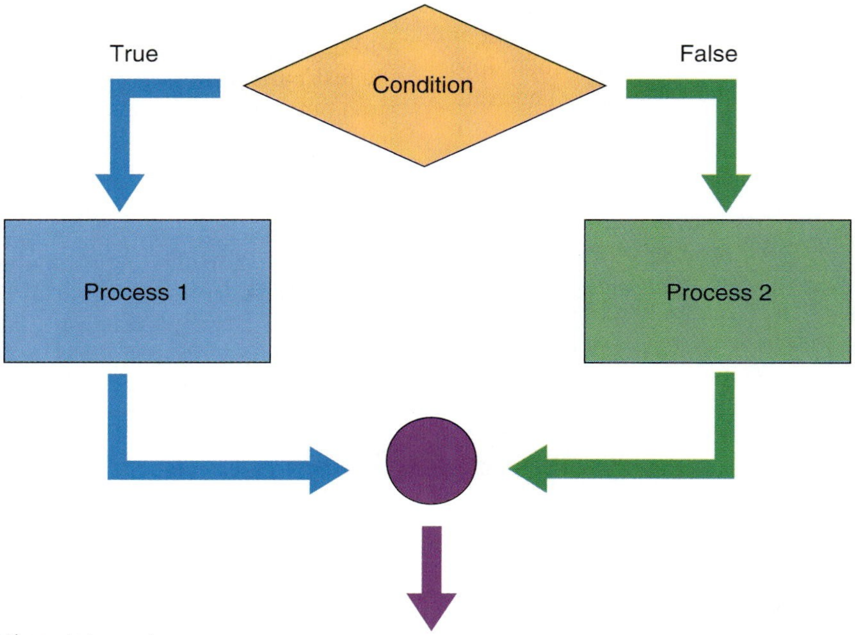

If-then statement

Branching

One key procedure that programmers use is branching in the form of an IF-THEN-ELSE statement that redirects, or branches, the flow of a program based on the outcome of a condition. For example, you can ask the user to answer yes or no to a question. If he answers yes (true) the program branches down one path. If he answers no (false), it branches down another.

Below is a flowchart and BASIC code for a program that converts Centigrade temperatures to and from Fahrenheit. You first input the temperature and then answer the question "Centigrade to Fahrenheit?" If you enter 1 (for yes), the program branches to the path that converts from Centigrade to Fahrenheit. If you enter 2 (for no), it branches to the path that converts from Fahrenheit to Centigrade.

1. **CLS** clears the screen.
2. **PRINT "Enter Temperature"** prompts you to enter the temperature to be converted.
3. **INPUT temp1** stores the temperature you entered in memory area *temp1*.
4. **PRINT "Enter 1 to go from C to F"** displays a prompt asking you to enter 1 if you want the number converted from Centigrade to Fahrenheit.
5. **PRINT "Enter 2 to go from F to C"** displays a prompt asking you to enter 2 if you want the number converted from Fahrenheit to Centigrade.
6. **INPUT dir** stores the number you enter in a memory area named *dir*.
7. **IF dir = 1 THEN** compares the number in *dir* to 1 and if they are equal, the next two steps are executed.

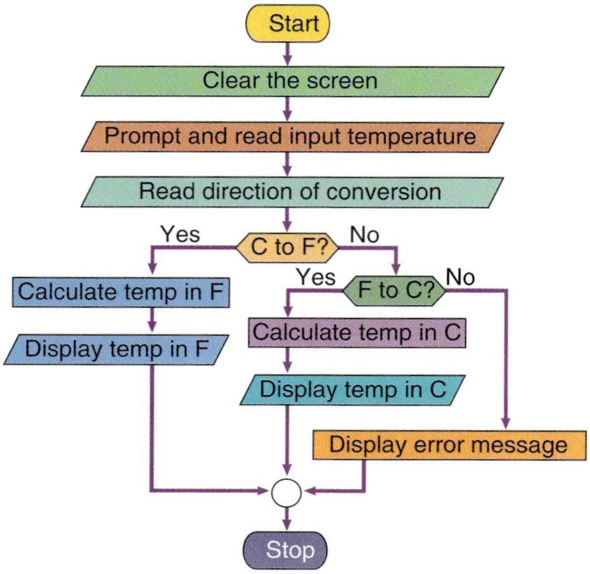

Flowchart

```
CLS
PRINT "Enter Temperature"
INPUT temp 1
PRINT "Enter 1 to go from C to F"
PRINT "Enter 2 to go from F to C"
INPUT dir
IF dir = 1 THEN
  temp2 = (temp1 * 9/5) + 32
  PRINT temp2; "F"
ELSE IF dir = 2 then
  temp2 = (temp1 – 32) * 5/9
  PRINT temp2; "C"
ELSE
  PRINT "Wrong entry"
END IF
END
```

Basic Code

8. **temp2 = (temp1 * 9 / 5) + 32** converts the number in *dir* from Centigrade to Fahrenheit and stores the result in memory area *temp2*.
9. **PRINT temp2; " F"** prints the number in *temp2* to the screen and adds a space followed by the letter *F*.
10. **ELSE IF dir = 2 then** compares the number in *dir* to 2 and if they are equal, the next two steps are executed.
11. **temp2 = (temp1** minus **32) * 5 / 9** converts the number in *dir* from Fahrenheit to Centigrade and stores the result in memory area *temp2*.
12. **PRINT temp2; "C"** prints the number in *temp2* to the screen and adds a space followed by the letter C.
13. **ELSE**. If the number in *dir* is not equal to 1 or 2, the next two steps are executed.
14. **PRINT "Wrong entry"**. This error message is displayed if the number in *dir* is not equal to 1 or 2.
15. **END IF** ends the IF-THEN-ELSE part of the program.
16. **END** ends the program.

Looping

Loops repeat a process over and over again until a condition is met and the process is completed. Each repetition of the loop is called an *iteration*. To the right is a simple example where the flowchart illustrates the process of checking the air pressure in your car's tires. After checking a tire, the program checks to see if four tires have been checked. If not, it loops you back to check another one. When it finds that four have been checked, it ends the program.

Below is a flowchart and BASIC code for a looping program that repeats your name the number of times you specify.

1. **CLS** clears the screen.
2. **PRINT "Enter your name"** prompts you to enter your name.
3. **INPUT name** stores the name you entered in the memory location named *name*.
4. **PRINT "How many times should I repeat it?"** prompts you to enter the number of times you want your name displayed.
5. **INPUT n** stores the number you entered in the memory location named *n*.

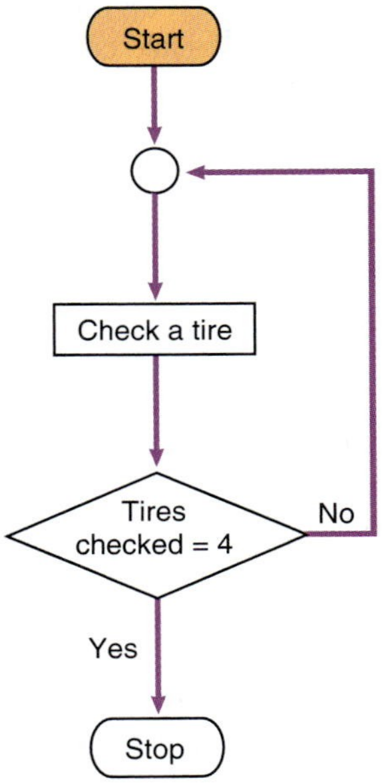

Loop

6. **FOR i = 1 to n** initially puts 1 in the memory location *i* and each time through the loop checks if *i* is greater than the value of *n*.
7. **PRINT i; " "; name** prints the current number followed by the name stored in memory area *name*.
8. **NEXT I** increments *i* by 1 and goes back to Step 6.
9. **END** ends the program.

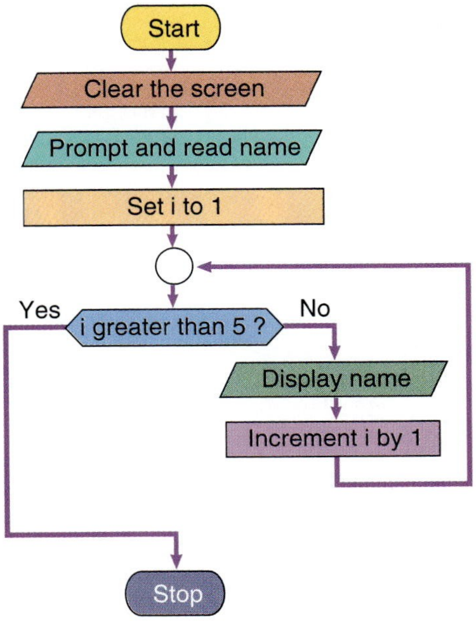

Flowchart

```
CLS
PRINT "Enter your name"
INPUT name
PRINT "How many times should I repeat it?"
INPUT n

FOR i = 1 to n
 PRINT i; " "; name
NEXT I

END
```

Basic Code

12.8 Programming Techniques-Functions and Decomposition

Programs can be broken up into sections so complex tasks are completed through a sequence of simpler steps. Two ways to do this are using functions and program decomposition or subroutines.

Subroutine

Functions

A programming language can be extended and customized through the use of functions. When you specify that the program perform any mathematical procedure, such as squaring or finding the square root, it is performing a function on a number. In a program, functions can be written once and then used over and over again as the need arises, without writing new code.

Below is a flowchart and BASIC code for a new program that converts Centigrade temperatures to and from Fahrenheit. After you input the temperature, the program branches to the function which performs the conversion.

1. **CLS** clears the screen.
2. **PRINT "Enter temperature in F"** prompts you to enter the temperature.
3. **INPUT temp1** stores the temperature you entered in a memory location named *temp1*.
4. **temp2 = FtoC(temp1)** uses the function *FtoC* to calculate the new value of the number in memory location *temp1* and stores the result in memory location *temp2*.
5. **PRINT temp2; " F"** displays the value in memory location *temp2* and adds a space followed by the letter *F*.
6. **END** terminates the program.

Program decomposition

Subroutines perform repetitive functions so new code doesn't have to be written each time a process is needed. They encapsulate similar functions into a single procedure. If you were writing a program to guide you in the repair of your house, each of the repairs might require its own unique series of steps. The steps you follow to run to the hardware store for supplies are always the same, so you write those steps as a subroutine and then refer to that subroutine from the main program whenever a trip is needed. When

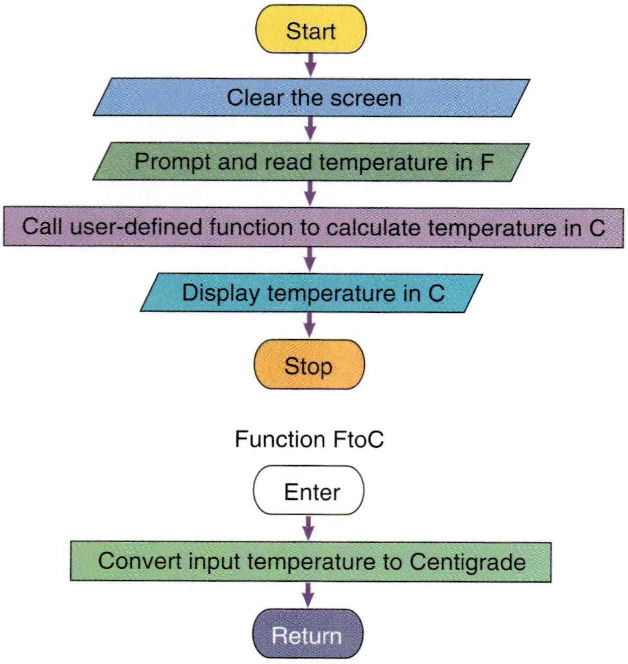

Flowchart

```
CLS

PRINT "Enter temperature in F"
INPUT temp1
temp2 = FtoC(temp1)
PRINT temp2; " F"

END

FUNCTION FtoC(t)

FtoC = (t -32) * 5/9

END
```

BASIC Code

each trip is completed, control returns to the main program.

Below is a flowchart and the BASIC code for a program that prints out a 10-line Fahrenheit to Centigrade conversion chart, starting from a specified temperature and going up in one degree increments. The main code asks you to enter the starting temperature and then it calls a subroutine that takes the starting temperature as input and prints out the 10-line chart. The subroutine uses a loop to make the chart and calls the FtoC function to do the actual calculation.

1. **CLS** clears the screen.
2. **PRINT "Enter starting temperature"** prompts you to enter the starting temperature for the chart.
3. **INPUT start** stores the temperature you enter in a memory area named *start*.
4. **PrintChart start** calls the subroutine that prints a 10-row table of temperatures starting with the temperature in *start*.
5. **END** ends the program.
6. **SUB PrintChart(S)** labels the subroutine that prints a 10-row table of temperatures starting with the temperature *S*.
7. **FOR i = S to S + 9** starts a loop where *i* has an initial value equal to *S* and is incremented by one each time through the loop till it reaches a value of *S + 9*.
8. **PRINT i, FtoC(i)** prints the current value of *I* (temperature in F) followed by the temperature in C (as calculated by the function *FtoC*).
9. **NEXT i** ends the loop and sends the program back to the beginning of the loop for the next value of *i*.
10. **END** exits the subroutine and sends control back to the main program.
11. **FUNCTION FtoC(t)** labels the function that calculates the temperature in centigrade corresponding to T degrees Fahrenheit.
12. **FtoC = (t** minus **32) * 5 / 9** converts Fahrenheit to Centigrade.
13. **END** returns the converted temperature to the calling program.

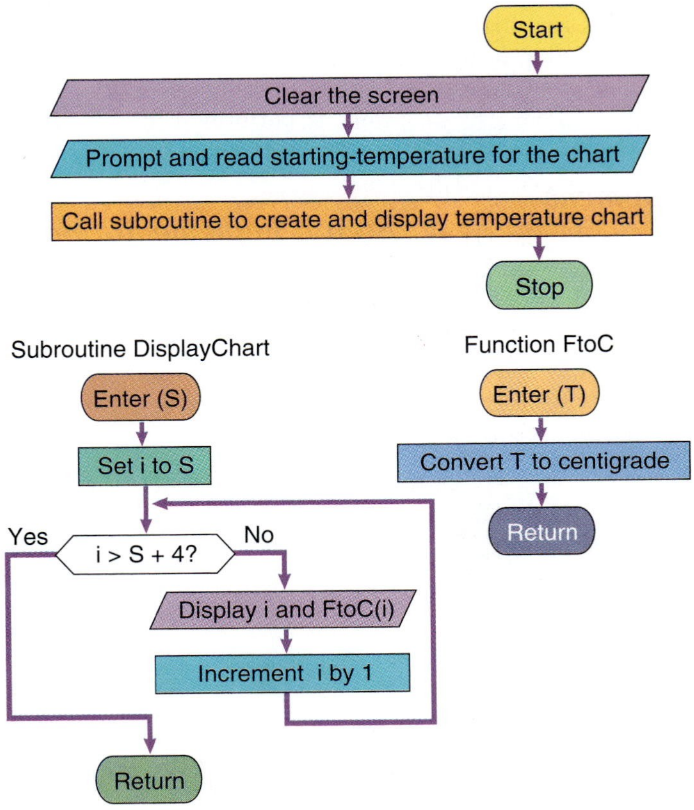

Flowchart

```
CLS
PRINT "Enter starting temperature"
INPUT start
PrintChart start
END

SUB PrintChart(s)
FOR i = S to S + 9
 Print i, FtoC(i)
NEXT i
END
FUNCTION FtoC(t)
FtoC = (t –32) * 5/9
END
```

BASIC Code

The programs that companies and organizations create are part of a much larger process of system analysis and design. System analysts study the organization's needs and operations and make detailed suggestions for improvements. The process they follow has five distinct steps: analysis, design, development, implementation, and maintenance.

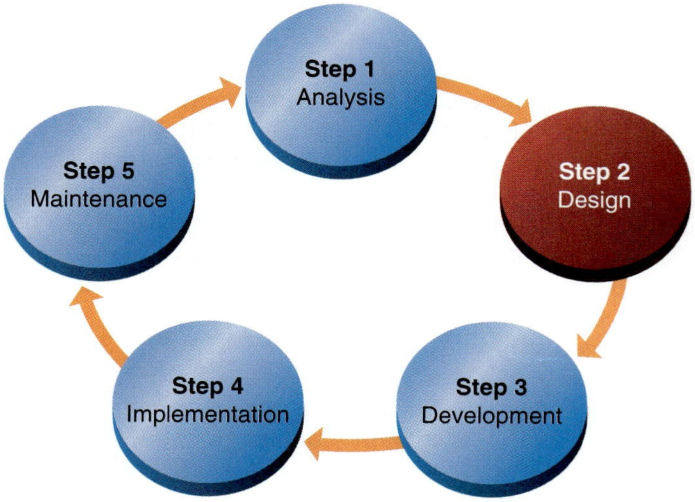

Design

Step 1 Analysis

When a change in an organization's procedures is first proposed, system analysts are assigned the task of studying the existing system or procedures. They analyze the needs of the organization, define the problem in detail, and propose alternative solutions. The analyst begins by gathering information from users and other sources. One tool used during this process is a data flow diagram that graphically illustrates the steps in a system so it can be seen at a glance how data flows and is processed. The analyst uses this information to prepare written recommendations that are submitted to management for consideration.

Step 2 Design

Once the system analyst's recommendations are approved, the design phase begins. Like all other creative processes, the design of a new system involves a lot of people and ideas. Once a consensus is achieved on what the system's design should look like, another report is prepared and presented to management for approval. If more than one design seems reasonable, the alternatives are included in the report so management can choose between them.

Step 3 Development

Next development is begun. The necessary hardware and software are acquired or developed and the system is tested. If the software and hardware are available commercially, they are purchased or leased. Although it is much cheaper to purchase commercially available software (called off-the-shelf software), these programs do not always fit the needs of the company developing the system. If not, custom software must be developed or a commercially available program must be modified by programmers in-house. If the work is performed by outside contractors it is called outsourcing.

Step 4 Implementation

Once the new system has been developed and tested, it is introduced into the organization's day-

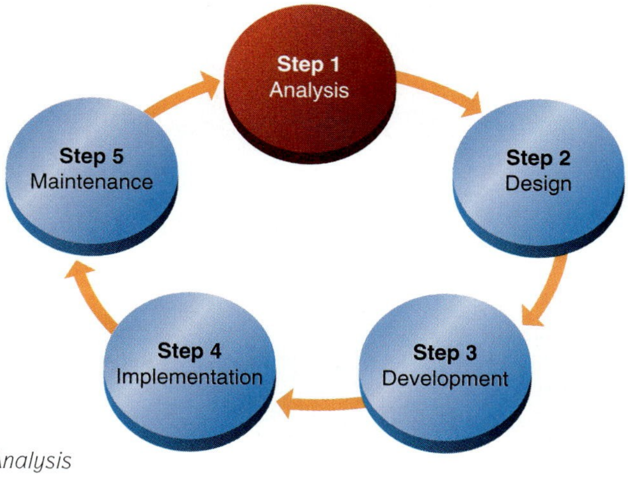

Analysis

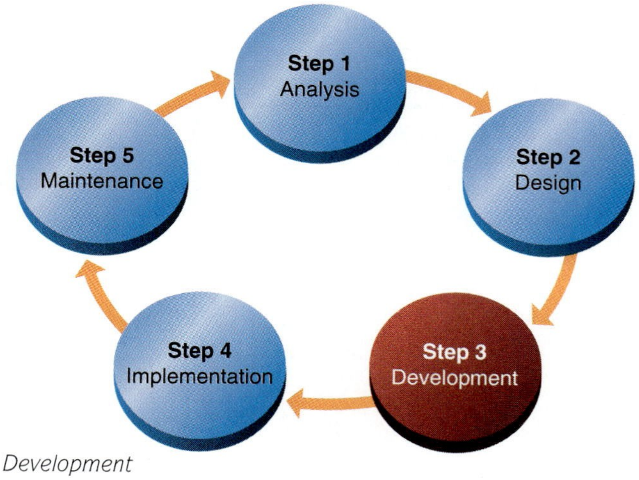

Development

to-day operations. This effort is an implementation. If the system is replacing an existing system it is a conversion. There are a number of ways to implement a new system.

- Direct implementation is essentially switching on the new system and switching off the old. If the new system has any problems, there is no backup. Obviously, this type of conversion is done only when there is no alternative.
- Parallel implementation initially processes part or all of the workload on both the old and new systems. If any problems arise, the workload can be temporarily shifted back to the old system. As the new system becomes more reliable and trusted, the old system is finally turned off.
- Phased implementation introduces the new system in stages. As each stage is proven and the bugs are worked out, the next stage is phased in. If problems arise, they have less disastrous results because they only affect a single stage of the operation. However, it can take a lot of time to implement the entire system.
- Pilot implementation is the least risky conversion. The new system is used to process only a small part of the workload. If it works, it may then be implemented company-wide. If it has problems, they can be worked out without affecting the organization's entire operation.

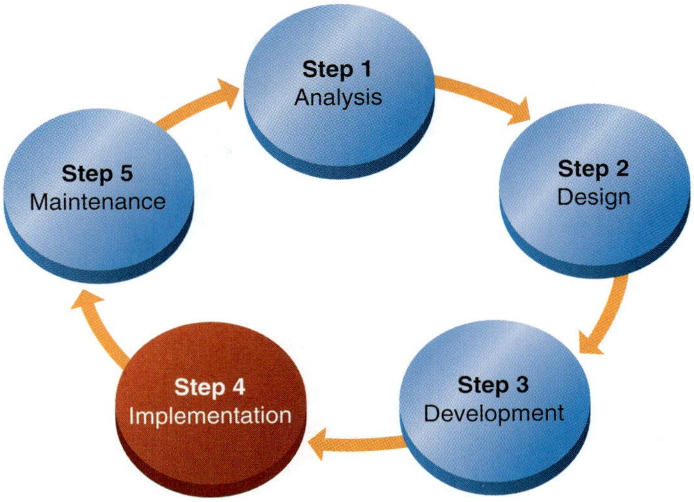

Implementation

Step 5 Maintenance

As the new system is implemented, maintenance begins monitoring and improving the system's performance. During this stage, which lasts as long as the system is in operation, problems are detected and fixed and changes are introduced to make the system run faster and better. Like a car, the system can be fine-tuned over time to give its best performance.

NOTHING IS CERTAIN

Industry surveys indicate that almost one-third of application development projects are canceled before they get started. Over half will exceed their budgets by substantial amounts. Only a little over 15% of projects are completed on time and on budget. $140 billion is spent in the U.S. each year on implementation.

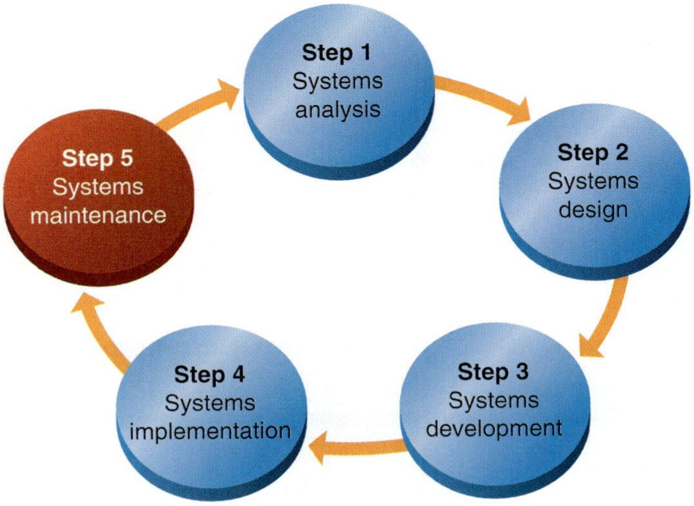

Maintenance

12.10 Enhancing and Testing Your Understanding

Summary

- Computers work because they are fed a series of step-by-step instructions called programs.
- Programs, also called software or code, are created by computer programmers who use word processors or editing programs to write them out just as you would write out a highly detailed and structured outline or report.
- John von Neumann proposed that if a program was stored in memory, program instructions could be easily changed just by loading a new program. Also as the program executed, it could easily change the instructions in memory. This is called the stored program concept.
- All computers have a built-in basic input/output system (BIOS) that allows the computer to load the operating system, then application programs.
- Many of the macro and query languages built into application programs allow you to complete small programming tasks on your own without the involvement of professional programmers.
- When a programmer writes (codes) a program, he or she uses a programming language.
- Languages are grouped into generation based on when they were first conceived.
- Languages are grouped by level based on how much they are like or unlike the language the computer itself uses called machine language. The levels include low-level, high-level, and very high-level languages.
- Every computer processor (CPU) is designed to understand and interpret a fixed set of instructions called the instruction set.
- Each type of processor has its own specific instruction set.
- A processor's instruction set, in conjunction with some rules about how the instructions can be combined, constitutes what is known as machine languages.
- To make programming easier, assembly languages were developed. Each numeric instruction is assigned a short name (called a mnemonic) that is easier to remember than a number. Assembly language allows you to assign names to memory locations instead of referring to them by number.
- CPUs can't understand assembly language. Therefore, a program called an assembler is used to translate assembly language into machine language. The assembler reads in each mnemonic instruction (called the source code) and using an internal chart converts each to its corresponding machine language numeric code. The resulting machine language program saved in a separate file is referred to as object code.
- After assembly languages came procedural languages that were easier to work with. Some of the most popular procedural languages, past and present, include FORTRAN, COBOL, BASIC, Pascal, C, C++, and Java.
- Compilers are translators used before a program is run to produce a complete machine language program that is stored on the disk so it can be executed later.
- Interpreters are used to do the translation on the fly. They read each instruction written in the high-level language and immediately translate it into instructions that the processor then executes.
- Java programs, called applets, are typically stored on a server. When you execute the program it is transferred to your computer. As it is transferred it is interpreted by a translator on your machine.
- A recent trend in programming methodology is known as object oriented programming (OOP) where the real world is represented by objects. An object is a combination of data structures and procedures that operate upon or extract information from these data structures.
- A flowchart is a graphical way of illustrating the steps in a process. It uses symbols connected by flowlines to represent processes and the direction of flow within the program.
- Pseudocode is simply an English-language-like way of writing programming code. In many ways it is like an annotated outline that you might prepare for a report.
- One key procedure that programmers use is branching in the form of an IF-THEN-ELSE statement that redirects, or branches, the flow of a program based on the outcome of a condition. For example, you can ask the user to answer yes or no to a question. If the answer is yes (true) the program branches down one path. If the answer is no (false), it branches down another.
- Loops repeat a process over and over again until a condition is met and the process is completed. Each repetition of the loop is called an iteration.
- Subroutines perform repetitive functions so new code doesn't have to be written each time a process is needed. They encapsulate similar functions into a single procedure.
- In large corporations, programming is just one step in a much larger process of systems analysis and design. This process has five distinct steps: analysis, design, development, implementation, and maintenance.

Review Questions

True/False

1. T F The generation of a language refers to when it was done on the time-line of program development.

2. T F The level of a language refers to how much it is like or unlike the actual language the computer itself uses to process data.

3. T F Computer programs are very detailed lists of precise instructions that describe how data is to be structured in the computer's memory and what processing logic is to be used on the data.
4. T F A procedural language is called a first-generation and low-level language.
5. T F Each processor can only understand any instructions you give it.
6. T F For a program written in a procedural language to run, it must first be converted to machine language using a program called a translator.
7. T F Translators for programs such as C, called compilers, convert source code into object code before the program can be run.
8. T F In object-oriented programs, objects are a combination of data structures and the procedures that operate on those data.
9. T F Subroutines are used in programs so certain procedures are coded only once and then referred to whenever needed.
10. T F System analysis and design is used to evaluate and improve any process and may or may not result in programs being written.

Fill-In the Blank

1. John von Neumann proposed that programs be stored in memory. This is called the __________.
2. All computers have a built-in __________ program that is executed the moment you turn on the computer.
3. Languages are grouped into __________ based on when they were first conceived.
4. Languages are grouped by __________based on how much they are like or unlike machine language.
5. Every computer processor (CPU) is designed to understand and interpret a fixed set of instructions called the __________.
6. CPUs cannot understand assembly language. Therefore, a program called a (an) __________ is used to translate assembly language into machine language.
7. The assembler reads in the __________ and converts it to __________.
8. __________are translators used before a program is run to produce a complete machine language program that is stored on the disk so it can be executed later.
9. __________are used to do the translation on the fly. They read each instruction written in the high-level language and immediately translate it into instructions that the processor then executes.
10. Java programs, called __________, are typically stored on a server. When you execute the program it is transferred to your computer.

Multiple Choice

1. A flowchart might include the symbols for ___.
   a. The beginning and end of every algorithm
   b. A calculation required by the algorithm
   c. Indicating when information is to be entered or output
   d. All of the above
2. The first program executed when a computer starts up is ___.
   a. The operating system
   b. The basic input/output system (BIOS)
   c. An application program you specify
   d. None of the above
3. The first programming languages were ___.
   a. Assembly languages
   b. Procedural languages
   c. Object-oriented languages
   d. Machine languages
4. Every processor has its own ___.
   a. Instruction set **b.** Procedural language
   c. Machine language **d.** Both a and c
5. ___ repeat a process over and over again until a condition is met and the process is completed.
   a. Subroutimes **b.** Functions
   c. Loops **d.** IF-Then statements
6. Languages are grouped into __________ based on how much they are like or unlike machine language.
   a. Levels **b.** Generations
   c. Both a and b **d.** Neither a nor b
7. A popular procedural programming language is ___.
   a. Machine language **b.** Assembly Language
   c. Cobol **d.** All of the above
8. The only language that doesn't need a translator to run is ___.
   a. Machine language **b.** Assembly Language
   c. Cobol **d.** Java
9. A translator converts ___.
   a. Object code to source code
   b. Source code to object code
   c. Both a and b
   d. Neither a nor b
10. When a program is translated on the fly, it's done with a(n) ___.
   a. Interpreter **b.** Compiler
   c. Assembler **d.** All of the above

Research Projects

1. Use the Internet or magazines to locate business applica tions written using the Java programming language. These are published by lots of companies, especially Lotus and Corel. What features do the publishers stress? What do reviewers say about these products?
2. Prepare a flowchart that illustrates the steps you might follow to mail a postcard. Be sure to include these two steps:
   - Do you have a postcard? If yes, what? If not what?
   - Do you have a stamp? If yes, what? If not what?

CHAPTER

13 PERSONAL, SOCIAL, AND

AN OVERVIEW

While there is no question that the new wave of information technology enhances life for many, it raises ethical questions that directly affect us all. As the microcomputer moves computing from its centralized mainframe origins to universal computing it presents real challenges and places new stress on organizations and individuals. When computing power was centralized, it was fairly secure. Now access is widely distributed and more and more data is being collected and stored, raising significant issues of privacy that have yet to be resolved. Nor are the effects on our health of using computers over long periods of time well understood, for the obvious reason that widespread computing hasn't been around that long. Short-term and more immediate health problems are clearly documented, but can be prevented. Legal issues about intellectual property rights, copyrights, and even libel on the Internet are being defined in courts of law.

It wasn't long ago that most information about you was hard to get. Someone had to physically go somewhere and convince someone to share information. With more and more data being digitized, there are fewer barriers to access. With the press of a few keys, an increasingly complete profile of you can be generated from a desktop computer. A "Digital Detective" has advertised his services on the Internet, including tracing social security numbers, locating people, obtaining consumer credit reports, finding if someone has filed for bankruptcy, getting driving records, and finding out who owns what real estate. His ad's closing paragraph should make us all ponder. "Here's to successful snooping! Get the goods on your friends and enemies alike."

It needn't be deliberate snooping. A woman physician recently gave birth in a leading Boston hospital. Ten of her colleagues, anxious to know how the mother and child were doing, logged onto the computer system and checked her medical records. Her complete medical profile, was there for them all to read. To state it mildly, she was shocked.

We seem to be on the verge of redefining what personal privacy means. Imagine if you stored your records in locked drawers, one drawer for each category: medical, driving, insurance, criminal, financial, educational, and so on. Now imagine that you unknowingly gave someone a single key that fit each and every lock: That's what you do every time you give someone your social security number, a rapidly evolving national identity number that can be used as a computer key to track your every move from birth to death.

In this chapter we explore some of the larger personal, social, and ethical issues, hoping to whet your appetite to learn more and to take the necessary actions to protect your own health and privacy.

OBJECTIVES

After completing this chapter, you will be able to:

- Explain how to avoid the major health issues associated with computing.
- Describe some major ethical issues facing computer users.
- Explain intellectual property rights and how to avoid infringing on them.
- Explain some major types of computer crime and how to counteract them.
- Describe cryptography and its uses.
- Be more aware of the burning issues caused by computers in a free society.

Personal *adj.* 1. of, pertaining to, or coming from a particular person.

Social *adj.* 1. living or disposed to live in a community, rather than in isolation.

Ethical *adj.* 1. pertaining to or dealing with morals; pertaining to right and wrong in conduct.

Issue *n.* 1. a point, matter, or dispute, the decision of which is of special or public importance.

Ethical Issues

13.1 Computers and Your Health

The medical and physical effects of working long hours on computers are not fully known. Some problems, however, have become commonplace. Complaints generally concern vision problems and muscle strain. You can avoid most, if not all, of these problems.

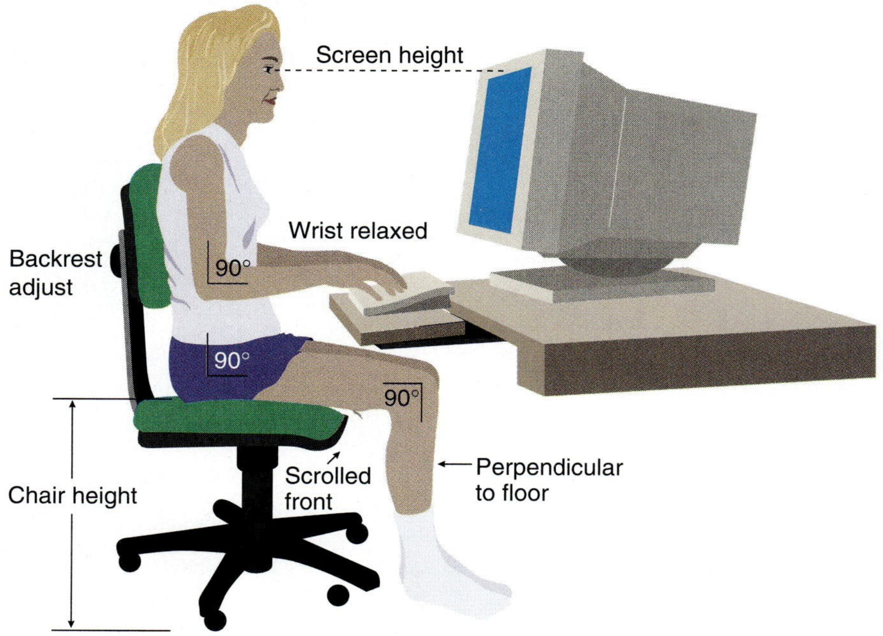

Sitting for comfort and health

Ergonomics

Ergonomics is the study of the interaction between people and machines. As a user, you should be aware of some of the things that researchers in this field recommend to avoid problems that arise from working on computers.

Your eyes were made for most efficient seeing at a far distance. Working at a computer calls for intense concentration on a task close at hand, usually no more than a couple of feet away. When your eyes change focus from far, their natural state, to near, several different muscles are called into action. A muscle inside the eye changes the shape of the eye's lens to focus sharply and clearly on the display screen. Other muscles turn both eyes inward, pointing them together at the same character on the screen, and still other muscles move the eyes quickly from one character or word to another.

There are signs of problems that should warn you to take the time to think through your working environment. These symptoms include headaches, blurred vision at both near and far viewing distances, itching and burning eyes, eye fatigue, flickering sensations, and double vision.

Lighting and glare control can make a difference. The following recommendations are designed to maximize comfort, accuracy, and productivity and to minimize eye fatigue and other complaints:

- Although lighting needs vary from person to person, check that overall illumination for computer equipment is less than the customary office lighting level. Display screen brightness should be three or four times greater than room light. You can lower the level of room lighting by using fewer bulbs or fluorescent lights and by replacing cool white fluorescent tubes with cool white deluxe tubes that provide less light but a more comfortable and pleasing atmosphere.
- Adjust the characters on the display screen to contrast well with the screen background.
- Minimize reflected glare on display screens by placing the screens so that windows and other sources of light are behind you. Do not sit facing an unshaded window or other bright light source. Make use of drapes and shades to reduce glare. Small hoods can be attached to extend above the display screen to shield it from overhead light if necessary. You can also use nonreflective surfaces or antiglare filters that fit over the screen.
- Use localized lighting like flexible lamps for other desk work as required. These lamps should be shielded and must be placed to avoid glare on the display screen.
- Avoid white or light-colored clothing if it causes a reflection on the screen.
- Take rest breaks and you can often alleviate many symptoms. Because computer work generally requires intense concentration on the document and screen, rest is important. The National Institute of Occupational Safety and Health (NIOSH) recommends a fifteen minute break after two hours of continuous work for users having moderate visual demands or moderate workload (less than 60 percent of your time looking at the screen) and a fifteen minute break every hour for users having high visual demands, high workloads, or repetitive work tasks.
- Use an adjustable chair, which can be a vision aid by enabling you to sit at a proper angle to the display screen. Generally, the top of the display screen should be 10 degrees above, and the center of the screen 20 degrees below, your

straight-ahead seeing position. The distance from your eyes to the screen should be 14 to 20 inches.
- Place your reference material as close as possible to the display screen to avoid frequent large eye and head movements. It should also be placed the same distance from your eyes as the display screen so you don't have to continually adjust focus as you look back and forth between them. A copy stand is very useful for this.

In addition to vision problems, anyone who has worked at a computer for long hours can tell stories about aches and pains. Some damage lasts for days or weeks and some is even permanent. The tragedy of these injuries is that most of them could be prevented with a little understanding of their causes.

When you type on a keyboard, you repeat the same movements over and over again using the same muscle groups in your hands, arms, and shoulders, and it's possible to suffer a repetitive stress injury. Somewhat common to assembly line workers and meat packers, these injuries are increasingly affecting computer users. One of the most common of such injuries, carpal-tunnel syndrome, swells tissues, pinching a nerve, causing a dull ache to excruciating pain in the wrist, hand, or arm. At the first indication of such an injury, you should consult a physician or other expert. There is some evidence that many of the supposed remedies such as wrist rests compound problems by affecting circulation. In some cases, simply taking stretching breaks or adjusting the height of your chair in relation to the keyboard can minimize the problem somewhat. Take early symptoms seriously because the damage can become serious.

Ergonomic keyboards designed to reduce or eliminate repetitive stress injuries to the wrists and arms have gentle slopes and shapes to remove the stress put on the wrists and arms by the normal flat keyboard.

Electromagnetic radiation

All electronic devices emit electromagnetic radiation (EMR) but the strength of the radiation, and any possible harmful effects, falls off rapidly as you move further from the device, especially the display screen. Questions about the effects of long exposure to this radiation have been asked for years, but not answered to everyone's satisfaction. There is some anecdotal evidence, however, of an increase in the rate of miscarriages, skin rashes, and eye problems. A report from Congress's Office of Technology Assessment states: "The emerging evidence no longer allows one to categorically assert there are no risks. But it does not provide a basis for asserting that there is a significant risk". To reduce any risks, manufacturers have introduced low-emission monitors that emit much lower electro-magnetic radiation than standard models. In many places, the use of these low-emission monitors is being mandated.

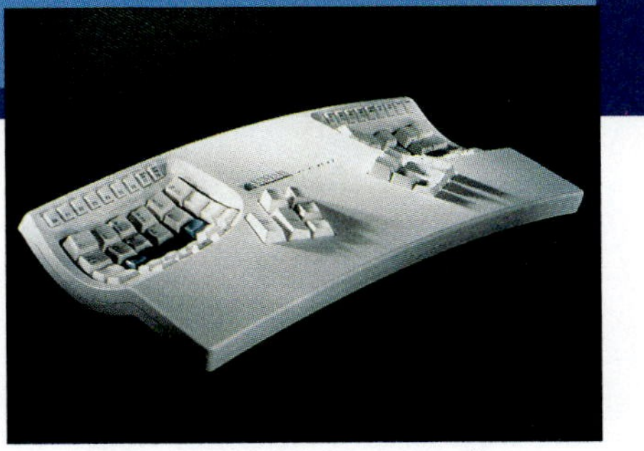

Ergonomic keyboard courtesy of Microsoft

VDT User Vision Checklist

Your workspace and vision care habits: Do they measure up?

- Correct angle and distance from screen to eyes.
- Reference material placed near the screen.
- Reference material and screen same distance from eyes.
- Screen brightness properly adjusted.
- Proper overall room lighting.
- Windows and other sources of bright light shielded.
- Proper lamps for reference material.
- Sources of screen reflection eliminated.
- Fifteen minute break every two hours for moderate users.
- Fifteen minute break every hour for frequent users.

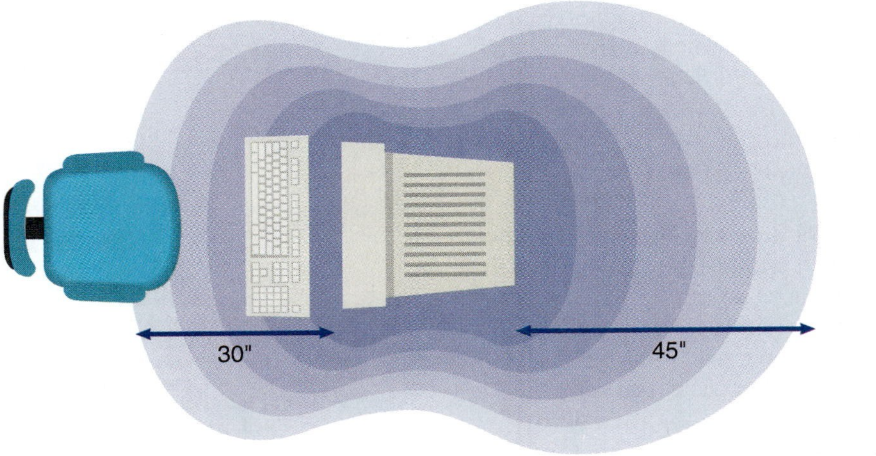

Electromagnetic fields

13.2 Computers and Ethics:

When you work at or around computers, there are always temptations. Some people just have the urge to look at personal data about fellow employees. "Does John make more than I do?" Others are motivated by good intentions. "If I copy this software and put it on my home computer I can work on these projects at home." Some are driven by more sinister motivations. "I'll just change some of the data so my boss looks bad." As in the rest of life, things you can do with a computer range from white to black with a middle gray area where you have to make personal decisions based on your own ethics and beliefs. If ever tempted, as being human we all may be, think through the implications of what you are about to do. If you are unsure whether something is ethical or not, it probably isn't. In general, ask others for advice in ambiguous situations and above all else, get approval from those above you in the organization or talk to mentors. This still doesn't absolve you of personal responsibility, but it gives you more information on which to base your own decision.

The Ten Commandments of Computer Ethics

The Computer Ethics Institute in Washington, DC, has proposed the following ten commandments of computer ethics:

1. Thou shalt not use a computer to harm other people.
2. Thou shalt not interfere with other people's computer work.
3. Thou shalt not snoop around in other people's computer files.
4. Thou shalt not use a computer to steal.
5. Thou shalt not use a computer to bear false witness.
6. Thou shalt not copy or use proprietary software for which you have not paid.
7. Thou shalt not use other people's computer resources without authorization or proper compensation.
8. Thou shalt not use other people's intellectual output.
9. Thou shalt think about the social consequences of the program you are writing or the system you are designing.
10. Thou shalt always use a computer in ways that demonstrate consideration and respect for your fellow humans.

Viruses

One of ongoing problems in the computer field is the introduction of viruses by antisocial users. A virus is a small program, either stored on a disk by itself or appended to an existing file. You get viruses when you use disks from other users or download files over a network such as the Internet.

A virus hiding in a program is called a Trojan horse. When the file is loaded or the Trojan horse program is run, the virus loads itself into the computer's memory. Once there, it can secretly attach itself to other files or programs or store itself on any other disks run on the computer, including the hard disk. What happens next depends on the intent of the vandal who created the virus.

- The virus may cause problems immediately.
- It may count specific occurrences, for example, how many times it is copied, and then cause damage.
- It may look at the computer's clock and cause damage on a specific date.
- It may reproduce itself and then cause damage. Like a biological virus, a computer virus can infect other files and then spread.

The instances of viruses causing damage are increasing. Once introduced, viruses are hard to detect and remove. For individual users, the best defense is to use only commercial programs and not to exchange files with other users. Using a virus scan program will help you detect the presence of viruses on your system. The screen below shows the web site of a major developer of anti-virus programs.

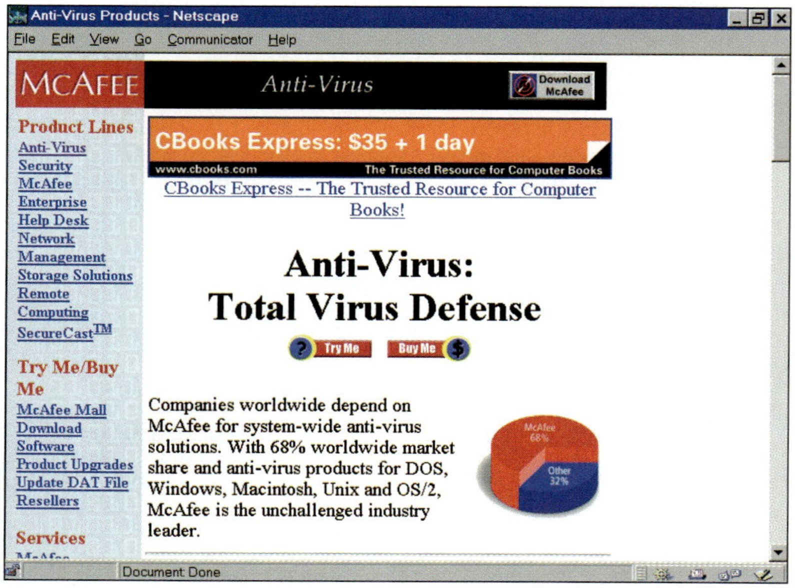

List of viruses in an antivirus program courtesy of McAfee

Leading viruses

New viruses appear almost every day but here are some that have been around long enough to become well known.

- Jerusalem was first seen in 1987 and now has 250 variations or strains.
- Monkey is a stealth boot virus that hides the hard disk from the computer when it's booted from a floppy disk.
- SATAN Bug prevents log-in access to the file server
- NATAS (Satan spelled backward) infects the boot area of the disk.
- Stoned displays on the screen the phrase "Your PC is Now Stoned"
- Joshi freezes your PC on January 5th until you enter the phrase "Happy Birthday Joshi."
- Cansu displays a V-shaped symbol on the screen every eighth time the computer is turned on.
- Michelangelo wipes out data on March 6, the artist's birthday.
- Green Caterpillar puts a crawling worm on the screen that moves about rearranging characters and altering their colors.

Browser security

When you're accessing the Internet, files are continually being downloaded to your computer. At other times, you specifically choose to download programs or other files. Both dramatically increase the risk of infecting your computer with a virus. To prevent viruses from being transferred to your system over the Web, security is being built into Web browsers. Microsoft's Internet Explorer employs a process called Authenticode. Using this technology, the publisher of a program digitally signs it. The browser can read that signature to identify the publisher and verify that the file hasn't been tampered with. When you download a file, the certificate seen above appears on your screen so you can decide whether or not to proceed.

Browser security
http://home.microsoft.com

Macro viruses

Until recently, viruses were distributed only through program files that were executed on a computer. However, as we mentioned in an earlier chapter, most application programs let you create macros, small programs that automate tasks. These macros are stored as a part of the application's documents and are transferred along with them. Just as these macros can be used to automate document procedures, they can also be designed to harm your system. The first such virus was the Word macro virus in 1995. No longer are documents safe to download or transfer and the same care must be given to them as you give to programs.

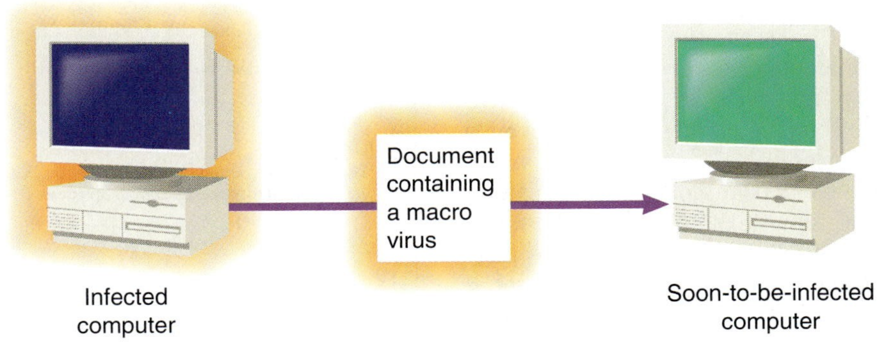

Macro virus

13.3 Intellectual Property Rights

In most countries around the world, it is recognized that writers, artists, programmers, sculptors, and entertainers have a right to their own work. Generally these rights are protected by copyright laws. In the United States, they are protected in the U.S. Constitution in which Article I, Section 8, grants the right to copyright works so as "To promote the progress of science and useful arts, by securing for limited times to authors and inventors the exclusive right to their respective writings and discoveries."

Copyrights and plagiarism

When you find things in places like the Web that are interesting, you may have a tendency to want to print them out or save them on your disk. In most, but not all cases, this is perfectly legal and ethical. Problems begin to arise, however, when you decide to use some of the text in a report or a graphic in a presentation. Now you are using the materials for other than your own personal use. This raises two dangerous questions: copyright infringement and plagiarism.

Almost any material that you find in print or electronic form is copyrighted, the rights to use it belonging solely to the owner of that copyright. Even uncopyrighted materials are protected. Using the materials without written permission violates the owner's rights and subjects you and your school or organization to penalties and embarrassment.

Plagiarism, the representation of someone else's work as your own may not carry as great legal penalties but the moral stigma attached is enormous. A student may be expelled from college for plagiarizing. As an example, the paragraphs in the following section on this page "What are copyrights?" are adapted from the U.S. Library of Congress's page on the Web. Including this material in this text without written permission is legally OK because many (but not all) government materials fall into what is called the public domain. (See next page). Secondly, the author avoids a charge of plagiarism because he credits the source of the text and does not claim it to be his own. Remember, you can be guilty of plagiarism inadvertently by simply failing to cite the source of an idea or certain words.

What are copyrights?

Copyright is a form of protection provided by the laws of the United States (title 17, U.S. Code) to the authors of "original works of authorship" including literary, dramatic, musical, artistic, and certain other intellectual works. This protection is available to both published and unpublished works. Section 106 of the Copyright Act generally gives the owner of copyright the exclusive right to do and to authorize others to do the following:

- To reproduce the copyrighted work in copies or phonorecords
- To prepare derivative works based upon the copyrighted work
- To distribute copies or phonorecords of the copyrighted work to the public by sale or other transfer of ownership, or by rental, lease, or lending
- To perform the copyrighted work publicly, in the case of literary, musical, dramatic, and choreographic works, pantomimes, and motion pictures and other audiovisual works
- To display the copyrighted work publicly, in the case of pictorial, graphic, or sculptural works, including the individual images of a motion picture or other audiovisual work.

Copyright symbol

It is illegal for anyone to violate any of the rights provided by the Act to the owner of copyright, that is, to do any of the things above without permission. There are some specified exemptions from copyright liability. One major one is the doctrine of "fair use."

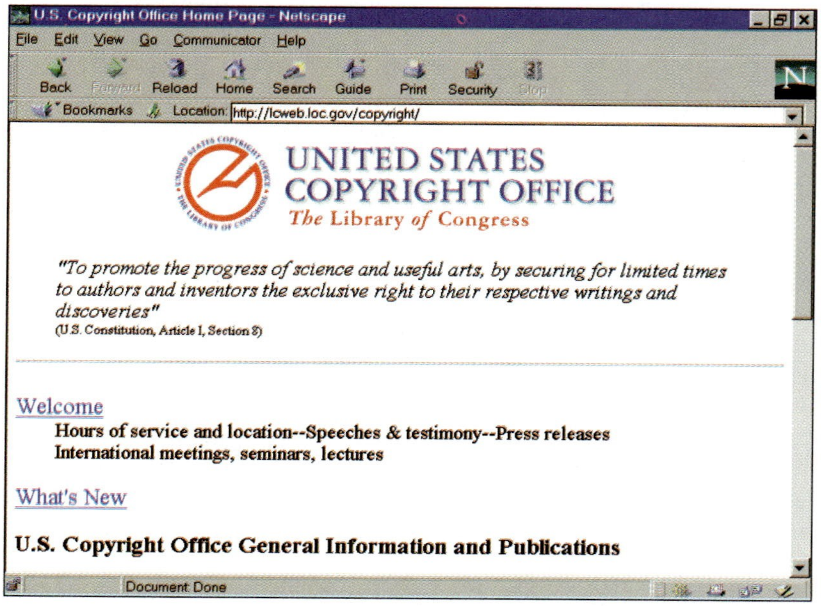

Copyright office
http://lcweb.loc.gov/copyright/

What is fair use?

Is copying that article from a Web magazine or newspaper into an e-mail message to a friend fair use? No, you're infringing the owner's copyright. The copyright law says "...the fair use of a copyrighted work, including such use by reproduction for purposes such as criticism, comment, news reporting, teaching (including multiple copies for classroom use), scholarship, or research, is not an infringement of copyright." Even for these uses, whether a specific use is fair or not depends on a number of factors.

Fair Use
- Criticism
- Comment
- New stories
- Teaching
- Scholarship
- Research

Fair Use

1. The purpose and character of the use, including whether such use is of a commercial nature or is for nonprofit educational purposes.

2. The nature of the copyrighted work.

3. The amount and substantiality of the portion used in relation to the copyrighted work as a whole.

4. The effect of the use upon the potential market for or value of the copyrighted work.

If you have questions about "Fair use," see the legal office of your school or organization.

What is public domain?

When something is in the public domain, you're free to use it any way you see fit. However, you are still expected to credit the source and not claim it as your own. How do you know if something is in the public domain? Partly it is common sense. Recent ads, logos, cartoon characters, illustrations, or photographs are almost certainly not in the public domain. However, 18th-century photographs and illustrations most likely are. In that gray area from 1900 through 1970 or so, some things remain protected while others don't. What is protected and what isn't depends on what type of property it is and when it was first copyrighted. If you have questions, you have to search the records of the U.S. Copyright Office yourself, or hire a qualified researcher (or the Copyright Office itself) to do the search for you. Even then, the Copyright Office states "Copyright searches cannot be considered conclusive . . . but at least will show a good faith effort. The responsibility of determining whether to use an item or not rests with you." Just to muddy the waters for you, even though something hasn't been registered with the Copyright Office doesn't mean it isn't protected by common law copyright.

Theft of software

When you walk into a computer store and pay $100 or more for a program, you may think you have bought the program, but usually you have bought the license, or right, to use the program and its documentation. The physical materials still belong to the publisher. Read these licenses carefully; they spell out your rights in detail. Most specify that you can use the program only on one computer and cannot make copies for distribution to others. You can, however, make copies for your own use because you should never run the program from the original disk.

Users usually do not have the right to make copies of software for distribution to others. Doing so infringes on the publisher's copyright and is a federal offense. Called software piracy, this practice costs software companies lost revenues, and they are increasingly taking legal action to prevent the distribution, sale, and use of these disks, especially in colleges and large corporations. Colleges and corporations are being held accountable for students and employees who illegally copy programs.

A site license allows a school or company either to run programs on networks without having a copy for each computer or to make a limited number of copies for use within a single department or location. Site licenses reduce the organization's total software costs, lessen the likelihood of violating the publisher's legal rights, and make it easier on all network users because they do not need individual program copies.

Who's the more likely software pirate?

Software theft

13.4 Computer Crime

Computer crime, waste, and abuse are a growth industry. Some estimates are that computer crime grows 35 percent and costs over $4 billion dollars a year. One obvious reason is the potential payoff. The average computer crime yields an estimated $560,000; the typical bank robbery, $19,000. As Willie Sutton responded when asked why he robbed banks, "It's where the money is." Also, the computer criminal is less likely to get caught or convicted. It's estimated that only 1 percent of the crime is detected and, if detected, the likelihood of criminal conviction is less than 10 percent.

Trojan horse—After a painting by Henri Motte, Corcoran Gallery, Washington D.C./The Bettman Archive

The butler did it!

You might think a computer criminal is some lonely misfit in a rundown house or apartment. The truth is quite different. He or she looks much like you. The typical computer criminal is an employee who is a legitimate and nontechnical end-user of the system. Employee crime, waste and abuse account for an estimated 70 to 80 percent of the annual loss related to computers. Dishonest and disgruntled employees cause an estimated 20 percent of the total computer-related loss.

Trap doors and salami techniques

Here are just some examples of the types of computer crimes and abuses that people try to pull:

- ♦ Data diddling. Information is changed during input or output. For example, at input, documents may be forged, valid disks exchanged, and data falsified.
- ♦ Browsing. Employees look in others' files for personal information. Access is gained by finding the password, disks left unattended, or using the person's own machine.
- ♦ Trojan horse. Altering a computer program to include an unauthorized function.
- ♦ Trap door. Accessing data through a hidden software or hardware mechanism that allows protection to be circumvented.
- ♦ Salami technique. Taking so little data (slices) at a time that it isn't obvious, for example, having the computer rounding down payments and diverting the few cents rounded off to a separate account.

Motivations for Computer Crime

- Personal or financial gain
- Entertainment
- Revenge
- Personal favor
- Challenge
- Accident
- Vandalism

- Superzapping. Using the program available for an emergency in many data centers to bypass all system controls. Using this "master key" the employee can access any data on the computer at any time.

And these are only the ones who got caught!

Computer crime is going on everywhere, maybe in your own school or office. Here are just a few cases that have occurred recently.

- A payroll clerk, notified of a beneficiary's death, opened a bank account using the beneficiary's name and social security number. The beneficiary was not removed from the computer's eligibility lists, but a computer input form changed the address and requested direct deposit of the benefits to the payroll clerk's new bank account.
- A major loss occurred with the diversion of government equipment. Fictitious requisitions were prepared for routine ordering at a major purchasing center. The requisitions directed shipment of communications equipment to legitimate private corporations holding government contracts. Just prior to the delivery date, one of the conspirators would call the corporation to alert them to the "error" and arrange "proper" delivery of the equipment to the conspirators.
- Three data clerks, using a remote terminal, entered phony claims into the computer to receive over $150,000 in benefits and then deleted records of these transactions to avoid being caught.

THE TOP 10

The 10 most common techniques used to commit computer-related fraud and abuse include:

Computer-Related Fraud

1. Entering unauthorized information.
2. Manipulating authorized input information.
3. Manipulating or improperly using information files and records.
4. Creating unauthorized files and records.
5. Overriding internal controls.

Computer-Related Abuse

1. Stealing computer time, software, information, or equipment.
2. Entering unauthorized information.
3. Creating unauthorized information files and records.
4. Developing computer programs for nonwork purposes.
5. Manipulating or improperly using computer processing.

Your role

Surveys show that only a very small percentage of computer-related fraud and abuse involves the deliberate damage or destruction of equipment, software, or data. Most abuses involve manipulating, creating, and wrongly using information. Preventing such abuse depends to a large extent on observant employees who report it to the proper authorities.

Be on the lookout for:

- Unauthorized use of computer time.
- Unauthorized use of or attempts to access data files.
- Theft of computer supplies, software, or hardware.
- Damage to data, hardware, or software.
- Unauthorized possession of computer disks, tapes, or printouts.

Be on the lookout for

- Unauthorized use of computer time
- Unauthorized use of or attempts to access data files
- Theft of computer supplies, software, or hardware
- Damage to data, hardware, or software
- Unauthorized possession of computer disks, tapes, or printouts

Detecting computer crime

13.5 Cryptography

There's an electronic war going on out there. As you might expect, there are the usual bad guys who want to read your mail to get corporate secrets or to steal credit card numbers and passwords. Unfortunately, a very ambivalent role is played by governments. There are some people in every government who want to read your mail. They'd like us all writing on postcards instead of using envelopes. Cryptography is a way to encode your messages so no one but you or the intended recipient can read them.

The Internet Privacy Coalition

To protect computer privacy, active groups are being formed. One of the big new players is the Internet Privacy Coalition. The mission of this group is to promote privacy and security on the Internet through widespread public availability of strong encryption and the relaxation of export controls on cryptography. This group has been founded by a diverse group of organizations including the American Bankers Association, American Civil Liberties Union, American Library Association, Association for Computing Machinery, U.S. Public Policy Office Electronic Frontier Foundation, Institute of Electronics and Electrical Engineers, Nortel-Northern Telecom, and Wired Magazine.

Web privacy supporter
http://www.privacy.org/ipc/#Members

It's Not Safe To Phone Either

Like e-mail, phone conversations are subject to eavesdropping. PGPfone (Pretty Good Privacy Phone) is a software package that turns your desktop or notebook computer into a secure telephone. It uses speech compression and cryptography protocols to give you the ability to have a real-time secure telephone conversation via a modem-to-modem connection. It also works across the Internet!

Who needs it

If you think your e-mail is safe, think again:

- E-mail messages are easy to intercept and automatically scan for specific words. International communications are scanned on a large scale by the National Security Agency. Words such as "bomb" or "drugs" which you might use in a legitimate or harmless context are sure to trigger their computers' interest.
- If your computer is connected to a local area network, any technician using a LAN analyzer can see and read everything that's being sent and received.
- If your laptop computer is lost or stolen; a competitor can read your e-mail and other files.

Lined up against the bad guys and the occasional zealots in government are an almost united high-technology industry and a few individuals like Phil Zimmerman. These people believe that communications between parties should be private and protected against eavesdropping by snoopers of any kind. Zimmerman wrote a shareware program called PGP (Pretty Good Privacy) that allows people to encrypt, or protect, their e-mail. Because he did this in the United States, where encryption technology is highly controlled by the government and the defense department, he was investigated for three years before the government backed off. Since this powerful, popular encryption program is widely used and so well known, we'll use it as our example of encryption technology.

Single-key cryptography

People have tried to keep messages private for centuries. The problem has always been that both parties needed the same code to encipher and decipher thee message. Let's say both might have a code dictionary of words and the codes that represent them. If one of them wanted to send the message "Offer increased to $1 billion" (this is called plaintext), he would look up each word in the code book and send the message as 3694 1563 7260 8808 3043 (this is called the encrypted or enciphered message). The recipient would open her copy of the same code book and look up the numbers to find what word each represented.

Plaintext	Codenumber
offer	3964
increased	1563
to	7260
one	8808
billion	3043

This system, called single-key cryptography because the same key is used to encrypt and decrypt it, has the big problem that log books can be stolen or intercepted. Anyone that has a copy can read your mail.

Public-key cryptography

PGP (Pretty Good Privacy) is based on public-key cryptography, a technology that uses two related complementary keys, your private key and a public key. Here is how it works:

1. You send your public key to your correspondent. You don't care if it is intercepted. Anyone can have access to it as far as you are concerned. You can publish it in newspapers, post it on billboards, or tape it to your forehead. Anyone that has it can send you encrypted mail. But once it's encrypted, even they can't read it.

2. Your correspondent writes you a message using her word processing or e-mail program. In its original form it is called plaintext.

3. Your correspondent now uses your public key to encrypt the message and sends it to you. Again you don't care who intercepts it because only you have the private key needed to decode it. The resulting encrypted and signed file would look something like the one shown on the right.

4. You use your private key to decrypt the message. Since you are the only one with your private key, no one else can read the message, not even the person who encrypted it.


```
-----BEGIN PGP PUBLIC KEY BLOCK-----
Version: 2.7.1
mQA9Aiz4/LgAAAEBgNX2Kle/2epzDvG4ZLWpebifSxd21Um6pKltG33XV6bQ3
tpA
k1QndiIllOZBe/z1HQAFEbQEdGVzdA==
=qFxi
-----END PGP PUBLIC KEY BLOCK-----
```


1. You send your public key to your correspondent, courtesy of PGP

Alice:

Lets get together at lunch tomorrow and discuss your possible employment here at ACME Hardware.

Best Regards,
Bob

2. Your correspondent writes you a message, courtesy of PGP


```
-----BEGIN PGP MESSAGE-----
Version: 2.7.1
hDwCSDC8VmC+9h0BAX9jpGKyhtBHrn+PHTo2JEBngpyGYZkC0aDEy5p+7EBhRNLI
Q+OXE6vKdTerXMQkXRumAAAA4Iuv6QYM/ErI/3M0HRgO7XJHFV1rUCnKXLv7/6zy
aFtLopRSChJfkMxTt0timsFLo23wDG5yhFG7/fHEz3Rio2f33aeaRDei13R3+4Vg
I0ghO+s88WiRGtamllqdqukUBM8MEQc3Zb1tevI3Y5igzApW8he3OsT82o/Zd4iU
d7N/K7xJdHnV1dmaYj5k+mbW8k4gd5AoqIkTNBccNAZRe4w7z7SdBA7YRWJ/bLk5
GgKU91TLvnytn7A5jfSJ7OUR11RNELFJq+YKzvFHVg6a8iWekPe2wPX7umOV106E
YqEF
=ULXZ
-----END PGP MESSAGE-----
```


3. Your correspondent encrypts the message with your public key and sends it, courtesy of PGP

Alice:

Lets get together at lunch tomorrow and discuss your possible employment here at ACME Hardware.

Best Regards,
Bob

4. You decrypt the message with your private key, courtesy of PGP

Digital signatures

To ensure that the message you get is really from the person you expect, she can sign it with her private key. This creates an encrypted file that can't be duplicated by any other means. Anyone can use your public key to read that signature and verify that it's from your correspondent and that it hasn't been altered since she signed it. A signed document can't be forged so the sender cannot later deny having sent it. This ability to authenticate a message's source and accuracy is the key to widespread electronic commerce. Encryption and digital signatures have made credit-card charges over the Internet feasible.

Behind the scenes

In reality, public-key encryption is much slower than single-key encryption so PGP uses a faster two-step process.

1. The message is first encrypted with a powerful single-key encryption algorithm. During this process a temporary random key called a session key is automatically created just for this one document and then used to encipher the plaintext file.

2. The recipient's public key is used to encipher this temporary random conventional key.

When the message arrives, the recipient's program uses his or her private key to decrypt the message's session key and then uses that key to decrypt the message.

13.6 The Burning Issues

In any free society, people's beliefs fall along the whole spectrum as to what role government has to play in the affairs of its citizens' lives. Politicians, often ignorant of computing technology themselves, are asked to vote on burning issues of our new information society that will have a lasting impact on your life and the lives of your children. As a member of a free society, it's your responsibility to be informed on all issues that affect your rights as a citizen, to develop opinions about the issues, and then act on your opinions by at least expressing them to your elected officials. Freedom and dignity didn't just happen; they had to be fought for. Freedom and workplace dignity won't just continue; they have to be worked at. There is always a tendency of those in power in government or business to whittle away at freedoms in the name of profits, efficiency, or law and order. This whittling can be powerful, turning huge trees into toothpicks over time. Most of the issues brought on by the new information technology cross party lines. You'll find people in all major parties taking different sides on each issue.

The Electronic Freedom Foundation launched a blue ribbon campaign to protest new censorship laws. It's symbol was a blue ribbon found on many Web pages.

http://www.eff.org/blueribbon.html#intro

Issue #1 National identity numbers

Computers make it possible to collect an amazing amount of data about you. When you use a credit card, buy a ticket, make a phone call, deposit money in the bank, make a withdrawal from an automatic teller machine, you are contributing to a record from which your movements, needs, and desires can be deduced. When all this data is stored in relational databases that share a common field, namely your social security number, they can be tied together to create a moving picture of your life.

Until recently, anyone interested in your medical records had to visit all of your doctors and each of the hospitals you have visited. They had to get by an assortment of protective receptionists and medical office record staff to open file drawers to see your records. Now they just have to log onto a computer, search your name, and voila, there it is, ready to be read, printed, or e-mailed to anyone else around the globe. In some cases, patients no longer tell their own doctors things they don't want their insurance company to know.

Side 1. All databases need at least one field that's unique to all of the records stored in it. Using an existing number like the social security number makes it easier to ensure the database is accurate and makes it easier to tie one database to another.

Side 2. Yes it makes it easy, but it also makes it dangerous. There is a certain amount of privacy in having all of your files held separately by different people. Once they can be so easily combined, governments, business, and individuals can read your life like an open book. You may not want your medical insurer to have access to your grocery store purchases. "Sorry Mr. Smith, we're canceling your insurance because you consume too much ice cream." The only way to hide would be to pay cash and not register anywhere.

Social security card courtesy of Scott Goodwin Photography

Issue # 2 The electronic supervisor

An expert in computer security has been quoted as saying, "You're not paranoid, they really are watching you." True or not, the possibility exists for your every computer activity to be monitored. In businesses, computer technology makes possible the continuous collection and analysis of management information about work performance and equipment use. Such statistics might include number of keystrokes made, types of transactions completed, or time spent for each transaction. The number of monitored workers can be expected to grow as computers begin to be used in more jobs, for example retail sales, and as computers are introduced in a greater variety of workplaces.

Side 1. This information can be useful to managers in managing resources, planning workloads, and reducing costs. It can be advantageous to employees as well, by providing timely feedback on performance and an objective basis for evaluation.

Electronic supervision

Side 2. These monitoring devices invade employees' privacy, cause stress, and can be used unfairly by some employers. They reduce the worker's dignity.

Issue #3 Censorship and free speech

Governments around the world have become alarmed by the Internet. Generally the concern is expressed in terms of the unregulated distribution of pornography, a legitimate issue in itself where children are conerned. You can expect this debate to deepen and spread to other issues as more and more people become connected.

Side 1. Distribution of pornography is so easy on the Internet we have to protect our kids from it. Because the Internet is international, child pornography also finds its way to the screen. There must be criminal penalties for the distribution of pornography on the Internet.

Side 2. Government should let the Internet alone. Any attempts to regulate it will complicate it and slow it down. "The price of liberty is eternal vigilance." Pornography is a phoney issue. Once the censors get a crack in the door they will begin to violate our First Amendment rights.

Issue #4 Privacy in communications

When you send e-mail, transfer files, or complete any other kind of computer transaction, your message can be encrypted so it can't be read by technically competent people at many points along the line. Only the person with the right "key" can open the message to read it.

Side 1. The F.B.I. and other government agencies object to this total confidentiality because they can't read the messages. They need to be able to read anyone's mail in their war against spies, terrorism, drugs, and pornography. They support special processes by which they can gain access to a special key to open mail when granted the right to do so by a court.

Side 2. You can't trust the security of the system because anyone may be able to get access to the key that unlocks your mail. And do you really believe that the government can't find an obliging judge who'll grant almost any request?

Sources to follow

There are many sources on the Web where you can follow the ongoing debates about social issues in computing. Here is just a sampling.

The Electronic Frontier Foundation states: "The Electronic Frontier Foundation is a nonprofit civil liberties organization working in the public interest to protect privacy, free expression, and access to public resources and information online, as well as to promote responsibility in new media."

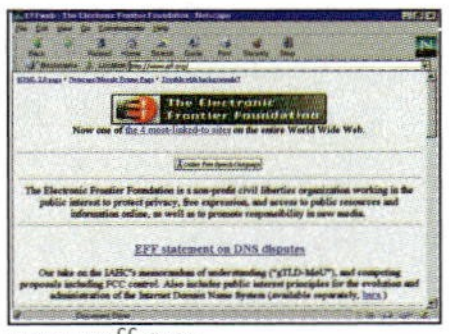
www.eff.org

The Inter-net Privacy Coalition states: "The mission of the Internet Privacy Coalition is to promote privacy and security on the Internet through widespread public availability of strong encryption and the relaxation of export controls on cryptography."

http://www.privacy.org/ipc/

The Center for Democracy and Technology is a nonprofit public interest organization based in Washington, DC. CDT's mission is to develop and advocate public policies that advance constitutional civil liberties and democratic values in new computer and communications technologies.

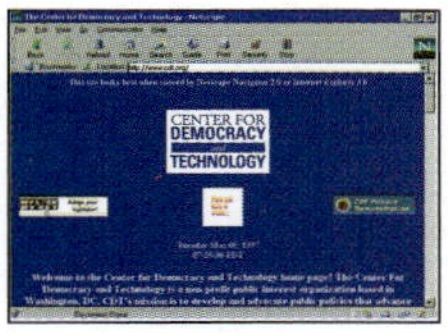

http://www.cdt.org

CPSR is a public-interest alliance of computer scientists and others interested in the impact of computer technology on society. As technical experts, CPSR members provide the public and policymakers with realistic assessments of the power, promise, and limitations of computer technology. As concerned citizens, they direct public attention to critical choices concerning the applications of computing and how those choices affect society.

http://www.cpsr.org

NATIONAL SECURITY

The Director of the U.S. Central Intelligence Agency reported to Congress that the U.S. is increasingly vulnerable to "cyber attacks" and other forms of information warfare. *The Wall Street Journal* quotes him as saying such attacks "could not only disrupt our daily lives, but also seriously jeopardize our national or economic security." He feared information warfare could disrupt air-traffic control, power plants, banks, international commerce and fund transfers, or send false orders to deploy military forces. He said "the electron in my judgment is the ultimate precision-guided munition."

Escrow keys

13.7 Enhancing and Testing Your Understanding

Summary

- The medical and physical effects of working long hours on computers are not fully known. However, muscle and eye strain are common complaints.
- Ergonomics is the study of the interaction between people and machines.
- Signs of problems that should warn you to think through your working environment include headaches, blurred vision, itching and burning eyes, eye fatigue, flickering sensations, and double vision.
- Adjust the characters on the display screen to contrast well with the screen background and minimize reflected glare.
- Use localized lighting such as flexible lamps for desk work.
- Avoid white or light-colored clothing if it causes a reflection on the screen.
- The National Institute of Occupational Safety and Health (NIOSH) recommends a fifteen minute break after two hours of continuous work with moderate visual demands or workload and a fifteen minute break every hour of work with high visual demands, high workloads, or repetitive tasks.
- Generally, the top of the display screen should be 10 degrees above, and the center of the screen 20 degrees below, your straight-ahead seeing position. The distance from your eyes to the screen should be 14 to 20 inches.
- Place your reference material as close as possible to the display screen, and at the same distance.
- Repeating the same movements over and over again can cause repetitive stress injury. One of the most common such injuries, carpal-tunnel syndrome, causes tissues to swell pinching a nerve.
- If you are unsure whether something is ethical or not, it probably isn't. Ask others for advice in these situations and above all else, get approval from those above you in the organization.
- A virus is a destructive small program that you can encounter when you use disks from other users or download files over the Internet.
- A virus may cause problems immediately, it may count specific occurrences before acting, it may look at the computer's clock and cause damage on a specific date, or it may reproduce itself and then cause damage.
- The best defense against viruses is to use only commercial programs and not to exchange files with other users.
- Viruses can be distributed through document files using macros.
- In most countries around the world, it is recognized that the works of writers, artists, programmers, sculptors, and entertainers are protected by copyright laws.
- In most cases, you are not free to use materials you find on the Internet in a report or a graphic in a presentation.
- Using copyrighted material without written permission violates the owner's rights and subjects you and your school or organization to penalties and embarrassment.
- When you use others' materials you must credit your source or you could be guilty of plagiarism, the representation of someone else's work as your own.
- Most software licenses specify that you can use the program only on one computer and cannot make copies for distribution to others. You can, however, make copies for your own use.
- A site license allows a school or company either to run programs on networks without having a copy for each computer or to make a limited number of copies for use within a single department or location.
- If you think your e-mail is safe, think again. E-mail messages are easy to intercept and automatically scan for specific words.
- To secure messages, you encrypt or encipher them.
- As a member of a free society, it's your responsibility to be informed on all issues that affect your rights as a citizen, to develop opinions about them, and then act on those opinions by at least expressing them to your elected officials.

Review Questions

True/False

1. **T** **F** There is nothing you can do about physical complaints arising from computer usage. They are just part of the process.

2. **T** **F** Light reflecting off the screen can be very distracting and lead to headaches and vision problems.

3. **T** **F** A virus cannot infect a document.

4. **T** **F** When a virus is activated, you always know it immediately because of some message on the screen or other unexpected event.

5. **T** **F** Copyright is a form of protection to the authors of "original works of authorship" including literary, dramatic, musical, artistic, and certain other intellectual works.

6. T F Copyright protection is available to both published and unpublished works.

7. T F Famous paintings can almost always be copied and used without permission because they are so old.

8. T F It is illegal for anyone to violate any of the rights provided to the owner of a copyright.

9. T F To secure copyright, you must file a registration with the Copyright Office.

10. T F Electronic performance monitoring (EPM) systems are solely for the employee's benefit.

Fill-In the Blank

1. If you begin to get pain in your wrists, you may have __________.
2. All electronic devices emit _________ but it has never been proved harmful.
3. __________ are small software programs able to replicate themselves without your permission or knowledge.
4. __________ viruses reside on the part of the hard drive that the computer reads each time it's started. If the boot code is infected, the virus is loaded into memory.
5. Viruses distributed through documents are called __________ viruses.
6. __________ viruses avoid detection by anti-virus tools by working ahead of the detection program restoring files to their original uninfected state. When the file is then closed, it is reinfected.
7. In special cases, copyrighted materials can be used with out permission under a provision called _________.
8. Using other people's materials without crediting them is called _________.
9. The phrase __________ refers to an adversary's attempt to exploit, corrupt, or destroy our information and information systems while protecting their own.
10. When sending data over networks your only protection from prying eyes is __________.

Multiple Choice

1. Ergonomics is the study of __.
   - **a.** Cost reductions in manufacturing
   - **b.** The interaction between people and machines
   - **c.** Artificial intelligence
   - **d.** Making computers faster
2. The National Institute of Occupational Safety and Health (NIOSH) recommends a fifteen minute break after ___ of continuous work for users having moderate visual demands or moderate workload (less than 60 percent of your time looking at the screen).
   - **a.** One hour **b.** Two hours
   - **c.** Three hours **d.** Four hours
3. When your system picks up a virus, you'll know it when ___.
   - **a.** Something happens immediately
   - **b.** A specific number of occurrences happen
   - **c.** The computer's clock reaches a certain date
   - **d.** Any of the above
4. Copyright gives the owner of the copyright the exclusive right to ___.
   - **a.** Reproduce the work in copies or phonorecords
   - **b.** Prepare derivative works
   - **c.** Distribute copies of the work to the public.
   - **d.** All of the above
5. When you buy an application software package, you have the right to __.
   - **a.** Use it only for yourself
   - **b.** Make a backup copy for your own use
   - **c.** Give it away when you are done with it
   - **d.** All of the above
6. Signs of problems about your working environment include ___.
   - **a.** Headaches
   - **b.** Blurred vision at both near and far viewing distances
   - **c.** Itching and burning eyes, eye fatigue, flickering sensations, and double vision.
   - **d.** All of the above
7. The best lighting for computer work has ___.
   - **a.** Overall illumination less than the customary office lighting level
   - **b.** Display screen brightness set to three or four times greater than room light
   - **c.** No glare on the screen
   - **d.** All of the above
8. The center of the display screen should be ___ your straight-ahead seeing position
   - **a.** 10 degrees above **b.** 20 degrees below
   - **c.** 10 degrees below **d.** 20 degrees above
9. The only materials you can be sure are in the public domain are ___.
   - **a.** Cartoons older than 10 years
   - **b.** Books older than 26 years
   - **c.** Paintings from the 1400s
   - **d.** None of the above
10. To copyright your own work, you must ___.
    - **a.** File with the Library of Congress
    - **b.** Publish the work in print or on the Internet
    - **c.** Either a or b **d.** Neither a nor b

Research Projects

1. Examine your work space at home, school, or work and list things you could do to make it a better place to work.
2. Try to locate some published material that is not protect ed by copyright. Explain how you know that.
3. List reasons that support or oppose the government's having keys that give them access to your e-mail. (Provide some reasons for each position.) Then, take a side on this issue and explain why you have taken it. You can't quibble because you either want them to have access or you don't. Explain why.
4. Watch for the next time someone asks for your social security number. Do you think it's a legitimate request? What happens if you refuse to give it?

INDEX